CW00749685

The Scottish Parliament 1639–1661

To my parents

THE SCOTTISH PARLIAMENT 1639–1661

A Political and Constitutional Analysis

JOHN R. YOUNG
Department of History
University of Strathclyde

JOHN DONALD PUBLISHERS LTD
EDINBURGH

John Donald Publishers Ltd.,
138 St Stephen Street, Edinburgh,
EH3 5AA.

ISBN 0 85976 412 5

British Library Cataloguing in Publication Data
A catalogue record for this book is available from the British Library.

Typeset by WestKey Ltd., Falmouth, Cornwall
Printed and bound by Redwood Books, Trowbridge, Wiltshire

Acknowledgements

This monograph is based on my doctoral thesis conducted in the Department of Scottish History at the University of Glasgow between 1989 and 1993. I would like to thank my former supervisor Allan MacInnes, now Burnett-Fletcher Professor of History at the University of Aberdeen, for his encouragement, advice, and assistance throughout the progress of the thesis. In particular, I benefited from his detailed historical knowledge of the nature of the Covenanting Movement. Dr Lionel Glassey of the Department of Modern History at Glasgow University was the internal examiner of my thesis. Dr Glassey taught me as an undergraduate student and I owe him a debt of gratitude for his teaching enthusiasm and academic encouragement towards myself and other students of his Special Subject class of 1988.

Volumes two and three of my doctoral thesis contain appendices of tabular parliamentary data. Two individuals deserve special thanks for their help in the production of these volumes. Firstly, I would like to thank Daina Whitelaw of Buchanan International Ltd, Glasgow, for the efficient production of these appendices, often at very short notice. Secondly, Professor Archie Duncan, formerly Professor of Scottish History at Glasgow University, is to be thanked for financial provision which helped towards the production costs.

Appreciation is also duly accorded to the postgraduate students in the Scottish History department at Glasgow University, 1989–1993, especially Dr Ewen Cameron, Dr Fiona Watson, Andrew 'Mackie' MacIlop, and Ronnie Lee. Their collective intense and lively discussions have increasingly emphasised to myself the sustained value of Scottish historical scholarship as we approach the new millennium.

The production of this monograph was made possible through a Postdoctoral Research Fellowship in the Research Centre in Scottish History at the University of Strathclyde. I wish to thank my colleagues at Strathclyde for their academic support and encouragement, especially Professor T.M. Devine, Professor J.F Macmillan, Dr Richard Finlay, and Dr Simon Adams. Within the wider historical community, I also wish to thank Professor Keith Brown, external examiner of my thesis, and Dr John Scally for their constructive criticisms of various aspects of my conclusions.

The librarians and archivists of Glasgow University Library, Edinburgh University Library, the Scottish Records Office, the National Library of Scotland, the British Library, and Strathclyde Regional Archives are also thanked for their professional services and expertise. Appreciation is also accorded to the Marquis of Bute and the Duke of Atholl for permission to consult their private collections. The professional expertise of Russell Walker of John Donald Publishers Ltd has also been most helpful in the completion of this book.

Finally, I wish to express my gratitude to my parents and family, to whom this book is dedicated, for their continued support throughout my education.

Glasgow, 1996 J.R.Y.

Contents

Abbreviations and Conventions

AHR	*American Historical Review*
APS	*Acts of the Parliaments of Scotland*, T. Thomson & C. Innes (eds.), volumes v-vii, (Edinburgh, 1814–1872)
BL	British Library
CJ	*Journals of the House of Commons*, 3, 15 March 1642–24 December 1644
CSPD	*Calendar of State Papers Domestic* (1639–1661), 16 volumes, W.D. Hamilton & M.A. Everett Green (eds.) (London, 1923–1931)
CSPV	*Calendar of State Papers and Manuscripts, Relating to English Affairs and Collections of Venice, and in other Libraries of Northern Italy*, volumes XXIV-XXXII, A.B. Hinds (ed.) (London, 1923–1931)
EHR	*English Historical Review*
EUL	Edinburgh University Library
GUL	Glasgow University Library
HJ	*The Historical Journal*
HMC	Historical Manuscripts Commission
LJ	*Journals of the House of Lords*, 4, 1628–42
NLS	National Library of Scotland
Records of the Kirk	*Records of the Kirk of Scotland, containing the Acts and Proceedings of the General Assemblies*, A. Peterkin (ed.), (Edinburgh, 1838)
RCGA	*Records of the Commissioners of the General Assemblies of the Church of Scotland, 1646–52*, A.F. Mitchell & J. Christie (eds.), three volumes, SHS, 1892–1909
RCHS	*Records of the Scottish Church History Society*
RPCS	*Register of the Privy Council of Scotland*, P.H. Brown (ed.), 2nd series, volumes i-viii, (1625–1660) (Edinburgh, 1899–1906)
SHR	*Scottish Historical Review*
SHS	Scottish History Society
SRA	Strathclyde Regional Archives
SRO	Scottish Records Office
	The Scots Peerage, Sir J. Balfour Paul (ed.), nine volumes, (Edinburgh, 1904–1914)
TRHS	*Transactions of the Royal Historical Society*
Dates:	Old Style dates used in contemporary Britain are retained throughout. The new year is taken to begin on 1 January according to Scottish usage, not 25 March (English usage)
Money:	The merk was valued at two-thirds of the pound Scots (£), twelve of which were equivalent to a pound sterling. All monetary value are Scots unless otherwise stated.

Introduction

This monograph encompasses two interrelated themes. Firstly, it is a study of the operation of the Covenanting Movement within the institutional confines of the Scottish Parliament during an era of military, political, and social conflict throughout the Three Kingdoms of the British archipelago. The Scottish Parliament was used by the Covenanters as the appropriate constitutional forum and political structure in which to redefine the relationship between the monarchy and the Scottish political nation following a period of unsatisfactory absentee kingship since 1625. Following the Union of the Crowns of 1603, the structural relationship between the two kingdoms of Scotland and England and the effective government of Scotland had been stabilised and maintained by James VI and I himself, principally by his willingness to co-operate with and listen to the advice of the more influential Scottish nobles. This system collapsed following the death of James VI and I in 1625, and the ascendancy of his son Charles I to the throne. Within 13 years of Charles I coming to the throne, the political nation in Scotland rebelled in a national revolt in 1638–39 as the result of national, constitutional, economic, and religious grievances against Charles I as King of Scots, but who was essentially an anglicised monarch. In essence, this represented a dual challenge, based on the organisation of the Covenanting Movement, not only to the personal authority of Charles I himself, but also to the nature and extent of the royal prerogative within the kingdom of Scotland itself. The origins and explanations behind the Covenanting rebellion have been documented by other historians, most notably Allan MacInnes, Maurice Lee, and David Stevenson. This study commences with the opening of the first Parliament convened under the auspices of the Covenanters in 1639 and concludes with the reactionary Restoration Parliament of 1661.

Yet the Covenanting Movement was not homogeneous and was composed of radicals and conservatives. Certainly there was no standard, uniform Covenanter, and although the labels of radical and conservative are not watertight, a 'radical mainstream' was in existence from 1638–1651 and operated through what has recently been described as 'oligarchic centralism'. In addition, pragmatic Royalists have been defined as those Royalists who subscribed Covenanting oaths and obligations (especially the National Covenant and the Solemn League and Covenant) in order to secure access to public office, especially Parliament. Following parliamentary ratification of the abolition of the clerical estate in 1640, the Three Estates now consisted of nobles, commissioners of the shires, and commissioners of the burghs.

The second major theme of the monograph focuses on the political and constitutional development of the Scottish Parliament itself. With the exception of the period 1689–1707, the Scottish Parliament underwent unparalleled constitutional development and political maturity during the era of Covenanting hegemony. The last two major studies of the Scottish Parliament were written in the early twentieth century. At the outset of what has become the standard text on the Scottish Parliament, Professor Robert Rait openly stated that H.M. Register House in Edinburgh (now the Scottish Records Office) contained a bulk of manuscript material 'which must be rendered in printed form before they can be efficiently utilised for the purposes of historical investigation'. Rait's reluctance to undertake manuscript analysis of parliamentary sources was criticised by a reviewer (Professor Tout) in 1925. Therefore my own monograph has attempted to utilise such manuscript evidence, especially manuscript committee registers. I have also concentrated on printed parliamentary rolls and parliamentary committee membership data in the *Acts of the Parliaments of Scotland.* All analytical data referred to in the text is based on tabular parliamentary data (mostly from these three categories) contained in volumes two and three of my doctoral thesis.

Writing in 1924, Professor Rait stated that he hoped that his own work 'may serve to advance the study of a neglected topic and may stimulate students to undertake some of the vast amount of research which is still necessary'. If this monograph enhances our understanding of the Scottish Parliament, during one of its most important periods of development, then it will have fulfilled some of Professor Rait's hopes.

NOTES

1. A.I. MacInnes, *Charles I and the Making of the Covenanting Movement 1625–1641* (Edinburgh, 1991); M. Lee, *The Road to Revolution: Scotland Under Charles I 1625–37* (Urban & Chicago, 1985); D. Stevenson, *The Scottish Revolution 1637–1644* (Newton Abbot, 1973).
2. A.I. MacInnes, 'Early Modern Scotland: the Current State of Play', *SHR*, 73, (1994), *Proceedings of the 1993 Strathclyde Conference*, 37–39, 42; A.I. MacInnes, 'The Scottish Constitution, 1638–51: The Rise and Fall of Oligarchic Centralism', in J. Morrill (ed.), *The Scottish National Covenant in its British Context 1638–51*, (Edinburgh, 1990), 106–133.
3. R.S. Rait, *The Parliaments of Scotland* (Glasgow, 1924); C.S. Terry, *The Scottish Parliament: Its Constitution and Procedure, 1603–1707* (Glasgow, 1905).
4. Rait, *The Parliaments of Scotland*, vii–viii.
5. Review by Professor Tout of *The Parliaments of Scotland*, SHR, 22, (1925), 95–96.
6. Rait, *The Parliaments of Scotland*, vii–viii.

1

The 1639 Parliament

> And now qu'hen come it this grate parliament Long wished for and in grate expectatione for all belivied, and wer right confident Yet it should setle this distracted Natione And pute ane End all our greiffes and feares. To see ane End pute to oure grate debait By this so longed for present parliament for setling all thinges both in kirke and stait.[1]

Throughout the evolution of the Covenanting Movement as a vehicle of protest against the administration and policies of Charles I, the question of a 'free' Parliament, primarily as a reaction against the experience of the 1633 Parliament, had emerged as an integral component of the demands of the Covenanting leadership. The issue had been incorporated within the National Covenant, the central document of Covenanting ideology.[2]

Despite the fact that royal assent for the summoning of a General Assembly and Parliament was not accepted until September 1638, the momentum of events had accelerated and intensified the struggle between the Crown and the Covenanters. The Glasgow Assembly held in November and December 1638 had abolished the episcopal structure of the government of the Church of Scotland and demanded legal ratification of its proceedings in the next ensuing Parliament, (wherein lay the civil power, Parliament being the ultimate judiciary in the kingdom). Following the termination of the First Bishops' War in 1639, Charles I had recognised in the Pacification of Berwick (June 1639) that Parliament should finally convene on 24 August 1639 (to be preceded by another session of the General Assembly). This followed the prorogation by royal warrant of two successive diets of Parliament on 15 May and 23 July, with only the officials of Parliament present. Prorogation had been forced under a veil of threats from John Stewart, 1st Earl of Traquair, King's Commissioner.[3]

Prior to the session of Parliament commencing on 31 August 1639, (plans for a session on 12 August having been likewise abandoned), the Covenanters had organised their personnel to a sufficiently high degree as to provide a solid base from which to infiltrate and control Parliament, given the appropriate opportunity. From November 1637 the direction of the movement had been under the control of the Tables, a corps of the political elite of the Covenanters to provide co-ordination and leadership, with each of the political estates represented (nobles, gentry, and burgesses,) plus the ministry. The Fifth Table (the executive table) provided the ultimate tier of organisation and leadership. Such efficiency of organisation had enabled an informal meeting of the Estates to take place on 9 May 1639, described as 'the noblemen, lords of parliament, commissioners of shyres, and commissioners of burrowes for the parliament', to provide a forum for the discussion of military preparations for the First Bishops' War.[4]

Just as the Tables had co-ordinated and controlled the elections to and proceedings of the Glasgow Assembly,[5] it is evident from the run-up to and progress of the 1639 session of Parliament that a broad range of issues had been taken on board by the Covenanting leadership to be settled in Parliament, issues which were to be finally incorporated in the Scottish constitutional settlement of 1640–1641. These proposals can be interpreted as forming a specific manifesto, and several of the proposals were sent to the members of the estates elected to the Lords of the Articles sitting in closed session throughout the autumn and winter of 1639.

The demands can be differentiated into four identifiable groupings. Firstly, parliamentary ratification of the religious settlement carried out by the Glasgow Assembly was sought. Secondly, the modification of the Lords of the Articles and its abolition as an instrument of royal authority and influence (as had been experienced in the 1633 Parliament) was advocated. Thirdly, the remodelling of the constitution of Parliament, relating especially to control over the appointment of Officers of State, Privy Councillors, and Ordinary Lords and Extraordinary Lords of the Court of Session and the safeguarding of the legitimacy and authority of future Parliaments, (by the compulsory holding of Parliaments every two to three years) was required. Fourthly, the return of the Incendiaries, the five individuals who in particular faced the wrath of Covenanting hatred and had been prominent in Charles I's Scottish administration was demanded (Traquair, Treasurer and King's Commissioner, Sir Robert Spottiswood, President of the Court of Session, Sir John Hay, Clerk Register, Walter Balcanqual, the author of the notorious *Large Declaration*[6], and John Maxwell, Bishop of Ross). Traquair was well aware of the fact that 'these people (the Covenanters) have somewhat else in there thoughts than religion.'[7]

Parliamentary sanction of Covenanting policy as expressed in the Glasgow Assembly (including the abolition of episcopacy and the clerical estate) remained at the forefront of the Covenanting agenda, as the principal means of providing legal protection to the religious settlement and enhanced credibility by ratification by the supreme court of the realm. Franceso Zonca, the Venetian Ambassador in London, noted that the Covenanters 'could not rely upon the royal promise for the abolition of the liturgy book unless it was suppressed by decree of parliament.'[8]

Nevertheless, as evident from examination of the second and third areas of the Covenanting agenda, the sanction of the religious settlement was only to provide one aspect of parliamentary business. Rather, it was constitutional concerns that were to predominate, the Covenanters being determined that religious revolution was to be complemented by constitutional revolution, checks and balances being placed on absentee monarchy and the abuse of the royal prerogative.[9]

The two prime spheres identified for constitutional amendment were the abolition of the clerical estate in Parliament and modification of the electoral procedure of the Lords of the Articles, the body which traditionally represented the means by which the Crown bulldozed legislation through Parliament. The Lords of the Articles had been restructured in 1621 to facilitate royal management of that Parliament. The same procedure had been followed in 1633. In 1621 those bishops and nobles elected to the Articles had chosen the representatives of the other two estates (shires and burghs), and this procedure had been followed in 1633 with the bishops electing the eight noble members of the Articles, and the nobles duly elected the eight respective members of the commissioners of shires and burghs. There was also the added presence the Officers of State, who were essentially royal appointees. It was the electoral power of the bishops in Parliament and their corresponding control of the composition of the Articles, complemented by their role as crown nominees in the Privy Council and other public offices, that required their removal. The manner of the electoral composition of the Lords of the Articles, based on the bishops and amenable Royalist nobles, ensured that 'all depended upon them, and they upon his Majesty'.[10]

The noble members of the 1633 Lords of Articles had been mainly courtiers. Moreover, the Parliament of 1633 had provided no meaningful forum for discussion and the parliamentary members were merely obliged to vote either way on the legislation constituted by the Articles, with Charles duly noting the names of those disobliging members voting against the constructed body of legislation.[11]

As early as June 1639 Covenanting proposals were being articulated to secure diets of Parliament at regular intervals (every two to three years) and rumours were circulating that if the king would not summon them then the nobility would do so of its own accord. Such demands were justified on two grounds; the king's personal absence from the country, which hindered the airing of native complaints and grievances, and the prevention of the 'disorders' committed by the corrupt councillors of the post-1625 regime. Such justifications were in reality merely a guise for keeping constitutional checks on an absentee monarch. Likewise, the appointment of Privy Councillors, Officers of State, and officers of the Court of Session was to come under the sphere of parliamentary control. Previous appointments to both these bodies, 'where men are placed at everie courtiers desyre' had only served the 'courts pleasure without regard to kirk or kingdome'. Future appointments were to revert to the former system of joint consultation between king and Parliament when Parliament was current.[12]

Apart from constitutional concerns a high premium was placed upon the return of the Incendiaries who, according to Covenanting propaganda, had been the cause of the troubles in Scotland on account of their 'evil' advice and misrepresentation of policy. Those 'Incendiaries and false informants against the kingdom who (out of malice) have caused thes commotions for their own private ends' were to face the censure and punishment of Parliament.[13]

From a different perspective, Royalists were well aware of Covenanting aspirations and Traquair had been issued with specific instructions on how to proceed when the Estates finally convened on 31 August 1639. Although the session had been scheduled for 26 August it had been held over for five days due to the General Assembly's continued sitting. Charles was adamant that the granting of a free Parliament was not to constitute ratification of legislation derogatory to royal authority. Royal concern was focused on two particular areas. Firstly, it was faced with the problem of how to deal with the abolition of episcopacy by the Glasgow Assembly, with the consequent removal of a Royalist voting block within Parliament, (the bishops had been already instructed not to attend the forthcoming session of Parliament). Secondly, it was forced to consider the issue of the constitution of the Committee of the Articles. Royal communications to Traquair stressed that the legislation which had been passed in the General Assembly was not to be repeated in Parliament under any circumstances. In particular, although royal assent had been given to the abolition of episcopacy by the General Assembly, Traquair was under strict instructions that any previous acts establishing episcopal government of the Kirk were not to be repealed in Parliament, with specific reference to the legislative clause which deemed episcopacy to be unlawful in the Kirk, and not merely contrary to the constitution of the Kirk. If royal refusal to consent to the rescinding of previous parliamentary legislation in favour of episcopacy provided a 'rupture' between the Crown and Parliament then religion was to be made the cause and not the delicate issue of royal power within Parliament.

Under the cloak of religion, however, attention centred on which grouping was to control power within Parliament. Monarchial interest made it imperative that some form of substitute should be implemented to replace the bishops' votes. Charles accepted the feasibility of a plan of which James, Graham, 5th Earl of Montrose, was the 'leading spirit' that a body of fourteen ministers, or if that was not possible, fourteen laymen, who were to be 'king's men' nominated by the Crown, should form the appropriate replacement. Not only were these fourteen to have the bishops' places and votes, but they were also to be present on the Articles and have the power of election of the noble component of the Articles. If this option was rendered impossible then 'wee ought to haue the nomination of those lordes which the bishops had.' On the other hand, if successful then the nomination of the appropriate individuals was to be left to Traquair. Traquair's instructions regarding the Lords of the Articles were clear; their power was not to be defined at this time, and any discussion thereof was to be avoided, as were attempts to constitute and define the power of any other judicatories. Any contrary manoeuvres were to interpreted 'att nothing, but the overthro of royall authorati.'[14]

It was against this background that the Scottish Parliament convened on 31 August 1639, the day after the dissolution of the General Assembly which had ratified the legislation of the 1638 Glasgow Assembly. The scene was now set for a constitutional clash between the Crown and the Covenanters.

The First Session of the Second Parliament of Charles I, 31 August–14 November 1639

1. The Composition of the First Session of the Second Parliament of Charles I

The Estates assembled in a newly-constructed Parliament House, located next to St Giles in the heart of Edinburgh.[15] Fifty nobles, 47 gentry representing 25 shires, and 52 burgesses representing 51 burghs (149 individuals in total) formed the parliamentary membership of the 1639 as per 31 August 1639 (see appendix 2a). In terms of numerical composition per estate, the 1639 Parliament witnessed a reduction of two nobles, a rise of two gentry, and a rise of one burgess (yielding a total rise of one) compared to the 1633 Parliament.

Sixteen of the 50 nobles (32%), 11 of the 47 gentry (23%), and 28 of the 52 burgesses recorded in the parliamentary rolls of 31 August 1639 are also listed in the membership details for the opening day of the Glasgow Assembly, 21 November 1638. The momentum of constitutional defiance had therefore been maintained in terms of the personnel of the Covenanting Movement attending the 1639 Parliament and had been supplemented by the addition of grass-roots activists from the shires and burghs.

In addition, 31 of the 50 nobles (62%), 15 of the 47 gentry (32%), and 12 of the 52 burgesses (23%) recorded in the parliamentary rolls of 31 August 1639, had also been recorded in the rolls of the 1633 Parliament as per 20 June 1633. Gentry and burghal common membership over both sessions was therefore almost identical and probably contained elements of a disaffected political grouping who had been alarmed at the king's behaviour in the 1633 Parliament. The elections of the commissioners of shires and burghs had undoubtedly been sanctioned by the Tables. The high retention of nobles over both sessions is unsurprising given the instability of the political environment in 1639.[16]

2. The Proceedings of the First Session of the Second Triennial Parliament of Charles I

When the session opened, debate immediately emerged over the election of the Lords of the Articles. Given the absence of the bishops, Traquair and a grouping of (unspecified) Royalist nobles defended the royal prerogative, in a private session of a meeting of the nobility in an inner room of the House. They argued that the noble element of the Articles should be determined by the king, whilst the Covenanting nobles advocated self-regulation and the election of their representatives by themselves. The proceedings of this meeting were documented by the William Graham, 1st Earl of Airth, formerly 7th Earl of Menteith, former President of the Privy Council, 1628–30 and Justice-General of Scotland until 1633. Menteith had also managed the 1630 Convention for the Crown. Airth had been authorised by Charles to assist Traquair in Parliament and also attempt to galvanise a Royalist party. After a long and intense debate, the nobles resolved that if they consented to Traquair appointing their representatives to the Articles, then a protestation would be issued stating that such a move would not be prejudicial to the choosing of their representatives in future Parliaments (which was duly done). As a concession to the Covenanting leadership on its compromising stance, Traquair agreed that he himself should nominate such nobles as should satisfy the Covenanting nobles. Thereafter, the whole of the nobility proceeded to choose the shire and burgh representatives. Whilst this was in progress, representatives of both the shires and the burghs (in essence from the Tables) entered and demanded to air their views, handing in a joint protestation of the right of their respective estates to elect their own members upon the Articles. By this time, however, the choice of the Articles had been made, and it is clear that the choice of the representatives of the political estates of the gentry and burgesses to the Lords of the Articles had been determined by the nobility. Upon this issue dissension had emerged between Covenanting and Royalist nobles. Archibald Campbell, 8th Earl of Argyll, the most powerful chieftain in the Highlands, protested that this manner of election was not to prejudice the rights of the gentry and burgesses in future Parliaments. Argyll advocated the introduction of legislation by the Articles that each estate (nobles, gentry, and burgesses) should elect their own representatives to the Articles. On the other hand, George Gordon, 2nd Marquis of Huntly, the most notable grandee of the north-east and spokesman for the Royalist nobles present in Parliament, demanded that the mode of election of the gentry and burgess members should rest with the noble estate. Both Argyll and his kinsman John Campbell, 2nd Lord Loudoun, made a point of distancing themselves from Huntly's point of view with the shire and burgh representatives present. When the Estates reassembled as a whole, the composition of the Articles was communicated to the House, along with the orders for the Articles to attend daily in the Inner Parliament House. The Estates were ordered to continue to sit until the Articles had concluded their deliberations. The Articles defied Traquair, however, and refused to meet until 4 September.[17]

Of the eight nobles elected to the Articles only two (Huntly and David Carnegie, 1st, Earl of Southesk) were not associated with the Tables. The fact remains, however, that Covenanting domination of noble representation on the Articles was less than complete. This can be attributed to a reflection of a stronger Royalist contingent among the noble estate in general compared to the other two estates, (the ranks of the gentry and burgesses were filled with Covenanting activists). Notable radicals such as Argyll and John Leslie, 6th Earl of Rothes, secured inclusion. Argyll and Rothes constituted two of the leading Covenanting nobles in Parliament and were in the front-line of demanding constitutional change and a stronger assertion of Parliament's power vis-a-vis the monarchy. Both were vehemently opposed to episcopacy, and Rothes had a long track record of defiance of royal authority behind him. In the Parliament of 1621 he had refused to vote on the Five Articles of Perth and is reputed to have challenged the royal prerogative and the accuracy of voting in the 1633 Parliament.

A more conservative grouping of Covenanters and even some Royalists were in the ascendancy in the noble contingent of the Articles. Montrose, John Maitland, 1st Earl of Lauderdale, John, 10th Lord Lindsay, and William Keith, 6th Earl Marischal, can be identified as more conservative Covenanters willing to make some form of concessions to the king. Montrose was to be the leading figure in the formulation of the Cumbernauld Band of 1640, a reaction against the hardline activities of the radical nobles led by Argyll. Montrose had also been in correspondence with Charles since the Pacification of Berwick. Montrose had been elected to the Tables on 15 November 1637, was an enthusiastic supporter of the National Covenant and an important lay member of the Glasgow Assembly. Covenanting enthusiasm had manifested itself in his command of military divisions in the north of the country, which forced the town of Aberdeen to subscribe the Covenant. Montrose had captured Huntly and his son Lord Gordon in March 1639, with further military manoeuvres against James Gordon, 2nd Lord Aboyne, Huntly's second son, in June 1639. Nevertheless, Montrose had become increasingly alienated by the radicals in both the Glasgow Assembly and the General Assembly of 1639, particularly by the stand against the royal prerogative. Although he did not openly break with the mainstream Covenanters quite yet, he had been the architect of the Royalist design to replace the power of the bishops in Parliament with a body of fourteen 'king's men'. Marischal had played an active role in Covenanting affairs in Aberdeenshire in the First Bishops' War and was still deemed the dominant figure in Covenanting circles in the counties of Aberdeen, Banff, and Kincardine. Marischal had been a member of the 1633 Lords of the Articles and likewise was to sign the Cumbernauld Band. Lauderdale had also been included on the 1633 Lords of the Articles. He had recently been identified by James, 3rd Marquis of Hamilton, the king's foremost adviser on Scottish affairs, as a possible recruit to the Royalist camp.

Royal interests were not entirely absent in the composition of the Articles. Huntly had raised forces against the Covenanters in 1639 and remained the most powerful Royalist noble in Parliament. Southesk had actively opposed the introduction of the Prayer Book in Scotland, but did not favour armed resistance to the king and may be regarded as an old-guard Royalist. He possessed a full career of royal employment, especially under James VI. Hamilton had also identified and recommended Southesk's disposition to the royal service. Hamilton even advocated the employment of Southesk as Chancellor in 1638–39. It also appears that Airth, a supporter of the Court, attended the meetings of the Articles despite his non-inclusion on that body. Airth was similarly commanded to attend any other committees concerning parliamentary affairs when called to do so by Traquair. Any subsequent voting power based on this attendance would seem doubtful, however.

The four Officers of State on the Articles, Robert Ker, 1st Earl of Roxburgh (Privy Seal), Sir James Carmichael (Treasurer Depute), Sir John Hamilton of Orbiston (Justice Clerk), and Sir Thomas Hope of Craighall (King's Advocate), can rightly be regarded as forming a powerful voting block, although Hope of

Craighall was later to desert to the Covenanters and was under suspicion of covertly working for and advising the Covenanting leadership.[18]

Gentry and burghal membership of the Lords of the Articles was based on the Tables. Three burgess members, for example, Patrick Bell (Glasgow), Thomas Bruce (Stirling), and John Semple (Dumbarton), had represented their respective burghs as lay commissioners at the Glasgow Assembly and the General Assembly in session directly before the formal meeting of the Estates. Two of the gentry representatives, Sir William Douglas of Cavers (Roxburgh) and Sir Robert Grierson of Lag (Dumfries), had also enjoyed membership of the 1633 Lords of the Articles. This may well indicate the election of two shire and burgh members who had technical experience of the operation of the Articles under the royal administration in 1633. Such experience could possibly be put to good use in a parliamentary environment by the Covenanting leadership. One further representative from the shires on the Articles, Sir Robert Graham of Morphie (Kincardine/Mearns), was not recorded in the parliamentary rolls of 31 August 1639, although he had been commissioned to sit in Parliament. The complete dominance of gentry and burgh members clearly indicates on the one hand the depth of Covenanting support among the gentry and burgesses, and on the other hand, that the Covenanting nobles had proved numerically superior in the private session held by the noble estate to determine the Articles. It also indicates the failure of the emergence of a strong Royalist opposition among the nobles, which in turn ensured that Covenanting domination of the other two estates on the Articles would be secured. The common membership of two nobles and two gentry between the Articles of 1633 and 1639 emphasises the realpolitik of the Covenanting leadership in employing the skills of those individuals, albeit the two nobles were on the conservative wing of the movement, with the necessary technical skills at their disposal for the Articles to function on an efficient basis. Such skills could therefore be used to counter any disruptive measures/tactics employed by Traquair.

Gentry representation on the Articles tended to be concentrated within a broad geographic domain. Four represented shires predominantly on the east coast stretching from the Lothians to the Mearns; Sir Patrick Hepburne of Wauchton (Haddington), Sir George Dundas of that Ilk (Linlithgow), Sir Thomas Lyon of Auldbar (Forfar), and Sir Robert Graham of Morphie (Kincardine/Mearns). Two gentry on the Articles represented Borders' shires; Sir William Douglas of Cavers (Roxburgh) and Sir Robert Grierson of Lag (Dumfries and Annandale). The last remaining member, Sir Robert Innes of that Ilk, represented the more peripheral shires of Elgin and Forres (represented jointly in the 1639 Parliament), yet Sir George Stirling of Keir (Stirling) was located sufficiently close to the Lothians to be included as part of the broad Lothians domain. As a political conformation their composition appears to have been more on individual merit and quality, rather than a deliberate emphasis given to certain shires, although the majority were in close proximity to the capital. Significantly, none of the west coast shires merited representation. Lyon of Auldbar and Stirling of Keir formed part of the protest which had presented the joint petition of the gentry and burgesses to the meeting of the nobility and Traquair to determine the membership of the Articles. Effective political lobbying had secured membership of the Articles for Auldbar and Keir.

Consideration of the burghal element in geographical terms reveals a concentration of power between the west and east of the country. Three burghs (Glasgow, Dumbarton, and Irvine), constituted three of the most powerful burghs in the west, both in terms of the economic and financial muscle which they contributed to the Covenanting cause, and in the quality of personnel they provided, particularly Robert Barclay (Irvine) and John Semple (Dumbarton). A similar, if not identical situation prevailed on the east coast, Edinburgh, Aberdeen, Linlithgow, and Dundee constituting the dominant burghs and their representatives being major national Covenanting figures of their particular estate, especially John Smith (Edinburgh) and Alexander Jaffray (Aberdeen). The one remaining burgess member, Thomas Bruce, although a Covenanting activist, represented the burgh of Stirling, which produces a final geographic relationship of those burghs represented on the Articles. Thus, a 'three-one-three-one' formation emerges reading from west to east, with Stirling the linchpin in the centre, and Aberdeen lying on the outward eastward flank. Whether or not this constituted a deliberate policy option formulated by the Covenanting leadership, or was mere recognition of the economic might of those burghs and the particular quality of their respective representatives, or a combination of both, remains a matter of speculation. The end result, however, produced a highly effective means of ease of formulation of policy and efficient organisation of the major burghs as a distinct grouping within Parliament in general and a powerful voting block on the Articles in particular.[19]

Analysis of the composition of the Lords of the Articles therefore reveals that Covenanting voting strength on the legislation to be debated in closed session would ultimately rest with the shire and burgh representatives. Nevertheless, the Covenanters had succeeded in infiltrating the most important internal organ of Parliament as a means of controlling the legislation to be presented to the House. This was achieved despite the fact that they had failed to achieve modification in the electoral procedure of the Articles (the election of the representatives of the Articles by each estate), and that they had been forced to submit to the election of the nobles by Traquair.

As suggested by the divisions among the nobles, the Covenanters did not represent a homogeneous body and considerable tension existed between the separate estates. The Articles began their deliberations on 4 September with the debate over their manner of election still raging. Particular resentment existed among the gentry and on 2 or possibly 3 September the commissioners of the shires and those of the burghs had assembled in the Parliament House (although the Estates were not due to meet again until the Articles had completed their business) and proceeded to elect their own representatives to the Articles, in line with the tenor of their protestation of 31 August. This appears to have been an assertion of the principle of freedom of election of their respective representatives. The 'rival' nominations conformed to those already elected, although there was a move to have the representative of the burgh of Perth elected in place of that of Linlithgow. The gentry expressed concern over what had taken place in the private meeting between Traquair and the nobles. Fears were expressed that the gentry were going to be politically marginalised by the nobility as a political estate.

Historical enquiry into the Scottish constitutional settlement of 1641 has tended to concentrate on the respective Parliaments of 1640 and 1641 and has failed to fully explore the bulk of legislation designed in Articles in 1639 which was to receive full parliamentary ratification in 1640–41. It has also failed to recognise the key role played by the gentry and the burgesses in that process.[20]

Throughout the convocation of the Articles in closed session the gentry representatives in particular, but also those of the burgesses, were issued with a plethora of topics which required discussion by the Articles. These topics represented a fusion of national, constitutional, regional, and sectional interests. The Articles as a single grouping were constantly reminded that they were to be a strictly preparatory committee, which was to report to Parliament and not to the king.

Areas of constitutional concern focused on the need for a redefinition of both the election and parliamentary powers of the Lords of the Articles. Each estate was to elect its own members to the Articles and there was to be no 'publick conclusione' of legislation discussed therein. Rather, the role of the Articles was to be of a preparatory nature only and prior to voting on legislation by the full estates a copy of the material to be voted on was to be issued to each estate for digestion and discussion on the day before the final vote. Freedom of speech was to be ensured; on the day of voting, after the reading of each article, each member was to be entitled to vote according to his own mind. This constituted a reaction against the king's behaviour in the 1633 Parliament. Stricter parliamentary control over the officials of the House was required to be employed; the right of appointment of the clerk of Parliament was to be transferred from the king to the Estates, indicating a limitation of the royal prerogative. On the day of voting on legislation presented by the Articles, representatives from each estate were to subscribe the conclusions reached, as a means of ensuring total parliamentary control of all legislation passed. Ultimate power and sovereignty was to rest with the Estates, without whose consent any legislation concluded by the Articles alone would be rendered null and void.

Within a broader constitutional perspective, the relationship between Parliament and the Privy Council required revision and redefinition. Parliament was to be the dominant of the two bodies and Privy Councillors were to be liable to parliamentary censure. Once more, this constituted a reaction against the post-1625 Scottish administration, when the bishops had played a prominent role, as royal appointees, in the operation of the Scottish Privy Council. In addition, proxy voting (as had been apparent in the 1633 Parliament) was to be abolished with voting rights being deemed non-transferable, as were the voting rights of 'strangers', a particular reference to the acquisition of Scottish titles by Englishmen (again a reaction against the experience of the post-1625 years).

Constitutional and procedural initiatives overlapped in demands for the regulation and control of parliamentary membership. The composition of the Scottish Parliament was to be redefined. In line with the expulsion of the bishops from Parliament, the 'Three Estates' were to be legally reconstituted as noblemen, commissioners of shires, and commissioners of burghs. The redefinition of the Three Estates was likewise extended to voting rights within the House, with voting restricted to members of Parliament. The relative voting strength of the shires was to be increased by a corresponding decrease of that of the nobility; those nobles who held high office as statesmen (Officers of State) were to be limited to one vote only and not two. By 19 October, during the sitting of the Articles, this had been further articulated to increase the actual voting power of the gentry by giving each shire commissioner a unique vote and not merely one vote per shire per se. Thus the voting power of the gentry was to be doubled. The influence of the gentry on the Tables was therefore to be matched by an augmentation in parliamentary voting power.

Further concerns for far-reaching constitutional change manifested themselves in the demand that separate annual conventions should be held for both the nobles and the commissioners of the shires, modelled along the lines already adopted by the Convention of Royal Burghs. Despite arguing from a position of precedence (with the existence of the Convention of Royal Burghs), in reality this was merely a cover for the continuation of the Tables, a demand which was to take a different and more specific form with the establishment of the Committee of Estates in 1640.

Detailed procedural proposals were to be implemented. This was a reflection firstly of unpopular procedural methods employed in the 1633 Parliament and secondly of a desire to establish Parliament as an effective and efficient national institution. Any member of Parliament was to have the right of handling any bill or supplication to the Articles during the sitting of Parliament, and he was to receive an appropriate response on his specific bill or supplication. This proposal appears to have its origins in the apprehension that the Articles in the past had received and rejected what they pleased to the grievance of the kingdom. Any previous legislation hindering these proposals was to be repealed.

The political aspirations of the gentry were not limited to control over parliamentary membership and procedure. The personnel of the judiciary was to be subject to parliamentary regulation. Significantly, no Lord of Session was to be appointed without the prior advice (meaning approval) of the nobles and gentry in the House. The exclusion of the burgesses may well have been an attempt by the gentry to marginalise the burgesses or to demonstrate their political independence from that estate. Justices of the Peace were to be elected by the commissioners of the shires, with the respective commissioner of shire in Parliament choosing the Justice of the Peace for his own locality. Once more this marked an increased confidence and political aggressiveness on the part of the gentry.[21]

Given the divisions among the nobility and the commercial interests of the burghs (which dominated burghal supplications to the Articles), it is clear that much of the radical initiatives stemmed from the gentry. A leading English correspondent observed that the demands of the gentry aimed at such things 'as quite overturn the very constitution of all future Parliaments.'[22]

On 6 September the ratification of the acts of the General Assembly was passed in Articles and a further ratification rescinding all former acts in favour of bishops or episcopacy was delivered to the King's Advocate, Hope of Craighall. Traquair subscribed the National Covenant twice on 6 September, both as King's Commissioner and as a noble per se. In the process of doing so, Traquair established the precedent (however unintentionally) that Parliament and the lieges of the kingdom were also to subscribe the National Covenant.

The following day, on 7 September, the act concerning the constitution of the 1639 Parliament was likewise delivered to Hope of Craighall (Argyll had asserted the legality and validity of the Parliament immediately on the opening of the Articles on 4 September). This provides a further indication that the Covenanting leadership had a significant body of material already constructed for presentation to the Articles. On 17 September it was agreed that the acts concerning the 1639 Parliament to be a perfect judicatory in terms of composition, that the abolition of episcopacy and the civil power of churchmen, and that of the constitution of all future Parliaments, were to be drawn up by three separate enactments. Speculation arises relating to the act of the constitution of all future Parliaments. Two rival acts had been handed in on 12 September, one by the King's Advocate, Hope of Craighall on the instructions of Traquair, and another by the Covenanters (who are not specified but were almost certainly members of the Fifth Table). This induced a long and controversial dispute concerning the constitution of Parliament. Traquair desired that the ecclesiastical estate be replaced by abbots and priors, whilst the Covenanters sought their place to be taken by the gentry.

A compromise act was passed on 24 September, which proved unacceptable to several leading Covenanters. Although no details of this compromise act exist, pamphlet material indicates that doubt existed concerning the ability of this act to pass in Parliament, despite having gone through the Articles, on the grounds of the absence of a whole estate (the clergy); hence the need for the shires to be reconstituted as the third estate. Two days later, on 26 September, Loudoun accompanied by several Covenanting representatives (in effect the Tables), demanded the withdrawal of the compromise act whilst producing another of their own to be read in Articles. This latter act was designed to pass in the full Parliament.

Part of Traquair's strategy to provoke dissension and division amongst the Covenanters on the Articles had been to keep the Articles in session for as long as possible to the point whereby he might gain the support of a majority to enable a delay in deciding constitutional concerns. He also attempted to cultivate political support away from the Covenanting leadership over all three estates. Traquair obviously thought that this position had been achieved by 4 October when he announced that Parliament would meet on 8 October to vote on matters presented by the Articles. Traquair might also have calculated that he wanted to limit the extent of Covenanting gains. Direct evidence of voting behaviour in Articles is sparse but on 5 October Traquair demanded a vote on whether or not proposals for regulation of the power of the Lords of the Articles were to be referred to the king or voted on by Parliament.

Although the majority of the nobles (five out of eight) and all the Officers of State sided with Traquair in his demand for referral to the king and despite the fact that Traquair had successfully lured two gentry and one burgess to his mind, the combined strength of the gentry and burgesses in tandem with three nobles (Argyll, Lindsay, and Rothes), was sufficient to secure a vote in full Parliament on the act of the constitution of future Parliaments. The final voting analysis was as follows: fourteen for a vote in Parliament, twelve for referral to the king, with two members being absent (one shire and one burgh representive). Traquair went on the defensive after this crucial vote and did not hold the planned meeting of Parliament on 8 October. Instead he delayed such a meeting on eight occasions until 14 November.

The rescinding of previous acts in favour of episcopacy and the civil power of churchmen was extended on 18 September to cover their rights of riding to and voting in Parliament. The Act Recissory consequently passed through Articles on 24 September for presentation to the Estates.[23]

By 23 October a Covenanting delegation had approached Traquair and complained of the long sitting of the Articles. Nevertheless, the Articles continued to sit until 30 October. On 1 November Parliament commissioned Loudoun and Charles Seton, 2nd Earl of Dunfermline, former Gentleman of the Bedchamber to Charles I, to proceed to the king to seek his consent to the acts passed in Articles. Royal assent was refused on the grounds that the commission had not been signed by Traquair as King's Commissioner. Charles consequently ordered Traquair to prorogue the Parliament to 2 June 1640 (Loudoun and Dunfermline returned to Edinburgh on 29 November). In the intervening period Charles aimed to have subdued the Covenanters by physical force, thus enabling him to reverse Covenanting innovations in Kirk and State. After repeated postponements and a handout of honours to Royalist nobles on 31 October, a full meeting of the Estates was held on 14 November. At this diet Traquair immediately prorogued Parliament to 2 June 1640, despite Covenanting protestations that it was an unprecedented event for the Estates to be prorogued without their own consent and despite concerns voiced over the legality of the manner of prorogation. The senior clerk of Parliament had refused to obey instructions to declare the Parliament prorogued, as did the junior clerk, and Traquair had consequently taken the matter of prorogation into his own hands with the use of a private warrant. The Tables had been preparing for prorogation since 28 October. The Estates protested that they were a sitting Parliament and stressed the need for legislation to determine future nomination of the Articles by the separate estates. Furthermore, members of each estate were selected to remain in Edinburgh, with full parliamentary authority, to await the king's reply on their remonstrances and before dissolving. In effect, this constituted a continuation of the Tables and was referred to as the 'Committee', being the forerunner of the Committee of Estates formally sanctioned in 1640. The 'Committee' became more concerned with military preparations for the Second Bishops' War than awaiting fruitless replies from Charles.

Traquair himself had doubted the legality of prorogation and convinced the leading Covenanters, called before the Privy Council, that if the Estates willingly dissolved then the king would hear any of their representations, but if they continued to sit it would be under the pain of treason. Following the failure of the Loudoun-Dunfermline mission to gain access to the king, a further supplication was then delivered by William Cunningham of Brownhill to Charles on behalf of the Estates seeking his ratification of legislation passed in Articles, but Cunningham returned to Edinburgh on 23 December empty-handed.[24]

In spite of Traquair's threats and in light of the failure of the Cunningham mission, a decision was taken on 23 December by the parliamentary representatives remaining in Edinburgh (especially the nobles and the burgesses) to issue communications to all the nobles, commissioners of the shires, and commissioners of the burghs who had been present in the 1639 Parliament to convene in a full meeting of the Estates on 11 January 1640. The remit of the meeting was to decide on future policy options. The meeting actually took place on both 15 and 16 January 1640. Alexander Leslie, commander-in-chief of the Covenanting forces was also present, indicating that it was specifically military issues that were on the agenda, given the run-up to the outbreak of the Second Bishops' War. A contemporary pamphleteer commented on the 'Resolutione of the Parliamentaire Men'; 'neither armes nor allurements, neither threats nor promises can by divisione gayne dominion against the conscience of the Covenant of God'. The pamphleteer further noted that the Covenanters were determined to 'to take hold of the present opportunitie which god and the king hath putt in their hands'.[25]

Leslie appears to have played a leading role in the course of action to be taken. It was upon his initiative and advice that a commission was decided upon to go once more and present the grievances of the Estates. This commission of four was composed of Loudoun, Sir William Douglas of Cavers (Roxburgh), and Robert Barclay (Irvine), although Dunfermline was also included for his high diplomatic standing. Following an inconclusive meeting of the Privy Council, the commissioners left for Court on 31 January, where they succeeded in gaining a royal hearing. The deputation insisted to Charles that prorogation should be by act of Parliament or consent of the Estates, but refused to commit themselves fully on the extent of royal power on this particular. The deputation stressed that the Articles should be abolished and replaced by a parliamentary committee accountable to Parliament itself. This was well appreciated at Court as greatly diminishing the royal prerogative in Scotland. Furthermore, the Covenanters had manipulated the situation to their advantage by insisting that no governor of either England or Scotland was to be placed in any of the royal garrisons without the consent of Parliament; thus 'upon the death or removal of every governor a Parliament must be called or for ever continued,' a clear countermeasure against the repeated prorogations of Parliament.[26]

Conclusion

The Scottish constitutional settlement enacted in 1640–41 owes its origins to the work of the Tables in 1639. The gentry, in particular, and the burgesses were campaigning vigorously for constitutional reform. Whilst the noble representatives on the Lords of the Articles were split between radicals, conservatives and Royalists, gentry and burghal representation formed a solid phalanx of voting power to drive through the Covenanting agenda in the Articles. Such a programme of constitutional reform was a reaction against the experience of the post-1625 administration in general and the 1633 Parliament in particular. The employment of bishops in public office and partisan royal nominees was to cease. Effective political power was to be transferred from the Crown and invested in Parliament. By the close of the 1639 Parliament the Royalist party in Scotland was on the defensive. Charles I had been forced to prorogue the session in order to avoid further political advancement by the Covenanters.

NOTES

1. NLS Adv. MS 19.3.8, Sir James Balfour, Collection of Pasquinades, folio 24.
2. HMC, 11th Report, appendix, *The Manuscripts of the Duke of Hamilton* (London 1887), 95, 96; SRO Dalhousie Muniments, GD 45/1/53; NLS Wodrow Quarto LXXXVII, number 22, folio 130; NLS Wodrow Folio LXIV, number 7, folio 1; NLS Adv MS 19.1.17, Papers Concerning the Covenanters, 1637–86, folio 7; G. Donaldson & W.C. Dickinson (eds.), *A Source Book of Scottish History*, volume III, (1567–1707), (Edinburgh, 1961), 101; W.A. Balcanqual, *A Declaration concerning the Late Tumults in Scotland* (Edinburgh, 1639), 109, 122; G. Burnet, *The Memoirs of the Lives and Actions of James and William, Dukes of Hamiltons and Castleherald* (London, 1838), 126; J. Rushworth (ed.), *Historical Collections*, volume II (i), 753, 940; G.M. Paul (ed.), *Fragment of the Diary of Sir Archibald Johnston of Wariston, 1639*, (SHS, Edinburgh, 1896), 28, 72, 74; Stevenson, *Scottish Revolution*, 169; MacInnes, 'The Scottish Constitution, 1638–1651. 2, 5; J.D. Mackie, *A History of Scotland* (1st edn., Middlesex, 1964), 208.
3. *APS*, v, 248–249; NLS MS 2263, Salt and Coal: Events, 1635–1662, folio 165; NLS AdvMS 32.4.8, 'A Short History of The Reformation of Religion in Scotland, England & Ireland and of The Wars carried on by King Charles The First in these Three Kingdoms during his Reign', folio 4; K. Sharpe, *The Personal Rule of Charles I* (London, 1992), 808; Rait, *The Parliaments of Scotland*, 374.
4. NLS Deposit 175, Gordon of Cumming Papers, Box 81, folio 9; NLS Adv MS 19.3.8, Sir James Balfour, Collection of Pasquinades, folio 16; NLS Adv MS 29.2.9, Papers Concerning the Covenanters, folio 128; Rait, *The Parliaments of Scotland*, 374; P. Yorke, earl of Hardwicke (ed.), *Miscellaneous State Papers, 1501–1726*, volume II, 103, 134–35; W.D. Macray (ed.), *The Ruthven Correspondence* (Roxburghe Club, London, 1828), 57; Stevenson, *Scottish Revolution*, 166; D. Stevenson, *The Government of Scotland Under the Covenanters*, SHS, (1982), xxi; Donaldson, *Source Book of Scottish History*, III, 105, 114; A.I. MacInnes, 'Covenanting Revolution and Municipal Enterprise', *History Today*, volume 40 (May, 1990),

10; W. Makey, *The Church of the Covenant 1637–1651. Revolution and Social Change in Scotland* (Edinburgh, 1979), 23–4, 25.

5. D. Stevenson, 'The General Assembly and the Commission of the Kirk, 1638–51', *RCHS*, XIX (1977), 59; Makey, *The Church of the Covenant*, 45–6, 48, 50–1.
6. W.A. Balcanqual, *A Declaration concerning the Late Tumults in Scotland* (Edinburgh, 1639).
7. Hardwicke, *State Papers*, 118; *CSPV*, 1639, 559; NLS Adv MS 19.1.17, Papers Concerning the Covenanters, ff.3, 7; Rushworth, *Historical Collections*, II (ii), 942; *Fragment of the Diary of Sir Archibald Johnston of Wariston*, 72; Stevenson, *Scottish Revolution*, 152, 169; MacInnes, 'Covenanting Revolution and Municipal Enterprise', *History Today*, volume 40 (May 1990), 10; P. Donald, *An Uncounselled King. Charles I and the Scottish Troubles, 1637–1641*, (Cambridge, 1989), 206–207.
8. *CSPV*, 1636–1639, 418.
9. Donaldson, *Source Book of Scottish History*, III, 115; Stevenson, *Government Under the Covenanters*, xxi; Stevenson, *Scottish Revolution*, 117; MacInnes, 'The Scottish Constitution, 1638–51', 111.
10. NLS Wodrow Folio LXIV, number seven; MacInnes, *Charles I and the Making of the Covenanting Movement*, 87; D.G. Mullan, *Episcopacy in Scotland: The History of an Idea, 1560–1638* (Edinburgh, 1986), 173, 187, 196; G. Donaldson, *Scotland. The Shaping of a Nation* (Newton Abbot, 1974), 96; Terry, *The Scottish Parliament*, 110–1; Rait, *The Parliaments of Scotland*, 370–1; Sir Robert Gordon, 'Anent the Government of Scotland as it wes befor the late troubles', in W. MacFarlane, *Geographical Collections Relating to Scotland*, (SHS, Edinburgh, 1907), 398–9.
11. SRO RH2/2/14, Cosmo Innes Transcripts, volume II, number 30, Anent the Committee of parliament called the committee of articles, ff. 14–15; *Source Book of Scottish History*, III, 234; Terry, *The Scottish Parliament*, 110; Rait, *Parliaments of Scotland*, 279–80, 370–371; Sir David Dalrymple, Lord Hailes, *Memorials and Letters relating to the History of Britain in the reign of Charles I* (Glasgow, 1766), 47–48; MacInnes, *Charles I and the Making of the Covenanting Movement*, 87–89; C. Carlton, *Charles I. The Personal Monarch* (London, 1983), 186.
12. *CSPV*, 1638, 418; Rushworth, *Historical Collections*, II (ii), 942; NLS Wodrow Folio LXIV, number 39; *Fragment of the Diary of Sir Archibald Johnston of Wariston, 1639*, 73–74, 77.
13. NLS Adv MS 19.1.17, Papers Concerning the Covenanters, folio 171; *CSPV*, 1639, 562.
14. HMC, 9th Report, part ii, appendix, *Traquhair Muniments*, (London, 1887), 249–250; SRO Hamilton Papers, GD 406/1/1031; NLS Wodrow Folio LXIV, folio 10; NLS MS 2263 Salt and Coal: Events, 1635–62, folio 166; *APS*, v, 248–49; S.R. Gardiner, *The Fall of the Monarchy of Charles I, 1637–42*, two vols, (London, 1882), I, 249; S.R. Gardiner, *History of England from the Accession of James I to the Outbreak of the Civil War 1603–1642*, 10 vols, IX, 1639–1641, (London, 1884), 51; A.I. MacInnes, 'The Origin and Organization of the Covenanting Movement during the reign of Charles I, 1625–41; with a particular reference to the west of Scotland', (University of Glasgow, PhD thesis, 1987), two volumes, volume two, 287.
15. R.K. Hannay & G.P.H. Watson, 'The Building of the Parliament House', *The Book of the Old Edinburgh Club*, XIII, (Edinburgh, 1924), 1–78.
16. *APS*, v, 7–9, 251–252; A. Peterkin (ed.), *Records of the Kirk of Scotland, containing the Acts and Proceedings of the General Assemblies, 1630–54* (Edinburgh, 1838), 109–11. Archibald Campbell, 8th Earl of Argyll, is not recorded in the membership

rolls of the Glasgow Assembly, although he did play a part in its proceedings (eg. see Stevenson, *Scottish Revolution*, 123). Membership details for the 1639 General Assembly are incomplete. According to this roll, eight of the 50 nobles (16%), three of the 47 gentry (6%) and 14 of the 52 burgesses (27%) in the 1639 Parliament were also present in the 1639 General Assembly. Three burgesses present in the 1639 General Assembly had not attended the Glasgow Assembly; George Hempseid (Cullen), John Douglas (Elgin) and Duncan Forbes (Inverness). The analysed figures for common membership of the Parliaments of 1633 and 1639 include Officers of State, but do not include the proxy votes exercised in the 1633 Parliament. According to the dates of the parliamentary commissions for the shires and burghs, the bulk of elections had been held in August 1639, although eight commissions for the shires are dated between 2 and 8 October 1638. This indicates that preparations for a parliamentary session were being made in the run up to the Glasgow Assembly (SRO Parliamentary Commissions, PA 7/25/2–101).

17. *APS*, v, 252–253. Terry, *The Scottish Parliament*, 311; NLS Wodrow Folio LXIV, number 45; NLS MS 2263 Salt and Coal: Events, 1635–62, folio 166; SRO Breadalbane Muniments, GD 112/39/786; SRO Hamilton Papers, GD 406/1/1070; SRO Montrose Papers, GD 220/4/78; Gardiner, *History of England*, IX, 50–2; Gardiner, *The Fall of the Monarchy of Charles I*, volume one, 253; Rait, *Parliaments of Scotland*, 374–375; Stevenson, *Scottish Revolution*, 171; MacInnes, *Charles I and the Making of the Covenanting Movement*, 82–83; J. Gordon, *History of Scots Affairs, 1637–41*, J. Robertson & G. Grub eds., (Spalding Club, Aberdeen, 1841), II, 64; *Scots Peerage*, I, 133–136, VI, 164; Sharpe, *The Personal Rule of Charles I*, 777; M. Lee Junior, *The Road to Revolution: Scotland under Charles 1st, 1625–37* (University of Illinois, 1985), 44, 47, 108.
18. *APS*, v, 9–10, 252–254; *Scots Peerage*, IV, 546, VI, 57, 244–45, VII, 297–298, VIII, 65; Balfour, *Historical Works*, II, 360–61; Hardwicke, *Miscellaneous State Papers*, II, 115–116; Burnet, *The Memoirs of the Dukes of Hamilton*, 53; Stevenson, *Scottish Revolution*, 171; MacInnes, 'The Origin and Organization of the Covenanting Movement', PhD thesis, volume two, 288; *Memoirs of the Marquis of Montrose*, (Edinburgh, 1856), I, 252, 254–55; HMC, 11th Report, appendix, *The Manuscripts of the Duke of Hamilton* (London, 1887), 98.
19. *APS*, v, 9–10, 251–252, 252–54. *Dumbarton Common Good Accounts, 1614–60*, F. Roberts & I.M.M. Macphail eds, (Dumbarton, 1972); *Dumbarton Burgh Records, 1627–1746* (1860), 60. John Semple had been elected to the Tables from 1637 (*Ibid*, 5); *Charters and Documents Relating to the City of Glasgow, 1175–1649*, part 1, ed. J.D. Marwick, (Glasgow, 1897), ccclxxix; *Extracts from the Records of the Royal Burgh of Stirling, 1519–1666*, ed. R. Renwick (Glasgow, 1887), 181–182; *Aberdeen Council Letters*, II, 135. The geographic composition of the Articles of 1639 remained virtually identical for the shires, but witnessed a move towards the west at the expense of the east for the burghs. Makey asserts that Stirling of Keir and Douglas of Cavers were friends of Montrose (*The Church of the Covenant*, 51).
20. This particularly applies to Stevenson, *Scottish Revolution*, and MacInnes, 'The Origin and Organization of the Covenanting Movement' (PhD thesis). The political role of the gentry must also be reassessed in light of Keith Brown's emphasis on the Scottish aristocracy in *Kingdom or Province?* (London, 1992), and Roger Mason in 'The Aristocracy, Episcopacy and the Revolution of 1638' in *Covenant, Charter, andParty. Traditions of revolt and protest in modern Scottish History*, ed., T. Brotherstone (Aberdeen, 1989). Peter Donald in *An Uncounselled King*, 212–213, has

noted the importance of legislation prepared in the Articles in 1639 and the political importance of the gentry and the burgesses. Nevertheless, Laing noted the significance of legislation enacted in 1640–1 which had been prepared in the Articles of 1639; M. Laing, *The History of Scotland from the Union of the Crowns on the Accession of James VI to the Throne of England, to the Union of the Kingdoms in the Reign of Queen Anne*, four vols, (3rd edn., London, 1819), III, 184–187, 191.

21. NLS Wodrow Folio LXIV, numbers 8, 26 and 39; SRO Breadalbane Muniments, GD 112/39/786, GD 112/39/789; *CSPD*, 1639, 508–509; *CSPD*, 1639–1640, 6; *APS*, v, 247–258, appendix 593–618; *Aberdeen Council Letters*, II, 135, 148; Gordon, *History of Scots Affairs*, III, 63–82; Gardiner, *The Fall of the Monarchy of Charles I*, I, 257; Gardiner, *History of England*, IX., 53–4; Stevenson, *Scottish Revolution*, 172–174; MacInnes, 'The Origin and Organization of the Covenanting Movement, PhD thesis, volume two, 288–289. The main thrust of the supplications handed in by the burghs were concerned with economic and commercial interests.
22. *CSPD*, 1639, 508–509; Gardiner, *History of England*, IX, 53–4.
23. *APS*, v. appendix 593–618; SRO Hamilton Papers, GD 406/1/1070; NLS MS 2263 Salt and Coal: Events, 1635–62; NLS Wodrow Quarto LXXVI, Number 22, folio 129, Number 24, ff 132–133; NLS Wodrow Folio LXIV, Number 8; SRO Breadalbane Muniments, GD 112/39/789–91; SRO Airlie Muniments, GD 16/40/4; SRO RH2/2/14, Cosmo Innes's Transcripts, volume II, number 30; Balfour, *Historical Works*, II, 361–362; Gordon, *History of Scots Affairs*, III, 66–68; Stevenson, *Scottish Revolution*, 173–177; Rait, *Parliaments of Scotland*, 375; Baillie, *Letters and Journals*, I, 224. A large body of material passed through Articles which reflected Parliament's role as a dominant national institution. Parliament had not met for six years and a vast body of supplications had been submitted for consideration of a local, economic, judicial, educational and ecclesiastical nature. The increased political clout of the gentry was matched by demands for increased renumeration/expenses for parliamentary attendance.
24. *APS*, v, appendix 616, 255–58; SRO GD 406/M1/87; NLS MS 2263 Salt and Coal: Events, 1635–62, folio 167; *CSPV*, 1636–1639, 600; *RPCS*, 1638–43, 141–142; Balfour, *Historical Works*, II, 361–363, 364–368; Gordon, *History of Scots Affairs*, II, 74–78; *Scots Peerage*, I, 32, 311, 746, II, 464, III, 373; Rait, *Parliaments of Scotland*, 65–66; Stevenson, *Scottish Revolution*, 175–177; MacInnes, 'The Origin and Organization of the Covenanting Movement', PhD thesis, volume two, 288–289; Sharpe, *The Personal Rule of Charles I*, 836–7; The main royal handouts on 31 October were as follows; Hamilton's brother, William, was created 1st Earl of Lanark, James, Lord Ogilvie created 1st Earl of Airlie, Lord Dalziel created 1st Earl of Carnwath and Sir Patrick Ruthven, governor of Edinburgh Castle, was created Lord Ruthven of Ettrick.
25. NLS Wodrow Quarto LXXVII, Number 22; Rait, *Parliaments of Scotland*, 375.
26. NLS MS 2263 Salt and Coal: Events, 1635–62, folio 168; *CSPD*, 1639–1640, 534–535.

2

The Scottish Constitutional Settlement of 1640–41

> Wipe away those teares from your eyes (Countreymen)
> which you have shed for the departure of your King,
> for he is as welcome to his native Scots, as ever
> was the Sun to the frozen earth.[1]

Within a British perspective, events had turned to the Covenanters' advantage before the planned meeting of the Estates on 2 June 1640. Charles had been forced to call the English Short Parliament, the first session of Parliament in England since 1629, on 13 April to secure further military and financial support in the conflict with the Covenanters. The Short Parliament, however, had failed to be as amenable to royal wishes as Charles had hoped for, and had provided an excuse for Covenanting forces to be strengthened in preparation for the Second Bishops' War. In addition, the Tables had been issuing literature in England urging English commissioners to the Short Parliament to galvanise opposition to the Crown in terms of English grievances. The four Scottish diplomatic commissioners had been arrested prior to the opening of the Short Parliament, although Dunfermline, Douglas of Cavers (Roxburgh), and Robert Barclay (Irvine) (but not Loudoun) had returned to Edinburgh on 20 May. They were issued with an order from the king to prorogue the session of 2 June to 7 July. Lord Advocate Craighall, confined to his home since January 1640 in light of Royalist suspicion at Court of his Covenanting sympathies, was likewise ordered by Charles to assist in the prorogation.

However, the Estates sat in defiance of Charles's attempt at prorogation by mere royal proclamation and argued that prorogations had always taken place in Parliament. Craighall attempted to use a commission under the quarter seal, issued in August 1639 allowing himself and three others (Lord Elphinstone, Lord Napier, and the Justice-Clerk) to act as king's commissioner in Parliament in the absence of Traquair, as a legal basis to prorogue the House. When Craighall attempted to implement this the other two officials refused their consent, as they had received none from Traquair, which nullified any legality of this controversial commission. Craighall himself acknowledged this. On the part of the Covenanting leadership, the subsequent lack of legally constituted orders of prorogation amounted to 'a Tacite consent' and 'presumed allowance' that Parliament had a legal right to convene.[2]

The Second Session of the Second Parliament of Charles I, 2–11 June 1640

1. The Composition of the Second Parliament of Charles I

Thirty-six nobles, 43 gentry representing3 shires, and 52 burgesses representing 51 burghs (131 individuals in total) constituted the parliamentary membership as per 2 June 1640. In terms of numerical composition per estate, this constitutes a reduction of 14 nobles and four gentry compared to the 1639 Parliament. Burghal numerical composition remained identical over both sessions. Thirty of the 36 nobles (83%), 39 of the 43 gentry (91%), and 47 of the 52 burgesses (90%) present in Parliament, 2 June 1640, had also been included in the 1639 Parliament (see appendices 2a and 2b). Therefore there was a high retention of personnel between the two sessions, indicating efficient party management by the Covenanting leadership.[3]

2. The Proceedings of the Second Session of the Parliament of Charles I

In the absence of a king's commissioner, the Estates took the unprecedented step of electing their own President for the current session; the radical noble Robert Balfour, 2nd Lord Burleigh. The process of constitutional defiance continued unhindered. The Estates sat for only nine days, but enacted sixty items of legislation (53 of which were public acts) in the parliamentary ratification of constitutional revolution. This corresponded to the constitutional agenda issued by the Covenanting oligarchy/Tables from 1638–39 and presented in Articles from 2 September to 30 October 1639.[4]

Following the election of Burleigh as President, the Estates wasted no time in sweeping through the most important piece of legislation; the Act anent the Constitution of the present and all future Parliaments (which had caused so much controversy in Articles). The legitimacy of the June 1640 session was sanctioned as a 'compleit and perfyte Parliament' and was to have the 'samene power and authoritie and Jurisdictione as absolutlie and fullie As any Parliament formerlie'. The three estates were redefined as consisting of Noblemen, Barons (in reality the gentry), and Burgesses. Voting rights were restricted to these three political groupings. The fact that the gentry were the driving force on the Tables was recognised by the doubling of the voting strength of the gentry. Previously the voting powers were invested solely in the shire, even although each shire was represented by two commissioners. Now each commissioner of the shire was entitled to an individual vote.[5]

As an integral component of the reconstitution of the three estates, the clerical estate was abolished and the civil power of any ecclesiastical dignitaries (archbishops, bishops, abbots, priors, or prelates) in Parliament was rescinded. Legislation of the Parliaments of 1597 (the Act anent Parsons and Prelates representing the Third Estate) and 1606 (the Act anent the restitution of the Bishops and their reconstitution as the Third Estate) were rescinded. The voting powers of the shire commissioners had been expanded at the expense of the clerical estate.[6]

The assertion of parliamentary independence continued with further voting regulation. Proxy votes were abolished and a financial criterion was applied to all 'strangers' (ie foreign noblemen, meaning Englishmen) possessing voting rights. This constituted a reaction against the 1633 Parliament where 19 nobles had been represented by proxies. Traditionally lordship of Parliament was directly related to ownership of land, but in 1627 Charles had conferred three Scottish peerages on Englishmen; Thomas Fairfax as Lord Fairfax of Cameron, Thomas Barrett as Lord Barrett of Newburgh, and Walter Aston as Lord Aston of Forfar. Lord Falkland and his successors had also been declared as naturalised Scottish subjects. No granting of land was involved in all cases. This was rectified by the 1640 Parliament. No foreign nobleman was henceforth entitled to parliamentary membership unless he possessed at least 10,000 merks (£6,667 Scots) worth of land in Scotland.[7]

Apart from the abolition of the clerical estate as a legal component of Parliament, further ratification of the Glasgow Assembly's proceedings included a broad scope of ecclesiastical issues. Both the Act anent the Ratification of the Acts of the Assembly and the Act of Recissory (abolishing all previous legislation detrimental to presbyterianism and replacing the functions of the bishoprics with that of the presbyteries) received parliamentary ratification on 6 June. Further ecclesiastical legislation dealt with two issues; the problems of churches formerly under the control of bishoprics which had now become vacant, and the plantation of kirks. Compulsory subscription of the National Covenant and the Confession of Faith was required by all the lieges of the kingdom. Subscription was deemed necessary for the holding of all public office and can be interpreted as a weapon of party management to exclude all opponents of the National Covenant.[8]

The bulk of legislation enacted concerned itself with procedural innovation. The reform of procedure within the House was designed to make the Estates more responsible for their own proceedings and regulation. It was a direct reaction against previous Crown management of parliamentary business through the Lords of the Articles and constitutional intimidation as evidenced in the Coronation Parliament. At the beginning of each parliamentary session all books, registers and parliamentary records were to be exhibited to the assembled estates and were to be made available for inspection at any required time during a parliamentary session. In future all grievances were to be given in open Parliament, and not to the Clerk Register as previously established by an enactment of 1594 (which was annulled). The use of the Committee of Articles/Lords of Articles was deemed to be optional and not mandatory in all subsequent Parliaments:

> All subsequent parliaments may according to the importance of effaires for the tyme either choose or not choose severall Committies for Articles as they shall thinke expedient.[9]

If employed, the remit of such a committee(s) was strictly limited to that of a preparatory nature, and the estates were given the freedom to elect their own representatives to it/them separately. Any such preparatory committees were not only limited in dealing with matters presented in open Parliament, but were also compelled to report all their deliberations back to the Estates for discussion before voting. All related voting was similarly to take place in open Parliament.[10]

The expedient of an optional Committee of Articles appears to have been employed on 2 June (four days prior to the enactment of the relevant legislation) with the establishment of the session committee for 'Reveising the paperis agitat in Articles' in 1639. This marked a fundamental step in the constitutional process and was elected 'by the haill bodie of the Estatis promiscouoslie togidder and not seperatlie by ilke ane of thrie estatis apairt'[11], for revising all the papers and supplications handed in during the Articles in 1639. Composed of four per estate, the committee was dominated by radicals who thus gained control in the priority of bills and overtures which were to be presented to the House. Three of the leading radical nobles, Argyll, Rothes, and Balmerino secured inclusion and led the committee. Argyll and Rothes, plus two gentry and two burgesses on the committee, had been members of the 1639 Lords of Articles. Technical expertise had been matched with Covenanting enthusiasm to provide an efficient grouping of human resources to process parliamentary legislation.[12] Acting as a reformed Lords of the Articles, therefore, the constitutional ideal of election by each estate was already in practice (on 2 June) before receiving full parliamentary sanction of the reconstitution of the Articles as an optional expedient (6 June).

Complementing the unprecedented reconstitution of the Articles by the authority of the Estates themselves and strengthening the magnitude of constitutional revolution, the Triennial Act (6 June) and Act 43 (10 June) asserted the sovereignty of Parliament as the ultimate court of the realm and the right of Parliament to convene on a regular basis and on its own authority. Under the terms of the Triennial Act, a 'full and frie' Parliament was to be held at least every three years. The motive behind this was the restoration of the practice of frequent Parliaments before the departure of James VI to England in 1603. It was also designed to hinder a return to arbitrary government. Before the conclusion of any future Parliaments the time and venue of the next Parliament were to be determined by the king's commissioner, with the approval of the Estates, and was to be constituted in the final legislative enactment of such Parliaments. Therefore the Estates could convene in future without the formality of a royal summons. In British terms, the Scottish Triennial Act provided a constitutional precedent for its English counterpart enacted in the Long Parliament.

The upholding of the enactments of Parliament as the supreme national legislature was enshrined in Act 43, which ordained all subjects and lieges of the country to 'obey menteene and defend the conclusiones Actes and constitutiones' of the current parliamentary session of Parliament. All were required to subscribe a band declaring the legality of the parliamentary session. In view of the requirement of compulsory subscription of the National Covenant, these combined measures ensured that only adherents to the Covenanting cause could gain access to public office.[13]

Nevertheless, the legislative programme was not restricted to the remedying of past abuses and the introduction of procedural innovations. Act 24 (8 June), the Act constituting a Committee of Estates to sit until the next session of Parliament, not only signifies parliamentary approval of the conduct of the Tables from 1637–1640, but also marks the initiation of a parliamentary committee as a provisional government between parliamentary sessions.

Justified as a temporary expedient on the grounds that the country was under the threat of 'utter exterminoun and totall distructione' and in consequent need of an institution to order, govern and direct the kingdom in light of this threat, the Committee of Estates was given remarkbly wide powers. Full power was given by Parliament to the committee to preserve and maintain the armed forces. It was also accorded powers for dealing with civil and public order, thereby circumventing the Privy Council, the College of Justice, and other judicial bodies (although this was strenuously denied in the terms of the commission). Stringent fiscal and economic powers were included in the remit of the committee, with full authority to borrow and levy money for public use, determine levels of taxation and collect any taxation revenue, and appoint auditors to examine and report on any appropriate accounts. The authority of the Committee of Estates as a national institution included further powers to order and direct all shires, burghs, presbyteries, stewarties, regalities, and all local committees.

Although the committee received its commission from Parliament and was ultimately answerable to the House, its composition was not restricted to parliamentary members. Full warrant was given to 'call and convene' any noble, laird or burgess or any other appropriate individual for their assistance where the committee thought it necessary and expedient. As an indication of an institution gearing itself towards war, all general officers of the army were given the right of attendance.[14]

Further legislation of the June 1640 session complemented the formal establishment of the Committee of Estates in preparation for war. On 4 June a session committee for the provision of the army was established, staffed by Covenanting activists from all three estates, with the notable inclusion of Burleigh and Lothian, supplemented by the General of the armed forces, Alexander Leslie. The committee was formed to maximise the use of existing economic resources to secure an efficient supply network for the army. On 4 June the Act for the Border Shires sanctioned the immediate mobilisation of Covenanting troops to resist any English invasion. Building upon retrospective legislation, Act 23 concerning the Common Relief, established a national system of collection for the tenth penny per head per rent in each presbyetry and burgh raised from 1639 as a contribution to the First Bishops' War. The leadership of personnel of the Covenanting armed forces was ratified on 9 June.[15]

The powers of the Exchequer were redefined. The Lords of the Exchequer were to be 'onlie Judges'. According to Balfour, this legislation was constructed with Traquair specifically in mind. As Treasurer in the 1630s Traquair had abused the Exchequer to look after the interests of his close political associates. The Act against Leasing Makers was similarly aimed against Traquair and the other four Incendiaries who had given 'bad informations to his Maiesty and counsell of England, contrarey to the treuthe and quhat was really done and acted by the couenanters.' The concept of treason was expanded to include all those who initiated or were involved in policy options prejudicial to the objectives of the Covenanting Movement. This is consistent with the requirement of compulsory subscription of the National Covenant and the Confession of Faith for the holding of public office and banding defending the authority and enactments of the June 1640 session.[16]

An overview of the legislative programme enacted in the June 1640 session in an assessment of the royal prerogative vis-a-vis the independence of the Scottish Parliament, reveals that the power of the former had been clearly diminished whilst that of the latter had been greatly enhanced. In the words of Sir James Balfour, the session exhibited

> the reall grattest change at ane blow that euer hapned to this churche and staite thesse 600 years baypast; for in effecte it ouerturned not onlie the ancient state gouernment, bot fettered monarchie with chynes and sett new limitts and marckes to the same, beyond wich it was not legally to proceed.[17]

The fact that the political initiative now lay firmly with the Covenanting leadership, led by the radicals, and that the Estates were determined to control their own proceedings, was reflected on 11 June when Parliament decided to reconvene of its own accord on 19 November 1640.[18]

3. The Appointment of Parliamentary Interval Committees

Twelve nobles, 16 gentry, and 12 burgesses (40 individuals in total) formed the membership of the Committee of Estates established on 8 June 1640.[19] Noble representation was dominated by radicals, particularly Rothes, Cassillis, Lothian, Wigtown, Balmerino, Coupar, and Burleigh. The omission of Argyll is due to his parliamentary commission to secure Covenanting interests against the Earl of Atholl, Lord Ogilvie, and the Farquharsons in the north of the country. Nobles on the conservative wing of the movement also secured inclusion. Montrose, Dunfermline, Napier, and Loure come into this category. Their inclusion probably amounts to a degree of flexibility amongst the Covenanting leadership in retaining a balance of nobles who had the king's ear and might be used in any subsequent relations with the Court.

Representation of the gentry amounted in total to 16, despite the fact that the committee had been deemed to consist of equal numbers (12 per estate). Three of the 16 were included in the judicial capacity as Senators of the College of Justice. Whilst gentry representation was dominated by Covenanting activists, eight of the 16 gentry (50%) were not members of Parliament as per 2 June 1640, three of whom were the Senators of the College of Justice. Of the additional five non-parliamentary gentry, the majority were from the south-west and the central belt. In overall terms, gentry representation was dominated by the east (eight gentry), but also included representation from the central belt (four gentry), the west (two gentry), and the Borders (two gentry).

By way of comparison, seven of the 12 burgess members of the Committee of Estates were not members of Parliament as per 2 June 1640, the majority of whom (five) represented eastern burghs. All non-parliamentary burgess members represented 'top ten' burghs as per the order of the burghs in the parliamentary rolls. Their respective burghs had been represented by other commissioners in the June 1640 session. Of the total burgh representation (12), only Montrose (number 13) and Jedburgh (number 23) lay outside the top ten burghs as per the June 1640 parliamentary rolls. Of these twelve, only three burghs (Glasgow, Ayr, and Jedburgh) did not come from the east coast. Overall burghal representation was based on the east coast stretching from Linlithgow to Aberdeen, but particularly concentrated on Edinburgh. Edinburgh, the capital, gained one third of burghal representation on the Committee of Estates. Two additional Edinburgh burgesses supplemented the capital's parliamentary commissioners. This can be explained by the fact that not only was Edinburgh the focus of political life, but also the centre of financial activity and capital accumulation. Edinburgh burgesses were particularly involved in financial speculation to provide a sound financial basis to the muscle behind the Covenanting Movement.[20]

Gentry and burghal representation was not directly related to parliamentary membership. This indicates that grass-roots activists were being brought on to the most important parliamentary committee established to date. In effect, the Committee of Estates was a formal institutionalisation of the Tables.

The Committee of Estates was not restricted to convening in Edinburgh. It was severed into two sections. One section was to remain in Edinburgh (or any other convenient place) as a provisional government. The other was to accompany the Covenanting armed forces on all military manoeuvres. The sections were to be divided in such a manner that neither 'the army nor the countrie at ant tyme shall want a competent nomber to sit and resid constantlie for determineing of all materis incumbent to them.' The numerical distribution of the split was as follows: 12 of each estate for both sections together (ie 36) and 18 for each section separately (i.e six per estate). The quorum for both sections was set at any seven 'promiscuouslie.' Each section had full power to govern itself per se and had control over any new members added to each section when Parliament was not in session. In the event of loss of personnel through death, any replacement members were to be nominated by the majority of the quorums at the camp or at Edinburgh (depending on which section the deceased member belonged to). Transactions of the respective quorums, in legal terms, were to have the 'full strenth of a valid and laufull decreet and sentance of what evir business or convenciency shall be prescrybit.' The only limitations placed on each section were any declarations of war and/or any concluding of peace negotiations; both these transactions required a minimum consent of both quorums in unison. Despite being separate administrative and legislative bodies, Adam Hepburne of Humbie was appointed Clerk to the Committee of

Estates in order to maintain an adequate level of contact between the two sections. His attendance and that of his deputies was made compulsory. Sir Archibald Johnston of Wariston, representative of the Kirk and close political ally of Argyll, was to be in constant attendance with the army section. He was given the responsibility of the preparation and construction of any legislative documents, treaties and public declarations. Wariston was not a member of Parliament at this time but appears to have been included for his legal expertise and to give a degree of allowance to the interests of the Kirk.[21]

4. The Operation of Parliamentary Interval Committees

Following the break-up of the Estates on 11 June, the attention of the Covenanting leadership was concentrated on preparations for the military invasion of England. Invasion duly took place on 20 August 1640, after the articles of war had been issued on 10 August.[22]

On 3 and 6 August the Edinburgh section of the Committee of Estates assembled along with those members of the army section presently in the country, along with the 'wholl ministers who were present her.' It was on these two days that the decision was formally taken for the invasion of England. This was a unanimous decision 'without any kynd of contradiction found first.' Although of an offensive nature, invasion was justified on the grounds that the country was engaged in a peculiarly defensive war, without which '(all uther meanes being denyed) this cuntrey cannot long subsist,'. It was further justified as the only way to prevent an invasion of Scotland.[23]

Both sections of the Committee of Estates were subsequently active in the nomination of the Scottish commissioners to participate in the peace negotiations at Ripon, which commenced on 2 October 1640. On 31 October and 4 November quorums of both sections had assembled with this remit specifically in mind. (The negotiations began at Ripon in October 1640, then transferred to London in December 1640 before being finally concluded in August 1641).

Analysis of those present reveals eight nobles, six gentry, and 10 burgesses. The bulk of nobles were on the radical wing of the movement (Rothes, Cassillis, Lothian, Burleigh, and Balmerino) and outnumbered a smaller grouping of conservatives (Montrose, Napier, and Lindsay). One of the six gentry, Sir John Couper of Hogar, was also present, although he was not listed in the original commission. This provides an illustration of non-parliamentary members being employed. Nine of the 10 burgesses were listed on the original commission.

The inclusion of Montrose on the quorum which elected the diplomatic representatives of Parliament is of particular interest given his involvement in the Cumbernauld Band of August 1640. The Banders constituted a reaction amongst many nobles against the domination of the movement by the central caucus of Argyll, Loudoun, Burgleigh, Balmerino and company. The Banders did not wish to see a further dimunition in the king's authority. Nevertheless, the involvement of Montrose was not disclosed until the turn of the year.

The Ripon contingent in all consisted of four nobles, three gentry and three burgesses. Rothes, Dunfermline, Loudoun and Lord Urquhart represented the nobility. Gentry and burghal membership was composed of Covenanting activists. In addition, General Alexander Leslie was included, both as a leading Covenanter and as a military representative. Alexander Henderson and Johnston of Wariston gained membership as representatives of the Kirk. The Ripon commissioners were entrusted with full power to conclude a treaty.

In total, the diplomatic grouping amounted to 13. The quorum was set at seven, with two per estate required to be present. The original grouping constructed on 31 August does not seem to have consisted of this 13 in total, but of 10, for on 3 November, Rothes, Drummond of Riccarton (Linlithgow), and Hugh Kennedy (Ayr) were admitted as three further commissioners to participate in the Ripon negotiations. On the other hand, Balfour states that there were eight Scottish negotiators at Ripon. This assessment is nevertheless in accordance with the guidelines laid down in the two respective commissions, with two of each estate and a total quorum of at least seven, but also with a further balance of two Kirk representatives.[24]

The growing importance and enhanced stature of Argyll as a national figure is reflected in his inclusion in the concluding stages of the Treaty of London, (August 1641) although he had not originally been charged with that responsibility. The negotiations at this point were at a particularly delicate stage and Rothes was determined to have Argyll present. Rothes shrewdly gained the assent of both the English commissioners and Charles I to Argyll's inclusion, which was subsequently approved by the Committee of Estates at Edinburgh.

Within the remit of parliamentary and constitutional concerns, four specific demands came to the fore on the part of the Scottish diplomatic negotiators. Firstly, royal assent to the legislation of the June 1640 session was to be secured. Secondly, the parliamentary enactments of the June 1640 session were to be published in the king's name. Thirdly, the Incendiaries were to be returned to Scotland to face parliamentary censure. This applied particularly to Traquair who under no circumstances was to participate in the peace negotiations, due to his 'malversation anent the proceidings' of the Parliament and General Assembly. Fourthly, financial reparations were demanded for the Scottish armed forces.

Due to the financial pressure of the Covenanting occupation of England, Charles had been forced to summon the English Long Parliament to meet on 3 November. This was only to provide a strong ally on the side of the Covenanters against the king. This is reflected in other six areas of constitutional concern. Conservators of the Peace were to be established to remedy any issues of disagreement between the two countries. The Conservators were to meet when the respective Parliaments were not in session. The Scots also demanded that triennial Parliaments should be held in both countries. This constitutes a clear move by the Scottish Covenanters to influence English parliamentary proceedings, given that a Triennal Act had already been passed in Scotland.

However, the demands of the Scottish diplomatic negotiators should not be interpreted as attempts to establish parliamentary union between the Parliaments or a 'supranational institution'. Rather, they should be viewed as an attempt to export the Covenanting revolution on a British basis and to give the Scottish Estates a greater role in British affairs. In addition, any future marriage of the Prince of Wales was to require the approval of both kingdoms and a greater number of Scotsmen were to acquire positions of influence at Court. Such arguments were wholly consistent with the fact that it had been the king's native kingdom that had enabled a Union of the Crowns in 1603 and that the erosion of Scottish influence around the king required rectification. Further demands were later articulated that the king should reside in Scotland for certain periods and that the Prince of Wales and his successors should receive part of their education in Scotland. This was advanced primarily as a means to overcome the effects of absentee monarchy and reinforce the Scottish identity of an increasingly British monarchy. Absentee monarchy had been detrimental and prejudicial to the nation in all spheres of national life and whilst the Covenanting revolution had revolved on the sovereignty of Scottish institutions, the monarchy was to be incorporated within this 'Scottishness' and made more in touch with the needs of the nation.[25]

The Committee of Estates was not only concerned with establishing a redefinition of the Union of the Crowns with the English Parliament during the peace negotiations. It was also involved in diplomatic initiatives on a European scale for the establishment of a tripartite confederation/league involving the Scottish Estates, the English Parliament and the Estates General of the United Provinces. An itemised agenda of seven articles was delivered to the Scots diplomatic commissioners on this matter which required discussion with the English commissioners.[26]

From the tenor of Article One, it would appear that the league/confederation was to be secured in general terms by the agreement of the Scots and English commissioners:

> that they concurre with thes of the kingdom of Ingland who are upoun yat treatie (i.e Ripon/London) to secure the conditionnes of that league and confedilacie to all his maties kingdomes.[27]

Even so, the committee at Edinburgh could give no 'particular directioun' to the 'generall conditionnes' of the confederacy (Article Two), but advised their diplomatic contingent to familiarise themselves with previous leagues between England and the Low Countries and/or France and/or Spain. Article Three stressed that 'diligent attendance to the forme and conceptioun' of any previous leagues between the kingdom of England and the United Provinces should be paid; principally to protect Scottish interests in the newly proposed confederation, but this also suggests that the proposals had gone beyond the stage of mere discussion and were on the point of being incorporated within a written document. Articles Four to Six focused specifically on the preservation of Scottish trading and economic privileges; protection of Scottish fishing rights (Article Five), ratification of burgh trading privileges in the Low Countries

(Article Six) and the consolidation of the office of Conservator within the Low Countries (Article Four).[28]

Trading and economic benefits resulting from such a league would certainly be advantageous and strong ties already existed. The Netherlands had provided the major source of arms and ammunition for the Covenanting forces during the Bishops' Wars. Thomas Cunningham, James Weir, and James Eleis, three Scottish factors at Campvere, likewise played an impotrant role in the traffic of Scottish commerce in the Provinces.[29]

The Dutch political system certainly offered attractions to the Covenanters with a strong emphasis on federalism and a Stadtholder with powers limited by the provincial estates. It also offered attractions to the ideal of centralised Covenanting oligarchy. Clement Walker, writing at a later date (1650) argued that Argyll was 'in conspiracy with certaine his Confederates' in order to 'transforme the Kingdome of Scotland into a Free State like the Estates of Holland.'[30]

Strengthening the evidence that a tripartite confederation was a serious diplomatic consideration, further enquiry reveals that a league with the Dutch had a strong attraction to the English Parliament. Giovanni Giustinian, the Venetian Ambassador in England in 1641–42, observed that there was 'a secret intention to approach the Dutch form of government, for which the people here show far too much inclination,' and later refers to the 'eagerness.... to bring the government into conformity with that of Holland.'[31]

An undated pamphlet of a speech given by a certain William Bennet, probably to the English Long Parliament, gives details of contemporary analysis of the European alliance system. Bennet advocated that, 'wee should enter into such a league with the Hollanders;' on the grounds that the Dutch will 'never enter into warre, or league, meerely for Religion.'[32] Bennet's argument ultimately centred on the European alliance system, but the fact remains that a closer relationship was being sought by English parliamentarians. An English parliamentary committee of the House of Lords, the 'Committee to meet about the Treaty with the States', was involved in negotiations for a 'Treaty of Confederation'. This appears to have been related to the fact that Charles himself was seeking a marriage alliance.[33]

Despite the fact that a tripartite confederation ultimately failed to emerge, conclusive evidence has nevertheless been provided which requires the institution of the Committee of Estates to be placed within a wider European perspective.

Continuations of Parliament, 19 November 1640–15 July 1641

When the Estates reconvened on 19 November 1640 no commissioner had been sent by the king. Given the fact that the military conflict had not yet been settled, the Estates agreed that Parliament should be continued to 14 January 1641. Burleigh was elected as President of Parliament in the absence of a commissioner (once more stressing the right of the Estates to determine their own proceedings).

Between 19 November and the king's attendance in Parliament from 17 August 1641, Parliament was prorogued on no less than three occasions (14 January, 13 April, and 25 May). Such prorogations were based on a communication of 31 December 1640 from the king requiring that the Estates should not meet again because he was unable to be present in person, and neither could he send a commissioner, due to the absence of many of the nobility. In actual fact the Covenanting leadership did not wish another full session of the Estates to take place until the peace negotiations had been satisfactorily concluded. Any peace treaty would therefore require parliamentary ratification.[34]

The Third Session of the Second Parliament of Charles I, 15 July–17 November 1641

Charles had intended to be present at the session commencing on 15 July and his attendance had also been expected by the Estates. This had been delayed by the English Parliament, however, because of difficulties in the ratification of the Treaty of London.

1. The Composition the Third Session of the Second Parliament of Charles I

Forty-three nobles, 49 gentry representing 28 shires, and 57 burgesses representing 56 burghs (149 individuals in total) formed the membership of the House. Noble attendance was greater than all previous sessions of Parliament, 1639–41, except for the 1639 Parliament. Gentry and burghal attendance levels were greater than all previous sessions of Parliament, 1639–41. Total parliamentary membership was higher than all other sessions, 1640–41, and was equal to that of the 1639 Parliament (see appendices 2a and 2b). Such figures indicate increased commitment and activism to the Covenanting cause in terms of parliamentary human resources. In terms of individual membership, 22 of the 43 nobles (51%), 15 of the 49 gentry (31%), and 12 of the 57 burgesses (21%) present in Parliament, 15 July 1641, had also sat in the previous parliamentary session (25 May). Individual membership figures also indicate that there was a grass-roots pool of human resources, particularly gentry and burgesses, that the leadership of the Covenanting Movement could draw on.[35]

2. The Proceedings the Third Session of the Second Parliament of Charles I

Following the re-election of Burleigh as President in the absence of a royal commissioner, Loudoun and Dunfermline, as principal diplomatic negotiators, moved that the Estates should prorogue until the king could be present and initiated a vote on the issue. The Estates voted against prorogation, but in accordance with the king's wishes, resolved 'not (to) proceed to any sentance act or determinatione till his Maties owne comeing'. The Estates resolved only to prepare business until Charles arrived, unless any urgent affairs should occur. Balfour asserts that this issue was carried by only 50 votes.[36]

Throughout this period the Estates continued the consolidation of the powers of Parliament and developed intricate procedural innovations. The remaining areas of parliamentary concern focused firstly on establishing the procedure by which the Incendiaries and Plotters (who had been imprisoned in May 1641 as signatories of the Cumbernauld Band for plotting against the radical leadership) were to be brought to trial and prosecuted. Secondly the House was concerned with the conclusion and subscription of the Treaty of London.

The determination of procedures for the regulating the order of the House was allocated to a session committee established on 16 July. Composed of six per estate, it was to consult with the Constable and Marischal, and the magistrates of Edinburgh. Radical interests were particularly served by Lothian and Patrick Leslie (Aberdeen).[37] By 19 July 13 articles for ordering the House had been agreed on and were communicated to the Estates. Article One emphasised the nature of the redefined three estates by stressing that only members of Parliament could remain in the House when the Estates were in session. This ideal was later implemented in practice on 3 August when the eldest sons of four nobles (Angus, Maitland, Montgomery, and Elcho) were removed from the House. The gentry and burgesses had refused to vote because this was contrary to the orders laid down on 19 July. According to the orders, a maximum of three parliamentary clerks and the Procurator of the Kirk were allowed admittance to serve the Estates, but enjoyed no debating or voting rights. On the other hand, Article Two permitted the attendance of all the members of the Committee of Estates, including any Lords of Session and non-parliamentary gentry and burgesses, along with any clerks of the Committee. By implication this suggests that the Committee of Estates might continue to meet when Parliament was in progress (despite the fact that the commission of 1640 expired on the first meeting of the next Parliament). It does not appear that this countenanced voting or debating rights (as per Article Seven). Lord Advocate Craighall was later allowed admission (17 August) on the basis that he was also advocate for the Estates. Nevertheless, Craighall was denied voting privileges and was only to speak when commanded by the Estates. Articles Four, 12, and 13 tightened up on non-attendance of members by establishing methods of ascertaining those members present and by setting down three tiers of fines per estate for non-attendance and latecomers. Article Four established the number of sessions per day (two) and their duration. This was designed to provide a more efficient structure for the deliberative and legislative process.

Prior to the arrival of the king in Parliament, the Estates had already set in motion the procedure that was to be implemented on all bills and overtures submitted to the House. Article Nine of the regulations had ordained that a consultation period of 24 hours was allowed for consideration of any overture by each of the estates separately (in effect the Tables). A session committee of 12 (four per estate) had been established on 28 July to consider all bills and overtures submitted. The leading Covenanting nobles were not members of this committee, which indicates that committee work was being spread throughout the noble estate.

All necessary supplications and citations were to be granted and the specific remit of the committee was to report back to the House on the subject matter of all such bills. On 3 August, this had been specified as the power to pass bills for citation only, with one of each estate to subscribe them. All other bills were to be reported to the House. In effect, all bills and supplications were to undergo a fourfold process that evolved from 19 July until the close of the 1641 Parliament. Depending on its individual nature, any bill/overture was to be submitted to a specialist committee for consideration, after an initial reading by the House (a whole plethora of which flourished between 17 August and 17 November). Thirdly, following consultation by a specialist committee each estate (in accordance with Article Nine) was to decide whether or not the bill was to proceed any further in the legislative process. Finally, the Estates were to reconvene to vote on appropriate legislation, each member of Parliament having a free vote (in accordance with the legislation of the June 1640 session).[38]

The Committee for the Bills has recently been described as a 'clearing house for standing and ad hoc committees' and the third stage of the above process has been represented as an assertion of the 'party discipline' of the Tables.[39] Whilst this legislative process did provide for a strong degree of control by the Covenanting leadership over all bills and supplications introduced into Parliament, it should be interpreted within a wider perspective of an increased parliamentary role for all three estates. It can be viewed as the introduction of a more efficient parliamentary procedure. The actual composition of the Committee for the Bills reveals that of the four noble representatives, Mar and Kinghorn had signed the Cumbernauld Band, implying an association with Montrose. The other two nobles, Elphinstone and Johnstone, had no strong association with the Covenanters. Noble representation was countered by a solid grouping of Covenanting support from the gentry and burgess representatives. Compared with the infamous Lords of the Articles, the Committee for the Bills was more of an institutional tool for the benefit of Parliament, although it did enable the Covenanting leadership ulitimately to control the progress of all bills and overtures.[40]

The determination of the Estates to control their own affairs continued to be asserted prior to 17 August. The quorums (attendance levels) for all committees was set at 50% of the total membership per committee. On 11 August a further parliamentary oath was initiated; each member of Parliament was required to uphold and defend the sovereignty of Parliament before any business was initiated. Subscription of the National Covenant was once more necessary for admission to Parliament. As perceived by Robert Baillie, this was designed to:

> make all the members of Parliament so fast to the Church and State as was possible, and to be without danger of temptation and Court corruption.[41]

As an instrument of party discipline, the oath of 11 August was a continuation of the process initiated in the June 1640 session whereby subscription of the National Covenant, the Confession of Faith, and the oath to recognise the legality of the June 1640 session was required.

Clarification was sought relating to the election of the President of Parliament. On 12 August it was enacted that in all future Parliaments the previous President was to continue in that post until the parliamentary oath was taken by all members. After subscription of the oath, a new President was to be elected. No President could continue in office without a fresh election being taken. This measure was to have immediate effect in the 1641 Parliament. Hence Burleigh who had held the office of President consecutively since June 1640 was replaced by Balmerino on 18 August (as a temporary nomination by the king until the manner of electing a President had been decided on). Balmerino had been tried for treason in 1634–5, having emerged as a critic of the king's policies, and was closely associated with Argyll. The fact that Balmerino had been nominated by the king indicates that Charles was on the defensive and was adopting a policy of conciliation. On 13 August it had been agreed that the 'publict bussiness' (ie constitutional concerns) was to take precedence over any other matters such as private petitions and grievances which required the attention of the Estates. Crucially, it was also agreed on 13 August that separate enactment should be made to exclude all Officers of State from Parliament. This was likewise to encompass all related voting rights and was in keeping with the exclusion of Officers of State from parliamentary committees since 1639. Any previous legislation passed in their favour was to be annulled.[42]

Parliamentary attention was also focused on the Incendaries and Plotters in the preparations for their trials. The Committee anent the Incendaries was established on 29 July. Consisting of six of each estate, its function was primarily to draw up a list of necessary witnesses to be cited and examined. The committee was led by three leading radical nobles; Argyll, Eglinton, and Cassillis.[43]

Viewing events within a British perspective as a whole, the Treaty of London had finally been ratified by the English Parliament on 7 August, and had received the royal assent on 10 August. This allowed Charles to finally attend the 1641 session of the Scottish Parliament in person. The session commencing on 15 July was closed on 14 August (no formal record of this was instituted, or failed to be recorded). A new session commenced on 17 August with the king present. Charles intended a short visit to deal with his 'Scottish problem' and possibly to seek Scottish aid or at least neutrality in a conflict with the English Parliament. He was accompanied to Edinburgh by a Joint Committee of the Lords and Commons.

3. The Composition of Parliament, 17 August 1641

Fifty-six nobles, 50 gentry representing 29 shires, and 57 burgesses representing 56 burghs (163 individuals in total) constituted the membership of Parliament as per 17 August. Attendance levels for all three estates were greater than all previous parliamentary sessions 1639–41 as was the total membership figure (163) (see appendices 2a and 2b). The increase in parliamentary membership, particularly the nobility, can be attributed to the fact that the king was now present in the House and had returned to his native kingdom for the first time in six years. Thirty-five of the 56 nobles (62%), 46 of the 50 gentry (92%), and 53 of the 57 burgesses (93%) were also recorded in the rolls of 15 July. That the retention rate of the gentry and burgesses was so high can be attributed to the fact that no new elections had been held. In strictly constitutional terms the proceedings commencing on 17 August did not constitute a new parliamentary session.[44]

4. The Proceedings of Parliament, 17 August to 17 November 1641

Upon his first formal contact with the Scottish Parliament since 1633, Charles stressed in his opening speech his willingness to 'settle and compose all differences' and ratify the enactments of the June 1640 session. This manoeuvre was met with hostility by the Covenanting leadership as an attempt by the Crown to reject the legality of both the meeting and proceedings of that session, as well as the parliamentary band of maintenance. Parliamentary observers stressed that:

> This if it had been yielded had been of Dangerous consequences for the putting of the Scepter to Acts is but a Ceremony signifying the Royal Assent, which to these Acts we have already in the Treaty. And the King's putting the Scepter to them now were to make them Acts of this present session of parliament and as much as if they had not been Laws sufficient force to bind the Subjects from the time wherein they were enacted.[45]

The lack of expertise of Charles in terms of man management was highlighted in his imprisonment of Sir William Cockburn of Langtoun (Berwick). Langtoun was imprisoned by the king for taking upon himself the right to exercise the office of Usher. Langtoun's imprisonment was taken 'extrem ill' by the Parliament. That a member of parliament should be removed from the House and imprisoned during a parliamentary session without the prior approval of the Estates was regarded as 'a dangerous preparative.'[46]

At this point, arguably, Argyll openly emerged as the dominant figure in Parliament. On 13 August the meeting of the nobility had taken place where it had been decided that all public business was to take priority in the parliamentary session. Argyll had been elected as President of that meeting, indicating the presence of a strong grouping of Covenanting nobles. Likewise, it was Argyll who took the initiative in the morning session of 17 August in securing Charles's agreement that a deputation of six should consult with the king if 'any thing debaitable' should be proposed in the House. This provided the occasion for a rapidly elected deputation of six, elected by each estate meeting separately. According to Robert Baillie, this grouping had been in existence since 13 August and the election would appear to be a matter of mere ratification. Argyll formed the leading figure in the deputation, which was dominated by activists, including Balmerino, President of Parliament. Lord Almont, ally of Montrose (Almont had signed the Cumbernauld Band), also secured membership. The deputation then secured a conference with Charles for discussion of two issues. Firstly, he was not to make any further reference to legislation of the 1640 session until the Treaty of London had been dealt with by Parliament (which the king agreed to). Secondly, it was demanded that those councillors who had advised the king to commit Langtoun without the consent of the Estates should be brought to trial (in reality a covert warning against the king's actions in the House).

When the Estates recovened on 18 August no time was wasted in asserting the legitimacy of Parliament to determine its own proceedings. This was enacted in three items of legislation consistent with the constitutional revolution of the June 1640 session and legislation prepared, but not voted on, from 15 July. Such a trend was in keeping with Parliament ratifying the past practices of the Covenanters (ie the 1640 Parliament ratified the legislation prepared by the Tables and the 1639 Lords of the Articles). The legality of the election of Burleigh as President from June 1640 onwards was approved, as was his replacement by Balmerino. This was based on a 'private promise' that the act establishing the election of President would be ratified before the close of the parliamentary session. The fact that the radical leadership continued to orchestrate parliamentary proceedings was reflected by the fact that the Committee of Estates continued to meet in secret until the third week of the parliamentary session.

In accordance with the terms of the new parliamentary oath agreed on 11 August, the ' Act anent the oath to be given by everie member of parliamente' was approved for the current parliamentary session and all future Parliaments. The oath was to be subscribed before the Estates could enact any legislation. This oath was duly signed by all members of Parliament on 31 August; a gap of 13 days before the implementation of the oath.

Subscription of the National Covenant, the Band of Maintenance, and the parliamentary oath was forced on the Marquis of Hamilton, the Earls of Roxburgh and Lanark, and Lords Yester and Ormont before the Estates on the same day 'before they sitt or voice.' This was in accordance with legislation enacted on 13 August which had barred all nobles from sitting and voting in the House unless they had subscribed all of the above oaths and bands. On 17 August, Hamilton, Lennox, Morton, Roxburgh, Annandale, Kinnoull, Lanark, and Carnwath (all adherents of the Court) had been refused access to the House. By 19 August all but two (Carnwath and Kinnoull) had pragmatically added their signatures.

Charles was forced to retract his imprisonment of Langtoun and agree that 'no member of the house of parliament shall be commited for ony misdemanor in tyme of parliat without the advyse of the estates in tymecomeing'.[47]

Within two days of attending the 1641 Parliament, Charles I had been forced on the defensive as the momentum of constitutional revolution continued and the Estates had immediately set the pattern that was to prevail until the close of Parliament on 17 November.

In total, 145 items of legislation passed through Parliament between 17 August and 17 November. The overwhelming bulk of these enactments (125), concerned the 'public business'. The concentration of attention on the public business had a knock-on effect on the legislative process concerning private affairs/petitions, a total of 220 of which were rushed through before the close of Parliament. This appears to have been a deliberate policy option. On 13 August the House had ordained that all public business was to be dealt with before any private measure could be introduced. The enactment of such a large amount of legislation was unprecedented compared to previous parliamentary sessions, 1633–1641.[48]

The concentration of historical analysis regarding Privy Councillors, Officers of State, and Sessioners in the August-November session of the 1641 Parliament has tended to obscure important procedural developments and other enactments of a constitutional nature. It was in this period that a complicated committee structure was evolving. Even when recognition has been given to the existence of a parliamentary committee structure, attention has been restricted to the foundation of the important interval committees established from 15–17 November. All were under Covenanting control and in essence constituted the break-down of the Committee of Estates into smaller, more specialised units. However, session committees also flourished, principally as a means to deal effectively with a mass of material submitted for legislation, but also as a by-product of the time-consuming debate over Officers of State, Privy Councillors, and Sessioners. By 19 October a session committee was certainly in operation with the aim of securing 'a faire accomodation of all things'. Consisting of six per estate, only two nobles (Glencairn and Lindsay) did not belong to the radical wing of the movement. Loudoun, Argyll, Cassillis, and Balmerino all gained membership and the gentry and burgess representatives were all 'men of knowne wisedome and integrity'.[49]

Consistent with the noted trend of the Covenanting leadership constantly revising and reneweing its previous legislation, a session committee was established on 19 August to revise all acts and articles presented in Parliament since 15 July 1641. Composed of four per estate, noble representation was based on the conservative wing of the Covenanting nobility (Roxburgh, Southesk, Mar and Elphinstone). No nobles and gentry included on this committee had been members of the Committee for Revising Papers Discussed in Articles of 2 June 1640. Only one burgess, Richard Maxwell (Edinburgh), was included on both committees. This would seem to indicate that committee work was being spread throughout all three estates. It would also appear that it was the committee established on 19 August that steered legislation through the House.[50]

That private legislation had to be rushed through the House was reflected on 11 November in the establishment of a specific session committee for ratifications to be enacted in Parliament. It is to this committee that credit must be given for the passage of 220 private measures in the final days of the parliamentary session. In effect, this committee was acting like the former Lords of Articles in putting forward measures for enactment en bloc. Composed of two per estate, both nobles (Southesk and Elphinstone) were also members of the committee established on 19 August. No common membership exists for the gentry and burgesses.[51]

Clearly these session committees played a crucial role in the effective operation of Parliament and the successful conclusion of all required legislation. Although the establishment of a Committee/Lords of Articles remained an optional expedient, the psychological barrier of using an institution so closely associated with the Crown rendered its implementation non-viable.

The constitutional combination of the Committee for Bills (28 July), the Committee for Revising Acts and Articles, and the Committee for Pursuing Ratifications must be interpreted as three separate, but interlinked, committees which had taken over much of the procedural and legislative functions which had previously been performed by the Lords of the Articles.

Public business legislation can be differentiated into three specific areas; firstly, the formal approval of the conduct of the Scottish diplomatic commissioners, secondly, the sanctioning of parliamentary control over the executive and judiciary and further internal procedural developments, and thirdly, the transfer of power from the Committee of Estates to newly-created specialised committees (both session and interval). Such specialised committees were dominated by activists and were designed to retain the government of the country in the hands of the Covenanting leadership after the close of Parliament.

Following the return of the diplomatic commissioners from London, Charles formally signed the Treaty of London in Parliament on 25 August. The treaty was duly ratified by the Estates on the following day. Although the differences between king and Parliament concerning the election of Officers of State had failed to be agreed on in the treaty, the Act of Pacification and Oblivion (incorporated in the treaty) did not apply to the five Incendiaries and four Plotters cited on criminal charges. A committee of three per estate was correspondingly established on 26 August to clarify with Charles a specific six point remit concerning matters 'not fullie determined in the treattie bot remitted to be determined be the king and parliament.' The committee's main sphere of interest centred on securing royal assent to publication of the acts of the June 1640 session (finally agreed to on 31 August), the trial and processes against the Incendiaries and Plotters, and the establishment of a diplomatic commission to preserve peace between England and Scotland. Noble representation was based solely on the radical wing of the Covenanting nobility and consisted of Argyll, Cassillis, and Lothian.[52]

Throughout the session political controversy ultimately focused on the appointment of Privy Councillors and Officers of State. The Covenanting leadership was determined that the holders of these offices should be elected by and accountable to Parliament. In keeping with the legislation of 1640, subscription of the National Covenant was to be required by all Officers of State, Privy Councillors, and Lords of Session. Four of the five Incendiaries cited to Parliament had been Officers of State and principal office holders during the Personal Rule. The election of these officers by the king alone had been the 'fountain of our evills, and was lyke to be a constant root of corruption, both in Kirk and State, if not seen to.' Historical precedent was also employed in the propaganda war between King and Parliament (prior to the Union of the Crowns officers of state had been appointed with parliamentary approval).[53]

Charles, on the other hand, regarded the appointment of such officers as a 'speciall part of his prerogative, a great sinew of his government, the long possession of the Kings in Scotland, the unquestionable right of the Kings in England.' The king cast a wary eye on the tense political situation in his southern kingdom and was under close political scrutiny by the Joint Committee of the Lords and Commons. Indeed, Charles was fearful of any limitation of his prerogative which might be taken as a precedent by a volatile English Parliament. The battle lines had been drawn, but it was the Covenanting leadership that was to triumph over the king. Given the increasingly alarming state of affairs in his English dominions and Ireland, Charles only had a finite amount of time available in Scotland and was being continually harassed by the English Parliament to return south. It was this factor that governed his final submission to Covenanting demands.[54]

Parliamentary control over the appointment of Officers of State, Privy Councillors and Lords of Session had been on the Covenanting agenda since 1639. At a meeting of the nobility on 31 August 1641 three points had been agreed on by 'way of opinioun'. Pragmatically, it was firstly agreed that the nominations to these offices belonged to the king but the nominations should also give 'most content and satisfactioune' to the Estates. Secondly, appointments were to be made with the advice and consent of the Estates when Parliament was in session, and during intervals of Parliament by consent of the Council. Thirdly, those appointed were to be liable and accountable to king and Parliament. Such limitations were designed to ensure that 'so far as is possible all ways of ambition and corruption may be stopped'.[55]

Judicial appointments of Senators of the College of Justice were also to be authorised by the king with the advice of Parliament. Once more this was aimed at prevention of a return to the reputed corruption of the College of Justice during the post-1625 administration. The rationale of such an argument rested on the absence of the monarch from the country which would cloud his knowledge of the suitabilty of individuals for these positions, but were also 'groundit upon the ancient Lawis and custome of this kingdome.'[56]

On 2 September 1641 a 'great committee' of 36 (12 of each estate) was elected by the Three Estates. Each estate elected its own representatives. The committee was charged with the responsibility of attending the king to discuss the problems relating to Officers of State, Councillors and Sessioners. No official reference exists in the Acts of Parliament of Scotland to this committee and no breakdown of membership is available. It may be supposed, however, that Covenanting activists filled its ranks although there was probably a spread of radicals and conservatives among the noble contingent.[57]

The committee attended the king on 3 September. Charles informed it of his decision that he would make all relevant appointments with the advice and approval of Parliament and in general adhered to the demands of the nobility. The king's paper containing his decision was then discussed and voted on by the Estates separately. The nobility concluded that the paper was satisfactory to the appropriate demand in the Treaty of London. Although the gentry found the paper to be satisfactory in 'ane greate parit,' they nevertheless articulated on what exactly advice and approval should constitute. Furthermore, any Officers of State, Councillors, and Sessioners appointed during intervals of Parliament were only to have tenure until the next Parliament. The next parliamentary session was to have power of veto over their appointments. Additionally, the consent of the majority of Privy Councillors was to be required concerning both the nomination and election of all Councillors. The Privy Council was to be legally called upon 15 days notice. The concerns of the burghal estate were in common with those of the gentry. A delegation of three per estate was dispatched to the king on 9 September to discuss the additional demands of the gentry and burgesses.

The legislation relating to the election of Officers of State, Councillors, and Sessioners passed through the House on 16 September. All the demands of the gentry and burgesses were incorporated within that act. It is therefore clear that it was the commissioners of the shires and burghs, and not the nobility, who constituted the dominant architects of the final form of the enactment. The gentry and burgesses remained at the cutting edge of constitutional revolution.

Following the passage of act on 16 September, Charles immediately submitted a list of nominees of Privy Councillors and Officers of State on 17 September. Fifty-eight names were submitted, 49 of which related to Privy Councillors, whilst nine related to Officers of State. Six of the 49 Privy Council nominations were English politicians of the Court who were to be employed in the capacity of supernumerary councillors. The employment of six English politicians was a device retained from the post-1625 administration (Charles had added nine Englishmen to the Privy Council of 1633). Of the remaining 43 nominations, seven gentry and all burgesses were significant Covenanting activists. This marks a significant increase from the post-1625 administration and indicates royal recognition of the political power of the gentry within the Covenanting Movement. The Provost of Edinburgh was included as the sole representative of the burghs. General Alexander Leslie, commander of the Covenanting armed forces, was included, not as a military representative, but in reality as a member of the nobility which he was shortly to be promoted into. The remaining 34 nominations constituted a solid block of pragmatic Royalist nobles, including Hamilton, Huntly, and Perth. Albeit in a minority radical nobles such as Argyll, Balmerino, and Cassillis also secured inclusion.

Controversy ultimately raged over the appointment of Chancellor, Treasurer and Clerk Register. The Chancellorship was vacant since the death of John Spottiswood, Archbishop of St Andrews. The Treasurership and the office of Clerk Register were also vacant due to the citations of Traquair (Treasurer) and Sir John Hay of Lands (Clerk Register) as Incendiaries. The Earl of Morton was nominated as Chancellor and Loudoun as Treasurer, whilst Sir Alexander Gibson of Durie was nominated as Clerk Register. When the composition of Privy Councillors and Officers of State was intimated to the Estates on 20

September, dissension immediately emerged. Charles was forced to concede that the total number of Privy Councillors and Officers of State would not actually exceed 52. Argyll took particular exception to the nomination of Morton, his father-in-law, as Chancellor. The argument continued for over a week until Morton personally announced that he did not wish to be considered for the post. Charles was forced to modify his nominations and against his better judgement, nominated the radical Loudoun as Chancellor and the conservative Lord Almont as Treasurer. Loudoun was also a Campbell and a kinsman of Argyll. Almont's nomination was strongly opposed by Argyll and rejected by the Estates. Although Almont was on the conservative wing of the movement, it was suspected that his sympathies leaned towards the Crown. An English correspondent, Thomas Webb, noted that the opposition to Morton was led by adherents of Argyll, that is the radicals. Baillie noted that the majority of the Estates wanted Argyll as Treasurer. Yet, a certain individual called 'Hirst', an English spy circulating in Edinburgh, observed that Morton and Argyll were:

> hott in competition for the Chancellorship, the prime place of the kingdom: the King preferring the first, and the Parliament the other.[58]

The nomination of Loudoun as Chancellor was a pragmatic concession by Charles to the Covenanting leadership whilst avoiding the political nightmare of putting Argyll into such an important office of state. The nomination of Almont was flatly rejected by the Estates on Argyll's instigation (due to Almont's association with Montrose and his signing of the Cumbernauld Band). Rather than leave the Treasury in Argyll's hands (as the majority wished), Charles was forced to establish a Treasury Commission, which was to endure until the next Parliament.

Considerable confusion existed concerning how the policy of 'advice and approval of Parliament' should be implemented. The gentry advocated that voting on the nominations of Officers of State should be determined by voting billets (a move which was rejected), in effect a secret ballot. The nominations were ultimately decided by the Estates meeting separately to discuss the issue and then voting in open Parliament.

By 13 November Charles had been forced to modify his original list of nominees. Seven pragmatic Royalist nobles had been rejected as Privy Councillors (Huntly, Airth, Home, Tullibardine, Galloway, Dumfries, and Carnwath), and replaced by seven Covenanting nobles, four of whom were radicals (Sutherland, Yester, Lothian, and Burleigh). Leslie remained in the new list as the newly-created Earl of Leven. In total, the reconstituted Privy Council consisted of 52 members, six of whom were English courtiers. The total membership of the reconstituted Privy Council consisted of 29 nobles, 12 gentry, and one burgess. Despite the amendments, the Privy Council was still dominated by pragmatic Royalist nobles. Only nine nobles were noted radicals. Twenty-three Councillors had served in the previous Privy Council. Nevertheless, in common with all members of the Estates and Lords of Session, all Privy Councillors were required under oath to defend and uphold not only the

National Covenant, but also acknowledge the 1641 Parliament to be free and lawful and subscribe to protect the legality of its enactments.

The Privy Council had virtually ceased to function in 1640–41 and following the formal close of Parliament on 17 November real power lay with the interval parliamentary commissions (Common Burdens, Brotherly Assistance, Conservators of the Peace) and not with the Privy Council.

Of the nine Officers of State, six retained offices. Roxburgh continued as Lord Privy Seal, Lanark as Secretary of State, Craighall as King's Advocate, Sir John Hamilton of Orbiston as Justice Clerk, Sir James Carmichael as Treasurer Depute, and Sir James Galloway as Master of Requests. Gibson of Durie was appointed as Clerk Register, despite the popular belief that it would go to Johnston of Wariston and in spite of the opposition of Argyll to Durie. Indeed, there was a proliferation of literature against Durie, 'most whereof manie wondered Durie gott the prize.' Loudoun gained the Chancellorship, and according to Baillie, the Treasury was put into commission until the Covenanters could get it into Argyll's hands.[59]

Parliamentary control over judicial appointments also reached the statute books on 13 November. Henceforth, the tenure of office of both Ordinary and Extraordinary Lords of Session were to be *ad vitam vel culpam*. In effect, this represented the defeat of Charles's attempts to have the tenure of Sessioners based on the principle of *ad beneplacitum* in the earlier years of his reign.

Of the 15 Ordinary Lords of Session, 11 were retained from the post-1625 administration. The four remaining places were filled by active Covenanters; Sir John Leslie of Newton, Sir Thomas Hope of Kerse, Hepburne of Humbie, and Johnston of Wariston. Of the four Extraordinary Lords, Argyll and Angus kept their places, whilst Balmerino and Lindsay filled the two other offices vacated by Traquair and the former Bishop of Ross. Radical nobles therefore filled the majority of places of Extraordinary Lords. No President of the Court of Session was specified and the election was to be performed by the Session itself (which took place in January 1642 with the election of Sir Andrew Fletcher of Innerpeffer). All judicial officials were bound to subscribe the same Covenanting bands and oaths as Councillors and members of Parliament.[60]

The de facto political significance of judicial and executive appointments and the necessary subscription of Covenanting oaths was to inflict severe damage on the royal prerogative in Scotland. It was the Scottish Parliament that now effectively controlled national executive and judicial appointments. Within Parliament, the radical wing of the Covenanting Movement controlled the political agenda.

The outbreak of the Irish Rebellion had occurred while the 1641 Parliament was still in session. The British dimension of this conflict had facilitated constitutional agreement between Crown and Parliament over the Officers of State crisis. In order to formulate parliamentary policy on the Irish crisis and establish closer diplomatic channels with the king, a delegation was formed on 18 October. Radical nobles dominated the delegation (Leven, Loudoun, and Lothian). Almont was also included, although this probably amounted to no more than token recognition of conservative interests and the king's personal favour. Baillie noted that Argyll was the dominant influence of this commission, although he was not included on it, and that the committee 'in two or three nights did agree all things privatelie with the King, most according to Argyle's mind.'[61]

Legislation enacted during the two month constitutional controversy of autumn and winter 1641 established further ground rules concerning parliamentary procedure. All members of Parliament were granted the right of attending and sitting in any committees of Parliament. Any member could be called to participate in the proceedings of any committee (19 August). The parliamentary timetable was reorganised on a more effective basis to maximise both the time and human resources available (19 August). On 11 November, legislation was enacted which provided a national structure of financial renumeration for expenses incurred by the gentry during the parliamentary session. Therefore the political muscle of the gentry was reflected in the commissioners of the shires securing an improved parliamentary parliamentary package. As a result of the doubling of shire voting power in 1640, the gentry were now a real political force to be reckoned with in Parliament. £5 per day was allowed per head per day from the first to the last day of Parliament inclusive. A travelling allowance of £5 per day was also allocated. Furthermore, all freeholders, heritors and liferenters were to be liable for the expenses of the commissioners of the shires through taxation. It would appear that the County Franchise Act of 1587 which imposed taxation on freeholders in the shires was not being adhered to.[62]

Royal recognition of the political ascendancy of the Covenanters was reflected in the handout of offices and pensions to leading Covenanters. Argyll was created a Marquis and Leslie created Earl of Leven. Loudoun and Lindsay were promoted as Earls, promotions which had been suspended for their opposition to Charles in the 1633 Parliament. Johnston of Wariston and Gibson of Durie were knighted, whilst Alexander Henderson was given office in the chapel-royal. Loudoun and Argyll received pensions of £12,000 sterling (£144,000 Scots) per annum. Johnston of Wariston received £2,400 sterling (£28,800 Scots) per annum. The General of the Artillery, Alexander Hamilton, received £9,600 sterling (£115,200 Scots) per annum and the young Earl of Rothes £10,000 sterling (£120,000 Scots) per annum. According to a contemporary source, these concessions and favours were given out on the king's understanding that,'as soon as the late Storm should be perfectlty calm'd they would repeal whatever was now unreasonably exorted from him'.[63]

The prime motive of Charles, however, was to secure Scottish Covenanting neutrality in the English Civil War. Charles wanted to avoid the nightmare scenario of the Covenanters aligning themselves with his enemies in England in a military alliance. Mismanagement of multiple monarchies over the 'Three Kingdoms' was now beginning to haunt Charles I.[64]

At the close of the session on 17 November 1641 it was ordered that the First Triennial Parliament should convene on the first Tuesday of June 1644. Technically this was under the terms of the 1640 Triennial Act.[65]

5. The Committee Structure of Parliament, 1639–41

Analysis of the committee structure of Parliament is based on seven session committees and seven interval committees, in combination with the Lords of the Articles (yielding a maximum of 15 committees). The bulk of session committees were issued with remits relating to parliamentary procedure.[66]

Thirty-nine nobles formed the noble field analysed. Radical membership was concentrated on six nobles (the number of committees is given in brackets); Argyll (eight), Cassillis, Eglinton (both five), Loudoun, Balmerino and Burleigh (all six), Cassillis and Eglinton (both five). Conservative interests among the nobility were not absent and were represented primarily by Lindsay (eight), Lauderdale and Southesk (both six), and Glencairn (five). Both groupings were particularly dominant on interval committees, although the overall balance was still in favour of the radicals. The remaining 29 nobles analysed were nominated to four or less committees.

Gentry analysis is based on a field of 40 gentry. Two gentry secured membership of a total of seven committees; Sir William Forbes of Craigievar (Aberdeen) and Sir George Dundas (Linlithgow). Sir Robert Grierson of Lag (Dumfries) was included on six committees, whilst six further gentry were nominated to five committees. Sir Robert Innes of that ilk (Elgin), Sir Patrick Hepburn of Wauchton (Haddington), Sir Thomas Hope of Kerse (Clackmannan), Sir David Home of Wedderburne (Berwick), William Rigg of Ethernie (Fife), and Sir Alexander Erskine of Dun (Forfar) constituted this grouping of gentry. In comparison with the nobility, gentry common membership included a broader degree of session committees. The remaining 31 gentry analysed were nominated to four or less committees.

Thirty-five burgesses constituted the total burghal field analysed. Four burgesses were included on a total of six committees each; Patrick Bell (Glasgow), Robert Barclay (Irvine), John Semple (Dumbarton), and James Sword (St Andrews). Six further burgesses secured nomination to a total of five committees. John Smith (Edinburgh), James Fletcher (Dundee), John Scott (Montrose), Patrick Leslie (Aberdeen), George Bell (Linlithgow), Alexander Douglas (Banff), and George Garden (Burntisland) formed this grouping. The remaining 24 burgesses analysed were included on four or less committees.[67]

Near parity therefore existed in the numbers of nobles and gentry employed compared to the burgesses. Near parity also existed in the numbers of nobles (10), gentry (9) and burgesses (11) who were nominated to a significant number of committees. Radical nobles combined with the above gentry and burgesses to form a caucus which appears to have been controlling the proceedings of parliamentary session and interval committees. Indeed, at the time of the debate concerning the manner of bringing to trial of the Incendiaries and Plotters, Baillie observed that the 'leading men of the Barrons and Burrowes did daylie consult with Argyle.' The above gentry and burgesses were probably among the individuals Baillie was referring to. It is also highly likely that such meetings took place on a regular basis.[68]

6. The Appointment of Parliamentary Interval Committees

Three categories of interval committees were established before the close of the 1641 session of Parliament; financial, diplomatic and judicial. All were under the auspices of the Covenanting leadership and continued the work of the Committee of Estates as the governing force in the country until the next session of Parliament. These interval committees represented a breakdown of the Committee of Estates into more specialised units with a broader field of membership.

The Treasury Commission consisted of four nobles and one laird. Radicals secured 50% of the noble representation (Argyll and Loudoun), the remainder consisting of Glencairn and Lindsay. Baillie stressed that both Glencairn and Lindsay were allied to Hamilton. According to Baillie's analysis, Lindsay and Glencairn were pragmatic Royalists, although Lindsay's prominence within the Covenanting Movement would suggest that he was a conservative. Sir James Carmichael was included in the capacity of Treasuer Depute. Attempts by Loudoun to have three further gentry (Johnston of Wariston, Hepburne of Humbie, and Sir Archibald Campbell) included on the commission failed. Radical control of the Treasury Commission was not therefore totally complete, but at the time the commission was regarded as only a temporary expedient until the office could be gained by Argyll.[69]

The Commission for Regulating the Common Burdens and the Commission for Receiving the Brotherly Assistance from the English Parliament were the other two interval committees with financial remits. Both were established on 15 November and had common memberships of 14 of each estate (42 in total). Leven and Hepburne of Humbie, former clerk to the Committee of Estates, were also added to both commissions.

Both committees enjoyed identical membership. Seven of the 14 nobles were noted radicals (Argyll, Loudoun, Eglinton, Cassillis, Lothian, Balmerino, and Burleigh). Although the remaining seven nobles were primarily conservatives, the 14 gentry and 14 burgesses were primarily allied to the radical nobles under the leadership of Argyll. In overall political terms, both commissions were controlled by the radical wing of the movement. Pragmatic Royalist nobles who were included on the reconstituted Privy Council did not gain membership of either committee. Two of the 14 gentry and and five of the 14 burgesses were not members of Parliament as per 17 August 1641. Neither was Hepburne of Humbie. Five radical nobles, one laird, and two burgesses had also been members of the 1640 Committee of Estates. This indicates not only that non-parliamentary grass-roots activists were being brought on to interval committees, but also that there was a depth of human resources which the radical leadership could draw on to staff interval committees.

The Common Burdens had a specific remit of establishing financial order following the Bishops' Wars. All arrears of taxes were to be accounted for, secured loans were to be payed for, and valuations for the tenth and twentieth pennies were to be completed. The remit of the Brotherly Assistance Commission was to deal with the £220,000 sterling (£2,64 million Scots) due from the

English Parliament in equal instalments over a two year period and determine how this sum should be disbursed.[70]

Two separate diplomatic commissions were established on 16 November; the Commission for conserving the Articles of the Treaty and the Commission anent the Articles referred to consideration by the Treaty. The former commissioners became known as the Conservators of the Peace, appointed to meet with commissioners from the English Parliament for conserving the peace treaty, whilst the latter commission was particularly concerned negotiations with the English Parliament on issues which had failed to be settled by the Treaty of London. Such issues revolved round including discussions on the establishment free trade between the kingdoms, as for determining the level of Scottish forces to participate in the Irish Rebellion. The Commission anent the Articles was a more specialised committee concerned with the wider British dimension of the Irish Rebellion and the English Civil War.

The Conservators of the Peace consisted of 17 nobles, 18 gentry, and 18 burgesses. Radical nobles were outnumbered by pragmatic Royalists and conservatives. Argyll, Loudoun, Eglinton, Lothian, Leven, and Balmerino formed the minority grouping. The remaining 10 nobles were all pragmatic Royalists and conservatives. The gentry and burghal contingents nevertheless ensured that overall political control rested with the radicals. No pragmatic Royalist noble gained access to the Committee anent the Articles. This constituted the major diplomatic grouping that was solely to continue negotiations with the English Parliament. All members of the Committee anent the Articles were also Conservators of the Peace. Exclusive of the inclusion of the conservative Lindsay, the remaining noble representation was radical (Balmerino and Lothian). Gentry and burghal members were all radicals, including Johnston of Wariston (Edinburgh). Radical strength was supplemented by the presence of Argyll and Loudoun as supernumeraries. Four nobles, four gentry, and six burgesses had also been included on the 1640 Committee of Estates. The low retention rate of personnel can be attributed to two factors. Firstly, the Committee for Conserving the Articles of the Treaty was the only committee to which such a large number of pragmatic Royalists gained access. Secondly, the 1640 Committee of Estates was smaller in composition compared to that committee for Conserving the Articles of the Treaty.[71]

The Commission for Plantation of Kirks and Valuation of Teinds was established as the appropriate means for the disposal of patronage rights following the abolition of episcopacy and the extension/redefinition of parish boundaries and for the valuation of teinds for subsequent redistribution. It was composed of 14 per estate. All 14 nobles, 14 gentry, and 14 burgesses were also members of the Commission for the Common Burdens and the Commission for the Brotherly Assistance. Hence a radical caucus was in control of three crucial parliamentary commissions. Membership was supplemented by five Officers of State, four of whom were gentry and three Senators of the College of Justice, who were also gentry. Total noble membership therefore amounted to 15, whilst that of the gentry amounted to 20; a reflection of the fact that teind revaluation was primarily for the benefit of the gentry. Only one noble (Southesk) and one laird (Lord Advocate Craighall) had also been members of the commission of 1633. Comparison with the 1633 commission reveals that whilst membership levels of the nobility remained virtually constant, both the gentry and burgesses had made significant gains.[72]

The method by which the Incendiaries and Plotters were to face trial had provided another sphere of controversy in parliamentary proceedings. Hamilton, as the king's formost Scottish political adviser in the late 1630s, had escaped censure primarily through his newly established political relationship with Argyll. 'The Incident', a Royalist plot hatched in October and aimed at the deposition of Argyll, Hamilton, and Lanark, had forced a political rehabilitation between Hamilton and Argyll in the interests of self-preservation. As a result of 'The Incident', parliamentary protection was quickly enacted in the interests of Hamilton which prevented him from facing any future charges of treason.[73]

Charles had favoured trial by full Parliament for the Incendiaries and Plotters but his credibility had been seriously undermined by his suspected involvement in 'The Incident'. Instead the 'greater number of voices' in the House was for trial by committee and on 16 November an appropriate commission was established. Six per estate formed its membership. Radical strength was dominant within noble representation (Loudoun, Weymes, Burleigh, and Coupar). Forrester and Lauderdale were conservatives and pragmatic Royalists failed to gain representation. Gentry and burghal contingents once more backed up the radical nobles. One of the six gentry and two of the six burgesses were not members of Parliament as per 17 August 1641. Two further gentry (Hepburne of Humbie and Gibson of Durie) secured membership as Senators of the College of Justice. The inclusion of the two Senators yielded a numerical imbalance in the composition of the committee in favour of the gentry and away from the nobility and burgesses. Both Humbie and Durie had been included on the 1640 Committee of Estates, as had two of the nobles and one burgess. Only two members of the committee, Loudoun and George Gray (Haddington), had served on the Committee anent the Incendiaries instituted on 29 July 1641. The earlier commission had been primarily concerned with ensuring that the Incendiaries would actually face trial and censure by the Estates, whilst the latter was the formal committee that would try the Incendiaries and Plotters.[74]

Conclusion

The Scottish constitutional settlement enacted in 1640–41 severely curtailed the royal prerogative and transferred political power firmly into the hands of Parliament (through control of the executive and judiciary). Parliamentary affairs were controlled and managed by a core of radical nobles, gentry, and burgesses. Sophisticated procedural developments reformed the internal organisation of the House and provided a more efficient basis for the sifting through of a vast bulk of legislation. Historical discussion of the English Civil War in parliamentary terms has concentrated on the constitutional enactments of the Long Parliament and has tended to ignore the fact that the June 1640 session of the Scottish Estates provided a powerful precedent for the actions and reforms undertaken by the Long Parliament. The Scottish constitutional settlement ultimately provided a constitutional model on which the English Long Parliament could draw, and also merits recognition within a wider European perspective.

NOTES

1. *A Relation of the Kings Entertainment into Scotland, on Saterday the 14 of August 1641. As also the Copy of a Speech which the Speaker for Scotland spake to His Majesty* (1641), 3.
2. NLS MS 2263 Salt and Coal: Events, 1635–62, folio 169; NLS Adv.MS 32.4.8, 'A Short History of The Reformation of Religion in Scotland, England & Irleind and of the Wars carried on by King Charles The First in these Three Kingdoms during his reign', ff 4–5; *CSPV*, 1640–1642, 53; *CSPD*, 1640, 208, 307; *Diary of Sir Thomas Hope of Craighall, 1634–45*, T. Thomson ed., (Bannatyne Club, Edinburgh, 1843), 117; Balfour, *Historical Works*, II, 373; Burnet, *The Memoirs of the Dukes of Hamilton*, 166–167; *The Memoirs of Henry Guthry*, 67–72; Gordon, *History of Scots Affairs*, III, 100–86; J. Spalding, *The History of the Troubles and Memorable Transactions in Scotland and England, 1624–45*, J. Skene ed., (Bannatyne Club, Edinburgh, 1828–1829), I, 213–214; Donaldson, *James V–James VII*, 327; Stevenson, *Government Under the Covenanters*, xxii; Stevenson, *Scottish Revolution*, 192–193; MacInnes, *Charles I and the Making of the Covenanting Movement*, 195; Rait, *The Parliaments of Scotland*, 340–341; A.I MacInnes, 'The Long Road to Edgehill', *The Sunday Mail Story of Scotland*, 16, (Glasgow, 1988), 446; C. Russell, *The Crisis of Parliaments. English History 1509–1660* (Oxford, 1971), 326–327; R. Lockyer, *The Early Stuarts. A Political History of England 1603–1642* (London, 1989), 235; M.C. Fissel, *The Bishops' Wars. Charles I's campaigns against Scotland 1638–40* (Cambridge, 1994), 1–2; J. Scally, 'The Political Career of James, third Marquis and first Duke of Hamilton (1606–1649) to 1643' (University of Cambridge, PhD thesis, 1993), 292–3.
3. *APS*, v, 251–252, 258–25. Two of the gentry recorded in June 1640 had been replaced by other commissioners in April and May 1640. On 2 April Harry Montgomery of Giffan had been commissioned for the shire of Ayr to replace Cunningham of Cunninghamhead who was ill. On 30 May Sir William Cockburn of Langtoun had been commissioned for the shire of Berwick to replace Home of Blackadder who was also ill. However, both Cunningham of Cunnighamhead and Home of Blackadder are recorded in the parliamentary rolls of 2 June 1640 and may have recovered from illness by that date (Ibid, 258–259; SRO, Parliamentary Commissions, PA 7/25/4, PA 7/25/6). Two burgesses were commissioned in May 1640 to replace the commissioners for their respective burghs; Alexander Wilkieson (Lauder) and James Scott (Montrose). Both burgesses are included in the parliamentary rolls of 2 June 1640 (*APS*, v, 258–259; SRO PA 7/25/79, PA 7/25/82).
4. *APS*, v, 259–299; Balfour, *Historical Works*, II, 373; Rait, *The Parliaments of Scotland*, 65–66; Gardiner, *History of England*, IX, 152.
5. *APS*, v, 260–261; Balfour, *Historical Works*, II, 374; MacInnes, *Charles I and the Making of the Covenanting Movement*, 196.

6. *APS*, v, 260–261; Rait, *The Parliaments of Scotland*, 66; Terry, *The Scottish Parliament*, 10–11.
7. *APS*, v, 7–9, 296–297; Rait, *The Parliaments of Scotland*, 66, 186–187.
8. *APS*, v, 270–271, 271–276, 276–277, 290–292; Rait, *The Parliaments of Scotland*, 66. The Court of Session was modified to two meetings per annum. The distinction between Spiritual and Temporal Lords of Session was abolished. Since the reign of James V and the establishment of the College of Justice the Lords of Council and Session had been split equally between the two groups. Henceforth all churchmen were barred from being Lords of Session (*APS*, v 266, 297).
9. *APS*, v, 270, 278–279; Balfour, *Historical Works*, II, 374; Rait, *The Parliaments of Scotland*, 66, 186–187, 286; W. Ferguson, *Scotland's Relations with England* (Edinburgh, 1977), 118.
10. *APS*, v, 278–279; Ferguson, *Scotland's Relations with England*, 118; Terry, *The Scottish Parliament*, 112–113; A. Hughes, *The Causes of the English Civil War* (London, 1991), 51.
11. *APS* v, 262.
12. Ibid, 252–254; 262. Sir Patrick Hepburne of Wauchton (Haddington), Sir George Stirling of Keir (Stirling), Sir John Smith (Edinburgh), and James Fletcher (Dundee) were the gentry and burgesses who had been members of the 1639 Lords of the Articles.
13. Ibid, 290; Balfour, *Historical Works*, II, 378; Ferguson, *Scotland's Relations with England*, 118; Lynch, *Scotland. A New History*, 272; Rait, *The Parliaments of Scotland*, 66–7, 315; J.P. Cooper (ed.), *The Decline of Spain and the Thirty Years War, 1609–59*, The New Cambridge Modern History, volume IV, (Cambridge, 1970), 570.
14. *APS*, v, 282–284; Stevenson, *Scottish Revolution*, 194–197; Stevenson, *Government Under the Covenanters*, xxi-xxvi; MacInnes, 'The Origin and Organization of the Covenanting Movement', PhD thesis, volume two, 292–293.
15. *APS*, v, 264, 280–282.
16. Balfour, *Historical Works*, II, 376, 378; MacInnes, *Charles I and the Making of the Covenanting Movement*, 197.
17. Balfour, *Historical Works*, II, 379; Stevenson, *Government Under the Covenanters*, xxi-xxvi; Stevenson, *Scottish Revolution*, 194–197; *CSPD*, 1640, 289, 307, 329, 449; Burnet, *The Memoirs of the Dukes of Hamilton*, 168; *Proceedings of the Short Parliament of 1640* (Camden Society, 4th series, 1977), 117–118; R. Menteith of Salmonet, *The History of the Troubles of Great Britain* (1734), 57–58; Rusworth, *Historical Collections*, II (ii), 1042–1212; Donaldson *James V–James VII*, 327; Ferguson, *Scotland's Relations with England*, 118–119; Rait, *The Parliaments of Scotland*, 341, 377; Terry, *The Scottish Parliament*, 89, 107–112, 118–121; Hughes, *The Causes of the English Civil War*, 51; Brown, *Kingdom or Province?*, 119–120.
18. *APS*, v, 299; MacInnes, *Charles I and the Making of the Covenanting Movement*, 210.
19. *APS*, v, 282–284.
20. Ibid; J.J. Johnston Brown, 'The Social and Economic Influences of the Edinburgh Merchant Elite, 1600–1638', (University of Edinburgh, PhD thesis, two volumes, 1985), charts the commercial and political careers of prominent Edinburgh burgesses such as John Smith, Edward Edgar, Archibald Sydserf, and William Dick.
21. *APS*, v, 282–284; MacInnes, *Charles I and the Making of the Covenanting Movement*, 196; Gordon, *History of Scots Affairs*, III, 181–184; Rait, *The Parliaments of Scotland*, 377.

22. Of the surviving records, the first recorded transactions of the Committee of Estates are dated 3 August 1640, although the Committee probably met regularly between 11 June and 3 August. (EUL, Transactions of the Committee of Estates of Scotland, August 1640–June 1641, Dc 4.16, folio 1). MacInnes, *Charles I and the Making of the Covenanting Movement*, 197.
23. EUL, Transactions of the Committee of Estates of Scotland, August 1640–June 1641, Dc 4.16, folio 1.
24. Ibid; NLS Salt and Coal: Events, 1635–62, MS 2263, folio 173; *APS*, v, 282–284, 335–336; Sir John Borough, *Notes of the Treaty carried on at Ripon between King Charles and the Covenanters of Scotland, A.D. 1640*, (Camden Society, 1869), 3–9, 13–18; Balfour, *Historical Works*, II, 407; *CSPD*, 1640–1641, 155; Rushworth, *Historical Collections*, II (ii), 1285; *The Memoirs of Henry Guthry*, 89; Stevenson, *Scottish Revolution*, 207; W.C. MacKenzie, *The Highlands and Islands of Scotland* (revised edn. Edinburgh, 1949), 226; Rait, *The Parliaments of Scotland*, 68; Hardwicke, *Miscellaneous State Papers*, 190; *Extracts from the Records of the Burgh of Aberdeen, 1625–1642*, ed., J. Stuart (Scottish Burgh Records Society, 1872), 245; L. Kaplan, *Politics and Religion During the English Revolution: The Scots and the Long Parliament, 1643–1645* (New York, 1976), xii-xiii; E.J. Cowan, *Montrose. For Covenant and King*, (London, 1977), 92–94, 97–98.
25. EUL, Transactions of the Committee of Estates of Scotland, August 1640–June 1641, Dc 4.16, ff 70–73; NLS Denmilne MSS XIII, 33.1.1, numbers 11 and 27; *CSPD*, 1640–1641, 131, 144, 244–46; *CSPV*, 1640–1642, 101–102; Menteith of Salmonet, *History of the Troubles of Great Britain*, 68–69; Balfour, *Historical Works*, II, 410; Baillie, *Letters and Journals*, I, 306; Makey, *The Church of the Covenant*, 64–65; B.P. Levack, *The Formation of the British state: England, Scotland and the Union 1603–1707* (Oxford, 1987), 48, 148; C.L. Hamilton, 'The Anglo-Scottish Negotiations of 1640–1', *SHR*, 41, (1962), 84; D. Stevenson, 'The Early Covenanters and the Federal Union of Britain' in *Scotland and England 1286–1815*, ed. R.A. Mason (Edinburgh, 1987), 164–167; MacInnes, *Charles I and the Making of the Covenanting Movement*, 198; MacInnes, 'The Scottish Constitution, 1638–1651', 117–118; J.S. Morrill, *The Nature of the English Revolution*, (London, 1993), 262.
26. EUL, Transactions of the Committee of Estates of Scotland, August 1640–June 1641, Dc 4.16, folio 93, 'Articles from the Comittee of estats to ther commissioneris at court anent ye league wt ye estats of ye United Provinces'. MacInnes, *Charles I and the Making of the Covenanting Movement*, 199.
27. EUL, Transactions of the Committee of Estates of Scotland, August 1640–June 1641, Dc 4.16, folio 73.
28. Ibid.
29. *The Journal of Thomas Cunningham of Campvere, 1640–1654*, ed., E.J. Courthope (SHS, 3rd series, 1927).
30. Clement Walker, *Relations and Observations, Historicall and Politick, upon the Parliament* (1650), 8. This pamphlet is included in the SRO Fraser MacKintosh Collection, GD 128/40/7a. Also included in GD 128/40/7a is *An Appendix to the History of Independency Being A brief description of some few of Argile's proceedings before and since he joyned in confederacy with the Independent Iunto in England. With a Parallel betwixt him and Cromwell. And A Caveat to all his seduced Adherents.* Included in this document are further references to a confederacy with the Dutch on pages 150–151. Samuel Rutherford, *Lex Rex* (1644), 211–212; D.H. Pennington, *Seventeenth Century Europe* (1972), 45–46, 212.

31. *CSPV*, 1640–1642, 220; *CSPV*, 1642–1643, 209.
32. *To the Honourable The Knights, Citizens and Burgesses, Now assembled in Parliament. The humble Propositions of William Ball, alias Bennet, Gentleman. Concerning the Forts of this Kingdome with some other Considerations of State* (undated), 12.
33. MacInnes, *Charles I and the Making of the Covenanting Movement*, 211–212; Gardiner, *History of England*, IX, 244; *Lords Journals*, 4, (1628–1642), 176, 178, 180; C. Carlton, *Charles I: The Personal Monarch* (London, 1984), 223.
34. *APS*, v, 300–307, 620–623. Twenty-two nobles, 22 gentry, and 35 burgesses (119 individuals in total) were present in Parliament, 19 November 1640. Parliamentary membership as per 14 January 1641 was identical to that of 19 November 1640. The membership of 13 April 1641 consisted of 11 nobles, 13 gentry, and five burgesses (29 individuals in total). Sixteen nobles, 22 gentry, and 22 burgesses (60 individuals in total) sat in Parliament, 25 May 1641. Levels of parliamentary attendance were therefore far lower than the June 1640 session. Gentry and burghal levels, with the exception of one set of burgess data, outstripped the attendance levels of the nobility (Ibid). Twenty of the 22 nobles (91%), 15 of the 22 gentry (68%), and 20 of the 35 burgesses (57%) present in Parliament, 19 November 1640, had also sat in the June 1640 session. All 20 nobles, 23 of the 31 gentry (74%), and all 35 burgesses present in Parliament, 14 January 1641, had also sat in the November 1640 session. Seven of the 11 nobles (64%), nine of the 13 gentry (69%), and three of the five burgesses (60%) present in Parliament, 13 April, had also sat in the January 1641 session. Eight of the 16 nobles (50%), eight of the 22 gentry (36%), and only one of the 22 burgesses (4%) in the session of 25 May 1641, had also sat in the April 1641 session. NLS Treaties at Newcastle and London, 1640–41, ff 101–102, 112–112; NLS Salt and Coal: Events, 1635–62, MS 2263, folio 174; NLS Denmilne MSS XIII 33.1.1, number 37; SRO Hamilton Papers GD 406/1/1369; EUL Instructions to the Committee of Estates of Scotland, 1640–41, Dc 4.16, ff 64–65, 69; Balfour, *Historical Works*, II, 425; Rushworth, *Historical Collections*, III (i), 383; *Diary of Sir Thomas Hope of Craighall, 1634–45*, T. Thomson ed., (Bannatyne Club, Edinburgh, 1843), 122; Rait, *The Parliaments of Scotland*, 327, 340, 342.
35. *APS*, v, 251–308.
36. *APS*, v, 310–311; Balfour, *Historical Works*, II, 10; NLS Salt and Coal: Events, 1635–62, MS 2263, ff 175–176; SRO Hamilton Papers, GD 40D/1/1381, GD 406/1/1386; NLS Wodrow Folio LXXII, numbers 258, 270; *CSPV*, 1640–1642, 153, 177; *Diary of Sir Thomas Hope of Craighall*, 148.
37. *APS*, v, 312. The Constable and Marischal were formal Officers of Parliament. The Constable was responsible for the maintainance of authority outwith the Parliament; he superseded the judicial authority of ordinary law court relating to certain criminal offences ('riot, disorder, blood and slaughter') within four miles of any meeting of Parliament. The Marischal was responsible for maintaining authority within the House when an assembled Parliament was in session (Rait, *The Parliaments of Scotland*, 513–514).
38. *APS*, v, 312–314, 318, 332, 643–722. The process by which all bills and overtures were subjected has been fully documented by MacInnes in 'The Origin and Organization of the Covenanting Movement', PhD thesis, volume two, 402–403. It should be noted, however, that this process was not incorporated or established in any single piece of legislation. Balfour, *Historical Works*, II, 11, 22, 27, 31–32; Baillie, *Letters and Journals*, I, 398; Rushworth, *Historical Collections*, III (i), 383, 381; NLS Salt and Coal: Events, 1635–62, MS 2263, folio 176; Stevenson, *Government Under*

the Covenanters, xxxiv; Rait, *The Parliaments of Scotland*, 377; Terry, *The Scottish Parliament*, 186–189; Despite the fact that noblemen's heirs had been barred from the House, evidnece indicates that Lords Carnegie, Fleming, Angus, Maitland, Montgomery, and Elcho were stil attempting to flout these rules; see C. Beattie, 'The Political disqualification of noblemen's heirs in seventeenth century Scotland', *SHR*, 59, (1980), 174–175.

39. MacInnes, 'The Origin and Organization of the Covenanting Movement', PhD thesis, volume two, 463.
40. *APS*, v, 318; Stevenson, *Scottish Revolution*, 207; *The Memoirs of Henry Guthry*, 89.
41. Baillie, *Letters and Journals*, I, 384–385; APS, v, 309–329, 642; Menteith of Salmonet, *History of the Troubles of Great Britain*, 77; MacInnes, 'The Origin and Organization of the Covenanting Movement', PhD thesis, volume two, 463.
42. *APS*, v, 309–329, 642; Balfour, *Historical Works*, II, 26, 36, 38; Baillie, *Letters and Journals*, I, 389; Rait, *The Parliaments of Scotland*, 510; MacInnes, 'The Origin and Organization of the Covenanting Movement', PhD thesis, volume two, 463.
43. *APS*, v, 319.
44. Ibid, 308, 331–332; Stevenson, *Government Under the Covenanters*, 174; Gardiner, *History of England*, X, 18, 27; *Lords Journals*, 4, (1628–1642), 366, A. Fletcher, *The Outbreak of the English Civil War* (London, 1981), 47–48.
45. GUL Murray Collection, 147, Notes of What Passes in the Parliament, 1641, ff 1–3; SRO Leven and Melville Papers, GD 26/7/163; Baillie, *Letters and Journals*, I, 386; Rait, *The Parliaments of Scotland*, 66, 342; *APS*, v, 330–332, 643.
46. GUL Murray Collection, 147, Notes of What Passes in the Parliament, 1641, folio 3; Baillie, *Letters and Journals*, I, 389.
47. GUL Murray Collection, 147, Notes of What Passes in the Parliament, 1641. ff 4–5; SRO Airth Writs GD 37/319; *APS*, v, 332–333, 329; Balfour, *Historical Works*, II, 44–46; Baillie, *Letters and Journals*, I, 20; *Memoirs of the Marquis of Montrose* (Edinburgh, 1856), I, 254–255; Rushworth, Historical Collections, III (i), 389; *The Nicholas Papers, Correspondence of Sir Edward Nicholas, Secretary of State*, G.F. Warner ed., (Camden Society), I, 20, 24; Stevenson, *Scottish Revolution*, 233, 263; MacInnes, 'The Origin and Organization of the Covenanting Movement', PhD thesis, volume two, 398; MacInnes, *Charles I and the Making of the Covenanting Movement*, 200–201, 201–202; Scally, 'The Political Career of James, third Marquis and first Duke of Hamilton,' PhD thesis, 307.
48. *APS*, v, 329, 332–588; Baillie, *Letters and Journals*, I, 398.
49. *The Truth of the Proceedings in Scotland containing the Discovery of the Late Conspiracie. With divers other Remarkable Passages. Related in a Letter written from Edinburgh, 19th October 1641* (1641), 5. The committee of October 1641, consisting of six per estate is not listed in *APS*.
50. *APS*, v, 262, 644; Baillie, *Letters and Journals*, I, 398.
51. Ibid, 333–334, 382.
52. Ibid, 334–45. On 25 August, Cassillis, Lauderdale, Southesk, and Loudoun had been appointed to revise the treaty prior to parliamentary ratification. A political balance therefore existed between radical and conservative nobles. Gentry and burgesses were also represented. It does not appear that the delegations of 25 and 26 August constituted formal parliamentary session committees.
53. Baillie, *Letters and Journals*, I, 389.
54. Ibid; Gardiner, *History of England*, X, 18, 29.
55. *APS*, v, 653.

56. Ibid, 654.
57. Ibid.
58. *A Declaration of the Proceedings in the Parliament of Scotland* (1641), 2; GUL Murray Collection, 147, Notes of What Passes in the Parliament, 1641, 15–18, 22, 24; SRO Supplementary Parliamentary Papers, 1606–42, 96(1)-(4), 95; NLS Copies of State Papers and Political Pamphlets, Adv MS 34.2.10, ff 290–293; *The Nicholas Papers*, I, 51–52; Carte, *A Collection of Original Letters and Papers Concerning the Affairs of England*, 2–5, 6–8; S.R Gardiner, *The Fall of the Monarchy of Charles I, 1637–42* (London, 1882), I, 256–259; Stevenson, *Scottish Revolution*, 236–237, 238; MacInnes, *Charles I and the Making of the Covenanting Movement*, 202–203; Carlton, *Charles I. The Personal Monarch*, 186; C.V Wedgwood, 'Anglo-Scottish Relations, 1603–40', *TRHS*, fourth series, XXXII, (1950), 41.
59. *APS*, v, 332–425, 643–721; Balfour, *Historical Works*, II, 148–152; Stevenson, *Scottish Revolution*, 237; MacInnes, 'The Origin and Organization of the Covenanting Movement', PhD thesis, volume two, 407–408, 410; Laing, *History of Scotland*, 216. The nine radical nobles on the Privy Council were Loudoun, Argyll, Sutherland, Eglinton, Cassillis, Lothian, Balmerino, Burleigh, and Yester; Brown, *Kingdom or Province?*, 122, fails to recognise that the Privy Council was infact marginalised and that real power lay with the interval committees, as was witnessed by later events, 1641–43. The interval committees constituted a breakdown of the Committee of Estates into specialised bodies with wider scope of membership.
60. Menteith of Salmonet, *History of the Troubles of Great Britain*, 78; Stevenson, *Scottish Revolution*, 290; D. Stevenson, 'The Covenanters and the Court of Session 1637–1650', *Juridicial Review*, 1972, 239–240; P.G.B McNeill, 'The Independence of the Scottish Judiciary', *Juridicial Review*, 1958, 140.
61. *APS*, v, 332–425, 643–71; Baillie, *Letters and Journals*, I, 396; NLS Adv MS 32.4.8, 'A Short History of The Reformation of Religion in Scotland, England & Irleind and of The Wars carried on by King Charles The First in these Three Kingdoms during his reign', folio 9; Scally, 'The Political Career of James, third Marquis and first Duke of Hamilton', PhD thesis, 313.
62. *APS*, v, 332–445, 643–71. Whilst Parliament was sitting it was enacted that all other judiciaries could not sit (such as Sheriff Courts, Baron Courts, and Burgh Courts). The legislation of the June 1640 session was also to be published and circulated. Balfour, *Historical Works*, II, 53–145; Rait, *The Parliaments of Scotland*, 206; Terry, *The Scottish Parliament*, 44, 69.
63. G. Crawford, *The Lives and Characters of the Officers of the Crown and the State in Scotland* (1726), 207; APS, v, 396; Terry, *The Scottish Parliament*, 83; MacInnes, 'The Origin and Organization of the Covenanting Movement', PhD thesis, volume two, 410; D. Stevenson, 'The King's Scottish Revenues and the Covenanters, 1625–1651', *HJ*, 17, (1974), 30.
64. The political ineptitude of Charles who was responsible for his own misfortunes as a 'British' monarch governing three kingdoms has been convincingly argued with vigour by Fissel, *The Bishops' Wars*, 289–299.
65. *APS*, v, 268, 588.
66. Ibid, 252–428.
67. Ibid.
68. Baillie, *Letters and Journals*, I, 393.
69. *APS*, v, 428; Baillie, *Letters and Journals*, I, 54; SRO Hamilton Papers GD 406/1/1487.

70. *APS*, v, 282–284, 331–332, 392, 395. Sir William Cunningham of Caprington (Ayr), George Douglas of Bonjedburgh (Roxburgh), Thomas Durham (Perth), John Binnie (Edinburgh), George Bell (Linlithgow), John Kennedy (Ayr), and James Anderson (Coupar) were not members of Parliament as per 17 August 1641. The five nobles who had been included on the 1640 Committee of Estates were Cassillis, Lothian, Lindsay, Balmerino and Burleigh. Hepburne of Humbie, James Sword (St Andrews), and James Scott (Montrose) formed the grouping of gentry and burgesses also included on that committee. MacInnes, *Charles I and the Making of the Covenanting Movement*, 203, 204; Stevenson, *Scottish Revolution*, 240–241.
71. *APS*, v, 282–284, 404–405. The four nobles who had been members of the 1640 Committee of Estates were Dunfermline, Lothian, Lindsay, and Balmerino. The four gentry who had been members of the 1640 Committee of Estates were Sir Patrick Hepburne of Wauchton (Haddington), Sir Patrick Hamilton of Little Preston (Haddington), Sir Thomas Hope of Kerse (Clackmannan), and Sir David Home of Wedderburne (Berwick). The six burgesses who had been members of the 1640 Committee of Estates were Edward Edgar (Edinburgh), John Smith (Edinburgh), Richard Maxwell (Edinburgh), James Sword (St Andrews), John Rutherford (Jedburgh), and Hugh Kennedy (Ayr). MacInnes, *Charles I and the Making of the Covenanting Movement*, 204.
72. *APS*, v, 35–39, 392, 395, 400–401; MacInnes, *The Making of the Covenanting Movement*, 204. The 1633 Commission for Plantation of Kirks and Valuation of Teinds had been composed of 14 nobles (including five Officers of State), nine clerics, 13 gentry (including four Officers of State), and nine burgesses.
73. Scally, 'The Political Career of James, third Marquis and first Duke of Hamilton', PhD thesis, 307–308; Gardiner, *History of England*, X, 23.
74. *APS*, v, 319, 331–332, 408. Sir John Hamilton was the remaining laird who was not a member of Parliament as per 17 August 1641. The two burgesses on the committee who were not members of Parliament as per 17 August 1641 were George Bell (Linlithgow) and James Sword (St Andrews). The two nobles who had been included on the 1640 Committee of Estates were Burleigh and Coupar. James Sword (St Andrews) was the one burgess who had been included on the 1640 Committee of Estates. MacInnes, *Charles I and the Making of the Covenanting Movement*, 204.

3

The Consolidation of the Radical Oligarchy: Government by Parliamentary Interval Committees and Radical Dominance, 1641–1644

Within a British perspective, and in the intricate triangular relationship of the 'Three Kingdoms', the outbreak of the Irish Rebellion and the English Civil War were to have a profound significance on Scottish domestic politics and the cohesion of the Covenanting Movement. The Scottish Parliament through the vehicle of its interval committees (under the management of the radical leadership), became embroiled in both the Irish Rebellion and the English Civil War as a means of exporting the Covenanting 'revolution' on a British basis.[1]

The operation of Parliamentary Interval Committees, 1641–44

Despite the reconstitution of the Scottish Privy Council on 13 November 1641, the political resources of the radical leadership were focused on the three most important parliamentary interval committees; the Commission for the Common Burdens, the Commission for the Brotherly Assistance, and the Conservators for the Peace. Analysis of the sederunts of the Privy Council and the above three commissions provides a crucial insight into their inter-relationship in terms of political significance and of membership.

Although defined by separate parliamentary commissions, the Commission for the Common Burdens and the Commission for the Brotherly Assistance had identical membership and in fact sat as a single commission (hence a single commission with two specific financial remits). The Common Burdens-Brotherly Assistance Commission and the Privy Council immediately convened on 18 November (Privy Council) and 19 November (Common Burdens-Brotherly Assistance) following the close of Parliament on 17 November. In both cases, sederunts commenced on 19 November.[2]

Inspection of both attendance records of Privy Council membership reveals that in the period to June 1643 recognised radical nobles dominated proceedings. Two hundred and eight sederunts of the Privy Council are recorded. Argyll, Loudoun, Cassillis, Leven, Eglinton, Balmerino, and Burleigh formed this radical grouping. Conservative/pragmatic Royalist influence was centred on Glencairn, Southesk, and Lauderdale. Other noted conservative/pragmatic Royalist nobles have relatively low attendance records, particularly, Hamilton, Lanark, and Lennox.[3]

Despite the theoretical balance in terms of membership between the various groupings of nobles on the Privy Council, radicals dominated and the conservatives/pragmatic Royalists were marginalised. As early as 18 November 1641 five radical nobles (Argyll, Loudoun, Eglinton, Balmerino, and Leven), had been commissioned by the Privy Council to draw up instructions to be sent to the Scottish Parliament concerning the Scottish contribution for the suppression of the Irish Rebellion.[4]

Fifteen gentry had been included on the Privy Council (as a reflection of the growing political importance of the gentry 1638–41), but only five were in attendance on a semi-regular basis. Of these four were officers of state; Gibson of Durie (Clerk Register), Hope of Craighall (Lord Advocate), Hamilton of Orbiston (Justice-Clerk), and Carmichael of that ilk (Treasurer Depute). They were supplemented by Hepburne of Wauchton (Haddington).[5] These gentry provided backup to the radical nobles on the Privy Council.

Therefore the reconstituted Privy Council of 1641 to 1643 was less of a Royalist body than has been traditionally assumed and was under the direction of influential radical nobles. The Privy Council had been the traditional vehicle of government and administration of the nation. However, the Covenanting leadership bypassed the Privy Council, whilst still retaining a marked presence in its meetings, and superseded it through the two interval committees of the Common Burdens-Brotherly Assistance Commission and the Conservators of the Peace.

It was these two bodies, controlled by the radical Covenanting leadership, that were to undertake the crucial financial, economic, military, and diplomatic decisions affecting Scottish military intervention in Ireland and diplomatic negotiations regarding possible Scottish intervention in the English Civil War.

The continuance of the Irish Rebellion soon overshadowed the original remit of the Commission for the Common Burdens and the Brotherly Assistance. From early 1642 onwards it became involved, with the conjunction of the Privy Council, in the transportation of 10,000 Scottish troops to Ireland (which was to be paid for by the English Parliament).[6]

In total the Common Burdens and Brotherly Assistance Commission met on 97 occassions (as per recorded sederunts) to 8 November 1644. Radical commitment was evident with regard to noble attendance. Argyll, Cassillis, Balmerino, Loudoun, and Eglinton were prominent attenders. Conservative/pragmatic Royalist interests were still maintained, on a lesser basis, by Glencairn, Southesk, Lauderdale, and Lord Forrester.

Gentry attendance was focused on Sir Gilbert Ramsay of Balmaine (Mearns), Sir John Wauchope of Niddrie (Edinburgh), and Sir Charles Erskine of Bandeth (Stirling). Compared to the gentry, burghal attendance levels involved the employment of a wider field of personnel. John Binnie (Edinburgh), George Garden (Burntisland), Patrick Leslie (Aberdeen), James Sword (St Andrews), and John Semple (Dumbarton) were to the fore in attendance of the burghal members of the Brotherly Assistance/Common Burdens commission.[7]

As per the terms of the original commissions of 15 November 1641, the quorum was set at 12, with a minimum attendance of three of each estate. On five occassions the actual quorum was less than 12. This would seem to indicate that radicals were continuing to control proceedings despite the fact that these meetings were inquorate. At nine further diets occassions, the rule that there must be at least three of each estate present was not adhered to. Nevertheless, at 92 diets the quorum of the commissions was greater than or equal to 12 (95%).[8]

Three subcommittees were established by the Common Burdens-Brotherly Assistance Commission between November 1641 and January 1642. Two were issued with related financial remits concerning public finances; firstly for the preparation of public accounts and secondly for the recording of all accounts and debts. Increased tension over the Irish troubles manifested itself in the establishment of a specialised military subcommittee on 21 January 1642. It was issued with three remits; on the required levels of arms and ammunition to be sent to Ireland, on pay levels for army officers, and the manufacture of magazine and weapons. In line with an increased Scottish commitment to the Irish Wars, the Commission as a whole authorised on 28 March the borrowing of £14, 000 sterling (£168, 000 Scots) to support the Scottish battalions in the invasion of Ireland.

Conservative/pragmatic Royalist nobles were allowed access to the two financial subcommittees; Southesk, Forrester, and Lauderdale. Radical noble interests were maintained by the presence of Burleigh. However, radicals prevailed on the crucial military subcommittee through the shrewd employment of Cassillis and Burleigh. Radical dominance was secured by the gentry and burgess members, several of whom enjoyed common membership of several of the subcommittees. This can be applied to Erskine of Bandeth (Stirling), Wauchope of Niddrie (Edinburgh), and Rigg of Ethernie (Fife) for the gentry. The corresponding burghal grouping consisted of John Binnie (Edinburgh), George Garden (Burntisland), and James Sword (St Andrews). It was supplemented by other radical burgesses, notably George Bell (Linlithgow) and Patrick Leslie (Aberdeen).[9]

The British dimension of the Great Rebellion led also to regular meetings of the Conservators of the Peace in 1642–43 as the principal Scottish diplomatic agency concerning the troubles in England and Ireland, principally to establish closer contact with the English Parliament.

The Conservators of the Peace first met, and accepted their commissions, on 23 September 1642. Between 22 September 1642 and 7 July 1643 they met on 33 occassions. Noble representation was dominated by radicals. Argyll attended 32 of the 33 diets and Balmerino 30. Loudoun, Leven, and Eglinton also had high attendance figures. Lauderdale also attended 32 diets, but conservatives and pragmatic Royalists were clearly outnumbered. Although Hamilton was present on 25 occassions, no forum was available for a Royalist party to emerge within this commission. Nobles associated with the Court have correspondingly low attendance figures. Lennox did not attend at all and Morton, Roxburgh, and Kinnoull only turned up for one diet. Lanark, on the other hand, is recorded in 10 sederunts. Pragmatic Royalists and conservatives were outflanked or simply declined to attend in recognition of radical political strength.[10]

Loudoun appears to have been President of this commission. On 22 February 1643 Argyll was chosen to be President of all meetings whenever Loudoun was absent on public business in England. Argyll was subsequently President on five occassions. This represents a spread of leadership among the leading radical nobles between Loudoun, Argyll, and Balmerino (Balmerino had been voted President of the Common Burdens-Brotherly Assistance Commission on 19 November 1641), although Argyll remained the dominant individual.[11]

The pattern of gentry attendance among the Conservators of the Peace illustrates a small dominant grouping. Hepburne of Wauchton (Haddington), Morton of Cambo (Fife), Hamilton of Little Preston (Haddington), Hope of Kerse (Clackmannan), Johnston of Wariston (as representative of the Kirk), and Erskine of Dun (Forfar), formed this close-knit grouping. A similar trend is reflected in the attendance records of the burgesses representatives, although it was based in a more widespread employment of personnel; William Glendoning (Kirkcudbright), Robert Barclay (Irvine), Thomas Bruce (Stirling), James Sword (St Andrews), John Semple (Dumbarton), Sir John Smith (Edinburgh), Edward Edgar (Edinburgh), and Robert Cunningham (Kinghorn). Of the four burgesses on the commission as a whole who were not members of Parliament as per 17 August 1641, all have low attendance levels apart from Edward Edgar (Edinburgh).[12]

The quorum of the Conservators of the Peace was set at 12, with three of each estate to be always present. In line with the nature of the commission, attendance levels were high and these minimum limits were surpassed at every diet.[13]

In essence, a great degree of interaction existed between the Common-Burdens-Brotherly Assistance Commission and the Conservators of the Peace. Of a combined total membership of 113, eight nobles, six gentry, and eight burgesses (yielding a total of 23 individuals) enjoyed common membership of both commissions. Five of the nobles (Argyll, Loudoun, Leven, Eglinton, and Balmerino) were noted radicals, whilst the remaining three (Lauderdale, Glencairn, and Lindsay) represented a conservative and pragmatic Royalist grouping. Innes of that ilk (Elgin), Grierson of Lag (Dumfries and Annandale), Dundas of that ilk (Linlithgow), Forbes of Craigievar (Aberdeen), Home of Wedderburne (Berwick), and Erskine of Dun (Forfar) enjoyed membership of both commissions. All were leading radicals among the gentry representatives. Radical strength also prevailed among the common grouping of burgesses; Patrick Bell (Glasgow), Robert Barclay (Irvine), John Semple (Dumbarton), James Sword (St Andrews), William Glendoning (Kirkcudbright), Thomas Durham (Perth), Patrick Leslie (Aberdeen), and George Bell (Linlithgow).[14]

The political significance of this interaction was twofold. Firstly, the Common Burdens-Brotherly Assistance Commission and the Conservators of the

Peace Commission (both controlled by the radicals under Argyll) formed the appropriate forum for the calling of the Convention of Estates of June 1643. Secondly, it enabled the radicals led by Argyll to outmanoeuvre the conservatives and pragmatic Royalists led by Hamilton in their attempts to use the Privy Council as the vehicle for a revival in Royalist fortunes in Scotland.

The outbreak of the English Civil War, in conjunction with the continuing Irish troubles, had led to rival appeals for aid (in effect military and financial) from both Charles and the English Parliament. These rival appeals found appropriate sympathy with the Scottish political elites. The Privy Council constituted the institution through which any Royalist stance in favour of the king could be taken, given the greater number of conservative and pragmatic Royalist nobles included in its commission. On the other hand, the Conservators of the Peace and the Common Burdens-Brotherly Assistance Commission represented the institutions through which an alliance or military alignment with the English Parliament would occur.[15]

Hamilton returned to Scotland in June 1642 in attempt to promote the King's fortunes and initiate a more concrete conservative and Royalist grouping. Following his return, Hamilton first attended the Privy Council on 5 July, and then 7 July, 1642. With the outbreak of civil war in England in August 1642, Hamilton appears on the Privy Council on a regular basis from August 1642 until February 1643. Subsequently he was present on only eight occassions until his last appearance on 20 June, before the holding of the Convention of Estates on 22 June 1643.[16]

There was no sustained attempt to forge a conservative/pragmatic Royalist revival on the Privy Council in reaction to radical political strength on the interval committees. Of this grouping, only Glencairn and Lanark took part in Council proceedings on a regular basis, whilst Southesk's attendance declined.[17]

Hamilton and his conservative/pragmatic Royalist faction achieved only one significant success on the Privy Council and even this was overturned within a short space of time. On 20 December 1642 a meeting of the Privy Council took place to discuss the printing of a letter from Charles justifying his conduct towards the English Parliament. The printing of a rival declaration from the English Parliament was also discussed. Acting on the instructions of the king, Hamilton, Lanark and Southesk advocated the printing of the King's letter only. Argyll, Loudoun, and Balmerino countered this move, but failed to secure a majority of votes. The King's letter alone was ordered to be printed by a vote of 11 to 9.[18]

By 10 January 1643 Argyll had secured a majority of votes to reverse the decision of 20 December and the publication of the English Parliament was authorised to be printed.[19] At the meeting of the Conservators of the Peace on 10 January it was decided to petition the king to call a Parliament in Scotland.[20] Of a total of 32 Conservators of the Peace (consisting of 10 nobles, 14 gentry, and eight burgesses) present at this meeting, seven declared that 'they were not in thair judgement against the calling of a Parliamt bot onelie against the tyme of supplicatting for it presentlie'.[21] Unsurprisingly, noble opposition emanated from Hamilton, Glencairn, Lanark, and Callander. Gentry opposition came from Douglas of Cavers (Roxburgh), Erskine of Dun (Forfar), and Graham of Morphie (Mearns). The fact that three gentry dissented does not necessarily imply an alignment with Hamilton; all had been present in the final session of the 1641 Parliament and their dissension may have been only related to the time of supplication for a Parliament. The opposition of Hamilton and Lanark, on the other hand, was more to do with principle and strategy.[22]

On 28 February 1643 the Privy Council issued an appeal for voluntary contributions to ensure the maintenance of the Scottish army in Ireland. Initiated by the radical leadership, the appeal was met by an immediate response. A tripartite meeting took place between the Privy Council, the Conservators of the Peace, and the Commissioners of the Common Burdens-Brotherly Assistance, on 3 and 4 March 1643, respectively.[23]

Constitutionally these were meetings of three separate commissions. In practice they were essentially assemblies of the radical caucus. Argyll, Leven, Eglinton, and Balmerino were members of all three commissions. Lauderdale was also a member of all three commissions. Cassillis, Burleigh, and Southesk were both Privy Councillors and Common Burdens-Brotherly Assistance commissioners. Lauderdale and Southesk were clearly outnumbered. Only Innes of that ilk (Elgin) and Sir John Smith (Edinburgh) were members of all three commissions for the other two estates. Smith was included by virtue of the inclusion on the Privy Council of the office of the 'provost of Edinburgh' as the sole representative of the burghal estate on that body. Hepburne of Wauchton (Haddington) and Morton of Cambo (Fife) were both Privy Councillors and Conservators of the Peace. Home of Wedderburne (Berwick), Hamilton of Little Preston (Haddington), John Semple (Dumbarton), and James Sword (St Andrews) were both Conservators of the Peace and Common Burdens-Brotherly Assistance commissioners. Further gentry and burgesses who were members of the Common Burdens-Brotherly Assistance Commission were noted activists, including Wauchope of Niddrie (Edinburgh), Ramsay of Balmaine (Mearns), and Erskine of Bandeth (Stirling) for the gentry, with John Binnie (Edinburgh) and George Garden (Burntisland) for the burgesses.[24]

In response to the appeal of 28 February, 14 individual sums were contributed on 3 March for the maintenance of the Scottish army in Ireland. Although of a limited amount (ranging fron £50–£200), financial commitment was particularly marked from the gentry and burgesses. Eight gentry and four burgesses accounted for 12 of the contributions. The bulk of the contributions came from noted activists including Wauchope of Niddrie (Edinburgh), Ramsay of Balmaine (Mearns), and Sir Archibald Johnston of Wariston for the gentry and John Binnie (Edinburgh) and James Sword (St Andrews) for the burghs. That there was conservative backing for the Scottish military commitment can be evidenced by the contributions of Lord Forrester (£300) and Lindsay (£500). The latter figure was pledged by Cassillis and Hepburne of Humbie on behalf of Lindsay. On 4 March 1643 the decision was taken to borrow £20,000 sterling (£240,000) to support the Scottish divisions.[25]

In the period 6 March to 28 April 1643, total voluntary contributions by Privy Councillors, commissioners of the Common Burdens-Brotherly Assistance and the Conservators of the Peace amounted to £118,999 19s 12d. This comprised contributions from 13 nobles, 16 gentry, and three burgesses.[26]

Argyll headed the financial contibutions of the nobility with £12,000, a sum double that of any other noble. By 10 August 1643 Argyll had lent a massive sum of £81,377 10s 5d for the supply of the Scottish army in Ireland. Investments from the nobility were supplied primarily, but not exclusively, by radicals. Balmerino, Lothian, Cassillis, Eglinton, Leven, and Loudoun supplied £6,000 per head, whilst Burleigh forwarded £3,600. Lauderdale, Lindsay, and Glencairn also contributed £6,000 each.[27]

Contributions from the gentry and burgesses were on a lesser scale, although Hepburne of Wauchton (Haddington), Innes of that ilk (Elgin), and Morton of Cambo (Fife) each supplied £6,000. Contributions once more stemmed from activists and included Johnston of Wariston, Lord Advocate Craighall, Hepburne of Humbie (£2,400), Wauchope of Niddrie (£1,333 6s 8d), and Ramsay of Balmaine (£1,200). Two noted radical burgesses James Sword (St Andrews) and George Garden (Burntisland) each supplied £600.[28]

By early March 1643 the radicals under the leadership of Argyll had successfully neutralised any potential political strength of Hamilton and his followers on the Privy Council. The fact that financial contibutions were almost exclusively from radicals who were active in the committee structure of Parliament indicates that political loading of committees with committed radicals was taking place.

Radical political ascendancy on the Privy Council was confirmed on both 11 and 12 May when the radical faction secured the calling of a Convention of Estates for 22 June. The continuance of the Irish rebellion and the rival demands from the King and the English Parliament for Scottish military aid in the English Civil War called for a meeting of the Scottish Parliament to formulate and define Scottish policy towards the British Civil Wars. Under the terms of the Scottish Triennial Act of 1640, the king was not officially obliged to call a Parliament before June 1644 (though he could do so if he wished). Charles refused to call a Parliament before the appropriate date, probably on the grounds that it would be used by Argyll to secure a closer understanding or alliance with the English Parliament.[29]

The radical leadership was anxious to maintain strict legality in the process of calling a Convention of Estates, in order that its manner of calling could not be challenged by Hamilton and his cohorts. Firstly, the Privy Council had met on 11 May 1643 to secure the authorisation of the calling of a tripartite diet of the Conservators of the Peace, the Common Burdens-Brotherly Assistance Commission and the Privy Council.[30]

The events of the Council diet of 11 May emphasised once more radical strength. Initially the Council appears to have voted in favour of a tripartite meeting. Thereafter a vote was taken on the procedure to be followed after consultation with the other two commissions; that is, were the Conservators of the Peace and the Common Burdens-Brotherly Assistance commissioners to be present with the Privy Councillors 'in tyme of voiceing'?[31] Thirteen Councillors voted in favour of allowing the admittance of the Conservators of the Peace and the Common Burdens-Brotherly Assistance commissioners. One Councillor voted against and four abstained.

The crucial vote was then taken on the necessity of summoning a Convention of Estates. Eighteen Councillors voted in favour of the motion, whilst two abstained. Now that the principle of calling a Convention had been secured, the agenda swiftly moved to its timing and whether or not the king was to be notified. Consideration was also given to whether or not the Convention should be delayed until the King was informed and his opinion known. Twelve Councillors voted in favour of deciding the date of the Convention immediately, three voted that the King should be informed before its calling and one abstained. Following the vote Lord Advocate Craighall declared that he could not vote on the calling of a Convention because the royal prerogative on this issue should not be questioned. Hamilton immediately backed up Craighall and argued that no meeting of the Estates could be called without a royal warrant.[32]

Two tripartite diets were subsequently held on 11 and 12 May. That the radicals were to be challenged was evidenced by the presence of leading conservative and pragmatic Royalist nobles on 11 May; Hamilton, Southesk, and Glencairn. Following the satisfactory conclusion of business for raising money for the Scottish army in Ireland, matters immediately turned to the urgency of a Convention of Estates as the appropriate forum for discussion of the Irish business. Hamilton, Southesk, and Lord Advocate of Craighall argued that calling of a Convention was outwith the remits of the three commissions. The numerical superiority of radical personnel ensured that the motion to call a Convention was carried.[33]

However, when the discussion moved on to the specific power of the joint meeting to actually call a Convention of Estates matters became more 'hotlie handled'.[34] The debate became so intense that the meeting was continued to 12 May.[35]

The three bodies met in 'full number'[36] on the morning session of 12 May. It was resolved that 'all ye thrie judicatories aucht and might concurre consult and resolve joyntly' on the expediency of a Convention of Estates being called in respect of the 'presnt condition (of) the publict affaires of this kingdome.' It was also agreed that the commissioners were entitled to determine the date of the Convention; this was scheduled for 22 June 1643.[37]

According to Baillie, 'of all the three bodies, not 10 were opposit.'[38] Baillie identified the conservative/pragmatic Royalist noble opposition as Hamilton, Southesk, Callander, Glencairn, Morton, and Dunfermline. The opposing gentry were all Officers of State; Lord Advocate Craighall, Carmichael of that ilk (Treasurer Depute), Hamilton of Orbiston (Justice Clerk), and Gibson of Durie (Clerk Register).[39] Of a total of 38 members of all three commissions present, only 10 dissenters emerged on the voting count (according to Baillie), illustrating the dominance of radicals.[40] The opposition of the four Officers of

State may well rest with the legality of the means of calling the Convention (that is, without a royal warrant) and not with the issue of a Convention in general.

When the three bodies reassembled in the afternoon session no time was wasted in preparing legislation for calling the Convention. A letter was prepared for delivery to Charles informing him of the decision. That Hamilton and his faction had been outwitted is evident from the absence of six conservative and pragmatic Royalists nobles in the afternoon session (Hamilton, Morton, Glencairn, Lauderdale, Southesk, Dalhousie, and Callander). Their absence was supplemented by three of the gentry Officers of State and who had sided with Hamilton in the morning session (Carmichael of that ilk, Lord Advocate Craighall, and Hamilton of Orbiston). Only one laird, Hepburne of Wauchton (Haddington), was absent in the afternoon session. Radical party discipline was maintained over both sessions.[41]

Two conclusions can therefore be reached regarding the calling of the Convention of Estates of 1643. Firstly, Hamilton had been outmanoeuvred on the Privy Council prior to the two tripartite diets of 11 and 12 May. This marks the final failure of Hamilton from June 1642 onwards to revive the Privy Council as a vehicle for a resurgence in the king's fortunes. Secondly, it was the radical leadership who orchestrated the summoning of the 1643 Convention of Estates and who controlled the proceedings of the construction of the legislation calling the Convention.

Having succeeded in securing the summoning of the Convention, the next step by the radical leadership was to attempt to secure the attendance of Hamilton and other conservatives/pragmatic Royalists at the Convention on 22 June. Hamilton and Morton were informed on 13 May that they were to 'keipe this dyet preceisly'.[42] This can be viewed as a shrewd attempt to enhance the legality of the Convention by the presence of Hamilton and others of his political ilk.

The expected Royalist backlash had commenced by 22 May. Charles informed the radicals that his approval of the summoning of the Convention had been refused. Charles correctly interpreted the calling of the Convention as an usurption of his royal prerogative. Rather than openly order that the Convention was not to be held when he was well aware that the radical leadership would do so anyway, Charles ordered all his supporters to hinder the Convention by all means possible and that all those 'right affected to us should be present at it; but to doe nothing there, but onely protest against their meiting'. In terms of a damage limitation exercise and acting on the advice of Hamilton, Charles had agreed by 10 June that the Convention could meet but it was to limit itself to closely defined remits, namely the consideration of the supply of the Scottish army in Ireland and discussion of options for a more speedy payment of the Brotherly Assistance. Hamilton's conciliatory role is consistent with his earlier behaviour in 1638–39 in attempting to have a working relationship with the radicals as opposed to the king's more partisan approach. In this particular instance Hamilton was particularly aware that the radicals would convene the Convention of Estates whether Charles approved or not.[43]

The Convention of Estates, 22 June–28 August 1643

By the time the Convention assembled, the exposure of the Antrim Plot and the involvement of both the king and prominent Scottish Royalists negated any possibility of the prevention of closer relationship between the Estates and the English Parliament. Letters discovered on the Earl of Antrim following his capture by the Scottish army in Ireland had revealed a Royalist plot involving the Earls of Nithsdale and Montrose, the Marquis of Huntly and Lord Aboyne to encourage insurrection in Scotland, whilst an army of Irish Catholics was to be deployed to assist the King in England.[44] The 1641 massacre of the Ulster Protestants remained fresh in the Protestant psyche and the employment of an Irish Catholic military force, in conjunction with Catholic Highlanders, aroused fears over the safety of 'British' Protestantism (which according to the Covenanters was to take a presbyterian form), as well as threatening Covenanting strategic interests in Scotland, necessitated an alliance on the side of the English Parliament:

> The common danger eminent to both Kirkes and Kingdomes doth invite us to helpe them, for as we have exprest in many Declarations, we and they sale in one bottome, dwell in one house, are members of one body, that according to their owne Principles, if either of the two Nations or Kirkes be ruinnated the other cannot long subsist, if the Parliament of England be destroyed, and Popery be set up there, it is a leading case to this Kingdome and Kirke, for we have the same friends and foes, the same Cause, and must run the same hazard, and many yeares experience hath taught us, what influence Popery and Prelacy in England may have upon Scotland ...[45]

The integrity of the King had now been fatally compromised and with it the opportunity for Hamilton and the conservatives/pragmatic Royalists to resist the radicals in the Convention.

1. The Composition of the 1643 Convention of Estates

The alarm raised by the Antrim Plot may well explain the high attendance level of the Estates when the Convention assembled on 22 June. With a total composition of 154, its membership was virtually identical to that of a Parliament.[46] Baillie stressed that the Convention 'was a most frequent meeting, never a Parliament so great.'[47] Of the parliamentary sessions held between 1639 and 1641 only the session commencing on 17 August 1641 had a greater total membership (163) and even this was marginal. The membership of the 1643 Convention was also greater than the 1639 Parliament (149) and the June 1640 session (131) (see appendices 2a and 2b). The 1643 Convention was therefore virtually equivalent to a plenary session of Parliament, limited only by lack of a royal warrant.

Forty-five nobles, 13 gentry, and 25 burgesses (83 individuals in total) who sat in the 1643 Convention had also been members of previous parliamentary sessions, 1639–41. On the other hand, 10 nobles, 34 gentry, and 30 burgesses

(74 individuals in total) present in the 1643 Convention had not been members of parliamentary sessions, 1639–41. Given the political background of the manner of summoning the 1643 Convention, not only could the radical leadership maintain party discipline, but also the strength of the Covenanting Movement in the Scottish localities ensured that there was a pool of manpower on which the leadership could draw for factional purposes.[48]

2. The Proceedings of the 1643 Convention of Estates

The legislative programme of the 1643 Convention consisted of only 23 enactments (16 concerning the public business and seven relating to private legislation).[49] The proceedings of the Convention can be split into four specific areas; constitutional/ legal, military, judicial, and diplomatic.

The controversy which had arisen in the tripartite meetings of 11 and 12 May over the calling of the Convention remained unabated and continued for several days concerning the powers of the Convention when it opened on 22 June. Factional confrontation swiftly recommenced. Hamilton, wary of Argyll's intentions, advocated that the powers of the Convention had been defined and restricted by the King's letter of 10 June. Argyll, on the other hand, argued that the Convention had been called on the authority of the Privy Council, the Conservators of the Peace and the commissioners for the Common Burdens and Brotherly Assistance; therefore the Convention had no restriction of power.[50]

The argument was to be resolved by a session committee established on 24 June, which was to determine the exact nature of the constitution of the Convention. Each estate elected its own representatives of nine per estate (giving a total membership of 27). Factional division among the nobility concerning the Convention is reflected in its representatives to the committee. Only two radical nobles, Argyll and Balmerino, secured election, whereas the strength of the conservative/pragmatic Royalist alliance within the noble estate was reflected in the nomination of Hamilton, Morton, Roxburgh, Southesk, Lanark, Callander, and Lauderdale. Gentry and burghal representation was aligned to Argyll and compensated for limited radical personnel within the noble representatives. Johnston of Wariston (Edinburgh), Sir John Smith (Edinburgh), Patrick Leslie (Aberdeen), and Robert Barclay (Irvine) are notable examples of this contingent. According to Baillie, 'all the Barrones and Burghs, without exception of one, were for the common weell.'[51] A contemporary pamphleteer also observed that 'most of our Gentry & Comminality are firm unto the Parliament of England'.[52] Indeed common membership existed with the radical Commission of the Kirk, established on 5 August 1642, and consisted of Argyll, Hepburne of Wauchton (Haddington), Winraham of Libberton (Edinburgh), and John Semple (Dumbarton).[53]

After two days' deliberation the session committee presented an act concerning the constitution of the 1643 Convention to the House on 26 June. One particular clause aroused the most controversy. It stated that the Convention was a 'Lawfull free and full Convention' which had power to 'treate Consult and determine in all matters that sall be proposed unto thame als freelie and amplie as any Convention quhilk has beene within this kingdome at any time bygane.'[54] This implied that the Convention would infact overstep the powers granted to it by Charles in his letter of 10 June. The inclusion of this clause indicates that the conservative and pragmatic Royalist nobles, despite their numerical superiority over Argyll and Balmerino on the session committee, had been overwhelmed by the combined voting strength of the gentry and burgesses.

The voting power of the shires and burghs was similarly evident when the act was put to the vote of the House. Burnet states Hamilton, 18 other nobles (who are not specified but undoubtedly represented the contingent of conservative/pragmatic Royalist nobles), and one laird voted against the act.[55] After the vote was taken, Hamilton and his brother Lanark, withdrew from the Convention. Hamilton refused to give instructions to the conservative and pragmatic Royalist nobles whether or not they should leave the Convention or stay for the remainder of the proceedings.

Hamilton's political defeat at the hands of Argyll and the parliamentary support from the shires and burghs, followed by his withdrawal from the Convention, left the conservatives and pragmatic Royalists leaderless and in disarray. Radical parliamentary control of the Convention was complete.[56]

Attention swiftly turned to military matters and a session committee of twelve was established for supplying the Scottish army in Ireland. Forward planning on the part of the radical leadership had ensured that heavyweights from all three estates were being held back for the session committee established on 1 July for the trial of the Earls of Traquair and Carnwath. The dominant radical noble on the Irish committee was Burleigh. Common membership with the 1642 Commission of the Kirk rests with Weymes, Winraham of Libberton (Edinburgh), and Hepburne of Wauchton (Haddington). Once more this provides an indication of the interaction with the radical Commission of the Kirk. Libberton and Wauchton had also been included on the committee to determine the constitution of the Convention. Therefore it would appear that radical interests were being represented by Burleigh and these two gentry in particular on the committee concerning the Scottish army in Ireland. Of the burghal representatives, Hugh Kennedy (Ayr) was a noted radical. The strength of the radicals amongst the gentry and burghal estate ensured that radical gentry and burgesses could safely be included on the Committee for Furnishing the Scottish Army in Ireland. The geographic composition of the committee reflected an east coast bias of gentry and burghal representation. Major west coast shires and burghs such as Glasgow, Renfrew, and Dumbarton, who provided quality radical personnel were excluded, although Ayr and Dumfries secured inclusion. This phenomenon is surprising given their strategic and logistical importance of the location of the west coast in relation to Ireland.[57]

The trial of the Earls of Traquair and Carnwath (both Incendiaries) was regarded as being of sufficient importance to warrant the inclusion of leading radical nobles, led by Argyll. The inclusion of radicals is unsurprising given the fact that the whole object of the committee was to punish Incendiaries.

The fact that two nobles were specified for punishment indicates an attempt by radical nobles to strenghten their position within the noble estate. The citation of Traquair and Carnwath perhaps served not only to punish those Incendiaries involved in the post-1625 administration, but also to check any attempts towards conservatism among the nobility. This is particularly significant in light of the withdrawal of Hamilton and much of his conservative/pragmatic Royalist grouping from the Convention. The fear of citation and the possible loss of estates was therefore used to ward off any moves towards a growth in conservatism.

Four per estate, plus one supernumerary, formed the membership of the Committee for the Trial of the Earls of Traquair and Carnwath. Only one conservative noble, Lauderdale, was included on the committee. The dominant radical grouping of nobles consisted of Argyll, Loudoun, and Cassillis. Loudoun was included as a supernumerary to bolster the numbers of the nobility in relation to the other two estates. Gentry and burghal representation enhanced and supplemented the radical nature of the committee. Radical interests among gentry representation appear to have been managed by Johnston of Wariston (Edinburgh), the close political ally of Argyll. Robert Barclay (Irvine) and James Sword (St Andrews) were the leading radicals representing the burghal estate. Two burgesses on the committee were not members of the Convention of Estates as per 22 June 1643. Neither Thomas Durham nor James Sword were commissioners for their respective burghs for the 1643 Convention. Both had been prominent members of Parliament for the burgesses in the period 1639–1641. Non-parliamentary personnel therefore gained access to session committees of the 1643 Convention and is in line with the practice employed in 1639–41.[58]

Analysis of the remainder of the Convention rests on the establishment of a fiscal and administrative structure geared towards military involvement in the English Civil War, and diplomatic proceedings leading to the agreement of the Solemn League and Covenant on 26 August 1643.

On 19 July a further session committee was established, to determine the level of loan and tax to be levied on the country for the sum of £800,000 Scots advanced for military aid. Controlled by Argyll, Balmerino, and Burleigh, the radical contingent amongst the nobles was supplemented by Sutherland, Eglinton, and Cassillis. Nevertheless noble membership was not exclusively radical. Lauderdale, Marischal, and Southesk represented conservative interests. Southesk's inclusion suggests that he may well have been moving towards a more conciliatory stance towards the Convention. The gentry representatives were fronted by Hepburne of Humbie (Haddington), leading a grouping of gentry in general gaining their first experience of parliamentary session committees. Time-served radical burgesses including Robert Barclay (Irvine) and Patrick Leslie (Aberdeen) composed the majority of the burghal representation. Two burgesses included on the committee were not members of the 1643 Convention; Thomas Durham (Perth) and James Airth (Pittenweem). Whilst gentry representation was predominantly based on the inclusion of gentry who had no previous parliamentary experience, burghal representation was based on the inclusion of active parliamentary burgesses.[59]

It was this session committee that relied on the precedent of 1640 and formulated the Act for the Loan and Tax of 15 August 1643 (£80,000 of loan and £120,000 of tax). A further precedent of 1640 was employed on 26 August in the Act for the Committees of War in the shires. Local committees of war were established throughout the country, staffed by radical gentry, as the central unit of local administration and government for the levying of troops and raising of supplies, and for the imposition of ideological conformity. In essence, these committees of war represented the re-establishment of the administrative organ which had proved so successful in the Two Bishops' Wars of 1639–1640.[60]

As early as 11 July the ramifications of the exposure of the Anrtim Plot and the threat to presbyterian hegemony had led to the formation of a session committee to 'consider of the remedies of the dangers to religion'. The committee was composed of eight per estate and was dominated by radicals. Argyll, Cassillis, Leven, and Balmerino were noted radical nobles, whereas Marischal, Dunfermline, Lauderdale, and Lindsay, were conservatives. In common with the session committee of 24 June concerning the constitution of the Convention, the shire and burgh representatives therefore played a crucial role. In addition, Argyll, Cassillis, and Winraham of Libberton (Edinburgh) were also members of the Commission of the Kirk established on 5 August 1642. The deliberations and conclusions of the session committee of 11 July clearly had an important bearing on subsequent Anglo-Scottish relations.[61]

The crucial diplomatic negotiations which were to lead to the signing of the Solemn League and Covenant and the treaty of military assistance with the English Parliament on 26 August were dominated by radicals. Balmerino, Hope of Kerse (Stirling), Johnston of Wariston (Edinburgh), Sir John Smith (Edinburgh), and Robert Barclay (Irvine), were commissioned by the Convention on 9 and 10 August to negotiate with the English commissioners from both Houses of Parliament on a closer relationship between the two countries and Parliaments within the context of the British Civil Wars. The conservative noble Lindsay was also commissioned as part of this grouping. All members of this diplomatic grouping had been included on the previous session committee of 11 July to 'consider of the remedies of the dangers of religion'. In essence, the diplomatic commissions of 9 and 10 August to negotiate with representatives of the English Parliament were subcommittees of the larger session committee of 11 July. This also emphasises the extent to which the gentry and burgess representatives on the session committee of 11 July had been to the fore in providing additional voting power to the four radical nobles on that committee.[62]

As early as 14 July the Convention had sent a representative to London, Robert Meldrum of Burghlie, to hurry the departure of English parliamentary representatives to Edinburgh. Meldrum of Burghlie was not a member of the 1643 Convention, although he was later to represent the shire of Fife in several sessions of the First Triennial Parliament. By the end of July the Convention had ordered the levying of military forces to contain any Royalist insurrection against the forthcoming treaty with the English Parliament. The English commissioners duly arrived in the capital on 7 August with the aim of securing Scottish military aid for their cause. Negotiations subsequently took place between representatives of the Convention (named above), representatives of the General Assembly (dominated by the ministry and radical lay elders), and the English commissioners from the English Parliament. By 17 August the Solemn League and Covenant had been agreed on and approved by the Convention of Estates. Whilst the Solemn League and Covenant was dispatched to London for ratification, negotiations then moved to the details of the treaty for Scottish military intervention on the side of the English Parliament in its struggle with Charles I. Argyll kept in close correspondence with the English radicals over the passage of the Solemn League and Covenant through both Houses of Parliament. The Convention of Estates had approved the treaty by 26 August.[63]

The Solemn League and Covenant, however, should not be regarded as a move towards a closer parliamentary union between England and Scotland. Scottish parliamentary independence was to be maintained. Article Three of the Solemn League and Covenant pledged to 'preserve the rights and priviledges of the parliamentes and the liberties of the kingdomes.'[64] Ultimately the Solemn League and Covenant was concerned with the transportation and imposition of the Scottish revolution on a British basis as the appropriate means of defending that revolution, in religious, military, and constitutional terms. In light of the Antrim Plot, Charles could no longer be trusted to accept Covenanting hegemony in Scotland.

Although the Solemn League and Covenant had been agreed on within 10 days of the arrival of the English commissioners in Edinburgh, and the military treaty within 20 days, it was born out of essentially different circumstances on the parts of the English Parliament and the Scottish Convention. The Scots were certainly aware that their fortunes were linked to the success of the English Parliament in its struggle against the king, whilst the English Parliament was likewise aware of the necessity of Scottish military assistance in securing that success.[65] Nevertheless, 'the English pressed chiefly a Civil League, and the Scots a Religious one.'[66] In return for military assistance, the Covenanters sought the imposition of presbyterianism on a pan-British basis for the English and Irish Churches, which were to be reformed in terms of doctrine, worship, discipline, and government.[67]

3. The Committee Structure of the 1643 Convention of Estates

The analysed committee structure of the 1643 Convention consists of seven session committees and one interval committee. Thirty-two nobles, 57 gentry, and 47 burgesses constitute the total field analysed. Such figures indicate that the gentry and burgesses could draw on a greater pool of human resources than the nobility, primarily due to the extent of radicalism within the former two estates.

Consideration of the committee structure of the Convention of Estates plays an important role in two areas of membership of parliamentary session and interval committees. Firstly, it allows analysis of the extent to which committees were being controlled and managed by a core of nobles, gentry and burgesses. Secondly, it provides a means of determining the extent to which non-members of the Convention were playing an active role on the session committees. Nevertheless, political control of individual committees rested with the radicals. Only six of the 32 nobles analysed (19%) were included on three or more committees.

Noble common membership, unsurprisingly, was dominated by radicals; Balmerino (six committees), Argyll (five committees), Cassillis and Burleigh (four committees). That conservative and pragmatic Royalist interests were not completely nullified is reflected in the inclusion of Lauderdale and Lindsay on four committees each and Marischal on three committees.

Johnston of Wariston (Edinburgh) (six commmittees), Hope of Kerse (Stirling), and Hepburn of Humbie (Haddington) (five committees each) were to the fore in terms of gentry common membership. Winraham of Libberton (Edinburgh) and Erskine of Scottiscraig (Fife) were included on four committees. Grierson of Lag (Dumfries), Brodie of that ilk (Elgin), and Hepburn of Wauchton (Haddington) each secured nomination to three committees. Only seven out of 57 gentry analysed (12%) were included on three or more committees. Burghal trends were consistent with those of the gentry. Robert Barclay (Irvine) was commissioned to sit on seven committees and Sir John Smith (Edinburgh) on six. James Dennistoun (Edinburgh), Thomas Durham (Perth), Patrick Leslie (Aberdeen), and Thomas Bruce (Stirling) formed a grouping elected to four committees. Alexander Douglas (Banff) secured membership of three committees.

Based on the cut-off point of three or more committees, a core of seven nobles, seven gentry, and seven burgesses were numerically dominant within the 1643 Convention of Estates. That proceedings were controlled by this core grouping is emphasised with reference to the appropriate representation in relative terms per estate; six of the 32 nobles (19%), seven of the 57 gentry (12%), and seven of the 47 burgesses (15%) analysed gained formal access to three or more committees. Gentry representation on session committees adhered to membership of the 1643 Convention, whilst three burgesses included on session committees were not members of the Convention.[68]

A new Committee of Estates was established on 26 August consisting of 22 nobles, 22 gentry, 21 burgesses, and two supernumeraries (both of whom were nobles). The total membership of the new committee therefore amounted to 67. Twelve of the 22 nobles (54%), 10 of the 22 gentry (46%), and 10 of the 21 burgesses (48%) were included only on the Committee of Estates and were not elected to any session committees. Five gentry and six burgesses from this grouping were not infact members of the 1643 Convention. Six nobles, 10 gentry, and 11 burgesses included on the Committee of Estates also secured membership of more than one session committee.

Whilst session committees were being controlled by a core of nobles, gentry, and burgesses, the vast bulk of each parliamentary estate was being deployed to the Committee of Estates. Gentry and burgesses who were not members of the Convention were being brought on to the 1643 Committee of Estates.[69]

4. The Appointment of Parliamentary Interval Committees

The Committee of Estates had been revived on 26 August (the same day that the treaty of military assistance with the English Parliament was agreed on) to undertake military prepartions for the forthcoming invasion of England and the subscription of the Solemn League and Covenant. It was to be the real governing force in the country as the Convention prorogued itself to a second session in January 1644. The prorogation established a constitiutional precedent (no Convention hitherto had been prorogued to a second session), but more importantly avoided the problem of securing royal assent to a second summons. Hence the momentum of events remained with the radicals.[70]

The 1643 Committee of Estates witnessed an increase of 12 nobles (including supernumeraries), six gentry, and nine burgesses (a total rise of 27), in terms of numerical membership per parliamentary estate, compared to the previous Committee of Estates of 1640. Seven nobles, four gentry, and five burgesses (16 in total) were included on both committees. Five of the seven nobles were radicals; Cassillis, Lothian, Burleigh, Balmerino, and Coupar. Lindsay and Dunfermline, on the other hand, belonged to the conservative wing. The absence of both Argyll and Loudoun on the common membership of the nobles is best explained by the fact that in 1640 both had been included on diplomatic commissions. Hepburne of Wauchton (Haddington), Home of Wedderburne (Berwick/Roxburgh), Hamilton of Little Preston (Edinburgh), and Douglas of Cavers (Roxburgh) were included on both commissions and all had been prominent in the committee structure of Parliament, 1639–1641, as well as the 1643 Convention. This suggests an alignment with the radical nobles. Sir John Smith (Edinburgh), George Porterfield (Glasgow), Hugh Kennedy (Ayr), John Rutherford (Jedburgh), and James Sword (St Andrews), constituted the five burgesses included on both commissions. Hamilton of Little Preston, Home of Wedderburne, James Sword, and George Porterfield were not members of the 1643 Convention for their respective shires and burghs. Six gentry and seven burgesses in total on the 1643 Committee of Estates were not members of the 1643 Convention. As was apparent in 1640, radical activists from the shires and burghs were being brought in to serve on the most important parliamentary interval committee, the Committee of Estates.[71]

5. The Operation of Parliamentary Interval Committees

The Committee of Estates held its first meeting in Edinburgh on 28 August 1643. Its main focus of business was to oversee preparations for the military invasion of England. On 26 August the Convention had commissioned committees to sit in the shires to prepare for war. Five days later instructions were issued by the Committee of Estates to the shire colonels and the committees of war for the training of men and the appointment of subordinate officers. By 24

November a joint meeting of the Committee of Estates and the Privy Council had granted the military commissions for the forthcoming invasion. Leven was commissioned as General, Sir Alexander Hamilton as General of the Artillery, and Hepburne of Humbie as Treasurer and Commissar General. Although officially a joint meeting, the proceedings were essentially the work of the Committee of Estates. Of a total of 30 individuals present, 14 were Privy Councillors, but 10 of the 14 Privy Councillors were also members of the Committee of Estates and included Argyll, Loudoun, Leven, Cassillis, and Balmerino. Dunfermline and Lauderdale were also in attendance but radical nobles were in the ascendancy.[72]

As in 1640 the Committee of Estates divided itself on 1 December into two sections, one to remain in Edinburgh and the other to accompany the army.[73] The Edinburgh section was composed of seven nobles, 10 gentry, and 12 burgesses (29 individuals in all). Its quorum was set at nine, with two per estate always required to be present. Superior numbers were directed towards the army section, which was composed of 15 nobles, 11 gentry, and 10 burgesses (36 in total). Gentry and burghal membership remained almost equal between the two sections, although the army section deployed the services of eight additional nobles. The fact that the manpower employed on the 1643 Committee of Estates was loaded towards the army section therefore indicates the importance of the parliamentary alliance with the English Parliament. It provides a further indication of the importance of British political and religious links. The quorum levels of the army section were identical to those of its Edinburgh counterpart. Two supernumeraries, both radical nobles (Loudoun and Leven), were included on both commissions, and members of either sections could attend the proceedings of the other section.[74]

Leading conservative/pragmatic Royalist nobles were contained within the Edinburgh section. Although Lauderdale and Glencairn were included on the Edinburgh section, they were outnumbered by the combination of Burleigh and Balmerino, with the supernumeraries Chancellor Loudoun and General Leven. Sir James Lockhart of Lee (Lanark) was nominated to the Edinburgh section for the gentry, despite the fact that he was neither a member of the 1643 Committee, nor a member of the 1643 Convention. Eastern burgesses dominated the Edinburgh section.

Radical manpower was particularly apparent on the army section. The dominant figure was Argyll, backed by Eglinton, Cassillis, and Lothian. Johnston of Wariston (Edinburgh) managed radical interests among the gentry representatives. Three western burgesses on the army section were particularly radical in political nature; Robert Barclay (Irvine), George Porterfield (Glasgow), and Hugh Kennedy (Ayr).[75]

The emphasis on military matters in the work of the Committee of Estates is reflected in the establishment of four subcommittees between 25 November and 4 December 1643; a committee for Hepburne of Humbie's accounts, a committee for the pay of the army, a committee for the artillery, and a committee for military discipline. Nobles appear to have taken a leading role in the staffing of these subcommittees. The membership of the army pay committee consisted solely of seven nobles, three of whom were influential radicals (Loudoun, Leven, and Eglinton). The remaining personnel was conservative/pragmatic Royalist, of whom Dalhousie was the major figure. This marks a departure from the usual procedure where subcommittees were in general staffed by equal numbers from all three estates. No burgesses, however, gained access to the artillery subcommittee, which was controlled by radicals (Cassillis and Balmerino). Gentry representation focused on Winraham of Libberton (Edinburgh) and Hepburne of Humbie (Haddington). Despite the inclusion of Lauderdale (who had also been nominated to the committee for Humbie's accounts) on the committee for military discipline, political control rested with the radicals in the form of Leven and Johnston of Wariston (Edinburgh). Robert Douglas, a minister of Edinburgh, also secured admission.[76] That representatives of the Kirk were being admitted to subcommittees of the Committee of Estates is a reminder of radical interaction between parliamentary committees and the Commission of the Kirk.

The Committee of Estates sat as one from 28 August until 1 December. The Edinburgh section then sat from 2 December until 31 May 1644. Consistent with its role as an interval committee, the Edinburgh section therefore sat throughout the proceedings of the second session of the Convention of Estates from 3 January 1644 until shortly before the Convention was dissolved on 3 June and the new session of Parliament commenced on 4 June. Therefore the Edinburgh section appears to have had a managerial role over the proceedings of the 1644 Convention. In strict constitutional terms the 1643 Commission was valid until the meeting of the First Triennial Parliament (June 1644).

Only one diet of the army section took place (on 4 December) prior to the meeting of the second session of the Convention of Estates on 3 January 1644. Following the invasion of England in early January 1644, sederunts of the army section are recorded on a regular basis from 5 January until 23 November. As the army section was obviously accompanying the Scottish army in England, sederunts are thus recorded not only throughout the second session of the Convention of Estates, but also throughout the session of Parliament from 4 June until 29 July 1644, and also following the prorogation of Parliament when a new commission had been issued to a new Committee of Estates.[77]

Membership details of the 1643 Committee were modified by the 1644 Convention of Estates. Additions were made on 2 February (four nobles, four gentry, and three burgesses) and 16 April (three nobles, one laird, and two burgesses). No reasons are given for the total addition of seven nobles, five gentry, and five burgesses.The Convention did not specify to which section of the Committee of Estates these individuals were to be allocated.[78]

Sederunts of the Edinburgh section indicate dominant noble attendance by Loudoun and Lauderdale; Loudoun attended 107 of 124 diets (86%) and Lauderdale 84 (68%). Argyll was present at 49 diets (40%), although he had been voted as President of the army section on 4 December. Argyll's sphere of influence was clearly not restricted to the army section. The remainder of noble attendance was dominated by radicals; Burleigh, Cassillis, Balmerino and Leven. Chancellor Loudoun appears to have been acting President of the Edinburgh section, although no formal vote was taken on this (unlike the army section).[79]

Two gentry with the most impressive attendance records were not members of the Convention of Estates, 1643–44; Ramsay of Balmaine 75 diets (60%) and Durham of Pittarrow 70 diets (56%). Johnston of Wariston (Edinburgh) was present at 60 diets (48%). Two further gentry were neither members of the 1643 Committee nor the 1643 Convention. Although both were later added to the Committee on 2 February 1644, one of them, Sir Archibald Campbell was territorially aligned to the House of Argyll. Five further gentry who were not included in the original commission nor in later additions to the Committee of Estates attended various diets, but on an irregular basis.

Burghal attendance was dominated by Edinburgh burgesses, notably James Stewart 92 diets (74%) and Sir John Smith 64 diets (52%). Three further Edinburgh burgesses who were not included in the original commission nor in later additions to the Committee of Estates attended various diets. All three had not been members of the 1643 Convention.[80]

Analysis of the quorums for the Edinburgh section reveals that at 10 out of the 42 diets (24%) held between 29 August and 1 December the total quorum was less than the specified 15. Furthermore, at 11 of the above 42 diets (26%) the rule that four of each estate were required to be present was broken. On various other occasions all three estates, either collectively or individually, were represented by less than four members each.[81]

Between 1 December and 16 May 1644 at only one out of 82 diets was the total quorum less than the specified nine decided on 1 December. On only one occassion (the same diet where the total quorum was less than nine) was the specified rule of compulsory attendance of two members per estate not adhered to. Empirical data therefore indicates that following the division of the Committee on 1 December 1643 the rules regarding the quorums of the Edinburgh section were more rigidly adhered to. Human resources were being efficiently managed.[82]

Ninety-four sederunts of the army section are recorded between 1 December and 23 November 1644. Thirteen of the 94 sederunts constitute meetings of the Committee of Both Kingdoms, the Anglo-Scottish body established to co-ordinate efforts between the Scottish and English Parliaments in the English Civil War.[83]

Attendance data suggests that noble radical interests were served primarily by General Leven (77 diets; 82%), whilst those of the conservatives and pragmatic Royalists were served by Crawford-Lindsay (66 diets; 70%). Argyll, President of the army section, attended only 27 of its meetings (29%) of the army section, although it should be borne in mind that he was also orchestrating the Edinburgh section, as well as the Common Burdens-Brotherly Assistance commission. His role as President appears to have been taken over by Crawford-Lindsay, who presided at 33 diets.

Callander and Forrester were added to the army section by the 1644 Parliament on 26 July. Callander had been appointed Lieutenant General of the Covenanting forces by the Convention of Estates on 16 April thus enabling him to sit on the Committee of Estates. Callander's inclusion as per 26 July 1644 was not in a military capacity but as a member of the noble estate per se. However, at 39 of the 94 recorded sederunts (42%) of the army section he is recorded in a military capacity.[84]

Hepburne of Humbie (Haddington) attended 71 of 94 diets (76%), Sir Harry Gibb 65 out of 94 diets (69%), and Winraham of Libberton (Edinburgh) 44 diets (47%). Gibb had been one of three gentry added to the army section by the 1644 Convention on 5 January, none of whom were members of the Convention, 1643–44. Two further gentry, Sir John Meldrum (of Baglillie Easter) and John Kerr of Lochtour (Roxburgh) attended various diets of the army section although they were not included in the original commission nor in any later additions to the Committee of Estates in general or the army section in particular. Meldrum was not a member of the Convention, 1643–44. A further laird in this category, Sir Charles Erskine of Cambuskenneth (Stirling), attended one diet of the army section. His presence can be explained, however, by the fact that he was one of the commissioners named to go to England, firstly by the Convention of Estates on 9 January 1644, which was renewed by the 1644 Parliament on 16 July.[85]

Attendance levels of the burgesses on the army section are relatively low. Within this limited context burghal attendance was dominated by George Porterfield (Glasgow), Thomas MacBirnie (Dumfries), James Rae (Edinburgh), and David Simpson (Dysart). Of these four, only David Simpson had sat in the Convention of Estates 1643–44. The low attendance record of the burgesses suggests a token representation of the burgesses on the army section. The role of the burgesses was primarily financial; to mobilise capital and raise cash. The burgesses were thus probably included on the army section to maintain the balance of the three estates.[86]

At 27 of the 94 diets (29%)of the army section the total quorum level of nine established on 1 December 1643 failed to be met. At 34 diets (36%) the rule that two of each estate must be present was not adhered to and at 24 of these diets it was the burghal estate which was at fault.[87] Unlike the Edinburgh section, quorum levels were not as rigidly enforced on the army section. The services of the burghal estate were therefore primarily employed on the Edinburgh section.

Throughout the second session of the Convention of Estates (3 January to 3 June 1644) both sections of the Committee of Estates continued to meet separately. Whilst in progress the 1644 Convention regulated the quorums and membership of the Committee. Legislation of 25 January stipulated that despite the divisions into the Edinburgh and army sections, both sections were part of the Committee of Estates as a whole and any member of either section could attend and vote in the other section. This may have been an attempt on the part of the nobility as an estate to check the noted radicalism of the gentry and burgesses. Thus Mure of Rowallan (Ayr), a member of the Edinburgh section, attended the diet of the army section on 12 February 1644.[88] The quorum of the army section had been originally set at nine, with two of each estate being present. The 1644 Convention redefined the terms of the quorum of the army section on 30 January. The quorum level redefined to seven with no requirement of attendance per estate. Such a change in policy was deemed neccessary not only due to the fact that in reality urgent decisions had to be made before a full meeting of the section could be convened, but also that a new legal requirement for attendance levels had to be set to ensure the continued legality of the committee's proceedings.[89]

The first sederunt of the army section is recorded on 17 January and seven sederunts are recorded in the period to 1st February. At five of these diets the original quorum figure of nine was surpassed and the attendance requirement of two per estate was adhered to and surpassed apart from the attendance levels of the burgesses.[90] On 2 February the legislation of 30 January was applied to the Edinburgh section. Of the 65 sederunts of the Edinburgh section between 29 August 1643 and 26 January 1644, the original quorum figure of nine was surpassed at all diets and the attendance requirement of two per estate was adhered to bar three diets.[91]

The change in the quorum levels by the 1644 Convention may be due to the desire to ensure that the legality of the Convention's proceedings and those of the Committee of Estates could not be challenged at a later date. Hence, the change in quorum regulations (even though they were generally being followed) allowed for a greater degree of scope (especially regarding the attendance levels per estate) in ensuring that that legality could not be challenged. The emphasis on the legality of the Convention's proceedings was reinforced on 2 February by the ratification of the commission to the 1643 Committee of Estates and the approval of its proceedings. An earlier enactment of 6 January 1644 had only approved the proceedings of the Committee of Estates to that date.[92]

Two sets of additions were made by the 1644 Convention to the Committee of Estates; 2 February and 16 April. Noble additions consisted primarily of conservatives/pragmatic Royalists, especially Lanark who had taken up the mantle as the parliamentary representative of the House of Hamilton. None of the gentry additions of 2 February and 16 April were members of the 1644 Convention. Edinburgh burgesses, for example Sir William Dick, accounted for the majority of burghal additions. None of the burgesses added on 16 April were members of the 1644 Convention. All these subsequent additions are surprising in the sense that the quorum levels had been more loosely defined and also given the fact that the original quorum rules were being adhered to anyway.[93]

6. The Operation of the Privy Council *vis-a-vis* Parliamentary Session and Interval Committees, 1643–1644

The 1643 Convention of Estates commenced its proceedings on 22 June. From 4 July, however, diets of the Privy Council were held throughout the duration of the Convention (although on a less regular basis than the Convention itself) until 10 August and continued as a whole until 2 January 1644 (ie until the opening of the 1644 Convention on 4 January).[94]

Corresponding to a maximum possible attendance level of 33 diets, analysis of the Privy Council sederunts is valuable in three respects. Firstly, it illustrates those Councillors in attendance during the 1643 Convention. Secondly, it illustrates those Councillors active in the committee structure of the Convention of Estates. Thirdly, it also identifies those Councillors in attendance following the prorogation of the Convention on 26 August until the eve of the 1644 Convention.

Radical dominance is apparent with regard to all three criteria. Argyll, Loudoun, Cassillis, Balmerino, and Lauderdale formed the dominant attenders at Privy Council diets. Despite the fact that Lauderdale was chosen as President of the Council on 27 September 1643, signifying the radicals' desire to accomodate the conservatives at present and avoid their alienation, it was the dominant clique of radical nobles that managed the agenda. Gentry attendance on the Council was low, bar that of Hepburne of Wauchton (Haddington). The low attendance records of the gentry members on the Privy Council emphasise the fact that it was a clique of radical nobles which was dominating the proceedings in general of that body.[95]

The trend of non-commissioned personnel attending the proceedings of parliamentary interval committees was also reflected in the Privy Council. At the diets of 4 and 7 July 1643, four non-commissioned gentry and three non-commissioned burgesses attended both meetings of the Council. Sir Thomas Hope of Kerse (Clackmannan), Sir William Scott of Harden (Selkirk), Sir John Charteris of Amisfield (Dumfries), and Johnston of Wariston (Edinburgh) constituted the four gentry, with Robert Barclay (Irvine), Alexander Douglas (Banff), and Thomas Durham (Perth) were the three burgesses. Johnston of Wariston and Robert Barclay were noted radical activists.[96]

The most important business discussed on 4 July was that of the exclusion of the Earl of Carnwath from office. Therefore influential radical gentry and burgesses appear to been brought on to ensure the safe passage of this Carnwath's case through the Council. Their presence at the next diet on 7 July may likewise have been a precaution and safeguard against a conservative revolt or backlash on the Council for business conducted on 7 July was limited to the issue of witchcraft.[97]

Sederunts of the Privy Council run from 4 July 1643 until 4 January 1644. No attempt was made by the conservative and pragmatic Royalist nobles to use the Council for a Royalist revival. The 'act anent the Covenant' of the Committee of Estates of 12 October called for compulsory subscription of the Solemn League and Covenant.[98] Sixteen nobles, five gentry, and one burgess subscribed the Solemn League and Covenant on 2 November (the earliest date at which Privy Councillors could do so). The 16 nobles included the radicals Loudoun, Argyll, Eglinton, Cassillis, Yester, Balmerino, and Burleigh but also included the influential conservatives, Lauderdale and Lindsay. Hepburn of Wauchton was among the five gentry who signed on 2 November. Sir John Smith, Provost of Edinburgh, signed the Solemn League and Covenant as the only burgess on the Privy Council.[99]

By 6 November 1643 the Committee of Estates had ordered Hamilton, Morton, Roxburgh, Kinnoull, Southesk, and Lanark to appear within 10 days and sign the Solemn League and Covenant. Eleven further nobles and two gentry, who were all in England at this time, were allowed an extended period until 12 January 1644 to appear and sign. The 11 nobles included Lennox, Montrose, Tullibardine, Traquair, and Carnwath. The fact that both Carnwath and Traquair were Incendiaries and had been investigated by the Convention of Estates, but were being allowed an extended period to sign, may indicate a degree of influence on the part of conservative nobles on the Council. It is more likely, however, that the radical nobles were seeking some form of accomodation with the conservatives for the time being. By 16 November only Southesk had signed the Solemn League and Covenant as one of the six nobles ordered to do so within the 10 day period. The remaining five were then declared as enemies of religion, and their incomes were to be put to public use. Although Roxburgh signed the Solemn League and Covenant in December, none of the Scottish nobles in England had signed by 12 January deadline and their incomes were confiscated.[100]

Several conclusions can be reached regarding the diets of the Privy Council from 4 July 1643 to 4 January 1644. Firstly, no attempt was made by Hamilton and the conservative and pragmatic Royalist nobles to hijack the Council during the sitting of the 1643 Convention. Hamilton and Lanark, in common with other conservative and pragmatic Royalist nobles, have very low attendance levels on the Council during this period. Secondly, following the prorogation of the Convention, the Committee of Estates outmanoeuvred any possible Royalist threat in political and constitutional terms by demanding wholescale subscription of the Solemn League and Covenant and taking retaliatory action against those nobles who refused to conform. Thirdly, even before this decision was taken on 6 November, no conservative or pragmatic Royalist revival took place on the Council. Fourthly, the relatively low attendance levels of the gentry and the Provost of Edinburgh on the Privy Council illustrates that the gentry and burgesses as a whole were being primarily employed on the parliamentary interval committees; the Committee of Estates, the Conservators of the Peace, and the Common Burdens-Brotherly Assistance commission.

Conclusion

Following the session of Parliament ending on 17 November 1641 the momentum of the radicals was maintained by parliamentary interval committees. Not only were conservatives and pragmatic royalists on the Privy Council outflanked by Argyll and the radical nobles, backed by the gentry and burgesses, but the parliamentary interval committees (composed of these same elements) remained the real driving force behind the Covenanting cause. It was these committees that succeeded in the calling of the 1643 Convention of Estates and were the force behind the Solemn League and Covenant. Detailed cross-analysis of the relationship between the Privy Council, parliamentary interval committees, session committees of the Convention of Estates, and movements and continuity of personnel between sessions of Parliament/Convention of Estates has demonstrated not only the dominance of a caucus of radical nobles, gentry and burgesses, but also the entrance of new radical blood, especially at the 1643 Convention of Estates. Moreover, the influence of Hamilton and the conservatives and pragmatic Royalists in the 1642–1643 period, especially within the Privy Council, has been traditionally overemphasised in historiographical terms.

NOTES

1. A discussion of the tripartite relationship between the three kingdoms in the British Isles in the seventeeth century is presented by David Stevenson in 'The Century of the Three Kingdoms', *Scotland Revisited*, ed. Jenny Wormald (London, 1991), 107–118; Lynch, *Scotland, A New History*, (London, 1991), 272–273; C. Russell, *The Causes of the English Civil War*, (Oxford, 1990), 119, argues quite rightly that the overriding need for Scottish security lay behind the design of implementing the Scottish Covenanting revolution on a British basis; Stevenson, *Government Under the Covenanters*, xxx.
2. *APS*, v, 392, 395; *RPCS*, 2nd series, vii, 142–149, SRO PA 14/1, Register of the Committee for the Common Burdens and the Commission for Receiving the Brotherly Assistance, 19 November 1641–10 January 1645, ff 1–266; SRO PA 14/2, Proceedings of the Scots Commissioners for Conserving the Articles of the Treaty, 22 September 1642–8 July 1643, ff 1–72.
3. *RPCS*, 2nd series, vii, 149–449.
4. Ibid, 149.
5. Ibid, 149–449.
6. SRO PA 14/1, ff 1–266; D. Stevenson, 'The Financing of the Cause of the Covenants, 1638–51', *SHR*, 51, 1972, 96; *APS*, vi, i, 190–191.
7. SRO PA 14/1, ff 1–266. Lord Forrester had sat in Parliament for Edinburgh in 1625 and 1628–33 as Sir George Forrester of Corstorphine. He was created Lord Forrester of Corstorphine on 22 July 1633 (*Scots Peerage*, iv, 91–93).
8. *APS*, v, 392, 395; SRO PA 14/1, ff 1–266.
9. SRO PA 14/1, ff 2, 15–16, 17, 68–69; Stevenson,'The Financing of the Cause of the Covenants', 97.
10. SRO PA 14/1, ff 1–72.
11. Ibid, folio one; SRO PA 14/2, ff 36, 1–72.
12. SRO PA 14/2, ff 1–72; *APS*, v, 331–332.
13. SRO PA 14/2, ff 1–72; *APS*, v, 404.
14. SRO PA 14/2, folio one; *APS*, v, 392, 395, 404.
15. Stevenson, *Scottish Revolution*, 256–257; Stevenson, *Government Under the*

Covenanters, xxx; Lynch, *Scotland Revisted*, 273; MacInnes, 'The Scottish Constitution, 1638–1651', 122. *RPCS*, 2nd series, vii, 288–450.

16. Ibid, 149–450.
17. MacInnes, 'The Scottish Constitution, 1638–1651', 122; Stevenson, *Scottish Revolution*, 256–257; Burnet, *The Memoirs of the Dukes of Hamilton*, 209; *RPCS*, 2nd series, vii, 359–363; Donaldson, *James V–James VII*, 330; Donaldson, 'The Solemn League and Covenant', *The Sunday Mail Story of Scotland*, 17, (Glasgow, 1988); E.J. Cowan, 'The Solemn League and Covenant', *Scotland and England, 1286–1815*, ed. Roger Mason, (Edinburgh, 1987), 187; Baillie, *Letters and Journals*, II, 58–60.
18. MacInnes, 'The Scottish Constitution, 1638–1651', 122; Stevenson, *Scottish Revolution*, 259; *RPCS*, vii, 372–374; Donaldson, *James V–James VII*, 330, neglects the role of the parliamentary interval committees and that of the gentry and burgesses; Cowan, 'The Solemn League and Covenant', 187.
19. SRO PA 14/2, folio 21.
20. Ibid.
21. Ibid.
22. *RPCS*, 2nd series, vii, 400, 406–407; SRO PA 14/1, ff 208–210; SRO PA 14/2.
23. Ibid.
24. *RPCS*, 2nd series, vii, 407.
25. Ibid, 83–84.
26. Ibid.
27. Ibid.
28. *APS*, v, 588; SRO PA 14/1, ff 223–225; SRO PA 14/2, ff 59–61; Menteith of Salmonet, *History of the Troubles of Great Britain*, 80.
29. *RPCS*, 2nd series, viii, 93.
30. Ibid.
31. Ibid, 93.
32. *RPCS*, 2nd series, viii, 93; SRO PA 14/1, ff 223–224; SRO PA 14/2, folio 59.
33. Baillie, *Letters and Journals*, II, 68.
34. SRO PA 14/1, folio 224; SRO PA 14/2, folio 59.
35. SRO PA 14/1, folio 224.
36. *RPCS*, 2nd series, vii, 93–94; SRO PA 14/1, folio 225.
37. Baillie, *Letters and Journals*, II, 68.
38. Ibid.
39. Ibid, 68; SRO PA 14/1, ff 224–225; SRO PA 14/2, folio 61; *RPCS*, 2nd series, vii, 93–94.
40. Ibid.
41. SRO Hamilton Papers, GD 406/1/10787; NLS Morton Chartulary, ii, folio 32.
42. SRO Hamilton Papers, GD 406/1/1884 and 1887; Laing, *History of Scotland*, 252.
43. MacInnes, 'The Scottish Constitution, 1638–1651', 123; Stevenson, *Scottish Revolution*, 270; Cowan, 'The Solemn League and Covenant', 189; L. Kaplan, 'Steps to War: the Scots and Parliament, 1642–1643', *Journal of British Studies*, ix, 1970, 58; W.M. Campbell, *The Triumph of Presbyterianism* (Edinburgh, 1958), 34, 47; Baillie, *Letters and Journals*, II, 80; *A Declaration of the Lords of His Majesties Privie Councell, And Commissioners for conserving the Articles of the Treatie: For the Information of His Majesties good Subjects of this Kingdome* (Edinburgh, 1643), 1–5.
44. *A Declaration of the Reasons for assisting the Parliament of England, Against the Papists*

and Prelaticall Army. By the General Assembly of the Kirke of Scotland (London, 1643), (2)-(3), (3), (6); D. Stevenson, *Alasdair Maccolla and the Highland Problem in the Seventeenth Century* (Edinburgh, 1980), 98.

45. *APS*, vi, i, 3–4; Rait, *The Parliaments of Scotland*, 157.
46. Baillie, *Letters and Journals*, II, 72.
47. *APS*, v, 251–252, 258–259; *APS*, vi, i, 3–4.
48. *APS*, vi, i, 5–57.
49. Baillie, *Letters and Journals*, II, 76–77; Burnet, *Memoirs of the Dukes of Hamilton*, 233–234; Rushworth, *Historical Collections*, II (ii), 466.
50. Baillie, *Letters and Journals*, II, 72; *APS*, vi, i, 6.
51. *Plaine Scottish, or Newes from Scotland* (London, 1643), (2).
52. *APS*, vi, i, 6; *Records of the Kirk*, 330–331.
53. *APS*, vi, i, 6.
54. Burnet, *Memoirs of the Dukes of Hamilton*, 234; Rushworth, *Historical Collections*, II (ii), 466.
55. Ibid.
56. *APS*, vi, i, 7–8.
57. Ibid, 8.
58. Ibid, 3–4, 18–19.
59. Ibid, 39–40, 51–57.
60. Ibid, 13; *Records of the Kirk*, 330–331.
61. *APS*, vi, i, 13, 23–24.
62. Ibid, 3–4, 43–51, 150–151; *Commons Journals*, 3, (March 1642–December 1644), 219–220; Stevenson, *Scottish Revolution*, 282–287; Makey, *The Church of the Covenant*, 70; Donaldson, *James V–James VII*, 331; Argyll and Bute District Archives, Argyll Papers, TD 40384.
63. *APS*, vi, i, 150–151; *The Analysis, Explication and Application, of the Sacred and Solemne League and Covenant, For the Reformation, and Defence of Religion, the Honour and Happinesse of the King, and the Peace and Safety of the three Kingdomes of England, Scotland, and Ireland* (London, 1643), 1.
64. Russell, *The Causes of the English Civil War*, 119; Stevenson, *Scottish Revolution*, 284; D. Stevenson, 'The Early Covenanters and the Federal Union of Britain', in *Scotland and England 1286–1815*, ed. R. A. Mason (Edinburgh, 1987), 163–181; Levack, *The Formation of the British State*, 110, 199; Ferguson, *Scotland's Relations with England*, 126; MacInnes, 'The Scottish Constitution, 1638–1651', 123–124; Stevenson, *Alasdair Maccolla and the Highland Problem*, 98; *Scotlands Alarme: Or, Some considerations tending to demonstrate the necessity of our speedie marching to the assistance of our Brethren in England, notwithstanding all difficulties, reall or pretended* (Edinburgh, 1643), 2; *A Declaration of the Reasons for assisting the Parliament of England, Against the Papists and Prelaticall Army. By the Generall Assembly of the Kirke of Scotland* (London, 1643), 2–3, 6.
65. Baillie, *Letters and Journals*, II, 90.
66. *APS*, vi, i, 150–151; Cowan, *Montrose for Covenant and King*, 143.
67. Ibid.
68. Ibid, 3–59, 57–58.
69. Ibid, 57–58; Rait, *The Parliaments of Scotland*, 157, 343.
70. *APS*, v, 282; *APS*, vi, i, 3–4, 57–58.
71. SRO PA 11/1, Register of the Committee of Estates, 28 August 1643–26 July 1644, ff 8–12, 64–72; Stevenson, *Scottish Revolution*, 293, 295.

72. SRO PA 11/2, Register of the Committee of Estates, 4 December 1643–23 November 1644 (Army), folio 3.
73. Ibid.
74. SRO PA 11/2, folio 3; *APS*, vi, i, 3–4, 57–58.
75. SRO PA 11/1, ff 72, 82, 87, 89. Lord Gordon was the brother of the Royalist Lewis, eighth Earl and third Marquis of Huntly, but had been persuaded by Argyll to ally himself with the Covenanters. In light of the Northern Rebellion, Gordon's inclusion may have been initiated by the radicals in order to watch over his movements and actions, especially since he was later to side with the Royalists after Inverlochy (*Scots Peerage*, iv, 548–549).
76. SRO PA 11/1, ff 5–86, 86–238; SRO PA 11/2, ff 1–113; *APS*, vi, i, 59, 60–95, 95–283.
77. *APS*, vi, i, 83, 92. Elcho and Angus were two of the noble additions of 2 February. Both had been barred from Parliament on 3 August 1641. Legislation of 19 July 1641 had barred noblemen's heirs from the House, However, their additions were not strictly constitutional illegal as the Committee of Estates was technically an interval committee with powers to add such individuals as it wished (Beattie, 'The Political Disqualification of Noblemen's Heirs in Seventeenth Century Scotland', 176).
78. SRO PA 11/2, ff 1–113.
79. Ibid; *APS*, vi, i, 3–95; *Registrum Magni Sigilli Regum Scotorum, 1634–1651*, J.M. Thomson (ed.), (Edinburgh, 1897), 57–58, 858–859.
80. SRO PA 11/1, ff 5–238; SRO PA 11/2, folio 3; *APS*, vi, i, 57–58.
81. SRO PA 11/1, ff 5–238; SRO PA 11/2, folio 3.
82. SRO PA. 11/2, ff 1–113. L. Mulligan, 'The Scottish Alliance and the Committee of Both Kingdoms, 1644–46', *Historical Studies Australia and New Zealand*, 14, (1970), 173; L. Mulligan, 'Peace Negotiations, Politics and the Committee of Both Kingdoms', *HJ* 12, (1969), 3; Ferguson, *Scotland's Relations with England*, 127.
83. SRO PA 11/2, ff 1–113; *APS*, vi, i, 92.
84. SRO PA 11/2, ff 1–113; *APS*, vi, i, 3–95, 57–58, 63, 71, 158–159.
85. SRO PA 11/2, ff 1–113. Alexander Hamilton, General of the Artillery, attended 59 out of 94 diets on the army section (63%), William Baillie of Lethem, Lieutenant General of the Foot 15 diets (16%), David Leslie, and General Major of the Horse 20 diets (21%).
86. Ibid.
87. *APS*, vi, i, 73; SRO PA 11/2, folio 20.
88. *APS*, vi, i, 74; SRO PA 11/2, folio 3.
89. SRO PA 11/2, ff 8–16.
90. *APS*, vi, i, 83; SRO PA 11/1, ff 5–119.
91. *APS*, vi, i, 63–64, 83.
92. Ibid, 69, 83, 92.
93. *RPCS*, 2nd series, viii, 1–22, 63.
94. Ibid, 1–22, 63. Out of 33 diets, Loudoun and Argyll attended on 30 (91%) and 28 occassions (85%). At a slightly lower level, Lauderdale was present on 22 occassions (67%), and Cassillis and Balmerino on 21 occassions each (64%). Hepburne of Wauchton (Haddington) attended on 18 diets (55%).
95. Ibid, 63–64.
96. Ibid.
97. SRO PA 11/1, ff 36–39.

98. *RPCS*, 2nd series, viii, 10.
99. SRO PA 11/2, ff 52–54, 55–57, 60, 61–62, 87, 91, 94–95; SRO PA 11/1, ff 92–93, 98–99, 102, 106, 107; Stevenson, *Scottish Revolution*, 291–292; *Two Speeches spoken at a Common Hall Oct. 27 1643. Wherein is shew'd the readynesse of the Scots to assist the Kingdome and Parliament of England to the vtmost of their power* (London, 1643), 4–5.

4

Parliamentary Management by the Radical Oligarchy: the 1644 Convention of Estates and the 1644 Parliament

The 1644 Convention of Estates, 3 January–3 June

The political trend of dominance and exercise of political power by the radical oligarchy had been apparent not only throughout the 1643 Convention of Estates, but also in the operation of parliamentary interval committees 1643–1644. The Privy Council had been successfully sidelined by the radical leadership and compulsory subscription of the Solemn League and Covenant had been required. It was against this political background that the 1644 Convention convened.

1. The Proceedings of the 1644 Convention

The 1644 Convention did not sit on a continuous basis. Its deliberations were held over four distinct blocks; 3–11 January, 25 January–2 February, 10–16 April, and 25 May–3 June.[1] The primary purpose of the Convention was to provide the formal forum to ensure that the necessary administrative, economic, and fiscal measures were taken to maximise the finite resources available for the benefit of the Scottish armed forces in the invasion of England. Of 40 enactments passed, 36 were public acts, a reflection of the emphasis on public affairs. All three ratifications passed also fell within this category.[2]

The decision to invade England and the appointments in the command chain of the leadership of the Scottish armed forces had already been taken by the Committee of Estates on 24 November. As early as 26 August the first session of the Convention had re-established the committees of war in the shires, the vehicle employed in 1640, as the central forum for local recruitment and administration. Further instructions had been issued to these committees and their colonels by the Committee of Estates on 1 September.[3]

Preparations for military invasion accelerated throughout the first block of diets (3–11 January). The kingdom was formally declared to be under a state of defence on 4 January. The army section of the Committee of Estates was ordered by the Convention on 8 January to proceed to the Borders to assist the forces in prepartion for the expedition into England. Military resources were rationalised by the Convention on 11 January when it ordered the withdrawal of Scottish forces from Ireland. The strategic implications of such a logistical move led the Edinburgh section of the Committee of Estates to reverse the decision on 22 February. The Edinburgh section of the Committee was therefore operating in a managerial capacity over the Convention and the protection of the west coast of Scotland from invasion by Irish Catholic rebels was paramount. Leven duly crossed the English border with an invading force on 19 January.[4]

Throughout the Convention a process of rationalisation of the fiscal, financial, and administrative infrastructure was underway to maximise available resources to initiate and sustain military invasion.

Finance was to be raised through use of the excise. Accordingly a session committee was established on 4 January to determine the most economical means of its uplifting. Three per estate formed its membership. Radical interests were managed by Balmerino, whilst those of the conservatives were represented by Lauderdale. The financial muscle of the burghs, combined with their skilled technical expertise in mercantile life, ensured the inclusion of representatives of Edinburgh, Perth, and Aberdeen. Alexander Foullis was appointed Collector Depute of the Loan and Tax to assist Hepburne of Humbie in his duties as Collector General. The committee was officially superseded on 27 January with the formation of a new excise committee, but this time with the specific remit of obtaining credit for the supply of arms. That the latter committee was more formal was reflected in its composition of 16 (five per estate with Chancellor Loudoun as supernumerary). Only four individuals served on both committees; Lauderdale, Crombie of Kemnay (Aberdeen) and the burgess representatives of Edinburgh and Aberdeen. Factional strength of both the radicals and conservatives/pragmatic Royalists was supplemented by the inclusion of Cassillis and Burleigh on the one hand and Glencairn and Lauderdale on other hand. The work of the committee resulted in an act of 2 February for raising of money for a present supply to the armies in England and Scotland.[5]

Two further session committees were established by the Convention with the specific purpose of raising finance to support Scottish military involvement in the king's British dominions; the committee for raising money to support the Scottish army in Ireland (30 January) and the committee for money (25 May). The first was composed of 16 (five from each estate and the Chancellor as supernumerary) with the task of raising money to support the Scottish army in Ireland. The remit of the committee for money was not specifically related to financial aid for the military campaigns; revenue was to be raised for the public use as a whole. Six nobles, six gentry, and four burgesses formed its membership. The political balance of the nobility on both committees was weighted towards the conservatives/pragmatic Royalists. Lauderdale served on both committees. He was backed primarily by Glencairn on the committee of 30 January and Lanark, Forrester, and Barganie on the committee for money of 25 May. Loudoun and Burleigh represented the radicals on the former committee, whilst Cassillis appears to be the sole radical noble on the latter.[6]

Diplomatic ties with the English Parliament were to go hand in hand with military assistance. Military alliance between the two kingdoms dictated the need for close consultation in military, diplomatic, civil, and religious matters. On 9 January Chancellor Loudoun, Lord Maitland, Johnston of Wariston

(Edinburgh), and Robert Barclay (Irvine) were dispatched by the Convention to oversee the imposition of the Solemn League and Covenant in England, particularly concerning the uniformity of religion between the two kingdoms. Maitland's inclusion was controversial as legislation of 19 July 1641 had barred noblemens' heirs from parliamentary proceedings (Maitland was Lauderdale's son). Uniformity of religion proved a most contentious issue with the negotiators of the English Parliament who were well aware that the abolition of episcopacy 'tooke from the king his Royall power in manie points of Jurisdiction, soveraignty and supremacie in the affairs and causes of Church and state'.[7]

When the Scottish commissioners reached London their role had not yet been determined. Division existed within the English Parliament not only over the role of the Scots, but on how the daily running of the war should be implemented. The fact that the Scots had now become involved in the war emphasised that some form of Anglo-Scottish executive body was required for the effective operation in the campaign against the king. The forum of a Committee of Both Kingdoms was instituted to oversee the co-ordination of the war effort. Gerolamo Agostini, the Venetian Secretary in England, observed that the Committee was in essence 'a Council of State composed of the two nations'.[8]

In common with the Solemn League and Covenant, in essence the mother of the Committee of Both Kingdoms, the Committee was born out of essentially different Scottish and English needs. For the Scots the Committee ensured a greater formal involvement in the conduct and co-ordination of the English Civil War, whilst for the English Parliament it represented an institution which could deal with the differing demands of the Scots, the king, and the military situation. Nevertheless, the Committee of Both Kingdoms was primarily an English institution based on the Committee of Safety established in July 1642. Indeed, whilst the Committee of Both Kingdoms could institute and enact on behalf of the English Parliament, it possessed no such power from the Scottish Parliament, and was primarily concerned with English interests.[9]

Twenty-seven members sat on the Committee of Both Kingdoms during 1644 and 1645. Of this number only six were Scots but the majority of them were radicals. Loudoun, Maitland, Johnston of Wariston, and Robert Barclay were supplemented in their numbers by the arrival in September 1644 of Erskine of Cambuskenneth (Clackmannan) and Hugh Kennedy (Ayr). Loudoun did not attend until September 1644 (along with Erskine and Kennedy) and relieved Wariston who was then free to return to Scotland. The small number of Scots as a grouping was not large enough, however, to balance the 20 English members from 1644–1645.[10]

In line with attempts to impose the Solemn League and Covenant in England, further moves were being taken by the Convention to ensure a more rigid subscription of the Solemn League and Covenant within Scotland. On 4 January the Committee of Estates was ordered to summon all relevant persons before the 1644 Parliament who had not yet subscribed the Covenant. The Act anent Non-covenanters' Estates of 4 January also stipulated that the estates and rents of those who refused to subscribe the Solemn League and Covenant were to be uplifted for public use. Legislation of the Committee of Estates of 12 October 1643 had stated that the rents and goods of the Earl of Lanark were to be confiscated for public use. Lanark was not to be employed in any public office in Scotland. Lanark appeared before the Convention on 16 April and swore the Solemn League and Covenant. This gained Lanark entry to the Convention (and committee membership), parliamentary voting rights, and access to public office. Indeed, Lanark was nominated to the Committee of Estates on the same day that he subscribed the League and Covenant. Likewise, on 16 April the Convention recommended the Committee of Estates to 'tak some speedie course for uplifting the rents of non-covenanters'.[11] Lanark's admission to the Convention was not to be used as an excuse to slacken the radicals' pursuit of wholescale subscription of the League and Covenant.

The rising of Sir John Gordon of Haddo and other lairds in the north-east of Scotland, backed by the Royalist Marquis of Huntly, disrupted the proceedings of the Convention. The second block of the Convention had commenced on 25 January and ended on 2 February, whereupon the next meeting of the Convention was deemed to be on 10 April. The rising in the north-east occurred between these two dates and the Convention of Estates reconvened on 10 April to deal with the insurrection. The Edinburgh section of the Committee of Estates had already issued orders to the committees of war in the north to round up their forces.[12]

Argyll returned to Edinburgh from the army at Newcastle specifically to attend the third block of the Convention (10–16 April). The reaction of the Convention to domestic disorder was the establishment of three session and two interval committees to deal not only with the rising in the north but also with the securing of the country in general. The Committee for the Present Expedition (10 April), the Committee anent Irish Affairs (11 April), and the Committee for a Posture of Defence formed the grouping of session committees, whilst the Committees for the North and South (16 April) were the two interval committees.

The Committee for the Present Expedition was to consider the terms and form of commissions, instructions, and directions for the forthcoming military expedition to the north, as well as securing peace in the Borders. Five nobles, four gentry, and four burgesses (13 in total) formed its membership. Although Lauderdale was included, radical nobles were the controlling force in the form of Argyll, Cassillis, and Burleigh.

The Committee anent Irish Affairs was established 'to heere the officeris of the armie in Ireland'. Its membership was composed of seven nobles, six gentry, and six burgesses (19 members in total). Two regiments of the Scottish forces had returned from Ireland; one was to be sent to the north to extinguish the rebellion and one was to be sent to the south to guard the Lowlands and the Borders. The purpose of consulting the officers of the officers recently returned from Ireland, therefore, may well have been to secure their military advice and opinions relating to a possible Irish Catholic assault on the west coast of Scotland. Political balance existed between the leading radical and conservative/

pragmatic Royalist nobles, with Lauderdale, Lanark, and Callander representing the conservatives and pragmatic Royalists and Cassillis, Balmerino, and Burleigh the radicals. Lanark may have been included to involve him in the consultation process. Despite the presence of three leading conservatives/pragmatic Royalists, the decisions would ultimately be made by the radicals backed by the gentry and burgesses.

The Committee for a Posture of Defence was issued with three remits; firstly, to ensure that the kingdom's defences were properly secured, secondly, to secure the Borders, and thirdly to consider the munitions in Dumbarton Castle. Clearly, the tightening up of the country's defences was being undertaken on all fronts by the Convention. Although the committee was composed of five per estate, noble representation was dominated by conservatives and pragmatic Royalists (Callander, Glencairn, and Lanark). Once again, Argyll had to rely on the political backing of the gentry and burgesses.[13]

By 16 April the Committee for the Present Expedition had reported its conclusions to the Convention. The two vital interval committees were correspondingly established on 16 April to accompany the two military regiments to the north and south respectively. The Convention also made various military appointments. Argyll was placed at the head of the force to suppress the northern rebellion, Earl Marischal was appointed Commander of the Horse in the northern expedition, with Lord Elcho as Commander of the Foot.[14]

The membership of the Committee for the North consisted of eight nobles, 16 gentry, three military officials, and seven burgesses (34 in total). The gentry clearly provided the backbone of the committee. Gentry and burghal representation reflected the northern nature of the committee and all eight nobles had their geographic domain in the north-east. Hence the committee was essentially regional in terms of membership. This was further emphasised by the fact that only one of the gentry, Sir James Scott of Rosyth (Clackmannan), was a member of the 1644 Convention. By way of comparison, three of the seven burgesses were Convention members; George Jamieson (Coupar), Andrew Gray (Montrose), and John Auchterlony (Arbroath).[15]

The Committee for the South was the larger of the two committees with 15 nobles, 28 gentry, and seven burgesses (yielding a total membership of 50). Conservative and pragmatic Royalist membership included Callander, Glencairn, Cassillis, Lauderdale, and Lanark. Gentry and burghal representation reflected the committee's southern nature. Only one laird, Sir William Home of Aitoun (Berwick), was a member of the 1644 Convention. None of the burgesses on the committee enjoyed Convention membership. The trend of employment of non-parliamentary gentry and burgesses continued unhindered.[16]

According to the commissions of the Committees for North and South all members of the Committee of Estates were allowed membership of both committees. It is also clear, however, that both committees were Committees of Estates in their own right. Burleigh was appointed President of the northern committee despite the fact that he had not been included in its membership. In turn, this also suggests that Argyll's appointment by the Convention as the leader of the northern expedition was primarily a military appointment, or that his military duties were preceding political and administrative considerations. The greater concentration of manpower on the Committee for the South indicates that the primary aim was to tighten the security of the country as a whole (which is consistent with the remits of several of the session committees formed by the Convention), whilst the role of the Committee for the North was to ensure that the forces led by Argyll achieved the suppression of the rebellion. Despite the theoretically large pool of human resources at the disposal of both these committees, the quorum of both committees was set at seven with no specification at the number per estate required to attend. This may well be attributable to the realisation that inclusion on a parliamentary commission per se did not neccessarily correspond with actual attendance. Both sections of the Committee of Estates were also sitting at that time and the northern rebellion was still unsuppressed.[17]

The fourth block of the Convention stretched from 25 May until 3 June. When the Convention reconvened a committee for processes was formed. Its purpose was to prepare the processes of those summoned to the 1644 Parliament (commencing on 4 June). Whether this applied only to those involved in the northern rebellion or also to those who still refused to subscribe the Solemn League and Covenant was not clarified. Conservatives and pragmatic Royalists secured all noble representation with the inclusion of Lauderdale and Lanark. Radical interests were primarily employed by Johnston of Wariston (Edinburgh) and the Provost of Edinburgh.[18]

3. The Committee Structure of the 1644 Convention of Estates

Eleven session and four interval committees have been analysed. Thirty-four nobles, 20 gentry, and 18 burgesses constitute the total field of membership of session committees, whilst 48 nobles, 69 gentry, and 39 burgesses form the corresponding field of interval committees.[19] It was the gentry who therefore achieved the greatest augmentation (49) in terms of interval committee membership compared to that of session committees. The corresponding rises for the nobility and burgesses were 14 and 21 respectively. This indicates once more the existence of a large pool of extra-parliamentary personnel in the Scottish localities which could be employed with ease, particularly on interval committees.

The growing prominence of conservative and pragmatic Royalist nobles in parliamentary affairs is reflected in committee analysis. Lauderdale is included on eight out of 11 session committees, and Lanark on five. Although Lanark did not initially subscribe the Solemn League and Covenant and did not gain formal entrance to the Convention until 16 April, he is included on three session committees prior to that date. The readiness of Lanark to co-operate with the Convention may have been an attempt to preserve an important role for the House of Hamilton in the Scottish and British political arena given the fact that his brother Hamilton was currently imprisoned by Charles I in England. On the other hand, Lanark may well have learned the lesson of the 1643 Convention when the walkout of himself, Hamilton and other pragmatic Royalists left the Convention under the control of the radicals. The willingness of the Convention to allow Lanark inclusion on so many committees may well have been a calculated manoeuvre to associate the Hamiltons with the Convention's illegal and unconstitutional enactments (as deemed by the king and the Royalists) including the 1643 Convention. Radical noble manpower on session committees was concentrated on Cassillis and Burleigh (five out of 11 session committees). Argyll and Loudoun secured nomination to only two session committees each, probably due to their other commitments. Both were heavily involved with the more important work of the Committee of Estates and Argyll was President of the army section as well as leading the expedition against Haddo and Huntly in the north. It is probable, however, that the influence of Loudoun and Argyll was employed on the session committees of which they were not members. It may also be the case that the Convention rubberstamped the work of the Committee of Estates, just as the Parliaments of 1640–1641 legalised the proceedings of the Tables and the Committee of Estates of 1640.[20]

Gentry representation on session committees was focused on Balfour of Denmilne (Fife), Hepburn of Wauchton (Haddington), Dundas of that ilk (Linlithgow), and Crombie of Kemnay (Aberdeen).[21] Analysis of burgess participation on the session committees of the Convention is restricted by the information listed in the parliamentary register; only the names of the burghs and not individual burgesses are listed in the majority of committees. Out of 11 session committees only four individual burgesses are actually named; Sir William Dick, Archibald Sydserf, James Stewart (all Edinburgh), and George Garden (Burntisland). None of these three burgesses are named in the attendance rolls of the Convention. The burgh of Edinburgh is included on eight session committees. On the three remaining session committees where the burgh of Edinburgh is not named, Archibald Sydserf and Sir William Dick are included on two session committees and James Stewart on the remaining one. The burghs of Dundee and Glasgow are included on four session committees, but it is clear that Edinburgh was dominating burghal representation, in keeping with its status as the capital.[22]

No more than eight nobles were nominated to two or more interval committees. They consisted primarily of two groups of radicals and conservatives. Cassillis and Loudoun were the leading radicals, with Lauderdale, Lanark, and Glencairn for the conservatives and pragmatic Royalists. Conservative and pragmatic Royalist nobles were therefore playing a prominent role on interval as well as session committees.

Similarly, no more than six gentry and three burgesses gained access to two or more interval committees; Johnston of Wariston (Edinburgh), Wauchope of Niddrie (Edinburgh), Grierson of Lag (Dumfries), Kerr of Cavers (Roxburgh), Scott of Harden (Selkirk), and Hamilton of Orbiston for the gentry, with Robert Barclay (Irvine), George Jamieson (Coupar), and Gideon Jack (Lanark) for the burgesses.

The noted trend of service on committees by extra-parliamentary gentry and burgesses is further emphasised by data extracted from interval committee analysis. Forty-four of the 69 gentry (64%) and 25 of the 39 burgesses (64%) on interval committees were not members of the 1644 Convention. The bulk of the 44 gentry were employed on the Committee for the North (19) and that for the South (20).[23] In comparison, the majority of the 25 burgesses were employed on the Committee of Estates (15).[24]

The First Session of the First Triennial Parliament, 4 June–29 July 1644

The 1644 Convention officially ended on 3 June in accordance with preparations for the First Session of the Triennial Parliament on 4 June. No special summons was required as the session was valid according to closing legislation of the 1641 Parliament and the 1640 Triennial Act. The Edinburgh section of the Committee of Estates had concluded its preparations on 31 May 1644, probably with a view to undertake the management of parliamentary proceedings.[25]

1. The Composition of the 1644 Parliament

Forty-one nobles, 44 gentry representing 25 shires and 43 burgesses representing 42 burghs constituted the membership of the 1644 Parliament. Total membership therefore amounted to 128.[26] Attendance levels of all Three Estates were generally lower than all previous parliamentary sessions, 1639–41, and were only higher than the June 1640 session (see appendices 2a and 3a).[27]

A grouping of 36 nobles, 12 gentry, and 19 burgesses (67 individuals in total) had served in the 1643 Convention. This amounts to 52% of the membership of the 1644 Parliament. Taking this analysis one step further reveals that 23 nobles, 18 gentry, and 18 burgesses (59 individuals in all) in the 1644 Parliament had served in various diets of the 1644 Convention; this amounts to 46% of the 1644 parliamentary membership. Interpretation of both data suggests a common core of parliamentary personnel, 1643–1644, primarily of radical affiliation.[28]

2. The Proceedings of the 1644 Parliament

Parliamentary proceedings were composed of 104 enactments (74 relating to public business and 30 relating to private legislation) and 45 ratifications.[29] Parliamentary proceedings focused on seven main areas: constitutional matters, procedural development, the punishment of those involved in domestic insurrection, the supplying and provision of the Scottish forces on a British basis, diplomatic correspondence with the Scottish commissioners in England, the rehabilitation of the House of Hamilton in the Scottish Parliament, and the renewal of parliamentary interval commissions to govern the country before the next session of Parliament.

Immediately after the calling of the parliamentary rolls, Balmerino, in the capacity of President of the last session of the 1641 Parliament, read the 1641 Act anent the President of Parliament and the 1640 Triennial Act to the

Estates, and then further enquired if a Commissioner had been sent by the king to convene the session. No such Commissioner had been sent. Thereafter, Lauderdale was voted President of the 1644 Parliament by the Estates, according to the strict interpretation of the 1641 legislation regarding the election of the President of Parliament in all succeeding Parliaments. According to such legislation, following the taking of the parliamentary oath by the Estates, either the Lord Chancellor or any other nominated by the King and the Estates (conjunctively) should be appointed President of Parliament. The President of the preceding Parliament would remain as President until the parliamentary oaths had been administered and until another President had been chosen by the Estates. However, Loudoun, Lord Chancellor, was not chosen as President (although he was present in Parliament on 4 June); the position went to Lauderdale. In essence, Lauderdale was elected without the agreement of Charles. The choice of Lauderdale is consistent with his growing influence, particularly in relation to his role in the 1644 Convention. His election to the office of President is probably also related to the fact that Loudoun was primarily concerned with diplomatic negotiations with the English Commissioners in London. It may also have been a move to present a more moderate stance by Parliament in relation to possible peace negotiations with the King, since the election of Argyll would have been regarded as too extreme (although Argyll was the main political operator). This is consistent with the elections of Presidents of Parliament, 1640–41.[30]

The significance of the constitutional legality of the 1641 Constitutional Settlement was further emphasised on 7 June by the 'Ordinance anente the Initial Wordes to be prefixed To everie Act of this Parliament' (ie the 1644 Parliament). Accordingly the text incorporated in each act read as follows:

> THE ESTATES of Parliament now presently conveind be vertue of the last Act of the last Parliament Haldine be his Matie and the Thrie Estates in Anno 1641.[31]

Hence any legislation enacted by the 1644 Parliament owed its legality to the 1640 Triennial Act (which received royal sanction as part of the 1641 Settlement) and the closing act of the 1641 Parliament. This is particularly important since no King's Commissioner had been sent to the 1644 Parliament.

The requirement of parliamentary sanction of the constitutional proceedings of 1643–44 (ie the summoning and sitting of the 1643 Convention, the signing of the Solemn League and Covenant and the military treaty with the English Parliament, and the 1644 Convention of Estates), had resulted in the establishment of a parliamentary session committee on 6 June to 'considder vpon the Way of approbatione of the Calling of the Conventione of Estates And all there proceidings and what hes flowed fra them'.[32] Two per estate formed its membership. Its radical orientation was reflected in the inclusion of both Burleigh and Balmerino, adherents of Argyll who themselves had been party to the events leading to and proceedings of the Convention.[33] The committee took over a month to conclude its findings and reported its conclusions to the House on 15 July. Four separate issues were incorporated in one enactment passed by the House. The calling of the 1643 Convention was approved and, by implication, its prorogation to a second session (the 1644 Convention). The Solemn League and Covenant was similarly approved and ratified, as was the original approval by the 1643 Convention and the General Assembly. The ordinance of 12 October 1643 requiring compulsory subscription of the Solemn League and Covenant for civil and religious office was similarly ratified, as was the military treaty with the English Parliament. Financial devices employed by the 1643 and 1644 Conventions to raise revenue (such as the loan and tax of 1643 and the raising of the excise) also secured ratification. The delay of the committee in taking over a month to report and legisalation being enacted once more emphasises the overriding need and desire for the legality of the constitutional events of 1643–44 to be secured.[34]

Procedural innovation in the 1644 Parliament rested on two important areas; the necessary formation of a parliamentary organ (or organs) to consider and prepare all legislation to be presented to Parliament, and a greater regulation concerning membership of parliamentary committees. Following the abandonment of the Lords of the Articles as a constitutional device, various committees had been employed in 1640–41 to deal with supplications, petitions, overtures, and ratifications.[35] The consideration of business in the 1644 Parliament was split and concentrated on two parliamentary session committees; the Committee for Bills and Ratifications (6 June) and the Committee for Overtures (19 June). A more efficient administrative parliamentary structure was being established. This procedural development is nevertheless consistent with the trends observed in 1640–41.[36]

The Committee for Bills and Ratifications consisted of two per estate. The increasing accommodation of conservative and pragmatic Royalist nobles within a parliamentary context was reflected in the inclusion of Glencairn. The leading figure on the committee, he made the report of the committee to the House on 13 June.[37]

As a reflection of its administrative nature, the Committee for Bills and Ratifications was issued with three remits. Firstly, all bills, supplications, and ratifications to be presented to Parliament were to be revised and considered. Secondly, the committee was empowered to grant warrants for citation of parties to appear before Parliament or the Committee of Estates (this applied to the latter in the case of Parliament rising before the appearance of any such parties). Thirdly, the committee was not empowered to determine on any bills, supplications and ratifications, but could reject any bill thought 'not competent to be received'. Only Parliament could determine on any such legislation.[38]

The Committee for Overtures was composed of four per estate. Only one laird and one burgh were also included on the Committee for Bills and Ratifications; Falconer of Halkerton (Kincardine) and the burgh of Linlithgow. Although conservative and pragmatic Royalist interests were served by Lanark, those of the radicals were managed by Cassillis and Burleigh. In common with the Committee for Bills and Ratifications, the primary role of the Committee for Overtures was administrative. All acts and overtures to be presented in

Parliament were to be considered and reports made. It was not specified whether or not the committee had a determinative remit, but considering the powers of the Committee for Bills and Ratifications this would seem unlikely.[39]

A further preparatory committee had been established on 11 June, although its nature was more revisionary; the Committee for considering the Commissions in the previous Parliament (ie the parliamentary session ending on 17 November 1641). Four per estate formed its membership. The influential radical nobles, Balmerino and Burleigh, were its leading members. Balmerino headed the committee and reported its findings to the House on 12 June. Two burgesses, George Bell (Linlithgow) and George Garden (Burntisland) were also members of the Committee for Bills and Ratifications. George Bell was also a member of the Committee for Overtures. Once more, the remit of this committee was not of a determinative nature; it was to revise and consider the commissions granted by the last session of the 1641 Parliament and to report to the House. The formation of this committee was probably due less to concerns of the legality of the 1641 commissions and more to a desire to revise and adapt, where appropriate, the terms of any relevant commissions which might be renewed by the 1644 Parliament. Although unspecified, the remit of the committee was probably restricted to the parliamentary interval commissions of 1641; the Common Burdens-Brotherly Assistance Commission, the Conservators of the Peace Commission, and the Plantation of Kirks and Valuation of Teinds Commission.[40]

The regulation of membership of parliamentary committees, both session and interval, was determined by legislation enacted on 26 July, three days before the close of Parliament.[41] According to Sir James Balfour, this was initiated and carried through Parliament by the gentry and burgesses.[42] This would appear to indicate that the nobility were interfering in the election of gentry and burgesess to committees.[43] Hence there was a reaction from the shires and burghs against contrived noble dominance of committees. New legislation set down rules governing the election of all committees of Parliament and Convention of Estates for the gentry and burgesses. Gentry and burghal members were to be chosen by Parliament from a list established by the commissioners of the shires and burghs. Both estates were to elect their own representatives; if any of the other estates wanted to add further names to that list then the additions were to consist of any of the present members of Parliament or 'other wayes that they shall be such as are capable to be Commissioners for each estate'.[44] Such further additions would not be allowed unless approved of by the present commissioners. If any of the additions were not members of Parliament then 24 hours notice had to be given to the relevant estate or estates as an approval or non-approval deadline. Furthermore, any of the three estates could add to the list of the other two. This rule had been already in practice by 5 July when all three estates had made additions. Sir John Smith (Edinburgh), for example, added Dundas of Maner (Linlithgow) to the list of gentry, whilst Burleigh added Alexander Douglas (Banff) to the burghal list.[45]

Although the legislation of 26 July tended to link membership of parliamentary committees with membership of the Parliament in session at the time of the initiation of such committees, non-members of Parliament were included in several interval committees commissioned on or after 26 July before the close of Parliament. Sixteen gentry and 18 burgesses included on the Committee of Estates (26 July) were not members of Parliament as per 4 June. Six gentry on the Committee for the Irish affairs (27 July) and 10 gentry on the Committee for the Exchequer (29 July) were non-parliamentary members.[46] In total, 64 out of 91 gentry analysed (70%) and 36 out of 56 burgesses analysed (64%) included on 11 interval committees were not members of Parliament. Interval committees which have been analysed were constituted between 19 June and 29 July. Two possible explanations can be forwarded for the high proportion of non-parliamentary gentry and burgesses employed on interval committees. Either the rules established on 26 July were being flouted, or those non-members employed had been included by the initiative of the gentry and the burgesses themselves or had at least met with their approval.[47] According to Sir James Balfour the act of 26 July was only passed after a continuation and a 'longe debait' between the nobility and the other two estates. The act met with hostility from the nobility who regarded it as 'ane directe violatione of the liberties of parliament'.[48] The passage of the act was probably therefore due to the combined voting strength of the gentry and burgesses. The act anent the choosing of commissioners out of the members of Parliament can therefore be interpreted as an attempt by the gentry and the burgesses to control their membership on parliamentary committees outwith or at the expense of the nobility. It also provides a further indication of grass-roots radicalism amongst the gentry and burgesses, as evident from 1639 onwards.

The punishment of ringleaders involved in the recent Northern Rebellion accounted for a large portion of parliamentary business. Almost immediately following the opening of the session, a session committee was formed on 5 June to regulate the processes of those cited to the Parliament. Three per estate constituted its membership. Despite the inclusion of Cassillis, the interests of conservative and pragmatic Royalist nobles were to the fore in the inclusion of Lanark and Perth. Two nobles, two gentry, and one burgess had been included on the Committee for Processes during the 1644 Convention.[49]

A similar session committee was set up on 5 June with a more specified remit of examining those cited as witnesses in the process against Lord Banff for his part in domestic insurrection. Two representatives from each estate constituted the membership of the committee. Both nobles (Linlithgow and Elphinstone) were conservatives and indicate a desire on the part of the radical nobles to involve the conservatives in the judicial process against the rebels. One laird (Francis Hay of Balhousie) and the two burgesses (John Semple and Alexander Douglas) were also included on the committee for regulating the processes of those cited to the Parliament. Therefore an efficient use of human manpower was being applied in terms of the gentry and burgesses.[50]

Following the establishment of the more general committee for regulating the processes of those cited to the Parliament, the House ordained on 7 June that examination by that committee of those presently in custody for rebellion in the north and the south was to commence. Sir James Balfour asserts that this was due to the pressure of the gentry led by Johnston of Wariston (Edinburgh) as 'speaker for the barrons'.[51] Acting on instructions from the parliamentary gentry, Wariston demanded that justice be administered on the main protagonists in the rebellions. Their processes were to be dealt with immediately by the committee for regulating processes. The committee's findings were then to be presented to the House. This request was endorsed by the House at once.[52]

By 12 June a further session committee was formed to deal with the northern rebels. The punishment of rebels had been restricted to Sir John Gordon of Haddo and seven other gentry. The new committee, the Committee for trying of the Delinquents, was given wide powers. Any of the accused and any witnesses could be summoned to appear before the committee. However, Parliament discharged the committee from pronouncing any sentence of censure or punishment. Report was to be made to the House before 19 June of the appropriate recommended punishment, but Parliament reserved the 'soll and only power of censureing and punishing of them in ther owne hand'. The commission was prorogued on 28 June to 4 July, and then on 5 July to 13 July.[53]

Four per estate formed the membership of the Committee for trying of the Delinquents. Noble membership was primarily conservative and pragmatic Royalist with only one radical included. In addition, three judicial members (all gentry) were included; Hamilton of Orbiston (Justice-Clerk), Alexander Colville of Blair, and James Robertson of Bedlay (Justice Deputes).[54] The latter were included in the commission 'not as ordinarie Judges in ye office of Justiciarie But as Comissionares delegat be ye saids Estats of Parliament.'[55] In terms of common membership, only two nobles (Linlithgow and Elphinstone) were also members of the committee dealing with Lord Banff, whilst there was no common membership with the committee for regulating the processes of those cited to the Parliament.[56]

Dundas of Maner (Linlithgow) reported the conclusions of the committee for trying of the Delinquents to the House on 25 June (six days later than the terms of the original commission). It found one of the main protagonists, Sir John Gordon of Haddo, guilty of high treason who should be punished with the loss of his life, land, and goods.[57] On 29 June two queries were presented by the judges delegated for the delinquents to Parliament for clarification. Firstly, the House was asked to determine the punishment for the crimes of raising of armies and invasion of the kingdom. The House decided that the appropriate punishment for such crimes was loss of life, lands, and goods. Five nobles (primarily conservatives and pragmatic Royalists) and one laird abstained from voting; Mar, Morton, Marischal, Home, and Roxburgh, and Sir John Sinclair of Hirdmeston (Haddington). Secondly, the House was asked its opinion on the appropriate punishment for holding house against the authority of the Estates. Parliament decided that punishment should be loss of life, land, and goods. Six nobles (primarily conservatives and pragmatic Royalists) were not in agreement with this decision; Marischal, Morton, Home, Perth, Roxburgh, and Lord Elphinstone. Marischal abstained from the vote and Elphinstone voted that punishment should be by death only. Four nobles (primarily conservatives and pragmatic Royalists) either abstained or voted in the contrary in both votes; Marischal, Morton, Home, and Roxburgh.[58] These decisions by Parliament were incorporated in the Act against these that takes up arms and holds house against the kingdom and Estates of the country of 29 June.[59]

A second session committee concerning the punishment of delinquents was established on 2 July. This dealt with the Earl of Hartfell, Sir John Charteris of Amisfield and the Provost of Dumfries (who is not specified). These would appear to be the individuals to be tried for insurrection in the south. Its membership was composed of two nobles, three gentry, and three burgesses. Significantly, the inclusion of Lanark indicates the accommodation of the interests of the conservative and pragmatic Royalist factions of nobles. Lanark was also included on the Committee for regulating the processes of those cited to the Parliament; apart from this no common membership exists with the other judicial session committees. Such membership data indicates an attempt for unity among conservatives and radicals, particularly Lanark's inclusion as the leading figure amongst the conservatives and pragmatic Royalists.[60] The decree of forfeiture against Sir John Gordon of Haddo reached the statute book on 16 July.[61]

The concentration of parliamentary business on judicial affairs continued with the establishment of a Committee for trying the relevancy of the summons of those cited to the Parliament on 19 July. Four of each estate plus Colville of Blair, Justice-Depute, formed its membership. Elphinstone, for the nobility, and Colville of Blair, had also been members of the Committee for trying of the Delinquents of 12 June. Two out of three nobles, two out of three gentry, and all three burgesses included on the committee for regulating the processes of those cited to the Parliament of 5 June were also included on the committee of 19 July. Noble common membership was split between radicals (Cassillis) and conservatives/pragmatic Royalists (Lanark). The radical orientation of this particular committee is marked by the inclusion of Balmerino for the nobility and Johnston of Wariston (Edinburgh) for the gentry. The remit of the committee was to consider and advise on all summons issued and statements given in to Parliament of those who were presently incarcerated.[62]

On 22 July Balmerino from the committee for regulating of processes reported the conclusions of that committee concerning the Earls of Crawford and Forth and Lord Eythin, all of whom were employed in the king's armies in England.[63] All were adjudged of high treason and forfeiture of their lives and property was recommended. This was voted on and passed by Parliament on 25 July. The title and dignity of the Earl of Crawford was awarded to the Earl of Lindsay, who had regarded it as traditionally belonging to the Lindsays.[64]

Crucially, Huntly and Montrose, the leading protagonists in the rebellion, escaped forfeiture of life, land, or goods. Both had already been excommunicated and their incomes confiscated until such time as they sign the Solemn League and Covenant. Such leniency may have been necessary to avoid alienating the conservative and pragmatic Royalist nobles which would have occurred if Huntly and Montrose had been captured and executed.[65]

Three of the 'lesser' individuals whose cases had been considered by the Committee for trying of the delinquents, George Gordon of Geicht, Robert Lindsay of Maynes, and John Sturgioun of Torrarie, had not had judgement passed by the end of the parliamentary session of 29 July. Therefore, a separate interval commission was initiated to deal with their cases. Three gentry and two burgesses included on this commission had been members of the original Committee for the Delinquents. One further burgess included on the latter committee was not a member of Parliament as per 4 June. Three judicial officials were also included on both committees. As with the terms of the Committee for trying of the Delinquents, the terms of the new interval commission stated that these judicial officials were included as full commissioners and not merely in a legal capacity. No nobles included on the interval committee had sat on the Committee for trying of the Delinquents. Indeed, whereas four nobles had sat on that session committee only two nobles were included on the interval committee.[66]

Five days previously, on 24 July, the commission for trying of the Delinquents of 12 June had been renewed by the Estates, this time as an interval committee. The membership was identical bar the replacement of three nobles. Yester, Kirkcudbright, and Loure were to replace the three nobles on the original commission. Yester and Loure constituted the noble element on the more specific commission for trying of Gordon of Geicht, Lindsay of Maynes, and Sturgioun of Torrerie. Thus, a rationalisation in terms of membership was being undertaken for those judicial parliamentary interval committees whose origins and specific remits lay in the parliamentary session committees.[67]

In common with the proceedings of the 1644 Convention, the supplying and provision of the Scottish armed forces on a British basis occupied the attention of the 1644 Parliament and was of paramount importance.

Two session committees were appointed on 5 June for dealing with financial affairs, principally for the raising of revenue; a committee anent the borrowing of money and a committee for the levy. The commission for the committee anent the borrowing of money was only to endure until 8 June; this was subsequently continued to 11 June. Six of each estate formed its membership. A comparison in membership with the Committee for money of 25 May of the 1644 Convention reveals that four nobles and six gentry were also included on the Committee anent the borrowing of money of 5 June, with Lanark and Cassillis the leading figures. The remaining members of the committee included the radicals Burleigh and Balmerino. Therefore a high concentration of personnel employed in the 1644 Convention was similarly employed on 5 June, especially among the gentry and even if they were not members of Parliament. This suggests a retention of financial expertise.[68]

Four of each estate formed the membership of the Committee for the Levy. Noble membership was primarily radical and included Argyll and Lothian. Johnston of Wariston (Edinburgh) was the dominant radical included in the gentry membership.[69] The Ordinance anent the Committees of War of 6 June ratified and continued the membership of the Committees of War in the shires. The committees named by Argyll for the shires of Kincardine, Aberdeen, and Banff were similarly approved. The only exceptions in the renewal of the above committees applied to those cited to the Parliament or who were under caution to appear before the Parliament. The commissioners of the shires sitting in Parliament were instructed to inform their local committees of such exceptions.[70] The relationship between the central and local administrations was further strained by legislation enacted on 11 June. Each committee of war was instructed to send two of its members with its clerk to Parliament with all acts and orders of its committees on the grounds that the war committees had failed to provide their required quotas of horse and foot.[71] On 12 June the Earl of Callander's commission as Lieutenant General of the Scottish armed forces in Scotland and England was renewed.[72] According to Sir James Balfour, a session committee had been established on 5 June to determine and revise on the nature and powers of the commission granted to Callander previously and the terms of renewal. Argyll and Lothian were the dominant radical nobles on that committee.[73]

A new commission for the committee for borrowing of money was issued on 11 June (the original commission having been twice continued to 8 and then 11 June). Five nobles, six gentry, and six burgesses constituted the membership of the new committee. Chancellor Loudoun and the President of Parliament, Lauderdale, were also included as supernumeraries. Four nobles, three gentry, and three burgesses included on the committee of 11 June had sat on the earlier committee. Although Lanark was one of these four nobles, he was outflanked by Cassillis and Burleigh. Three nobles (including Cassillis and Lanark), three gentry, and one burgess had also sat on the Committee for Money of 25 May in the 1644 Convention.[74]

A general session committee concerning all matters relating to the Scottish army in Ireland was likewise formed on 11 June. Seven nobles, seven gentry, and six burgesses constituted the membership. Three nobles, two gentry, and four burghs included on the committee had sat on the Committee anent the Irish affairs of 11 April in the 1644 Convention. Cassillis and Burleigh represented radical interests, whilst Lanark represented those of conservatives and pragmatic Royalists. Of the remaining four nobles on the Committee concerning the army in Ireland, Argyll and Lothian were the leading radicals. Glencairn was the one noted pragmatic Royalist included among the remaining noble membership.[75]

By 13 June orders were being issued to the Committees of War for the raising of forces and finance. Lord Elcho was ordained to execute all acts and ordinances of the late Committee for the North regarding the collection of the loan and tax within the sheriffdoms of Aberdeen, Banff, and Kincardine. On 14 June, for example, four warrants were issued to the Committees of War for the sherrifdom of Perth for putting out of forces, and Aytoun of that ilk (Fife) was similarly issued with a warrant for putting out the forces in Fife.[76]

Callander was issued with instructions from Parliament on 18 June for his invasion of England to enforce the Solemn League and Covenant. As well as military instructions, the pursuit of leading Royalists and any of their adherents in arms against the Parliaments of both kingdoms was ordered. Particular reference was made to the Earls of Crawford, Montrose, and Nithsdale, and Lords Aboyne and Ogilvie.[77]

The uplifting of the excise had been used throughout the 1644 Convention to finance Scottish military expeditions on a British basis. The 1644 Parliament turned to consideration of the excise to secure further revenue on 9 July. Six from each estate, plus Chancellor Loudoun, formed the membership of a new excise committee. Three nobles, two gentry, and four burghs included on the new committee had also been members of the previous excise committee of 27 January in the 1644 Convention. This grouping included the radicals Cassillis and Burleigh and the conservative Lauderdale. The remaining noble members of the new committee were both radicals (Argyll and Lothian) and were supplemented by Johnston of Wariston (Edinburgh). The committee had reported to the House by 15 July when Parliament voted in favour of the excise as the necessary means of building up a stock of credit.[78]

The rehabilitation of the House of Hamilton, which had commenced with Lanark's growing influence in the 1644 Convention, was complete by 22 July 1644. Out of 18 parliamentary session committees analysed between 5 June and 19 July, Lanark was included on 10, the highest figure for any member of the nobility.[79] On 22 July an Act and declaration in favour of James, Duke of Hamilton, and other peers and subjects imprisoned in England denounced the imprisonment of the Duke of Hamilton and other Scottish peers in England without trial. If any trial of Hamilton was to take place then he was to be returned to Scotland to await such trial. On 22 July Parliament ratified Lanark's appointment as the sole Secretary of State. Lanark had been appointed to this post by the 1641 Parliament in consultation with the King. Sir James Galloway, Master of Requests, had usurped the office and title of Secretary and the King had further replaced Lanark by Sir Robert Spottiswood. The Estates nevertheless upheld Lanark's appointment.[80] Such moves helped to accommodate the conservative and pragmatic Royalist nobles in the help being given to the English Parliament.[81]

In common with the close of the 1641 Parliament, a bulk of ratifications passed through the 1644 Parliament on the closing day of the session. Sir James Balfour states that these had already been approved by the Committee for Bills and Ratifications (as per the terms of its commission of 6 June). Parliament was then continued to the first Tuesday in January 1645.[82]

3. The Committee Structure of the 1644 Parliament

Eighteen session committees and 11 interval committees have been analysed. Twenty-seven nobles, 62 gentry, and 22 burgesses were nominated to 18 session committees, whereas 50 nobles, 91 gentry, and 56 burgesses secured membership of 11 interval committees. Such a large field of membership is unsurprising given the fact that Parliament had not met for three years and that the Scots were now heavily involved in the English Civil War. In common with previous trends more personnel over all three estates was employed on interval committees. In this particular instance, the burghal estate exhibited the greatest rise (34) in comparison to both the nobility (23) and the gentry (29). Eight of the 62 gentry (13%) and two of the 22 burgesses (9%) included on session committees were not members of Parliament as per 4 June 1644. In comparison, 65 of the 91 gentry (71%) and 36 of the 56 burgesses (64%) elected to interval committees were not members of Parliament as per 4 June 1644. Therefore employment on session committees, in general, adhered to parliamentary membership. The employment of so many non-parliamentary gentry and burgesses on interval committees provides a clear indication of Covenanting strength in the Scottish localities and an efficient use of human resources on a parliamentary basis.[83]

Five judicial committees, four financial committees, four executive committees, three diplomatic committees, and two military committees constituted the breakdown of the 18 parliamentary session committees. The 11 interval committees consisted of three diplomatic committees, three financial committees, two military committees, one executive committee, one ecclesiastical committee, and one judicial committee.[84]

Radical nobles dominated the power balance of the 18 session committees as a whole and was concentrated on Burleigh (nine), Cassillis (eight), Balmerino (seven), and Argyll (six). Conservative and pragmatic Royalist interests were served primarily by Lanark who secured nomination to the largest number of session committees (10) of any noble.

Conservative and pragmatic Royalist nobles, particularly Lanark and Linlithgow, were assigned an influential role on the five judicial session committees; Lanark served on three and Linlithgow on two. Noble radical interests on judicial session committees were focused on the services of Cassillis (two). Whilst conservative and pragmatic Royalist interests on the four financial session committees were represented by Lanark, Lauderdale, and Barganie (two each), they were outflanked by Cassillis and Burleigh (three each) along with Loudoun and Balmerino (two each). Conservative and pragmatic Royalist strength on the three financial interval committees was represented by Lanark and Lauderdale and supplemented by Forrester (two each). The influence of Loudoun and Burleigh on the financial session committees was matched on the financial interval committees; Loudoun was elected to all three and Burleigh to two. The ascendancy of radical noble strength was also reflected on the four executive session committees; Burleigh served on three and Balmerino on two. Where conservative and pragmatic Royalist nobles were included, they were marginalised to a single committee each.

A greater degree of political balance is apparent on the three diplomatic session committees. Argyll was included on all three committees, whilst Lothian and Balmerino were nominated to two. On the other hand, Lanark was also included on all three committees, with Morton and Roxburgh securing membership of two each. Nevertheless, radicals were dominant on the most important diplomatic session committee, that relating to the articles of peace and the renewal of the diplomatic commission to England. The political balance of noble representation on the three diplomatic interval committees, however, was weighted in favour of the radicals. Argyll served on all three commissions, whilst Leven, Loudoun, and Lothian each served on two. Conservative and pragmatic Royalist influence on the diplomatic interval committees rested with Glencairn (two). Futhermore, noble membership of the military session committees was essentially radical. Argyll, Lothian, and Burleigh were included on both committees.[85]

Gentry membership of the 18 session committees as a whole was based on seven gentry; Johnston of Wariston (Edinburgh) and Shaw of Greenock (Renfrew) (six each), MacDowall of Garthland (Wigtown) (five), Hamilton of Little Preston (Edinburgh), Dundas of Maner (Linlithgow), Hay of Balhousie (Perth), and Forbes of Craigievar (Aberdeen) (four each). Forbes of Craigievar and Hamilton of Little Preston also gained access to five of the 11 interval committees. Gentry membership of interval committees as a whole was also supplemented by a grouping of five gentry, each of whom was elected to four interval committees; Wauchope of Niddrie (Edinburgh), Grierson of Lag (Dumfries), Home of Wedderburne (Berwick), Innes of that ilk (Elgin), and Hamilton of Orbiston (Renfrew), Justice Clerk.

Gentry membership of the five judicial session committees was centred on Hay of Balhousie (Perth) (three), Cochrane of Cowdoun (Ayr), and Belshes of Toftis (Berwick) (two each). In addition, Colville of Blair, Justice Depute, was also included on two judicial session committees. Gentry membership of the four financial session committees was also centred on three gentry; Hamilton of Little Preston (Edinburgh), Balfour of Denmilne (Fife), and Hamilton of Orbiston (Renfrew) (two each). The fact that neither Balfour of Denmilne nor Hamilton of Orbiston were members of Parliament as per 4 June 1644 suggests that their inclusion was dependent on possession of a required level of financial expertise. Hamilton of Little Preston, Hamilton of Orbiston, and Falconer of Halkerton (Kincardine) were each elected to two of the three financial interval committees, as were Sir James Carmichael of that ilk, Treasurer Depute, and Hope of Craighall, as Senator of the College of Justice.

Falconer of Halkerton (Kincardine) and Dundas of Maner (Linlithgow) dominated gentry membership of the four executive session committees. Both secured membership of two such committees. The three diplomatic session committees exhibit a common membership grouping of six gentry; Johnston of Wariston (Edinburgh) (all three), Hamilton of Little Preston (Edinburgh), Falconer of Halkerton (Kincardine), Carnegie of Pittarrow (Kincardine), MacDowall of Garthland (Wigtown), and Erskine of Cambuskenneth (Clackmannan) (two each). Johnston of Wariston, political ally of Argyll, was the only laird nominated to more than one of the three interval diplomatic committees. Agnew of Lochnaw (Wigtown) was the only laird included on both session committees with a military remit, whilst Wauchope of Niddrie (Edinburgh) was the only laird with common membership of both interval military committees. Niddrie had not been a member of Parliament as per 4 June 1644.[86]

Six burgesses were to the fore in burghal common membership of session committees as a whole; James Bell (Glasgow) (eight), George Bell (Linlithgow) (seven), John Semple (Dumbarton), and Alexander Douglas (Banff) (six each), John Lepar (St Andrews) and Sir John Smith (Edinburgh) (five each). Robert Cunningham (Kinghorn), along with Semple and Douglas, were included on five of the 11 interval committees as a whole. Smith, James Bell, in addition to James Sword (St Andrews), Robert Barclay (Irvine), and William Glendoning (Kirkcudbright), each were nominated to four interval committees.

John Semple (Dumbarton), Alexander Douglas (Banff), and Sir John Smith (Edinburgh) formed the core membership of the five judicial committees. Five burgesses constitute the common grouping of burgesses included on the four financial session committees; James Bell (Glasgow) (three), George Bell (Linlithgow), Robert Cunningham (Kinghorn), Thomas Halyburton (Dundee), and John Osburne (Ayr) (two each). Burghal common membership of the three financial interval committees was based on Sir John Smith (Edinburgh) and John Semple (Dumbarton) (two each). Burghal control of the four executive session committees was based on George Bell (Linlithgow) (three), George Garden (Burntisland), and John Lepar (St Andrews) (two each).[87]

The three diplomatic session committees (in terms of the burghal estate) were staffed primarily by five burgesses; Patrick Leslie (Aberdeen) and James Bell (Glasgow) (all three), Sir John Smith (Edinburgh), George Bell (Linlithgow), and John Semple (Dumbarton) (two each). Burghal common membership of the three diplomatic interval committees was based on Sir John Smith (Edinburgh), Hugh Kennedy (Ayr), and Robert Barclay (Irvine). Neither Kennedy nor Barclay were members of Parliament as per 4 June 1644. Only two burgesses were included on both session committees with a military remit; Sir John Smith (Edinburgh) and George Jamieson (Coupar).[88]

The numerical strength of the shires and burghs had therefore ensured that membership of session committees in the 1644 Parliament could be spread/devolved to specific groups of gentry and burgesses. Burghal membership of session committees, however, was concentrated with a more defined grouping. Extra-parliamentary gentry and burgesses were employed virtually exclusively on interval committees, which tended to be controlled by distinct gropuings of gentry and burgesses. Conservative nobles were allowed access primarily to financial interval committees. With the exception of Glencairn, they were not allowed membership of the crucial diplomatic interval committees, which remained the domain of the leading radical nobles, gentry, and burgesses.

4. The Appointment of Parliamentary Interval Committees

Four main interval commissions from the 1641 Parliament were renewed by its 1644 counterpart; the Committee for Plantation of Kirks and Valuation of Teinds, the Committee for the Common Burdens, the Commission for the Conservators of the Peace, and the Commission for the Exchequer. Additions were made by the 1644 Parliament to the Committee for Plantation of Kirks and Valuation of Teinds and the Committee for the Common Burdens due to the death or infirmity of five of its members (three gentry and two burgesses). Four per estate were also added to the Committee for Plantation of Kirks and Valuation of Teinds. Conservative and pragmatic Royalists interests were recognised by the addition of Lanark to the committee.[89]

Increased diplomatic activity *vis-a-vis* the king and the Englsh Parliament occupied the attention of the Estates from 4 June to 29 July. Current peace negotiations and proposals had been referred to a session committee of 11 June, the Committee for Propositions of Peace. Twelve per estate formed its membership. Argyll, Balmerino, and Burleigh were included for the radicals, although there was strong conservative/pragmatic Royalist grouping based on Glencairn, Lanark, Callander, Morton, Perth, and Roxburgh. Radical interests among the gentry were particularly represented by Johnston of Wariston (Edinburgh).[90]

A further diplomatic session committee, dominated by radicals, was established on 22 June with two specific remits; to debate further on specific individuals to be included in the terms of the peace proposals, and to consider the renewal of the commission of the Scottish commissioners to be sent to England. Three nobles, five gentry, and four burghs who sat on the Committee for Propositions of Peace secured membership of this committee. This included Argyll, Balmerino, and Johnston of Wariston (Edinburgh) for the radicals, with Lanark for the conservatives/pragmatic Royalists.[91]

The latter committee had reported to Parliament by 28 June on both remits. Twenty individuals were included in the clauses of the peace proposals for subscription of a declaration against the Solemn League and Covenant and the 1643 Convention of Estates and those involved in the rebellions in the north and south of Scotland. They included Huntly, Crawford, Montrose, and Nithsdale. Instructions were also laid down for the commissioners who were to go to England, principally for their work with the Committee of Both Kingdoms and the English Parliament.[92]

The Scottish commissioners to be sent to England were named on 16 July (in constitutional terms this was a parliamentary interval committee). Three per estate, plus Lord Maitland as supernumerary, constituted the membership. Maitland's inclusion was in contravention of legislation of 19 July 1641 which barred heirs of noblemen from parliamentary membership. Maitland had been commissioned by the General Assembly in 1643 to attend the Westminster Assembly of Divines in London, and had also been commissioned by the 1644 Convention in a diplomatic capacity. Noble representation of the parliamentary diplomatic commission was exclusively radical and consisted of Chancellor Loudoun, Argyll, and Balmerino. In addition Johnston of Wariston (Edinburgh) was the leading gentry representative and all burgess representatives were noted radicals. Two nobles, one laird, and one burgess included on the commission had formed the membership of the commissioners sent by the Convention of Estates on 9 January 1644. According to the commission of 16 July Loudoun, Balmerino, Johnston of Wariston (Edinburgh), and Erskine of Cambuskenneth

(Clackmannan) were ordered to depart for England immediately. Argyll, Dundas of Maner (Linlithgow), and Sir John Smith (Edinburgh) were to depart as when required by the nature of any appropriate business under discussion or when commanded to do so by the Committee of Estates in Scotland or by the Committee with the army in England. Maitland and Robert Barclay (Irvine) were already in London. On 4 July the House had elected the three gentry representatives, whilst the nobility and burgesses had been elected on 5 July.[93] Parliament stipulated on 19 July that the Scottish commissioners in England were to be part of the Committee of Estates and that those members who failed to attend when required would be fined. The radicals had clearly succeeded in securing the nominations, over all three estates, for the diplomatic dealings with the English Parliament.[94]

The second commission for the Northern Business was issued on 19 July (the first having been commissioned by the 1644 Convention on 16 April). The Committee for the Northern Business was accorded the status of a Committee of Estates and was to take control of the armed forces in the north. Its remit was essentially of military and judicial nature; it was to suppress any potential insurrection, administer the processes of malignants, and censure non-subscribers of the Solemn League and Covenant. The Committees of War were to be subject to the authority of the committee, which was to extend throughout the sheriffdoms of Aberdeen, Banff, Elgin and Forres, Inverness, Nairn, Sutherland, Caithness, and Cromarty.[95]

The Committee for the Northern Business was composed of 14 nobles, 28 gentry, and 15 burgesses (57 individuals in total). The gentry formed the backbone of the committee, whereas noble and burghal membership was almost equal. Burleigh was appointed as President, although he was not specified as a committee member under the noble estate. Gentry and burgess membership was determined by their northern geographical location. In terms of membership per estate, the commission of 19 July constitutes a rise of six nobles, two gentry, and eight burgesses compared to the Committee for the North of 16 April 1644. Twenty-six of the 28 gentry (93%) and nine of the 15 burgesses (60%) included on the commission were not members of Parliament as per 4 June 1644. The high rate of employment of non-parliamentary personnel can be explained by the local remit of the committee. Noted radical personnel, such as Alexander Douglas (Banff), George Jamieson (Coupar), and Patrick Leslie (Aberdeen) still secured membership. Six nobles, six gentry, and three burgesses, plus three burghs included on the Committee for the North of 16 April were also included on the Committee for the Northern Business of 19 July. Membership was determined by primarily by geographical location and allowed for a continuity of personnel.[96]

A new Excise Commission was issued on 29 July, in the form of a parliamentary interval committee.The membership per estate was reduced by 50% to three per estate compared to the membership of the Committee anent the Matter of the Excise of 9 July. Three nobles and one burgess who sat on the former committee of 9 July were included on the interval committee. This grouping of three nobles consisted of two radicals (Balmerino and Burleigh) and one conservative (Lauderdale). Chancellor Loudoun was included as a supernumerary on both committees. Radical common membership was further accentuated by the presence of Sir John Smith (Edinburgh) on both committees.[97]

A new commission for the Committee of Estates was issued on 26 July. Three supernumeraries (all nobles), 27 nobles, 32 gentry, and 33 burgesses (yielding a total of 95 individuals) formed the membership of the 1644 Committee of Estates. Sixteen of the 32 gentry (50%) and 19 of the 33 burgesses (58%) were not members of Parliament as per 4 June 1644. The three supernumeraries appear to have been included due to the positions they held; Chancellor Loudoun, Leven, General, and Callander, Lieutenant General. In common with the 1643 Committee of Estates, its 1644 counterpart was split into two sections, an Edinburgh section and an army section. The 1644 Committee of Estates exhibited a rise of eight nobles, 10 gentry, and 12 burgesses (30 in total) compared to the numerical composition of the 1643 Committee.[98]

The Edinburgh section of the 1644 Committee of Estates was composed of 13 nobles, 21 gentry, and 24 burgesses (58 in total). In comparison, the army section consisted of 16 nobles, 11 gentry, and nine burgesses (36 in total). The most influential nobles on the Edinburgh section were Lauderdale and Lanark, Balmerino, and Burleigh. Hence there appears to have been a political balance between radicals and conservatives/pragmatic Royalists. The same scenario may have also applied on the army section; Argyll and Cassillis for the radicals, with Crawford-Lindsay and Glencairn for the conservatives/pragmatic Royalists. However, Lanark and Lauderdale may have been marginalised to the Edinburgh section and balanced by Balmerino and Burleigh. This suggests that there was a deliberate policy option to marginalise the influence of the conservatives and pragmatic Royalists on each section and deliberately keep apart the core of conservative nobles.

Seven of the 21 gentry (33.3%) on the Edinburgh section on the Edinburgh section were not members of Parliament as per 4 June 1644. Only two of the gentry included on the army section were parliamentary members; Kerr of Cavers (Roxburgh) and Scott of Harden (Selkirk). The remaining nine gentry had been prominent in Parliament and the Convention of Estates, 1639–1644. Ten of the 24 burgesses (42%) on the Edinburgh section and all nine burgesses on the army section were non-parliamentary members. All nine burgesses on the army section had been prominent in Parliament, Conventions of Estates, and Committees of Estates, 1639–1644.[99]

A core grouping of 26 of the 32 nobles (81%), 19 of the 32 gentry (59%), and 20 of the 33 burgesses (61%) included on the 1644 Committee had been included on the 1643 Committee or in the additions by the 1644 Convention.[100] A further grouping of seven nobles, five gentry, and six burgesses (18 in total) had also been included on the 1640 Committee of Estates. Cassillis, Dunfermline, Lothian, Crawford-Lindsay, Balmerino, Burleigh, and Coupar were the seven such nobles. All had also been included on the 1643 Committee.

Lord Advocate Craighall, Nicholson of Carnock (Stirling), Hepburne of Wauchton (Haddington), Home of Wedderburne (Berwick), and Hamilton of Little Preston (Edinburgh) formed the grouping of five gentry. Three of these five gentry had also been included on the 1643 Committee; only Hope of Craighall and Nicholson of Carnock did not meet this criterion. Edward Edgar (Edinburgh), Thomas Paterson (Edinburgh), George Porterfield (Glasgow), Hugh Kennedy (Ayr), John Rutherford (Jedburgh), and James Sword (St Andrews) formed the corresponding grouping of six burgesses. Four of the six burgesses were also included on the 1643 Committee of Estates; only Edward Edgar and Thomas Paterson did not meet this criterion.[101]

Parliament stated on 29 July that the 1644 Committee was to have full authority to appoint a Committee of Processes, whose members were to be chosen out of the Committee of Estates. The Justice Clerk and two Justice Deputes were to be included as members. This committee was to report to the next session of Parliament.[102]

The Committee for Irish Affairs was established on 27 July. It was to proceed to Ireland and join with commissioners from the English Parliament for joint consultation on the Irish campaign. Its commissioners were included on the Edinburgh section of the Committee of Estates and were to attend the diets of that section when present in Edinburgh. The Committee for Irish Affairs can therefore be interpreted as the section of the Committee of Estates to accompany the forces in Ireland (as was the case with the 1643 Committee of Estates). In conjunction with the commissioners from the English Parliament the Commission for Irish Affairs can also be interpreted as a section of the Committee of Both Kingdoms specifically for the military theatre in Ireland. Five nobles, five gentry, three burghs, and four military officials formed the membership. Noble membership was dominated by radicals with the inclusion of Argyll, Leven and Lothian. Leven and Lothian were included in the capacities as General and Lieutenant General respectively. Glencairn appears to have been included not only as a concession to the conservatives/pragmatic Royalists, but also as a recognition of his own geographic and territorial interests. Gentry and burghal membership both exhibited a west coast bias, due to the proximity of the west coast to Ireland.[103]

The Exchequer Commission was issued on the last day of the session, 29 July. This was a renewal of an earlier commission. Sir James Galloway, disgraced on account of the rivalry over the office of Secretary, was omitted and Loudoun was added. Three nobles and 11 gentry constituted its membership. All three nobles held institutional posts; Loudoun, Chancellor, Roxburgh, Keeper of the Privy Seal, and Lanark, Secretary. Bar Loudoun, conservative and pragmatic Royalist nobles thus had a strong footing within the Exchequer Commission. Similarly, 10 of the 11 gentry held institutional posts. Three were Officers of State and six gentry were Senators of the College of Justice. Scott of Scotstarvit was included as Director of the Chancellory. Only Lockhart of Lee did not hold an institutional post and he was not a member of Parliament as per 4 June 1644. The Commissioners of the Exchequer were to assist the new Treasurer, Crawford-Lindsay, and Carmichael of that ilk, Treasurer Depute.[104]

The 1641 Parliament had created five Treasury commissioners. The 1644 Parliament conferred the office on one Commissioner only, Crawford-Lindsay, with Carmichael of that ilk remaining Treasurer Depute. The Treasury Commission therefore also exhibited a shift towards conservatism. Both had been included on the 1641 Commission for the Treasury. Therefore, it would appear that the Commissioners of the Exchequer were to be subordinate to the Treasurer.[105]

5. The Operation of Parliamentary Interval Committees

The Edinburgh section of the Committee of Estates convened on 30 July and sat until 6 January 1645.[106] Eighty-four sederunts are recorded for the Edinburgh section of the Committee of Estates. Lauderdale's political status continued to grow and was reflected in his attendance at 81 of the 84 diets (96%), the highest figure of any noble. His nearest challenger was Balmerino who attended 48 diets (57%). The remaining 14 nobles on the Edinburgh section (including supernumeraries) attended 20 or less diets. In addition, 12 nobles included on the army section of the Committee of Estates attended various diets of the Edinburgh section, including Cassillis (38, 45%) and Crawford-Lindsay (32, 38%). Five further nobles who were not included on either section of the Committee of Estates attended various diets of the Edinburgh section. Lauderdale's dominance among the nobility in terms of attendance is paralleled by the fact that he is recorded as President of the Edinburgh section in 66 sederunts.[107]

Gentry attendance on the Edinburgh section was based on Ramsay of Balmaine (65, 77%), Sir Archibald Campbell (54, 64%), and Sir John Hope of Craighall (49 diets 58%). The remaining 18 gentry on the Edinburgh section all have attendance rates less than 50%. Six further gentry included on the army section of the Committee of Estates attended various diets of the Edinburgh section (all have low attendance figures). Five additional gentry who were not included on either section of the Committee of Estates attended various diets of tbe Edinburgh section.

Only one burgess, James Stewart (Edinburgh), had a significant record of attendance. Stewart was present at 51 diets (61%). The remaining 23 burgesses on the Edinburgh section attended less than 50% of diets. In addition, five burgesses included on the army section of the Committee of Estates attended various diets of the Edinburgh section. All have low attendance figures apart from Archibald Sydserf (Edinburgh) with 44 (50%) and Sir John Smith (Edinburgh) with 45 (54%). The quorum levels of the Edinburgh section (seven, with at least one per estate) were adhered to and surpassed at all diets.[108]

Twelve sederunts of the Privy Council are recorded between 11 September 1644 and 4 January 1645. Balmerino attended 11 diets, whilst Cassillis and Lauderdale attended nine. They were closely followed by Crawford-Lindsay (eight) and Burleigh (seven). Those nobles who were to the fore in the 1644 Parliament and on the Committee of Estates were therefore also dominant on the Privy Council. The attention of Argyll and Loudoun was concentrated on the work of the Committee of Estates and the Scottish diplomatic mission in England. Lauderdale's growing political stature was reflected in his role as President of the Privy Council. Conservatives and pragmatic Royalists did not dominate that body, however, and the grouping of radical nobles may have checked any further swings towards conservatism. Gentry attendance was based on that of Hepburne of Wauchton and Carmichael of that ilk, Treasurer Depute.[109]

Conclusion

Scottish political, diplomatic, and military intervention in the English Civil War, which resulted in insurrection and rebellion within Scotland formed the focus of attention of the 1644 Convention of Estates and the 1644 Parliament. The 1644 Parliament witnessed a growing rapprochement between conservative/pragmatic Royalist nobles and radical nobles. In particular, Lanark, representing the House of Hamilton and also the most influential parliamentary figure among the conservatives and pragmatic Royalists, secured membership on crucial session and interval committees. Nevertheless, radical nobles dominated the most important session and interval committees and were backed by the gentry and burgesses. The flexing of political muscle by the gentry and burgesses as a 'Scottish Commons' was indicated not only by the presence of Johnston of Wariston as speaker for the gentry and Dundas of Maner as spokesman of the Committee for Delinquents, but also by the pressure by the parliamentary gentry for punishment of those who had been in rebellion. The trend towards rehabilitation of conservative and pragmatic Royalist nobles who were prepared to co-operate with the radicals was to be severely tested by the outbreak of full-scale civil war within Scotland during 1645.

NOTES

1. *APS*, vi, i, 60–95.
2. Ibid.
3. *APS*, vi, i, 51–57; SRO, PA 11/1, ff 9–12; PA 11/2, ff 64–72.
4. *APS*, vi, i, 60–80; SRO PA 11/1, folio 135; D. Stevenson, *Revolution and Counter-Revolution in Scotland, 1644–1651*, (London, 1977), 1; Donaldson, *Source Book of Scottish History*, III, 131.
5. *APS*, vi, i, 61, 62–63, 74, 81.
6. Ibid, 74, 93.
7. NLS, Wodrow Folio LXVII, number 29; APS, vi, i, 70–71; Stevenson, *Revolution and Counter-Revolution in Scotland*, 3; Beattie, 'The Political Disqualification of Noblemen's Heirs in Seventeenth Century Scotland', 175–176.
8. *CSPV*, 1643–1647, 73; Stevenson, *Revolution and Counter-Revolution in Scotland*, 4; Brown, *Kingdom or Province?*, 127; Mulligan, 'The Scottish Alliance and the Committee of Both Kingdoms, 1644–46', 173; Mulligan, 'Peace Negotiations, Politics and the Committee of Both Kingdoms', 3–4.

9. SRO, Leven and Melville Papers, GD 26/7/166; W. Notestein, 'The Establishment of the Committee of Both Kingdoms', *AHR*, 17, 1912, 477–478; Mulligan, 'The Scottish Alliance and the Committee of Both Kingdoms, 1644–46', 14, 173; L. Glow, 'The Committee of Safety', *EHR*, 80, 1965, 289–313; Ferguson, *Scotland's Relations with England*, 127.
10. Mulligan, 'Peace Negotiations, Politics and the Committee of Both Kingdoms'4; Mulligan, 'The Scottish Alliance and the Committee of Both Kingdoms', 174.
11. *APS*, vi, i, 61, 89, 92.
12. Ibid, 73–83; Stevenson, *Revolution and Counter-Revolution in Scotland*, 6–8.
13. *APS*, vi, i, 83–92, 84–85; *Diary of Sir Thomas Hope of Craighall*, 204.
14. *APS*, vi, i, 89–92. Elcho, was constitutionally barred from the House as a noblemen's heir by virtue of legislation of 19 July 1641. However, his appointment here was essentially a military one.
15. Ibid, 60–95, 90–91. Nine gentry and three burgesses had been included on the shire committees of war established on 26 August 1643 (Ibid, 51–57).
16. Ibid, 60–95, 91–92. Sixteen gentry and three burgesses had been included on the shire committees of war established on 26 August 1643.
17. Ibid, 90–92. Although the Marquis of Argyll led the northern expedition he was still technically subordinate to the Earl of Callander, the commander-in-chief of the armed forces within Scotland. The Earl of Callander was in charge of the forces to secure the south and Borders of Scotland; *APS*, vi, i, 89–92; Stevenson, *Revolution and Counter-Revolution in Scotland*, 7. Although the Committees for the North and South were Committees of Estates in their own right, in comparison to earlier Committees of Estates 1640–1643, in essence they appear to be sub-committees of a larger Committee of Estates.
18. *APS*, vi, i, 93.
19. Ibid, 60–95.
20. Ibid, 60–95; Stevenson, *Revolution and Counter-Revolution in Scotland*, 4.
21. *APS*, vi, i, 60–95.
22. Ibid.
23. Ibid, 60–95. These figures take account of the additions to the Committee of Estates throughout the 1644 Convention.
24. Ibid.
25. Ibid, 94–95; SRO PA. 11/1, folio 238. *Diary of Sir Thomas Hope of Craighall*, 206. Rait, *Parliaments of Scotland*, 71, 316; Spalding, *Memorialls of the Troubles*, II, 378.
26. *APS*, vi, i, 95–96.
27. *APS*, v, 251–332; *APS*, vi, i, 3–4, 95–96.
28. *APS*, vi, i, 3–96.
29. Ibid, 95–283.
30. Ibid, 95–97. Menteith of Salmonet, *History of the Troubles of Great Britain*, 167; Spalding, *Memorialls of the Troubles*, II, 378. Constitutional considerations continued on 5 June with the approval of the 1641 legislation relating to the ordering of the House and decisions on disputed elections relating to the commissioners of the shires in Lanark in favour of radical interests.
31. *APS*, vi, i, 99.
32. Ibid, 98–99.
33. Ibid, 3–96, 98–99.
34. Ibid, 148–157. Menteith of Salmonet, *History of the Troubles of Great Britain*, 167.
35. *APS*, v, 262, 318, 333, 382; Stevenson, *Government Under the Covenanters*, 187.

36. *APS*, vi, i, 98, 114; Balfour, *Historical Works*, III, 173, 189.
37. *APS*, vi, i, 3–4, 60–95, 98; Balfour, *Historical Works*, III, 184.
38. *APS*, vi, i, 98.
39. Ibid, 3–4, 60–95, 98, 114.
40. Ibid, 95–96, 98, 102, 114; Balfour, *Historical Works*, III, 173, 181, 183, 189.
41. Ibid, 215; Balfour, *Historical Works*, III, 238. Rait, *Parliaments of Scotland*, 379.
42. Balfour, *Historical Works*, III, 238.
43. Stevenson, *Government Under the Covenanters*, xxxix.
44. *APS*, vi, i, 215.
45. Ibid; Balfour, *Historical Works*, III, 205–206.
46. *APS*, vi, i, 95–96, 211–246.
47. Ibid, 113–283.
48. Balfour, *Historical Works*, III, 238.
49. *APS*, vi, i, 93, 98.
50. Ibid, 98. Balfour, *Historical Works*, III, 172–173.
51. Balfour, *Historical Works*, III, 177.
52. Ibid, 178.
53. *APS*, vi, i, 104, 131, 138.
54. Ibid, 103–104.
55. Ibid.
56. *APS*, vi, i, 3–4, 60–95, 98, 103–104.
57. Balfour, *Historical Works*, III, 196.
58. Ibid, 200.
59. *APS*, vi, i, 132–133.
60. Ibid, 98, 103–104, 136. Balfour, *Historical Works*, III, 203, lists a different membership for the noble and burghal estate compared to *APS*. His list includes Argyll and Cassillis. I have accepted the official parliamentary version.
61. *APS*, vi, i, 161–166. Balfour, *Historical Works*, III, 219–220. Prior to the decree of forfeiture, an attempt had been made on 16 July to delay the pronouncing of sentence against Haddo; this petition had been presented to Parliament but had been rejected after debate and a vote.
62. *APS*, vi, i, 98, 103–104, 174.
63. This information is based on the comments of Sir James Balfour, (*Historical Works*, III, 230). However, Balmerino was not a member of the Committee for regulating the processes of those cited to the Parliament as per 5 June 1644,(*APS*, vi, i, 98). Balmerino was a member of the Committee for trying the relevancy of the summons of those cited to the Parliament and it may have been in that capacity that he was reporting to the House (*APS*, vi, i, 174).
64. *APS*, vi, i, 215–220. Balfour, *Historical Works*, III, 230–231, 235–236. Stevenson, *Revolution and Counter-Revolution in Scotland*, 10. Spalding, *Memorialls of the Troubles*, II, 387–391.
65. Stevenson, *Revolution and Counter-Revolution in Scotland*, 10.
66. *APS*, vi, i, 3–4, 95–96, 103–104, 245–246.
67. Ibid, 103–104, 199, 245–246.
68. Ibid, 93, 95–96, 98, 100.
69. Ibid, 98.
70. Ibid, 99; Balfour, *Historical Works*, III, 174.
71. Ibid.
72. Ibid.

73. Balfour, *Historical Works*, III, 172. This committee is not listed in *APS*, vi, i.
74. *APS*, vi, i, 93, 95–96, 98, 101; Balfour, *Historical Works*, III, 181.
75. Ibid, 84, 102. Balfour, *Historical Works*, III, 181, contains several variations in terms of membership from *APS*, vi, i, 102. In addition, whereas only six burghs are listed in *APS*, vi, i, 102, seven burghs are listed in Balfour, *Historical Works*, III, 181. This achieves a balance of seven per estate.
76. *APS*, vi, i, 105, 111; Balfour, *Historical Works*, III, 182, 184.
77. *APS*, vi, i, 112.
78. Ibid, 61, 74, 142. Balfour, *Historical Works*, III, 211, 217. Variations in membership exist between these two sources. The official parliamentary version has been accepted.
79. *APS*, vi, i, 98–174.
80. Ibid, 181–182, 182–183; Stevenson, *Revolution and Counter-Revolution in Scotland*, 10; Balfour, *Historical Works*, III, 229. If the Duke of Hamilton was to be tried as an English peer then he was to be judged by the English Parliament.
81. Stevenson, *Revolution and Counter-Revolution in Scotland*, 10.
82. *APS*, vi, i, 98, 283; Balfour, *Historical Works*, III, 244.
83. *APS*, vi, i, 95–283.
84. Ibid.
85. Ibid; Balfour, *Historical Works*, III, 244. The number of committees each individual was included on is given in brackets. No noble common membership exists with the two military interval committees.
86. *APS*, vi, i, 95–283.
87. Ibid. No burgesses were included on the Excise Commission (an interval committee). Therefore Smith and Semple secured access to a maximum number of financial interval committees for the burghal estate.
88. Ibid. No common membership exists for the burgesses on the two military interval committees.
89. Ibid, 95–96, 198–199, 199, 208.
90. Ibid 102; Balfour, *Historical Works*, III, 180.
91. Ibid, 102, 124.
92. Ibid, 126–129.
93. Ibid, 70–71, 158–159; Balfour, *Historical Works*, III, 177, 204, 206;.Beattie, 'The Political Disqualification of Noblemen's heirs in Seventeenth Century Scotland', 175–176.
94. *APS*, vi, i, 174. Balfour states that the Scottish commissioners at London were to be supernumeraries on the Committee of Estates (*Historical Works*, III, 247). This is not specified in the parliamentary records. Stevenson, *Revolution and Counter-Revolution in Scotland*, 9.
95. *APS*, vi, i, 174–177.
96. Ibid, 90–91, 174–177.
97. Ibid, 95–96, 142, 237–245.
98. Ibid, 57–58, 212–213. Two nobles, Barganie and Elibank, are listed for the nobility in the Edinburgh section but are not named in the preceding total commission. Therefore, the amended figure for the nobility is 29 and the amended total figue is 97. The three supernumeraries are not named in either the Edinburgh or the army section. The comparative figures for the 1643 and 1644 Committees include supernumeraries.
99. Ibid, 57–58, 212–213.

100. Ibid.
101. *APS*, v, 282; Ibid, vi, i, 57–58, 212–213.
102. *APS*, vi, i, 245; Balfour, *Historical Works*, III, 242.
103. *APS*, vi, i, 222; SRO PA. 11/1, folio 3. None of the members of the Committee for Irish Affairs were members of the Committee for Both Kingdoms.
104. *APS*, vi, i,95–96, 235–236; Balfour, *Historical Works*, III, 242.
105. *APS*, v, 428; *APS*, vi, i, 235–236.
106. SRO PA.11/3, Register of the Committee of Estates, 29 July 1644–6 January 1645, ff 6–172.
107. Ibid; *APS*, vi, i, 212–213; SRO PA.11/3, ff 6–172.
108. *APS*, vi, i, 158–159, 212–213. SRO PA 11/3, ff 6–172. A separate analysis of the attendance trends of the army section cannot be carried out; the sederunts of the 1644 section are included as a continuation of the army section of the 1643 Committee of Estates until 23 November 1644.
109. *RPCS*, 2nd series, viii, 27–43.

5

Parliamentary Management by the Radical Oligarchy: the Civil War Campaign against Montrose, January to November 1645

The Second Session of the First Triennial Parliament, 7 January–8 March 1645

By the time the parliamentary session convened the run of military successes by James Graham, 5th Earl and 1st Marquis of Montrose against the Covenanting armies continued unabated, commencing with the Battle of Tippermuir on 1 September 1644. The services of the Gaelic warlord of Clan Donald, Alasdair MacColla, were employed to supreme effect in alliance with Montrose, using the infamous 'Highland Charge'. Indeed, the military conflicts of the Scottish civil war campaign represented an attack on the lands and supremacy of the Clan Campbell and the House of Argyll.[1] Faced with the reality of full-scale civil war, the radical leadership was faced with no other policy option but to continue the working relationship with the conservatives and pragmatic Royalists, primarily to avoid an alignment with Montrose.

1. The Composition of the Second Session of the First Triennial Parliament

Forty-three nobles, 44 gentry representing 45 shires, and 47 burgesses representing 46 burghs formed the membership of Parliament, 7 January 1645. The total parliamentary membership amounted to 134. Compared to the 1644 Parliament, the session exhibited a rise of two nobles and four burgesses. Gentry membership, in numerical terms, remained identical (see appendices 3a and 3b). A core grouping of 31 of the 43 nobles (72%), 22 of the 44 gentry (50%), and 21 of the 47 burgesses (45%) had also been present in the 1644 Parliament (as per parliamentary rolls). Seventy-four of the total membership of 134 (55%), 7 January 1645, had been present in the previous session.[2]

2. The Proceedings of the Second Session of the First Triennial Parliament

Following the calling of the parliamentary rolls those nobles, gentry, and burgesses who had not sat in the First Session of the First Triennial Parliament (4 June–29 July 1644), were required to subscribe the parliamentary oath. Thereafter the rules established by the 1641 Parliament concerning the election of the President of Parliament were followed. Lauderdale was re-elected as the new President of Parliament (according to the 1641 legislation each session must have a new President, in constitutional terms). The House also ordained that no other President could be elected during the duration of the First Triennial Parliament. Hence Lauderdale would be President in all future sessions. No commissioner had been sent by the King but Parliament 'did not cair muche' for this.[3] By 11 January, however, Lauderdale had become seriously ill and had been absent from the House on a regular basis. This forced Parliament to initiate further procedural innovation. A new office of Vice-President was created, with Crawford-Lindsay its new incumbent.

Following the death of Lauderdale on 17 January, Crawford-Lindsay was appointed as President and was to continue in that office until the close of the session. Legislation enacted on 20 January stated that the promotion of Crawford-Lindsay from Vice-President to President had been in accordance with the terms of the 1641 act concerning the election of parliamentary Presidents. No attempt was sought for royal approval.[4]

Parliamentary proceedings were dominated by military affairs and the punishment of malignants. Of a total of 94 enactments, 65 concerned public business and 29 dealt with private affairs. Twenty-eight ratifications were also passed.[5]

The two crucial session committees which were formed were the Committee for Managing the War and the Committee for Bills, Overtures, and Ratifications. On 10 January the Committee for Managing the War was established to oversee and supervise the war within Scotland and also in England and Ireland. Concentrating such powers as recruitment, provision, and governing of Scottish forces within the committee would thus allow Parliament to proceed with the other important issues which required attention. In essence, the Committee for Managing the War was a revamped Committee of Estates in the form of a parliamentary session committee. Indeed, only one noble, one laird, and one burgess had not been included on the 1644 Committee of Estates.

The Committee for Managing the War was only to sit for the duration of the parliamentary session and was ultimately answerable to the House. Six per estate formed its membership. Noble representation was primarily conservative and pragmatic Royalist and included Lanark, Crawford-Lindsay, and Tullibardine. Cassillis was the only noted radical included in the parliamentary noble representation. Radical interests among gentry membership were managed by Johnston of Wariston (Edinburgh). Sir John Smith (Edinburgh) and Patrick Leslie (Aberdeen) were the noted radical burgesses with parliamentary track records. Five further nobles and one laird were included in military and administrative capacities; Lauderdale as President of Parliament, Leven as Lord General, Callander, as Lord Lieutenant General, Argyll as the head of the armed forces in the North, Lothian as Lieutenant General of the Scottish forces in Ireland, and Hepburne of Humbie as General Commissioner. The noble element of this grouping was therefore composed primarily of the leading radicals (bar Callander and Lauderdale). Further additions of two per estate were made on 21 January. Whilst conservative and pragmatic Royalist influence was boosted by the addition of Glencairn, it was also offset not only by the addition of Balmerino but also that of the noted radical burgess Robert Barclay (Irvine). All additions had been included on the 1644 Committee of Estates bar the two additional gentry. Following the death of Lauderdale no other noble replaced him as one of the supernumeraries, probably because Crawford-Lindsay, the new President of Parliament, was included on the commission anyway. Although Lanark and Glencairn were included, the role of the noble supernumeraries was crucial, particularly Argyll, Leven, and Lothian. In addition, Balmerino and Cassillis added to the strength of radical nobles led by Argyll. Despite the inclusion of conservatives and pragmatic Royalists, the ultimate political balance of the Committee for Managing the War was weighted towards the radical faction.[6]

The Committee for Bills, Overtures, and Ratifications was established on 11 January. In comparison to the 1644 Parliament, it merged the remits of overtures with bills and ratifications. No common membership exists with the Committee for Bills and Ratifications of the 1644 Parliament. Sir William Carmichael (Lanark) and Falconer of Halkerton (Kincardine), however, had been members of the Committee for Overtures in the 1644 Parliament.

Two further sets of additions were made on 24 January and 6 February. The first additions consisted of two radical nobles (Kinghorn and Torphichen) and two radical burgesses, Alexander Douglas (Banff) and Robert Cunningham (Kinghorn). The conservative/pragmatic Royalist Southesk was included in the latter additions, as were three gentry and two burgesses. In terms of overall membership, conservatives and pragmatic Royalists dominated the noble membership. This may well indicate an attempt to rehabilitate those groupings within Parliament, thereby avoiding a political alignment with Montose. Such a manoeuvre was crucial following Montrose's stunning rout of Covenanting forces at Inverlochy on 2 February.

The Committee for Bills, Overtures, and Ratifications was accorded four remits; firstly, to revise and consider all bills, supplications and overtures for the parliamentary session; secondly, it was empowered to cite parties to Parliament; thirdly, it could reject legislation which it saw fit; fourthly, it was to report to Parliament, except in those cases where the consent of both parties had been obtained.[7]

The proceedings of the Second Session of the First Triennial Parliament were focused primarily on three areas; financial affairs, the punishment of malignants, and military matters.

A session committee was established on 11 January to consider the problems of borrowing money and malignants' rents. Details of all money borrowed from private individuals since 1643 were to be examined as were the accounts of the 1643 Loan and Tax. The membership of the committee itself consisted of five per estate, plus three supernumeraries. Noble representation was mainly conservative/pragmatic Royalist, including Glencairn and Barganie, but also included the radical Balmerino. Only one member of the committee, Sir John Smith (Edinburgh), had been a member of the Committee for Managing the War of 10 January and the Committee for Bills, Overtures, and Ratifications. The shires and burghs provided the three supernumeraries; Balfour of Denmilne (Fife) for the gentry, with Sir William

Dick of Braid (Edinburgh) and James Stewart (Edinburgh) for the burgesses. None of the supernumeraries were members of Parliament as per 7 January 1645. The constitutional position of the supernumeraries is interesting in the sense that they were not allowed voting rights on the committee and their role was merely of an advisory nature.[8]

Of the three most important session committees established, personnel was not concentrated within a small group of nobles, gentry, and burgesses. The spread in the staffing of these session committees can perhaps be attributed to the need for solidarity during a time of civil war.

The Exchequer Commission was renewed on 1 February and was to last until the next parliamentary session. Membership remained identical to the previous commission of 29 July 1644. On 28 February Hepburne of Humbie was appointed by the Estates to collect maintenance due to finance the army in accordance with the act of maintenance.[9]

Joint consultation between the Committee for Managing the War and the Committee for Borrowing Malignants' Rents had resulted in agreement by 6 March that a 'constant' committee of 12 or 13 'able and sufficient men' should be appointed to deal with the inbringing and distribution of money and the regulation of the burdens of the kingdom.[10] Such a committee was to ensure that the levels of of regiments of horse and foot were to be maintained. This new committee would therefore constitute a new common burdens commission combined with a delegation of powers from the Committee for Managing the War. Four per estate, supplemented by three supernueraries, formed the committee membership. Only three of its members, all of whom were burgesses, had also been included on the session committee anent the borrowing of money and malignants' rents of 11 January. Sir John Smith (Edinburgh), John Kennedy (Ayr), and George Garden (Burntisland) formed this burghal grouping. Radical strength was monopolised in terms of noble representation which was based on Argyll, Cassillis, Balmerino, and Burleigh. Chancellor Loudoun, Crawford-Lindsay, President of Parliament, and Hepburne of Humbie, General Commissioner, were included as supernumeraries.[11]

Consideration of the punishment of malignants and rebels was invested in a Committee of Processes established on 16 January. Eight per estate, supplemented by three judicial officials, formed its membership. The supernumeraries were not included in a judicial capacity but as parliamentary commissioners per se. Two nobles (Cassillis and Weymes), six gentry, two burgesses, and the three judicial officials had been included on the Committee for Regulating Processes and the Committee for Trying Delinquents of the 1644 Parliament. Five nobles, including Lanark, were displaced from the 1644 committees, and all were conservatives or pragmatic Royalists. Despite the fact that Annandale and Dalhousie were included on the committee of 16 January, there was a shift in political balance among the nobles away from the conservatives/pragmatic Royalists, with the inclusion of Balmerino, Burleigh, Weymes, and Frendraucht. The inclusion of conservatives/pragmatic Royalists was therefore a token presence, probably initiated to avoid their alienation in a time of civil war. Radical strength was complemented by Johnston of Wariston (Edinburgh) for the gentry and a phalanx of radical burgesses; Patrick Leslie (Aberdeen), John Kennedy (Ayr), William Glendoning (Kirkcudbright), David Simpson (Dysart), and Gideon Jack (Lanark).[12]

Nine individuals were forfeited by Parliament on 11 February for insurrection and invasion in the south of the country. The most prominent of these nine were the Earls of Montrose and Nithsdale and the Viscount of Aboyne. This followed the Battle of Inverlochy on 2 February. Fourteen further individuals (including Montrose) were further forfeited for insurrection and invasion in the north. All were found guilty of high treason.

Sir James Balfour asserts that only two members of Parliament present in Parliament on 11 February abstained from the vote; Southesk (Montrose's father-in-law) and Dalhousie. Balfour states that 26 nobles were present in the House on 11 February and that only a few gentry and burgesses present on the opening day of the session were absent. Forty-four gentry and 47 burgesses are recorded in the parliamentary rolls on 7 January. Accepting Balfour's figures, somewhere in the region of 117 members of Parliament were present in the House on 11 February and around 115 voted in favour of forfeiture. Traquair was fined 40,000 merks (£26, 667 Scots) on 1 March and was ordered to be confined within his own lands.[13]

The forfeiture of malignants and rebels provided a useful avenue to secure additional finance for the Covenanting leadership. With this purpose in mind, a Committee for Selling Forfeited Lands was formed on 25 February. It was to establish the market value of the lands, rents, and other resources of forfeited individuals. The committee was composed of two per estate. Noble membership was exclusively radical and consisted of Cassillis and Balmerino. The committee was required to report back to the House before the end of the session. If it had not concluded its deliberations before that time then it was to report to the Committee of Estates.[14]

By the time the parliamentary session closed on 8 March not all processes against malignants had been concluded. Ninety-five cases of either summons or processes were then remitted to the Committee of Estates for consideration.[15]

The discussion of military matters and related issues formed the third important area of the work of the Second Session. The Committee anent the Losses of 15 January was formed to provide a systematic study of the extent of losses suffered at sea and on land, the manner of the losses, and the extent of repairs required. Six per estate, plus the President of Parliament as supernumerary, formed its membership, Conservative/pragmatic Royalist nobles and radical nobles both secured inclusion, although the balance was tilted in favour of the former. This provides a further indication of the the desire of the radicals to secure a working relationship with the conservatives/pragmatic Royalists during the civil war.[16]

On 24 January a committee was established to accompany Lieutenant General William Baillie of Lethem on the military expedition within the country. The committee was to sit at Perth or at any other place appointed by Lieutenant General Baillie. The commission was to endure until discharged by Parliament or the Committee of Estates. Four per estate, plus two supernumeraries, formed its membership. The composition of the committee, centred on the east and north-east, reflected Perthshire as the main theatre of civil war. Burleigh was the one noted radical noble included on the committee and Tullibardine the one noted conservative/pragmatic Royalist. Of the total membership, only two burgesss, William More (Aberdeen) and George Jamieson (Coupar), had been included on the Committee for the North of 19 July 1644.[17]

The renewal and/or new nomination of the Committees of War in the shires was delegated from Parliament to the consideration of the Committte of Estates established on 8 March 1645.[18]

By the time the parliamentary session ended on March three types of bills and supplications had not been fully dealt with by Parliament; firstly, those bills which had been considered by the Committee for Bills and Supplications but had not yet been reported in Parliament; secondly, those bills and supplications which had received citations but had not yet been called, thirdly, those bills and supplications which had not yet been called or heard at the committee stage or in in Parliament. All three categories were remitted to the consideration of the Committee of Estates.[19]

3. The Committee Structure of the Second Session of the First Triennial Parliament

Eleven parliamentary session and interval committees have been analysed. Three of these committees were both session and interval committees; the Committee for assisting Lieutenant General Baillie, the Committee for the Exchequer, and the Committee for selling Forfaulted Lands. The remaining eight committees consisted of six session and two interval committees.[20]

Forty-six nobles, 61 gentry, and 47 burgesses formed the field of parliamentary human resources employed on these committees. Whereas noble and burgess levels were virtually identical, it was the gentry, once again, who provided the backbone of committee personnel. Thirty of the 61 gentry (49%) and 23 of the 47 burgesses (49%) were not members of Parliament as per 7 January 1645. Extra-parliamentary gentry and burgesses continued to be employed in large numbers.

Legislation enacted on 10 January had stipulated that the President of Parliament was to sit and vote on all parliamentary committees and to preside when present. Following Lauderdale's death, Crawford-Lindsay was appointed as President on 18 January. Therefore Crawford-Lindsay (as the new President) was included on all committees established prior to 18 January. In terms of political affiliation, radical noble representation was based primarily on Balmerino (six committees), Cassillis (five), Loudoun and Burleigh (four each), and Argyll (three). Prior to his death Lauderdale was included on five committees, although it is doubtful that he took part in any committee proceedings. In addition to Crawford-Lindsay, conservative/pragmatic Royalist representation was focused on Lanark and Tullibardine (four committees each), supplemented by Glencairn and Southesk (three committees each).

Political polarisation was undoubtedly taking place in terms of noble committee membership. Balmerino, Cassillis, and Burleigh secured collective membership of almost identical committees and were joined by Argyll and Loudoun on the two interval committees. At the other end of the political spectrum, Lanark and Tullibardine were included on identical committees and were joined by Southesk and Glencairn on the two interval committees. They could also rely on the political sympathies of Crawford-Lindsay. Crucially, Lanark, Hamilton's spokesman in Parliament, secured access to three of the most important session and interval committees; the Committee for Managing the War, the Committee for the Exchequer, and the Committee of Estates. From a radical perspective, Lanark's inclusion was undoubtedly aimed at establishing a working relationship with the conservatives/pragmatic Royalists, as opposed to allowing them to establish an alliance with Montrose. Conservative and pragmatic Royalist influence, whilst recognised, was still subordinate to the managerial agenda of the core of the radical nobles who could draw on the support of the other two estates.[21]

The greater number of gentry employed allowed for a spread of gentry membership on the 11 committees. In terms of total membership, the committee structure was dominated by Dundas of Maner (Linlithgow), Hay of Balhousie (Perth), Hamilton of Orbiston (Renfrew), and Cochrane of Cowdoun (Ayr), all of whom served on four committees. All four were included on the Committee for Processes and the Committee of Estates, and all bar Hamilton of Orbiston gained membership of the interval committee for the inbringing and distributing ofmonies. Orbiston was included on the Exchequer Commission instead. Individual lairds could also exert influence on individual committees. Johnston of Wariston (Edinburgh), for example, was included on only three committees; the Committee for Managing the War, the Committee for Processes, and the Committee of Estates. Wariston's influence, however, was far greater than this figure suggests.[22]

Burghal common membership was focused on Sir John Smith (Edinburgh) (seven committees) and Patrick Leslie (Aberdeen) (five committees). A further grouping of four burgesses gained access to four committees each; John Kennedy (Ayr), George Garden (Burntisland), and Alexander Douglas (Banff). All burgesses included on three or more committees were members of the Committee of Estates.[23] The combined strength of the gentry and burgesses within the committee structure formed a powerful alliance with the radical nobles which guaranteed parliamentary supremacy in light of an increased profile of the conservative/pragmatic Royalist nobles.

4. The Appointment of Parliamentary Interval Committees

Two interval committees were appointed; the Committee anent the borrowing of Money and Malignants' Rents on 6 March and the Committee of Estates on 8 March.[24]

The Committee of Estates commissioned by Parliament on 8 March was composed essentially of four sections; the Scottish diplomatic mission in London, an Edinburgh section, a section to accompany the army in England, and a section to accompany the army in Scotland.

Four nobles, three gentry, and three burgesses formed the membership of the Scottish diplomatic grouping in London. One of these nobles (Argyll) was also included on the army section (England) while another (Balmerino) was included on the Edinburgh section. Balmerino was the leading noble on the Edinburgh section and Argyll was the dominant figure on the army section (England). The army section (Scotland), however, was controlled by conservative/pragmatic Royalist nobles and included Lanark and Crawford-Lindsay. The Edinburgh section was composed of those residue nobles, gentry, and burgesses who were not appointed for the army section (England), the army section (Scotland), nor the diplomatic section. In total, the Committee of Estates of 8 March consisted of 40 nobles, 38 gentry, and 39 burgesses (117 members in total). Near parity existed in membership per estate. Only one noble (Roxburgh) and two gentry (Gibson of Durie, Clerk Register, and Hepburne of Humbie) included in the total membership were not allocated to any of the four sections. In common with established trends, 14 of the 38 gentry (37%) and 18 of the 39 burgesses (46%) included on the Committee of Estates were not members of Parliament as per 7 January 1645.[25]

Thirty-one of the 40 nobles (78%), 25 of the 38 gentry (66%), and 26 of the 39 burgesses (67%) included on the Committee of Estates of 8 March 1645 had also been members of the previous 1644 Committee of Estates. Therefore there was a high retention of personnel between the two committees, The political momentum was maintained by the radicals.[26]

5. The Operation of Parliamentary Interval Committees

The Edinburgh section of the Committee of Estates first met on 10 March. Sixty sederunts are recorded between 13 March and 2 July 1645. It was based in Edinburgh from 13 March to 27 May, although diets were often held outwith Edinburgh due to the plague. In those circumstances it convened at Linlithgow (29 and 30 May and 19 June–2 July), Stirling (5 and 15 June), and Perth (9–12 June).[27]

Radical nobles dominated the proceedings of the Edinburgh section. Cassillis attended 39 of the 60 diets (65%), Burleigh attended 33 diets (55%), and Balmerino attended 32 diets (53%). Conservative/pragmatic Royalist influence was served primarily by Barganie who was present at 30 diets (50%). Seven nobles who were included on the army section (England) also attended various diets of the Edinburgh section. All have low attendance records bar Argyll who attended 24 diets (40%) of the Edinburgh section. Argyll was clearly the most influential noble on both sections and was clearly exercising his political authority over the Edinburgh section. Four conservative/pragmatic Royalist nobles who were members of the army section (Scotland) similarly attended diets of the Edinburgh section. This group consisted of Lanark, Tullibardine, Glencairn, and Balcarras, although they all have low attendance records. Only one noble (Annandale) who was not a member of the 1645 Committee of Estates attended any diets of the Edinburgh section. Annandale was present at 16 diets in total (27%).

In the absence of Chancellor Loudoun, Balmerino was to preside in the Edinburgh section. Argyll was to preside in the army section (Scotland) when the Chancellor was absent. In the event, Loudoun was not present at any of the proceedings of the Edinburgh section between 13 March and 2 July. Balmerino was President at 26 of the 60 meetings (43%), whilst Argyll was President at only five of the 24 diets (21%) which he attended of the Edinburgh section.[28]

Gentry and burghal attendances on the Edinburgh section were relatively low. Only two gentry and two burgesses attended more than 50% of diets. All four were not members of Parliament as per 7 January 1645; Sir Archibald Campbell (48 diets, 80%), Hope of Craighall (40 diets, 67%), Archibald Sydserf (Edinburgh) (42 diets, 70%), and Robert Farquhar (Aberdeen) (34 diets, 57%). Sydserf and Farquhar were members of the army section (Scotland).

Eight additional gentry included on the army section (England) and eight gentry on the army section (Scotland) also attended proceedings of the Edinburgh section. Four gentry were prominent within these categories; Hepburne of Humbie (20 diets, 33%) and Wauchope of Niddrie (Edinburgh) (18 diets, 30%) as members of the army section (England), with Sinclair of Hirdmeston (Haddington) (11 diets, 18%) and Hay of Balhousie (Perth) (10 diets, 17%) as members of the army section (Scotland).[29]

Seven burgesses who were members of the army section (Scotland) likewise attended proceedings of the Edinburgh section. In addition to Archibald Sydserf and Robert Farquhar, this grouping consisted of Alexander Douglas (Banff), John Douglas (Elgin), Patrick Leslie (Aberdeen), Robert Arnot (Perth), and George Jamieson (Coupar). James Rae and James Sword, both of whom were members of the army section (England), also attended several diets of the Edinburgh section.

Sederunt analysis clearly indicates that there was considerable cross-liaison between the various sections of the Committee of Estates, with the Edinburgh section as a base. Movement was concentrated towards the Edinburgh section from both the army sections. Movement was especially marked by gentry and burgess members, who exhibited a high degree of flexibility. Taken in conjunction with Argyll's movement between sections, this may well indicate an aspect of effective radical management of the various sections of the Committee of Estates. The commission of 8 March had set the quorum of the Edinburgh section at seven with one per estate required to be present. These rules were adhered to at all 60 diets. The transfer of personnel from the other sections had enabled the parliamentary quorum legislation to be fulfilled.[30]

On 17 March the Edinburgh section established eight committees of war for the shires of Haddington, Fife, Wigtown, Stirling, Clackmannan, Forfar, and Edinburgh. This suggests that the existing committee structures in those shires were failing to operate properly. It may also indicate that those committees of war required purging. Furthermore, on 11 April the Edinburgh section established a Committee anent Malignants to consider the citations of malignants. Annandale, Lanark, and Barganie were included as the noble membership of that subcommittee. The fact that all noble members were conservatives/pragmatic Royalists may be explained by the fact that it would seem less likely to alienate the conservatives/pragmatic Royalists if they were actually involved in the process of considering citations. The parliamentary alienation of conservatives/pragmatic Royalists and a rapprochement with Montrose was to be avoided at all costs. In any case, the decisions of the subcommittee would have to be approved by the appropriate section of the Committee of Estates as a whole.[31]

The Third Session of the First Triennial Parliament, 8 July–11 July 1645

By the time the parliamentary session convened, Montrose remained undefeated on the battlefield and had recently scored further victories at Auldearn (9 May) and Alford (2 July). The political threat of an alignment between Montrose and the conservatives/pragmatic Royalists remained a real one.

1. The Composition of the Third Session of the First Triennial Parliament

The session convened at Stirling instead of the traditional venue of Edinburgh due to the widespread plague in the capital. Thirty-four nobles, 21 gentry representing 14 shires, and 20 burgesses representing 19 burghs (75 members in total) formed the parliamentary membership as per 8 July 1645. Twenty-six of the 34 nobles (77%), 19 of the 21 gentry (90%), and all 20 burgesses had sat in the previous parliamentary session as per 7 January 1645 (as per parliamentary rolls). The Third Session witnessed a reduction of nine nobles, 23 gentry, and 27 burgesses (yielding a total reduction of 59) compared to the Second Session (see appendices 3a and 3b). Attendance levels appear to have been effected by the plague, especially relating to shire and burgh representation, as well as commitments relating to the civil war.[32]

2. The Proceedings of the Third Session of the First Triennial Parliament

Parliamentary affairs were dominated by the conduct of the civil war. Of the 18 acts passed, 16 dealt with public affairs. Crawford-Lindsay was elected to continue as President of Parliament.

In line with the procedure established in the Second Session, a Committee for Managing the War was established on 8 July. It owed its origin to the Committee for Managing the War of 10 January 1645. A core of five nobles, three gentry, and three burgesses (11 members in total) served on both committees. Argyll, Cassillis, Crawford-Lindsay, Tullibardine, and Balcarras formed the grouping of five nobles. Hence there was a balance in this common membership between radical nobles and conservatives/pragmatic Royalists. Whereas Crawford-Lindsay had been included on the committee of 10 January as one of the six nobles representing the noble estate, he was included as a supernumerary on the committee of 8 July in the constitutional capacity as President of Parliament. Whereas Argyll had been included on the committee of 10 January as a military official, he was included on the committee of 8 July as one of the six nobles representing that estate.

The exclusion of military officials included in the commission of 10 January can be attributed to the fact that by July 1645 the military campaign in the civil war was actually underway. In line with the terms of the commission of 10 January, the Committee for Managing the War of 8 July was subject to the authority of Parliament to which it was answerable.[33]

Close correlations in membership are apparent between the Committee for Managing the War of 8 July and the Committee of Estates of 8 March. All seven nobles (including the supernumerary), all six gentry, and three of the six burgesses on the Committee for Managing the War had been included on the Committee of Estates. In addition, the three burghs whose representatives as per 8 July had not been included on the Committee of Estates had been represented by other burgesses on that committee. In terms of the total membership of the Committee for Managing the War (19) of 8 July, eight members had been included on the army section (Scotland), five on the Edinburgh section, two on the army section (England), one on the diplomatic section, and three were non-members. In effect, the Committee for Managing the War was a subcommittee of the Committee of Estates.[34]

The Committee anent the Northern Business was established on 10 July to draw up a list of individuals to whom pardon could be awarded by Seaforth after 'reall proofe or assurance givine be these persones for thair dewtifull cariage to ye cuntrie'.[35] All persons already forfeited were exempt from pardon. Membership of the committee consisted of two per estate. Noble membership was balanced between Argyll and Lanark. In common with those committees concerning the punishment or citation of individuals, Lanark was included as the conservative/pragmatic Royalist spokesman, albeit Argyll was the dominant figure. Argyll's inclusion, supplemented by the gentry and burgess members, ensured that pardons could only be issued with the agreement of the radicals, given the fact that both Seaforth and Lanark were conservatives/pragmatic Royalists.[36]

The Third Session terminated on 11 July when Parliament was continued to 24 July and was to convene at Perth. However, the Committee of Estates had the authority to bring forward the session if need be and alter the location.[37]

3. The Committee Structure of the Third Session of the First Triennial Parliament

Two session committees and two interval committees have been analysed. Both session committees had military remits, as did one of the interval committees. The other interval committee had a financial remit. Thirteen nobles, 11 gentry, and 13 burgesses formed the field of parliamentarians employed on these committees. Two gentry and four burgesses were not members of Parliament as per 8 July 1645.[38]

Argyll's dominant influence was reflected in his inclusion on all four committees, the only noble to do so. Cassillis, Burleigh, and Tullibardine were included on three committees each. One laird, Dundas of Maner (Linlithgow), and one burgess, Patrick Leslie (Aberdeen), each secured membership of three committees.[39]

4. The Appointment of Parliamentary Interval Committees

On 10 July the House continued the commission granted to the Committee of Estates on 8 July until 24 July. Parliament then created a new subcommittee of that Committee of Estates to remain with the army at Perth until the next parliamentary session to be held on 24 July. In theory, this created five sections of the Committee of Estates formed on 8 March as Parliament continued the whole commission (the Scottish diplomatic mission, the Edinburgh section, the army section (Scotland), the army section (England), and the new section to remain at Perth). Legally and constitutionally, the new section to remain at the army at Perth was distinct from the army section (Scotland).

Four nobles, three gentry, and three burgesses included in the new army section to remain at Perth had also been included in the army section (Scotland) of 8 March. The most noted of the four nobles was the conservative/pragmatic Royalist Tullibardine. In addition, two nobles who were not members of the army section (Scotland) but were members of other sections of the Committee of Estates, were included in the new army section to remain at Perth. Both these nobles were leading radicals; Argyll was President of the army section (England) and Burleigh was a member of the Edinburgh section. Argyll and Burleigh both appear to have been included on the new Perth section to oversee the management of radical interests.

Two gentry and two burgesses included on the new Perth section had not been included in the full commission to the Committee of Estates of 8 March. Both burgesses and one of the lairds were not members of Parliament as per 8 July. Of the total membership (17) of the committee to reside at Perth, nine had been included on the army section (Scotland), two on the Edinburgh section, one on the army section (England), and six were not members of the Committee of Estates. Given the remit of the committee, the geographical composition of the committee to remain with the army at Perth naturally reflected a dominance of eastern gentry and burgesses.[40]

On 10 July the Commission for the Exchequer and the interval committee for inbringing of monies and for regulating the public accounts and burdens were both continued to 24 July. No additions were made in terms of membership.[41]

The Fourth Session of the First Triennial Parliament, 24 July–7 August 1645

1. The Composition of the Fourth Session of the First Triennial Parliament

Thirty-eight nobles, 38 gentry representing 23 shires, and 34 burgesses representing 33 burghs (110 members in all) formed the parliamentary membership of the Fourth Session as per 24 July. The Fourth Session witnessed a rise of four nobles, 17 gentry, and 14 burgesses (yielding a total rise of 35). The attendance level of the nobility was therefore on a near par with the Third Session, whilst the rise in the gentry and burgesses was almost identical (see appendices 3a and 3b). Twenty new gentry and 22 new burgesses were in attendance and provides a further indication of grass-roots radicalism among the shires and burghs. This suggests not only that noble attendance was being reduced due to events on the battlefield, but also that that the other two estates were now prepared to attempt to take on an enhanced parliamentary role as evidenced in the numerical increase in gentry and burgesses from the previous session.[42]

2. The Proceedings of the Fourth Session of the First Triennial Parliament

The Fourth Session convened at Perth and its legislative programme consisted of 37 acts, 34 of which related to public business and four ratifications. Military affairs and the conduct of the civil war campaign continued to dominate the parliamentary agenda.[43]

The Committee for the Prosecution of the War and the Committee for Provision of the Army of 29 July collectively formed the two most important session committees. In essence, the remits of the Committees for Managing the War of 10 January and 8 July had been more closely delegated to two specialised session committees.

The Committee for the Prosecution of the War was composed of six per estate. Three nobles, three gentry, and three burgesses who had been included on the Committee for Managing the War of 8 July also gained membership of this committee. Noble common membership was primarily radical (Argyll and Cassillis), but also included Marischal. Of the three remaining noble members of the new committee, Eglinton was a noted radical whilst Lanark and Tullibardine were conservatives/pragmatic Royalists. Hence there was an overall balance between radicals and conservatives/pragmatic Royalists in terms of noble representation. All noble and gentry members of the Committee for Prosecuting the War had been included on the renewed Committee of Estates of 10 July. Of the six burgesses included on the Committee for Prosecuting the War, five had been included on the previous Committee of Estates. In common with established trends, the Committee for Prosecuting the War was essentially a subcommittee of the Committee of Estates.[44]

The Committee for the Provision of the Army of 29 July consisted of two nobles, four gentry, and two burgessses. Gentry representation was therefore double that of the other two estates. Moreover, two of the four gentry were not members of Parliament as per 24 July 1645. Noble representation was balanced between radicals (Burleigh) and conservatives/pragmatic Royalists (Loure). Common membership between the Committee for the Provision of the Army and the Committee for Managing the War of 8 July extended to only one burgess, George Jamieson (Coupar). Common membership with the renewed

Committee of Estates of 10 July extended only to Burleigh and Hay of Balhousie (Perth).

The geographical composition of the Committee for the Provision of the Army was determined by the location of the current parliamentary session (Perth) and the fact that the army was based in the vicinity. This is in common with earlier Edinburgh based committees when parliamentary sessions were held in the capital. The actual military jurisdiction of the committee appears to have been under some doubt until 5 August. A report from the Committee for Prosecuting the War was presented to the House on that date. Following debate on the report and then a vote, it was enacted that the

> directing of the warr shall be be the parliament or Comittie of parliament And the Actuell manageing and executing of the directiones To bee the Comander in cheefe As will be ansuerable to the parliament or yr Committy.[45]

The destruction of land and property caused by the civil war was an issue of considerable importance. A session committee was established on 4 August to assess the extent of loss and damage in the area around Perth. Three per estate formed its membership. Only one radical noble was included (Burleigh) compared to two conservatives/pragmatic Royalists (Tullibardine and Perth). Two of the three gentry representatives were not members of Parliament as per 24 July 1645. In keeping with the local remit of the committee, gentry and burghal membership consisted of personnel from the surrounding localities, including Robert Arnot (Perth) and George Jamieson (Coupar).[46]

The Committee for Examining Deficients was formed on 5 August to examine and scrutinise deficiencies in the quotas of the former levies. Consisting of two per estate, noble membership was balanced between conservatives/ pragmatic Royalists (Glencairn) and radicals (Burleigh). Once again, gentry and burghal representation was exclusively eastern and was related to the location of the army.[47]

In order to compensate for the financial losses suffered in the north of the country, five nobles from this area were warranted by Parliament on 7 August to uplift the rents of malignants within their specific domains.[48]

At the close of the Fourth Session of the First Triennial Parliament on 7 August the Estates adhered to the recent trend of remitting those bills and supplications handed into Parliament, but not fully dealt, with to the consideration of the Committee of Estates.[49]

3. The Committee Structure of the Fourth Session of the First Triennial Parliament

Four parliamentary session committees and four parliamentary interval committees have been analysed. Two military committees, one judicial committee, and one diplomatic committee constituted the four session committees. The four interval committees were composed of one financial committee and three regional administrative committees.[50]

Fifteen nobles, 32 gentry, and 13 burgesses constituted the field of parliamentary human resources employed within the committee structure of the Fourth Session. Burleigh was to the fore in noble membership and was included on five out of eight committees. Loudoun, Crawford-Lindsay, Perth, and Tullibardine were each members of three committees. The figures of Perth and Tullibardine are higher in relative terms compared to the rest of the nobility because they were included on localised committees. Both Perth and Tullibardine were included on identical committees.[51]

Balfour of Denmilne, Meldrum of Burghlie (Fife), Dundas of Maner (Linlithgow), Haldane of Gleneagles (Perth), and Hay of Balhousie (Perth) secured membership of three committees. Balfour of Denmilne was not a member of Parliament as per 24 July 1645. Dundas of Maner was not included on any of the regional Perthshire committees and therefore played an important role on the national committees. Nineteen gentry on the Committee for the lands in Perthshire possessed, burned or wasted by the enemy were not members of Parliament as per 24 July 1645. This amounts to 59% of the total gentry analysed. Burghal membership was focused on Sir John Smith (Edinburgh) and Robert Arnot (Perth) each of whom was included on three committees.[52]

Whilst there is near parity between the noble and burghal membership fields, the greater numbers employed for the gentry can be explained by the vast amount of regional gentry included on the regional Perthshire committees. Geographically the trend of eastern dominance continued (although not exclusively), a phenomenon not unsurprising given that the parliamentary session was being held at Perth.[53]

Two sets of four nobles were also members of the Committee anent the Excise and the Committee for the Exchequer renewed on 7 August. Loudoun, Lauderdale, Balmerino, and Burleigh were included on the former committee and Crawford-Lindsay, Loudoun, Roxburgh, and Lanark on the latter. Incorporating these two sets of membership into the analytical structure yields a total of 10 committees for the noble estate. Loudoun and Burleigh served on six out of 10 committees, Crawford-Lindsay served on five, Lanark served on four committees, while Lauderdale, Roxburgh, and Balmerino served on only two committees each. Thus there was a balance between radical and conservative/pragmatic Royalist nobles at the upper end of this scale, with a slight bias in favour of the radicals. One laird analysed was also a member of the Committee for the Excise renewed on 7 August; Balfour of Denmilne. One laird analysed was also a member of the Committee of the Exchequer renewed on 7 August; Hamilton of Orbiston (Renfrew), Justice-Clerk. Therefore the amended committee structure figures for these two gentry are four for Balfour of Denmilne and two for Hamilton of Orbiston. No burgesses were included on the Committee for the Exchequer. One burgess analysed was a member of the Committee anent the Excise renewed on 7 August, probably to represent the interests of the burghal estate on that commission. Sir John Smith (Edinburgh) was the relevant burgess. Therefore the amended figure for Sir John Smith is four out of 10 committees.[54]

4. The Appointment of Parliamentary Interval Committees

Two separate but related regional parliamentary interval committees were established by the Estates on the final day of the session, 7 August; a committee for the burned, lands in Perthshire and a committee for trying the lands in Perthshire possessed, burned or wasted by the enemy. Both were staffed by regional personnel. The former was composed of three nobles, one laird, and one burgess, whilst the latter was composed of two nobles and 22 gentry. Perth and Tullibardine served on both committees and only two of the 22 gentry were members of Parliament as per 24 July 1645.[55]

Within a wider political and British perspective the Fourth Session was also concerned with the progress of the Scottish diplomatic commissioners in England. Chancellor Loudoun was present in Parliament on the opening day of the session (24 July). On 3 August a session committee was initiated to consider diplomatic issues and correspondence produced by Loudoun relating to proceedings with the English Parliament and the Scottish army. Two per estate, plus two supernumeraries, constituted the membership of this committee. Noble representation was exclusively conservative (Lauderdale and Lanark were the two nobles). Crawford-Lindsay, President of Parliament, and Chancellor Loudoun were included as supernumeraries. Consideration of the supernumeraries does not alter the political balance of the noble members in favour of conservatism. Radical strength, however, was present in the form of the two burgess members, Sir John Smith (Edinburgh) and Patrick Leslie (Aberdeen).

Two nobles, one laird, and one burgess included on the session committee were also members of the Scottish diplomatic contingent commissioned by the Estates on 8 March 1645 to treat with the English commissioners and were part of the Committee of Estates commissioned on 8 March. Parliament ordained on 6 August that additional diplomatic commissioners should be dispatched. Three nobles, three gentry, three burgesses, and one supernumerary account for the membership of the new diplomatic commission. Only one of the new diplomatic commissioners, Sir Alexander Wedderburne (Dundee) for the burgesses, was not a member of the Committee of Estates as per 8 March 1645. The additional noble representation was in favour of the conservatives/pragmatic Royalists (Lanark, Crawford-Lindsay, and Marischal). Radical strength was once more apparent in the inclusion of the remaining two burgess members; William Glendoning (Kirkcudbright) and John Kennedy (Ayr).

Lanark's inclusion on both the crucial diplomatic committees of 3 and 6 August indicates the fact that the radicals continued to have a working relationship with the conservatives/pragmatic Royalists during an era of instability and civil war. Nevertheless, the diplomatic commission as a whole was still controlled by radicals, despite the inclusion of leading conservative/pragmatic Royalist nobles to assist them in their diplomatic commission.[56]

On the final day of the session, 7 August, Parliament continued the commission of the Committee of Estates which had expired on 24 July and ordered the committee to meet after the dissolution of Parliament. The commission for the Committee for inbringing of Monies and for regulating the Public Accounts and Burdens was renewed as was the commission to the Committee for the Exchequer and the commission to the Committee for the Excise.

Parliament modified the original commission to the Committee of Estates of 8 March. The section of the Committee of Estates to accompany the Scottish army in Scotland was officially abolished and it was deemed that there should be only one section of the committee within Scotland. The army section within Scotland was therefore absorbed into the Edinburgh section. Although Edinburgh had been abandoned due to the plague the main section of the Committee of Estates was still referred to as the Edinburgh section as per the terms of the commission of 8 March.

Four additions to the Committee of Estates of two gentry and two burgesses were similarly made on 7 August. Both gentry were not members of Parliament as per 24 July 1645. In essence the Edinburgh section was merged with the section of the Committee of Estates to accompany the army in Scotland into a new section of the Committee of Estates to accompany the army in Scotland. This policy option provided a more efficient means of concentrating resources against Montrose.[57]

5. The Operation of Parliamentary Interval Committees

Parliament had ordered the Committee of Estates to convene immediately after the dissolution of the parliamentary session. However, no sederunts of the main section of the Committee of Estates are recorded between 2 July and 21 October 1645.

Montrose's victory over Covenanting forces at Kilsyth on 15 August not only had the effect of dispersing the Covenanting army but also of dispersing the Committee of Estates. Individual meetings of the Committee of Estates have been identified as taking place at Duns on 26 August, at Floors on 29 August, and Mordington on 3 September. Covenanting fortunes were reversed when a Covenanting force which had returned from England crushed Montrose's army at the Battle of Philiphaugh on 13 September. Philiphaugh marked a turning point in the civil war campaign. Defeat forced Montrose to withdraw to the Highlands. Victory at Philiphaugh secured Covenanting control of Scotland, albeit the last vestiges of Royalist resistance in the Highlands were not mopped up until the summer of 1647. Further meetings of the Committee of Estates took place near Stirling on 20 September, at Perth on 21 and 26 September, and at Duns in early October. The Committee of Estates was at St Andrews by 14 October and proceedings were being recorded by 16 October although sederunts were not recorded until 21 October when the committee met at Glasgow. The significance of Montrose's defeat at Philiphaugh should not be restricted to the military arena. Montrose had been commissioned by Charles I to indite a Parliament to be held in Glasgow on 20 October 1645. Montrose was to be the King's Commissioner in this Parliament and was empowered to appoint a Vice-Chancellor in the absence of the Chancellor and also Officers of State if the present incumbents refused to attend. Montrose's military successes had thus been translated into organised Royalist plans for a constitutional revival in Scotland.[58]

Twenty-two sederunts of the Committee of Estates are recorded between 16 October and 21 November. As noted, the Committee of Estates convened at St Andrews on 16 and 17 October. From 21 October until 8 November the Committee of Estates then convened at Glasgow. From 15 November until 21 November the Committee then held its proceedings at St Andrews in anticipation of the Fifth Session of the First Triennial Parliament which commenced at St Andrews on 26 November.

Fourteen nobles, 21 gentry, and 24 burgesses did not attend any of the 22 diets. Attendance data illustrates a balance between conservative/pragmatic Royalist nobles and radical nobles. Crawford-Lindsay attended 21 diets (96%) and Glencairn 14 diets (64%), whilst Burleigh attended 15 diets (68%) and Eglinton 13 diets (59%). No laird attended more than 50% of the committee's meetings; Crawford of Kilbirnie (Ayr) has the highest attendance figure with that of 11 (50%). Only one burgess attended 50% or more diets; George Jamesion (Coupar) attended 12 diets (54%).

Several commissioners who were members of the Committee of Estates in a diplomatic capacity also attended various diets. This was based around a grouping of prominent radical nobles, gentry, and burgesses; Argyll (15 diets, 68%), Johnston of Wariston (Edinburgh) (10 diets, 46%), and Robert Barclay (Irvine) (five diets, 23%). The conservative Lauderdale, however, was also present at 10 meetings (46%).

Attendance levels had been greatly affected by the aftermath of the civil war campaign. According to parliamentary legislation of 7 August the quorum of the reconstituted Committee of Estates to accompany the army was deemed to be promiscuous. Therefore the reconstituted committee was no longer governed by the quorums established on 8 March.[59]

Following the defeat of Montrose at Philiphaugh the Committee of Estates concentrated on the punishment of those who had collaborated with Montrose. One contemporary source, James Burns, merchant and bailie of Glasgow, commented that those 'who were most forward for Montrose ran great hazard of life and fortune'.[60] Glasgow was fined £20,000 by the Committee of Estates for collaboration with Montrose after his victory at Kilsyth. Between 21 and 22 October William Rollock, Alexander Ogilvie younger of Inverquharity, and Sir Philip Nisbet were executed for assisting Montrose. No trial was required as the three had already been forfeited by Parliament.

A Committee anent Delinquents was established by the Committee of Estates on 23 October to investigate the behaviour of 12 nobles and gentry towards the rebels. The 12 under investigation included the Earl of Queensberry, Lord Loure, Sir David Murray of Stanehope, and Sir Alexander Murray of Blackbarony. Both Loure and the two gentry had limited previous parliamentary experience. The Committee anent Delinquents was to decide whether or not the 12 under investigation were to be processed or fined. Where fining was deemed to be appropriate the level of fining was to be established. Two of each estate formed the membership of the Committee anent Delinquents. Both nobles on the Committee anent Delinquents were conservatives/pragmatic Royalists (Lauderdale and Lanark).

Lanark's inclusion again indicates the desire not to alienate the conservatives/pragmatic Royalists. Radical representation was particularly focused on George Porterfield (Glasgow). On 27 October the quorum of this subcommittee was set at four.[61]

The Committee anent Delinquents reported to the Committee of Estates on 27 October. Seven conclusions were incorporated in the Act anent some Delinquents passed by the Committee of Estates on 27 October. Firstly, those delinquents whose crimes were worthy of their estates and fortunes being allocated for public use but who were not to be processed to death, were to be fined five years' rents according to established valuations. Secondly, those delinquents who were to be fined on this basis but whose rents had not been valued, were to have their valuations carried out by the Committee of Estates. Thirdly, if the fortunes of relevant delinquents consisted of money or goods then such delinquents were to fined a third of their stock of money and moveable goods. Fourthly, banishment, confinement, or imprisonment could be imposed by the Committee of Estates. Fifthly, if any concealment of part of a delinquent's rental or estate was found then that delinquent was to incur a fine of two years' rent over and above the fine. Sixthly, the payment of fines was to be made in instalments of three; one third to be paid immediately, a second third to be paid at Candlemas, and the remaining third at Lammas. On 31 October the Committee of Estates ordained that one third of fines due by delinquents had to be paid within 10 days of intimation of sentence, otherwise their estates would be forfeited and they would be liable to confinement, imprisonment, or banishment. The recommendations of the Committee anent Delinquents established a precedent not only for the 1646 Act of Classes but also for the 1649 Act of Classes, in terms of fining tiers.

Three localised subcommittees were formed; the Committee for Malignants in Perthshire on 28 October, the Committee for Examining Compliers with the Rebels in Lanark, Ayr, and Renfrew on 8 November, and the Committee for Trial of Malignants in Fife by 21 November. All three subcommittees consisted of local personnel and were controlled by radicals. These subcommittees operated independently from the shire committees of war and were answerable to the Committee of Estates.[62]

A Committee for the Processes as a subcommittee of the Committee of Estates was formed on 19 November and consisted of one noble, two gentry, and one burgess. The political orientation of the committee was radical and included Burleigh and Johnston of Wariston (Edinburgh). The powers of the committee entailed the prosecution of the trials of delinquents and examining parties and witnesses. However, a Committee for the Processes had been in existence as early as 27 October. No full details of membership are given. Meldrum of Burghlie (Fife) was included as a representative of the gentry and Robert Farquhar (Aberdeen) as a representative of the burgesses. The quorum was set at five. On 29 and 31 October the Committee for the Processes was reporting to the Committee of Estates concerning those cited to appear before the committee and the manner of fining. Therefore the committee established on 19 November may been a subcommittee of a larger Committee for the Processes.[63]

The destruction caused by the military campaign throughout the country also attracted the attention of the Committee of Estates and led to the establishment of four specific committees; the Committee for trying the losses of the inhabitants of Lanarkshire, the Committee for trying the losses of the inhabitants of Stirlingshire, the Committee for trying the losses of the shire of Nithsdale and the stewartry of Annandale (established on 8 November), and the Committee for trying the losses of the inhabitants of Kinross-shire and related parishes (21 November).[64]

The regional bias towards the west and the central belt in the establishment of the various subcommittees may have been due to caution on the part of the radicals in ensuring that grass-roots radicalism and their power base was maintained. This had particular relevance considering the fact that the two recent major battles had taken place within the west.

Wider diplomatic considerations required the attention of the Committee of Estates, notably the management of the war in Ireland. It had been agreed that a Committee of Both Kingdoms should constitute the appropriate means of such management. Commissioners had already been appointed by the English Parliament. Three Scottish commissioners were appointed on 7 November; Argyll, General Robert Monro, and Cochrane of Cowdoun (Ayr). Likewise on 7 November, Lauderdale was ordered to return to London in the capacity of one of the Scottish diplomatic commissioners in England. This was to enable Chancellor Loudoun to return to Scotland for the next parliamentary session, and Balmerino was unable to attend through illness. By 15 November Lauderdale had not yet left for London and was being pressed by the Committee of Estates to do so given the lack of Scottish diplomatic commissioners currently in London.[65]

Conclusion

Three parliamentary sessions of the First Triennial Parliament have been analysed along the lines of legislation covered, membership of parliamentary session and interval committees, and the work of the Committee of Estates within the context of a Scottish Civil War. Between 1 September 1644 (the Battle of Tippermuir) and 15 August 1645 (the Battle of Kilsyth), Montrose and the MacCollas defeated Covenanting military forces on six occassions. Events on the battlefield affected parliamentary proceedings. The radicals initiated a closer working relationship with the conservatives and pragmatic Royalists within Parliament primarily to avoid the nightmare of a rapprochement between these groupings and Montrose. Particular attention was made in giving Lanark an increased parliamentary role. Not only was Lanark the influential leader and spokesman of the conservative and pragmatic Royalist nobles, but perhaps more importantly he was the spokesman of the House of Hamilton in general and of his brother James in particular. From the radicals' perspective a political alignment between the Hamiltons and Montrose was to be avoided at all costs. In common with the parliamentary trends to date, radical nobles backed by gentry and burgesses continued to control the parliamentary agenda in terms of legislation and the composition of committees. With the defeat of Montrose at Philiphaugh the Committee of Estates commenced a more rigorous programme of punishment of collaborators with Montrose. This programme would be pursued with greater intensity by the Fifth Session of the First Triennial Parliament which convened on 26 November 1645.

NOTES

1. S. Reid, *The Campaigns of Montrose. A Military History of the Civil War in Scotland 1639 to 1646* (Edinburgh, 1990), 34–134; McKenzie, *The Highlands and Isles of Scotland*, 232–233; J.M. Hill, *Celtic Warfare 1595–1763* (2nd edn., 1995), 45–63. In particular, see the relevant chapters of Stevenson, *Alasdair Maccolla and the Highland Problem.*
2. *APS*, vi, i, 95–96, 284–285.
3. Spalding, *Memorialls of the Troubles*, III 436; *APS*, vi, i, 285–286; Balfour, *Historical Works*, III, 246–247.
4. *APS*, vi, i, 288, 296; Menteith of Salmonet, *History of the Troubles of Great Britain*, 193–194; Balfour, *Historical Works*, III, 250, 256; *Diary of Sir Thomas Hope of Craighall*, 211; NLS, MS. 2263, History of Events 1635–1662, folio 186. As with the opening of the 1644 Parliament a dispute emerged concerning the election of the commissioners of the shire of Lanark on 8 January. Two commissions had been issued; one to Sir William Carmichael and James Hamilton of Dalserf, and the other to Sir James Lockhart of Lee and Hamilton of Woodhall. The first commission in favour of Sir William Carmichael and Hamilton of Dalserf was approved on the grounds that when it had been issued in June 1644 it had included a clause instructing them to vote and consult in all things until the conclusion of Parliament. The latter commission issued to Lockhart of Lee and ( ) Hamilton of Woodhall did not contain this provision. Furthermore, Sir John Smith, Provost of Edinburgh, and spokesman for the burghs protested on the presence of a commissioner of the Stewartry of Kirkcudbright whilst the shire of Wigtown was represented by two commissioners of the shires. The Estates ordained that until the matter was fully explored by Parliament the commissioner for the stewartry, John Gordon of Cardines, was allowed to sit and vote in the House. Hence an extra member for the gentry in relation to the other two estates was entitled to sit.
5. *APS*, vi, i, 284–429.
6. Ibid, 212–214, 287, 297. Balfour, *Historical Works*, III, 249, states that the Committee was to be called the Committee for Dispatches; Stevenson, *Government Under the Covenanters*, xxxv; Stevenson, *Revolution and Counter-Revolution in Scotland*, 27.
7. *APS*, vi, i, 98, 114, 288–289, 299, 311; Balfour, *Historical Works*, III, 252.
8. *APS*, vi, i, 284–285, 287, 288, 288–289. There is a clash in terms of membership between *APS* and Balfour, *Historical Works*, III, 250. The official parliamentary version has been accepted.
9. *APS*, vi, i, 235–236, 303–305, 306, 355–357; Balfour, *Historical Works*, III, 265.
10. *APS*, vi, i, 371.
11. Ibid, 284–285, 371–372, 383–385.
12. Ibid, 98, 103–104, 290–291.

13. Ibid, 284–285, 371–372, 383–385; Balfour, *Historical Works*, III, 286; *Scots Peerage*, VI, 253; *The Memoirs of Henry Guthry*, 175. Carnwath was forfeited on 25 February and Huntly on 8 March.
14. *APS*, vi, i, 284–285, 344–345.
15. Ibid, 402; Balfour, *Historical Works*, III, 292.
16. *APS*, vi, i, 289–290.
17. Ibid, 284–285, 297–298.
18. Ibid, 380–383, 384.
19. Ibid, 401.
20. Ibid, 287–385.
21. Ibid.
22. Ibid.
23. Ibid.
24. Ibid, 380–383. The interval committee for malignants' rents has already been discussed earlier in the chapter.
25. Ibid, 284–285, 380–383. One burgess from the Committee for Money was to be included on the army section (Scotland). This burgess was not identified nor named. *The Memoirs of Henry Guthry*, 183, lists the political balance among the nobility on the various sections. Guthry also states that after the Battle of Inverlochy Crawford-Lindsay was appointed President of the Privy Council in recognition of the growing political power of the Hamiltonian faction (*Memoirs*, 182).
26. Ibid, 212–214, 284–285, 380–383.
27. SRO PA 11/4, Register of the Committee of Estates 10 March 1645–31 March 1646 ff 1–128
28. Ibid; *APS*, vi, i, 380–383. The other six nobles on the army section (England) who attended diets of the Edinburgh section were Coupar, Buccleuch, Yester, Dunfermline, Dalhousie, and Eglinton. All have low attendance records.
29. SRO PA 11/4, ff 1–128; *APS*, vi, i, 284–285, 380–383.
30. SRO PA 11/4, ff 1–128.
31. Ibid, ff 12–14, 45.
32. *APS*, vi, i, 284–285, 429–430; *The Memoirs of Henry Guthry*, 190; Stevenson, *Revolution and Counter-Revolution in Scotland*, 28.
33. *APS*, vi, i, 287, 429–433.
34. Ibid, 380–383, 430–431.
35. Ibid, 435.
36. Ibid, 429–430, 435.
37. Ibid, 440; Balfour, *Historical Works*, III, 297.
38. *APS*, vi, i, 429–430, 430–433.
39. Ibid, 430–433.
40. Ibid, 380–383, 429–433.
41. Ibid, 433; Balfour, *Historical Works*, III, 295.
42. Ibid, 429–430, 440–441.
43. Ibid, 440–474.
44. Ibid, 430–431, 442.
45. Ibid, 380–383, 430–431, 440–441, 442–443, 448.
46. Ibid, 440–441, 447.
47. Ibid, 450.
48. Ibid, 462–465. Marischal, Findlater, Erroll, Frendraught, and Fraser formed this grouping of five nobles.

49. Ibid, 466. The act anent the remitting of Bills to the Committee of Estates refers to Committee of Bills in the session of Parliament, 24 July to 7 August. However, no record of this committee or details of its membership exists.
50. Ibid, 442–470.
51. Ibid.
52. Ibid, 440–441, 442–470.
53. Ibid.
54. Ibid, 237–245, 303, 440–441.
55. Ibid, 440–441, 469–470, 470.
56. Ibid, 380–383, 440–441, 457.
57. Ibid, 440–441, 460–462; Stevenson, *Government Under the Covenanters*, 1. Sir Harry Gibb was added to the gentry representatives on the Committee of Estates, whilst Balfour of Denmilne replaced Sir Archibald Campbell. Sir Alexander Wedderburn (Dundee) replaced Alexander Halyburton (Dundee) and James Pedie (Montrose) replaced Robert Taylor (Montrose) for the burgesses on the Committee of Estates.
58. SRO PA 11/4, ff 127–130. Stevenson, *Government Under the Covenanters*, 1–2. Stevenson, *Revolution and Counter-Revolution in Scotland*, 43. *Records of the Kirk*, 441; *Aberdeen Council Letters*, III, 13. NLS, MS 2263, History of Events, 1635–1662, incorrectly states that the proposed Parliament was to be held at Glasgow on 20 Septmber. SRO, Montrose Papers, GD 220/3/131, lists the commission from Charles I to Montrose although it should be noted that this commission does not contain the time and place of convocation. Reid, *The Campaigns of Montrose*, 134–162; Lynch, *Scotland, A New History*, 275; C. Russell, *The Crisis of Parliaments, English History 1509–1660* (1990 edition, Oxford), 360; *The Memoirs of Henry Guthry*, 196–197. Guthry states that after Kilsyth Hamilton of Orbiston, Justice Clerk, and Archibald Primrose, clerk to the Committee of Estates, had aligned themselves to Montrose and were attempting to draw Lanark along with them.
59. Stevenson, *Government Under the Covenanters*, 5–56, 57–60; *APS*, vi, i, 460.
60. 'Memoirs of the Civil War and During the Usurpation, by James Burns, Merchant and Bailie of the City of Glasgow, from the (Year) 1644 till the (Year) 1661', in J. Maidment (ed.), *Historical Fragments, Relative to Scottish Affairs, from 1635 to 1664*, (Edinburgh, 1833).
61. Stevenson, *Government Under the Covenanters*, 7, 8–9; Stevenson, *Revolution and Counter-Revolution in Scotland*, 43; *APS*, vi, i, 313–23; W.S Shepherd, 'The Politics and Society of Glasgow, 1648–74', (University of Glasgow, PhD. thesis, 1978), 22.
62. Stevenson, *Government Under the Covenanters*, 15, 18, 24.
63. Ibid, 15–16, 19, 22, 52–53.
64. Ibid, 46, 47, 56; *APS*, vi, i, 380–383. Two members of the Lanarkshire committee were also included on the Stirlingshire committee; Dundas of that ilk (Linlithgow) and Dundas of Maner (Linlithgow).
65. Ibid, 34, 38–39, 48.

6

Parliamentary Management by the Radical Oligarchy: Purging and the Punishment of Collaborators, November 1645–November 1646

> The Lord hath given you a fitt opportunity for purging and reforming the Kingdome according to your Covenant[1]

The Fifth Session of the First Triennial Parliament, 26 November 1645–4 February 1646

The Second, Third, and Fourth Sessions of the First Triennial Parliament had witnessed the emergence of a working relationship between radical and conservative/pragmatic Royalist nobles, primarily to avoid the latter grouping becoming aligned to Montrose. Nevertheless, the military defeat of Montrose at Philiphaugh had swung the political balance of events more firmly towards the radicals. It was against this background of events that the Fifth Session convened.

1. The Composition of the Fifth Session of the First Triennial Parliament

The parliamentary session convened at St Andrews due to the continuance of the plague in the vicinity of the capital. Punishment of collaborators formed the main focus of parliamentary business. One hundred and two enactments were passed, 68 of which concerned public business, as well as 10 ratifications. Thirty-three nobles, 37 gentry representing 20 shires, and 32 burgesses representing 32 burghs (102 members in total) formed the parliamentary membership. Twenty-four nobles, 13 gentry, and 15 burgesses (52 members in total) had also been present in the previous session commencing on 24 July. Numerical analysis in terms of composition per estate indicates a drop of five nobles, one laird, and two burgesses compared to the Fourth Session (see appendices 3a and 3b).[2]

2. The Proceedings of the Fifth Session of the First Triennial Parliament

Parliamentary representation of burghs which had collaborated with Montrose had been restricted by the Committee of Estates. The burghs of Edinburgh, Linlithgow, and Glasgow were initially barred from sending commissioners to the Parliament at St Andrews. The burgh council of Glasgow had been purged by the Committee of Estates on 30 September 1645 on the orders of the Earl of Lanark. The office of Provost was filled by George Porterfield and 31 council places were purged. Moreover, George Porterfield represented the burgh of Glasgow in Parliament, 26 November 1645. Porterfield was also a noted radical aligned to Argyll. Therefore the installation of the Porterfield faction on Glasgow Burgh Council nullified the earlier parliamentary bar applied to the burgh of Glasgow.[3]

Following the calling of the parliamentary rolls and before the parliamentary oath could be taken, dissension immediately emerged over the composition of the Parliament. Johnston of Wariston (Edinburgh) stated that his answering of his name did not imply his acknowledgement of the constitution of Parliament until he was tried concerning compliance with the rebels. In a long speech to the House Wariston referred to the parliamentary presence of malignants and delinquents. Before Parliament was formally constituted Wariston implored that Parliament 'wold make ane serious searche and enquirey after suche as wer eares and eyes to the enimies of the comonwealthe'.[4] Therefore Wariston argued that Parliament should be dissolved until 27 November and that each estate should meet separately to consider 'quhat corrupted members amongest them, quho had complayed with the publicke enimey of the stait, ather by themselues, or by ther agents or frindes'.[5] Following Wariston's speech, debate emerged concerning the manner of procedure and form of trial of such individuals and how they were to be removed from the House. It was agreed that once the House had dissolved the Estates should consider the issue separately. When the Estates reassembled as a whole on 27 November, Parliament was again adjourned, until 28 November, and the Estates were to consider the issue further. Each parliamentary estate was to call before it any suspected malignants and delinquents and examine their comments. The insistence on the procedural and legislative integrity of each of the three estates separately, which was initiated by the gentry, can be interpreted as a means of resisting noble domination of the procedural and judicial agenda of Parliament *vis-a-vis* malignancy. This phenomenon is not only consistent with the procedure established by Parliament in 1640–41 for scrutinising legislation, but can also be traced to the administrative organisation of the Tables in 1638–39.[6]

On 28 November Parliament appointed a session committee of four of each estate to consider those malignants who were members of Parliament and to examine the commissions of those commissioners of the shires and the burghs. Noble membership was dominated by leading radicals in the ratio of 3:1 compared to the conservatives/pragmatic Royalists (Argyll, Cassillis, and Lothian compared to Crawford-Lindsay). Johnston of Wariston (Edinburgh) was also included as one of the four gentry members. Burghal membership included the radicals Robert Cunningham (Kinghorn), Robert Barclay (Irvine), and George Garden (Burntisland). Of the total membership, only two gentry had not been included on the Committee of Estates initiated on 8 March 1645. By 29 November the committee had reported its conclusions. Following the swearing of the parliamentary oath on 29 November, legislation was enacted which stipulated that all members coming to Parliament were to be tried for collaboration with Montrose before they could sit or vote in the House.

Furthermore, the commissioners of the burghs were to be called in the parliamentary rolls by their names and not according to burgh; this would facilitate the process of identifying collaborators.[7]

Wariston's actions of 26 November can be regarded as a deliberate political manoeuvre intended to force the House's hand on the issue of parliamentary membership *vis-a-vis* collaboration with Montrose. In short, it made inevitable the establishment of the committee of 28 November.

On 29 November Parliament laid down rules of membership concerning four session committees; the Committee for Dispatches, the Committee for Processes, the Committee for the Bills, and the Committee for hearing the Commissioners of the Burghs of Edinburgh, Linlithgow, St Andrews, and Jedburgh. Six per estate were to be represented on the Committee for Dispatches and the Committee for Processes. The General Officers of the army were included as supernumeraries on the Committee for Dispatches. The Committee for Bills was to consist of three per estate, as was the Committee for the Commissioners of the burghs of Edinburgh, Linlithgow, St Andrews, and Jedburgh. The President of Parliament, Crawford-Lindsay, was to be supernumerary in all committees. After hearing the report of that committee, on the same day the Estates ordained that John Lepar (St Andrews) was entitled to sit and vote in Parliament as commissioner for his burgh.[8]

The Committee for Dispatches was appointed on 1 December for managing the army within and outwith the country during the parliamentary session and was answerable to Parliament. The official parliamentary register indicates that no common membership would be allowed to exist between the Committee for Dispatches and the Committee for the Processes during the session. However, Chancellor Loudoun, was to remain as supernumerary on both committees. Therefore the combined voting strength of the gentry and burgesses in the House had restricted a possible monopoly of power by the nobility on both committees.[9]

Only one noted radical noble (Argyll) secured membership of the Committee for Dispatches, although Loudoun was also included as a supernumerary in his capacity as Chancellor. Tullibardine and Lanark were the noted conservative/pragmatic Royalist nobles included, along with Crawford-Lindsay in the capacity of President of Parliament. All the nobles on the Committee for Dispatches had been included on the Committee of Estates of 8 March. By way of comparison, only two gentry were members of the Committee of Estates as per 8 March and only two burgesses on the Committee for Dispatches were not members of the Committee of Estates of 8 March.[10]

Four Committees for the Dispatches had therefore been established from the First to the Fifth sessions of the First Triennial Parliament. Although classified under a variety of names, the remit of each of the committees was essentially identical. Common membership between these committees was focused on the nobility. Argyll served on all four committees and was backed by Loudoun. Nevertheless, the rehabilitation of conservative and pragmatic Royalist nobles is evidenced by the presence of Lanark and Crawford-Lindsay within this common grouping of nobles. None of the six gentry appointed on 1 December had been included on any of the four committees appointed since January 1645. As is evident from the trends recorded from previous analysed committee structure data, the gentry and burgesses had a strong grass-roots base to draw on, while conservative/pragmatic Royalist nobles had to be brought in to work beside the radicals.[11]

Six per estate formed the membership of the Committee for Processes of 1 December. Noble membership was dominated by radicals (in particular by Cassillis and Burleigh) and only one noted conservative/pragmatic Royalist (Glencairn) gained membership. The radical orientation of the committee was supplemented by the presence of Johnston of Wariston (Edinburgh). Colville of Blair and Robertson of Bedlay, Justice Deputes, were included and possessed the same powers as the rest of the Commissioners for the Processes. All six nobles included on the committee had been included on the Committee of Estates of 8 March. Including supernumeraries, four of the eight gentry and four of the five burgesses on the committee were members of the Committee of Estates of 8 March. Although the quorum was set at nine with two of each estate required to be present, the two Justice Deputes were not to be counted in the total number for the quorum. Hence the quorum was dependent on attendance by the representatives of each parliamentary estate. In common with the Committees of Processes established by other sessions of the First Triennial Parliament, the committee was to proceed in the trials of rebels cited to the Parliament.[12]

Three Committees for the Processes had now been established between the First and the Fifth Sessions of the First Triennial Parliament. Common membership between the Committees for Processes of 5 June 1644 and 1 December 1645 focused on Cassillis and Cochrane of Cowdoun (Ayr). A large degree of common membership exists between the Committees for the Processes of 16 January and 1 December respectively. The political orientation of that common membership was primarily radical. It consisted of Cassillis, Weymes, and Burleigh for the nobility, Johnston of Wariston (Edinburgh), Dundas of Maner (Linlithgow), and Cochrane of Cowdoun (Ayr) for the gentry, with John Kennedy (Ayr) and William Glendoning (Kirkcudbright) for the burgesses.[13]

The Committee for Bills and Ratifications of 1 December 1645 was composed of three per estate. Noble and burghal membership was linked to the Committee of Estates of 8 March 1645, whereas only one laird was included on both committees.[14] Of the three Committees for Bills and Ratifications established between the First and Fifth sessions, there was limited common membership. No nobles and no burgesses served on all three committees. Falconer of Halkerton (Kincardine) served on all three committees. No common membership exists for the burgesses between the Committee for Bills and Ratifications of 11 January and 1 December.[15]

Membership details of the Committee for Dispatches, the Committee for the Processes, and the Committee for Bills and Ratifications were issued on 1

December. Contemporary sources indicate that between 29 November and 1 December considerable lobbying took place regarding the membership of those committees. A first vote on the membership of the Committee for Dispatches and the Committee for Processes had taken place on 29 November. Only three of the nobles included on the Committee for Dispatches on 29 November remained on that of 1 December; Argyll, Lanark, and Tullibardine. Five of the gentry included on the Committee for Dispatches on 29 November remained on 1 December and only MacDowall of Garthland (Wigtown) had been replaced. No details of burgess representation on 29 November are given. The membership of the Committee for Processes on 29 November was identical to the membership of the Committee of the Processes on 1 December. On 1 December there was a 'grate debait in the housse, wich lasted aboue 3 houres'[16] in which Glencairn, Cassillis, and Lanark attempted to be included on both the Committee for Dispatches and the Committee for Processes. Therefore both radical and conservative/pragmatic Royalist nobles were attempting to bolster their particular political factions within the noble representation on these two committees. This manoeuvre was strongly opposed by the commissioners of the shires and the commissioners of the burghs. Following a vote in the House it was ordained that the three nobles, one laird, and one burgess who had been included on both committees at the first election on 29 November were to sit on the Committee for the Processes only. This grouping consisted of Marischal, Glencairn, and Cassillis for the nobility, MacDowall of Garthland (Wigtown) for the gentry, and John Kennedy (Ayr) for the burgesses. Undoubtedly, it was these proceedings that led to the ordinance of 1 December separating the two memberships of the Committees for Processes and Dispatches. The parliamentary gentry and burgesses had succeeded in curtailing the power of the nobility and is indicative of the former's radicalism in particular. These developments would also tend to indicate that the noble estate had been attempting to dominate the legislative agenda within Parliament.[17]

Additions to the membership of the Committee for Processes were later made by Parliament on 13 January 1646. This was at the request of the Committee of the Processes itself for the purposes of examining parties and witnesses. Balfour of Denmilne and Sir John Hope of Craighall, Lord of Session, were specifically asked by the gentry to be included on the Committee of Processes. This was granted by the Estates despite the fact that neither Balfour of Denmilne nor Hope of Craighall were members of Parliament as per 26 November 1645. James Sword (St Andrews) was also added along with Colville of Blair, Justice Depute. James Sword was not a member of Parliament as per 26 November 1645. Colville of Blair had been included as a member of the Committee for Proceses on 1 December. His further addition on 13 January 1646 may be due to his lack of attendance at committee diets between 1 December and 13 January. The additions of 13 January 1646 constituted in essence a subcommittee of the Committee for the Processes. The supplementary members of 13 January were only required to deal with the examination of witnesses and parties.[18]

Further powers were awarded to the Committee for the Processes on 31 January. Individuals fined by the Committee for the Processes during the session of Parliament or by appropriate commissioners appointed with jurisdiction for the period after the parliamentary session were to be subject to tighter parliamentary control regarding the payment of fines. If insufficient security was provided by those persons fined by the Committee for the Processes then those individuals were to be imprisoned. The Committee for the Processes was also awarded the power of sequestration of delinquents' rents and estates.[19]

Recommendations from the Committee for Dispatches were followed throughout the parliamentary session until 4 February 1646. Firstly, the army was reorganised; regiments were sent to England as reinforcements. Four thousand three hundred foot and six troops of horse were to be stationed in eight garrisons north of the Clyde and Forth. Eight thousand four hundred men in total formed what has been termed 'a mobile army' to seek out the rebels in the north of the country.[20] Secondly, new committees of war were established in the shires on 2 February. Thirdly, the new Committee of Estates established on 3 February was to raise 10,000 men to reinforce Scottish armed forces on a British basis. Fourthly, military appointments to the Scottish forces were made on 4 February. Middleton was placed at the head of the force to pursue the rebels within Scotland; the offer had orginally been made to Callander whose excessive demands resulted in the transfer of the position to Middleton. James Hepburne was appointed as General Major of the foot.[21]

Having established the three most important session committees by 1 December 1645, Parliament could now concentrate on punishing the malignants and rebels in greater detail. On that date a new session committee was established to consider the behaviour of the Earls of Mar and Perth and the commissioners of Edinburgh and Linlithgow towards the rebels. It was composed of three nobles, three gentry, and four burgesses. The examination of the commissioners of Edinburgh and Linlithgow had been included in the remit of a previous session committee formed on 29 November. Therefore the commissioners of Edinburgh and Linlithgow were still under suspicion of malignancy. The inclusion of the conservative/pragmatic Royalist noble Dalhousie was balanced by Kirkcudbright and Yester. One of the three gentry members, Maxwell of Newark, was not a member of Parliament as per 26 November. Of the four burghal members, only one did not represent a burgh which was not under suspicion. Sir John Smith (Edinburgh), Robert McKean (Edinburgh), and George Bell (Linlithgow) constituted the representatives of the three burghs under examination. Furthermore, all three were not members of Parliament as per 26 November 1645. All nobles included on the committee were members of the Committee of Estates of 8 March 1645. Only one laird on the committee, Belshes of Toftis (Berwick) had been included on the Committee of Estates of 8 March. This indicates that new gentry were being brought in and illustrates the commitment of grass roots radicalism. All burgesses included on the committee had been included on the Committee of Estates of 8 March. Chancellor Loudoun and Crawford-Lindsay, President of Parliament, were included as supernumeraries on the committee of 1 December. As Sir John Smith (Edinburgh), Robert McKean (Edinburgh), and George Bell (Linlithgow) were included in the parliamentary burghal representation with the same voting rights as the representatives of the nobility and the gentry, this committee may have been employed by the radical leadership to whitewash any aspersions or doubts of malignancy against the commissioners of the respective burghs (under the supervision of Loudoun and Crawford-Lindsay). Moreover, it may have been employed as a constitutional precedent as a means of ensuring that further session committees could be formed during the session to examine malignant tendencies among members of Parliament. The remit of the committee regarding those under suspicion was 'anent the clearing of their carriage before they sit and vote as members of Parliament.'[22] In the naming of the session committee no differentiation was made between commissioners of the shires and commissioners of the burgh. However, commissioners were present for the shires of Edinburgh and Linlithgow in Parliament on 26 November; Johnston of Wariston (Edinburgh), Foullis of Colington (Edinburgh), Dundas of Maner (Linlithgow), and John Hamilton of Boghall (Linlithgow). The fact that no burgess representatives for Edinburgh and Linlithgow were present in Parliament on 26 November reinforces the assertion that the committee was to consider the burgess representatives of Edinburgh and Linlithgow only, and not the gentry representatives for those shires.[23]

Delinquents and Malignants were classified within three specific tiers of punishment according to the severity of their crimes. Those whose crimes fell within the first class were to be fined between four and six years' rent and barred from all public office until peace was properly restored. The latter included a bar from sitting or voting in Parliament and the Privy Council, being included as an Officer of State, or having vote in the election of Commissioners of Shires and Commissioners of the Burghs. Replacements for those removed from any public office would be provided by Parliament or parliamentary committee. Banishment, confinement, or imprisonment could also be imposed within the first class. Those whose crimes fell within the second class were to be fined between two to four years' rent and barred from all public office at least until the next session of Parliament. Those barred from public office within the second class included representation in Parliament or membership of any parliamentary committees. Those whose crimes fell within the third class were to be fined between half a year's rent to two years' rent. In cases of lesser importance the fine under the third class could be dispensed with and censure imposed. Those individuals whose crimes fell within the third class were to have their cases remitted to the judges to consider whether or not suspension was appropriate.[24]

The Act of Classes of 8 January 1646 therefore constituted the major item of legislation designed to punish and purge malignants and delinquents. Designed ostensibly to deal with those rebels captured at Philiphaugh, the scope of the Act of Classes also extended to individuals who had been sentenced, fined, or confined by Parliament or its committees since the Act of Oblivion of

1641. Those who had joined with the rebels in previous battles but were not included within the remit of the Act of Classes could be remitted to the determination of Parliament or appropriate parliamentary committees.[25]

Although the Act of Classes received parliamentary sanction on 8 January 1646, it had been under overt parliamentary discussion since 31 December 1645. The first class of the Act of Classes was considered by the Estates on 31 December and probably prior to this as well. Intense pressure on the part of Loudoun, Cassillis, Lanark, Lothian, Burleigh, Johnston of Wariston (Edinburgh), Cochrane of Cowdoun (Ayr), and Dundas of Maner (Linlithgow) secured the incorporation of important legislation concerning the remit of the first class. Lanark was the only conservative/pragmatic Royalist among this grouping and illustrates his willingness to have a working relationship with the radicals. The House 'vnanimously enacted'[26] that those within the first class who were not to be forfeited or executed were to be fined between three and six years' rent. When the final Act of Classes was passed on 8 January 1646 the level of fining for the first class had been extended to four to six years' rent. Furthermore, the House voted in favour of incorporating an extension to the first class in two important respects. Firstly, that 'this acte should be extendit and stricke aganist all relapses and delinquents'[27] since the 1641 Act of Oblivion. Secondly, banishment, imprisonment or confinement could be imposed within the first class, as well as fining, for those Parliament should 'thinke to demeritt a heigher censur then ther fynes, and might proue dangerous instruments to the peace of the countrey.'[28]

The second and third classes of the Act of Classes had been remitted to the consideration of the Estates separately on 6 January. When the full Parliament met on the morning session of 7 January a minor addition was made to the second class (those who had advanced the rebels' cause by holding public meetings or convening meetings were to be included within that class) and the third class was 'quolly assented too by the housse, without a contradictorey wotte'.[29] In the afternoon session exclusion from public office was agreed on and it was ordained that no proscribed noble, gentry, or burgess was to have a vote in Parliament until peace was concluded and that none of the three classes was to have any involvement in the election of parliamentary commissioners.[30]

Four death sentences were passed by Parliament against malignants on 16 January. Nathaniel Gordon, William Murray (brother of the Earl of Tullibardine), Andrew Guthrie (the son of the former Bishop of Moray), and Sir Robert Spottiswood were to be forfeited of life, lands, and goods. The date of execution was set for 20 January. Reports on all four cases were made from the Committee for the Processes to the House. The Committee for the Processes had found all four guilty of high treason.[31]

The case of Nathaniel Gordon was the first to be dealt with by the Estates. Having been found guilty of high treason by the Committee for the Processes, the full Parliament voted in favour of his execution, but only after a three hour debate. This would suggest that the case against Gordon was far from clear-cut. Chancellor Loudoun voted against the forfeiture of Gordon's life, land, and goods. It is not clear whether or not Dunfermline, Cassillis, Lanark, and Carnwath voted against the forfeiture of Gordon, but at the very least they were uncertain about technical aspects of the case. Of all the gentry present only Beaton of Creich (Fife) found the case against Gordon not proven. Having been found guilty of high treason by the Committee for Processes, the report of that committee against William Murray was read twice to the House, which then voted in favour of Murray's forfeiture and execution. Tullibardine, Murray's brother, was not present in the House when the vote was taken. Five nobles and two gentry voted that Murray should be imprisoned for life and his lands and goods forfeited; Eglinton, Glencairn, Kinghorn, Dunfermline, and Buccleuch for the nobility and Falconer of Halkerton (Kincardine) and Frederick Lyon of Brigton (Forfar) for the gentry. The report of the Committee for Processes against Andrew Guthrie finding him guilty of high treason was also read to the House. Cassillis and Dunfermline voted in favour of the imprisonment of Guthrie for life with the forfeiture of his lands and goods. Chancellor Loudoun abstained in the vote against Guthrie. The vast majority of members present, however, voted for the execution of Guthrie. The report by the Committee for the Processes against Sir Robert Spottiswood, the last of the quartet to be forfeited and ordered to be executed by Parliament on 16 January, was based on two points. The first concerned Spottiswood's role in the delivery and prosecution of the commission from Charles I to Montrose. The House voted that execution constituted the appropriate punishment for such behaviour. The second point concerned the capture of Spottiswood at the Battle of Philiphaugh. Forfeiture of land and goods was voted as the appropriate punishment for fighting with the rebels. Four nobles voted in favour of life imprisonment and forfeiture of land and goods; Eglinton, Cassillis, Dunfermline, and Carnwath. Two further nobles, Loudoun and Lanark, craved the pardon of the House in the case of Spottiswood, but abstained from the final vote. One laird and one burgess voted in favour of saving the life of Spottiswood; Patrick Maxwell of Tailing (Forfar) for the gentry and Robert Farquhar (Aberdeen) for the burgesses.

Deviation in voting patterns from the consensus in the House regarding the four executions was most marked in the noble estate. A total of nine nobles did not vote in favour of all four executions. Dunfermline, Cassillis, Lanark, Eglinton, and Carnwath voted against execution in more than one case and favoured life imprisonment with forfeiture of land and goods. Chancellor Loudoun abstained in two cases. Voting patterns among the nobles therefore cut across radical and conservative lines (although this is dependent on the total number of nobles present; information which is not available). However, it is clear that it was the voting strength of the gentry and burgesses which had forced the decisions through.[32]

Whilst the punishment of maliganants and delinquents formed the most crucial area of parliamentary business discussed between 26 November 1645 and 4 February 1646, a reassessment of the effectiveness of the Covenanting military leadership during the period of Montrose's victories was undertaken.

In particular, the conduct at the Battle of Kilsyth was closely scrutinised. On 18 December 1645 a session committee was established to consider three specific remits. Firstly, the conduct of Lieutenant General Baillie (as the commander of the Covenanting forces at the battle) and the officers of the army present at the battle was to be examined. Secondly, the conduct of the Committee of Estates as constituted at that time was likewise to be examined. Thirdly, the extent and manner of the losses suffered at Kilsyth were to be considered. The committee was then to report back to Parliament which would then take any appropriate action. The formation of this committee owes its origin to a petition from Lieutenant General Baillie himself desiring a trial concerning his carriage at Kilsyth. Five per parliamentary estate plus the General Officers of the army formed the membership of the Committee anent the Battle of Kilsyth and Lieutenant General Baillie.[33]

The political orientation of noble representation on the committee was radical (and included Cassillis and Eglinton) with only one noted conservative/pragmatic Royalist noble securing membership (Glencairn). In addition, Johnston of Wariston (Edinburgh), was included as one of the five gentry members, whilst noted radicals such as Robert Barclay (Irvine), John Kennedy (Ayr), and William Glendoning (Kirkcudbright) were included. The committee had reported back to Parliament by 29 January.

The Estates absolved Lieutenant General Baillie of any blame for the defeat at Kilsyth, but did not mention the conduct of the Committee of Estates. Of the 15 parliamentary members on the Committee anent the Battle of Kilsyth and Lieutenant General Baillie, 14 were members of the Committee of Estates as per 8 March 1645 or as per later additions on 7 August 1645. Only David Beaton of Creich (Fife) for the gentry had not been a member of the Committee of Estates then in session. Therefore there appears to have been a whitewash of the role of the Committee of Estates in the defeat at Kilsyth *vis-a-vis* the actions of the military leadership at Kilsyth.[34]

The concentration of attention on the punishment of malignants and delinquents did not obscure the fact that action was required to deal with the issue of reparations for those whose lands and estates had been ravaged during the course of the civil war in Scotland. Such an issue was devolved to a parliamentary session committee established on 12 December 1645; the Committee anent the Losses. It was to establish a uniform device which could be applied nationally for an effective reparations scheme. The committee was only to concern itself with the estates of individuals who had been loyal to the Covenanting cause. Four nobles, five gentry, six burgesses, and two supernumeraries (both nobles) constituted the membership of the Committee anent the Losses. Noble membership was based on radicals (Eglinton, Buccleuch, and Kirkcudbright). The two supernumeraries, Chancellor Loudoun and Crawford-Lindsay, President of Parliament, supplemented the numbers of the nobility to six, giving a greater parity with the other two estates. Only one noble, two gentry, and two burgesses included on the Committee of the Losses were not members of the Committee of Estates of 8 March 1645. The Committee for the losses sat throughout the session of Parliament from 12 December until 4 Februrary. The commission to the Committee for the Losses was then renewed on 4 February and the committee would then convene as a parliamentary interval committee until the next session of Parliament.[35]

Throughout the parliamentary session Parliament continued to regulate its own affairs and initiated constitutional and procedural legislation. Low levels of parliamentary attendance are indicated by legislation enacted on 20 December 1645. No member of Parliament was to be allowed to leave a diet of Parliament without having received permission from the appropriate parliamentary official. Shires and burghs which had not sent commissioners of the shires or commissioners of the burghs to the Fifth Session were to be written to, elections were to be held, and then the elected commissioners were to be sent to Parliament as quickly as possible. Such a phenomenon probably reflects the economic and financial effects of a civil war campaign throughout parts of the country which hindered several shires and burghs from dispatching parliamentary representatives. Lack of attendance by parliamentary members was further addressed by an ordinance issued on 2 February 1646 concerning members leaving in numbers before the dissolution of Parliament on 4 February. A three tier level of fining was applied to such members; 300 merks per noble, 200 merks per individual gentry, and one hundred merks per individual burgess. In common with the Second Session commencing on 7 January 1645, the Fifth Session also appointed a Vice-President of Parliament. Due to the absence of Crawford-Lindsay, the present incumbent of the office of President, Cassillis was appointed Vice-President of Parliament on 26 December 1645 and was to continue in that post during the absence of Crawford-Lindsay. Greater regulation of burghal representation was enacted on 12 January 1646. Robert Hill had represented the burgh of Queensferry in the First to Fourth Sessions of the First Triennial Parliament. John Milne is recorded in the parliamentary rolls as representing the burgh of Queensferry on 26 November 1645 (the opening day of the Fifth Session). Parliament ultimately proved of the change in commissioner but stipulated that during the current session there was to be no change in commissioners of the burghs without Parliament's approval. Therefore it would appear that the burgh of Queensferry had changed its parliamentary commissioner during the Fifth Session without Parliament's approval.[36]

The Fifth Session was dissolved on 4 February 1646 and the Sixth Session was to meet on the first Tuesday of November 1646. Twenty-three bills and 101 supplications were remitted to the Committee of Estates and the Committee for Monies. The concentration of parliamentary business on judicial matters had obviously left insufficient time for the House to consider all legislation submitted to it.[37]

3. The Committee Structure of the Fifth Session of the First Triennial Parliament

Twelve parliamentary session committees and five parliamentary interval committees have been analysed. Of the 12 session committees, four had financial remits, three had remits relating to parliamentary commissions and malignancy, whilst two were concerned with military affairs. The three remaining session committees possessed diplomatic, judicial, and procedural remits respectively. Of the five interval committees, four were concerned with financial affairs, and one was an executive committee.[38]

Twenty-five nobles, 25 gentry, and 23 burgesses were employed on the 12 session committees, whereas the five interval committees were staffed by 26 nobles, 48 gentry, and 26 burgesses. Parity per estate is apparent in the membership levels of the session committees. Furthermore, the staffing levels of the nobility and the burgesses are virtually retained in the interval committees, albeit there is a slight increase. Once again, however, gentry levels witnessed a significant increase between session and interval committees, with a rise of 23. Five gentry (20%) and five burgesses (22%) included on session committees were not members of Parliament as per 26 November 1645. The comparative figures for interval committees are 28 gentry (58%) and nine burgesses (35%). Twenty-three of the 28 non-parliamentary gentry were members of the regional committee, the Committee anent the Losses of the Sheriffdom of Aberdeen. These 23 gentry may well account for the exact increase of 23 gentry between session and interval committees. Twelve of the 25 nobles (48%), 20 of the 25 gentry (80%), and 11 of the 23 burgesses (48%) were included on only one session committee each. By way of comparison, 20 of the 26 nobles (77%), 40 of the 48 gentry (83%), and 19 of the 26 burgesses (73%) included on interval committees secured membership of only one interval committee. This corpus of empirical data indicates dominance of both session and interval committees by a small grouping of nobles, gentry, and burgesses.[39]

Legislation enacted on 29 November and 1 December 1645 stated that the Chancellor and the President of Parliament were to be included on all parliamentary session committees. Therefore Chancelllor Loudoun and Crawford-Lindsay, President of Parliament, were theoretically included on the maximum of 12 parliamentary session committees.

Common membership of the noble estate on parliamentary session committees was primarily radical, but also included a conservative/pragmatic Royalist element. Cassillis served on four session committees in total, Glencairn and Yester on three, whilst Argyll, Eglinton, Lothian, Burleigh, Kirkudbright, Marischal, Lanark, and Dalhousie each served on two.

Johnston of Wariston (Edinburgh), Ruthven of Frieland (Perth), and MacDowall of Garthland (Wigtown) each gained membership of three committees. Two further gentry were included on two session committees as a whole; Lockhart of Lee (Lanark) and Ramsay of Balmaine (Kincardine). Burghal common membership of session committees, on the other hand, was concentrated within a wider grouping. Sir Alexander Wedderburne (Dundee) was included on six session committees in total, whilst John Kennedy (Ayr) and George Garden (Burntisland) served on four. Three further burgesses, Robert Cunningham (Kinghorn), William Lyon (Brechin), and Robert Barclay (Irvine) each served on three session committees. In terms of total membership of session committees, the above nobles, gentry, and burgesses form the dominant grouping.[40]

Within the structure of parliamentary session committees, a significant relationship over all three estates existed between the membership of the Committee for Processes, session committees dealing with parliamentary commissions and malignancy and the diplomatic committee concerning Crawford-Lindsay's possible inclusion on the diplomatic interval commission. Noble common membership within this relationship was primarily radical and was focused on Cassillis and Burleigh, although it did also include Glencairn. Where noble common membership exists between the Committee for Processes and any of the session committees dealing with parliamentary commissions and malignancy, that common membership was radical (Cassillis and Burleigh). Gentry common membership within this context was based on Johnston of Wariston (Edinburgh) and Dundas of Maner (Linlithgow). George Garden (Burntisland), Robert Cunningham (Kinghorn), and Robert Barclay (Irvine) formed the comparative burghal grouping.

No laird gained membership of all four financial session committees. Only one laird, Ramsay of Balmaine (Kincardine), was included on more than one financial session committee, and only one laird, Ruthven of Frieland (Perth), gained membership of more than one session committee relating to parliamentary commissions and malignancy. Only one laird, MacDowall of Garthland (Wigtown), gained membership of both the judicial and the diplomatic session committees respectively.

No burgess gained membership of three or more financial session committees. Four burgesses gained membership of two out of four financial session committees; John Johnstone (Dumfries), William Lyon (Brechin), George Garden (Burntisland), and Robert Farquhar (Aberdeen). Only one burgess, Sir Alexander Wedderburne (Dundee), gained membership of more than one session committee relating to parliamentary commissions and malignancy.

Burghal common membership of financial session committees was greater than that of the nobility and the gentry. On the other hand, there was no common membership on financial session committees nor military session committees for the nobility (bar the two supernumeraries). The discussion of financial affairs was spread throughout the noble estate as a whole, possibly in an attempt to maintain the fragile radical-conservative/pragmatic Royalist alliance within that estate. Common membership of gentry and burghal representation on the two military session committees was centred on Beaton of Creich (Fife) and Sir Alexander Wedderburne (Dundee).[41]

No noble served on more than two interval committees. A total of six nobles were nominated to two interval committees each and there was a balance between radical and conservative nobles; Eglinton, Lothian, Kirkcudbright, Dunfermline, Buccleuch, Balcarras, and Kirkcudbright. Argyll had been dispatched to Ulster and this may account for a lower figure than expected on the parliamentary interval committees. No nobles included on the Committee for Monies, Processes, and Excise were included on any other interval committee.[42]

In common with the nobility, no laird was included on more than two interval committees. However, a core grouping of eight gentry did secure access to two interval committees; Dundas of Maner (Linlithgow), Kerr of Cavers (Roxburgh), Ruthven of Frieland (Perth), Forbes of Craigievar (Aberdeen), Hepburne of Humbie, Treasurer of the Army, Home of Wedderburne (Berwick), Ramsay of Balmaine (Kincardine), and Maxwell of Tailing (Forfar).

Burghal common membership of interval committees was spread over a greater field compared to both the nobility and gentry. Robert Farquhar (Aberdeen) and John Johnstone (Dumfries) were members of three interval committees, Robert Arnot (Perth), Sir Alexander Wedderburne (Dundee), Alexander Jaffray (Aberdeen), William Glendoning (Kirkcudbright), and John Auchterlony (Arbroath) were each members of two interval committees.

Both the gentry and burgesses openly breached parliamentary legislation concerning membership of the Committee for Monies, Processes, and Excise, whilst the nobility did not. Such a breach provides further evidence of a challenge to the political power of the nobility over the other two estates. Legislation of 29 January had stipulated that no member of the Committee for Monies could sit on any other parliamentary committee. However, one laird, Forbes of Craigievar (Aberdeen), secured membership of both the Committee for Losses and the Committee for Monies, Processes, and Excise. Alexander Jaffray (Aberdeen), for the burgesses, was included on the Committee for Monies, Processes, and Excise as well as the Committee anent the Losses of the Sherriffdom of Aberdeen.[43]

Membership of interval committees over all three estates was, in general, related to membership of the Committee of Estates (with the exception of the regional interval committee, the Committee anent the Losses of the Sherriffdom of Aberdeen). The noble estate was the most noted among the three estates in terms of this phenomenon. All three nobles, all four gentry, and three of the four burgesses on the Committee for Clearing the Accounts with England were also included on the new Committee of Estates. Three of the four nobles, two of the five gentry, and four of the six burgesses on the Committee for the Losses were also included on the Committee of Estates.[44]

4. The Appointment of Parliamentary Interval Committees

Five parliamentary interval committees were appointed (one of which was a regional committee); the Committee for Monies, the Committee anent the Losses of the Sherriffdom of Aberdeen, the Committee for Hepburne of Humbie's Accounts, the Committee for clearing the Accounts with England, and the Committee of Estates. In addition, the parliamentary session committee of 12 December 1645, the Committee anent the Losses, was renewed as an interval committee on 4 February 1646.[45]

Acting on a petition from Forbes of Craigievar and Forbes of Echt, the commissioners of the shires for Aberdeen, a parliamentary interval committee was appointed on 3 February to consider the losses suffered by the shire of Aberdeen. This was in common with localised parliamentary committees established by earlier sessions of Parliament (for example, the Committee for trying the Lands in Perthshire of 4 August 1645).[46]

Fining of malignants on a national basis was remitted to a specialised parliamentary interval committee, the Committee for Monies, established on 3 February 1646. Following the four death sentences passed against malignants on 16 January, the radical orientated Commission of the Kirk had been strongly advocating that the same course should be followed for other malignants. The policy of further executions was refused by the noble estate and the Commission of the Kirk could only be placated by the initiation of a policy of heavy fining of malignants. The establishment of the parliamentary interval committee of 3 February therefore owes its origins to this development. The full remit for the Committee for Monies was essentially that of fining and processing of malignants, the raising of monies, and the farming of the excise. Therefore different financial agendas were incorporated within the one parliamentary committee allowing an efficiency of financial administration and expertise (for example, the powers of previous Committees of the Excise being invested in that committee). The distribution of public money was to be under the monopoly of the Committee for Monies. However, the powers of the Committee for the Exchequer were not incorporated within the Committee for Monies and the Commission for the Exchequer was renewed on 2 February to continue until the next parliamentary session. Legislation enacted on 4 February empowered the Committee for Monies to forfeit the lands and estates of any individuals fined within the first and second class of the Act of Classes who were refusing to pay their fines, as well as individuals who were fined by the Committee for Monies following the close of the parliamentary session. On 29 January Parliament had formulated three stipulations concerning the Committee for Monies. Firstly, no member of the Committee for Monies was to be included on any other parliamentary committee. Secondly, six per parliamentary estate (yielding a total of 18 members) were to constitute the membership of that committee. Thirdly, the Committee for Monies was to be split into two sections the Committee for the Monies (North) and the Committee for Monies (South); 12 members were to be on the Committee for Monies (South) and six on the Committee for Monies (North). The membership of the Committee for the Monies had been agreed on by 30 January although the committee had been redefined to seven per parliamentary estate. According to Sir James Balfour, it had been decided on 22 January that seven per estate were to be on the Committee for Monies and that those commissioners were to be on no other committee; this may well have represented a shift in power away from the nobility. Gentry and burghal voting strength appear to have combined to check noble domination of the Committee for Monies and direct political power to the other two parliamentary estates. When the commission was officially issued on 3 February seven per parliamentary estate were confirmed as the parliamentary membership complemented by Hepburne of Humbie in the capacity as Treasurer of the Armies. Twelve members (four per parliamentary estate) were allocated to the southern section of the Committee for Monies, whilst nine members (three per parliamentary estate) were allocated to the northern section of the Committee for Monies. Therefore the increase of one per estate from the official parliamentary record of 29 January appears to have been allocated to the Committee for Monies (North) resulting in a total membership of nine as opposed to six. Hepburne of Humbie was allocated to the southern section resulting in a total membership of 13.[47]

Noble membership of the northern section of the Committee for Monies was local based and consisted of Marischal, Findlater, and Arbuthnot. One of the gentry representatives and two of the burgess representatives were not members of Parliament as per 26 November 1645. The quorum of the Committee for Monies (North) was set at five with no stiplulation on compulsory attendance per estate. The geographical radius of the Committee for Monies (North) was that of the sheriffdoms of Forfar, Mearns, Aberdeen, Banff, Murray, Nairn, Inverness, Cromarty, Sutherland, Caithness, and Orkney. Hence geographical remit was matched by geographical parliamentary membership on the Committee for Monies (North).[48]

Noble membership of the southern section of the Committee for Monies was also radically orientated, with Cassillis and Burleigh included, with only one conservative/pragmatic Royalist noble (Tullibardine) gaining membership. Radical personnel also included George Jamieson (Coupar) and George Garden (Burntisland). The geographical radius of the Committee for Monies (South) was that of the remainder of the country south of the sheriffdoms under the remit of the Committee for Monies (North). However, the Committee for Monies (South) was dominated by east coast gentry and burgesses.[49]

The southern section of the Committee for Monies was to reside at Edinburgh and the quorum of that committee was set at seven. No compulsory attendance per estate was stipulated. Although the Committee for Monies had been split into two geographic sections, these two sections were infact part of the one committee. Thus the two sections were ordered to keep regular correspondence with one another, as well as with the Committee of Estates. Ultimately answerable to Parliament, members of both sections were allowed to attend the diets of the other section.[50]

The reassessment of financial affairs on a Scottish and British basis as a result of military commitments manifested itself in the appointment of two parliamentary committees. A parliamentary session committee had been appointed on 12 December to audit the accounts of Hepburne of Humbie as Treasurer of the Army. On 4 February an interval committee was established to meet after the close of the parliamentary session to attempt to settle financial transactions with the English Parliament.[51]

No common membership exists between the Committee for Hepburne of Humbie's accounts and the Committee for the English Accounts. Three per parliamentary estate formed the membership of the former committee. Noble membership of the session committee appears to have been orientated towards the conservatives/pragmatic Royalists (Dalhousie, Kellie, and Yester). Three nobles, three gentry, four burgesses, and five military officials formed the membership of the Committee for the English Accounts. Of the three noble members, Lothian was the only noted radical, although James Sword (St Andrews) and William Glendoning (Kirkcudbright) secured membership among the burgess representatives.[52]

A new commission was issued to the Committee of Estates by Parliament on 3 February. A total of 18 nobles, 17 gentry, 16 burgesses, and one military official (52 individuals) were included in four sections of the Committee of Estates. One section of the Committee of Estates was to reside constantly within Scotland, another section was to accompany the Scottish army in England, another section was to accompany the Scottish army in Ireland, and a fourth section was to negotiate with the English Parliament. The composition of the Committee of Estates as per 3 February 1646 represents a drop of 21 nobles, 22 gentry, and 23 burgesses compared with the Committee of Estates of 8 March 1645. The reduction in numbers (spread almost evenly over all three estates) was obviously effected by Parliament's ruling that members of the Committee for Monies could not serve on any other interval committee. Eighteen nobles, 10 gentry, and 14 burgesses (42 individuals in total) included in the Committee of Estates of 8 March 1645 or in later additions of 6 and 7 August 1645 were also members of the new Committee of Estates of 3 February 1646. Conservatives/pragmatic Royalists formed only a small proportion of the nobles on both commissions; Dalhousie and Lanark.[53]

Three per estate were included on the section of the Committee of Estates to accompany the Scottish army in England. Lothian was the only noted radical noble who secured access to this section and he was outflanked by Dunfermline and Balcarras.[54] Two nobles, two gentry, two burgesses, and one military official were included on the section of the Committee of Estates to accompany the Scottish army in Ireland. Noble membership was balanced between radicals (Kirkcubdright) and conservatives/pragmatic Royalists (Glencairn), although burghal membership was exclusively radical; George Porterfield (Glasgow) and John Kennedy (Ayr).The quorum of the section of the Committee of Estates to accompany the Scottish army in Ireland was deemed to 'promiscuous' although three of the committee was required to be present.[55]

No exact details of membership of the section of the Committee of Estates to reside in Scotland are provided in the parliamentary commission. Extraction of the respective members of the sections to accompany the Scottish army in England and the Scottish army in Ireland nevertheless reveals a rump of seven per estate on the section of the Committee of Estates to reside in Scotland. Noble membership of this section was primarily radical (including Loudoun, Eglinton, and Weymes) but also included a conservative/pragmatic Royalist element (the major influences being Lanark and Dalhousie). Conservative and pragmatic Royalist nobles were thus isolated on the 'Edinburgh' section, where a close watch on them could be kept. Two of the burgesses (both from Edinburgh) were not members of Parliament as per 26 November 1645.[56]

Also included on the Committee of Estates of 3 February were the Scottish diplomatic commissioners negotiating with the English Parliament. Four nobles, three gentry, and three burgesses had been included on the original commission of 8 March 1645. The political orientation of this grouping of nobles was radical (Argyll, Loudoun, and Balmerino), with only one conservative/pragmatic Royalist noble (Lauderdale) included. The radical orientation of the diplomatic section of the Committee of Estates was enhanced by the inclusion of Johnston of Wariston (Edinburgh) as one of the three gentry representatives within this common grouping. During the Fourth Session of the First Triennial Parliament additions had been made to the Scottish diplomatic contingent on 6 August 1645 of three per estate. The noble additions were primarily conservative/pragmatic Royalist but also included a radical element. The commission issued to the Committee of Estates on 3 February 1646 does not differentiate between the membership of the diplomatic contingents of 8 March and 6 August 1645, although the grouping listed on 8 March was clearly the major one. Furthermore, according to the new commission of 3 February 1646 Crawford-Lindsay was listed as one of three supernumeraries for the nobles and Loudoun and Lanark were included on the section of the Committee of Estates to reside in Scotland. None of the gentry added to the diplomatic grouping on 6 August 1645 were included in any other of the sections of the Committee of Estates on 3 February. Of the three burgessses added to the diplomatic grouping on 6 August 1645, Sir Alexander Wedderburne (Dundee) was included on the section of the Committee of Estates to reside in Scotland, John Kennedy (Ayr) was included on the section of the Committee of Estates to accompany the Scottish army in Ireland, and William Glendoning (Kirkcudbright) was included on the section of the Committee of Estates to accompany the Scottish army in England. It would therefore appear that the diplomatic commissioners appointed on 6 August had been appointed for a temporary period only and that the main grouping remained those commissioners named on 8 March 1645. Radicals continued to have dominant political control of the diplomatic section.[57]

Indeed, when the House agreed the membership of the Committee of Estates on 3 February 'a grate debait'[58] emerged concerning the renewal of the diplomatic commission to the English Parliament. Glencairn and Lanark 'with muche hait and contentione'[59] attempted to have Crawford-Lindsay included as a supernumerary on the diplomatic commission. Hence conservative/pragmatic Royalist nobles were attempting to bolster their numbers on the diplomatic section. It was put to the vote whether or not Crawford-Lindsay should leave the House until the motion was decided on. A majority voted that Crawford-Lindsay should not leave the House. Thereupon a vote was taken whether or not the issue should be decided by parliamentary session committee; a majority of the House voted in favour of parliamentary session committee. Three per estate constituted the membership of that committee. Both Glencairn and Lanark themselves were included on that committee along with the radical Cassillis, whilst Johnston of Wariston (Edinburgh) galvanised the organisation of the gentry and burghal members. The conclusion of the parliamentary session committee was that no alteration should be made to the original diplomatic commission of 8 March 1645. Two important details can be interpreted regarding this episode. Firstly, the fact that Glencairn and Lanark had been the instigators of the move to have Crawford-Lindsay installed on the commission and had then been included on the session committee to decide the issue suggests that a majority of the noble estate was in favour of Crawford-Lindsay being installed (the nobility having elected Glencairn and Lanark to be on that session committee). Thus the noble estate seemed to favour a more balanced grouping of radical and conservative/pragmatic Royalist nobles to deal with the English Parliament (and possibly also to challenge the power of Argyll on the diplomatic committee). Secondly, it also indicates that there was sufficient opposition from the gentry and burgess representatives to Crawford-Lindsay's inclusion to defeat the motion at the committee stage. Johnston of Wariston (Edinburgh) was one of the diplomatic commissioners included on 8 March 1645 and probably led some form of opposition at the committee stage, considering that the remaining gentry and burgesses on the session committee were important radicals, such as George Porterfield (Glasgow) and John Kennedy (Ayr). Moreover, Johnston of Wariston acted as the spokesman and political agent for Argyll within the other two estates.[60]

The commission to the Committee of Estates of 3 February included three supernumeraries for the nobility, two supernumeraries for the gentry, and one supernumerary for the burgesses. The supernumeraries appointed for the nobility and gentry were based on military and administrative functions, but also included Crawford-Lindsay in the capacity of President of Parliament. None of these individuals had been allocated to the sections of the Committee of Estates to reside in Scotland, to accompany the army in England or to accompany the army in Ireland. Whilst the supernumeraries could sit in any of these three sections, the effect of the barring of Crawford-Lindsay as a supernumerary from the diplomatic commission was to bar all the other supernumeraries too. Hence no supernumerary could sit with the diplomatic commissioners negotiating with the English Parliament.[61]

The renewal of the diplomatic commission of 8 March 1645 also presented problems regarding gentry representation. Dundas of Maner (Linlithgow) was included on the original diplomatic commission, renewed on 3 February. He was also included on the Committee for Monies initiated on the same day. Parliament had stipulated on 31 January that should Dundas have to leave for London on diplomatic business then the Committee for Monies was to choose another member of the gentry to replace him.[62]

5. The Operation of Parliamentary Interval Committees

Following the dissolution of the Fifth Session on 4 February, the first recorded meeting of the section of the Committee of Estates to reside in Scotland is on 27 February. Details of the diets of that section of the Committee of Estates are provided from 27 February until 31 March 1646.[63] From 27 February until 7 March that section of the Committee of Estates convened at Linlithgow probably due to the plague and from 12 March until 31 March at Edinburgh.

Twenty-two sederunts in total are recorded. Crawford-Lindsay attended 18 diets (82%), Lanark 14 diets (64%), and Dalhousie 10 diets (46%). Conservative and pragmatic Royalist nobles were therefore the dominant noble attenders on the Edinburgh section and would appear to be exerting political influence. Nobles included on the other sections of the Committee of Estates often attended the proceedings. Glencairn, a member of the Committee of Estates (Ireland), was present on seven occasions (32%), whilst Dunfermline, a member of the Committee of Estates (England), attended five diets (23%). Argyll was included on the Committee of Estates as one of the Scottish diplomatic commissioners in London and was present on three occasions (14%). Barganie attended nine diets (41%) despite the fact that he had not been included on any sections of the Committee of Estates as per 3 February. At the first diet on 27 February Crawford-Lindsay was nominated and elected as President of the Committee of Estates (Scotland) in the absence of Chancellor Loudoun. Crawford-Lindsay is recorded as President at 15 diets (68%). Chancellor Loudoun did not attend any of the diets of the Committee of Estates (Scotland) between 27 February and 31 March 1646. Glencairn is recorded as President at five diets, Crawford-Lindsay being absent.[64]

Analysis of gentry representation on the Committee of Estates (Scotland) reveals five gentry attending on a regular or semi-regular basis; Foullis of Colington (Edinburgh) 19 diets (86%), Ramsay of Balmaine (Kincardine) 16 diets (73%), Beaton of Creich (Fife) 14 diets (64%), Belshes of Toftis (Berwick) 13 diets (59%), and Lockhart of Lee (Lanark) attended 10 diets (46%). Maxwell of Newark attended six diets (27%) despite the fact that he had not been included in any sections of the Committee of Estates as per 3 February 1646. Maxwell of Newark was not a member of Parliament as per 26 November 1645.[65] Burghal attendance was based on Archibald Sydserf (Edinburgh), who attended 21 diets (96%), and Thomas Bruce (Stirling) who attended 19 diets (86%). Sydserf was not a member of Parliament as per 26 November 1645. Sir John Smith (Edinburgh) was included on the diplomatic section of the Committee of Estates, although he also attended two diets of the Committee of Estates (Scotland). The fact that it was only the nobility who were cross-attending sections compared to the other two estates, might have been an attempt on the part of the nobility to check the radicalism of the other two estates, particularly the gentry.[66]

Under the terms of the commission of the Committee of Estates issued on 3 February, the quorum of the Committee of Estates (Scotland) was set at nine with two of each estate required to be present. This rule was not adhered to at only one of the 22 diets. Therefore the rules laid down by Parliament relating to the quorum of the Committee of Estates (Scotland) were adhered to in general.[67]

The Committee for Monies (South) first met and accepted its commission on 7 February 1646. From 7 to 9 February the committee met at St Andrews, from 5 to 7 March at Linlithgow, and from 12 March until 26 October at Edinburgh. Ninety-five sederunts are recorded for the period as a whole.

Noble attendance was focused on the radicals; Cassillis 77 diets (81%) and

Burleigh 56 diets (59%). Tullibardine, on the other hand, attended 58 diets (61%). In addition, the three nobles on the Committee for Monies (North) attended sessions of the Committee for Monies (South). On 7 February Cassillis was elected President of the Committee for Monies (South). When Cassillis was not present Burleigh was President on nine occasions (10%) and Weymes of Bogie (Fife) was President on five occasions (5%). At four of the diets where Buleigh was President Weymes of Bogie (Fife) was also prest at the diet. When Bogie was listed as President, Marischal, Coupar, Burleigh, and Arbuthnot were present over the period of all five diets. Therefore when Cassillis was absent, Weymes of Bogie (Fife) took precedence over the noble members present, even when the leading radical noble Burleigh was in attendance. The appointment of a laird as President of an important parliamentary interval commission ahead of other noble members indicates the political strength of the gentry *vis-a-vis* the noble estate. It also provides an indication of the grass-roots radicalism of the gentry in general.[68]

Gentry attendance on the Committee for Monies (South) was based on Hope of Craighall, 71 diets (75%), Cochrane of Cowdoun (Ayr) 61 diets (64%), Dundas of Maner (Linlithgow) 55 diets (58%), and Weymes of Bogie (Fife) 49 diets (52%). Hope of Craighall was not a member of Parliament as per 26 November 1645. Although Weymes of Bogie has the lowest attendance record of the gentry on the Committee for Monies (South) the fact that he was often President of the committee indicates that he was the most influential laird on the committee. Hepburne of Humbie attended 22 diets (23%) in the capacity as Treasurer of the Army. Three gentry included on the Committee for Monies (North) attended various diets of the Committee for Monies (South); Forbes of Echt (Aberdeen) 16 diets (17%), Arbuthnot of Findowrie eight diets (8%), and Forbes of Craigievar seven diets (7%).[69]

Burghal attendance was concentrated on James Campbell (Dumbarton) 77 diets (81%), James Stewart (Edinburgh) 76 diets (80%), George Garden (Burntisland) 63 diets (66%), and George Jamieson (Coupar) 40 diets (42%). James Stewart was not a member of Parliament as per 26 November 1645. The three burgesses on the Committee for Monies (North) attended various sessions of the Committee for Monies (South); Robert Lockhart (Edinburgh) 71 diets (75%), Alexander Jaffray (Aberdeen) six diets (6%), and James Pedie (Montrose) five diets (5%). Robert Lockhart and Alexander Jaffray were not members of Parliament as per 26 November 1645.[70]

The terms of the commission to the Committee for Monies stated that the quorum for the southern section was to be seven although no requirement was placed on attendance per estate. The quorum for the southern section was met at all diets.[71]

Between 6 March and 30 October 1646 the Committee for Monies (South) ordained 386 individuals to lend sums between 200 and 900 merks.[72] Fourteen individual cases were considered for fining by the Committee of Estates during July 1646, the details of which are recorded in the Register of the Committee for Monies (South). Of the 14 cases considered, 12 resulted in fines and two were discharged. One of the 12 cases which resulted in fining was later discharged. The level of fines imposed ranged from £1,440 Scots to £6,667 Scots. Three fines imposed were less than £3,000 Scots, whilst the other nine were in the region of £3,000 to £6,667 Scots.[73] Within a wider perspective covering the period 9 January to 28 October 1646 and also relating to fining during the parliamentary session, it has been calculated that 151 individuals were fined during this period amounting to £901,818. By November 1646, however, £332,111 13s 4d of this total had still not been paid.[74]

The Committee for Monies (North) sat at Dundee from 9 March until 8 May, at Edinburgh from 16 to 18 May, at Dundee from 22 May until 5 June, and at Aberdeen from 12 October until 28 October 1646. Fifty-six sederunts are recorded in total. Findlater attended 49 diets (88%), Arbuthnot 41 diets (73%), and Marischal 25 diets (45%). Three of the nobles on the Committee for Monies (South) also attended various sessions of the Committee for Monies (North). Coupar attended 12 diets (21%), Burleigh nine diets (16%), and Tullibardine one diet only. Chancellor Loudoun attended one diet although he was not a member of the Committee for Monies. Marischal is listed as President at 19 diets, whereas Findlater is listed as President at 13 diets (Marischal was not present at these diets).[75]

Robert Arbuthnot of Findowrie, a non-member of Parliament as per 26 November 1645, attended 50 diets (89%), whilst Forbes of Echt (Aberdeen) attended 48 diets (86%), and Forbes of Craigievar 13 diets (23%) respectively. The four gentry on the Committee for Monies (South) attended one diet each only.[76] Analysis of burghal attendance on the Committee for Monies (North) reveals that Alexander Jaffray (Aberdeen), a non-member of Parliament as per 26 November 1645, attended 55 diets (98%). James Pedie (Montrose) attended 40 diets (71%) and Robert Lockhart (Edinburgh) eight diets (14%). Although Robert Lockhart had been included on the Committee for Monies (North), he sat on the Committee for Monies (South); this was in accordance with the commission issued on 3 February. Three burgesses on the Committee for Monies (South), George Jamieson (Coupar), James Stewart (Edinburgh), and James Campbell (Dumbarton), also attended various diets of the Committee for Monies (North).[77]

The terms of the commission to the Committee for Monies stated that the quorum of the northern section was to be five with no requirement placed on attendance per estate. This quorum was adhered to at all diets.[78]

Between 17 March and 5 June 1646 the Committee for Monies (North) ordained 69 individuals to lend money. Between 15 October and 28 October it also ordained 106 individuals to lend money. As was the case with fining, this constituted an additional source of raising revenue at a time of recent civil war.[79]

A comparison between cross-attendance of the various sections of the Committee of Estates and cross-attendance of the two sections of the Committee for Monies suggests that the radicalism of the gentry and burgesses on the latter committee had gone unchecked by the nobility. In any case the nobles on the Committee for Monies were primarily radicals. Evidence of the radicalism of the gentry is enhanced by the fact that Weymes of Bogie was often President of the Committee for Monies (South).

Conclusion

On the eve of the Sixth Session of the First Triennial Parliament on 3 November 1646, the military campaign of Montrose and the rebels had been effectively neutralised. The Fifth Session had initiated the process of purging malignants from civil office and of fining individuals according to three tiers of malignancy. Purging and fining were to be continued during the Sixth Session from 3 November 1646 to 27 March 1647. The emergence of a Scottish Commons, as noted earlier, in the form of the parliamentary power of the gentry and burgesses, became more marked during the Fifth Session. Johnston of Wariston continued his role as speaker for the gentry. The power of the noble estate in comparison to the gentry and burgesses had been checked in three ways. Firstly, the combined voting strength of the gentry and burgesses prevented the inclusion of Glencairn, Lanark, and Cassillis on both the Committee for Dispatches and the Committee for Processes. Secondly, it was that combined voting strength which was the driving force behind the passing of the four death sentences against malignants. Thirdly, the appointment of Weymes of Bogie as President of the southern section of the Committee for Monies provides a striking example of the political power of the gentry in operation. The drawing of the English Civil War to a conclusion and the role of Charles I vis-a-vis both the Scottish and English Parliaments were to have an equally divisive effect on the power relationship between the radicals and conservatives/pragmatic Royalists. The Fifth Session had witnessed a closer working relationship between conservative and pragmatic Royalist nobles and radical nobles. During the Sixth Session that relationship would be redefined gradually, but not exclusively, in the formers' favour.

NOTES

1. BL Add MS 37, 978, Letter-Book of the Commissioners of Scotland, 1645–1646, folio 20.
2. *APS*, vi, i, 440–441, 474–475, 474–612.
3. Ibid, 474–475; Shepherd, 'The Politics and Society of Glasgow, 1648–74', PhD. thesis, 33–34; 'Memoirs of the Civil War and During the Usurpation, by James Burns, Merchant, and Bailie of the City of Glasgow, from the (Year) 1644 till the (Year) 1661', ed. J. Maidment, *Historical Fragments, Relative to Scottish Affairs, from 1635 to 1644* (Edinburgh, 1833), 13.
4. *APS*, vi, i, 475; Balfour, *Historical Works*, III, 311. The official parliamentary register lists Wariston's speech as taking place on 27 November. However, Balfour's account is more consistent with events as recorded in *APS* and his own *Historical Works*, 26 to 28 November.
5. Balfour, *Historical Works*, III, 311.
6. Ibid, 313.

7. *APS*, vi, i, 380–383, 460, 475. Balfour, *Historical Works*, III, 314. Robert Barclay (Irvine) is listed in Balfour but not in *APS*.
8. *APS*, vi, i, 476.
9. Ibid, 478.
10. Ibid, 380–383, 460, 474–475, 477–478.
11. Ibid, 287, 430–431, 442, 447–478.
12. Ibid, 380–383, 476–477. Balfour states that Colville of Blair and Robertson of Bedlay, Justice Deputes were included as supernumeraries, (*Historical Works*, III, 316). However, this is not indicated in *APS* which states that the Justice Deputes were included as ordinary members.
13. *APS*, vi, i, 98, 290–291, 476–477.
14. Ibid, 380–383, 474–475, 478.
15. Ibid, 98, 288–289, 299, 478.
16. Balfour, *Historical Works*, III, 318.
17. Ibid, 318–319. According to Balfour's account of these proceedings, Lanark and not Marischal was included on both the Committee for Dispatches and the Committee for Processes on 29 November. However, the lists of membership provided by Balfour for 29 November have Marischal on both committees. Dunfermline, Frendraught, and Balcarras replaced the three relevant nobles on the Committee for Dispatches on December. Hamilton of Beill (Haddington) replaced MacDowall of Garthland (Wigtown) on the Committee for Dispatches. Gabriel Cunningham (Glasgow) replaced John Kennedy (Ayr) on the Committee for Dispatches. No other details of burgess membership on the Committee for Dispatches on 29 November are available apart from John Kennedy (Ayr).
18. *APS*, vi, i, 474–475, 517.
19. Ibid, 549–550.
20. Stevenson, *Revolution and Counter-Revolution in Scotland*, 47.
21. *APS*, vi, i, 559–563, 570–572, 581–582; Balfour, *Historical Works*, III, 470–471, Stevenson, *Revolution and Counter-Revolution in Scotland*, 47.
22. *APS*, vi, 474–475, 476, 478.
23. Ibid, 474–475, 478.
24. Ibid. Restrictions were imposed regarding the level of fining within each class. Those within the first class were to be fined a maximum of a third of the value of their estates or moveable goods and a minimum of two thirds of their estates or moveable goods (these figures are within the context of fines between four and six years' rents). Those within the second class were to be fined a maximum of two thirds of their moveable goods or money and a mimimum of a third of their moveable goods or money (these figures are within the context of fines between two and four years' rents). Those within the third class were to be fined a maximum of a third of their moveable goods or money and a minimum of a quarter of their moveable goods or money (these figures are within the context of half a year's fine to two years' fine).
25. *APS*, vi, 503–505.
26. Balfour, *Historical Works*, III, 346.
27. Ibid, 347; *APS*, vi, i, 503–505.
28. Balfour, *Historical Works*, III, 347.
29. Ibid, 353–354.
30. Ibid, 354.
31. Ibid, 358–362; *APS*, vi, i, 521–532; Stevenson, *Revolution and Counter-Revolution in Scotland*, 47; *The Memoirs of Henry Guthry*, 211.

32. Balfour, *Historical Works*, III, 358–362.
33. Ibid, 331, lists the noble and gentry representatives as being elected on 12 December; *APS*, vi, i, 490.
34. *APS*, vi, i, 380–383, 460–461, 490, 546.
35. Ibid, 380–383, 484–485, 572–573. Patrick Maxwell of Newark was not a member of Parliament as per 26 November 1645.
36. *APS*, vi, i, 288, 491–492, 494, 517, 564.
37. Ibid, 602, 611–612; Balfour, *Historical Works*, III, 372.
38. *APS*, vi, i, 475–583.
39. Ibid. The five non-parliamentary gentry included on session committees were Balfour of Denmilne (Fife), Hope of Craighall, Maxwell of Newark (Perth), and Colville of Blair and Robertson of Bedlay, Justice Deputes. The six non-parliamentary burgesses were Sir John Smith (Edinburgh), Robert McKean (Edinburgh), George Bell (Linlithgow), James Sword (St Andrews), and Gabriel Cunningham (Glasgow).
40. Ibid, 475–579.
41. Ibid, 474–475, 475–579.
42. Ibid, 567–583. Stevenson, *Revolution and Counter-Revolution in Scotland*, 47.
43. Ibid, 474–475, 567–583.
44. Ibid, 567–583. Dunfermline, Lothian, Balcarras, Kerr of Cavers (Roxburgh), Ruthven of Frieland (Perth), Hepburne of Humbie, Treasurer of the Army, Home of Wedderburne (Berwick), John Johnstone (Dumfries), William Glendoning (Kirkcudbright), and John Auchterlony (Arbroath) formed the common grouping included on both the Committee for Clearing the Accounts with England and the Committee of Estates. Eglinton, Buccleuch, Kirkcudbright, Ramsay of Balmaine (Kincardine), Maxwell of Tailing (Forfar), Robert Arnot (Perth), Sir Alexander Wedderburne (Dundee), Robert Farquhar (Aberdeen), and John Johnstone (Dumfries) formed the common grouping on both the Committee for Losses and the Committee of Estates.
45. Ibid, 567–570, 570–572, 572–573, 573–574, 583.
46. Ibid, 203, 470, 474–475, 572–573, 573–574. In line with the concept of a localised committee the vast majority of the membership of the Committee anent the Losses of the Sheriffdom of Aberdeen were non-parliamentary members. Out of a total membership of 32, 17 (13 gentry and four burgesses) had been included on the Committee of War for the Sheriffdom of Aberdeen of 24 July 1644. No nobles were included on the commission of 3 February and of the 23 gentry on the committee none were members of Parliament as per 26 November 1645. Forbes of Craigievar (Aberdeen) and Forbes of Echt (Aberdeen) were not included on the committee.
47. Ibid, 546, 563, 567–570, 580; Balfour, *Historical Works*, III, 365, 366; MacInnes, 'The Scottish Constitution, 1638–51', 125; Stevenson, 'The Financing of the Cause of the Covenants', 107–108.
48. *APS*, vi, i, 474–475, 567–570. Robert Arbuthnot of Findowrie, Robert Lockhart (Edinburgh), and Alexander Jaffray (Aberdeen) were not members of Parliament as per 26 November 1645.
49. Ibid, 474–475, 567–570.
50. Ibid, 567–570.
51. Ibid, 485, 583.
52. Ibid.
53. Ibid, 380–383, 457, 460, 460–461, 570.
54. Ibid, 570.

55. Ibid.
56. Ibid, 474–475, 570. Sir William Dick and Archibald Sydserf were not members of Parliament as per 26 November 1645.
57. Ibid, 380–383, 457, 474–475, 570.
58. Balfour, *Historical Works*, III, 371.
59. Ibid.
60. Ibid, 371; *APS*, vi, i, 579.
61. *APS*, vi, i, 474–475, 570, 579. General Leven, Lieutenant General Callander, and Crawford-Lindsay, President of Parliament formed the supernumeraries for the nobility. Gibson of Durie, Clerk Register, and Hepburne of Humbie, Treasurer of the Army, formed the supernumeraries for the gentry. John Lepar (St Andrews) was included as supernumerary for the burgesses.
62. Ibid, 550, 567–570, 570.
63. SRO PA 11/4, Register of the Committee of Estates, 27 February–31 March 1646, ff 180–215. SRO PA 7/4/6, Minutes of the Committee of Estates, 20 March–2 April 1646, records six diets of the Committee of Estates separately from those in SRO PA 11/4.
64. *APS*, vi, i, 570; SRO PA 11/4, ff 180–215.
65. *APS*, vi, i, 474–475, 570; SRO PA 11/4, ff 180–215.
66. Ibid.
67. SRO PA 11/4, ff 180–215.
68. SRO PA 14/3, Register of the Committee for Monies (South), 3 February 1646–26 October 1646, ff 25–375. The three nobles on the Committee for Monies (North) who attended diets of the Committee for Monies (South) were Findlater, Arbuthnot, and Marischal. Findlater attended 30 diets (32%), Arbuthnot nine diets (10%), and Marischal 26 diets (27%).
69. Ibid, 25–375; *APS*, vi, i, 474–475.
70. Ibid.
71. SRO PA 14/3, ff 25–375.
72. Ibid, 399–423; Stevenson, 'The Financing of the Cause of the Covenants', 109.
73. SRO PA 14/3, ff 501–507.
74. Stevenson,'The Financing of the Cause of the Covenants', 109.
75. *APS*, vi, i, 567–570; SRO PA 14/4, Register of the Committee for Monies (North), 9 March–28 October 1646, ff 24–324.
76. *APS*, vi, i, 474–475; SRO PA 14/4, ff 24–324.
77. *APS*, vi, i, 474–475, 567–570; SRO PA 14/4, ff 24–324.
78. SRO PA 14/4, ff 24–324. Following the dissolution of the Fifth Session on 4 February, the Privy Council convened on 19 occassions before the commencement of the Sixth Session on 3 November 1646. Six nobles attended 50% or greater of the Council's diets; Burleigh 13 diets (68%), Dalhousie 12 diets (63%), Glencairn 11 diets (58%) and Marischal, Cassillis, and Crawford-Lindsay 10 diets (53%) each. Cassillis was listed as President at six diets and Glencairn and Lanark were listed as President at one diet each. Glencairn and Lanark were listed as President when Cassillis was absent. Four gentry attended 50% or greater of the Council's diets. Sir Thomas Hope of Craighall attended 13 diets (68%), Gibson of Durie and Hepburne of Wauchton 11 diets (58%), and Carmichael of that ilk 10 diets (53%). Sir John Smith, Provost of Edinburgh, attended 12 diets (63%). On 16 July 1646 the Council expressed its desire to Charles I that he should sign the National Covenant.

7

The Disposal of Charles I and the Rise of Conservatism, November 1646 to March 1647

The traitor Scot
Sold his King for a groat.[1]

The Sixth Session of the First Triennial Parliament, 3 November 1646–27 March 1647

By the time the Sixth Session convened on 3 November 1646 such a serious breach had emerged in the relationship between the Scottish and English Parliaments concerning the king that the parliamentary alliance was becoming increasingly strained. Under the jurisdiction and protection of the Scottish army in England, Charles I had consistently refused to reach an accomodation with Scottish negotiating demands (primarily the subscription of the National Covenant and the imposition of presbyterianism within England). In attempting to employ a balancing act with the Scottish Parliament and the rival power groups within the English Parliament, Charles only succeeded in alienating Scottish protection for himself as the price for maintaining the Anglo-Scottish parliamentary alliance. The Houses of Parliament had also claimed sole jurisdiction relating to the disposal of the king as per the crucial vote of 24 September 1646. In September 1646 the English Parliament also agreed to pay £400,000 sterling (£4,8 million Scots) to the Scottish army to leave England (half to be paid before the Scottish army left). The interim period of such a large sum being raised by the English Parliament and then being paid to the Scottish army allowed for a negotiating period concerning the disposal of the king. Hamilton had returned to Scotland following his release from Pendennis Castle in Cornwall. On 16 September the Committee of Estates, currently under the control of Hamilton and Lanark due to the absence of Argyll and Johnston of Wariston in England, had decided to suspend the issue of the king until the Sixth Session. Such a decision raised doubts that a private deal had been struck between Hamilton and Argyll concerning the king. Throughout October 1646 the Scottish diplomatic commissioners emphasised that the king was to be disposed of by joint advice and consultation with the Scottish and English Parliaments. It was against this background of events that the Scottish Parliament assembled on 3 November 1646.[2]

1. The Composition of the Sixth Session of the First Triennial Parliament

The Sixth Session was composed of 48 nobles, 50 gentry representing 28 shires, and 56 burgesses representing 48 burghs (yielding a total membership of 154). Compared to the Fifth Session, the Sixth Session witnessed a rise of 15 nobles, 13 gentry, and 24 burgesses (a total rise of 52). The total membership was higher than any of the previous sessions of the First Triennial Parliament and was equal to that of the 1643 Convention of Estates. The membership figures per estate of 3 November 1646 were similarly the highest compared to all previous sessions of the First Triennial Parliament (see appendices 3a and 3b). Thirty of the 48 nobles (62%), 23 of the 50 gentry (46%), and 20 of the 56 burgesses (36%) had also been recorded in the parliamentary rolls of the Fifth Session.[3]

Of the 28 shires represented on 3 November, 22 sent two commissioners whilst the remaining six sent only one commissioner each (Caithness, Banff, Kirkcudbright, Clackmannan, Sutherland, and Peebles). Eight of the 48 burghs were represented by two commissioners each. Allowing for the fact that the burgh of Edinburgh was legally entitled to be represented by two commissioners, seven burghs were clearly in breach of parliamentary regulations relating to burghal representation. The burghs of Dundee, Linlithgow, St Andrews, Haddington, Anstruther Easter, Dunbar, and Crail formed this burghal grouping. The parliamentary minutes of 3 November contain no evidence of any action being taken by the other two estates against the burgesses, such as ordering the removal of each one of the excess seven burgesses. This phenomenon may not only be interpreted as an attempt by the burghal estate to strenghten its parliamentary position *vis-a-vis* the nobility and the shires, but may also be regarded as an attempt by either the radicals or conservatives/pragmatic Royalists to bolster their parliamentary numbers. The Duke of Hamilton writing to Sir Robert Moray on 3 November describing that day's proceedings in Parliament also made no observation on this breach of parliamentary regulations. Fletcher of Innerpeffer (Forfar) appears to have been working as a parliamentary whip/ political manager for the Hamiltonians throughout November and December 1646 and was manoeuvring to galvanise parliamentary support among the gentry and burgesses to defend the king. Combined with Hamilton's lack of commentary on the breach in regulations by the burgesses, it may have been the case that the breach was initiated by the conservatives/pragmatic Royalists to bolster their numbers. On the other hand, the radicals may have secured the sending of dual commissioners for these burghs in order to gain increased numbers to fend off a conservative/pragmatic Royalist parliamentary revival.[4]

The only controversy which took place related to the stewartry of Kirkcudbright. On 6 November Edward Edgar (Edinburgh), acting as the spokesman for the burgesses, protested against the commissioner for the stewartry sitting in Parliament. No parliamentary commission had been received from the stewartry. William Grierson of Bargattoun (Kirkcudbright) had nevertheless represented the stewartry as a commissioner of the shire and had been included in the parliamentary rolls of 3 November. The Estates ordered that they would take the matter to their consideration and in the interim Grierson of Bargattoun was to be allowed to sit and vote in Parliament. It would appear that the commissioner for the stewartry of Kirkcudbright continued to sit throughout the session.[5]

Taken in tandem with the burghal estate breaching parliamentary rules, the controversy over the stewartry of Kirkcudbright indicates growing tension between the gentry and the burgesses. It marks a transition in the strength of the burghal estate against the other two estates. On the one hand, the burgesses had violated parliamentary rules which had provoked no adverse reaction from the nobility and gentry. On the other hand, the burgesses were quick off the mark to complain against the gentry when they had attempted (successfully) to bolster their numbers. These developments must be placed within the context of the noted emergence of a Scottish Commons and indicates the flexing of political muscle by the burgesses against the parliamentary power of the gentry.

2. The Proceedings of the Sixth Session of the First Triennial Parliament

By the time the Sixth Session convened, the Scottish diplomatic commissioners at London had already been pressing for a prorogation of Parliament.[6] On the one hand, this may have been in order to finalise negotiations with the English Parliament before presentation to the Scottish Parliament. On the other hand, there was also a desire to find appropriate financial and fiscal remedies to improve the condition of the country. According to Hamilton, the Estates

> were all unanimous that this Parliamt should not be prorogued till some remedie were found for ye easing of this Kingdomes of the heavy burdens they now lye under.[7]

Nevertheless, the crucial issues of the disposal of the king and the removal of the Scottish army from England were not discussed by the full Parliament for over a month. Instead the attention of the Estates was concentrated on the administration of the country.[8]

After the calling of the parliamentary rolls and the subscription of the parliamentary oath, 11 parliamentary members who were attending the First Triennial Parliament for the first time were required to subscribe that oath. This grouping consisted of one noble, six gentry, and four burgesses. On 10 November 10 further new members were required to subscribe the parliamentary oath. All were included in the parliamentary rolls of 3 November and consisted of one noble, three gentry, and six burgesses. In total, two nobles, nine gentry, and ten burgesses (21 in all) subscribed the parliamentary oath for the first time. Parliamentary discipline was being enforced.[9]

On 7 November the House ratified alterations in membership to the judiciary according to the 1641 act concerning Officers of State, Privy Councillors, and Lords of Session. On 30 October the king had nominated Johnston of Wariston to the office of Lord Advocate to replace Sir Thomas Hope of Craighall who had died. Similarly, since the close of the Fifth Session Charles had made several other judicial nominations. Gibson of Durie, Clerk Register, had been nominated as an Ordinary Lord of Session in place of Erskine of Innerteill. Lockhart of Lee and Belshes of Toftis had also been nominated as Lords of Session, whilst Weymes of Bogie was nominated as a Privy Councillor.[10]

Several batches of session committees were appointed in the period before Parliament turned its attention to the issue of the king. The first batch was appointed on 10 November to activate the process of parliamentary business. Four session committees were established on this date, three of which dealt with matters of a retrospective nature; the Committee for the Common Burdens, the Committee for Revising the Acts of the Committees of Estates, Processes, Monies, and Excise, and the Committee for the Accounts of Hepburne of Humbie.[11]

The Committee for the Common Burdens was essentially the successor to earlier session committees known as the Committee for Dispatches and the Committee for Managing the War which had operated during previous sessions of the First Triennial Parliament. It was not a financial committee in the sense that the previous Committees for Common Burdens had been.[12] The committee's remit was to consider the 'burdens and pressures' given in by all three estates relating not only to the condition of Scotland but also to England and Ireland. Given the current state of Anglo-Scottish relations, it is clear that the main emphasis of the Committee for the Common Burdens lay with the disposal of the king and the withdrawal of the Scottish army from England. Powers were granted from the Estates allowing the committee to answer letters remitted to it and to make dispatches without recourse to the full Parliament. Therefore the Committee for the Common Burdens and not the full Parliament was deemed the appropriate forum for discussing Anglo-Scottish relations on a British basis.[13]

Ten per estate formed the membership of the Committee for Common Burdens. The quorum was set at 14 with four per estate required to be present. Seven of the 10 nobles were conservatives/pragmatic Royalists (Hamilton, Lanark, Glencairn, Tullibardine, Roxburgh, Findlater, and Marischal), whilst three were radicals (Argyll, Cassillis, and Balmerino). Conservatives/pragmatic Royalists therefore enjoyed a majority of noble representation. Chancellor Loudoun and Crawford-Lindsay, President of Parliament, were included as supernumeraries, as were all general officers of the army who were not members of Parliament. Hence the addition of Loudoun and Crawford-Lindsay did not alter the political balance between radical and conservative/pragmatic Royalist nobles. However, the noted radical laird, Johnston of Wariston (Edinburgh), was included as one of the shire representatives. Burghal representation included noted radicals such as George Porterfield (Glasgow) and John Semple (Dumbarton). The Estates also stated that any member of Parliament was entitled to attend committee proceedings and had 'liberty to represent any overture that is sitting'.[14]

Throughout the session, the Committee for Common Burdens was referred to as the 'grand Comitte'.[15] The Committee for Common Burdens may therefore be regarded as the adoption of the institution of the Committee of

Estates on a smaller basis to sit during the session with a closely defined remit. Four nobles, eight gentry, and five burgesses had been members of the Committee of Estates of 4 February 1646. Noble common membership was split between radicals (Argyll and Balmerino) and conservatives/pragmatic Royalists (Lanark and Glencairn). Noted radicals such as Johnston of Wariston (Edinburgh) and George Porterfield (Glasgow) formed part of the gentry and burghal common grouping. Five nobles, three gentry, and two burgeses had also been included on the Committee of Dispatches formed during the Fifth Session on 1 December. Of these five nobles, Chancellor Loudoun and Crawford-Lindsay (President) were included as supernumeraries. Of the three remaining nobles, two were conservatives/pragmatic Royalists (Tullibardine and Lanark) and one was a radical (Argyll).[16]

The Committee for Revising the Acts of the Committee of Estates and the Committee for Processes, Monies, and Excise marked the second retrospective session committee fromed on 10 November. Therefore legislation of two interval committees established at the close of the Fifth Session was delegated to the consideration of a single session committee. The session committee was issued with three remits. Firstly, it was to scrutinise all acts of these committees and then report to the House. Secondly, consideration was to be given to any overtures for introducing new legislation which the committee thought expedient. Thirdly, it was to co-operate with the Lord Advocate, Johnston of Wariston (Edinburgh), and other legal officials in deciding whether or not any acts or overtures considered by the Committee for Monies (the interval committee) should be rejected before presentation to the House.[17]

Four per estate, plus two supernumeraries, formed the membership of the Committee for Revising the Acts of the Committee of Estates and the Committee for Processes, Monies, and Excise. The quorum was set at seven with two per estate required to be present. Three of the four nobles were conservatives/pragmatic Royalists (Buchan, Haddington, and Southesk) and one was a radical (Sutherland). Chancellor Loudoun and Crawford-Lindsay (President) were included as supernumeraries. Any member of Parliament was allowed to attend the committee's proceedings and was also allowed 'access and liberty to represent any overture that is sitting'.[18]

The Committee for the Accounts of Hepburne of Humbie marked the third session committee of a retrospective nature established on 10 November. Its role was to examine the financial statements and accounts of Hepburne of Humbie as Treasurer of the Army. It was composed of three per estate plus two supernumeraries (Chancellor Loudoun and Crawford-Lindsay). The quorum was set at five with one per estate required to be present. Noble representation was conservative/pragmatic Royalist. No common membership exists between the noble and gentry representatives and the previous Committee for the Accounts of Hepburne of Humbie of 12 December 1645. However, two burgesses, John Kennedy (Ayr) and George Garden (Burntisland), were included on both committees. The committee had reported to the full House by 9 December when Humbie's preparation and auditing of accounts was approved.[19]

The fourth session committee established on 10 November was concerned with the administration and organisation of bills and ratifications presented to Parliament. This adhered to the trend throughout previous sessions of the First Triennial Parliament. The Sixth Session passed 332 acts (193 of which were public acts and 139 private acts) and 45 ratifications. The full title of the committee was the Committee for Bills, Ratifications, and Losses. As well as receiving and considering all bills and ratifications, the committee was ordered to revise and consider all reports of commissions granted for trial of losses. During the Fifth Session these two specific remits had been allocated to two separate session committees; the Committee for Bills and Ratifications of 1 December 1645 and the Committee anent the Losses of 12 December. The latter committee had its commission renewed on 3 February 1646 as an interval committee and had sat between the Fifth and Sixth Sessions. That the division of such remits was not followed during the Sixth Session may well be due to the fact that the interval committee had operated efficiently in the implementation of its remit.[20]

The Committee for Bills, Ratifications, and Losses consisted of four per estate. The quorum was set at seven with two per estate required to be present. No common membership exists with the Committee for Bills and Ratifications of 1 December 1645. Two nobles (Eglinton and Buccleuch) had been included on the Committee anent the Losses of 12 December. Radical noble strength on the Committee for Bills, Ratifications, and Losses was focused on Eglinton, Buccleuch, and Coupar, whilst that of the conservatives/pragmatic Royalists was based on Dalhousie. In addition, Chancellor Loudoun and Crawford-Lindsay were included as supernumeraries.[21]

Procedural innovation was also employed by the Estates in terms of the committee structure of Parliament. Two items of parliamentary procedure were introduced on 10 November. Firstly, Chancellor Loudoun and Crawford-Lindsay, President of Parliament, were to sit as supernumeraries on all committees. This may be interpreted as a form of parliamentary executive control. Secondly, all members of Parliament were granted access to the proceedings of any committee and were free to represent any relevant overture.[22] This could have been adopted as a means of disrupting factional management of committees. The conservatives/pragmatic Royalists may have initiated and secured this ploy in order to disrupt radical organisation on committees by 'storming' committee proceedings with a body of conservative/pragmatic Royalist personnel. On the other hand, such an option would also be open to the radicals to disrupt the proceedings of committees which were being controlled by the conservatives/pragmatic Royalists.

On 25 November the House amended the various quorums of the session committees established on 10 November. The original quorum of the Committee for Common Burdens had been set at 16 with four per estate required to be present. This was modified on 25 November to two per estate, although the total figure of 16 was to remain. This indicates that the rules of 10 November governing attendance per estate were not being adhered to by the Committee for Common Burdens. In particular, it indicates that there was a deficiency in attendance by one or more of the three estates. The quorums of the Committee for Revising the Acts of the Committee of Estates and the Committee for Monies, and the Committee for Bills, Ratifications, and Losses had originally been set at seven with two per estate required to be present. The quorum of the Committee for the Accounts of Hepburne of Humbie had been set at five with one per estate required to be in attendance. The quorums of all three committees were modified on 25 November to one per estate (no totals were given). Once more, this indicates a lack of attendance at committee diets.[23]

Following the close of the day's proceedings on 10 November, Hamilton informed Sir Robert Moray that the Parliament 'is now fully consisted, our Committees named, and well chosen'.[24] Hamilton's commentary appears to indicate that the radicals had failed to secure overall control of those committees appointed and that the conservatives/pragmatic Royalists had been well-represented. Radical nobles were concentrated on the Committee for Common Burdens, but did not have exclusive membership within the noble estate. On the other session committees appointed radical nobles were in a minority. Given that the trends from 1639 onwards had revealed the voting strength of the gentry and the burgesses, it was perhaps this phenomenon that Hamilton was referring to. It also appears that the conservatives/pragmatic Royalists had been securing support within the other two estates.

Four days later on 14 November the Estates continued the Committees for War in the shires and ordered that 'the meetings and exercise of the committees of war should not be interuppted by the sitting of this session of parliament'.[25] The Committees for War were ordered to keep regular diets. For those commissioners of the shires who were members of the Committees for War in their respective shires, parliamentary attendance was to take priority over attendance at the shire level as they had been elected by their shires for parliamentary representation. This may well have been a device initiated by the conservatives/pragmatic Royalists to prevent radicals from lobbying Parliament and the capital.

The second batch of session committees was established on 28 November. Two committees were formed; the Committee for Processes, Monies, and Excise and the Committee for the Irish Business. Three per estate formed the membership of the former committee. This contrasts with a membership of seven per estate in the interval committee of 3 February 1646, the Committee for Processes, Monies, and Excise. Common membership between the two committees rested with Cassilis and Tullibardine and did not include any gentry or burgesses. However, one burgess, John Kennedy (Ayr), had been included on the Committee for Processes (session committee) of 1 December 1645. A warrant issued on 9 December 1646 also allowed John Kennedy to receive and give out public money. This warrant was only to be valid until the end of the current parliamentary session.[26]

The Committee for Processes, Monies, and Excise was issued with three remits. Firstly, it was to summon individuals who had not lent money for public use or had previously lent money and had since been repaid. Both categories were to be asked for further financial loans for public use. Secondly, the committee was to summon all delinquents who had not yet been tried for compliance with the rebels. Such delinquents were to tried and censured by the Act of Classes. Thirdly, the committee was to meet with the magistrates of Edinburgh to secure use of their excise to provide meal and maintenance for several regiments of the army. On 2 December the committee was ordered to secure an exact account of the previous excise.[27]

The Committee for the Irish Business was composed of three per estate. Burleigh was the one radical noble included. Gentry and burghal membership was based on the west coast, within the close geographic remit of Ireland. It was centred on Wigtown and Ayr for the shires and Irvine for the burghs.[28]

Prior to the discussion of the disposal of the king, the third batch of session committees was appointed on 3 and 10 December. Four per estate formed the membership of the Committee anent the Excise of 3 December. One laird, Dundas of Maner (Linlithgow), and two burgesses, John Kennedy (Ayr) and Edward Edgar (Edinburgh), had been included on the Committee for Processes, Monies, and Excise of 28 November. Of the four noble members, Lothian and Balmerino were noted radicals, whilst Glencairn and Marischal were conservatives/pragmatic Royalists. Marischal had been included on the interval committee of 3 February, as had Dundas of Maner. Whereas the Committee for Processes, Monies, and Excise had been ordered to account for the previous excise, the Committee anent the Excise was faced with the task of settling the current level of excise.[29]

The Committee for calling Subcollectors to Account and the Committee anent the Losses were the two session committees appointed on 10 December. The former committee consisted of three per estate and contained a strong conservative/pragmatic Royalist element among the nobility (Winton, Loure, and Barganie). Nevertheless, radical burgesses such as George Garden (Burntisland) and Gideon Jack (Lanark) also secured inclusion. Chancellor Loudoun and Crawford-Lindsay were included as supernumeraries. The committee's function was to examine the subcollectors concerning public money and it was to act in liaison with the Committees for War in the shires.[30]

The Committee anent the Losses was composed of four per estate with Loudoun and Crawford-Lindsay included as supernumeraries. The quorum was set at six with one per estate required to be present. Of the four noble members, two were noted radicals (Lothian and Burleigh). The Highlands and the Borders were represented in greater proportion than usual in terms of shire and burghal representation, reflecting the extent to which those areas had been effected by the civil war campaign. Only one committee member, John Forbes (Inverness), had been included on the Committee for Bills, Ratifications, and Losses of 10 November 1646. However, two nobles and one laird had been included on the Committee anent the Losses of 12 December 1645 (renewed as an interval commission on 3 February 1646). This grouping consisted of Loudoun, Crawford-Lindsay, and Falconer of Halkerton (Kincardine).[31]

The Committee anent the Losses was to consider 'the losses of the kingdom both by sea and land and receiving in, revising and considering of the supplications of parties given in thereanent'.[32] The formation of this committee raises several scenarios given the fact that its remit had been previously incorporated within that of the Committee for Bills, Ratifications, and Losses of 10 November. A separate session committee may have been established to deal with losses because of the amount of bills and ratifications which had been handed in and which required attention in the period between 10 November and 10 December. On the other hand, the extent of supplications relating to losses may have been so great as to warrant the formation of a separate session committee.[33]

Prior to the issue of the discussion of the king, the only matter of controversy which occurred was that of the parliamentary ratification of the agreement which had allowed Montrose to go into exile. The House ratified the agreement by a majority of 20 votes on 27 November, which also included a list of pardons granted by Middleton. Hamilton observed that the ratification of this agreement by the Committee of Estates was secured only 'after many houres dispute'.[34] This was in face of strong opposition from the Commission of the Kirk and illustrates an increasingly marginalised position on the part of the General Assembly and the Commission of the Kirk. The parliamentary radicals led by Argyll had also opposed the motion. On the other hand, it also illustrates the strengthened position of the conservative/pragmatic Royalist nobles, who had obviously gained the backing of a sufficient number of gentry and burgesses to secure the passage of the controversial legislation through the House. It would appear that the tactics and methods of parliamentary management which had been employed by the radicals throughout the 1640s were now being effectively exploited by the conservatives/pragmatic Royalists. Gentry and burghal voting power was now being galvanised for conservative political ends.[35]

The controversial issue of the position of the king was finally to raise its head on 15 and 16 December when crucial decisions were made by the Committee for Common Burdens. Before the Sixth Session convened, the Committee of Estates had decided that the issue of the king should be concluded by Parliament. Following the ratification of the agreement of 27 November which allowed Montrose to go into exile and the ratification of Middleton's pardons, tentative steps were made by conservatives/pragmatic Royalists to encourage Hamilton to initiate discussion of the king's position. This was described by contemporaries as the 'main business'.[36] This move appears to have emanated from the gentry who were unhappy with the present negotiations with the king and who strove to safeguard his position as King of Scots. Fletcher of Innerpeffer (Forfar) had sounded out the opinions of a large number (but not all) of the commissioners of shires and burghs and found that the majority wanted to secure the king's safety. Fletcher's conclusions were reported to Hamilton. Fletcher stressed, however, that if the issue was raised immediately in the House then a majority of 30 could be secured in favour of the king, but if the matter was delayed then such a majority would be severely reduced because the 'Argilians and the commissioners of the church intrigued so bussily'.[37] Contemporaries therefore commented on and were acutely aware of the organisational and parliamentary management skills of the radical leadership. Indeed, one week after Fletcher had conducted his original soundings, he reported that many commissioners he had previously consulted had now changed their minds and a maximum majority of only 15 votes could now be secured. In spite of advice from Hamilton of Orbiston, Justice Clerk, Hamilton refused to initiate discussion of the king at this time. Hamilton made no formal mention of the king's position until 15 December and this was only because correspodence had been received from the Scottish diplomatic commissioners at London stating that agreement had almost been reached on the payment of £200,000 sterling (£2,4 million Scots) from the English Parliament. This was to be in exchange for the withdrawal of the Scottish army from England and the surrender of the king to the English Parliament without any conditions. Hamilton's obvious reluctance to take the initiative on this crucial issue, despite advice to the contrary, was now beginning to backfire.

On 15 December the Committee for Common Burdens determined that a declaration supporting monarchical government should be issued. The king's title to the English crown was also to be supported and Charles was to be allowed to travel freely to London. Given the balance of power between radicals and conservatives/pragmatic Royalists among the nobility on the Committee for Common Burdens, it would therefore appear that the radicals under Argyll had been outmanoeuvred by Hamilton. Conservative/pragmatic Royalist nobles had secured the backing of enough gentry and burgesses on the Committee for Common Burdens to secure a majority when the vote was taken on 15 December. However, when the committee reconvened on 16 December it was agreed that the king must consent to all the Newcastle Propositions, the crux of which (from the Scottish negotiating perspective) centred on the king's acknowledgement of presbyterian church government in Scotland and England. Royal refusal of the Newcastle Propositions was to have three important repercussions. Firstly, the government of Scotland would be settled without the king and his regal sanction would be suspended. Secondly, Charles would not be allowed to come to Scotland. Thirdly, Scotland would not engage itself in England to protect the king even if he were deposed. In light of the decisions taken by the Committee for Common Burdens on 15 December several scenarios present themselves regarding the voting patterns of 15 and 16 December.

Firstly, the diet of 15 December may have been poorly attended, particularly by the gentry and burgesses. Hamilton may then have seized on this opportunity to secure the agreement of 15 December concerning monarchical government. On 16 December Argyll may have then galvanised the customary support of the gentry and burgesses for the radicals to obtain a high turnout on 16 December. Backed by the radical nobles, Argyll may then have used the support of the gentry and burgesses to push through the stringent demands agreed on 16 December. In any event, the decision of 16 December was a close and bitter one. According to Lanark, the full Parliament attended the diet of 16 December and the debates were of an intense and heated nature. This points to a full turnout of the Committee for Common Burdens. A crucial factor in swinging the vote in favour of the radicals appears to be a declaration from the Commission of the Kirk which was read to the Committee for Common Burdens. Seven of the 12 nobles (including supernumeraries), two of the 10 gentry, and two of the 10 burgesses included on the Committee for Common Burdens were also members of the current Commission of the Kirk established on 13 February 1645. Of these seven nobles, four were conservatives/pragmatic Royalists (Crawford-Lindsay, Glencairn, Tullibardine, and Lanark) and three were radicals (Argyll, Cassillis, and Balmerino). Gentry common membership consisted of Johnston of Wariston (Edinburgh) and MacDowall of Garthland (Wigtown), whilst John Semple (Dumbarton) and William Glendoning (Kirkcudbright) formed the common burghal grouping. The declaration of the Kirk stressed that the king must first subscribe the National Covenant before being allowed to return to Scotland and that the enemies of the Covenant (an obvious reference to Hamilton) were attempting to discredit the Covenant and the Anglo-Scottish alliance under the pretext of preserving the king. Given the alliance between the radicals and the Kirk and the predominance of conservatives/pragmatic Royalists in terms of noble common membership between the Committee for Common Burdens and the Commission of the Kirk, the intervention of the Kirk appears to have had the desired effect in securing the support of the majority of gentry and burgesses on the Common Burdens committee.[38]

The decision of 16 December was ratified by the House on 24 December, although a final attempt was made to secure royal agreement to the Newcastle Propositions. Seven diplomatic commissioners were named on 24 December for this purpose. If the king still refused to budge, however, then the commissioners were authorised to arrange the subsequent disposal of the king with the English Parliament. This diplomatic grouping was distinct and separate from the main contingent based in London and its commission was only to endure until the army was withdrawn from England. Two per estate, plus one supernumerary, formed the membership of the diplomatic mission of 24 December. Noble membership was balanced between radicals (Lothian) and conservatives/pragmatic Royalists (Balcarras). Hepburne of Humbie was included as a supernumerary and was not a member of Parliament as per 3 November 1646. The quorum of the residue of Scottish commissioners at London was set at two due to the fact that several of the commissioners named were currently at Newcastle and others were being sent there. Although named on 24 December, the parliamentary commission was not issued until 31 December.[39]

The culmination of events concerning the disposal of the king centred on three dates; 16 January, 30 January, and 3 February 1647. In the interim between 24 December and 16 January negotiations with the king continued. Whilst this was taking place, Parliament considered the elections of the burgh councils of Glasgow and Aberdeen (although Parliament did not legislate on Aberdeen until 6 February). The annual election of Glasgow Burgh Council had been due to take place in October 1646. This had been delayed by warrant of the Committee of Estates until such time as Parliament could consider the issue. In the meantime, the council was to be continued under the control of the radical burgess George Porterfield and his faction. Porterfield was the current parliamentary representative for Glasgow. The continuance of the Porterfield faction in power, backed by the Committee of Estates, threatened to marginalise the conservative opposition on the council. The conservatives then rushed through an election in which Porterfield was maintained in power but all other offices were filled by conservatives (26 movements in office took place). Throughout November and December 1646 the Porterfield faction, supported by the presbytery of Glasgow and the Commission of the Kirk, petitioned Parliament against this conservative coup. Therefore, on 26 December the House overturned the conservative election and ruled that there should be a return to the membership format dominated by the Porterfield faction. This was confirmed by an official election of January 1647 for Glasgow Burgh Council which secured the Porterfield faction in office (25 movements in membership took place).[40]

Parliament similarly intervened in the election of Aberdeen Burgh Council. A process had been submitted to the Committee of Estates and then on to Parliament relating to the previous election of the council. The House declared on 6 February that the election had been influenced by the presence of rebels at the time of election. Thus the election had been illegal and Aberdeen Burgh Council was elected by Parliament itself. Radicals such as Patrick Leslie, Robert Farquhar, and Alexander Jaffray were elected. In both cases of Glasgow and Aberdeen Burgh Councils Parliament had intervened to secure the ascendancy of radical cliques.[41]

The desire to supress conservatism as well as malignancy can be viewed as a counter-attack by the radicals against the growing parliamentary influence of the conservatives/pragmatic Royalists. This reassertion of radical influence was reflected in the formation of a session committee concerning malignancy. The Committee for Drawing up of the Proclamation against Malignants was established on 26 December. The committee was to revise all proclamations issued in 1641 in order to draw up a proclamation for parliamentary presentation concerning the rebels or those under censure from Kirk and State. It did not apply to those currently under parliamentary citation. The committee was composed of two per estate. Noble representation was based on conservatives/pragmatic Royalists (Glencairn and Southesk), although noted radicals such as Johnston of Wariston (Edinburgh) and John Semple (Dumbarton) were included for the shires and burghs. Whilst the shire and burgh nominees reflected the accustomed radicalism within these two estates, the inclusion of Southesk and Glencairn indicates the delicate power struggle underway between radicals and conservatives/pragmatic Royalists. The latter could not claim to be excluded from the committee, yet the combined voting strength of the shires and burghs could veto proposals which were not to the radicals' liking.[42]

By 16 January it had become clear that the king would not compromise and a vote was taken in the House to determine whether or not he should be left at Newcastle. News had already reached Edinburgh during the first week of January that an agreement had been reached between the Scottish diplomatic commissioners and the English Parliament to withdraw the Scottish armed forces and leave Charles in the custody of the English Parliament. On 16 January Crawford-Lindsay, President of Parliament, attempted to have the clause on which the vote was to be taken altered to

> Whither or not his Majestie who wes our Native King and had done so great things for the good of Scotland and thrown himselff upon ws for shelter should be delivered up to the Sectaries avowed enemies to his liffe and Government.[43]

Crawford-Lindsay's amended motion was not adopted, however, the original motion was voted on, and the Scottish Parliament voted in favour of leaving Charles I as King of Scots at Newcastle. Hamilton and Lanark recorded their disapproval and Crawford-Lindsay only agreed to sign the act in the constitutional capacity of President of Parliament and not of his own personal accord. Contemporary sources state that six nobles, four gentry, and three burgesses voted against the motion. Hamilton, Lanark, Kinghorn, Tullibardine, Elibank, and Spynie formed the opposing six noble votes. Falconer of Halkerton (Kincardine), Fletcher of Innerpeffer (Forfar), James Graham of Monorgrund (Forfar), and Sir Archibald Stirling of Carden (Stirling) formed the opposition vote from the shires. The commissioners of the burghs of Forfar, Brechin, and Tain all opposed the motion. As per 3 November 1646 no commissioners of the burghs of Tain and Forfar were recorded in the parliamentary rolls. George Steill (Brechin) was the one identifiable burgess who opposed the motion. Gentry and burghal opposition was therefore concentrated in Angus and the Mearns. It has also been estimated that around one third of the nobility were absent from the House when the vote was taken. The absence of such a large number of nobles has been attributed to several reasons. Firstly, some of the nobility were barred (presumably under the Act of Classes and other legislation) because they were Royalists and had not subscribed the National Covenant and/or the Solemn League and Covenant. Secondly, many nobles who would have been admitted to the House withdrew. Of this latter category, many knew that they were not going to vote to leave the king and interpreting the cause as a lost one, they withdrew in fear of their fortunes and estates if they were seen to be antagonising the parliamentary radicals and the Commission of the Kirk. The fact that Crawford-Lindsay had now aligned himself to Hamilton was emphasised in his correspondence with the king after 16 January. The Committee for Common Burdens ruled that this correspondence was a private one and was not addressed to Parliament. Therefore the Committee for Common Burdens refused to acknowledge the legality of the king's letters.

The final details concerning the disposal of the king were settled on 30 January and 3 February. On 30 January the Scottish army received the initial batch of £100,000 sterling (£1,2 million Scots) and on 3 February the second batch of the same amount was handed over by the English Parliament. Hence the difficult tripartite political and diplomatic situation revolving around the king had been resolved for the present. A close relationship with the English Parliament had been deemed more important than that with Charles I as King of Scots.[44]

The withdrawal of the Scottish army from England aroused controversy in the House as various factions argued over exactly what should now be done with this army when it returned home. Hamilton's argument rested on the fact that the army was required to assist the presbyterian reformation in England, although under this guise probably lay a desire to help the king militarily at some future point. Argyll, backed by the Commission of the Kirk, argued for disbanding of the army as he was wary of it being misused. The disbanding of the army was only advocated by the radicals in order to purge malignant officers and soldiers and replace them with those who had been approved by the radical leadership. Paradoxically, this may well explain the intense opposition of Hamilton and the conservatives/pragmatic Royalists to disbandment. Argyll's argument was carried and on 29 and 30 January the House ordered the army to be slimmed down to 1,200 horse, 6,000 foot, and two companies of dragoons. Although the command structure rested with Leven, effective overall control was exercised by Lieutenant General David Leslie assisted by General Majors John Middleton and John Holburne. Royalist sympathisers, as interpreted by the radicals, were excluded from the armed forces. Argyll had succeeded in securing the implementation of his policy concerning the armed forces.[45]

By 27 February the Committee for Common Burdens had settled the details concerning the disbanding of the army. On 27 February a session committee was formed to consider the accounts of the £200,000 sterling (£2,4 million Scots) transferred from the English to the Scottish Parliament. The remit of the committee was extended to consider complaints of officers and also to the complaints of soldiers towards their officers. Apart from illustrating discontent among the rank and file soldier, military discipline and control was being exerted by Parliament over the armed forces (throughout the 1640s Parliament had shown that the army was accountable to Parliament). Three per estate formed the committee membership. Of the three noble members, two were conservatives/pragmatic Royalists (Callander and Balcarras) and one was a radical (Eglinton). Callander was not included in a military capacity but as a noble member per se. No common membership exists with the interval committee of 4 February 1646, the Committee for Clearing the Accounts with England.[46]

Despite the fact that the disbanding of the army was not finally settled until 27 February, parliamentary affairs in the post-30 January period were concentrated on four areas; the extent of debt and burdens of the kingdom, financial renumeration to those who had lent money for public use or who were to be compensated, procedural developments, and the renewal of parliamentary interval commissions.

A revision of the financial affairs of the kingdom had been requested by Hamilton in Parliament. Acting on Hamilton's initiative, a new Committee for Common Burdens was established on 30 January. This was distinct and independent from the Committee for Common Burdens of 10 November 1646. The remit of the new committee was specifically of a financial nature, in keeping with the accustomed nature of previous Committees for Common Burdens. It was to examine the level of debts and burdens either owing by or to the public in the form of loaned money, loan and tax, or precepts in any other form. The committee's financial nature was emphasised by the fact that its membership was identical to that of the parliamentary interval committee of 3 February 1646, the Committee for Monies, Processes, and Excise. The commission of 3 February 1646 was renewed on 30 January 1647 and three additions were also made. In total, three nobles, two gentry, and one burgess were also members of the crucial Common Burdens committee of 10 November 1646. Two of the three nobles were conservatives/pragmatic Royalists (Tullibardine and Findlater) and one was a radical (Cassillis). Cassillis and Tullibardine, along with Cochrane of Cowdoun (Ayr) and Dundas of Maner (Linlithgow), were also members of the Committee for Processes, Monies, and Excise of 28 November 1646.[47]

Repayments of loans and compensation for destroyed land and/or loss of rents was a particular feature of the session throughout March 1647 until the close of the session on 27 March. This was clearly the work of three session committees; the Committee for Bills, Ratifications, and Losses, the Committee for Processes, Monies, and Excise, and the Committee anent the Losses. Two specific session committees were also formed in January 1647 to deal with the cases of General Major Middleton and the Duke of Hamilton.[48]

Two per estate formed the membership of the Committee for General Major Middleton's Recompense. The quorum was set at two and one per estate was required to attend. Noble membership was balanced between radicals (Cassillis) and conservatives/pragmatic Royalists (Glencairn). The radical Johnston of Wariston (Edinburgh) was included as part of the shire representation. Consideration was to be given to two issues; renumeration for Middleton's loyal service and payment of money owing to him for past arrears. In the case of Hamilton a separate session committee was not established to examine his case. Instead an earlier commission granted by the Committee for Processes, Monies, and Excise was renewed. The commission to that latter committee was likewise renewed and was to examine Hamilton's claim. Robert Hamilton of Torrens was added to the committee, although he was not a member of Parliament as per 3 November 1646.[49]

Yet the claims of Argyll to losses sustained at the hands of the rebels had required the formation of a separate session committee on 1 December 1646. Composed of three per estate, noble membership consisted of two conservatives/ pragmatic Royalists (Roxburgh and Southesk) and one radical (Cassillis). Gentry and burghal representation included radicals such as Johnston of Wariston (Edinburgh) and George Porterfield (Glasgow).[50] On 16 December 1646 a further session committee relating to losses was established, although its remit was of a regional nature. The Committee for Aberdeen, Stirling, Glasgow, and other distressed Shires and Burghs consisted of two per estate. Noble representation was balanced between radicals (Burleigh) and conservatives/ pragmatic Royalists (Southesk).[51]

Analysis of 47 items of legislation pased between 12 and 27 March provides a revealing breakdown of three forms of legislation relating to financial renumeration; firstly, relating to individuals who were to be compensated for money lent for public use, secondly, relating to those who had suffered losses due to the civil war campaign, and thirdly, relating to the reduction of fines. Twenty-three of the 47 enactments concerned the reparation of losses. The largest reparation figure awarded was that of £20,000 sterling (£240,000 Scots) to the free royal burghs for losses suffered by land and sea. This figure excluded a further £15,000 sterling (£180,000 Scots) awarded by an act of Parliament of 27 July 1644. The high amount of the awards provides a telling indication of the lobbying power and political strength of the burgesses within Parliament.

Of the remaining 22 enactments relating to losses, the value of compensation ranged from 1,000 merks (£667 Scots) to £5,000 sterling (£60,000 Scots). Hamilton was awarded £5,000 sterling (£60,000 Scots) and Tullibardine, Dunfermline, and Murray £2,500 sterling (£30,000 Scots) each. As per legislation of 26 and 27 march no exact sum is given for the amount of reparations to be paid to Argyll. However, it has been calculated that £180,000 Scots (£15,000 sterling) was paid to Argyll and £360,000 Scots (£30,000 sterling) to other Campbell chiefs. According to the contemporary observer Guthry, Argyll was to receive £30,000 sterling (£360,000 Scots) and his adherents £15,000 sterling (£180,000 Scots). Johnston of Wariston (Edinburgh) received £3,000 sterling (£36,000 Scots) as a reward for his commitment to the cause. Guthry also stated that radical ministers of the Kirk were financially rewarded but he also notes that this was kept secret, as were the amounts they received.[52]

In addition, 14 further enactments related to money paid back which had either been lent for public use/and or money that was due to those involved. Five enactments related to nobles, five related to gentry, and four related to burgesses. James Stewart, burgess of Edinburgh, and James Hamilton of Boigs were awarded £8,000 sterling (£96,000 Scots) which was to be spilt equally between them, for money which they had advanced for public use. George Jamieson (Coupar) received £32,830 Scots for money owed to him. Lauderdale was awarded £22,920 Scots, a sum due for previous contributions for public use, whilst Crawford-Lindsay received £23,799 Scots and Yester £20,000 Scots for the same purpose.[53]

Acting on reports from the Committee for Processes and Monies, three nobles and six gentry had their fines reduced. The Marquis of Douglas (having been imprisoned) had paid 25,000 merks (£16,667 Scots) of his fine. the committee recommended that he should pay a further 10,500 merks (£7,000 Scots) and that the remaining surplus should be discharged. Queensberry had been fined for delinquency and had already paid 60,000 merks (£40,000 Scots) and was due to pay a further fine of the same amount. In comparison to Douglas, the committee recommended that this should be discharged. Lord

Seaton had already paid half of his £40,000 Scots fine. It was recommended that he should only be liable for 12,000 merks (£8,000 Scots) of the the remaining £20,000. The surplus of fines to be paid by the six gentry were similarly to be discharged. Parliament accepted all such recommendations. Hence there was a general move to accommodate conservative/pragmatic Royalist nobles and gentry in their individual cases. Such a measure of financial rapprochement reflected the importance of avoiding political and parliamentary alienation of the conservatives/pragmatic Royalists. Of the 46 enactments relating to financial renumeration, 19 related to the nobility, 20 to the gentry, and six to the burgesses (of the remaining two enactments, one related to a sheriffdom and to the royal burghs).[54]

The House also enacted on 22 March that reparation of losses would not be paid to any individual who had complied with the rebels. This was in accordance with the Act of Classes and pointed to financial ruin for those who failed to comply with compulsory Covenanting oaths and obligations.[55]

The fact that the Committee for Monies and Processes was not singularly concerned with claims for losses is highlighted in two items of legislation passed on 15 March. Much of the committee's work focused on the processing of delinquents' cases. By 15 March the committee reported to the House that it was experiencing difficulties in processing the trials of delinquents. In particular, it was finding difficulty in having cases proven by witnesses. The Act of Classes had allowed the option of the death sentence as the ultimate punishment under the first class, but a trial was required before it could be decided whether or not an individual's crimes came under the first class. The Estates clarified the issue by abolishing the death sentence under the first class (suggesting political conciliation) and declared that delinquents could be examined and tried upon their own oaths. Despite the abolition of the death penalty under the first class, legislation enacted on 24 March still excluded those found guilty from all places of public trust. This applied to the Committees of War in the shires (established on 26 March) and such individuals as were barred from access from any Committee of War.[56]

Procedural developments also took place between January and the close of the session on 27 March. Five specific items of legislation were enacted. Firstly, on 19 January the House allowed the commissioners of shires and burghs to modify the membership of session committees which had been appointed to date. The gentry and the burgesses were ordered to choose alternative members to compensate for those original members who were failing to attend committee diets. The election of alternative members was to take place at separate meetings of the commissioners of shires and burghs. Those alternative members were to enjoy the same privileges as the original members. This allowed for increased parliamentary management of gentry and burghal membership of session committees. Secondly, on 21 January the Estates stated that at the close of each day's proceedings the parliamentary minutes were to be read in the House. Whether this was the result of demand from the Estates for increased parliamentary accountability or was merely a device to improve efficiency in the legislative process by reminding members of each day's work cannot be ascertained. Thirdly, on 3 February the Estates issued an ordinance concerning the commissioners of shires and burghs. It stated that from 3 February no commissioner of the shire or commissioner of the burgh could be changed, elected, called by the Clerk Register, or admitted to the House until a general parliamentary rule was established. The issue was to be considered by the Estates separately at their first possible convenience. This ordinance may have been a reaction against a possible abuse of the committee membership details of 19 January and is possibly related to the issue of the breach of parliamentary regulations on the opening day of the session. The commissioners of shires and burghs may have been putting forward alternative committee personnel who were not members of Parliament. Despite the ordinance of 3 February, the Estates permitted Archibald Sydserf, burgess of Edinburgh, as a replacement for Edward Edgar (Edinburgh) on all session committees that Edgar had been elected to. No reason is given for this, but one interpretation may suggest that the ordinance issued on the same day (3 February) had been breached to allow special treatment for Edinburgh. Alternatively, it might be argued that the ordinance did not technically apply to Edinburgh as the capital was entitled to send two commissioners and Edward Edgar may not have been in attendance prior to this date. Or, favour may have been shown to Edinburgh as it was the capital and the most powerful burgh in the kingdom. Earlier in the session, on 17 December 1646, the Estates had allowed William Purves (Dunbar) to replace James Lauder (Dunbar) and allowed Purves to sit on all committees to which James Lauder had been nominated. James Lauder had been elected as the first commissioner for Dunbar ahead of William Purves, but both are included in the rolls of Parliament of 3 November 1646. The fourth procedural development was enacted on 6 February and concerned the office of President of Parliament. Due to the absence of Crawford-Lindsay, the Estates nominated and elected Cassillis as President in his place. The use of the office of Vice-President, as employed in earlier sessions of the First Triennial Parliament, was therefore avoided. That Crawford-Lindsay had recently been appointed Treasurer may also have given rise to unease at concentrating too many offices in the hands of one powerful noble. That Crawford-Lindsay had presided in the first three sessions of the First Triennial Parliament and a new President had now been elected may also account for the fifth enactment relating to procedural development. Doubt clearly existed in the House concerning the exact format to be followed in the election of a new President. It had been stipulated that the House should make choice of the Lord Chancellor or any other the King and the Estates should appoint as President and that individual should remain President throughout the Parliament in which he was chosen and in the subsequent Parliament until the parliamentary oath had been taken and another President elected. According to the legislators, however, this rule did not specify whether or not a President could be changed during the course of several sessions of a current Parliament until the calling of a new Parliament.

Legislation of 27 March clarified the technicalities of this situation. The first act of all future sessions of Parliament, after the taking of the parliamentary oath, was to relate to the choice of a President. The chosen President would then preside in that session and would be President in the next session of Parliament until the parliamentary oath was taken and a new President elected. This clarification was probably required because Crawford-Lindsay had presided for so long and Cassillis had been chosen during a parliamentary session. Hence all current parliamentary members would be fully aware of the proper procedure regarding the election of the President of Parliament.[57]

Prior to the close of the parliamentary session, the Estates decreed that supplications which had been handed in to Parliament and had been considered by the appropriate committee, but had not yet been enacted, were to be remitted to the Committee of Estates. Supplications which were the remit of the Privy Council or the Court of Session were to be dealt with by those bodies and not by the Committee of Estates. Hence there was an attempt, perhaps by the conservatives and pragmatic Royalists, to restore the traditional authority and standing of the Privy Council and the Court of Session.[58]

The Sixth Session of the First Triennial Parliament, and with it the First Triennial Parliament itself, ended on 27 March. The Second Triennial Parliament was appointed to be held on the first Thursday of March 1648. The holding of a seventh parliamentary session had been discussed but this option had been rejected. Both the radicals and the conservatives/pragmatic Royalists favoured the calling of the Second Triennial Parliament, but for different reasons. Argyll and the radicals wanted a new Parliament in order to remove Crawford-Lindsay (who had gone over to Hamilton and the conservatives/ pragmatic Royalists) from the office of President of Parliament. The radicals were clearly worried by having a conservative/pragmatic Royalist President of Parliament who was also the Treasurer. If a seventh session had been called, then Crawford-Lindsay would have presided. Hamilton and the conservatives/pragmatic Royalists, on the other hand, favoured a new Parliament as new elections would have to be held for it. The conservatives/pragmatic Royalists were confident that they would have 'a larger number of knights and burgesses of their faction in a new Parliament than they have in the present one.'[59] Hamilton and his supporters were still clearly worried by the remaining extent of radical support within the House.

3. The Committee Structure of the Sixth Session of the First Triennial Parliament

Eighteen session committees and five interval committees have been analysed. Thirty nobles, 31 gentry, and 32 burgesses were nominated to serve on the 18 session committees. The comparative figures for the five interval committees were 30 nobles, 43 gentry, and 36 burgesses. Whilst near equality per estate is evident in the staffing of session committees, superior numbers of gentry were employed on interval committees. The bulk of the gentry were primarily concentrated on the Committee of Estates and the Committee for Plantation of Kirks and Valuation of Teinds.

Of the 18 session committees, eight had financial remits, five had remits relating to losses, and two had executive remits. The remaining three session committees were issued with military, judicial, and procedural remits respectively. Crawford-Lindsay, President of Parliament, and Chancellor Loudoun were included as supernumeraries on all session committees. With the exception of the two supernumeraries, no common membership exists between the two executive session committees for any of the Three Estates.

Conservative and pragmatic Royalist nobles were to the fore in terms of noble representation on session committees as a whole. Southesk was nominated to six session committees, Glencairn five session committees, and Lanark four session committees respectively. Radical influence was based on Cassillis (five session committees) and Burleigh (four session committees). Noble common membership of the eight financial session committees was primarily conservative/pragmatic Royalist. This 'grouping' centred on Winton, Loure, Barganie, Glencairn, Marischal, and Tullibardine. Cassillis was the only noted radical noble enjoying common membership of financial session committees. Limited noble common membership existed between the five session committees concerned with 'losses' and was based on Burleigh and Southesk, although Southesk did serve on three of those committees.

Overall total gentry membership of session committees focused on Cochrane of Cowdoun (Ayr) (six session committees), Johnston of Wariston (Edinburgh), Weymes of Bogie (Fife), and Dundas of Maner (Linlithgow) (five session committees each), and Brodie of that ilk (Elgin) (four session committees). In comparison to the nobility, gentry common membership of financial session committees was more pronounced. Dundas of Maner (Linlithgow) gained membership of four of the eight financial session committees, whilst Weymes of Bogie (Fife), Brodie of that ilk (Elgin), and Cochrane of Cowdoun (Ayr) were each included on three financial session committees. In common with the noble estate, however, gentry common membership of the five session committees relating to losses was also limited, but was based on the radical laird, Johnston of Wariston (Edinburgh).

Burghal membership of the eighteen session committees centred on John Kennedy (Ayr) (six session committees). John Semple (Dumbarton), Edward Edgar (Edinburgh), and John Hay (Elgin) each served on a total of four session committees. In line with the noted trend evident from noble and gentry common membership of financial session committees, burghal common membership of such committees was also limited. John Kennedy (Ayr) was included on three financial session committees, whilst Edward Edgar (Edinburgh), James Pedie (Montrose), and George Garden (Burntisland) were included on two financial session committees. Common membership of the five session committees relating to 'losses' was based solely on John Kennedy (Ayr), who served on two such committees.

Radical influence was reasserted in the noble representation of the five interval committees. Lothian and Chancellor Loudoun were elected to on three interval committees (60%). Eighteen nobles served on two interval committees and 10 served on one interval committee (17%). Seventeen of the 22 nobles (77%) who were included on the Committee for Plantation of Kirks and Valuation of Teinds were also included on the Committee of Estates. All nobles included on the Committee for the Exchequer were also included on the Committee of Estates. On the other hand, none of the nobles included on the Committee anent the Excise gained membership of the Committee of Estates.

Five gentry served on a total of three interval committees each; Johnston of Wariston (Edinburgh), Weymes of Bogie (Fife), Lockhart of Lee (Lanark), MacDowall of Garthland (Wigtown), and Fletcher of Innerpeffer (Forfar). Fourteen further gentry were included on two interval committees each and 24 were included on one interval. Seventeen of the 42 gentry analysed (40%) were not members of Parliament as per 3 November 1646. Sixteen of the 28 gentry (57%) included on the Committee for Plantation of Kirks and Valuation of Teinds were also included on the Committee of Estates. Four of the 10 gentry included on the Committee for the Exchequer and two of the three gentry on the Committee anent the Excise were also members of the Committee of Estates.

Burghal common membership of interval committees centred on William Glendoning (Kirkcudbright), who was included on three interval committees. Eight further burgesses were included on two interval committees and 27 were included on only one interval committee. Fifteen of the 36 burgesses analysed (42%) were not members of Parliament as per 3 November 1646. Ten of the 21 burgesses (48%) included on the Committee for Plantation of Kirks and Valuation of Teinds were also members of the Committee of Estates. None of the burgesses included on the Committee anent the Excise were included on the Committee of Estates and no burgesses were included on the Committee for the Exchequer.[60]

4. The Appointment of Parliamentary Interval Committees

Two parliamentary interval commissions, the Commission for Plantation of Kirks and Valuation of Teinds (24 March) and the Exchequer Commission (25 March), were renewed. A Committee anent the Excise Commission was formed on 10 March and a new Committee of Estates was established on 20 March.[61]

Five direct changes in membership took place in the Commission for Plantation of Kirks and Valuation of Teinds. Three previous gentry members, Douglas of Bonjedburgh, Sir Thomas Hope of Craighall, and Campbell of Auchinbreck, were now deceased, whilst Cunningham of Capringtoun was barred due to being charged with compliance with the rebels. John Maitland, 1st Earl of Lauderdale, was also now deceased. Direct replacements were provided for all these individuals. Beaton of Creich (Fife) replaced Douglas of Bonjedburgh, Brodie of that ilk (Elgin) replaced Campbell of Auchinbreck, Johnston of Wariston (Edinburgh) replaced Hope of Kerse, and John Maitland, 2nd Earl of Lauderdale replaced his father.[62] In addition, four further members per estate were added to the commission. Noble additions were conservative/pragmatic Royalist (Hamilton, Callander, and Barganie), but also included

Buccleuch.[63] The Exchequer Commission of 1 February 1645 was renewed on 25 March. Only one change in membership took place. Johnston of Wariston, Lord Advocate, replaced Sir Thomas Hope of Craighall, previous Lord Advocate.[64]

The Committee anent the Excise was instituted on 10 March. Two per estate formed the membership of the Committee anent the Excise. Noble representation was balanced between radicals (Burleigh) and conservatives/pragmatic Royalists (Southesk). One noble (Burleigh), one laird (Dundas of Maner), and both burgesses (George Jamieson and George Garden) had also been included on the parliamentary interval committee, the Committee for Monies, Processes, and Excise of 3 February 1646. Therefore there was a strong degree of continuity of personnel between the two committees. This may signify financial expertise on the parts of those individuals.[65]

A new Committee of Estates was formed on 20 March. The membership of this committee must be viewed in light of the growing tensions between the conservatives/pragmatic Royalists, led by Hamilton, and the radicals led by Argyll. On 11 March the diplomatic section of the Committee of Estates (constituted on 8 March 1645) to negotiate with the English Parliament was renewed. This contingent of the Committee of Estates was dominated by radicals. However, four of the commissioners were to be sent to England ahead of the remaining commissioners; Lauderdale, Erskine of Cambuskenneth (Clackmannan), Hugh Kennedy (Ayr), and Robert Barclay (Irvine) formed this grouping. It was significant that Lauderdale was to be sent ahead of the influential radicals Argyll and Balmerino. Following the earlier parliamentary decision to hand the king over to the jurisdiction of the English Parliament, Lauderdale had aligned himself more closely to Hamilton and Lanark. At the same time Lanark had terminated his working relationship with Argyll.[66] Jean de Montereul, the contemporary French diplomatic representative in Scotland, observed that a 'middle course' had been adopted in dispatching Lauderdale to England before the other nobles. It had been adopted to placate Hamilton and the conservatives/pragmatic Royalists who had failed to have the membership of the diplomatic section altered. According to this analysis, Lauderdale was the one noble on the diplomatic section 'least mistrusted' by Hamilton.[67] Nevertheless, although the strength of the conservatives/pragmatic Royalists was on an upward spiral throughout the parliamentary session, the radicals still had enough power to retain their control of the diplomatic section and indicates that they were still a powerful parliamentary grouping over all three estates. To counter this, however, new diplomatic instructions issued to be followed by the commissioners were of a more flexible nature. Presbyterian government and reformation were to be along the lines of the Solemn League and Covenant in England. If Charles finally accepted the Newcastle Propositions then the English Parliament was to restore him to his throne. If he refused the Scottish diplomatic commissioners were to prevent anything being implemented to his disadvantage. The tenor of these instructions was clearly that of the conservatives/pragmatic Royalists.[68]

Twenty-six nobles, 25 gentry, and 25 burgesses (76 members in total) formed the Committee of Estates established on 20 March. Numerical balance existed in the staffing levels of the three estates. The new committee witnessed a rise of seven nobles, eight gentry, and nine burgesses (24 in total), compared to the previous Committee of Estates of 3 February 1646.[69] Fifteen of the 26 nobles (58%), 12 of the 25 gentry (48%), and 12 of the 25 burgesses (48%) included on the Committee of Estates of 20 March 1647 had been included on the previous committee.[70]

With the exception of the Scottish diplomatic grouping to be sent to England, the Committee of Estates was not split into sections. The structure of the 1647 Committee of Estates did not maintain the accustomed form apparent from the 1640 Committee of Estates onwards. The membership of the 1647 Committee of Estates was also strongly based on parliamentary membership. Only one laird and six burgesses were not members of Parliament as per 3 November 1646. Three of the non-parliamentary burgesses, Sir John Smith (Edinburgh), Hugh Kennedy (Ayr), and Robert Barclay (Irvine), were on the diplomatic section and had probably been in London at the opening of the Sixth Session.[71]

The membership of the new Committee of Estates of 20 March altered the political balance between the radicals and conservatives/pragmatic Royalists in favour of the latter grouping. The conservatives/pragmatic Royalists, led by Hamilton, claimed that the majority of the Committee of Estates were aligned to himself. Even the radicals, led by Argyll, conceded that they were outnumbered within the noble representation. The radicals strongly argued, however, that they had the backing of half of the gentry and three quarters of the burgesses on the Committee of Estates.[72] The most telling indication that power had swung to the conservatives/pragmatic Royalists within the noble representation was provided by the notorious Traquair, one of the leading Incendaries of 1637–41. The rehabilitation of Traquair had commenced on 26 December 1646 when Parliament admitted him to sit and vote in the House, after appropriate approval by the Kirk and the Committee of Estates and his subscription of the parliamentary oath. Wariston had moved on 26 December 1646 that Traquair should be allowed to proceed to Newcastle to persuade Charles to sign the National Covenant. Parliament left it to Traquair whether he went or not. It would therefore appear that the radicals had allowed Traquair back into Parliament as they believed or had been persuaded that he could secure the king's signature on the National Covenant. Traquair's inclusion on the 1647 Committee of Estates had now demonstrated that the radicals had made a major strategic blunder.[73]

The influential grouping of conservative and pragmatic Royalist nobles (as per March 1647) included at least Hamilton, Morton, Tullibardine, Roxburgh, Traquair, Lanark, Callander, Lauderdale, Barganie, Crawford-Lindsay, and Glencairn. Radical nobles were clearly outnumbered. Accepting Montereul's analysis, the gentry were split between the radicals and conservatives/pragmatic Royalists and a greater majority of the burgesses were aligned to the radical camp.[74]

Conclusion

The crisis in Anglo-Scottish relations and the disposal of Charles I, now officially under the jurisdiction of the English Parliament, had produced crucial political repercussions in the parliamentary balance of power between conservatives/pragmatic Royalists and radicals. Previous parliamentary sessions of the First Triennial Parliament had witnessed a working relationship between conservatives/pragmatic Royalists and radicals, with conservative/pragmatic Royalist nobles gaining increased access to session and interval committees. The return of the influential Hamilton to Scotland and his return to parliamentary affairs provided a focal point which the conservatives/pragmatic Royalists could rally round and challenge Argyll. Nevertheless, Hamilton clearly blundered in his political judgement by refusing to take up the cause of the king during late November and early December 1646 when he was being advised to do so. By the time Hamilton decided to move on the issue a deal had already been struck between the Scottish diplomatic commissioners and the English Parliament. The refusal of Charles to accept the Newcastle Propositions had resulted in the crucial vote of 16 January (sanctioning the Scottish army to leave England and leave the king under the control of the English Parliament) and the payment of the arrears due to the Scots on 30 January and 3 February 1647. This destroyed any possible radical-conservative/pragmatic Royalist rapprochement and indicated the prevalent parliamentary strength of the radicals. By the close of the Sixth Session, conservative/pragmatic Royalist nobles were now in the driving seat and had succeeded in marginalising the radical nobles on the Committee of Estates. An unquantifiable number of gentry and burgesses, albeit a minority, had also swung over to Hamilton, although the majority of these two estates still adhered to Argyll. The scene was now set for a bitter power struggle between Argyll and Hamilton within the confines of the Committee of Estates; a battle that would be resolved in favour of the conservatives/pragmatic Royalists and would result in the Engagement of 1647–48.

NOTES

1. J.K Hewison, *The Covenanters. A History of the Church in Scotland from the Reformation to the Restoration*, volume one, (Glasgow, 1913), 441.
2. Stevenson, *Revolution and Counter-Revolution in Scotland*, 72–75; *CSPV*, 1643–1647, 292; *The Memoirs of Henry Guthry*, 231–234; Menteith of Salmonet, *The History of the Troubles of Great Britain*, 247; Burnet, *Memoirs of the Dukes of Hamilton*, 293; Clarendon, *History of the Rebellion*, IV, 212; *Some Papers Given in by the Commissioners of the Parliament of Scotland, To the Honourable Houses of the Parliament of England. In Answer to their votes of the 24 of September 1646. Concerning the disposing of His Majesties Chancellour of Scotland* (Edinburgh, 1646), 1–4; *Severall Speeches, Spoken by the Right Honourable The Earle of Loudoun, Lord high Chancellour of the Kingdome of Scotland: At a Conference with a Committee of the Honourable Houses in the Painted Chamber, October 1646* (Edinburgh, 1646), 33–45; *An Unhappy Game at Scotch and English* (Edinburgh, 1646), 1–2; Scally, 'The Political

Career of James, third Marquis and first Duke of Hamilton (1606–1649) to 1643', PhD thesis, 341.

3. *APS*, vi, i, 3–4, 95–96, 284–285, 429–430, 440–441, 474–475, 612–613. Despite the high attendance levels of 3 November 1646, Hamilton commented that the Estates had assembled on 3 November 'but in no frequent number in regard of the extraordinarie bade wedder' (SRO Hamilton Papers, GD 406/1/2098). Hamilton's comments must be taken in light of the fact that he had not attended the previous sessions of the First Triennial Parliament due to his imprisonment in England and had only been released in April 1646.
4. *APS*, vi, i, 612–613; SRO Hamilton Papers GD 406/1/2098; *The Memoirs of Henry Guthry*, 234.
5. *APS*, vi, i, 614.
6. SRO Hamilton Papers GD 406/1/2098.
7. SRO Hamilton Papers, GD 406/1/2099.
8. *APS*, vi, i, 612–856; Stevenson, *Revolution and Counter-Revolution in Scotland*, 76.
9. *APS*, vi, i, 612–613, 617.
10. Ibid, 615; *The Memoirs of Henry Guthry*, 233.
11. *APS*, vi, i, 616–617.
12. Stevenson, *Revolution and Counter-Revolution in Scotland*, 76; Stevenson, *Government Under the Covenanters*, 177.
13. *APS*, vi, i, 616; Stevenson, *Revolution and Counter-Revolution in Scotland*, 76.
14. *APS*, vi, i, 616–617.
15. SRO Hamilton Papers GD 406/1/2147
16. *APS*, vi, i, 477–478, 570, 616.
17. Ibid, 616.
18. Ibid.
19. Ibid, 617.
20. Ibid, 478, 484–485, 612–856, 616–617.
21. Ibid, 478, 616–617.
22. Ibid, 616.
23. Ibid, 616–617; 623.
24. SRO Hamilton Papers GD 406/1/2099.
25. *APS*, vi, i, 619.
26. Ibid, 476–477, 567–570, 624, 631–632.
27. Ibid, 624, 627.
28. Ibid, 624.
29. Ibid, 567–570, 624, 627–628.
30. Ibid, 632.
31. Ibid, 484–485, 572–573, 616–617, 632.
32. Ibid, 632.
33. Ibid, 616–617, 632.
34. Ibid, 623–624, 669–671; SRO Hamilton Papers GD 406/1/2104; Burnet, *Memoirs of the Dukes of Hamilton*, 294; Stevenson, *Revolution and Counter-Revolution in Scotland*, 76.
35. *The Memoirs of Henry Guthry*, 234.
36. Ibid.
37. Ibid.
38. SRO Hamilton Papers GD 406/1/2147; APS, vi, i, 616, 634; Burnet, *The Memoirs of the Dukes of Hamilton*, 306; *The Memoirs of Henry Guthry*, 234; Baillie, *Letters and*

Journals, III, 4–5; *Records of the Kirk*, 427–428; Stevenson, *Revolution and Counter-Revolution in Scotland*, 77–78; Brown, *Kingdom or Province?*, 130.

39. *APS*, vi, i, 635, 636–637, 638, 641–642, 645–646; Stevenson, *Revolution and Counter-Revolution in Scotland*, 78; *The Memoirs of Henry Guthry*, 234; *CSPV*, 1643–1647, 299–301.
40. Shepherd, 'The Politics and Society of Glasgow, 1648–1674', PhD thesis, 36–37; *APS*, vi, i, 639; *RCGA*, i, 63–64, 65, 103–104, 106, 111–112, 125–126, 126–128, 129, 140, 145, 186.
41. *APS*, vi, i, 688; *Aberdeen Council Letters*, III, 76–77; *RCGA*, i, 63–64, 65, 106, 134–135, 145, 186.
42. *APS*, vi, i, 639–640.
43. Ibid, 659–660; Burnet, *Memoirs of the Dukes of Hamilton*, 311; Stevenson, *Revolution and Counter-Revolution in Scotland*, 79.
44. *APS*, vi, i, 669; NLS Adv MS 22 1 15, ff 5–6; *The Memoirs of Henry Guthry*, 327–238; Stevenson, *Revolution and Counter-Revolution in Scotland*, 80; *Sir James Turner, Memoirs of His Own Life and Times*, T. Thomson (ed), (Bannatyne Club, 1829), 43.
45. *APS*, vi, i, 672–674, 676; *The Memoirs of Henry Guthry*, 240; Baillie, *Letters and Journals*, II, 511; Stevenson, *Revolution and Counter-Revolution in Scotland*, 82.
46. *APS*, vi, i, 669, 712.
47. Ibid, 567–570, 612–613, 616, 624, 675, 677.
48. Ibid, 616–617, 624, 632, 642, 675, 732–827.
49. Ibid, 612–613, 624, 643, 675.
50. Ibid, 625.
51. Ibid, 642.
52. Ibid, 732–827; A.I. MacInnes, 'The Impact of the Civil Wars and Interregnum: Political Disruption and Social Change within Scottish Gaeldom', in *Economy and Society in Scotland and Ireland, 1500–1939*, R. Mitchison and P. Roebuck (eds), (Edinburgh, 1988), 58–59. MacInnes lists the figures paid to Argyll and the other Campbell chiefs. The legislation of 26 March stated that the payment of Argyll's pension was to take priority over the payment of any other pensions. This was passed despite the opposition of Hamilton, Lanark, and Crawford-Lindsay. *The Memoirs of Henry Guthry*, 242, state that Hamilton was to receive £30,000 sterling (£360,000 Scots) for his losses. This was clearly a mistake on the part of the scribe.
53. *APS*, vi, i, 732–827.
54. Ibid.
55. Ibid, 771.
56. Ibid, 742, 780, 812–816.
57. Ibid, 612–613, 662, 677, 680, 686, 827–828; Stevenson, *Government Under the Covenanters*, 174–175.
58. *APS*, vi, i, 855.
59. J.G. Fotheringham (ed.), *The Diplomatic Correspondence of Jean de Montereul and the Brothers De Bellievre, French Ambassadors in England and Scotland, 1645–1648*, (SHS, Edinburgh, 1898), volume two, 80; APS, vi, i, 856.
60. *APS*, vi, i, 612–856.
61. Ibid, 727–731, 766–768, 778–779, 780.
62. Ibid, 199, 778–779.
63. Ibid, 612–613, 778–779. Lockhart of Lee (Lanark), Belshes of Toftis (Berwick), Weymes of Bogie (Fife), and Foullis of Colington (Edinburgh) were added for the gentry. Archibald Sydserf (Edinburgh), Sir Alexander Wedderburne (Dundee),

Robert Farquhar (Aberdeen), and John Short (Stirling) were added for the burgesses. Archibald Sydserf was not a member of Parliament as per 3 November 1646.

64. Ibid, 303–305, 780.
65. Ibid, 567–570, 727–731.
66. Ibid, 731, 766–768; Stevenson, *Revolution and Counter-Revolution in Scotland*, 85; *Montereul Correspondence*, volume two, 13; Burnet, *Memoirs of the Dukes of Hamilton*, 313.
67. *Montereul Correspondence*, volume two, 64.
68. Stevenson, *Revolution and Counter-Revolution in Scotland*, 85–86.
69. *APS*, vi, i, 570–571, 766–767.
70. Ibid, 546, 570–571, 766–767.
71. Ibid, 612–613, 766–767; *APS*, v, 282–284. Gibson of Durie, Clerk Register, was the one laird who was a non-member of Parliament, although he was an Officer of State. John Scott (Edinburgh), Archibald Todd (Edinburgh), and James Stewart, General Collector of the Excise, were the three remaining burgesses who were non-members of Parliament.
72. Stevenson, *Revolution and Counter-Revolution in Scotland*, 87; *Montereul Correspondence*, volume two, 70–81, 83. Montereul's breakdown of party allegiances is not entirely clear. Two points can be taken from his analysis. Firstly, the radicals only had the support of around eight nobles on the Committee of Estates. Secondly, the radicals also had the backing of the supernumeraries apart from one or two.
73. *APS*, vi, i, 638–639; Stevenson, *Revolution and Counter-Revolution in Scotland*, 87.
74. Party alignments cannot be quantified at this stage for the gentry and burgesses. Certainly radicals such as Johnston of Wariston were included, but many of the other gentry had parliamentary experience. The political alignment of the gentry can only be analysed in terms of the operation of the Committee of Estates, 1647–48 and analysis of the Engagement Parliaments. The assertion that 75% of the burgesses supported Argyll has further credibility as the many of the burgesses were leading radicals, such as Robert Barclay, John Semple, Archibald Sydserf, John Kennedy, George Porterfield, Hugh Kennedy, Robert Cunningham, and William Glendoning. What cannot be quantified, however, is how many nobles, gentry, and burgesses 'changed sides' as events developed.

8

The Ascendancy of the Conservatives and Pragmatic Royalists: the Engagement and the Engagement Parliament of 1648

> The affaires of this poore Kingdome, hath been of late, moulded in so many heads, gon through so many hands, translated into so many formes, and shapes, by men of such different principles, and interests, that its almost impossible to give an exact account, or true series of the managing of them, whereby any man may either satisfie himselfe, or others.[1]

From 1639 until 1647 it had been the Scottish Parliament and Scottish military intervention in England in alliance with the English Parliament which had been of primary importance in determining the political course of the English Civil War within the confines of the British archipelago. Following the close of the Sixth Session of the First Triennial Parliament, it had become increasingly apparent that Scottish influence, in British terms, was on the wane. The Independent faction, under Oliver Cromwell, was now the dominant power group in the English Parliament and had no intention of imposing the Solemn League and Covenant on the English kingdom. The kidnapping of Charles in June 1647 by the New Model Army, controlled by the Independents, tranformed Anglo-Scottish relations. It was to result in the Engagement Treaty of December 1647. Military invasion of England once more took place, this time to secure the king. It was an invasion led by the Scottish conservatives and pragmatic Royalists who had secured control of the Committee of Estates and were now the dominant force within the Scottish Parliament.[2]

The Operation of Parliamentary Interval Committees, March 1647–February 1648

Sederunts of the Committee of Estates are recorded between 30 March 1647 and 28 February 1648. Four subcommittees of the Committee of Estates were established, three of which were set up at the first meeting of the committee on 30 March 1647. The Committee for Losses, the Committee for Accounts, and the Committee for Farming the Excise were all established on 30 March 1647. The Committee for the Bills was formed on 6 July 1647.[3]

The Committee for Losses consisted of one noble, five gentry, and one burgess. Its political orientation was radical and included Balmerino, Johnston of Wariston (Edinburgh), and James Stewart (Edinburgh). Two of the other gentry, Belshes of Toftis (Berwick) and Weymes of Bogie (Fife), had been members of the Committee anent the Losses of 10 December 1646. An additional laird and ally of Hamilton, Fletcher of Innerpeffer (Forfar), had been included on the Committee for Bills, Ratifications and Losses, of 10 November 1646.[4]

The composition of the Committee for Accounts of 30 March 1647 was identical to that of the Committee anent the Excise, which sat as a parliamentary interval committee. The Excise Commission was to examine all public accounts remitted to the Committee of Estates and was then to report its conclusions to that committee as a whole. The Committee of Estates also established a subcommittee on 30 March 1647 which was to liaise and co-operate with the Excise Commission. The Committee for Farming the Excise was formed to take over one specific function of the Excise Commission, thus allowing that commission to concentrate on examining public accounts. Two per estate formed its membership. None of its members were included on the Excise Commission. One radical noble, Balmerino, and one conservative laird, Fletcher of Innerpeffer (Forfar), had been included on the Committee anent the Excise, of 3 December 1646. Of the remaining members on the Committee for Farming the Excise, Barganie and Lockhart of Lee (Lanark) were conservatives/pragmatic Royalists, whilst Sir John Smith (Edinburgh) was the only noted radical.

The Committee for Bills of 6 July 1647 consisted of only one per estate. None of the three members had been included on the Committee for Bills, Ratifications, and Losses of 10 November 1646. Noble representation (Barganie) and gentry representation (Cochrane of Cowdoun) was conservative/pragmatic Royalist, whilst James Stewart (Edinburgh) was a radical.[5]

The Committee of Estates was remarkably slow to react to the abduction of the king and political inertia is apparent. In May 1647 the Scottish diplomatic commissioners had announced that a coup by the New Model Army or the Independents would result in a Scottish invasion to secure the king. It was not until August 1647, several months later, that the Committee of Estates began to act, despite the fact that special diets had been held on 11 June to discuss the issue.[6]

On 10 August the committee stated that it would continue to convene on a permanent basis in Edinburgh until the situation in England concerning the king was satisfactorily resolved. Diets of the committee between 12 August and 19 August all centred on this issue. Argyll had returned to the capital from the west where he had been with the army since May. Argyll's return may have had the effect of forcing some sort of decision by the committee. On 19 August instructions were issued to those Scottish diplomatic commissioners presently in London (Lauderdale, Erskine of Bandeth, Hugh Kennedy, and Robert Barclay). The English Parliament was to be asked to take the king out of the control of the New Model Army to London and attempt to secure his assent to the Newcastle Propositions. Chancellor Loudoun and Lanark were to be sent to England to consult with the king; they were to inform him of the concern of the Committee of Estates for his safety and were to inform him that it was the committee's opinion that he should be restored to the English throne. In contradiction of the Scottish diplomatic warning of May 1647 relating to a military invasion of England, the Committee of Estates clarified the instructions which had been issued on 19 August. On 20 August the committee enacted that those instructions were not intended to infer a military engagement nor weaken the union between the two kingdoms. This was passed primarily because Hamilton managed to outmanoeuvre Argyll. Argyll had interpreted the diplomatic instructions as too royalist in nature. Hamilton counter-protested that the instructions should not be detrimental to the king's interest and it was this that secured the support of the majority of the committee, despite further attempts by Argyll to get it suppressed.[7]

The power struggle between Argyll and Hamilton on the Committee of Estates was intensified by the debate over whether or not the army should be disbanded, given the fact that the military campaign against the rebels had been concluded. Argyll argued in favour of retention of David Leslie's army principally because of the precarious situation of the king and the threat to the Solemn League and Covenant by the rise of Independency. On the other hand, Hamilton advocated that it should be disbanded as it was now an unnecessary burden on the country. Both arguments may well have been a disguise for more ulterior motives; Hamilton was probably wary of a military force which could be employed by Argyll in a future military takeover of the Committee of Estates.

Matters came to a head concerning the issue of the army on 8 September and 12 October. At the diet of 8 September the Committee of Estates voted in favour of Hamilton's policy option and the army was to be disbanded on 20 October. The Act for Disbanding the Army was formally enacted by the committee on 11 September. Argyll was absent at both diets of 8 and 11 September.

Eight nobles, 11 gentry, and six burgesses were present at the 8 September diet. Hamilton, Loudoun, Crawford-Lindsay, Glencairn, Traquair, Lanark, Callander, and Barganie all attended the diet. Despite the radical presence of Johnston of Wariston (Edinburgh), Sir John Smith (Edinburgh), James Stewart (Edinburgh), and John Kennedy (Ayr), the superior numbers of conservative and pragmatic Royalist nobles ensured that only a minority of gentry and burgess votes was required to secure Hamilton's motion.[8]

The factional struggle between Hamilton and Argyll continued and Hamilton's victory proved to be short-lived. A further meeting of the Committee of Estates was called for 12 October to reconsider the vote. The trial of strength between Hamilton and Argyll was resolved in Argyll's favour, but only after three days of intense debate. On 15 October it was determined that the army would not be disbanded until the Second Triennial Parliament met in March 1648. However, this motion was only passed by one vote and a reduction in pay was forced on the army.

Eighteen nobles, 23 gentry, and 18 burgesses attended the diet of 15 October (59 individuals in total). All nobles present at the diets of 8 and 11 September were also present on 15 October diet, except for Loudoun, Lanark, and Callander. The loss of these votes was vital to Hamilton and was worsened by the fact that Argyll was present on 15 October, reducing Hamilton's factional power even further. This is highlighted by the fact that all gentry and burgesses who had been present at the diets of 8 and 11 September were also in attendance on 15 October. A significant number of gentry and burgesses had realigned themselves to Argyll. Fourteen nobles, 17 gentry, and 16 burgesses (47 individuals in total) attended all diets from 12 to 15 October inclusive.[9]

Although Argyll had defeated Hamilton in the attempt to disband the army, the diplomatic negotiations with Charles were coming increasingly under the control of the conservatives and pragmatic Royalists. Lauderdale, Lanark, and Loudoun were now the three principal negotiators with the king, who had escaped to the Isle of Wight from the New Model Army. Lauderdale and Lanark were aligned to Hamilton and favoured an acceptable deal with the king. Although Loudoun was Argyll's traditional ally and kinsman, he was still sufficiently concerned about the king's fate as to secure a deal that would guarantee his safety. On 11 October the Committee of Estates had nevertheless made it clear that Argyll was free to join the Scottish diplomatic team negotiating with the English Parliament whenever those commissioners requested his presence. Therefore while negotiations with the king were controlled by the conservatives and pragmatic Royalists, the Scottish diplomatic commissioners at London were desperately attempting to secure the ends of the Solemn League and Covenant.[10]

After several months of secret negotiations the 'Engagement' was struck between Lanark, Loudoun, and Lauderdale and Charles I in December 1647. The Scots guaranteed to defend the rights and authority of the king from the New Model Army and the Independents. It was agreed that he should be allowed return to London from the Isle of Wight in order to reach an accommodation with the English Parliament. In return, Presbyterianism was to be imposed on England for a trial period of three years and free trade between the kingdoms was to be established. The legislation of the First Triennial Parliament was to be ratified and debts owed to the Scottish Parliament were to be paid. Charles was also to attempt to establish closer union between the two kingdoms. In what amounts to a remarkable degree of power in British terms, Scots were to be employed in equal numbers as the English in foreign negotiations, Scots were to be represented on the English Privy Council (Englishmen were also to sit on the Scottish Privy Council) and were to be employed in places of trust in the royal household. The king or the Prince of Wales was to reside in Scotland at intervals. Such executive terms are remarkably similar to Covenanting negotiating demands of 1640 and constitute the attempt of the conservatives/pragmatic Royalists to redefine Anglo-Scottish relations. For the third time within a decade, the political balance of the British archipelago had been redirected away from the dominant southern kingdom towards its weaker Scottish sister. The momentum of events had swung towards initiatives taken in Scotland and the Engagement agreement was to result in a full-scale military invasion of England in 1648 in favour of the king.[11]

The Committee of Estates itself was not formally informed of the signing of the Engagement until 2 January 1648. Sir John Chiesly, formerly an adherent of Argyll, but now an ardent supporter of the Engagement, carried out this task (Chiesly was rewarded by the king with the office of Master of Requests). Loudoun and Lauderdale reported to the Committee of Estates on 10 February and 15 February 1648. A majority of the committee approved the diplomatic conduct of Loudoun and Lauderdale and their signing of the Engagement Treaty. Approval was given despite strong opposition from the Commission of the Kirk and in particular from Argyll, Lothian, Balmerino, and Balcarras on the Committee of Estates. Concerns were also expressed that no parliamentary committee should have the power to engage the nation in war without full parliamentary approval. The Engagement settlement was thereby viewed by its opponents as an abuse of the powers and privileges of Parliament.

Eighteen nobles, 19 gentry, and 19 burgesses (56 individuals in total) attended the diet of 10 February. The comparative attendance figures for 15 February are 21 nobles, 19 gentry, and 19 burgesses (59 individuals in total). All nobles, gentry, and burgesses who attended the diet of 10 February also attended the diet of 15 February. The approval of the Engagement by the Committee of Estates marked the ascendancy of the conservatives over the radicals in terms of faction and the victory of the policy of Hamilton against Argyll in terms of personal rivalry. Nevertheless, the treaty was not to be implemented until approved by the Second Triennial Parliament (due to meet in March 1648).[12]

One hundred and seven sederunts of the Committee of Estates are recorded between 29 March 1647 and 28 February 1648. The quorum of the committee was set at nine and two per parliamentary estate were required to be present. These rules were adhered to in all 107 recorded sederunts. Attendance data reflects the importance of contemporary events and the intense factional struggle taking place. Argyll attended 70 of the 107 diets (65%) and Hamilton attended 48 diets (45%). Chancellor Loudoun was present at 64 diets (60%). Argyll's cause was aided by the presence of Cassillis (63 diets, 59%) and Eglinton (50 diets, 47%). This was supplemented by radical support from the gentry and the burgesses, notably Johnston of Wariston (Edinburgh) (84 diets, 79%), James Stewart (Edinburgh) (74 diets, 69%), Sir John Smith (Edinburgh) (73 diets, 68%), John Kennedy (Ayr) (67 diets, 63%), and John Semple (Dumbarton) (51 diets, 48%).

Conservative/pragmatic Royalist strength was primarily noble based and focused on Crawford-Lindsay (99 diets, 92%), Barganie (73 diets, 68%), and Traquair (51 diets, 48%). In addition, the noted conservative, Lockhart of Lee (Lanark) attended 80 diets (75%), whilst Fletcher of Innerpeffer (Forfar), one of Hamilton's parliamentary agents attended 67 diets (63%).[13]

A non-commissioned grouping of two nobles, two gentry, and one burgess attended various diets of the Committee of Estates. Lord Belhaven attended only one diet, that of 28 February 1648, which was the last recorded diet of the Committee of Estates of 1647–48. On the other hand, Tweeddale attended 34 diets (32%), including the crucial diets of 10 and 15 February 1648 when the

Engagement was approved of. Sir Archibald Stirling of Carden (Stirling) attended only one diet, that of 12 October 1647. Hamilton of Orbiston also attended only one diet. George Garden (Burntisland) attended one diet only, that of 12 August when the position of the king was under discussion. It would appear that conservatives were being brought on to secure the passage of the Engagement settlement, although George Garden was a noted radical burgess.

In the absence of Chancellor Loudoun, Crawford-Lindsay was President of the Committee of Estates on 40 occasions (37%). Hamilton was never recorded as President. The fact that Crawford-Lindsay was favoured as President as opposed to Hamilton indicates the exercise of realpolitik. Hamilton did not preside at any diets. This would have been too controversial a political move to make. It would be capitalised on by Argyll who could then pressure a sufficient number of gentry and burgesses to hesitate from withdrawing their support from the conservatives (however fragile that support may have been).

The key issue which would require the attention of the Second Triennial Parliament was identified by William Ross, a contemporary observer based in Edinburgh. Ross commented that 'When the Parliament sits here the great question will be, whether they will condescend for an Army to passe into the Kingdome of England.'[14]

The First Session (I) of the Second Triennial Parliament, 2 March–11 May 1648

The factional struggle continued into the arena of the elections to the First Session of the Second Triennial Parliament. The Engagement leadership successfully managed/interfered in the elections of the shire and burgh commissioners to secure a parliamentary majority. The radical parliamentary faction was now in a clear minority. Both Argyll and Hamilton had intervened in the election of the Provost of Edinburgh by Edinburgh Burgh Council. The Provost would automatically be entitled to attend Parliament as one of the two commissioners of the burgh and was extremely influential within the burghal parliamentary estate. Archibald Sydserf was re-elected as Provost, despite attempts by Argyll to have him removed. Archibald Sydserf had become a strong supporter of Hamilton and the Engagement settlement and had attended 78 out of 107 diets (73%) of the Committee of Estates between 29 March 1647 and 28 February 1648. Moreover, nobles who had deliberately avoided sitting in earlier Parliaments now took their places. Nineteen nobles recorded in the parliamentary rolls of 2 March 1648, had not been present in Parliament as per 3 November 1646.

Jean de Montereul, a French diplomatic representative in the pay of Cardinal Mazarin, who was present in Scotland at this time, made several observations on Scottish factionalism. Montereul identified three distinguishable factions. The radical faction, allied with the Kirk, strongly opposed the Engagement and continued to demand that the Charles should meet their religious terms. It also opposed the raising of an army to save the king. A second faction, led by Traquair and Callander favoured a direct miltary alignment with the king to restore him immediately to his English throne. A third faction favoured the raising of an army but only with the specific purpose of suppressing Independency in England. In spite of these different factions, Montereul stressed that 'the Hamilton faction is absolutely the most powerful in this Parliament.'[15]

1. The Composition of the First Session of the Second Triennial Parliament

Deficiencies exist in the parliamentary rolls for this session which limit extensive analysis (see appendices 4a and 4b).[16] Fifty-six nobles are recorded in the parliamentary rolls. This figure is higher than any of the six sessions of the First Triennial Parliament, but is also equal to noble attendance as per 22 June 1643 (the 1643 Convention of Estates) and the parliamentary session of 17 August 1641 (where Charles I was himself present). Compared to the final session of the First Triennial Parliament, there was a numerical increase of eight nobles (see appendices 2a, 2b, 3a, 3b, and 4a). These figures as a whole indicate the importance the nobility placed on the current session. Indeed, Baillie remarked that there were 'Never so many noblemen present in any of our Parliaments; near fyftie Earls and Lords'.[17] In this instance, Baillie's technical awareness was slightly off the mark.

Figures for the gentry and burgesses have been established on a maximum and minimum basis (see appendices 4a and 4b). A maximum of 53 gentry representing 29 shires or a minimum of 47 gentry representing 26 shires were present in Parliament, 2 March 1648. The corresponding figures for the burgesses are maximum of 57 burgesses representing 56 burghs or a minimum of 49 burgesses representing 48 burghs.[18] Minimum figures are indicative of those gentry and burgesses *definitely* listed in the rolls of 2 March 1648. Based on minimum attendance figures for the gentry and the burgesses, there was a reduction of two gentry and seven burgesses compared to 3 November 1646.[19]

Based on minimum attendance figures, 37 of the 56 nobles (66%), 22 of the 47 gentry (47%), and 25 of the 49 burgesses (51%) listed in the rolls of 2 March 1648 are also included in the previous rolls of 3 November 1646. This constitutes a core grouping between the two sessions. On the other hand, 25 of the 47 gentry (53%) and 24 of the 49 burgesses (49%) listed in the rolls of 2 March 1648 had *not* been present in Parliament on 3 November 1646. Compared to the staffing levels of November 1646 eight of the 26 shires listed in the 1648 rolls had replaced both commissioners with new personnel. Five shires witnessed no changes in membership over the two sessions, whilst six shires replaced one commissioner only. With the exception of the burgh of Edinburgh which could send two commissioners, 24 burghs retained the same commissioner of over both sessions, whereas 23 burghs elected a new commissioner.[20]

Empirical parliamentary evidence can be analysed in several ways *vis-a-vis* factionalism. Firstly, the majority of the nobles who sat in both sessions were pro-Engagement and were supplemented by the presence of 19 additional nobles. Secondly, it would also appear that the Hamilton faction had secured the support of not only a sizeable portion of the 22 gentry who had sat in both sessions, but also that of the 25 new gentry in the 1648 Parliament. Indeed, Johnston of Wariston only managed to get elected through the patronage of the Marquis of Argyll. He secured Wariston's election for the shire of Argyll by providing him with land that satisfied the necessary property qualification.[21] Thirdly, burghal membership as per 2 March 1648 was split between 'new burgesses' (compared to 3 November 1646) and those who had served in both sessions. Either the Hamilton faction could rely on the support of the majority of both groupings of burgesses or they had only been partially successful in the management of the burghal elections.

In common with Montereul, Robert Baillie, writing on 27 March 1648, attempted to assess the nature and extent of factionalism. This provides a useful gauge to measure the above scenarios. Baillie concluded that only eight or nine nobles were radicals. He identified this group as consisting of Argyll, Eglinton, Cassillis, Lothian, Arbuthnot, Torpichen, Ross, Balmerino, Coupar, Burleigh, and 'sometimes the Chancellour and Balcarras'.[22]

> All the rest, with more than halfe of the barrons, and almost halfe of the burgesses, especiallie the greater tounes, Edinburgh, Perth, Dundee, Aberdeen, St Andrews, Linlithgow, ran in a string after Duke Hamilton's vote.[23]

The marriage of contemporary commentaries and analysis of empirical parliamentary data has indicated the extent to which the Hamiltonians had penetrated the shires and burghs, the traditional domain of radicalism throughout the 1640s.

In terms of the operation of parliamentary politics, the radicals were further weakened, according to Baillie, because 'For us none did speak but Argyle and Warriston, and sometimes Cassillis and Balmerinoch'.[24] The opposing faction enjoyed the support of Hamilton, the Treasurer, Lanark, Lauderdale, Traquair, Glencairn, Cochrane, and Sir James Lockhart of Lee (Lanark), who were 'all able spokesmen'.[25] Baillie concluded that within a few days of the opening of the parliamentary session, 'we found the Parliament, two parts for one, otherwise affected than we wished'.[26]

2. The Proceedings of the First Session of the Second Triennial Parliament

The parliamentary legislative programme consisted of 64 enactments (47 relating to public legislation and 17 to private legislation) and 10 ratifications. Parliamentary proceedings focused on three specific areas; disputed elections to the Parliament, the ratification of the Engagement Settlement, and preparations for a military invasion of England.[27]

Following the calling of the parliamentary rolls and the subscription of the parliamentary oath, Hamilton secured an immediate victory in the appointment of the new President of Parliament. Despite the opposition of Argyll, Chancellor Loudoun was installed as President instead of the three other radical candidates (Balmerino, Cassillis, and Burleigh) approved of by his kinsman Argyll. Chancellor Loudoun was elected as President on a factional basis (to avoid having an ally of Argyll as President) and not on a constitutional basis of trying to merge the two offices.[28]

Seven cases of disputed elections were dealt with between 2 and 7 March. All were concerned with commissioners of the shires; Inverness, Berwick, Perth, Clackmannan, Wigtown, Banff, and Aberdeen. Only two disputed elections were actually approved by the House. MacDowall of Garthland and Agnew of Lochnaw had been originally been elected to represent the shire of Wigtown. A rival commission had been produced by Adair of Kinhilt and James Ross of Balneill. MacDowall of Garthland and Agnew of Lochnaw were present in Parliament as per 2 March. Parliament approved of the original commission. The commission granted to Sir Alexander Abercrombie of Birkinboig and John Lyon of Troupe to represent Banff was also approved of by the Estates. Both lairds were also present in Parliament on 2 March. New elections were ordered to be held in the cases of three shires; Perth, Clackmannan, and Inverness. Commission had been granted to Mercer of Adie and Ruthven of Frieland to represent the shire of Perth. A supplication had been presented to Parliament disputing this election. The 1587 Act relating to the land qualification of 40 shillings allowing a vote in the election of commissioners of the shires had been abused. The House rejected the commission and ordered a new election to be held. As per the parliamentary rolls of 2 March, Sir Patrick Ogilvie of Inchmartin and Sir Thomas Blair of Balthyok represented the shire of Perth. The fact that new elections were ordered by Parliament on 6 March suggests that once the new elections had been held, the names of the new commissioners may have been inserted in the parliamentary rolls. The commission of Erskine of Cambuskenneth and Meldrum of Tullibodie to represent the shire of Clackmannan was also rejected, because the 1587 Act had once more been abused, and new elections were ordered to be held. No commissioners for the shire of Clackmannan are recorded in the parliamentary rolls of 2 March. Two commissions had been produced for the shire of Inverness; one to Fraser of Brae and a Colonel Fraser and the other to Sir John MacKenzie of Tarbet and Hugh Rose of Kilravock. No commissioners for the shire of Inverness are recorded in the parliamentary rolls of 2 March. Both commissions were rejected and new elections were to be held. The gentry and freeholders of the shire were instructed to elect commissioners favourable to religion, crown and country. In the case of the shire of Berwick, the House approved the election of one of the commissioners, Sir Harry Home of Heidrig, but rejected the election of the other commissioner, Alexander Home of Plandergaist, on the grounds that he could not have been elected for the shire at the time of election as he did not possess the necessary qualifications. Both commissioners are present in the parliamentary rolls of 2 March.

In only one case of disputed elections was the issue remitted to the consideration of a parliamentary session committee. Two commissions had been produced for the shire of Aberdeen; one had been issued to Fraser of Phillorth and Udnie of that ilk, and the other had been issued to Forbes of Craigievar and Forbes of Echt. Fraser of Phillorth and Udnie of that ilk are recorded in the parliamentary rolls of 2 March. Acting on a protestation from Skene of that ilk and Kennedy of Kermukes relating to the abuse of electoral regulations by the sheriff of the shire, Earl Marischal, a session committee was established to consider the sworn oaths of Marischal, Fraser of Phillorth and Udnie of that ilk. Skene of that ilk and Kennedy of Kermukes had represented the shire of Aberdeen in the last session of the First Triennial Parliament. One per parliamentary estate formed the membership of the session committee established on 7 March. All were leading figures of their respective parliamentary estates; Glencairn represented the nobility, Hepburne of Humbie (Haddington) represented the gentry, and Sir Alexander Wedderburne (Dundee) represented the burgesses. On 8 March the commission granted to Fraser of Phillorth and Udnie of that ilk received parliamentary approval.[29]

Clear evidence therefore exists that the terms of the 1587 Act were being abused. On 4 March Parliament issued an ordinance relating to the election of commissioners. This legislation was constitutional and was not initiated on a factional basis. No noble, nor any other individual without voting rights regarding the election of commissioners of the shires, was allowed to attend the actual meeting of the gentry and freeholders of the shires when elections took place. In particular, those without the necessary property qualification had been participating in the electoral process. If such instructions were not followed, then any election contrary to them would be declared null and void. This suggests that several nobles were exerting pressure on the electors of the commissioners of the shires within their own geographic domain. The fact remains, however, that all disputed elections were settled in favour of the Hamilton faction. Paradoxically, this may suggest that it was the radicals who were abusing the terms of the 1587 Act.[30]

Following the settlement of all disputed elections, the conduct of the Scottish diplomatic commissioners in London was approved of on 9 March. This constituted parliamentary approval (but not ratification) of the Engagement settlement itself. On 10 March the quorum levels of all parliamentary session committees were settled. One per estate and an attendance of a majority of the total membership of any committee constituted the quorum levels. Thereafter, five parliamentary session committees were established on 10 March; the Committee for Dangers, Remedies, and Duties, the Committee for the General Commissioner and other Public Accounts, the Committee for Overtures and Laws, the Committee for Bills and Supplications, and the Committee for Revising the Books and Acts of the Committees of Estates and Excise.[31]

The Committee for Dangers, Remedies, and Duties was issued with three remits. It was to consider the imminent threats to religion, the Covenant, the king, and monarchical government. These were to be considered on a British basis (Scotland, England, and Ireland) and were not to be restricted to Scottish interests. Policy options were to be formulated by the committee for dealing with any such dangers. It was a 'close committee for the greatest affaires'.[32] In essence, the Committee for Dangers, Remedies, and Duties was the descendant of parliamentary session committees from sessions of the First Triennial Parliament such as the Committee for Managing the War and the Committee for Dispatches. Six per estate, plus one supernumerary, formed its membership. The Hamilton faction dominated noble representation and consisted of Hamilton, Crawford-Lindsay, Lanark, Lauderdale, and Callander. Argyll would not have been included on the committee, but it was Hamilton himself who supported Argyll's membership. It has been estimated that only five out of the total 18 members were of the Argyll faction. Argyll, Johnston of Wariston (Argyll), George Porterfield (Glasgow), and William Glendoning (Kirkcudbright) were identified as four of this grouping. The fifth member identified was not on the original committee. However, two of the gentry members were noted conservatives Fletcher of Innerpeffer (Forfar) and Lockhart of Lee (Lanark), whilst Archibald Sydserf (Edinburgh) was a conservative placeman. Chancellor Loudoun, President of Parliament, was included as a supernumerary. All six nobles, four of the six gentry, and five of the six burgesses had been included on the Committee of Estates of 20 March 1647. Contemporary pamphlets suggest that the Committee for Dangers had operated as a 'Sub-Committee' of the Committee of Estates at least during February 1648 and that it 'inclines to have an Army' in opposition to the Kirk.[33]

By 17 March the committee had reported to the House and its commission was renewed. Three changes in burghal membership took place. In addition, Loudoun was not named as a supernumerary in the renewed commission. George Porterfield (Glasgow), William Glendoning (Kirkcudbright), and John Short (Stirling), all of whom were adherents of Argyll, were purged from the committee. They were replaced by George Bell (Linlithgow), James Robertson (St Andrews), and Thomas MacBirnie (Dumfries). In relative terms, the Hamilton faction had increased its political muscle on the committee. The fact that the replacements were from different burghs indicates that the primary aim was political and was not based on non-attendance on the part of those burgesses. The renewed committee was also ordered to meet in secret behind closed doors. It was given power to have complete control over the manning of the garrisons of Berwick and Carlisle and only employ those who adhered to the Hamilton faction. This constituted a clear breach of Anglo-Scottish treaties of 1641 and 1643 by which neither country was authorised to garrison Berwick and Carlisle. It resulted in an ineffectual and unsuccessful protest by 47 (unspecified) members of Parliament. Baillie argued that this controversial motion concerning Berwick and Carlisle was quickly passed at this juncture because 'Lord Callander's partie' was threatening to desert Hamilton. This group, 'which is great', allegedly had a keen eye on the prize of Berwick.[34]

The Committee for the General Commissioner and other Public Accounts was to consider the accounts of the General Commissioner, Weymes of Bogie, and all other accounts and monies not already accounted for. Three per estate formed its membership. Noble membership was conservative/pragmatic Royalist (Ethie, Barganie, and Cochrane). With the exception of George Garden (Burntisland), no adherents of Argyll were included in the gentry and burghal representatives. Two of the nobles (Barganie and Cochrane) had been included on the Committee of Estates of 20 March 1647.[35]

The Committee for Overtures and Laws was to consider all overtures handed in to Parliament. Where appropriate, it was to draw up overtures for enactment. Noble membership was radical (Cassillis, Buccleuch, and Balmerino). Chancellor Loudoun was included as supernumerary. All three nobles, one laird and two burgesses had been included on the Committee of Estates of 20 March 1647. Cassillis, Buccleuch, and Balmerino may have been included in order to provide a parliamentary role for radical nobles, as all bar Argyll had been excluded from the main session committee. On the other hand, it also suggests that the radical nobles could not be completely ignored.[36]

Four nobles, four gentry, and three burgesses formed the membership of the Committee for Bills and Ratifications. Noble membership was exclusively conservative/pragmatic Royalist, and consisted of Tullibardine, Perth, Southesk, and Traquair. Chancellor Loudoun was included as a supernumerary. Two nobles, one laird, and all three burgesses had been included on the Committee of Estates of 20 March 1647. Only one burgess, John Forbes (Inverness), and Loudoun had been included on the Committee for Bills, Ratifications, and Losses of 10 November 1646.[37]

The remit of the Committee for Revising the Books and Acts of the Committees of Estate and Excise centred on the revision of all acts of the Committee of Estates and the Excise Commission since the close of the last session of the First Triennial Parliament. Three per estate formed its membership. Noble membership was conservative/pragmatic Royalist. One of the gentry members, Fullarton of Corsbie, was not a member of Parliament as per 2 March 1648. No member had been included on the Committee of Estates of 20 March 1647.[38]

Of the four session committees appointed on 10 March, the Committee for Dangers, Remedies, and Duties was clearly the most important. The dominance of the Hamilton faction on the committee and the breach of Anglo-Scottish diplomatic agreements on the renewed commission of 17 March marks an attempt by one particular faction to invest powers in a parliamentary committee outwith the control of the full Parliament. Indeed, Argyll and his faction argued that the powers awarded to the Committee for Dangers, Remedies, and Duties constituted a breach of the 1640 act which abolished the Lords of the Articles. After an official protest by Argyll was ignored, Argyll led more than 40 members of Parliament out of the House. This grouping was forced to return on pain of losing its seats. Even Chancellor Loudoun, President of Parliament, made it clear that he signed the renewed commission in an official and not a personal capacity. Nevertheless, it was estimated that the Hamilton faction had a parliamentary majority of between 30 and 36 votes over the Argyll faction. Despite moves to refuse Argyll and his followers to return to the House, Hamilton and Traquair succeeded in having the Argyll faction summoned to return. Primarily Hamilton and Traquair instigated this move to avoid presenting their enemies with a picture of divided opinion in Scotland, but they were probably also wary of Argyll raising an extra-parliamentary force which could possibly align itself with the Independents in England.[39]

The Hamilton faction, now in dominant control of parliamentary proceedings, faced strong opposition to the Engagement from the Kirk and moves were initiated to placate the Kirk and secure its support. Following the appointment of the most important session committees on 10 March, three per estate were appointed on to meet with the Commission of the Kirk to establish a mutual working relationship. This move was initiated by the gentry and the burgesses. Burleigh, Innes of that ilk (Elgin), and Sir Alexander Wedderburne (Dundee) were the three such commissioners. That a leading radical noble was included can partly be explained by the fact that the Commission of the Kirk would be more prepared to form a working relationship if initiated by one inclined to their own beliefs than by a leading noble member of the Hamilton faction. Indeed, shortly afterwards the original Committee for Dangers, Remedies, and Duties issued a declaration stressing that a military invasion was necessary in order to secure religious reform in England as opposed to saving the king. This had been nullified by the terms of the renewal of the commission to the Committee for Dangers, Remedies, and Duties on 17 March.

On 22 March a formal session committee was established to consider the opposition of the Commission of the Kirk. On the same date, Lauderdale and Lanark informed Charles in a confident manner that 'We can bodly say we have the Major Vote the Parliament clear'.[40] The Committee concerning the Desires of the Commission of the General Assembly was composed of eight per estate. Apart from Argyll, noble membership was composed of the leading conservative/ pragmatic Royalist nobles. Hamilton, Crawford-Lindsay, Roxburgh, Lauderdale, Traquair, Lanark, and Callander. Fletcher of Innerpeffer (Forfar) and Lockhart of Lee (Lanark) were noted conservative gentry members, whilst Johnston of Wariston (Argyll) was the only noted radical included. Archibald Syderf (Edinburgh) was the noted representative of the Hamilton faction included, whilst radical interests were served primarily by George Porterfield (Glasgow). Chancellor Loudoun was included as a supernumerary. All six nobles, all six gentry, and four of the six burgesses on the Committee for Dangers, Remedies, and Duties of 17 March were also included on the Committee concerning the Desires of the Commission of the General Assembly of 22 March. Loudoun was also included on both committees as supernumerary. Two of the radical burgesses removed from the original committee of 10 March, George Porterfield (Glasgow) and William Glendoning (Kirkcudbright), were also members of the committee of 22 March. This marks an increased role for the radicals, but is unsurprising given the radical nature of the Commission of the Kirk anyway. Two nobles, two gentry, and three burgesses included on the Committee concerning the Desires of the Commission of the General Assembly were actually included on the Commission of the Kirk of 31 August 1647. Argyll and Crawford-Lindsay, Johnston of Wariston (Argyll), MacDowall of Garthland (Wigtown), George Porterfield (Glasgow), John Kennedy (Ayr), and William Glendoning (Kirkcudbright) formed this grouping. They may have been included as an attempt to accommodate Argyll and his faction under the control of a parliamentary session committee controlled by Hamilton, as opposed to driving that faction further into the hands of the Kirk.[41]

The Commission of the Kirk and the Committee concerning the desires of the Commission of the General Assembly convened between 22 and 27 March. The Commission of the Kirk itself had been sitting throughout March and April. Parliament reported on 27 March and emphasised that invasion was necessary to secure Presbyterianism in England from the dangers of Independency, which in turn was necessary to free the king from the hands of the Independents. Indeed, the securing of religion was deemed the principal cause of Engagement. The king would also be obliged to give royal sanction to acts relating to the Solemn League and Covenant. Arguments were thus being subtly articulated to attempt to gain the support of the Kirk to work in tandem with the dominant parliamentary faction. Such propaganda was incorporated in legislation enacted on 11 April. Not only did it indicate a formal constitutional move to satisfy the Kirk, but it also marked an attempt to provide a justification for military invasion by exerting demands which the English could not possibly accept. According to such legislation, the establishment of Presbyterianism in England had been deliberately hindered, the Solemn League and Covenant had not been implemented by the English Parliament and negotiation with the king had been carried out without Scottish agreement. The New Model Army, under the control of the Independents, was to be disbanded and the king was to proceed to London. Propaganda document though it was, it nevertheless succeeded in winning over the parliamentary opposition to war with England. There were only four votes recorded against the act, including Argyll, Cassillis, and Johnston of Wariston. Therefore significant numbers of the Argyll faction had approved the act, primarily because of the clauses relating to religion. However, the concessions to the Kirk alienated the support of Callander and Traquair who abstained from the vote.[42]

Party discipline among the Argyll faction had been retained by 20 April. On that date Parliament issued a declaration which indicated that unless the demands of 11 April were met then a military invasion of England would be undertaken. This declaration was formulated and issued without consultation with the Kirk. The desire to secure religion was only a ploy to secure the support of the Kirk. When the declaration was passed, Argyll led over 40 of his faction out of the House.[43]

Attention could now be concentrated on the actual preparations for military invasion of the southern kingdom. On 18 April the Estates had placed the kingdom in a 'posture of defence'. According to Lanark, this was designed as a ploy, 'under pretence whereof we mean to raise our army'.[44] By this point, Lanark commented that Loudoun 'hath intirely deserted us, and not only joyned with them, but endeavours by all means imaginable to divide us among ourselves'.[45] New shire committees of war and shire colonels were established on 18 April. On 10 May the Burgh Council of Edinburgh was appointed as committee of war in its own right. In an attempt to secure the backing of the Kirk, any individuals found guilty under the first or second class of the 1646 Act of Classes were barred from inclusion on the shire committees. Nevertheless, several shires would appear to have been under financial and economic strain. On 23 March the Committee for the Overburdened Shires had been established to identify those shires which were finding difficulty in maintaining troops and companies of foot. The levying of a new army, composed of 27,750 foot and 2,760 horse, was not ordered until 4 May. In terms of military organisation, they were headed by appointees of Hamilton, Lanark, and Callander. The command structure of the military was purged quite simply because Hamilton and Lanark were well aware of the fact that 'the Scots Army was then headed, and conducted by those who were of another partie; Argile having the greatest influence on the most considerable Commanders.'[46] Maintenance levels for the army and orders for ammunition were issued on 9 May. Leven, who was hostile to the Engagement, was removed as General of the armed forces and was replaced by Hamilton himself. Callander was appointed Lieutenant General. Baillie noted that from a radical perspective, this marked an uneasy conciliation between Hamilton and Callander. Parliament was then adjourned to 11 May 1648 in order to enable members of Parliament to participate in the levying of troops.[47] The political significance of the new military command structure of the armed forces under the Hamiltons was not underestimated by contemporaries:

> For now the Hamiltons have not only the pen and the purse of Scotland, (the Dukes brother Lanerick being Secretary, and his brother in law, Treasurer)...But they have the sword settled in their hands by authority.[48]

3. The Committee Structure of the First Session of the Second Triennial Parliament

Twelve session committees and five interval committees have been analysed. Twenty-four nobles, 25 gentry, and 23 burgesses were included on the 12 session committees. Equality per estate existed in the staffing levels of session committees. Only nine nobles, 27 gentry, and 11 burgesses formed the total membership field of interval committees. Three gentry and two burgesses analysed for session committees were not members of Parliament as per 2 March, albeit all were included on only one session committee each. The corresponding figures for interval committees were 18 non-parliamentary gentry and two non-parliamentary burgesses. The skew in terms of non-parliamentary gentry on interval committees can be explained by the fact that three interval committees were regional and were composed of a majority of non-parliamentary gentry. Loudoun was included on all 12 session committees, primarily in the capacity of Chancellor and President of Parliament.

That radical influence, although limited, was still in existence, was reflected in the inclusion of Argyll, Cassillis, Johnston of Wariston (Argyll), and George Porterfield (Glasgow) on three session committees each. Furthermore, the two non-parliamentary burgesses included on one session committee each were both radicals; Sir James Stewart (Edinburgh) and Robert Barclay (Irvine). This would appear to be significant in that the radicals had succeeded in penetrating through the dominant Engager influence in the House.

In terms of the overall structure of session committees, Southesk (four session committees), Hamilton, Crawford-Lindsay, Lauderdale, Lanark, and Callander (three session committees each) were playing a prominent role. Foullis of Colington (Edinburgh), Dundas of Maner (Linlithgow), and Hepburne of Humbie (Haddington) gained access to four session committees. Four further gentry, including Lockhart of Lee (Lanark) and Fletcher of Innerpeffer (Forfar), were included on three session committees. In comparison, Sir Alexander Wedderburne (Dundee) was included on four session committees. Six further burgesses, including Archibald Syderf (Edinburgh), were included on three session committees.[49]

Limited common membership of the five interval committees is apparent over all three estates. This is unsurprising given the fact that three were regional committees. All nine nobles were members of only one interval committee. Seven were members of the Committee of Estates and the remaining two nobles belonged to the Excise Commission. Twenty six of the 27 gentry and nine of the 11 burgesses were members of only one interval committee. Weymes of Bogie, General Commissioner and Treasurer of the Army, Archibald Sydserf (Edinburgh), and Patrick Leslie (Aberdeen) were members of two interval committees in total. Bogie and Sydserf were members of identical interval committees (Excise Commission and the Committee of Estates).[50]

4. The Appointment of Parliamentary Interval Committees

Five parliamentary interval committees were appointed on 11 May; the Committee of Estates, the Excise Commission, the Commission for the Burned and Wasted Lands in Nairn, the Commission for the Burned and Wasted Lands in the Shire of Elgin and Forres, and the Commission for the Burned and Wasted Lands in Banffshire. The latter three interval committees had remits of a local nature and were primarily composed of non-parliamentary gentry. They were concerned with the calculation of the monthly maintenance within their respective geographic domains.

The Committee of Estates consisted of six per estate and three supernumeraries (one noble and two gentry). Hence total membership amounted to 21. Compared to the previous Committee of Estates established on 20 March 1647, the committee of May 1648 witnessed a reduction of 19 nobles, 17 gentry, and 19 burgesses (55 members in total, including supernumeraries). Such a notable scaling down in membership levels, virtually identical over all three estates, can be explained by several factors. Firstly, the majority of parliamentary members were involved in the levying of troops in their localities. Secondly, the committee was only to convene for a few weeks and was to take no major policy decisions. Thirdly, there was limited conservative/pragmatic Royalist dominance over the radicals and it was imperative that radical influence be minimised.[51]

Including supernumeraries, all seven nobles, six of the eight gentry, and three of the six burgesses had also been members of the Committee of Estates of 20 March 1647. Unsurprisingly, Engager heavyweights such as Lauderdale, Crawford-Lindsay, Callander, and Hamilton himself were all members.The need to maintain a close watch over the radical leadership was reflected in the inclusion of Argyll and Johnston of Wariston. On 11 May, after the commission had been issued, the House stated that David Douglas (Edinburgh) was to replace Archibald Sydserf (Edinburgh), Hamilton's placeman as Provost of Edinburgh. Given the political situation, it can be assumed that David Douglas was also suitable to Hamilton's political liking. Two members of the Committee of Estates were to be sent to Ireland, although the names of such commissioners are not specified. The Committee of Estates of 11 May 1648 was under the clear control of supporters of the Engagement.[52]

The Excise Commission was staffed by two per estate. Radical influence was also evident with the inclusion of Burleigh and George Garden (Burntisland), albeit Southesk and Archibald Sydserf (Edinburgh) were also present. Weymes of Bogie, General Commissioner and Treasurer of the Army, was included as a supernumerary. John Jossie, burgess of Edinburgh, was appointed Treasurer of the Excise. The previous Excise Commission had been incorporated into the powers of the Committee of Estates of 20 March 1647. In addition to Bogie and Sydserf, both gentry members, Dundas of Maner (Linlithgow) and Cockburn of Clerkington (Haddington), had also been included on the Committee of Estates of 20 March 1647.[53]

5. The Operation of Parliamentary Interval Committees, 12 May–27 May 1648

Nine sederunts of the Committee of Estates are recorded between 12 and 27 May. Argyll and Johnston of Wariston refused to take their seats on the Committee of Estates. Lanark attended all nine diets and Callander attended seven diets. Loudoun, Hamilton, Crawford-Lindsay, and Lauderdale all were present at six diets. Two nobles, Roxburgh and Traquair, who had not been included on the committee as per 11 May, also attended several diets. The noted conservative laird, Lockhart of Lee (Lanark), is recorded in seven sederunts. Innes of that ilk (Elgin) attended all nine diets although he was not commissioned to sit on the committee as per 11 May 1648. Archibald Sydserf (Edinburgh), attended eight diets, despite the fact that David Douglas (Edinburgh) had originally been appointed by Parliament on 11 May to replace Archibald Sydserf. On 23 May, however, David Douglas was appointed to replace John Kennedy (Ayr). John Kennedy (Ayr) was not commissioned to sit on the Committee of Estates as per 11 May and was associated with the radicals. Excluding those burgesses who attended diets although they were not officially commissioned to, the remaining four burgesses on the Committee of Estates attended no diets. Therefore, the proceedings of the Committee of Estates were dominated by Engager nobles and were backed by gentry and the Provost of Edinburgh.[54]

As part of the preparation for the invasion of England, military affairs formed the principal focus of the attention of the Committee of Estates. It was concerned with issues such as the raising of levies and negotiations relating to the movement of forces between Scottish armed forces in Ireland to the Scottish mainland. By 16 May, however, problems had arisen relating to the manning of the shire committees of war. Several nominees to the committees were refusing to accept their charges and give their oaths. The Committee of Estates therefore barred any such individuals from admittance to shire committees of war. On 19 May the Committee of Estates was notified that Balmerino had been appointed one of the colonels of the shire committee of Edinburgh but despite continual requests had refused to take his place. Foullis of Colington (Edinburgh), one of the other colonels of the shire, was therefore instructed to proceed with the raising of levies without the co-operation of Balmerino. On 23 May the Committee of Estates was also informed that the town of Glasgow had refused to carry out the levying of its quota of foot. Hence the Burgh Council of Glasgow was cited before the Committee of Estates. Two members of the Council, William Lightbodie and Peter Johnston, appeared before the Committee of Estates on behalf of the Burgh Council of Glasgow on 27 May. Both were to be committed to Edinburgh Tolbooth and the remainder of the Council was to be committed by 31 May under the pain of 10,000 merks as the punishment for not only refusing to obey the levy orders but also attempting to create open hostility to the Engagement. By 2 June over 50% of the members of the Burgh Council of Glasgow were imprisoned in Edinburgh Tolbooth. On 14 June a new election for the Burgh Council of Glasgow was held, controlled by the Committee of Estates, and the council which had been purged by the radicals in 1645 was reinstated. Such evidence indicates that support for the Engagement was by no means universal.[55]

The First Session (II) of the Second Triennial Parliament, 1 June–10 June 1648

1. The Composition of the First Session (II) of the Second Triennial Parliament

No parliamentary rolls are available for this parliamentary session. Therefore no comparisons can be made in terms of total membership, movement per estate and individual membership per estate between 2 March and 1 June 1648 (see appendices 4a and 4b).

2. The Proceedings of the First Session (II) of the Second Triennial Parliament

Twenty-six enactments (23 of which related to public business) and 13 ratifications constituted the legislative programme of the June 1648 session. The parliamentary session concentrated on the final preparations for military invasion of England and the appointment of a new Committee of Estates.[56]

In technical terms, the proceedings of 1 to 10 June did not constitute a new parliamentary session. Consequently, there was no requirement to elect a new President and Loudoun continued in that office. It also appears that the Committee of Estates was continuing to meet, regardless of whether or not this had been authorised by Parliament. This had a constitutional precedent with the Committee of Estates of 1643–1644 continuing to meet during the 1644

Convention of Estates. Reference is made in the parliamentary records of 1 June to the 'committee of 24' which was to receive and consider all supplications handed in to Parliament. In essence, this committee was therefore operating along the same lines as the Lords of the Articles and followed the procedure of what had happened unofficially in 1641. Additions of three per estate were also made to this committee. Noble additions were primarily conservative/pragmatic Royalist (Dunfermline and Barganie) but also included the radical Balmerino.[57]

Parliament authorised the Committee of Estates on 2 June to appoint two of each estate to form a session committee to assist the Commissioners of the Excise. It was also to be allowed to operate as an interval committee. No membership details are provided. Dispute had emerged by 10 June concerning the office of Clerks of the Excise. Gibson of Durie, Clerk Register, and James Campbell, current Clerk of the Excise, both disputed the rights of the other to hold the office. On 8 June two per estate had been appointed to hear the case, but it is unclear whether or not this constituted the session committee which was to assist the Commissioners of the Excise. In any event, the commissions of 1644 and 1646 granted to James Campbell to be Clerk of the Excise were repealed and the Clerk Register was given the right to choose the replacement.[58]

The act of the Committee of Estates of 16 May, which barred all those from membership of the shire committees of war who refused to accept their charges and administer the necessary oath, received parliamentary ratification on 6 June. On 8 June an ordinance was issued relating to the garrisons and provisioning of the armed forces. On 7 June the House had refused to consider concessions issued by the English Parliament (in essence the Newcastle Propositions), a move which finally alienated Chancellor Loudoun from the conservatives and drove him over to the Argyll faction with which he had previously been aligned. The rebuttal of 7 June stimulated the initiation of legislation on 9 June which emphasised that the preservation of the ends of the Covenant, the safety of the king and the continuance of the union between the two kingdoms were the principal reasons for invasion. This was directed primarily against the Kirk and was in response to petitions from presbyteries and synods in the localities. Hence the events of 7 June had illustrated that concessions from the English Parliament would not prevent a military invasion. Moreover, the legislation of 9 June stressed that the commands and orders of Parliament and the Committee of Estates were to be obeyed. Further legislation of 9 June was directed at the opposition of the Kirk to the Engagement. It was in direct response to legislation of the Commission of the Kirk of 5 June which had instructed presbyteries to censure ministers who preached in favour of the Engagement. According to parliamentary legislation of 9 June, those ministers who openly supported the Engagement were promised the security of their stipends and glebes during their lifetimes. Therefore open bribery was being practised in the cat and mouse struggle between Kirk and Parliament in the attempt to divide the Kirk and secure further support for the Engagement.[59]

All members of Parliament and all other subjects in the shires and burghs were required by legislation of 10 June to subscribe the oath which stated that the Engagement Parliament had been a 'free and lawful parliament'.[60] Hence the Hamilton faction employed earlier precedents from 1640–41 to attempt to secure national subscription of its political aims. At the close of the session all bills and supplications which had been presented to Parliament, but not yet been dealt with, were remitted to the Committee of Estates. All acts of the Committee of Estates which had sat during May 1648 were ratified on 10 June. The next parliamentary session was appointed to be held on the first Thursday in March 1650.[61]

3. The Committee Structure of the First Session (II) of the Second Triennial Parliament

No session committees were openly appointed during the session, possibly because the Committee of Estates was continuing to meet. One interval commission, the Committee for Plantation of Kirks and Valuation of Teinds, was renewed on 10 June. A new Committee of Estates was appointed on 9 June.[62]

Forty-six nobles, 56 gentry, and 56 burgesses in total were employed on the two interval committees. Eighteen nobles, 18 gentry, and seven burgesses were included on both interval committees. Seven of the 18 nobles were radicals; Argyll, Loudoun, Eglinton, Cassillis, Lothian, and Buccleuch, Balmerino. Johnston of Wariston (Argyll) was the only noted radical laird included on both committees. Two of the seven burgesses were noted radicals, George Garden (Burntisland) and Robert Cunningham (Kinghorn), whilst Archibald Sydserf (Edinburgh) was a noted conservative. Twenty-eight nobles, 38 gentry, and 49 burgesses were included on only one interval committee.

Parity per estate is apparent in the staffing levels of the gentry and burgesses, both of which outstripped that of the nobility. An identical number of nobles and gentry were included on both the Committee of Estates and the Committee for Plantation of Kirks and Valuation of Teinds, whilst only a small minority of burgesses were included on both committees.[63]

4. The Appointment of Parliamentary Interval Committees

The Commission for Plantation of Kirks and Valuation of Teinds initiated in 1641 and renewed in 1644 and 1647 was further renewed on 10 June 1648. Six gentry and three burgesses were added to the committee. One of the burghal additions, George Porterfield (Glasgow), was a noted radical.[64]

The new Committee of Estates of 9 June was composed of 36 nobles, 35 gentry, and 36 burgesses. It was supplemented by 13 supernumeraries, consisting of four nobles, five gentry, one burgess, and three military officials. Including supernumeraries, 40 nobles, 40 gentry, 37 burgesses, and three military officials (120 members in total) formed the membership of the Committee of Estates. Compared to the previous Committee of Estates of 11 May 1648, there was a rise of 32 nobles (including supernumeraries), a rise of 33 gentry (including supernumeraries), and a rise of 31 burgesses (including supernumeraries). The total rise in membership amounted to 99 members (including military officials who were included as supernumeraries on the commission of 9 June).[65]

With the exception of Thomas MacBirnie (Dumfries), all nobles, gentry, and burgesses were included on both Committees of Estates of 11 May and 9 June.[66] Opponents of the Engagement such as Argyll, Balmerino, Cassillis, and Johnston of Wariston were included on the Committee of Estates of 9 June, but they were in a clear minority compared to the majority of members who supported the Engagement. According to Burnet, Hamilton and his faction had secured a Committee of Estates which was 'sure to their Designs'.[67] Contemporary sources also indicate that the Committee of Estates of 9 June was invested with considerable powers. As well as being in control of levying forces, negotiating with the king and the English Parliament and having control over the collection of the excise, it also enjoyed full powers to supress domestic hostility and/or insurrection against the invasion of England. Any individuals involved in armed uprising against the authority and proceedings of Parliament and/or the Committee of Estates or involved in liaison or correspondence with the enemies of the Engagement were to be punished. All holders of public office in the shires and burghs were required to adhere to the commands of Parliament relating to the Engagement; any public office-holder who either failed or refused to do so was to be removed from office. The Committee of Estates was also to divide itself into two sections (as per 1643); one was to reside at Edinburgh and the other to accompany the army.[68]

5. The Operation of Parliamentary Interval Committees, 12 June–4 September 1648

Sixty-nine sederunts of the Committee of Estates are recorded between 12 June and 4 September 1648. Noble attendance was dominated by four conservative/pragmatic Royalist nobles; Crawford-Lindsay attended 61 diets (88%), Cardross 56 diets (81%), Lanark 52 diets (75%), and Southesk attended 45 diets (65%). Crawford-Lindsay presided at 55 diets. Only three gentry are recorded in more than 35 diets. Hamilton of Orbiston (Renfrew) is recorded in 48 sederunts (70%), Sir Harry Gibb in 38 sederunts (55%), and Udnie of that ilk (Aberdeen) in 37 sederunts (54%). Only two burgesses attended 35 or more diets; Archibald Sydserf (Edinburgh) and Edward Edgar each attended 38 diets (55%). Two nobles and two gentry who were not included in the commission to the Committee of Estates of 9 June attended various diets. The quorum level of nine, with two per estate required to be present, was adhered to at all diets.[69]

The Committee of Estates divided itself into an Edinburgh section and an army section on 3 July. Only details of membership of the army section are given in the committee register. Fifteen nobles, 11 gentry, nine burgesses, and three military officials constituted the membership of the army section. Hamilton, Callander, Crawford-Lindsay, and Lauderdale were the leading nobles on the army section. A residue of 25 nobles, 32 gentry, and 28 burgesses was left on the Edinburgh section.[70]

Twenty sederunts of the Committee of Estates are recorded prior to the division of the committee on 3 July. Of those nobles included on the army section, Crawford-Lindsay attended 19 of the 20 diets, Lanark 17 diets,

Barganie 12 diets, and Lauderdale 10 diets. Crawford-Lindsay attended 42 diets of the Edinburgh section after 3 July, whilst Lanark attended 35 diets. The comparative figures for Lauderdale and Barganie are nine and ten diets respectively.

Of those gentry included on the army section, Sir Harry Gibb, Weymes of Bogie, Dundas of Arnieston, Foullis of Collington, and Gibson of Durie all attended diets of the Edinburgh section. John Milne, John Jossie, Alexander Crawford, and John Auchterlony formed the corresponding grouping for the burgesses. Considerable cross-over existed in attendance between the army section and the Edinburgh section. Crawford-Lindsay, Lanark, Barganie, Sir Harry Gibb, John Milne, and John Jossie formed the central core of army section members involved in this cross-over.[71]

Conclusion

Following the close of the final session of the First Triennial Parliament on 27 March 1647, a power struggle ensued between the parliamentary factions of Argyll and Hamilton. This power struggle was ultimately decided in favour of Hamilton. By December 1647 the Argyll faction, now a minority on the Committee of Estates, had been outwitted. The conservatives and pragmatic Royalists had secured the signing of the Engagement Treaty to rescue Charles from the English Independents. This victory had been secured by winning over a majority of gentry and burgesses on the Committee of Estates. By the time the Engagement had been approved by the Committee of Estates, the conservatives/pragmatic Royalists were already intervening in the electoral process in the elections to the Second Triennial Parliament. When the Second Triennial Parliament met in March 1648, the Hamilton faction was now the dominant force, having successfully managed the elections, albeit there was still a radical presence within the House. In the parliamentary session from March to June 1648 preparations for a military invasion of England to secure the king, under the guise of protecting the Covenant, were undertaken despite strong opposition from the Kirk. A contemporary English pamphleteer lamented that 'the Covenant is made the stalking horse to every designe; And may be a Caution to all to take heed how Wee trust pollliticians with Religion'.[72] The rout of the Engagement army by Cromwell at the Battle of Preston in August 1648 paved the way for the Whiggamore Raid, the coup d'etat by western radicals, and the installation of a regime of extreme radicals; a regime propped up by the protection of Cromwell and his armed forces. The conservatives and pragmatic Royalists had been crushed in military terms and ousted from political power. The Engagement had failed.

NOTES

1. *The Scots Cabinet Opened. Wherein you have a short and full Account of the secret Transactions of the late affaires, by the Scots Commissioners with the King and Parliament,*

and the invisible steps, by which wee are brought to a new warre,(London, 1648), (1). This is a reference to England and the English Parliament, although I think the comments are also particularly apt for the Scottish context.

2. NLS MS 2263 History of Events 1635–1662, folio 196. Lynch, *Scotland, A New History*, 276; F.D. Dow, *Cromwellian Scotland 1651–1660*, (Edinburgh, 1979), 5; I. Donnachie and G. Hewitt (eds.), *A Companion to Scottish History*, (London, 1989), 67; A.I MacInnes, 'The First Scottish Tories', *SHR*, 67, (1988), 57.
3. SRO PA 11/5, Register of the Committee of Estates, 29 March 1647–28 February 1648, ff 3–218, 6, 40.
4. Ibid; *APS*, vi, i, 616–617, 632.
5. SRO PA 11/5, folio 6; *APS*, vi, i, 627–628, 727–731.
6. SRO PA 11/5, folio 40; *APS*, vi, i, 616–617.
7. SRO PA 11/5 ff 31, 59–72, 72, 75; Stevenson, *Revolution and Counter-Revolution in Scotland*, 91–92; Lynch, *Scotland, A New History*, 276; *Montereul Correspondence*, volume two, 240.
8. SRO PA 11/5 ff 77–78, 89; Stevenson, *Revolution and Counter-Revolution in Scotland*, 92–93.
9. SRO PA 11/5 ff 92–93, 113–119; Stevenson, *Revolution and Counter-Revolution in Scotland*, 93; *Montereul Correspondence*, volume two, 287–288, 294.
10. SRO PA 11/5 folio 113; Stevenson, *Revolution and Counter-Revolution in Scotland*, 94.
11. Stevenson, *Revolution and Counter-Revolution in Scotland*, 94, 97–98; Donaldson, *James V–James VII*, 336–337; Donnachie and Hewitt, *A Companion to Scottish History*, 67; Cowan, *Montrose for Covenant and King*, 259–260; Dow, *Cromwellian Scotland*, 5; Levack, *The Formation of the British State*, 201–202; S.R Gardiner (ed.), *Constitutional Documents of the Puritan Revolution*, (3rd edition, Oxford, 1906), 347–352.
12. SRO PA 11/5, ff 210–211; SRO Scott of Harden Papers, GD 157/1637; Stevenson, *Revolution and Counter-Revolution in Scotland*, 98–99; *Montereul Correspondence*, volume two, 392, 399, 407; *A Message from the Estates of Scotland to the English Commissioners at Edinburgh* (London, 1648), (2).
13. SRO PA 11/5, ff 3–218; Stevenson, *Government Under the Covenanters*, xlii.
14. *APS*, vi, i, 766–767; SRO PA 11/5, ff 3–218; *The Lord Loudoun's Speech to the English Commissioners at Edinburgh, with the Treaty between the Grand Committee of Scotland, and the Commissioners from the Parliament of England* (London, 1648), (5).
15. *Montereul Correspondence*, volume two, 288, 420; Burnet, *Memoirs of the Dukes of Hamilton*, 336; Rushworth, *Historical Collections*, IV.(ii), 1032; Clarendon, *History of the Rebellion*, IV, 321; Stevenson, *Revolution and Counter-Revolution in Scotland*, 100; *APS*, vi, i, 612–613, *APS*, vi, ii, 3–4; SRO PA 11/5 ff 3–218.
16. *APS*, vi, ii, 3–4.
17. Baillie, *Letters and Journals*, III, 35; *APS*, v, 251–252, 258–259, 300–301, 302, 303–304, 305–306, 308, 331–332, *APS*, vi, i, 3–4, 95–96, 284–285, 429–430, 440–441, 474–475, 612–613.
18. *APS*, vi, ii, 3–4.
19. *APS*, vi, i, 612–613; *APS*, vi, ii, 3–4.
20. Ibid.
21. *APS*, vi, ii, 3–4. Stevenson, *Revolution and Counter-Revolution in Scotland*, 100.
22. Baillie, *Letters and Journals*, III, 35. Baillie's comments were written on 27 March, more than three weeks into the parliamentary session.
23. Ibid.

24. Ibid.
25. Ibid.
26. Ibid, 37.
27. *APS*, vi, ii, 3–88.
28. Ibid, 5; Stevenson, *Revolution and Counter-Revolution in Scotland*, 100; Stevenson, *Government Under the Covenanters*, 175; *CSPD*, 1648–1649, 26.
29. *APS*, vi, i, 612–613; *APS*, vi, ii, 3–4, 5, 6, 6–7, 7, 7–8, 8, 9.
30. *APS*, vi, ii, 6; Stevenson, *Revolution and Counter-Revolution in Scotland*, 100; *Montereul Correspondence*, volume two, 420.
31. *APS*, vi, ii, 9, 10, 10–11, 11; Stevenson, *Revolution and Counter-Revolution in Scotland*, 100. NLS MS 8482, Minute Book of the Convention of Estates, ff 2–5, indicates that the committees were actually appointed on 9 March before being approved of by Parliament on 10 March.
32. Baillie, *Letters and Journals*, III, 37.
33. *APS*, vi, i, 766–767; APS, vi, ii, 10, 13. *News from Scotland: Or the Result of the Generall Assembly of that Kingdome in order to England's Peace* (London, 1648), (4), (6). Stevenson, *Revolution and Counter-Revolution in Scotland*, 101. Stevenson, *Government Under the Covenanters*, xxxv; *Montereul Correspondence*, volume two, 426; Thomas Kennedy was identified as the fifth member; this was obviously an error on the part of a foreign correspondent. The fifth member was probably John Short (Stirling) as he was removed from the original committee on 17 March along with George Porterfield and William Glendoning. NLS MS 8482, Minute Book of the Convention of Estates, 1648, ff 4–5, indicates that the Committee for Dangers, Remedies, and Duties, was known as the 'Committee for Dispatches'. Variations also exist in the membership details between this manuscript version and the official parliamentary record. Eight nobles are listed in the manuscript version, whereas only six are included in the parliamentary record. Cassillis and Mar are the two nobles not included in the parliamentary record. No details of gentry and burghal membership are given in the manuscript version.
34. *APS*, vi, ii, 10, 13; Stevenson, *Revolution and Counter-Revolution in Scotland*, 102; Baillie, *Letters and Journals*, III, 37–38, 40. Conflict in terms of noble membership of the renewed committee of 17 March exists between the official parliamentary record and manuscript minutes of Parliament listed in SRO RH2/8/15, Minutes of Parliament, 11 March to 8 April 1648. Hamilton is included in the parliamentary record but not the manuscript version, whereas Cassillis is listed in the manuscript version but not the parliamentary record. All other noble membership details remain the same. Only five gentry are included in the manuscript version.
35. *APS*, vi, i, 766–767; *APS*, vi, ii, 10. NLS MS 8482 Minute Book of the Convention of Estates, folio 5. Lord Cochrane had recently been promoted into the nobility. As Sir William Cochrane of Cowdoun, he had represented the shire of Ayr during the First Triennial Parliament.
36. *APS*, vi, i, 766–767; *APS*, vi, ii, 10–11. NLS MS 8482 Minute Book of the Convention of Estates, folio 5.
37. *APS*, vi, i, 766–767; *APS*, vi, i, 612–613; *APS*, vi, ii, 11.
38. *APS*, vi, ii, 766–767; *APS*, vi, ii, 3–4, 11. NLS MS 8482 Minute Book of the Convention of Estates, 1648, folio 5.
39. Stevenson, *Government Under the Covenanters*, xxxv; Stevenson, *Revolution and Counter-Revolution in Scotland*, 102; Rushworth, *Historical Collections*, IV (ii), 1049; *Montereul Correspondence*, volume two, 426. NLS MS 2263 History of Events,

1635–1662, folio 197. The vote concerning Berwick and Carlisle had been taken on 16 March, SRO RH2/8/15 Minutes of Parliament, 11 March 1648 to 8 April 1648.

40. Burnet, *Memoirs of the Dukes of Hamilton*, 340.
41. *APS*, vi, ii, 10, 13, 14–15; *Records of the Kirk*, 477–478; Stevenson, *Revolution and Counter-Revolution in Scotland*, 101. NLS 8482 Minute Book of the Convention of Estates, 1648, folio 7.
42. NLS MS 8482 Minute Book of the Convention of Estates, 1648, folio 23; SRO Hamilton Papers, GD 406/1/2378; *APS*, vi, ii, 17–18, 23–25; S.R Gardiner (ed.), *The Hamilton Papers*, (Camden Society, London, 1880) 29–30; *Montereul Correspondence*, volume two, 451; Stevenson, *Revolution and Counter-Revolution in Scotland*, 103–104; *Records of the Kirk*, 373–451.
43. *APS*, vi, ii, 40–42; *Montereul Correspondence*, volume two, 459.
44. Burnet, *Memoirs of the Dukes of Hamilton*, 343.
45. Ibid.
46. *The Scots Cabinet Opened*, (3)-(4).
47. *APS*, vi, ii, 16, 29, 30–39, 53–56, 58, 59–62, 66, 72, 87; Baillie, *Letters and Journals*, III, 45; Stevenson, *Revolution and Counter-Revolution in Scotland*, 105, 107.
48. *The Manifold Practises And Attempts of the Hamiltons, And particularly of the present Duke of Hamilton Now Generall of the Scottish Army to get the Crown of Scotland* (1648), (3)-(4).
49. *APS*, vi, ii, 3–87.
50. Ibid. No nobles were included on the three regional interval committees analysed; the Committee for the Burned and Wasted Lands in Nairn, the Committee for the Burned and Wasted Lands in the Shire of Elgin and Forres, and the Committee for the Burned and Wasted Lands in Banffshire.
51. *APS*, vi, i, 766–767; *APS*, vi, ii, 69–71. Stevenson, *Government Under the Covenanters*, 61.
52. *APS*, vi, i, 766–767; *APS*, vi, ii, 69–71.
53. *APS*, vi, i, 766–767; *APS*, vi, ii, 71.
54. Stevenson, *Government Under the Covenanters*, 82.
55. Ibid, 61, 66–67, 69, 71, 79–80; Shepherd, 'The Politics and Society of Glasgow, 1648–74', PhD thesis, 40, 41.
56. *APS*, vi, ii, 89–124.
57. *APS*, vi, ii, 89; Stevenson, *Government Under the Covenanters*, 62.
58. *APS*, vi, ii, 91, 109. The committee appointed to consider the case of Gibson of Durie and James Campbell is not officially listed in the parliamentary records as a session committee.
59. *APS*, vi, ii, 93–94, 107–108, 108–109; Stevenson, *Revolution and Counter-Revolution in Scotland*, 109.
60. *APS*, vi, ii, 106–107. *The Differences in Scotland Still on Foot. Or, The late Proceedings between the Parliament and Kirk* (London, 1648), 1–2. *Some Few Observations By the Committee of Estates of Parliament, Upon The Declaration of the General Assembly of the last of July* (Edinburgh, 1648), 3.
61. *APS*, vi, ii, 122, 123–124.
62. Ibid, 102–105, 114. On 6 June an interval commission, the Committee for Burned and Wasted Lands in the Shire of Inverness, was appointed to assess the extent of land which was not paying any duty in relation to the maintenance. This committee has not been included in the analytical structure as it was not of central importance to contemporary events.

63. Ibid.
64. Ibid, 114. Sir William Baillie of Lamington (Lanark), Dundas of Arnieston (Edinburgh), ( ) Murray of Polmais (Stirling), Sir Thomas Blair of Balthayok (Perth), Sir Alexander Morrison of Prestongrange (Peebles), and Sir Archibald Stirling of Carden (Stirling) constituted the six gentry additions. George Porterfield (Glasgow), James Lentron (St Andrews), and James Pedie (Montrose) constituted the three burghal additions.
65. Ibid, 69–71, 102–105.
66. Ibid.
67. Burnet, *Memoirs of the Dukes of Hamilton*, 351.
68. *APS*, vi, ii, 102–105; NLS MS 2263 History of Events 1635–1662, folio 200. The quorum of the Edinburgh section was set at nine, with two of each estate required to be present. The quorum of the army section was set at seven, with one of each estate required to be present. The membership of both sections was not issued as per 9 June 1648.
69. SRO PA. 11/6, Register of the Committee of Estates, 12 May–4 September 1648, ff 17–193; APS, vi, ii, 102–105. Lords Banff and Cochrane, Grierson of Lag (Dumfries), and Meldrum of Burghlie (Fife) formed the non-commissioned nobles and gentry who attended various diets of the committee. Meldrum of Burghlie was not a member of Parliament as per 2 March 1648, although he had represented the shire of Fife in the Second, Third and Fourth Sessions of the First Triennial Parliament (*APS*, vi, i, 284–285, 429–430, 440–441; *APS*, vi, ii, 3–4).
70. SRO PA. 11/6, folio 64; Stevenson, *Revolution and Counter-Revolution in Scotland*, 111. Hamilton was included in the capacity of General of the armed forces and Callander was included as Lieutenant General.
71. SRO PA. 11/6, ff 17–193.
72. *The Scots Cabinet Opened*, (10).

9

The Rule of the Radical Regime, September 1648–August 1649

> The Parliament that year 1649 mett and acted with as much zeal against the Engagers as the General Assembly had done, they concurred with them each inflicting their Censures upon that Party, according to the nature of their Power and Degree of their Offices.[1]

Following military defeat of the Engagement army at the Battle of Preston in August 1648, the power base of the Engagers within Scotland collapsed. The Whiggamore Raid of western radicals established a radical regime in Edinburgh, backed by Oliver Cromwell, whose political and military support was crucial to the regime's survival.[2] The first political move of the regime was to establish firm control of the Committee of Estates.[3]

The Operation of Parliamentary Interval Committees, September 1648–January 1649

Fourteen sederunts of the Committee of Estates are recorded between 22 September and 18 October.[4] Only eight of the 40 nobles, two of the 40 gentry, and three of the 40 burgesses included on the Committee of Estates of 9 June attended any of the 14 diets. All eight nobles were radicals; Argyll, Loudoun, Cassillis, Balmerino, Leven, Lothian, Eglinton, and Buccleuch. Erskine of Scottiscraig (Fife) and Johnston of Wariston (Argyll) were the two radical gentry in attendance and were supplemented by John Milne (Edinburgh), Robert Cunningham (Kinghorn), and George Garden (Burntisland) for the burgesses. In addition, five nobles, 11 gentry, and nine burgesses who had not been included in the original commission also attended diets. None of the 11 gentry and only two of the nine burgesses, James Campbell (Dumbarton) and Thomas MacBirnie (Dumfries), had been members of Parliament as per 2 March 1648. This non-commissioned grouping of 25 can be classified as radicals. Burleigh, Angus, Elcho, Torphichen, and Kirkcudbright formed the noble grouping. Three of the 11 gentry, Wauchope of Niddrie (Edinburgh), Winrham of Libberton (Edinburgh), and Dundas of Duddingston (Linlithgow), had their domains in the immediate vicinity of the capital. Furthermore, six of the non-commissioned burgesses were Edinburgh based; Sir William Dick, Sir James Stewart, Sir John Smith, Lawrence Henderson, James Roughead, and David Wilkie. Robert Barclay (Irvine) was another noted radical in attendance.[5]

Despite the attendance of non-commissioned nobles, gentry, and burgesses, there was a clear need to bring in additional personnel to strengthen the radical regime in its embryonic stages. In constitutional terms the commission to the Committee of Estates of 9 June was still valid. In light of the fact that the vast majority of that committee had been Engagers, in de facto political terms the Committee of Estates of 9 June was now defunct. In order to bolster its position, the radical rump legislated on 7 October to bring persons of 'good affection and qualification' (ie radicals) on to the committee.[6] Those individuals were to assist the committee in the ordering, directing, and governing of the public affairs of the kingdom. They were to have 'ample power ... as if they had been inserted nominated in the commission of Parliament'.[7] Eight nobles, 45 gentry, 25 burgesses, and two military officials (80 individuals in total) were added to the Committee of Estates.[8]

The Act Anent the Constitution of the Committee passed on 22 September defined the terms and conditions of membership. The Committee of Estates was deemed to consist of those persons who had been nominated on the original commission of 9 June and who had also opposed the Engagement in the 1648 Parliament. The committee was to operate under the advice of the parliamentary opposition to the Engagement. Committee membership was to be increased in the form of two representatives of the commissioners of the shires and one representative of the commissioners of the burghs. Those who had raised arms in support of the Engagement or had sworn oaths or declarations in favour of the Engagement were barred from committee membership, as were all who were aiding or assisting those joined in arms with Crawford-Lindsay, Glencairn, Lanark, Sinclair, and Gibson of Durie. This was designed to stop the growth of an Engager 'home guard' within Scotland.

In a separate item of legislation enacted on 22 September, the committee also set out the terms of election of commissioners of shires and burghs as well as the election of magistrates in the burghs. No adherents of the Engagement (including those who had sworn or subscribed oaths or declarations in favour of the Engagement) were to be elected to sit in Parliament nor to be admitted to any offices of public trust. On the assurance of the security of their lives, it was also ordered that the military forces of Engagers were to be disbanded, and they were to withdraw from public life. The insistence on the exclusion of Engagers came from Cromwell himself, although the policy was implemented by the radical regime.[9] In effect, this was in breach of the spirit of the Treaty of Stirling, whereby 'all differences betuixt the Parties (were) referred to parliament', and whereby conciliation had been agreed on,

> not only to Shun the Effusion of Scots Blood, but that the English might not intermeddle in their Quarrells, which was feared might not serve either for the Honour or Advantage of the Nation.[10]

The Second Session of the Second Triennial Parliament, 4 January–16 March 1649.

The parliamentary session can be differentiated into two subsessions, whilst still constituting a full parliamentary session in procedural and constitutional terms.

The Estates convened from 4 January to 3 February. On 3 February Parliament was adjourned, following the execution of Charles I in London, until 6 February 1649. The Estates actually reconvened, however, on 5 February. Details of all committees analysed have been considered with reference to two subsessions although they were constitutionally incorporated in the one parliamentary session.[11]

1. The Composition of the Second Session of the Second Triennial Parliament

In common with the First Session of the Second Triennial Parliament, deficiencies exist in the parliamentary rolls of 4 January 1649. Attendance data has been analysed in terms of maximum and minimum figures for the shires and burghs. Sixteen nobles, 46 gentry representing 26 shires, and 51 burgesses representing 50 burghs formed the minmum parliamentary membership as per 4 January 1649. Corresponding maximum figures amount to 52 gentry representing 29 shires, whilst those for the burghs are 58 burgesses representing 57 burghs (see appendices 4a and 4b).[12]

Comparison of the rolls of 2 March 1648 and 4 January 1649 illustrates that the attendance levels for the gentry and burgesses remain virtually constant, in terms of both maximum and minimum figures. However, there was a sharp drop of 40 nobles between the two sessions (see appendices 4a and 4b). Such figures provide further evidence to the assertion that the establishment of the radical regime constituted an anti-aristocratic reaction against the nobility who had been at the forefront of the Engagement. This phenomenon is also in marked contrast to the noble domination of the Engagement Parliament. One contemporary observer commented that 'hardly the fifth part of the lords of Scotland were admitted to sit in parliament, but those who did sitt were esteemed truely godly men; so were all the rest of the commissioners elected of the most pious of every corporation'.[13]

In terms of minimum attendance figures of 4 January, 14 of the 16 nobles (88%), 12 of the 46 gentry (26%), and 13 of the 51 burgesses (25%) had also been recorded in the rolls of 2 March 1648. This radical core grouping amounted to 39 individuals in total. Near parity per estate is apparent in common membership over both sessions.

Attendance data can also be analysed from another perspective. Forty-one of the 56 nobles (73%), 34 of the 47 gentry (72%), and 34 of the 49 burgesses (69%) (109 individuals in total) who are recorded in the rolls of the Engagement Parliament of 2 March 1648 do not appear in the rolls of 4 January 1649. This provides clear empirical evidence of purging in the shires and burghs, given the fact that the 1648 Parliament had been dominated by Engagers. Cromwell himself observed that the 'Committee of Estates have declared against all of that party's sitting in Parliament. Good elections are made in divers places, of such as dissented from and opposed the late wicked Engagement'.[14]

2. The Proceedings of the Second Session of the Second Triennial Parliament

The full parliamentary session has been examined in terms of two subsessions, 4 January to 3 February and 5 February to 16 March. The former subsession of 4 January to 3 February concentrated on establishing the legitimacy of the full session under the radical regime and laying the foundations for the punishment of Engagers and the purging of public offices. The latter subsession of 5 February to 16 March concentrated on the consequences of the execution of the king and the purging of office-holders who supported the Engagement.

The legislative programme of the first subsession (4 January–3 February) consisted of 26 enactments (23 of which concerned public business) and one ratification. After the calling of the parliamentary rolls, Chancellor Loudoun was elected President of Parliament. The Estates then stated that any disputed commissions produced by commissioners of the shires and/or commissioners of the burghs could be rejected by the House even after such commissioners had taken the parliamentary oath. Such a manoeuvre was undoubtedly aimed at removing any shire or burgh commissioners who did not adhere to the radical regime.[15]

The actual process of parliamentary business did not properly begin until 5 January. All members of Parliament were required to renew the Solemn League and Covenant. Cassillis, Johnston of Wariston (Edinburgh), and Sir James Stewart (Edinburgh) were appointed to inform the General Assembly of this resolution in name of Parliament. The Solemn League and Covenant was subscribed by all members of Parliament present on 12 January. The Act anent the Several Committees stipulated that any member of Parliament was entitled to full access to any parliamentary session committee. Such access did not include voting rights. In addition, Chancellor Loudoun, and President of Parliament, was to be a supernumerary on all committees. The Excise Commission was continued until such time as a new committee was appointed. In accordance with an act of the Committee of Estates of 14 October 1648, the Committees of War in the shires were to continue their meetings throughout the parliamentary session. Three parliamentary session committees were established on 5 January; the Committee for Dispatches, the Committee for Overtures and Laws, and the Committee for Bills and Ratifications. The specific quorums for these committees were not issued until 31 January and were set at a third of the total membership of each committee.[16]

Seven per estate formed the membership of the Committee for Dispatches. Noble membership was composed of hard core radicals led by Argyll, and included Cassillis, Eglinton, and Balmerino. Chancellor Loudoun and General Leven were included as supernumeraries. Gentry representation was led by Johnston of Wariston (Edinburgh), the leading ally of Argyll. All seven burgesses were major radical figures within the burghal estate, including Robert Barclay (Irvine) and James Sword (St Andrews).

Two nobles, one laird, and one burgess had also been members of the Committee for Dangers, Remedies, and Duties of 10 March 1648 in the

Engagement Parliament. This group consisted of Argyll, Loudoun (included as supernumerary on both committees), Johnston of Wariston (Edinburgh), and George Porterfield (Glasgow). Seven of the nine nobles (including supernumeraries), two of the seven gentry, and two of the seven burgesses on the Committee for Dispatches of 5 January 1649 had also been members of the Committee of Estates of 9 June 1648. Gentry and burghal representation within this context consisted of Johnston of Wariston (Edinburgh), Erskine of Scottiscraig (Fife), Hugh Kennedy (Ayr), and Robert Cunningham (Kinghorn). This provides evidence of a radical rump which had been retained from the Engagement Parliament.[17]

The Committee for Dispatches was to consider all business relating to the army in Scotland, to consider all affairs in England and Ireland relevant to the kingdom of Scotland, and was to report on the most appropriate policy options. In addition, the Committee for Dispatches was to liaise with the Commission of the Kirk and was to acquaint that body with any appropriate particulars. Infact three of the seven nobles, five of the seven gentry, and four of the seven burgesses on the Committee for Dispatches were members of the current Commission of the Kirk instituted on 11 August 1648. Close correlations in membership therefore existed between the Committee for Dispatches and the Commission of the Kirk. The Committee for Dispatches of 5 January 1649 can be interpreted as a joint Kirk-Parliament radical rump, staffed by leading radical nobles, gentry, and burgesses and led by Argyll. The parliamentary institution of the Committee for Dispatches, which had clear parliamentary precedents throughout the 1640s, was used to strenghten the formal links between Kirk and Parliament.[18]

The Committee for Overtures and Laws consisted of three per estate. It was led by Cassillis and Balmerino. Cassillis, Chancellor Loudoun (as supernumerary), and Robert Cunningham (Kinghorn) had also been included on the Committee for Overtures and Laws of 10 March 1648 in the Engagement Parliament. This provides further empirical evidence of radical parliamentary activity within the Engagement Parliament. Two of the three nobles (Cassillis and Balmerino) were also included on the current Commission of the Kirk of 11 August 1648. One laird, Halkett of Pitsirrane (Fife), and one burgess, Gideon Jack (Lanark), were also members of that Commission of the Kirk. Such evidence provides further indicators of liaison between Kirk and Parliament. Cassillis, Balmerino, Loudoun, and Robert Cunningham (Kinghorn) had also been members of the Committee of Estates of 9 June 1648.[19]

The Committee for Bills and Ratifications of 5 January was also composed of three per estate. Noble membership was not composed of first rank radicals. Chancellor Loudoun (as supernumerary) and John Hay (Elgin) had also been members of the previous Committee of Estates of 9 June 1648. No common membership exists with the Committee for Bills and Supplications of 10 March 1648 in the Engagement Parliament and the Committee for Bills and Ratifications of 5 January 1649. Only Loudoun was included on both committees but that was in the capacity as Chancellor and President of Parliament.[20] Two of the nobles (Torphichen and Coupar) were also included on the current Commission of the Kirk of 11 August 1648.

That the radical regime was intent on a programme of public retribution against the Engagers was made apparent immediately by Argyll and Johnston of Wariston in their speeches to the House on 5 January. Argyll's speech contained five heads aimed at the 'brecking of the malignants teith' and Wariston's speech, designed to complement Argyll's, 'wold brecke ther jawes'.[21] Five groups were idenitified by Argyll as worthy of punishment; firstly, the leading Engagers employed in public offices, secondly, those Engagers who had been employed on parliamentary committees, thirdly, malignants who had been formerly fined by Parliament but whose cases had since relapsed, fourthly, those who had been eager promoters of the Engagement, and fifthly, those who had petitioned for the advancement of the levy for the Engagement invasion of England. Argyll defined these five heads as classes and they were modified into a new Act of Classes. Nevertheless, this Act of Classes was not formally instituted until 23 January 1649.[22]

The process of establishing the constitutional legality of the current parliamentary session and repealing the legislation of the Engagement Parliament commenced on 9 January. The House ordained that all items of legislation were to be prefixed by a clause legally justifying the convening of the January 1649 session based on the power and authority of the legislation of the Committee of Estates.[23] The Act Ratifying the Act of Indiction of This Present Parliament of 11 January approved and ratified legislation of the Committee of Estates of 27 October 1648 which called for the convening of a new session before 10 January 1649. Furthermore, any individual questioning the legality and authority of the current parliamentary session would be punished under the pain of treason. The charge of treason was clearly being used for party purposes. Subsequent legislation enacted on 26 January required subscription of the band for securing the peace of the kingdom. This included the acknowledgement of the legality of the meeting and constitution of the current parliamentary session.

Following the passage of the Act Ratifying the Act of Indiction, a parliamentary session committee of three per estate was established to revise all acts of the previous Committee of Estates and the Excise Commission. This was despite the fact that the Act Ratifying the Act of Indiction had already ratified such legislation. The committee was to report with their opinion 'anent what they may find' to the Estates in order that the House may 'doe and determine as they shall think fit and expedient'.[24] The fact that the remit of the committee was so vague may have been a deliberate ploy. The remit of the committee did not differentiate between the period before and after the military defeat of the Engagers and the installation of the radical regime. Therefore the emphasis of the parliamentary session committee was probably inclined towards the legislation of the Committee of Estates before the Battle of Preston and prior to the Whiggamore Raid. All legislation passed in the Committee of Estates under the control of Engagers could then be repealed. This was facilitated by the passage of the Act Ratifying the Act of Indiction which had legalised the acts of the

Committee of Estates convening the parliamentary session on 4 January. Therefore the legality of convening the session could not be questioned.[25]

On 16 January all acts of the First Session of the Second Triennial Parliament, 2 March–10 June 1648, and all acts of the Committee of Estates between June and September 1648 were repealed. Hence all Engagement legislation was now null and void. It was also recognised in law that the Kirk had lobbied constantly against the Engagement and the military invasion of England. Petitions from shires and synods and the formal opposition of the General Assembly had been all ignored by the Engagement faction. Thus the Kirk was white-washed of any association with the Engagement. The Whiggamore Raid and the coup d'etat which established the radical regime was defended and approved of in legal and constitutional terms. Just as the dominant Engagement faction had used the procedures of Parliament and parliamentary committees (especially the Committee of Estates) for its own particular ends, so too did the radical regime employ exactly the same procedures to repudiate and repeal the legislation of the Engagement Parliament. In particular, it condoned armed uprising as the appropriate manner of removing an ungodly faction.[26]

The assertion that the 1649 Act of Classes was in existence as an item of legislation, but without parliamentary sanction as yet, is complicated by the fact that the 1646 Act of Classes was still in operation and was being used as a source of reference. The case of John Dickson of Hartrie indicates this complication. Dickson represented the shire of Peebles in Parliament as per 4 January 1649. On 11 January Cassillis rose in the House and questioned the right of any individual to sit and vote who had been found guilty under the Second Class of the Act of Classes. The House answered that no such individuals were entitled to sit and vote. Cassillis then moved that any such individuals then present in Parliament should be removed and barred from Parliament until they were cleared, otherwise Cassillis would name them publicly. At this point, Dickson of Hartrie, aware of the fact that he was about to be named, desired that the House consider that he had already been cleared by a Committee of Processes in March 1647 and had also been admitted at the last synod of Edinburgh and other Kirk judicatures. Two per estate were commissioned to consider Dickson's case. They were led by Cassillis and Burleigh, but also included the noted radical burgess Robert Barclay (Irvine), and were supplemented by Chancellor Loudoun as supernumerary. By 18 January the committee had reported to the House and Dickson of Hartrie was allowed to sit and vote.[27]

Although the basic terms of a new Act of Classes had been formulated by 5 January, the new act did not receive parliamentary sanction until 23 January. The 1649 Act of Classes had a constitutional precedent and was based on the 1646 Act of Classes. The 1649 act aroused the hostility of Engagers who felt that they had been deceived by the Treaty of Stirling which had promised them a free Parliament to defend their cause. Hence from the Engager perspective the 1649 Parliament was technically 'prelimited'. Four classes were laid down in the 1649 Act.

The First Class included five groups. The first group applied to all general officers of the Engagement forces who had fought at Mauchline Moor and/or Stirling. The second group applied to those who were principally active in the transportation of forces from Ireland to Scotland. The third group related to the leading promoters of the Engagement in Parliament, parliamentary committees, or otherwise. The fourth group was concerned with those who had been the chief promoters of the Montrose Rebellion. The fifth group applied to individuals who were guilty of any crimes under the 1646 Act of Classes but had still been active post-1646 and had promoted the Engagement.[28]

Exclusion from public office for life was the punishment accorded to those whose crimes came under the First Class. Exclusion from public office for individuals found guilty under the Second, Third, and Fourth Classes amounted to 10 years, five years, and one year respectively. In addition, those found guilty under the Second, Third, and Fourth Classes were required to repent publicly in the Kirk for their crimes in support of the Engagement before they could be readmitted to public office.

In comparison with the 1646 Act of Classes, the 1649 Act of Classes contained no provisions for the physical punishment of individuals and/or the confiscation of their private estates. Far from being a more moderate punitive item of legislation than the 1646 Act of Classes, the 1649 act had to be formulated and implemented within the legal constraints of the Treaty of Stirling which had guaranteed that Engagers would not be punished physically or materially in the form of their estates. Nevertheless, this restriction was partly circumvented by legislation enacted on 3 February which stated that Engagers would be responsible for the payment of the monthly maintenance from March to October 1648 (this should have been paid by non-Engagers).[29]

Complementary legislation was enacted on 23 January, although it was constitutionally and procedurally separate. It stated that all holders of public office were to be tried according to the Act of Classes. Where appropriate, such individuals were to be purged from public office.[30]

As well as establishing the constitutional legitimacy of the radical regime and laying the foundations for purging Engagers, Parliament acted to take account of the public debts of the kingdom. The Committee for Common Burdens, Accounts, Losses, and Monies was established on 18 January. In common with earlier such committees, it was to assess the level of public debt, scrutinise public accounts and establish ways of maximising revenue accumulation. Furthermore, the committee was to enquire into the extent of losses suffered by opposers of the Engagement either from Engagers themselves or by forces levied to oppose the Engagers. Therefore there was to be financial renumeration for the godly who had suffered in material terms for opposing the Engagement. Six per estate formed the membership of the committee. Burleigh appears to have been the leading noble on the committee. Chancellor Loudoun was included as a supernumerary.[31]

By 3 February the Committee for Common Burdens, Accounts, Losses, and Monies had reported to the House. Firstly, it was enacted that the western shires and burghs which had opposed the Engagement were exempted from paying backdated arrears of monthly maintenance due for the period 1 March to 31 October 1648 which had not been paid. The total amount of maintenance for this period remained unaltered but those who had supported the Engagement were to pay the amount due from the anti-Engagement western shires and burghs. In a separate item of legislation, the levels of monthly maintenance for February 1649 were issued on 3 February.[32]

Whilst the domestic political situation centred on the punishment of Engagers, in wider British terms the trial of the king dominated events. The radical regime neither favoured nor advocated the execution of Charles, but it was powerless to influence events. The relationship between the 'Three Kingdoms' and Charles I had swung in favour of the Cromwellian faction now dominant in the English Parliament.

Fourteen instructions were concluded by the Committee for Dispatches on 6 January and were enacted by Parliament on 9 January to be sent to the Scottish diplomatic commissioners in London; Lothian, Sir John Chiesly, and William Glendoning (Kirkcudbright). Although these instructions emphasised the alliance between the radical regime and Cromwell and were anti-Royalist in terms of monarchical power, they stressed the safety of the king's person as a condition of the handing over of the king to the English Parliament in January 1647. Nevertheless, a dispute had emerged on 6 January in the diet of the Committee for Dispatches and six ministers of the Commission of the Kirk. Parliament had ordained on 5 January that a fast should be held. At the committee diet on 6 January Johnston of Wariston (Edinburgh) moved that the fast should be observed by the whole Parliament (including diets of parliamentary session committees) and that discussion of the king's position should be delayed for three or four days. After heated debate it was carried that the preservation of the king's person was of such profound significance that the committee should immediately proceed to the drawing up of the diplomatic instructions. No records exist of the total number of committee members present on 6 January, but there were three adherents to Wariston's motion; Wariston himself, Ruthven of Frieland (Perth), and Argyll. In addition, David Dickson, one of the ministers present, sided with Wariston's motion. Nevertheless, once it was apparent that the motion had been defeated, Argyll quickly backtracked and argued for immediate discussion of the instructions. It would therefore appear that Argyll and Johnston of Wariston were attempting to delay the parliamentary process aimed at saving the king's life in order to facilitate the trial and subsequent execution.

When news of the king's execution reached Edinburgh, the parliamentary session was adjourned on 3 February until 6 February.[33] The second subsession convened on 5 February (one day earlier than planned) and continued until 16 March. It enacted 247 items of legislation (112 of which related to public business and 135 of which related to private business) and 16 ratifications.[34]

When the Estates reconvened the Scottish Parliament immediately proclaimed the Prince of Wales as Charles II, King of Great Britain, France, and

Ireland. By doing so the alliance between the radical regime and the English Parliament had now been formally broken. Paradoxically, it had been the Scottish Parliament in 1639 that had initiated the constitutional and political limitations on Charles I in British terms. Now in 1649 the Scottish Parliament once again took the initiative in British terms by proclaiming Charles as King of Great Britain, France, and Ireland. Nevertheless, admission to that office was not unconditional. Firstly, Charles was required to defend the National Covenant and the Solemn League and Covenant between the two kingdoms. Secondly, royal subscription of both covenants was required.[35]

Supplementary legislation of 7 February expanded on the parliamentary proclamation of 5 February. The Act anent the Securing of Religion and Peace of the Kingdom stressed that not only Charles II but also all his successors must give assent to all parliamentary legislation securing the National Covenant and the Solemn League and Covenant and legislation establishing presbyterian church government in all three kingdoms. Further confirmation was required that both Charles II and his family would not alter this legislation nor create any opposition to it. In addition, Charles II was to be required to discharge from his entourage any counsellors prejudicial to presbyterianism and opposed to both the National Covenant and Solemn League and Covenant. The influence of the Kirk was reflected by the fact that the determination of all civil matters was to reside with Parliament and the determination of all religious matters was to reside with the General Assembly. Therefore, although the legislation of 5 February had proclaimed Charles as king subject to general limitations, subsequent legislation of 7 February expanded on the specific limitations which would in reality reduce the future king to a figurehead monarch (in common with his father).[36]

The execution of Charles I and the subsequent abolition of monarchy in England effectively ended the Union of the Crowns. Yet the increased interaction of the three kingdoms of the British archipelago ensured that a viable Scottish monarchy could only be safeguarded within a wider British monarchical settlement. The Union of the Crowns therefore had to be restored, but Charles II was to be a covenanted king of three covenanted kingdoms, based on the export of a presbyterian reformation to England and Ireland. In short, covenanted monarchy and Britannic presbyterianism were the lynchpins at the heart of the revival of the Union of the Crowns by the Scottish radical regime.[37]

Yet the proclamation of Charles II as King of Great Britain, France, and Ireland did not command universal approval and had aroused 'doubt' and 'hesitation'. Two main reasons were advocated. Firstly, Charles might 'use his Sword to recover his Right to the Possession' of the kingdom, and his subjects might be encouraged to assist him in this thanks to the proclamation itself. Secondly, because his right of succession had been declared and asserted by parliamentary proclamation then it might well prove more difficult to secure his agreement to the limitations and conditions imposed on him. This in turn could furnish him with enough evidence to seek the support by arms of those who were 'disaffected to the present Constitution of the Government both in Church and State'.[38]

On the other hand, it was argued that a delay in proclamation would be profoundly dangerous. It might cause Charles to resort to 'desperate causes' to recover the kingdom. More importantly, it would also allow time to the English Commonwealth to 'employ all their Arts' to 'shake off the Monarchy and twin themselves into a Commonwealth'. Such an achievement the 'English would look upon as their greatest Security for their new commonwealth which they laboured to obtrude upon this nation'. That Charles was ultimately proclaimed as King (within a short space of time following his father's execution) was attributed to the appeal of monarchy among the people at large, the support of the nobility, and 'by the great Influence and Authority of the Marquis of Argyle upon the members both of Church and State'.[39]

The Scottish commissioners currently in London at this time, Sir John Chiesly and William Glendoning (Kirkcudbright), were to be sent to Holland to secure royal assent to the parliamentary conditions laid down before admission to the royal office could be allowed. Diplomatic instructions issued on 23 February stressed that the terms of the legislation of 7 February must be met. Despite the fact that Sir John Chiesly and William Glendoning were imprisoned by the English Parliament, new Scottish diplomatic commissioners were named on 6 March. Cassillis, Brodie of that ilk (Elgin), Winraham of Libberton (Edinburgh), and Alexander Jaffray (Aberdeen) were commissioned to sail to Holland. Three ministers, James Wood, Robert Blair, and Robert Baillie, represented the Kirk. By 6 March Chiesly and Glendoning had been released from imprisonment and they were to remain in London to negotiate with the English Parliament. They were also accompanied by Lothian.[40]

The legislative and procedural structure for the purging of office-holders established by the first subsession was used to full effect during the second subsession, 5 February–16 March. Widespread purging of office-holders took place. In constitutional terms Charles II had not yet been admitted to the royal office. This enabled Parliament to purge of its own accord without royal approval.[41]

Only two Officers of State were not purged from office. Chancellor Loudoun, currently President of Parliament, was not removed despite the fact that he had initially supported and been involved in the Engagement, although he had been made to repent publicly. Sir John Chiesly retained his post of Master of Requests. Three Officers of State who had retained their posts since 1637 were now removed from office; Roxburgh, Keeper of the Privy Seal, was replaced by the Earl of Sutherland, Hamilton of Orbiston, Justice Clerk, was replaced by Campbell of Cessnock, and Sir James Carmichael of that ilk, Treasurer Depute, was replaced by his son, Sir Daniel Carmichael of Hyndford. Carmichael of Hyndford is not recorded in the parliamentary rolls of 4 January. Of the remaining Officers of State, Lanark, Secretary, was replaced by Lothian, and Glencairn, Justice General, was replaced by Cassillis. Crawford-Lindsay was removed from the office of Treasurer and a new Treasury Commission was established in his place. Gibson of Durie, Clerk Register, was replaced by Johnston of Wariston. Wariston's former office of Lord Advocate was filled by Sir Thomas Nicholson of Carnock. Nicholson of Carnock is not recorded in the parliamentary rolls of 4 January.[42]

Eight new Ordinary Lords of Session and Senators of the College of Justice and two Extraordinary Lords of Session and Senators of the College of Justice were appointed to take account of the purging of the eight Senators of the College of Justice and Lords of Session from office under the 1649 Act of Classes. Fifteen Ordinary Lords of Session and Senators of the College of Justice and four Extraordinary Lords of Session and Senators of the College had been appointed by the 1641 Parliament. Hence the judicial appointments of 1649 constituted a leaner series of appointments.[43]

Johnston of Wariston was allocated a crucial role in the process of purging on 12 March. The purging of lesser offices was devolved to Johnston of Wariston as Clerk Register and to the Committee of Estates (and/or any appropriate subcommittee of the Committee of Estates appointed). Wariston was also to oversee the implementation of the Act of Classes after the close of the parliamentary session.[44]

New Sheriff Principals were appointed on 15 March for 16 shires. Twelve of the new Sheriff Principals were gentry and only four were nobles. The political and geographic influence of the House of Argyll was relected in the appointment of the Marquis of Argyll as Sheriff Principal of the shires of Inverness and Ross. Loudoun, Argyll's kinsman, was appointed for Ayrshire, and Sutherland was appointed Sheriff Principal for his own locality. Fife enjoys the repuatation as a traditional base of Covenanting radicalism, but unlike the majority of the shires where Sheriff Principals were appointed, the position was filled by a noble, Rothes. Of the 12 shires where gentry were appointed as Sheriff Principals, seven were also members of Parliament as per 4 January 1649. In one further instance a burgess, Alexander Douglas (Banff), was appointed to the office of Sheriff Principal for his own locality. The appointment of Sheriff Principals highlight the political muscle of the gentry in the Scottish localities.[45]

A new Privy Council was established on 16 March. Substantial vacancies had occurred due to death and also due to the fact that sentences of depositions had been pronounced against several Privy Councillors. Whereas 36 nobles, 14 gentry, and one burgess (51 members in total) had been included on the Privy Council of 13 November 1641, only four nobles and five gentry (nine members in total) were included on the new Privy Council of 16 March 1649. None of the nine members had been included on the previous Committee of Estates of 9 June 1648 and only three new Privy Councillors were members of the current Commission of the Kirk. The end result of purging, nevertheless, was to ensure that 'godly men were imployed in all offices, both civil and military'.[46]

The Commission of the Kirk acted as an effective lobbying agency throughout the parliamentary session and secured the enactment of legislation deemed appropriate to its interests. Most importantly, Parliament passed 'a most strange acte'[47] on 9 March abolishing patronage of church lands, on the insistence of the Kirk. The abolition of patronage weakened the rights of the nobility by cancelling grants of superiorities and feu duties made by Charles I to nobles in the aftermath of the Revocation Scheme. The original intention of that scheme had been to transfer the feudal superiority of former kirklands to the crown, but in reality new grants of superiorities ended up being issued to nobles. The cancellation of the king's grants had been a live issue since 1647–48. Petitions had been handed into Parliament in both 1647 and 1648 but had been rejected by the nobility, despite the support of a section of parliamentary gentry and burgesses. When the legislation was enacted Buccleuch and other unnamed members left the House in protest. Nevertheless, the act secured the support of Argyll, Loudoun, and Johnston of Wariston. Increased financial provision for ministers was secured on 14 March in the Act for Augmentation and Provision of Stipends. Social legislation relating to poor relief and moral reform relating to drunkenness, sexual relations, and the spread of witchcraft also formed a prominent feature of parliamentary legislation enacted throughout the session.[48]

Despite the fact that a bulk of legislation (247 acts and 16 ratifications) was enacted between 5 February and 16 March, a sufficient amount of supplications had not been considered by the close of the session. The problem was resolved on 13 March by the formation of a session committee, the Committee for Revising of Reports and Bills. Its membership consisted solely of three gentry. The committee was to assess bills and supplications which had been presented to two session committees; the Committee for Bills and Ratifications (5 January) and the Committee for Common Burdens, Accounts, Losses, and Monies (18 January). It was then to decide on which of those bills and supplications were worthy of parliamentary enactment. On 16 March the House stated that all supplications which had not been discussed or considered in Parliament were to be remitted to the Committee of Estates. Fifty-seven such supplications were submitted to the Committee of Estates on 16 March. This suggests that the Committee for Revising of Reports and Bills of 13 March had failed to deal with all relevant bills and supplications.[49]

At the close of parliamentary business on 16 March the Third Session of the Second Triennial Parliament was ordered to be held on 23 May 1649.[50]

3. The Committee Structure of the Second Session of the Second Triennial Parliament

The committee structure of the full parliamentary session has been analysed in terms of each subsession, 4 January to 3 February, and 5 February to 16 March.[51]

Fourteen nobles, 22 gentry, and 20 burgesses formed the total field of five session committees appointed betweeen 4 January and 3 February (no interval committees were appointed). All 22 gentry and 18 of the 20 burgesses were included on only one session committee. All gentry and burgesses analysed were members of parliament as per 4 January 1649, with the exception of Sir James Hope of Hopetoun.

Noble common membership was concentrated within a broader group of radicals than the other two estates, but both the gentry and burgesses could draw on a broader field of radical membership. Chancellor Loudoun (also President of Parliament) was included as a supernumerary on all five session committees. Although two radical nobles (Arbuthnot and Coupar) were included on three session committees, noble common membership was concentrated on six nobles who secured membership two session committees each (Sutherland, Eglinton, Cassillis, Cathcart, Torphichen, and Balmerino). James Sword (St Andrews) and Robert Cunningham (Kinghorn) were each included on two session committees for the burghal estate.[52]

The subsession dating from 5 February to 16 March has been analysed in terms of two parliamentary session and eight parliamentary interval committees. Analytical data has been merged to yield a maximum figure of 10. The total membership field consisted of 24 nobles, 42 gentry, and 40 burgesses. Thirteen of the 42 gentry (31%) and 16 of the 40 burgesses (40%) were non-members of parliament as per 4 January.

Although Chancellor Loudoun was entitled to sit on all session committees as a supernumerary, no nobles (nor burgesses) were included on the procedural committee, the Committee for Revising of Reports and Bills. Cassillis, Buccleuch, and Burleigh were nominated to the remaining session committee analysed (the Committee for Additional Excise). Argyll's dominant role was emphasised by his inclusion on six of the eight interval committees, whilst Cassillis and Burleigh each secured nomination to five interval committees. The Committee for Revising of Reports and Bills consisted of only three gentry. Yet no common membership exists with the other session committee (the Committee for Additional Excise) and of the eight gentry included on the two session committees all were included on only one interval committee. Interval committee membership for the gentry was concentrated on Campbell of Cessnock (Ayr) (five interval committees), Winraham of Libberton (Ayr), Ruthven of Frieland (Perth), Cunningham of Cunninghamhead (Ayr), and Hope of Hopetoun (four interval committees each). Interval committee membership for the burghal estate was based primarily on the services of Robert Barclay (Irvine) (five interval committees), Sir John Smith (Edinburgh), Alexander Jaffray (Aberdeen), George Porterfield (Glasgow), and Hugh Kennedy (Ayr) (four interval committees each).[53]

Session committees continued to be staffed, in general, by eastern gentry and burgesses, although there was a strong western presence on the Committee for Dispatches. There was also a strong western presence on the financial interval committee, the Committee for Money and Accounts. Although eastern gentry and burgesses were present in greatest numbers on the Committee of Estates, both the Borders and the west secured a strong body of representation. It appears, therefore, that the traditional dominance of the east was being challenged in the staffing of parliamentary committees. This is borne out by the fact that western gentry and burgesses were dominating common membership of both session and interval committees.

4. The Operation of Parliamentary Session Committees

Twelve sederunts of the Committee for Dispatches are recorded between 26 January and 8 March 1649. The committee's proceedings were well-attended. Argyll and Johnston of Wariston were present at all 12 diets, whilst Chancellor Loudoun, Sutherland, Winraham of Libberton (Edinburgh), and Alexander Jaffray (Aberdeen) each attended 11 diets.[54]

The Committee for Dispatches operated as a 'preparative committee for the full parliament' in terms of preparing legislation for the punishment, trial, and sentences of delinquents.[55] The main business recorded related to the threat of a Royalist uprising (which occurred when Inverness was captured by Sir Thomas MacKenzie of Pluscardine) and the threat of an Anglo-Scottish War following the proclamation of Charles II as King of Great Britain, France, and Ireland. The Pluscardine Rising occurred amidst fears of a Royalist-Engager military invasion from Holland and threatened the internal security of the radical regime. Information received from intelligence sources in England on 19 February resulted in a strengthening of the kingdom's defences. Argyll, Johnston of Wariston (Edinburgh), and Sir James Stewart (Edinburgh) were delegated to supervise the efficient collection of clandestine intelligence information 'using all means and ways'.[56]

A specialised subcommittee was established on 26 January to oversee the compulsory subscription of bands to keep the peace by Engagers and Royalists. The subcommittee was staffed by leading radicals; Argyll, Cassillis, and Balmerino for the nobility, Johnston of Wariston (Edinburgh), Winraham of Libberton (Edinburgh), and Brodie of that ilk (Elgin) for the gentry, and Sir James Stewart (Edinburgh), Robert Barclay (Irvine), and Alexander Jaffray (Aberdeen) for the burgesses. On 27 January eight individuals were ordered to appear before the full committee. They included Crawford-Lindsay, Glencairn, Innes of that ilk (Elgin), and Grierson of Lag (Dumfries). Brodie of that ilk was clearly involved in the enforcement of party discipline in his own locality. They were followed by the citation of 11 further individuals on 14 February. On 29 January all officers who had been involved in the Engagement were ordered to withdraw from the kingdom's garrisons.[57]

5. The Appointment of Parliamentary Interval Committees

Eight parliamentary interval committees were appointed, seven of which were appointed between 14 and 16 March. On 6 March commissioners were appointed to treat with the king.

The Committee for Money and Accounts was appointed on 14 March to consider the issue of public debt. Five per estate formed the membership of the committee. Noble membership was composed of the leading radicals (Argyll, Cassillis, Arbuthnot, Burleigh, and Torpichen). Gentry and burghal representatives were leading radicals within their respective estates. Campbell of Cessnock (Ayr) and Hope of Hopetoun were noted radical gentry members. Radical membership was particularly pronounced in terms of burghal membership; Robert Barclay (Irvine), George Porterfield (Glasgow), Hugh Kennedy (Ayr), Gideon Jack (Lanark), and Sir John Smith.[58]

A new Committee of Estates was commissioned on 14 March. Its membership consisted of 21 nobles (including two supernumeraries), 30 gentry (including four supernumeraries), and 29 burgesses (including three supernumeraries). Hence the total membership of the committee was 80. Compared to the previous Committee of Estates of 9 June 1648 (including supernumeraries), the committee of 14 March witnessed a reduction of 19 nobles, 10 gentry, and eight burgesses. Five of the 30 gentry (17%) and eight of 29 the burgesses (28%) included on the new Committee of Estates were not members of Parliament as per 4 January.

Seven of the 21 nobles, two of the 30 gentry, and six of the 29 burgesses (15 individuals in total) had also been included on the previous Committee of Estates of 9 June 1648. The Committee of Estates of 9 June 1648 had been dominated by Engagers from all three estates and the common grouping represents a radical rump of nobles, gentry, and burgesses.

The new Committee of Estates enjoyed a close relationship in terms of membership with the Commission of the Kirk established on 11 August 1648. Eleven of the 21 nobles (52%), 11 of the 30 gentry (37%), and 10 of the 29 burgesses (34%) were included on that commission. Only one of the nobles (Torphichen) on the Commission of the Kirk did not gain membership of the Committee of Estates of 14 March 1649. The noble section of the Commission of the Kirk was quite clearly integrated into the Committee of Estates.[59]

The Commission for the Plantation of Kirks and Valuation of Teinds was renewed on 15 March. Twenty-two nobles, 32 gentry (including five supernumeraries), and 23 burgesses (including one supernumerary) formed its membership. Ten of the 32 gentry (31%) and six of the 23 burgesses (26%) were not members of Parliament as per 4 January.

Seven of the 22 nobles (32%), seven of the 32 gentry (22%), and 11 of the 23 burgesses (48%) had been included on earlier Committees for the Plantation of Kirks and Valuation of Teinds dating from 15 November 1641 to the current date. Once again this provides an indication of the existence of a core of radical personnel, especially in terms of the burgesses. Eleven of the 22 nobles (50%), 13 of the 32 gentry (41%), and eight of the 23 burgesses (35%) included on the Committee for Plantation of Kirks and Valuation of Teinds were also members of the Commission of the Kirk established on 11 August 1648. In common with the membership trends established with the Committee of Estates, this indicates a nucleus of membership originating from the Commission of the Kirk.[60]

A Commission for Revising of the Laws was established on 15 March to consider the issue of legal reform. The relative lack of noble influence (in terms of influence per parliamentary estate) was reflected in the inclusion of only one noble out of 18 members, albeit that noble was Argyll. Neither of the two Extraordinary Lords of Session named on 12 March, Cassillis and Coupar, gained membership of this specialised legal commission. The remaining 17 members were included mainly in a legal capacity, although some were also current members of Parliament. This applies to Johnston of Wariston (Edinburgh), Clerk Register, Campbell of Cessnock (Ayr), Justice Clerk, and Winraham of Libberton (Edinburgh), Lord of Session. Nicholson of Carnock, Lord Advocate, secured inclusion on the committee, as did four Lords of Session including Hope of Hopetoun. They were backed up by a surplus group of parliamentarians consisting of Maxwell of Nether Pollok (Renfrew), Dickson of Hartrie (Peebles), and Robert Barclay (Irvine). Seven of the 18 members were included on the Commission of the Kirk of 11 August 1648, whereas only Argyll and Johnston of Wariston had gained membership of the previous Committee of Estates of 9 June 1648.[61]

Three financial interval commissions were established on 16 March; the Treasury Commission, a new Commission for the Exchequer, and a new Excise Commission. Although the Treasury and Exchequer Commissions were constitutionally separate and distinct, they enjoyed identical membership. Five nobles and one laird formed the membership of both commissions. Loudoun, Argyll, Eglinton, Cassillis, and Burleigh were the five nobles on both commissions. Sir Daniel Carmichael, Treasurer-Depute, was the one laird included on both commissions. With the exception of Loudoun and Carmichael of Hyndford, all were members of the current Commission of the Kirk. All bar Burleigh and Carmichael of Hyndford had been included on the Committee of Estates of 9 June 1648. Given the non-radical nature of the latter committee, this represents an efficient retention of influential radical personnel.[62]

Whereas membership of the Treasury and Exchequer Commissions had been numerically dominated by the nobility, gentry and burghal membership was more to the fore on the Excise Commission. The Excise Commission consisted of five nobles, eight gentry, and five burgesses. Three nobles and three burgesses of the session committee of 27 February, the Committee anent the Additional Excise, were also absorbed into the larger interval committee. Burghal membership was particularly radical, consisting of Sir James Stewart (Edinburgh), Alexander Jaffray (Aberdeen), and Robert Barclay (Irvine), and was supplemented by George Porterfield (Glasgow) and Hugh Kennedy (Ayr). Only two members of the Excise Commission had been included on the Committee of Estates of 9 June 1648, but two nobles, five gentry, and three burgesses were all members of the current Commission of the Kirk.[63]

6. The Operation of Parliamentary Interval Committees

Twenty-six sederunts of the Committee of Estates are recorded between 20 March and 22 May prior to the commencement of the Third Session of the Second Triennial Parliament on 23 May. Nine nobles, seven gentry, and nine burgesses did not attend any diets.

Proceedings were dominated by a relatively small group of nobles, gentry, and burgesses. Chancellor Loudoun (18 diets, 69%), Balmerino (17 diets, 65%), Argyll (11 diets, 42%), Burleigh, and Leven (both 14 diets, 54%) formed the dominant noble grouping. Dickson of Hartrie (Peebles) attended 23 diets (88%), Hope of Hopetoun and Johnston of Wariston (Edinburgh) each attended 19 diets (73%), Chiesly of Kerswell attended 14 diets (54%), whilst Dickson of Busbie (Lanark) attended 13 diets (50%) and Scott of Clerkington attended 12 diets (46%). Three gentry who were not commissioned as members of the Committee of Estates as per 14 March 1649 attended various diets; Scott of Thirlestane (Selkirk), Dundas of that ilk (Linlithgow), and Nicholson of Carnock (Stirling).

Either James Campbell (Linlithgow) or James Campbell (Dumbarton) was also present at 23 diets (88%). James MacCulloch (Whithorn) attended 16 diets (62%), Sir John Smith (Edinburgh) attended 15 diets (58%) and Sir William Dick (Edinburgh) 11 diets (42%).

As per the terms of the commission of 14 March 1649, the quorum was set at nine with two of each estate required to be present. These rules were adhered to at all 26 diets. Chancellor Loudoun presided at 15 diets.[64]

The Third Session of the Second Triennial Parliament, 23 May–7 August 1649

The Scottish diplomatic commissioners had set sail for Holland on 17 March following the close of the parliamentary session. It had been intended that a treaty with the king could be secured with the king and that such a treaty could then be approved and ratified by the Third Session of the Second Triennial Parliament. Nevertheless, when the diplomatic contingent reached Holland they encountered difficulties in the negotiation process. Charles II refused to recognise the 1649 Act of Classes and refused to subscribe the National Covenant or Solemn League and Covenant. By the time the Estates convened on 23 May no agreement had been reached.[65]

1. The Composition of the Third Session of the Second Triennial Parliament

In common with the First and Second Sessions of the the Second Triennial Parliament, deficiences exist in the parliamentary rolls relating to the precise attendance data of the opening day of the session. Twenty nobles are recorded in the parliamentary rolls of 23 May; this represents a rise of four nobles compared to the numerical membership of 4 January. Minimum attendance data amounts to 49 gentry representing 28 shires and 50 burgesses representing 49 burghs. Comparative analysis of minimum and maximum attendance data between 4 January and 23 May indicate that shire and burgh attendance remained more or less constant. In terms of total membership, the composition of the Estates, 23 May 1649, constituted a rise of five members (based on maximum figures) or a rise of six (based on minimum figures) compared to 4 January 1649 (see appendices 4a and 4b).

Significant correlations exist in terms of common membership between the two parliamentary sessions. Thirteen of the 20 nobles (65%), 38 of the 49 gentry (78%), and 46 of the 50 burgesses (92%) recorded in the parliamentary rolls of 23 May had also been recorded in the parliamentary rolls of 4 January 1649.[66]

2. The Proceedings of the Third Session of the Second Triennial Parliament

The legislative agenda of the Third Session comprised 298 enactments (153 of which related to public business and 145 private enactments) and 14 ratifications.[67] Chancellor Loudoun was re-elected as President after the calling of the parliamentary rolls.

Two parliamentary commissions were renewed on 23 May. The commission to the Committee for Money and Accounts (which also acted as the Excise Commission) which had been appointed as an interval commission on 14 March in the previous session was continued as a parliamentary session committee. No changes in the membership of that committee were announced. The Committees of War in the shires were also continued until such time as they were re-elected. The commission to the Committee for Bills and Ratifications appointed on 5 January was also continued on 30 May.[68]

The Committee for Dispatches was appointed on 23 May to oversee all business concerning the army in Scotland and all affairs in England, Holland, and Ireland which concerned Scottish interests. Seven per estate (including supernumeraries) formed the committee membership. A core grouping of three nobles, one laird, and five burgesses had also been included on the previous Committee for Dispatches of 5 January. All were leading radicals within their respective estates and were led by Argyll and Chancellor Loudoun. The retention of burgess personnel between both committees was particularly marked in comparison to the other two estates. This burgess grouping consisted of noted radical burgesses; Sir James Stewart (Edinburgh), George Porterfield (Glasgow), Robert Barclay (Irvine), James Sword (St Andrews), and Hugh Kennedy (Ayr).

With the exception of Wauchope of Niddrie (Edinburgh), all members of the Committee for Dispatches of 23 May had also been included on the Committee of Estates of 14 March.[69] Committee membership was largely based on the Commission of the Kirk of 11 August 1648. Four of the seven nobles, two of the seven gentry, and five of the seven burgess members of the Committee for Dispatches of 23 May were members of that commission.

Additional personnel were added to the Committee for Dispatches during the parliamentary session. Sutherland was added on 31 May and had been a member of the previous Committee for Dispatches of 5 January, as well as a member of the previous Committee of Estates of 14 March. The diplomatic contingent which returned from the Hague on 11 June was added to the committee three days later on 14 June.[70]

Indeed, the Scottish diplomatic commissioners negotiating with the king reported back the House on 11 June. No deal had as yet been reached and the parliamentary conditions of 5 and 7 February for admission to royal office had still not been met. The fundamental insecurity of the radical regime was increased by the presence of Montrose at the Hague who appeared to have a strong influence on the king. In addition, Lauderdale, Callander, Hamilton (previously the Earl of Lanark), Seaforth, St Clair, Napier, and William Murray were also at the Hague. Only William Murray represented Argyll's interests.

Montrose, St Clair, and Napier had all been advising the king to undertake a military invasion of Ireland, a ploy which Charles II himself favoured. However, the Cromwellian conquest of Ireland had effectively neutralised that policy option. The Scottish commissioners consistently opposed the presence of Montrose to the king and demanded his removal. Despite the fact that the proceedings of the diplomatic commissioners were approved by Parliament on 14 June, no agreement/treaty had been secured with the king. On 7 or 8 July a private meeting had taken place to discuss the issue. Loudoun, Argyll, Lieutenant General Leslie, Johnston of Wariston (Edinburgh), Chiesly of Kerswell (Lanark), and five ministers of the Kirk met with Cassillis and Winraham of Libberton (Edinburgh). It was concluded that they would be satisfied if the king adhered to the terms relating to religion and the Covenant. There were only three dissenters from this conclusion; Johnston of Wariston (Edinburgh), Chiesly of Kerswell (Lanark), and James Guthrie, the influential radical minister. It was observed that all three owed their allegiance to the English Commonwealth. On the closing day of the parliamentary session (7 August) Winraham of Libberton (Edinburgh) was dispatched to negotiate with the king once more. This was in spite of clandestine manoeuvres on the part of Argyll and William Murray (Argyll's representative at the Hague) to have Lothian sent alone. Such a manoeuvre was initiated by Argyll in the absence of both Loudoun and Johnston of Wariston and raised two possible scenarios for contemporary observers. Firstly, it was suggested that Argyll's own personal political ambitions were leaning towards a private agreement between himself and the king. On the other hand, it was also suggested that Argyll was considering intervening in the negotiations in order to deliberately scupper the diplomatic process and avoid an agreement with the king. The end result, however, was the defeat of Argyll's motion.[71]

The most significant facet of parliamentary business during the Third Session was the purging of the Scottish armed forces. Despite the the threat of a military invasion from Montrose and uncertainty about the intentions of Cromwell, the Kirk insisted on a systematic programme of purging. The Act for Purging the Army was passed on 21 June. Five Articles for the Purging of Officers and six Articles for the Purging of Soldiers were enacted. Although moral and religious offences as dictated by the Kirk were included, the main emphasis for purging of officers and soldiers lay with those who had been employed in the Engagement armies or had been involved in Huntly's Royalist rising in the north-east. Due to the fact that the orders of February 1649 had not been implemented, new provisions were made to levy over 10,000 men.[72]

Six session committees were appointed throughout the parliamentary session to deal with military matters and valuations in the shires relating to the raising of revenue. Two of these committees were essentially specialised session committees with local remits and were composed mainly of non-parliamentary personnel; the Committee for Trial of the Collectors of Perthshire and the Committee for Revaluation of the Parish of Ayr. The former committee consisted solely of 13 gentry, whilst the latter's membership consisted of only three gentry and five burgesses. Only one local member of Parliament was included on each of these committees.[73]

The remaining four military/valuation session committees were the Committee for Grievances (31 May), the Committee for Rectifying Valuations (1 June), the Committee anent the Rates of Money and Inbringing of Bullion (12 June), and the Committee to Compare the Maintenance with the Pay of the Army (14 June). Membership of these specialised committees was overwhelmingly based on membership of the Committee of Estates of 14 March, although close membership ties were also retained with the Commission of the Kirk of 11 August 1648. Five military officials were also included on the committee relating to army pay. Leading radicals from all three estates were included on these specialised committees, although this trend was especially marked in terms of noble and burgess membership.[74]

The issue of the distribution of the monthly maintenance levels on a national basis created dispute and disruption within the House. Legislation was enacted which redressed previous levels of maintenance which had ensured that the western shires had paid a larger proportion of the maintenance than their eastern counterparts. The maintenance was now to be raised on a more equitable basis, with the eastern shires paying an increased proportion. This was made possible by the fact that the western shires had been prominent in the Whiggamore Raid and many eastern nobles were now excluded from Parliament due to their involvement in the Engagement. Cassillis, Campbell of Cessnock (Ayr), and Chiesly of Kerswell (Lanark) were the leading figures behind the legislation of 27 July. This was despite the opposition of Burleigh, Balcarras, Lothian, and the commissioners of the shires for Lothian and Fife. When the legislation was passed, over half the members of Parliament present left the House and refused to return for over two weeks, leaving the western representatives in complete control of parliamentary proceedings. Western representation had become increasingly prominent on session committees throughout the parliamentary session. The power base of the radical regime was primarily in the south-west and had now struck out to secure its own financial interests.[75]

Inter-parliamentary dispute was not limited to the gentry. Westerns burgh challenged the financial privileges of Edinburgh in the Convention of Royal Burghs on 3 July. This occurred in the Convention of Royal Burghs on 3 July. The proportion paid per burgh of the total maintenance and other sundry taxes was increased from 28.75% to 36% for the burgh of Edinburgh, whilst the proportion for Glasgow and Irvine, as well as St Andrews was decreased. The muscle of George Porterfield (Glasgow), Robert Barclay (Irvine), and James Sword (St Andrews) was being clearly exercised in real political terms. A bitter dispute between the burghal estate and the nobility occurred on the closing day of the parliamentary session concerning the levels of interest rates. Interest rates were reduced from 8% to 6%. As it was the burgesses who formed the prominent group of money lenders within Scottish society, it was that group which was affected by such legislation. Cassillis was one of the leading figures behind the reduction in interest rates. The whole of the burghal estate, bar one or two lesser burghs, walked out of Parliament, and despite moves by Johnston of Wariston (Edinburgh) and Robert Douglas, representative of the Kirk, to have the close of Parliament delayed, the session ended without the presence of the burghal estate.[76]

Furthermore, the power base of the radical regime among the gentry and burgesses was reflected in legislation which weakened the number of the maximum number of possible nobles sitting in Parliament. In common with legislation of 19 July 1641, it was enacted on 6 August that no noble under the age of 21 could qualify for admittance to Parliament or the Privy Council. This suggests that nobles under this age were sitting/or attempting to sit in Parliament. Indeed, both Angus and Elcho had gained membership of the session committee, the Committee for Additional Excise of 27 February. The fact that so many nobles were now barred from public office due to their involvement in the Engagement may have led many noble families to send their eldest sons to Parliament to preserve family and geographical influence. In turn, this may have warranted a political reaction by the gentry and burgesses.[77]

On 7 August the Second Triennial Parliament was continued to the first Thursday in March 1650. All undetermined bills and reports had already been remitted to the consideration of the Committee of Estates on 3 August.[78]

3. The Committee Structure of the Third Session of the Second Triennial Parliament

Eight session committees and seven interval committees have been analysed. Seven nobles, 27 gentry, and 18 burgesses were nominated to the eight session committees. The comparative figures for the seven interval committees are 27 nobles, 49 gentry, and 38 burgesses. Fifteen of the 27 gentry (56%) and five of the 18 burgesses (28%) included on session committees were not members of Parliament as per 23 May 1649. The bulk of this non-parliamentary membership was based on two localised session committees, the Committee for the Revaluation of the Parish of Ayr and the Committee for the Trial of the Collectors of Perthshire. All 15 gentry were included on the two localised committees. Of these 15, only one, Ruthven of Frieland, was included on any other session committee. Four of the five burgesses were included on one of the localised committees.

In comparison, 15 of the 49 gentry (31%) and 14 of the 38 burgesses (37%) included on interval committees were non-members of Parliament. Nine of the 15 gentry and six of the 14 burgesses were included on the Committee of Estates. Seven of the 15 gentry and five of the 14 burgesses were included on the Committee for Plantation of Kirks and Valuation of Teinds. Five of the seven gentry and four of the five burgesses were included on both the Committee of Estates and the Committee for Plantation of Kirks and Valuation of Teinds. A core grouping of non-parliamentary personnel was therefore being deployed on the most important interval committees.

Noble common membership of session committees, although limited, centred on Lothian (four committees), Argyll and Burleigh (three committees each), and Cassillis (two committees). Gentry attendance was centred on Ruthven of Frieland (Perth), Chiesly of Kerswell (Lanark), Hope of Hopetoun (Stirling), and Campbell of Cessnock (Ayr). Burghal common membership was focused on Robert Barclay (Irvine), George Porterfield (Glasgow), Hugh Kennedy (Ayr), and Alexander Jaffray (Aberdeen). The remaining eight burgesses were included on one session committee each.[79]

Those nobles, gentry, and burgesses prominent on parliamentary session committees were also prominent in their inclusion on parliamentary interval committees. Argyll was nominated to six of the seven interval committees, whilst Cassillis and Burleigh were included on five interval committees. In addition, Eglinton and Arbuthnot were included on four interval committees, whilst five further nobles gained membership of three interval committees each. Campbell of Cessnock (Ayr) secured nomination to five of the seven interval committees. Winraham of Libberton (Edinburgh), Hope of Hopetoun (Stirling), Ruthven of Frieland (Perth), and Cunningham of Cunninghamhead (Ayr) each gained membership of four interval committees. Nine further gentry were included on three interval committees each. A similar trend is evident regarding burghal membership of interval committees. Robert Barclay (Irvine) was also a member of five interval committees. Sir John Smith (Edinburgh), George Porterfield (Glasgow), and Hugh Kennedy (Ayr) were all nominated to four interval committees. Two further burgesses were included on three interval committees each.[80]

Geographically, western gentry and burgesses were taking on a more prominent role, primarily because the power base of the radical regime was in that domain. In terms of membership per estate, the nobility were numerically dwarfed by the gentry and the burgesses from whom the dynamism of the radical regime emanated. Of all three estates, it was the gentry who were the dominant force in numerical terms.

4. The Appointment of Parliamentary Interval Committees

All parliamentary interval committees established by the Second Session were renewed on 7 August. In addition, a new Committee of Estates was appointed. Membership of the renewed committees remained unaltered, with the exception of the addition of Dickson of Hartrie (Peebles) to the Committee for Plantation of Kirks and Valuation of Teinds.[81]

The new Committee of Estates of 7 August consisted of 25 nobles (including one supernumerary), 44 gentry (including four supernumeraries), and 29 burgesses (including three supernumeraries). Its total membership amounted to 98. Compared to the previous committee of 14 March, there was a rise in membership of four nobles and 14 gentry. Burghal membership remained the same. The new committee, in terms of membership, was essentially a renewal of the previous commission supplemented by a grouping of additional nobles, gentry, and burgesses. All 21 nobles, 30 gentry, and 29 burgesses included on the previous committee of 14 March secured membership on the new committee. They were supplemented by four nobles and 14 gentry. Seven gentry and six burgesses on the new Committee of Estates were not members of Parliament as per 23 May. Panmure, Tweeddale, Forrester, and Balcarras were the four nobles who were added to the committee. All had been admitted to Parliament in early July 1649 despite their involvement in the Engagement. Their inclusion on the Committee of Estates of 7 August may have been to bolster the ranks of the nobility compared to the other two estates, especially given the fact that there was a low attendance of nobles throughout the parliamentary session. All 10 nobles, 20 of the 36 gentry (56%), and 12 of the 16 burgesses (75%) included on the Commission of the Kirk of 4 August 1649 were also included on the new committee.[82]

Conclusion

The defeat of the Engagers at the Battle of Preston and the Whiggmore Raid had resulted in the installation of a radical regime in Edinburgh. It was composed of a limited radical noble base, but its power base in terms of manpower emanated from the gentry (especially) and the burgesses. The execution of Charles I, carried out without the consent or approval of the Scottish Parliament, resulted in the proclamation of the Prince of Wales as Charles II as King of Great Britain, France, and Ireland. The conditions which were required to be met before the admission to royal office ensured that the future monarch would not only be a constitutional monarch, but also a covenanted monarch. Paradoxically, a process of wholescale purging of public offices removing those involved in the Engagement was initiated by the Committee of Estates and continued by Parliament. Such a policy was incorporated in the 1649 Act of Classes. Only those nobles, gentry, and burgesses who were successfully vetted by the radical leadership could hold public office. Officers of State, Ordinary and Extraordinary Lords of Session were all purged and a new radically based Privy Council was appointed. By the close of the Third Session of the Second Triennial Parliament, Charles II had not yet agreed to the parliamentary terms to secure admission to royal office. Moreover, there was a strong threat of some form of a Royalist invasion led by Montrose, fears which had been accentuated by the abortive Pluscardine Rising, at the same time when no accomodation with the king had been reached. The radical regime had now become isolated within the British archipelago as Cromwell was in the process of subjugating Ireland. The purging of the Scottish armed forces, at the insistence of the Kirk and with parliamentary sanction, was to have catastrophic results militarily and politically in 1650–51 as the covenanted kingdom of Scotland collapsed.

NOTES

1. EUL, Dc 5. 44, Alexander Hamilton of Kinkell, Memoirs of Scots Affairs from the Death of King Charles I to the Restoration, folio 77.
2. W.C. Abbott (ed), *The Writings and Speeches of Oliver Cromwell*, volume one, (Harvard, 1937), 659–664.

3. *A True Account of the great Expressions of Love from the Noblemen, Ministers and Commons of the Kingdom of Scotland unto Lieutenant General Cromwel, and the Officers and Soldiers under his command. Whose mutual love each to other is hoped to be the beginnings of a happy Peace to both Nations. Declared in a Letter to a Friend* (London, 1648) (3)-(4), (6)-(7), (8); *Scotlands Holy War. A Discourse Truly, and plainly remonstrating, how the Scots out of a corrupt and pretended zeal to the Covenant have made the same scandalous, and odious to all good men: and how by religious pretexts of saving the Peace of Great Brittain they have irreligiously involved us all in a most pernitious Warre* (London, 1651), (21), (31).
4. SRO PA 11/7, Register of the Committee of Estates, 22 September 1648–2 January 1649, ff 1–129. Twenty-seven further diets took place between 20 October 1648 and 2 January. No sederunts were recorded for these diets. Prior to 22 September subcommittees of the Commission of the Kirk were already meeting with the Committee of Estates (*RCGA*, ii, 35, 41, 59, 63).
5. Ibid, ff 1–129; *APS*, vi, ii, 3–4, 102–105.
6. SRO PA 11/7, ff 1–129, folio 11.
7. Ibid.
8. Ibid; APS, vi, ii, 102–105, 124–126.
9. SRO PA 11/7, ff 1, 7; Ferguson, *Scotland's Relations with England*, 134; Donaldson, *James V–James VII*, 339; Ian Gentles, *The New Model Army in England, Ireland and Scotland, 1645–1653* (Oxford, 1992), 265; Lynch, *Scotland, A New History*, 278.
10. EUL, Dc 5. 44, Memoirs of Scots Affairs, ff 19–22, 80–82.
11. *APS*, vi, ii, 124–156, 157.
12. Ibid, 3–4, 124–126.
13. Kirkton, *History of the Church of Scotland*, 22; *APS*, vi, ii, 3–4, 124–126. A.I MacInnes, 'Scottish Gaeldom, 1638–1651: The Vernacular Response to the Covenanting Dynamic' in *New Perspectives on the Politics and Culture of Early Modern Scotland*, eds. J. Dwyer, R.A. Mason and A. Murdoch (Edinburgh), 75.
14. APS, vi, ii, 3–4, 124–126; Abbott, *Writings and Speeches of Oliver Cromwell*, volume one, 669.
15. Ibid, 126–156, 126; Balfour, *Historical Works*, III, 374.
16. *APS*, vi, ii, 126–127, 127, 128, 128–129, 132, 152. Balfour, *Historical Works*, III, 375.
17. *APS*, vi, ii, 10, 102–105, 128.
18. *APS*, vi, ii, 128; *Records of the Kirk*, 514–515.
19. *APS*, vi, ii, 10–11, 102–105, 128. *Records of the Kirk*, 514–515. Balfour, *Historical Works*, III, 376.
20. Ibid.
21. Balfour, *Historical Works*, III, 377.
22. Ibid; Stevenson, *Revolution and Counter-Revolution in Scotland*, 130.
23. *APS*, vi, ii, 129. The full clause was as follows: 'The estats of parlement now pntly Conveened in yis second session of ye second Trienniall parlement be vertue of ane act of the Committee of estats who had power and auctie from ye last parlement for conveining the pliament'.
24. Ibid, 132.
25. Ibid, 130–132, 132.
26. Ibid, 129, 130–132, 138–139, 150–151.
27. Ibid, 132, 142. Brodie of that ilk (Elgin) and Winraham of Libberton (Edinburgh)

represented the gentry. Alexander Jaffray (Aberdeen) and Robert Barclay (Irvine) represented the burgesses.

28. Ibid, 143–147; EUL, Dc 5. 44, Memoirs of Scots Affairs, ff 78–79; Stevenson, *Revolution and Counter-Revolution in Scotland*, 130; Rait, *Parliaments of Scotland*, 72.
29. *APS*, vi, ii, 146–147, 153–154; Stevenson, *Revolution and Counter-Revolution in Scotland*, 130; MacInnes, 'The Scottish Constitution, 1638–51,' 126–127.
30. *APS*, vi, ii, 147–148.
31. *APS*, vi, ii, 141–142; Stevenson, 'The Financing of the Cause of the Covenants, 1638–51', 114.
32. *APS*, vi, ii, 153–154, 154–155; Stevenson, 'The Financing of the Cause of the Covenants, 1638–51', 114. The maintenance collected from Engagers for the period March to July 1648 was to be distributed among opponents of the Engagement in proportion to their losses.
33. *APS*, vi, ii, 127–128, 156; Balfour, *Historical Works*, III, 383–386. Legislation enacted prior to 3rd February was attributed to the previous reign (Rait, *Parliaments of Scotland*, 316). Sir John Chiesly and William Glendoning were not members of Parliament as per 4 January 1649.
34. *APS*, vi, ii, 157–376.
35. Ibid, 157; BL, Egerton MS 2542, Nicholas Papers, ff 1–2; Stevenson, *Revolution and Counter-Revolution in Scotland*, 132.
36. *APS*, vi, ii, 161; Stevenson, *Revolution and Counter-Revolution in Scotland*, 132; *RCGA*, ii, 196–198; Carte, *A Collection of Original Letters and Papers*, 180.
37. *The Desires of the Commissioners of the Kingdom of Scotland: That Both Houses of Parliament may sit in freedome for setling of Religion according to the Covenant. That King Charls the Second (Upon just satisfaction given) May be admitted to the Government of these Kingdomes. Together with their Protestation against all proceedings to the contrary* (1649), (5)-(6); *An Act for the Abolishing the Kingly Office in England, Ireland, and the Dominions Thereunto belonging* (London, 1648).
38. EUL, Dc 5. 44, Memoirs of Scots Affairs, ff 61–65.
39. Ibid, ff 67–68.
40. *APS*, vi, ii, 211–212, 232, 236, 300; Balfour, *Historical Works*, III, 392, states that Robert Barclay (Irvine) was also sent to Holland. Stevenson, *Revolution and Counter-Revolution in Scotland*, 133.
41. *APS*, vi, ii, 174–364; Stevenson, *Revolution and Counter-Revolution in Scotland*, 134.
42. *APS*, vi, ii, 124–126, 174–176, 176–178, 178–179, 179–181, 196–198, 199–201, 271–273, 273, 273–274, 274, 274–275, 316, 321. Cassillis had been offered the position of Joint Secretary with Lothian but he had refused to accepted. Campbell of Cessnock refused the position of Justice Clerk but this position was not filled until March 1651 when Sir Robert Moray took up the office, Stevenson, *Revolution and Counter-Revolution in Scotland*, 134. Balfour, *Historical Works*, III, 389–390.
43. *APS*, vi, ii, 181–183, 195–196, 196–198, 270–271, 283, 283–285; Stevenson, *Revolution and Counter-Revolution in Scotland*, 134; Balfour, *Historical Works*, III, 389–390; D. Haig and G. Brunton, *The Senators of the College of Justice* (1832), xx, 296–344.
44. *APS*, vi, ii, 277.
45. Ibid, 124–126, 316–317. The seven Sheriff Principals who were members of Parliament were William Douglas of Mouswall (Dumfries), Sir Charles Erskine of Alva (Cambuskenneth), Sir David Home of Wedderburne (Berwick), Sir Thomas

Ruthven of Frieland (Perth), John Lindsay of Edzell (Forfar), Sir John Sinclair of Dunbeath (Caithness), and William Forbes of Leslie (Aberdeen).

46. Kirkton, *History of the Church of Scotland*, 22; *APS*, vi, ii, 102–105, 124–126, 364. John, second Lord Balmerino, had died on 1 March 1649 (*Scots Peerage*), volume one, 568–569; *Records of the Kirk*, 514–515. Arbuthnot, Brechin, Coupar and John, third Lord Balmerino formed the grouping of four nobles on the Privy Council. Erskine of Cambuskenneth (Clackmannan), Home of Wedderburne (Berwick), Ruthven of Frieland (Perth), Adair of Kinhilt (Wigtown), and Forbes of Echt (Aberdeen) formed the grouping of five gentry on the Privy Council.
47. Balfour, *Historical Works*, III, 391; MacInnes, 'The Scottish Constitution, 1638–1651', 127.
48. Balfour, *Historical Works*, III, 391; *APS*, vi, ii, 261–262; Stevenson, *Revolution and Counter-Revolution in Scotland*, 137–139, 141. For a more detailed account of the Commission of the Kirk as a parliamentary lobbying agency and the nature of social and moral legislation enacted, see J.R. Young, 'Scottish Covenanting Radicalism, the Commission of the Kirk, and the establishment of the parliamentary radical regime of 1648–49', *RCHS*, (1995).
49. *APS*, vi, ii, 128–129, 141–142, 286, 364, 725–726, 124–376. Robert Hepburn of Keith (Haddington), John Dickson of Hartrie (Peebles), and Sir James Hope of Hopetoun formed the membership of the Committee for Revising of Reports and Bills. Hope of Hopetoun was not a member of Parliament as per 4 January 1649.
50. Ibid, 376; SRO Supplementary Parliamentary Papers, 1649, PA 7/6/62.
51. *APS*, vi, ii, 124–156, 157–376.
52. Ibid, 124–156.
53. Ibid, 157–376.
54. The register of the Committee for Dispatches, SRO PA 11/8, ff 1–7, has been calendared in Stevenson, *Government Under the Covenanters*, 83–94, where the full attendance data can be examined.
55. Ibid, 83–84, 84.
56. Ibid, 83–84, 89, 90, 90–91, 91–92, 92–93; Stevenson, *Revolution and Counter-Revolution in Scotland*, 145–148.
57. Stevenson, *Government Under the Covenanters*, 85–86, 86–87, 88.
58. *APS*, vi, ii, 124–126, 294–296. One laird, Sir James Hope of Hopetoun, and one burgess, Sir John Smith (Edinburgh), were not members of Parliament as per 4 January 1649.
59. Ibid, 102–105, 124–126, 290–292; *Records of the Kirk*, 514–515. The common membership between the Committees of Estates of 9 June 1648 and 14 March 1649 consisted of Argyll, Loudoun, Leven, Eglinton, Cassillis, Buccleuch, and Lothian for the nobility, Erskine of Scottiscraig (Fife) and Johnston of Wariston (Edinburgh) for the gentry, and Hugh Kennedy (Ayr), John Forbes (Inverness), George Garden (Burntisland), John Hay (Elgin), James MacCulloch (Whithorn), and Gilbert More (Banff) for the burgesses. Gilbert More was not a member of Parliament as per 4 January 1649.
60. *APS*, v, 400; *APS*, vi, i, 199, 778–779; *APS*, vi, ii, 114, 300; *Records of the Kirk*, 514–515. Loudoun, Argyll, Eglinton, Cassillis, Buccleuch, Lothian, and Burleigh formed the grouping of seven nobles included on previous Committees for Plantation of Kirks and Valuation of Teinds since 1641. The grouping of seven gentry included on previous committees consisted of Brodie of that ilk (Elgin), Johnston of Wariston (Edinburgh), Belshes of Toftis (Berwick), Sir John Hope of Craighall, Dundas of that

ilk (Linlithgow), Wauchope of Niddrie (Edinburgh), and Home of Wedderburne (Berwick). The grouping of 11 radical burgesses consisted of George Porterfield (Glasgow), Sir James Stewart (Edinburgh), Sir John Smith (Edinburgh), Thomas Bruce (Stirling), Robert Cunningham (Kinghorn), James Sword (St Andrews), John Semple (Dumbarton), William Glendoning (Kirkcudbright), Robert Barclay (Irvine), Alexander Douglas (Banff), and George Garden (Burntisland).

61. *APS*, vi, ii, 102–105 283, 299–300, 317. *Records of the Kirk*, 514–515. Eight new Lords of Session and two Extraordinary Lords of Session had been named on 12 March. Campbell of Cessnock was appointed Justice Clerk on 15 March.
62. *APS*, vi, ii, 102–105, 124–126, 321; *Records of the Kirk*, 514–515. Sir Daniel Carmichael was not a member of Parliament as per 4 January 1649.
63. *APS*, vi, ii, 102–105, 321; *Records of the Kirk*, 514–515.
64. Ibid, 290–292. SRO PA 11/8, ff 11–92.
65. Stevenson, *Revolution and Counter-Revolution in Scotland*, 151; Balfour, *Historical Works*, III, 393, 397; G.R Kinloch (ed.), *The Diary of Mr John Lamont of Newton, 1649–71* (Maitland Club, 1830), 2; J. Barclay (ed.), *Diary of Alexander Jaffray* (Aberdeen, 1856), 54; *CSPV*, 1647–1652, 93.
66. *APS*, vi, ii, 124–126, 377–378.
67. Ibid, 377–554.
68. Ibid, 128–129, 294–296, 378–379, 379, 380, 384.
69. Ibid, 128, 290–292, 379.
70. Ibid, 128, 290–292, 386, 414. Balfour, *Historical Works*, III, 408; *The Diary of Mr John Lamont of Newton*, 2.
71. *APS*, vi, ii, 411, 553, 727–732; Stevenson, *Revolution and Counter-Revolution in Scotland*, 151; Carte, *A Collection of Original Letters and Papers*, 238; *CSPV*, 1647–1652, 127; Baillie, *Letters and Journals*, III, 99; Balfour, *Historical Works*, III, 146–147.
72. *APS*, vi, ii, 447–448, 477, 506–508, 511, 527–528; Stevenson, *Revolution and Counter-Revolution in Scotland*, 152.
73. *APS*, vi, ii, Sir Thomas Ruthven of Frieland (Perth) was the member of Parliament included on the Perthshire committee. Hugh Kennedy (Ayr) was the member of Parliament included on the Ayrshire committee.
74. Ibid, 388, 389–90, 409, 414. Argyll, Lothian, and Burleigh were all included on both the Committee for Grievances and the Committee for Rectifying Valuations. George Porterfield (Glasgow) and Robert Barclay (Irivine) were prominent for the burgesses, as was Chiesly of Kerswell (Lanark) for the gentry.
75. Ibid, 501–502; Baillie, *Letters and Journals*, III, 98; Stevenson, *Revolution and Counter-Revolution in Scotland*, 154; Stevenson, 'The Financing of the Cause of the Covenants', 117.
76. Stevenson, 'The Financing of the Cause of the Covenants', 117–118; Stevenson, *Revolution and Counter-Revolution in Scotland*, 152; Stevenson, *Government Under The Covenanters*, xxxvi; Baillie, *Letters and Journals*, III, 98–99.
77. *APS*, vi, ii, 527.
78. Ibid, 519, 538.
79. Ibid, 377–554. No nobles were included on the Committee anent the rates of money and inbringing of bullion, and the two session committees with local remits
80. Ibid, 377–554.
81. *APS*, vi, ii, 537, 539.
82. Ibid, 290–292, 377–378, 536–537; *Records of the Kirk*, 549–550. Legislation of 19

July 1641 had barred heirs of noblemen from parliamenatry proceedings. Angus, Elcho, and Brechin all secured membership of the Committee of Estates. Yet their additions were not in contravention of the 1641 legislation as the Committee of Estates was free to include such members as it wished as an interval committee (Beattie, 'The Political Disqualification of Noblemen's Heirs in Seventeenth Century Scotland', 176).

10

The Rule of the Radical Regime, August 1649–September 1650

By the close of the Third Session of the Second Triennial Parliament on 7 August, the radical regime had conducted a thorough programme of purging of Engagers from public office. The regime now faced two increasingly dangerous external threats to its security. Within the context of the British archipelago, Cromwellian imperialism had succeeded in the subjugation of Ireland, whilst the threat of a military invasion by Montrose remained a real one.

The Operation of Parliamentary Interval Committees, August 1649–February 1650

A combined total of 49 sederunts are recorded in two committee registers between 10 August 1649 and 26 February 1650. Thirty-two sederunts are recorded between 10 August and 27 November, and 17 sederunts are recorded between 4 December and 26 February.[1] The committee convened at Edinburgh between 10 and 23 August, at Perth between 24 August and 3 September, before returning to Edinburgh from 7 September to 27 November. The movement of the committee of to Perth was undertaken primarily to force Highland Engagers to sign declarations denouncing the Engagement. As well as the concentration on Engagers, attention was also focused on purging minor officials from public office.

Attendance analysis of the committee between 10 August and 27 November indicates that it was the gentry who appear to have been dominating the committee proceedings. Both noble and burghal representation were based on a small caucus of nobles and burgesses. Chancellor Loudoun attended 23 of the 32 diets (72%) and presided at 20 diets. Lothian attended 17 diets (53%). The remaining 23 nobles attended 11 or less diets and six nobles did not attend at all. For the burghal estate, Sir John Smith (Edinburgh) is recorded at 21 diets (66%) and James MacCulloch (Whithorn) at 17 diets (53%). The remaining 27 burgesses attended 10 or less diets and three did not attend at all.

Gentry attendance was based on four individuals, none of whom were members of Parliament as per 23 May 1649; Johnston of Wariston (Edinburgh) 28 diets (88%), Belshes of Toftis (Berwick) 26 diets (81%), Hope of Craighall 21 diets (66%), and Dickson of Busbie (Lanark) 17 diets (53%). Two further lairds, Winraham of Libberton (Edinburgh) and Wauchope of Niddrie (Edinburgh) attended 20 diets (62%) and 18 diets (56%). The remaining 38 gentry attended 14 or less diets and one did not attend at all. As per the commission to the Committee of Estates of 7 August 1649 the quorum was set at nine with no specification on attendance per estate. This rule was adhered to at all diets of the committee over the whole period.[2]

In the period between 4 December and 26 February 1650 both noble and burghal attendance was spread within a broader field of personnel compared to the previous period. Chancellor Loudoun and Cassillis were present at all 17 diets recorded. Loudoun presided at 16 of these diets. Coupar attended 16 diets (94%), whilst Argyll, Lothian, and Balcarras each attended 14 diets (82%). Fourteen nobles are recorded in less than eight sederunts and seven did not attend at all. Either James Campbell (Dumbarton) or James Campbell (Linlithgow) attended 13 diets (76%). James MacCulloch (Whithorn) is recorded in 12 sederunts (70%), whilst Sir John Smith (Edinburgh), Robert Lockhart (Edinburgh), and Sir James Stewart (Edinburgh) are all recorded in 11 diets (65%). The latter three burgesses were not members of Parliament as per 23 May 1649. Excluding these six burgesses, 19 burgesses are recorded in less than eight sederunts and 10 burgesses did not attend at all.[3]

Gentry attendance, on the other hand, was concentrated within a smaller field in comparison to the noted gentry pattern in the former period. The majority of nobles, gentry, and burgesses in attendance between December 1649 and February 1650 had been in regular attendance between August and November 1649. Johnston of Wariston (Edinburgh) appears to have been the most influential laird on the committee. The leading political ally of Argyll, he attended 16 diets (94%). Two further lairds, Carmichael of Hyndford (Lanark) and Wauchope of Niddrie (Edinburgh) are both recorded in 14 sederunts (82%). Twenty-two gentry are recorded in less than eight sederunts and five did not attend at all.

Argyll had now taken on a more prominent role on the committee and Johnston of Wariston continued to be the most influential radical laird. Edinburgh burgesses dominated burghal attendance, primarily because the committee had returned to the capital.

On 8 January the Committee of Estates approved of a commission for purging the armed forces. This was fully ratified by the Committee of Estates on 22 January. The commission incorporated a subcommittee of the Committee of the Estates for purging. As per the Act for Purging the Army of 28 June 1649 of the Third Session, the commissioners for purging the army were not named but it would appear that the committee of 28 June constituted a parliamentary session committee. Purging of the armed forces had been a live political issue for the Commission of the Kirk since at least January 1649 and the subcommittee of the Committee of Estates appears to have been set up in response to a subcommittee of the Commission of the Kirk formed on 2 January. No common membership exists between the two committees and the subcommittee of the Committee of Estates was clearly the dominant one.

The membership of the Committee for Purging the Army of January 1650 was nominated and appointed by the General Officers of the army and other subordinate officers. In total there were 13 members of the Committee for Purging the Army. Argyll and Weymes were the only two nobles included.

Weymes was not a commissioned member of the Committee of Estates as per the commission of 7 August 1649. The remaining 11 members were all included in a military capacity, six of whom had served in either current or previous Parliaments; Sir James Halkett of Pitfirrane (Fife), Andrew Kerr of Greenhead (Roxburgh), William Kerr of Newton (Roxburgh), Arthur Forbes of Echt (Aberdeen), John Swinton of that ilk (Berwick), for the gentry, and Sir James Stewart (Edinburgh) for the burgesses. Membership of the Committee for Purging the Army was clearly based on the gentry.[4]

At the close of the Third Session of on 7 August, Parliament had overruled Argyll and authorised the dispatch of Winraham of Libberton (Edinburgh) to the Hague instead of Lothian. Although Libberton did not finally leave until 12 October, he was issued with instructions by the Committee of Estates on 12 September. Charles would be invited to come to Scotland if he acknowledged the legality of Parliament and the Committee of Estates and all other parliamentary conditions. By the time Libberton reached the Hague the king had moved to Jersey. Nevertheless, the fact that Cromwell had now succeeded in subjugating much of Ireland meant that an alliance/treaty with the Scottish Parliament was the only viable way for Charles to secure his thrones. Yet the king would not budge from his refusal to acknowledge the legitimacy of the radical regime in Scotland. All he was prepared to compromise on was the sending of Scottish diplomatic commissioners to Breda to negotiate a treaty on 15 March. The king's terms were included in correspondence directed to the Committee of Estates. Libberton returned to Scotland and informed the committee of these developments on 5 February.

The immediate response of the Committee of Estates was the formation of a subcommittee to consider the issue. A final decision was not reached by the full Committee of Estates until 21 February, when it was decided that diplomatic commissioners should be sent to negotiate a treaty with the king at Breda. Not only had the king gained the upper hand, but the decision was not reached without controversy and dissension. The majority of the full committee, led by Argyll and Chancellor Loudoun, advocated the sending of commissioners, whereas Cassillis, Johnston of Wariston, and Swinton of that ilk, younger, all argued against. Cassillis and Wariston had been members of the subcommitee of 5 February which also indicates that no unanimity had been reached in the subcommittee.

The latter grouping, allied closely to the Kirk, was backed by several ministers who attended the diet. They were defeated despite attempts to delay the decision until the meeting of the next parliamentary session and despite the fact that they had produced evidence of correspondence between the king and Montrose concerning an invasion of Scotland. This indicates that the influence of the Kirk, regarding this particular decision, had been sidelined. Moreover, Argyll had been specifically appointed by the Committee of Estates on 13 February (*one week after 5 February*) to inform the Commission of the Kirk of the contents of the king's letter to the Committee of Estates. In response to Argyll's information, a specialised subcommittee of the Commission of the Kirk was formed on 13 February to meet with the subcommittee of the Committee of Estates to discuss these issues.

It was also agreed on 21 February, however, that the diplomatic commissioners could not conclude a treaty on their own and any agreement would be subject to parliamentary ratification. The commissioners were duly named by the Committee of Estates on 22 February. All had been included in the Commission of the Kirk of 4 August 1649. Therefore the Kirk had managed to salvage back its influence in the naming of the commissioners. Two nobles, one laird, and one burgess named on the diplomatic commission of 22 February had also been members of the subcommittee of 5 February. Cassillis, Lothian, Brodie of that ilk (Elgin), and Sir John Smith (Edinburgh) formed this grouping. Cassillis had therefore been nominated as a commissioner, despite his opposition to the principle of sending diplomatic commissioners.[5]

The Fourth Session of the Second Triennial Parliament, 7–8 March 1650

1. The Composition of the Fourth Session of the Second Triennial Parliament

As with the previous three sessions of the Second Triennial Parliament deficiencies exist in the parliamentary rolls relating to the attendance of shire and burgh commissioners (refer to appendices 4a and 4b). The minimum parliamentary membership as per 7 March 1650 consisted of 23 nobles, 29 gentry representing 16 shires, and 25 burgesses representing 24 burghs. Corresponding maximum figures amount to 57 gentry representing 30 shires and 58 burgesses representing 57 burghs. Minimum attendance figures over all three estates present the most realistic scenario. According to Sir James Balfour, 'scarsse halffe of the Commissioners of Shyres and Burrowes (were) present'.[6] Minimum attendance figures per estate indicate a rise of three nobles, a reduction of 20 gentry, and a reduction of 25 burgesess, compared to the previous parliamentary session of 23 May 1649. Nineteen of the 23 nobles (83%), 15 of the 29 gentry (52%), and 24 out of the 25 burgesses (96%) listed in the parliamentary rolls of 7 March 1650 had also been included in the parliamentary rolls of 23 May 1649. Ten of these burgesses were included in five dual commissions (two commissioners were named on an either or basis but only one commissioner could actually sit in Parliament). In terms of common membership, there was a high retention of personnel among the ranks of the nobility and the burgesses between the two parliamentary sessions, with a circa 50% retention rate among the gentry.[7]

2. The Proceedings of the Fourth Session of the Second Triennial Parliament

Eight enactments (seven of which related to the public business) constitute the legislative programme of the parliamentary session. After the calling of the parliamentary rolls and the subscription of the parliamentary oath, Chancellor Loudoun was re-elected as President. Following the formal reading of the king's letter had been made to the House, the commission to the Scottish diplomatic commissioners to negotiate at Breda was approved.

The limited parliamentary agenda of 7 March was continued on 8 March with the issue of the diplomatic remit and negotiating terms for the Breda commissioners. On a broader pan-European diplomatic front, Parliament attempted to involve the Prince of Orange in the negotiating process before the commissioners reached Breda. Correspondence sent by Parliament to the Prince of Orange advocated that the Prince should persuade Charles II to accept the demands of the Scottish Parliament.

Twelve separate diplomatic instructions for the commissioners were approved of by Parliament on 8 March. The subscription of the National Covenant and the Solemn League and Covenant was required, the legality of all sessions of the 1649 Parliament was to be acknowledged, as was the the separation of civil and ecclesiastical powers. In addition, all commissions granted by the king to Montrose were to be cancelled and Ormond's treaty with the Irish Catholic confederates was to be nullified. The negotiating period for securing a treaty at Breda was set at 30 days, although the commissioners could actually stay for another 10 days if necessary. Moreover, the commissioners were required to secure the king's signature to a treaty in Holland. If this was not possible, then the king's signature was to be gained before he landed in Scotland otherwise he would be refused access to the royal office. Parliament further ordained that if the Committee of Estates wished to alter any of the instructions sent to the commissioners then six days notice of any alteration was required as was a quorum of 20 with at least five of each estate being present. Moreover, any new instructions issued were not to be contrary to the instructions presently issued. Where matters of religion were concerned, the consent of the Moderator of the Commission of the Kirk was required upon six days prior notice. Therefore Parliament, and not the Kirk, was exerting a large degree of policy control over the most important parliamentary interval committee. Once again, the influence of the Kirk in the formulation of factional policy had been sidelined.[8]

Parliament was ordered to reconvene on 15 May in the hope that in the interim a treaty could be agreed on at Breda and that such a treaty could be ratified during the Fifth Session.[9]

3. The Committee Structure of the Fourth Session of the Second Triennial Parliament

Due to the short-term nature of the session, no session committees were appointed. Only one interval committee was appointed (the diplomatic contingent for Breda), albeit the commission to the Committee of Estates of 7 August 1649 was renewed with additions. All members of the diplomatic grouping had been members of the Committee of Estates of 7 August 1649.[10]

4. The Appointment of Parliamentary Interval Committees

The previous Committee of Estates of 7 August 1649 was renewed on 8 March with 10 additions. The effect of the additions of 8 March was to strengthen the numerical superiority of both the gentry and burgesses over the nobility. The original committee of 7 August 1649 had consisted of 25 nobles, 44 gentry, and 29 burgesses (all including supernumeraries). As per 8 March the renewed committee was now composed of 26 nobles, 50 gentry, and 32 burgesses. These figures provide an indication of the limited extent of radicalism within the nobility compared to the other two estates. The 10 additions were made up of one noble, six gentry, and three burgesses. The influence of the House of Argyll was enhanced by the addition of Lord Lorne, son of the Marquis of Argyll. Lorne's inclusion was not illegal as per the legislation of 19 July 1641 barring noblemen's heirs, as the Committee of Estates could appoint any further membership that it wished. Only one of the additions, Colville of Blair, Justice Depute, was a member of the Commission of the Kirk established on 4 August 1649. Blair was not a member of Parliament as per 7 March 1650.[11]

The Fifth Session of the Second Triennial Parliament, 15 May–5 July 1650

In the interim period between the close of the Fourth Session and the commencement of the Fifth Session several crucial developments had taken place. Firstly, the internal security to the radical regime had been shaken by Montrose's invasion of the Scottish mainland via Orkney. Following his defeat at Carbisdale on 27 April, Montrose was now held in secure imprisonment. Secondly, the defeat of Montrose had dictated that the only realistic possibility of the king securing his thrones lay in a political accommodation with the radical regime. Although such an accommodation had been reached by 1 May, Charles had not agreed to subscribe the Covenants nor disregard the treaty with the Irish Confederates.

Factionalism had emerged among the Scottish diplomatic commissioners throughout the negotiations. Dissension was apparent as early as the first meeting with the king on 19 March. Lothian and Winraham of Libberton argued that Hamilton, Lauderdale, and other former Engagers should be brought into the negotiating process. The election of Cassillis as President of the diplomatic commissioners ultimately weakened the extreme radicals and the Kirk for Cassillis could only vote if the votes of the other commissioners were equally tied. Therefore the more moderate commissioners secured a permanent voting majority. Despite the fact that Cassillis and Brodie signed the invitation of 29 April for Charles to come to Scotland (which was accepted on 1 May), in conjunction with the three ministers at Breda they urged the Kirk to prevent the agreement being ratified by Parliament, primarily because the king had still not signed the Covenants. Therefore although an agreement had been reached, it had been the parliamentary commissioners and not the king who had been forced to compromise.[12]

1. The Proceedings of the Fifth Session of the Second Triennial Parliament[13]

The legislative programme of the Fifth Session consisted of 41 enactments (29 of which were public enactments and 12 of which were private acts) and 13 ratifications. After the subscription of the parliamentary oath Chancellor Loudoun was re-elected as President.[14]

Eighteen members of the king's entourage in Holland were barred from entering the country by Parliament on 18 May. All were required to give satisfaction to Kirk and State before rights of entry would be granted. Twelve nobles, including Hamilton, Traquair, and Lauderdale, and six gentry constituted this grouping. Lauderdale was later allowed to stay in the country until mid-August and as late as 13 September Chancellor Loudoun was complaining to the king that many of those ordered to leave had not yet done so.[15]

Two parliamentary session committees were established on 16 May; the Committee for Prisoners, Processes, Fines, and Forfaultures and the Committee for Dispatches. The principal remit of the former committee was to deal with the prisoners captured in Montrose's abortive rebellion. This was modified on 6 June, however, when the House stated that all members of the Committee for Processes were to be included on the Committee for Fines and vice versa. This suggests that either there was a separate Committee for Processes in operation independent of the Committee for Prisoners, Processes, Fines, and Forfaultures, or the latter committee had split into two sections and was now being formally remerged.

Three per estate formed the membership of the Committee for Prisoners, Processes, and Fines. In terms of the total committee membership only one noble and one laird had not been included on the Committee of Estates of 8 March. However, Chiesly of Kerswell (Lanark), Colville of Blair, Justice Depute, James Campbell (Dumbarton), and Alexander Douglas (Banff) were all members of the Commission of the Kirk of 4 August 1649. Additions of one per estate were made to the committee on 20 May. Torphichen, Hope of Hopetoun (Stirling), and John Hay (Elgin) formed this additional membership. With the exception of Torphichen all had been included on the renewed Committee of Estates of 8 March, albeit none had been included on the Commission of the Kirk of 4 August 1649.[16]

Seven per parliamentary estate, plus Chancellor Loudoun as supernumerary, formed the membership of the Committee for Dispatches of 16 May. A core of four nobles, two gentry, and four burgesses had also been included on the previous Committee for Dispatches of 23 May 1649. This core contained leading radicals and consisted of Argyll, Buccleuch, Burleigh, and Chancellor Loudoun (supernumerary on both committees) for the nobility, Adair of Kinhilt (Wigtown) and Hope of Hopetoun (Stirling) for the gentry, with Sir James Stewart (Edinburgh), George Porterfield (Glasgow), Hugh Kennedy (Ayr), and James Sword (St Andrews) for the burgesses.

Including Loudoun as supernumerary, six of the eight nobles, six of the seven gentry, and five of the seven burgesses had been members of the Committee of Estates of 8 March. On the other hand, three nobles, three gentry, and five burgesses had all been included on the Commission of the Kirk of 4 August 1649. In terms of the membership of the Committee for Dispatches as per 16 May, only two nobles, one laird, and one burgess did *not* have membership links with either the Committee of Estates or the Commission of the Kirk. Roxburgh, Weymes, Swinton of that ilk (Berwick), and John Jaffray (Aberdeen) represented this 'non-grouping'.

The intense radical orientation of the committee was enhanced on 4 June by the addition of two western gentry and one western burgess, all of whom were of sound radical pedigree. Campbell of Cessnock (Ayr), Cunningham of Cunninghamhead (Ayr), and Robert Barclay (Irvine) formed this additional membership. All had been members of the Committee of Estates of 8 March. Both Campbell of Cessnock and Robert Barclay had served on the previous Committee for Dispatches of 23 May 1649 and were also members of the Commission of the Kirk of 4 August 1649.[17]

On 16 May the House appointed Argyll, Home of Wedderburne (Berwick), and Sir James Stewart (Edinburgh) to liaise with the Commission of the Kirk. Both Argyll and Home of Wedderburne were actually members of the Commission of the Kirk established on 4 August 1649. However, this grouping did not constitute a parliamentary session committee. Parliament was to appoint an official and formal committee to liaise with the Kirk and the Kirk was to do likewise.[18]

Two procedural session committees were established to ensure the efficient passage of parliamentary legislation; a Committee for the Bills (21 May) and a Committee for Overtures and Laws (23 May). Both committees consisted of three per estate and in both cases membership was more closely linked to the Committee of Estates than the Commission of the Kirk. With the exception of Weymes, all members of the Committee for Bills had been included on the Committee of Estates of 8 March. Two of the three nobles, two of the three gentry, and one of the three burgesses on the Committee for Overtures and Laws had also been members of that Committee of Estates. The only member of the Committee for the Bills included on the Commission of the Kirk of 4 August 1649 was Eglinton, whereas only Burleigh and Thomas MacBirnie (Dumfries), and John Corsan (Kirkcudbright) were the Commissioners of the Kirk included on the Committee for Overtures and Laws.

Limited common membership also existed between the two procedural committees themselves. Buccleuch, Weymes, and Dickson of Hartrie (Peebles) were members of both the Committee for Bills and the Committee for Overtures and Laws. Membership of both committees appears to have been partly based on specialised knowledge and/or parliamentary experience. Two gentry members of the Committee for Bills, Dickson of Hartrie (Peebles) and Hepburn of Keith (Haddington), had also served on the previous Committee for Bills established on 30 May during the Fourth Session. Moreover, Hope of Hopetoun (Stirling) had also served on that committee and was also a current member of the new Committee for Overtures and Laws. These close ties of membership may explain the decision of the House on 18 June to merge the Committee for Bills and the Committee for Overtures and Laws into a single session committee. Such specialised experience may have ensured that the legislative workload could be dealt with by a single committee.[19]

Three financial session committees were appointed throughout the Fifth Session; the Committee for Valuations, the Committee for Oaths in Matters of Excise, and the Committee for the General Commissioner's Affairs. The Excise Commission was also continued on 16 May and additions were made on 4 June. Balcarras and Campbell of Cessnock (Ayr) had been included on the Committee of Estates of 8 March, whilst Campbell of Cessnock and John Corsan (Kirkcudbright), the remaining committee member, had been included on the Commission of the Kirk of 4 August 1649.

Five per estate formed the membership of the Committee for Valuations established on 29 May. Membership was closely related to both the Committee of Estates and the Commission of the Kirk. Three of the five nobles, four of the five gentry, and four of the five burgesses had been members of the previous Committee of Estates of 8 March. Two nobles, four gentry, and three burgesses had also been included on the Commission of the Kirk of 4 August 1649 and all of this latter grouping were members of the Committee of Estates. The core grouping therefore consisted of Eglinton, Burleigh, Ruthven of Frieland (Perth), Adair of Kinhilt (Wigtown), Chiesly of Kerswell (Lanark), Forbes of Echt (Aberdeen), James Sword (St Andrews), Robert Barclay (Irvine), and Alexander Douglas (Banff).[20]

Three per estate formed the membership of the Committee for Oaths in Matters of Excise appointed on 29 May. All three nobles, two of the three gentry, and two of the three burgesses had been included on the recommissioned Committee of Estates of 8 March; Argyll, Burleigh, Balcarras, Carmichael of Hyndford (Lanark), Dundas of Duddingston (Linlithgow), Sir James Stewart (Edinburgh), and James Sword (St Andrews). Similarly, two per estate were members of the Commission of the Kirk of 4 August 1649. All had also been included on the Commission of the Kirk of 4 August 1649 with the exception of Balcarras, Dundas of Duddingston (Linlithgow), and John Jaffray (Aberdeen). Scott of Harden (Selkirk) was the remaining committee member included on the Commission of the Kirk.[21]

The Committee for the General Commissioner's Affairs was appointed on 1 June. It dealt with the affairs of Sir James Stewart (Edinburgh) in the capacity of General Commissioner. Three per estate formed its membership. All three nobles, two of the three gentry, and two of the three burgesses had been included on the recommissioned Committee of Estates of 8 March 1650. By way of comparison, only Burleigh and Ruthven of Frieland (Perth) had been included on the Commission of the Kirk of 4 August 1649. Subsequent additions of leading western gentry and burgesses were made on 18 June. Campbell of Cessnock (Ayr) was added for the gentry as was Hugh Kennedy (Ayr) for the burgesses. In addition, James Sword (St Andrews) replaced Alexander Bower (Dundee) who had been absent from the committee's proceedings.[22]

The punishment of those involved in Montrose's abortive invasion was delegated on 30 May to the Committee anent Accessories to the Late Rebellion in the North, composed of four per estate. All had been included on the recommissioned Committee of Estates of 8 March except for Weymes, Brisbane of Bishopton (Renfrew), and John Corsan (Kirkcudbright). A radical grouping of one noble and three burgesses had been included on the Commission of the Kirk of 4 August 1649. Eglinton, Sir James Stewart (Edinburgh), Hugh Kennedy (Ayr), and John Corsan (Kirkcudbright) formed this grouping.[23]

Significantly, the Committee anent Accessories to the Late Rebellion was appointed after the case of Montrose had been dealt with and after he had been tried and executed. The case of the leading protagonist had clearly taken priority. Legislation sanctioning the execution of Montrose was passed on 17 May. A parliamentary delegation of one per estate accompanied by three ministers of the Kirk was sent to the Tolbooth on 18 May to inform Montrose to come to the House to receive his sentence. Burleigh, Hope of Hopetoun (Stirling), and George Porterfield (Glasgow), all noted radicals, formed the membership of the parliamentary delegation. Nevertheless, Montrose's execution was delayed until 20 May apparently because a further parliamentary delegation, staffed by leading radicals from all three estates, was needed to examine Montrose on information relating to Hamilton. Burleigh, Hope of Hopetoun (Stirling), Johnston of Wariston (Edinburgh), Clerk Register, Nicholson of Carnock (Stirling), Lord Advocate, and Sir James Stewart (Edinburgh) formed the membership of this second parliamentary delegation. Montrose's sentence was read to Parliament on 20 May and he was executed the following day.[24]

Continued diplomatic negotiations with the king and the levying of forces to meet the threat from Cromwell constituted the most important components of the parliamentary agenda of the Fifth Session. New diplomatic instructions were issued to the Breda commissioners on 17 May. These clarified and expanded on the agreement reached between the king and the diplomatic commissioners on 1 May. Parliamentary ratification of the invitation to come to Scotland was dependent on the king accepting all former demands made by Kirk and Parliament, and the Covenants were to be subscribed. The factional interest of the radical regime was also enforced and those found guilty under the 1646 Act of Classes and the 1649 Act of Classes (in effect Royalists and Engagers) were to be refused access to the king. The regime likewise exercised its own interests within the wider British archipelago. Not only was the treaty with the Irish Confederates to be disregarded, but Scottish efforts to help the king recover his English and Irish thrones did not imply that Scotland would declare war on his behalf, except with the approval of Kirk and Parliament.

In the event Charles was faced with no viable option but to accede to the regime's demands and he eventually signed the Covenants at Speymouth on 23 June. The Treaty of Breda received parliamentary ratification on 4 July and the coronation was scheduled for the opening of the Sixth Session of the Second Triennial Parliament to be held on 15 August 1650.[25]

The role and conduct of Archibald Campbell, eighth Earl and first Marquis of Argyll, in bringing the uncrowned king home from Breda had proved crucial. Argyll's motives in this were subjected to scrutiny by contemporary commentators. Two main opinions were articulated by one scribe. Firstly, Argyll was the driving force behind the king's return quite simply to 'prevent his punishment for complyance in ye late kings death'. Argyll's behaviour at the diet of 6 January 1649 of the Committee for Dispatches when Wariston attempted to delay the drawing up of diplomatic instructions for the Scottish commissioners in London (during the trial of Charles I) must be borne in mind regarding these allegations. His conduct at that diet suggests that there was a possibility that both Argyll and Wariston were trying to delay attempts to save the king's life. The second opinion, belonging to 'more moderate men', assigned Argyll's actions to 'ambition' and the desire to be the king's 'onely creature'. The scribe's own personal view was that Argyll was 'much for a king upon easier tearmes, if a king will come his way, and acknowledge him ye onely instrument'.[26] Further evidence was supplied to question Argyll's previous motives and actions. It was alleged that when Charles I was still located at Newcastle in the mid-1640s that Argyll was in correspondence with his wife, Queen Henrietta Maria, to persuade the king 'to betake Himselfe wholy to Argylle'. In return, Argyll would safeguard the king's safety and restoration. Now in 1650 it was alleged that Argyll had a 'greate interest' and correspondence with the Queen Mother and the French Court, as well as meeting with a French agent in Edinburgh (the brother of the diplomat Jean de Montereul). The intended result of this was to secure the agreement of Charles to the 'present State of Scotland'. The Prince of Orange, Lauderdale, and the rest of the 'Scotts Lords' at the Hague similarly adhered to this notion. Moreover, it was also alleged that Argyll was in correspondence with all of those 'Scots Lords'.[27] Another scribe attributed Argyll's enthusiasm for bringing the king home to the necessity of the continuance of monarchy in Scotland, despite the faults of Charles I; a necessity that had been highlighted by the abolition of monarchy in England. Therefore the uncrowned Charles II should return to Scotland for 'if the family of the Stuarts were passed by it was uncertain where the Monarchy would subsist'.[28]

The levying of armed forces proved to be an issue of major contention in the House. Initial opposition from the shires and burghs to the nobility's desire for a new levy, through fear that a new army would be Royalist in sympathy, soon evaporated when it became clear that an English invasion was imminent. When the Act of Levy was passed on 25 June there were only six votes in opposition. The opposition vote consisted of four gentry and two burgesses, all of whom appear to have been ideologically aligned to the English Commonwealth. Hope of Hopetoun (Stirling), Swinton of that ilk, younger, (Berwick), Glendoning of Galstoun (Kirkcudbright), and Chiesly of Kerswell (Lanark) constituted the gentry opposition vote, whilst burghal opposition came from Sir James Stewart (Edinburgh) and John Jaffray (Aberdeen). Orders for a second levy, (double that of August 1649) which amounted to a total figure for the armed forces of over 36,000 men, were enacted on 3 July.

Prior to the new levies, it had nevertheless been enacted on 21 June that purging of the armed forces should continue. Moreover, it was ordained on 22 June that none of the army officers were to be allowed membership of a purging committee. A Committee for Purging the Army was subsequently formed as a session committee on 28 June, and operated as a parliamentary interval committee after 5 July. Its commission was to endure until the Sixth Session.

The Committee for Purging the Army was composed of five per estate. It was staffed by leading radicals from all three estates. With the exception of two burgesses, all members of the Committee for Purging the Army had been members of the renewed Committee of Estates of 8 March. Three of the five nobles, three of the five gentry, and four of the five burgesses were also members of the Commission of the Kirk established on 4 August 1649. The Commission of the Kirk had been lobbying for further military purging from 23 May and the formation of the purging committee can be viewed as a victory for the Kirk. Hope of Hopetoun (Stirling), Chiesly of Kerswell (Lanark), and Sir James Stewart (Edinburgh) all secured inclusion, despite the fact that they had all voted in opposition to new levies being raised. In addition, Eglinton, Cassillis, Burleigh, Brodie of that ilk (Elgin), Johnston of Wariston (Edinburgh), George Porterfield (Glasgow), Alexander Jaffray (Aberdeen), and Robert Lockhart (Edinburgh) formed the remaining commissioners of the Kirk on the committee.[29]

Purging was not limited to the armed forces, but was also applied to parliamentary members themselves. A specialised session committee was established on 8 June to revise the commissions of shire and burgh members and to vet individual members. This appears to have been at the instigation of the Commission of the Kirk who wanted to increase purging levels to Parliament. On 23 May the Commission had approved a lobbying remonstrance for Parliament, which included demands for purging of judicatories as well as the army. Although three per estate were included on the committee, only details of gentry membership are provided. All three were members of the Commission of the Kirk established on 4 August 1649; Forbes of Echt (Aberdeen), Swinton of that ilk (Berwick), and Chiesly of Kerswell (Lanark).

The voting strength of the shires and burghs had combined to defeat the nobility in determining that Callander should not be allowed to stay in the country. He had arrived in the capital in May and the nobles in Parliament advocated that he should be allowed to remain. It was the votes of the gentry and burgesses on 25 May that forced his expulsion.[30]

2. The Committee Structure of the Fifth Session of the Second Triennial Parliament

Nine session committees and five interval committees have been linked to provide a total analytical structure of 14 committees. Eighteen nobles, 27 gentry, and 22 burgesses form the total field of membership for these 14 committees.

Weymes, Buccleuch, and Balcarras were each included on eight committees. Burleigh was nominated to seven committees and Eglinton was included on six committees. The remaining 13 nobles were included on three or less committees and four nobles gained membership of only one committee. Gentry committee membership was based largely on Hope of Hopetoun (Stirling) (seven committees), Chiesly of Kerswell (Lanark), and Ruthven of Frieland (Perth) (six committees each). Four further gentry secured nomination to five committees, whilst one laird was included on four committees. The remaining 19 gentry were included on three or less committees and nine gentry were included on only one committee. Only one burgess, Sir James Stewart (Edinburgh), gained membership of seven committees. George Porterfield (Glasgow) and Hugh Kennedy (Ayr) were included on six committees, whereas Robert Barclay (Irvine) was nominated to five committees. Five burgesses were included on four committees. The remaining 13 burgesses were included on three or less committees and 10 burgesses were included on only one committee.[31]

A larger field of personnel was employed by the gentry in comparison to the other two estates. In general terms, gentry common membership was concentrated on the west and the Borders, whilst burghal common membership was focused on the west. Indeed, although the east was still well represented on committees, the Borders and the west still had a notable presence. This is consistent with the power base of the radical regime being located in the west and the south-west.

3. The Appointment of Parliamentary Interval Committees

The Excise Commission had been continued on 16 June and additions had also been made to the Exchequer Commission on 4 June. Both these commissions operated as interval commissions following the close of the parliamentary session. The Committee for Purging of the Army of 28 June operated as a parliamentary interval committee after 5 July.

Following the parliamentary ratification of the Treaty of Breda, 12 commissioners were appointed to proceed to the king once he had landed in Scotland. These commissioners were also incorporated within a parliamentary interval commission, and consisted of four per estate. Cassillis and Lothian were the most noted radical noble members. All gentry and burgess members were noted radicals. Three of the four nobles, three of the four gentry, and two of the four burgesses had also been included on the recommissioned Committee of Estates of 8 March 1650. Two nobles, two gentry, and two burgesses had also been included on the Commission of the Kirk of 4 August 1649. Therefore the committee to proceed with the king following his homecoming was essentially a subcommittee of the Committee of Estates, albeit close links with the Commission of the Kirk were retained.[32]

No official membership details are provided for a Committee of Estates established on 4 July. This committee was to be the 'Kings grate counsaill' until the next parliamentary session. The previous Committee of Estates of 8 March was continued and six additions of three nobles, one laird, and two burgesses were made on 4 July. None of the additions were members of the Commission of the Kirk established on 4 August 1649. Two quorums for the committee had been set; one of 13 for 'ordinarey affairs of the kingdome' and one of 21 for 'matters of grate consequence concerning the kingdome'. A vote was taken in the House whereby a quorum of 15 was decided on.[33]

On 5 July the Committee for Money and Accounts appointed on 14 March

1649 was recommissioned. Three of the five nobles on the original commission were replaced. Argyll, Cassillis, and Burleigh were replaced by Buccleuch, Weymes, and Balcarras. Replacement was not based on purging and it would appear that the services of Argyll and the other two leading radical nobles were required on more pressing business, namely the position of the king. Indeed the radical presence on the committee was enhanced by six additions, consisting of one noble, three gentry, and one burgess; Balmerino, Johnston of Wariston (Edinburgh), Dickson of Hartrie (Peebles), and Nicholson of Carnock (Stirling), Lord Advocate, and Sir James Stewart (Edinburgh). Of the six additions, membership was based on the Committee of Estates as opposed to the Commission of the Kirk. Only Weymes and Sir James Stewart had not been included on the Committee of Estates of 8 March, whereas only Johnston of Wariston and Sir James Stewart were members of the Commission of the Kirk established on 4 August 1649.[34]

Changes to the Exchequer Commission established on 14 March 1649 were also announced on 5 July. The original commission had been dominated by the nobility and had consisted of five nobles and one laird, but this dominance was redirected towards an exact balance between the noble estate and the shires with the addition of four gentry; Hope of Hopetoun (Stirling), Dickson of Hartrie (Peebles), Chiesly of Kerswell (Lanark), and Adair of Kinhilt (Wigtown). All had been members of the renewed Committee of Estates of 8 March, yet only Kerswell was a member of the Commission of the Kirk of 4 August 1649.[35]

4. The Operation of Parliamentary Interval Committees[36]

The formal rapprochement between Charles II and the Scottish Parliament had now aroused the hostility of the English republicans. Whilst the collapse of the king's Royalist cause in Ireland had ensured that Scotland now provided the sole opportunity of the king securing his thrones, paradoxically, this in turn had dictated that the security of the English Commonwealth and the ascendancy of Independency in England was now dependent on a the military defeat of the Scots as backers of Charles's restoration in the three kingdoms of the British archipelago.[37]

Cromwell and his army had crossed the Tweed on 22 July. In the period up to military defeat at Dunbar on 3 September, wholescale purging of the Scottish armed forces took place, weakening the military base for opposing Cromwell. The Committee for the Purging of the Army met on 2, 3, and 5 August. Over 80 members of the command structure of the armed forces were purged whilst the committee 'acted nothing against the enimey'.[38] Despite enjoying not only military superiority in numbers (20,000 to Cromwell's 11,000), but also a superior strategic position, the ministers present at the scene harried the commander of the armed forces, David Leslie, to abandon all superiority resulting in a rout by inferior numbers and the loss of circa 14,000 men (4,000 were killed and 10,000 captured).[39]

In the aftermath of Dunbar, the influence of the ministry continued unabated with demands for further purging of the army as well as the royal entourage. Military defeat had only strengthened the resolve of the ministry to purge the ungodly from God's chosen nation. The Act for Purging the King's Household was passed by the Committee of Estates on 27 September. Twenty-four members of the court (most of whom were English courtiers) were ordered to leave the court and the kingdom. Defeat at Dunbar emphasised the urgency of Parliament convening to deal with the national crisis. The Sixth Session had been scheduled to meet on 15 August, but given the threat of the Cromwellian forces, had been postponed until 10 September. At the diet of the Committee of Estates on 10 September the meeting of the Sixth Session was postponed on five occasions before being finally scheduled for Perth on 26 November.[40]

Attempts to stabilise the regime were not helped by the actions of the king himself. An emergency diet was convened by Chancellor Loudoun at Perth on 4 October after the incident known by as 'The Start' whereby the king fled from the protection of the Committee of Estates and attempted to join Middleton's Royalist force in the Highlands. All members of the Committee of Estates were ordered to attend, as were 'such as wer weill affected'.[41] In the event, the meeting was attended by only five nobles, eight gentry, two burgesses, and one minister. A delegation was sent from the Committee of Estates to locate the king and by 10 October he had returned to the jurisdiction of the committee.[42]

Conclusion

The radical regime strengthened its political and factional base within Parliament. Whilst correlation clearly exists between membership of parliamentary committees and the Commission of the Kirk, a close relationship in terms of membership also existed with the Committee of Estates. The political manpower of the radical regime remained concentrated in the west and the Borders, although there was also a noted eastern (especially Edinburgh) influence. Four months of continued diplomatic pressure and harassment of the king had been necessary before the Treaty of Breda could be ratified. Royal rapprochement with the radical regime was nevertheless an exercise in realpolitik and offered the only real possibility of Charles securing his English throne. Radical insistence on the purging of the Scottish armed forces, initiated and sustained by the Kirk, weakened military resistance to Cromwell's invading army, as witnessed at the fiasco of Dunbar, and was to facilitate the process of foreign occupation and subjugation by Cromwell in 1651.

NOTES

1. SRO PA 11/8, Register of the Committee of Estates, 8 August–27 November 1649, ff 99–202; SRO RH 2/1/42, Transcripts of the Committee of Estates, 4 December 1649–26 February 1650, pp. 1–173.
2. Ibid; *APS*, vi, ii, 377–378, 536–537; Stevenson, *Revolution and Counter-Revolution in Scotland*, 154.

3. SRO RH 2/1/42, 1–173; *APS*, vi, ii, 377–378, 536–537. One noble, Weymes, attended nine diets, and one laird, Andrew Agnew of Lochnaw younger, attended three diets, although they were not members of the committee as per 7 August 1649.
4. SRO RH 2/1/42, pp. 64, 87–88; *APS*, vi, i, 95–96, 284–285, 440–441, 612–613; *APS*, vi, ii, 3–4, 124–126, 377–378, 446–447; *RCGA*, ii, 150, 340; Stevenson, *Revolution and Counter-Revolution in Scotland*, 115. The commission of the sub-committee of the Committee of Estates for purging the army had expired by 18 February (*RCGA*, ii, 348, 361, 364–365).
5. SRO RH 2/1/42, 125, 166; *RCGA*, ii, 354–355, 367, 368–370; *Records of the Kirk*, 549–550; J. Nicholl, *A Diary of Public Transactions and Other Occurrences, Chiefly in Scotland, from January 1650 to June 1667* (Bannatyne Club, Edinburgh, 1836), 4; Stevenson, *Revolution and Counter-Revolution in Scotland*, 155–157.
6. Balfour, *Historical Works*, IV, 4; *APS*, vi, ii, 377–378, 555–556. Lord Torphichen is included in the parliamentary rolls for the nobility. Balfour, *Historical Works*, IV, 4, states that Torphichen was removed from the House on the insistence of Cassillis who pointed out that Torphichen was under the age of 21 and therefore could not sit in Parliament. However, Balfour, later states that Torphichen subscribed the parliamentary oath. Therefore it is unclear whether or not Torphichen was actually allowed to remain in the House.
7. *APS*, vi, ii, 377–378, 555–556.
8. Ibid, 556–561; SRO Supplementary Parliamentary Papers, 1650, PA 7/7/3; Balfour, *Historical Works*, IV, 5–6; Stevenson, *Revolution and Counter-Revolution in Scotland*, 157. The king was to be 'offered' £300,000 if he accepted the regime's demands. If he refused then the commissioners were 'to giue him no money at all' (Balfour, *Historical Works*, IV, 7).
9. *APS*, vi, ii, 561; Nicholl, *A Diary of Public Transactions*, 5.
10. *APS*, vi, ii, 556–556, 561.
11. Ibid, 536–537, 555–556, 561; *Records of the Kirk*, 549–550. One of the burgess additions, John Denholm, was not a member of Parliament as per 7 March 1650. He was probably the John Denholm who was appointed Commissary General at a later date on 17 October 1650 (Stevenson, *Government Under the Covenanters*, 195). Two additions were also made to the Privy Council; Lorne and Weymes were added for the nobility. Lorne's addition to the Privy Council was not illegal as the legislation of 19 July 1641 only applied to Parliament itself (Beattie, 'The Political Disqualification of Noblemen's Heirs in Seventeenth Century Scotland', 176).
12. EUL, Dc 5. 44, Memoirs of Scots Affairs, 184–185, Stevenson, *Revolution and Counter-Revolution in Scotland*, 159–160; *CSPV*, 1647–1652, 150.
13. No official parliamentary rolls have been recorded/surived for this session (*APS*, vi, ii, 562).
14. Ibid, 562–607. Burleigh was subsequently elected as Vice-President on 18 June, due to the absence of Loudoun. He was to retain this position until Loudoun returned.
15. Balfour, *Historical Works*, IV, 14; *The Diary of Mr John Lamont of Newton*, 17. D. Laing, (ed), *Correspondence of Sir Robert Kerr, first Earl of Ancrum and his son William, third Earl of Lothian*, volume two, 1649–1667, (Edinburgh, 1875), 303; Hewison, *The Covenanters*, volume two, 2.
16. *APS*, vi, ii, 536–537, 561, 563, 565; *Records of the Kirk*, 549–550.
17. *APS*, vi, ii, 379, 536–537, 561, 563, 573; *Records of the Kirk*, 549–550. SRO Supplementary Parliamentary Papers 1650, PA 7/7/10, Minutes of the Committee for Dispatches, 16 May–5 June 1650, records six sederunts. Four gentry who were

non-members of the committee each attended one diet; Johnston of Wariston (Edinburgh), Clerk Register, Hepburne of Humbie (Haddington), Forbes of Echt (Aberdeen), and Inglis of Ingliston.

18. *APS*, vi, ii, 562; *Records of the Kirk*, 549–550. On receiving the parliamentary delegation, a subcommittee of the Commission of the Kirk, consisting of 12 ministers and four lay elders, was formed on 16 May (*RCGA*, ii, 388–389).
19. *APS*, vi, ii, 384, 536–537, 561, 566, 567, 581; *Records of the Kirk*, 549–550.
20. *APS*, vi, ii, 536–537, 561, 563, 569, 571, 573; *Records of the Kirk*, 549–550.
21. *APS*, vi, ii, 536–537, 561, 569; *Records of the Kirk*, 549–550.
22. *APS*, vi, ii, 536–537, 561, 571, 581; *Records of the Kirk*, 549–550.
23. *APS*, vi, ii, 536–537, 561, 570; *Records of the Kirk*, 549–550. Balfour, *Historical Works*, IV, 35, states that the committee appointed on 30 May was to consider the extent of fines to be imposed on those who had taken oaths and subscribed bands to Montrose in Orkney, Shetland and Caithness. It is therefore possible that it is this committee, referred to as the Committee for Fines as per 6 June, that was merged with the Committee for Prisoners, Processes, Fines, and Forfaultures (*APS*, vi, ii, 574).
24. Balfour, *Historical Works*, IV, 12, 13–14, 15, 19.
25. *APS*, vi, ii, 601–602, 607; Stevenson, *Revolution and Counter-Revolution in Scotland*, 168–169; Abbott, *Writings and Speeches of Oliver Cromwell*, volume two, 280, 293; Balfour, *Historical Works*, IV, 12, 14, 41–44, 79.
26. BL Add MS 34, 713, Historical Collections, 1642–1796, ff 7–8. For a recent study of Argyll's political ideology, see E.J. Cowan, 'The Political Ideas of a Covenanting Leader: Archibald Campbell, Marquis of Argyll, 1607–1661', in R.A. Mason (ed), *Scots and Britons. Scottish Political Thought and the Union of 1603* (Cambridge, 1994), 241–262.
27. Ibid.
28. EUL, Dc 5. 44, Memoirs of Scots Affairs, ff 173, 173–177.
29. *APS*, vi, ii, 536–537, 561, 586, 587, 588–590, 594, 597–600. Stevenson, *Revolution and Counter-Revolution in Scotland*, 171; Balfour, *Historical Works*, IV, 57, 70, 71, 79–80; *Records of the Kirk*, 549–550; *RCGA*, ii, 411–412. The remaining members of the Committee for Purging the Army were Buccleuch, Balmerino, Cunningham of Cunninghamhead (Ayr), and Robert Foullis. For detailed consideration of the political ideology of Sir James Hope of Hopetoun see A.H. Williamson, 'Union with England Traditional, Union with England Radical: Sir James Hope and the Mid-Seventeenth-Century British State', *EHR*, 110, (1995), 303–322.
30. *APS*, vi, ii, 568; *Records of the Kirk*, 549–550; Stevenson, *Revolution and Counter-Revolution in Scotland*, 171; Balfour, *Historical Works*, IV, 25, 52; *RCGA*, ii, 411–412.
31. *APS*, vi, ii, 562–607.
32. *APS*, vi, ii, 536–537, 561, 563, 573; *Records of the Kirk*, 549–550.
33. Balfour, *Historical Works*, IV, 74; *APS*, vi, ii, 561, 602; *CSPD*, 1650, 234; *Records of the Kirk*, 549–550.
34. *APS*, vi, ii, 294–296, 561, 604; *Records of the Kirk*, 549–550; Balfour, *Historical Works*, IV, 78, only lists the changes in membership for the nobility and states that Balmerino replaced Chancellor Loudoun possibly in the capacity of supernumerary.
35. *APS*, vi, ii, 321, 561, 604; *Records of the Kirk*, 549–550.
36. No manuscript registers for the Committee of Estates are available/have survived.
37. Abbott, *Writings and Speeches of Oliver Cromwell*, volume two, 292–293; *A Declaration of the Army of England, Upon their March into Scotland* (London, 1650).

38. Balfour, *Historical Works*, IV, 89; Stevenson, *Revolution and Counter-Revolution in Scotland*, 171–172.
39. Stevenson, *Revolution and Counter-Revolution in Scotland*, 177–179; Abbott, *Writings and Speeches of Oliver Cromwell*, volume two, 312–332; C. Hill, *God's Englishman. Oliver Cromwell and the English Revolution* (London, 1970), 125. Hill notes that this was the first major military confrontation where Cromwell did not possess superior numbers.
40. Balfour, *Historical Works*, IV, 89–93, 96, 98, 109, 127, 129, 166; *Correspondence of Sir Robert Kerr, first Earl of Ancrum and his son William, third Earl of Lothian*, volume two, 302; Nicholl, *Diary of Public Transactions and Other Occurrences*, 23; NLS MS 2263, History of Events 1635–1662, ff 214, 215, 216.
41. Balfour, *Historical Works*, IV, 115; Donaldson, *James V–James VII*, 341.
42. Balfour, *Historical Works*, IV, 115.

11

The Patriotic Accommodation, 1650–1651

The Operation of Parliamentary Interval Committees, October-November 1650.

The proceedings of the Committee of Estates up to the opening of the Sixth Session of the Second Triennial Parliament on 26 November 1650 will be examined in terms of the extent of rapprochement between the various factions within Scotland in light of defeat at Dunbar and the growing threat to national independence from Cromwell and his forces, a threat which had come to realisation in the partial Cromwellian occupation of the kingdom.

In the immediate aftermath of defeat at Dunbar four separate and rival forces were now stationed in Scotland; the residue of the official Scottish army crushed at Dunbar, the extreme radical forces of the Western Association, a smaller Royalist rump in the north-east following the Atholl Rebellion, and the English Cromwellian forces. Plans for Charles to join with the Royalist forces in the north-east, known as 'the Start', had failed at the beginning of October. Having fled, Charles was captured by the Committee of Estates, and it had become clear not only that the king would have to co-operate with the Committee of Estates, still under the direction of the radicals, but that body would also have to co-operate effectively with the king.

Particular attention was initially centred on the extreme radical force in the west. On 14 October the committee ordered a delegation to consult with the western forces in order to 'solicit unity for the good of the kingdome'.[1] The geographic and political orbits of the Houses of Argyll and Kennedy were reflected in the inclusion of Argyll and Cassillis on the delegation. Ruthven of Frieland (Perth) and Brodie of that ilk (Elgin) represented the gentry, whilst burghal membership was based solely on Robert Lockhart (Edinburgh). Robert Douglas, minister, represented the Kirk. All delegates were members of the Commission of the Kirk instituted on 4 August 1649.[2]

At the next committee meeting on 15 October, Sir John Brown of Fordell (Perth), was commanded to proceed to the Royalist force in the north and on 16 October a 'grate dispute'[3] arose in the Committee of Estates whether or not there should be an Act of Indemnity for those who had been involved in the Atholl Rebellion of north-eastern Royalists. After discussion, a general Act of Indemnity was agreed on, although this did not receive legislative sanction from the Committee of Estates until 26 October, and was not officially proclaimed until 29 October. Sanction on this date appears to have been due to the the Northern Band and Oath of Engagement which was sent to Lieutenant General David Leslie on 26 October. The Band and Oath was subscribed by 11 hands, four of whom were Royalist nobles (Atholl, Seaforth, Huntly, and St Clair). The document was primarily nationalist in nature and was directed against English military occupation which would reduce the kingdom to the status of a province. Ultimately, it was designed to appeal to as broad a section of Scottish political groupings as possible. The conciliatory nature and tone of the document is stressed by its emphasis on national unity. It stressed its determination to defend the true religion as established in Scotland (presbyterianism), to defend the National Covenant and the Solemn League and Covenant, to defend the king's person, authority, and the royal prerogative, as well as upholding the privileges of Parliament. Indeed, as Middleton commented to Leslie, 'we are Scotishmen, we desyre to fight for our countrie; religion, king and kingdome are in hazard'.[4] However, on 4 November the northern rebels laid down their arms, accepted the Act of Indemnity and agreed a treaty with Leslie at Strathbogie.[5]

Whilst negotiations were proceeding with the northern rebels throughout October, the main concern of the Committee of Estates was directed towards the western armed forces. This had been recognised in the formation of the delegation of 14 October. After 'the Start' the Committee of Estates had ordered the Western Association armed forces to join with Leslie's troops, but it had refused to do so. Paradoxically, the Northern Band and Oath of Engagement emphasised national unity, but the Western Remonstrance issued on 17 October by the Western Association destroyed any immediate prospects of reconciliation between the various factions. Presented to the Committee of Estates on 22 October, the Western Remonstrance represents a hard line ideological stance of extremists in the heartlands of the radical regime. Certainly the Remonstrants were resolved to expel the English armed forces from Scotland, but they stressed that the king's cause in Scotland was an ungodly one and that the Scots should refrain from meddling in the affairs of the English Commonwealth. The Remonstrants pledged that they would not fight for the king until he had supplied concrete evidence of genuine repentance for his past sins and until he abandoned the company and councils of malignants. Geographically, the subscribers to the Remonstrance were confined to the south-west and no noble signature was secured. The leading figure behind the document was Sir George Maxwell of Nether Pollock (Renfrew), but it also secured the backing of other western gentry who had served in Parliament; Campbell of Cessnock (Ayr) and Chiesly of Kerswell (Lanark). Burghal support had strong backing on Glasgow Burgh Council, but also included Robert Farquhar (Aberdeen) and Sir James Stewart (Edinburgh), former General Commissioner and Treasurer of the Excise. The Committee of Estates reacted slowly to the presentation of the Remonstrance. Only on 19 November did the committee formally resolve to have a conference with the Commission of the Kirk to discuss the issue.

On 22 November Chancellor Loudoun reported on the progress of the joint discussions and on 23 November the matter was fully discussed by the Committee of Estates. During the morning session Argyll, Lothian, Balcarras, and Nicholson of Carnock, Lord Advocate, all denounced the Remonstrance as 'the opiner vpe of a breache for tolleratione and subuersione of the gouerniment, bothe ecclesiasticke and ciuill'.[6] The general political mood of the committee was hostile. All members of the Committee of Estates were ordered to declare that they had no part in the formulation of the Remonstrance or any other clandsetine involvement with it. All members present adhered to this declaration, bar Johnston of Wariston who refused to give his vote on the issue. Wariston also denied that he had been involved in the formulation of the Remonstrance itself. During the afternoon session the political mood against the Remonstrance was confirmed. Two per estate were appointed to construct the condemning the Remonstrance. That committee was led by Argyll.[7]

Legislation constructed by the subcommittee was presented to the Committee of Estates on 25 November. The Declaration of the Committee of Estates against the Western Remonstrance was voted on and passed, but only after intense debate. Particular controversy arose over the inclusion of the words 'scandalous', 'scandalous paper', and 'scandalous lybell'. Eglinton, a western noble, wanted the Remonstrance called treasonable, a scandalous paper and a libel. When it came to the vote, however, only 'scandalous' was carried. Six gentry, including Johnston of Wariston, and two burgesses wanted the whole issue referred to the Commission of the Kirk. Hope of Hopetoun (Stirling), Adair of Kinhilt (Wigtown), Scott of Harden (Selkirk), Dickson of Busbie (Lanark), and Carmichael of that ilk (Lanark), Treasurer Depute, were the remaining five gentry who advocated reference to the Commission of the Kirk. Significantly, all except Johnston of Wariston, had their geographic domains ranging from Stirling downwards to the south-west. Robert Lockhart (Edinburgh) and John Denholme (Edinburgh), General Commissioner, were the two dissenting burgesses. Of these six gentry only Hope of Hopetoun and Dickson of Busbie were not members of the Committee of the Kirk instituted on 4 August 1649, whilst John Denholme was not a burgess member of that commission. Fifteen gentry and 10 burgesses were present at the diet of the Committee of Estates on 25 November. Therefore six of the 15 gentry (40%) present and two of the 10 burgesses (20%) present challenged the prevailing consensus reached in the committee.[8]

Voting then took place on the various clauses of the act, which remained intact except for minor alterations. Hope of Hopetoun (Stirling) appears to have been particularly fervent as a dissenter and he suffered the wrath of Argyll for alleging that all the Committee of Estates was doing was destructive to the king and kingdom. In return, Argyll openly implied that Hopetoun was an adherent of Cromwell who plotted on his behalf. After all the clauses of the declaration had been voted on, the dissenters switched their political tactics and attempted to have the act (as distinct from the declaration) voted on as a single entity. This was refused and the tactic failed.

Argyll, Nicholson of Carnock (Stirling), Lord Advocate, and James Sword (St Andrews) were commissioned to inform the Commission of the Kirk of this decision of the Committee of Estates. Both Argyll and Sword were actually members of the current Commission of the Kirk, and the delegation was also to present the Commission with a paper which accused James Guthrie and James Gillespie, ministers, as being the main contrivers behind the Remonstrance.[9] According to Balfour, three nobles, six gentry, and three burgesses (12 dissenters in all) were opposed to this. In comparison to the earlier voting figures, only two gentry who had dissented at the earlier vote, Adair of Kinhilt (Wigtown) and Dickson of Busbie (Lanark), did not dissent on the second occasion.[10]

Balfour has recorded five sederunts of the Committee of Estates between 4 October and 25 November 1650.[11] Seventeen nobles, 25 gentry, and 18 burgesses (60 individuals in total) constituted the attendance field of the five diets. Noble and burghal attendance fields were almost identical, but that of the gentry outstripped the other two estates. Although a larger number of gentry was deployed, noble attendance was more concentrated. Five nobles attended all five diets (Loudoun, Eglinton, Lothian, Lorne, and Mauchline), whilst a further three attended four diets (Argyll, Cassillis, and Angus). This noble dominance was primarily radical and Lorne and Mauchline were the sons of Argyll and Loudoun respectively. Only noble attendance has been noted for the diet of 21 November, therefore the maximum attendance figure available to any laird or burgess is four. Nevertheless, only two gentry attended four diets; Hope of Hopetoun (Stirling) and Wauchope of Niddrie (Edinburgh). No burgess is noted in four sederunts. Patrick Ross (Perth), Sir John Smith (Edinburgh), and Sir William Dick (Edinburgh) are each recorded in three sederunts. Therefore it would appear that a core of predominantly radical nobles continued to control the agenda of the Committee of Estates between 4 October and 25 November 1650.[12]

Several conclusions can be reached in relation to the political developments of October and November 1650. Firstly, factional rapprochement was hindered by the behaviour and actions of the king himself. The hostility towards the king expressed in the Western Remonstrance is understandable in light of 'the Start' and hindered the moves towards national reconciliation expressed in the Northern Band and Oath of Engagement. Secondly, the bulk of the Committee of Estates did not adhere to the Western Remonstrance, although there was a rump that remained loyal to it. Thirdly, on the eve of the Sixth Session the threat posed by the Western Remonstrance had been dealt with in legislative and constitutional terms and the act against the Remonstrance now only required parliamentary sanction. Therefore, the dissenters had been defeated even before Parliament convened. Fourthly, radical nobles controlled the agenda of the Committee of Estates and had exercised a degree of realpolitik in attempting to subdue the west in order to strive to secure some form of national reconciliation.

The Sixth Session of the Second Triennial Parliament, 26 November–30 December 1650

The Sixth Session had been scheduled to meet on 15 August, primarily for the king's coronation. Balfour records four prorogations of that session by the

Committee of Estates, although according to the dates of prorogation this amounts to a figure of six. In addition, a contemporary scribe states that three meetings of Parliament actually took place, on 30 October, 20 November, and 22 November respectively, although these may have been mistaken for meetings of the Committee of Estates. However, Parliament did eventually formally convene at Perth on 26 November.[13]

1. The Composition of the Sixth Session of the Second Triennial Parliament

In common with the Fifth Session, no official parliamentary rolls have been recorded for 26 November 1650. Balfour, however, has noted the parliamentary data for all three estates for the opening day of the Sixth Session (see appendix 4a). The king was also in attendance on 26 November.

Balfour lists a minimum of 27 gentry representing 17 shires and 20 burgesses representing 19 burghs. Seven of the 17 shires were eastern, six were from the Borders, and two were central belt shires. Of the two remaining shires, only one was western, whilst the remainder was from the Highlands. Eastern influence was more marked in burghal representation; 17 of the 19 burghs were eastern and the two remaining burghs were western. Therefore the west had clearly been marginalised in terms of both gentry and burghal representation, although western shires and burghs may have declined to have sent commissioners as a protest against contemporary events.[14]

Thirteen of the 18 nobles (72%), eight of the 27 gentry (30%), and seven of the 20 burgesses (35%) recorded by Balfour in his parliamentary data for 26 November are also recorded in the parliamentary rolls of 7 March for the Fourth Session (no attendance data is available for the Fifth Session commencing on 15 May). Two conclusions can be drawn from this set of data. Firstly, a large degree of common membership prevailed within the noble estate but was extremely limited regarding the gentry and burgesses. Secondly, the lack of retention of personnel from the shires and burghs may be due to the exhaustion in terms of manpower and human resources following the defeat at Dunbar and the worsening in the financial and economic condition of the country. Although noble common membership was more marked than the other two estates, it was still dominated by radical nobles. Ten of the 13 nobles who sat in both sessions were radicals. The marginalisation of western influence is also highlighted by the fact that only one of the eight gentry and one of the seven burgesses represented western shires and burghs. Of the eight gentry who sat in both sessions, three represented eastern shires, two represented Borders' shires, and two represented the central belt. Six of the seven burgesses who sat in both sessions represented eastern burghs.[15]

2. The Proceedings of the Sixth Session of the Second Triennial Parliament

Forty-one enactments (32 of which related to public business and nine of which related to private affairs) formed the legislative programme of the Sixth Session, and the king was present throughout the session.[16] Following the calling of the parliamentary rolls, the parliamentary oath was subscribed by all members present. Chancellor Loudoun was challenged by Cassillis for the post of President of Parliament, although Loudoun secured re-election by a majority of 15 votes.[17]

The proceedings of the Sixth Session can be split into four distinct areas; the appointment of session committees, the regulation of parliamentary membership, the issue of the Western Remonstrance, and military preparations to defend the kingdom against the Cromwellian forces.

Three major session committees were appointed on 27 November; the Committee for the Affairs of the Army, the Committee for the Bills, and the Committee for Overtures. Two further session committees were appointed on later dates; the Committee for Grievances on 30 November and the Committee for Revising the Acts of the Committee of Estates on 14 December.[18]

Four per estate formed the membership of the Committee for the Affairs of the Army. Argyll, Cassillis, Eglinton, and Lothian represented the nobility and constituted a powerful radical grouping. All four nobles, two of the four gentry, and three of the four burgesses had also been included on the Committee of Estates of 7 March 1650. Membership problems were apparent by 9 December when two gentry were ordered to be elected to the committee to replace two unspecified gentry who had not been attending committee diets.[19]

The Committee for the Affairs of the Army was primarily a military and not an executive committee. Its function was to oversee the unification, strengthening and supplying of the armed forces. Only two radical nobles, Argyll and Eglinton, and two burgesses James Sword (St Andrews) and Alexander Bower (Dundee), had been included on the Committee for Dispatches of 16 May.[20] Yet the Committee for the Affairs of the Army was also accorded a wider role and was ordered to act as a negotiating body with the Commission of the Kirk with three specific remits. Both bodies were to co-operate on the details of the king's coronation, the provision of ministers for the king's family, and the grounds of exclusion from or admittance to the armed forces. All noble members of the Committee for the Affairs of the Army had been included on the Commission of the Kirk of 4 August 1649, but only one laird, Buchanan of that ilk (Stirling), and one burgess, James Sword (St Andrews), on the army session committee had been Commissioners of the Kirk.[21]

Appointments were made to two specialised procedural committees on 27 November. Three per estate formed the membership of the Committee for the Bills, whereas the Committee for Overtures consisted of four per estate. Common membership between the two committees was limited to one burgess, George Garden (Burntisland). Radical influence on the Committee for Bills was maintained by Burleigh, although Buccleuch and Balcarras were also selected. Buccleuch had also served on the Committee for Bills of 21 May in the Fifth Session. Of the 12 members of the Committee for Overtures, only Weymes and Hope of Hopetoun (Stirling) had served on the previous Committee for Overtures and Laws of 23 May in the Fifth Session. Burghal representation on the

Committee for Overtures of 27 November was based on a particular geographic domain; Robert Whyte (Kirkcaldy), Peter Walker (Dunfermline), William Walker (Dunfermline), and George Garden (Burntisland) formed this contingent from Fife. Representation included two burgesses from the same burgh (Dunfermline) and may indicate either that non-parliamentary burghal personnel were being employed on this particular session committee or that one particular burgh was in breach of parliamentary regulations by sending two commissioners.

Membership links with the Commission of the Kirk of 4 August 1649 were based on Burleigh and Scott of Harden (Selkirk) for the Committee for the Bills and Kerr of Cavers (Roxburgh) for the Committee for Overtures. The staffing of these two procedural session committees originated largely from the Committee of Estates of 7 March 1650. All three nobles and two burgesses, William Simpson (Dysart) and George Garden (Burntisland), included on the Committee for Bills had been members of the Committee of Estates. Similarly, in addition to George Garden, all four gentry on the Committee for Overtures, been included on the Committee of Estates of 7 March.

On 28 November the House laid down several criteria for the processing of Bills in Parliament. Bills presented directly to the Committee for Bills were to be dealt with by that body. Bills that were presented in Parliament were to be considered by the full Parliament, and not the Committee for Bills, but the House reserved the right to refer them to the Committee for Bills if deeemed necessary.[22]

Three parliamentary session committees had therefore been established on 27 November 1650. Diversification in the employment of parliamentary manpower is apparent in the staffing of these committees over all three estates, particularly in the light of the low attendance levels of 26 November. No noble or laird was included on more than one of these three central session committees.Only one burgess, George Garden (Burntisland), secured nomination to more than one of the batch of core session committees.

The Committee for Grievances was established three days later on 30 November. The policy remit of the committee was of a military nature and was limited to the consideration of the lack of military discipline exercised by officers and soldiers in the armed forces. Noble influence on the committee was limited and committee membership consisted of only one noble, four gentry, and three burgesses. The one noble member, Angus, was not a noted radical or conservative/pragmatic Royalist. Only one burgess, Sir John Smith (Edinburgh), had been a member of the previous Committee for Grievances established on 31 May 1649 in the Third Session. Only one laird, Wauchope of Niddrie (Edinburgh), and two burgesses, Sir John Smith (Edinburgh) and Patrick Ross (Perth), had been included on the Committee of Estates of 7 March 1650. Niddrie had also been a member of the Commission of the Kirk of 4 August 1649.[23]

On 2 December 1650 the House ruled that a session committee should be appointed to revise the legislation enacted by the previous Committee of

Estates. Yet it was not until 14 December that an appropriate committee was finally established. Three per estate formed its membership. Noble membership was composed of two conservatives/pragmatic Royalists, Linlithgow and Dunfermline, and one radical, Coupar. Coupar and all three burgees members had also been included on the Committee of Estates of 7 March 1650. Coupar represented the sole committee member included on the Commission of the Kirk of 7 August 1649.[24]

The regulation of parliamentary membership was an issue of immediate parliamentary attention and was dealt with on 27 November. The case of Robert Barclay (Irvine), a noted radical burgess, was used to exert parliamentary authority and discipline. Robert Barclay attended the parliamentary session without a valid and current parliamentary commission. After a vote was taken, the Estates resolved that no commissioner of the shires or burghs could sit and vote in Parliament without first producing the relevant parliamentary commission or an act of continuation of former commissions. On 27 November a session committee was established (of which no membership details are given) to deal with the problem of non-attendance by a significant number of commissioners of the shires and burghs, particularly those areas which were subject to enemy occupation. Hence it is clear that there was a low turnout of gentry and burgesses on 26 November. It was determined that the Clerk Register, Johnston of Wariston (Edinburgh), should write to such shires and burghs and command them to attend the parliamentary session with immediate effect. On 29 November the shires of the Lothians and Linlithgow (and other unspecified shires under enemy occupation) were ordered to elect parliamentary commissioners. Similarly, on 7 December the House ordered that parliamentary commissioners were to be elected by the burgh of Edinburgh. By 14 December such elections had clearly taken place, as Sir John Smith was admitted to the House and subscribed the parliamentary oath. He had earlier been appointed as General Commissioner on 3 December following the resignation of John Denholm. That appointment had been made by the Committee for the Affairs of the Army and had been ratified by Parliament. However, according to Balfour's data of the parliamentary rolls of 26 November, the burgh of Edinburgh was already represented by two commissioners, one of whom was Sir John Smith (the other was James Monteith). It would therefore appear that there may have been some problem with the parliamentary commissions for Smith and Monteith and that a new election had to be carried out to maintain the consistency of the legislation of 27 November and the case of Robert Barclay.[25]

Throughout the parliamentary session nobles who had been associated with the Engagement were gradually admitted to the House and became involved in parliamentary affairs. Many were still technically barred from doing so under the 1649 Act of Classes. This parliamentary process can be traced from 29 November to 27 December and all cases required the approval of the Commission of the Kirk prior to parliamentary sanction. Six nobles and two gentry had acts of banishment against them repealed; Lauderdale, Callander, Hamilton (formerly the Earl of Lanark), Montgomery, Carnegie, and Seaforth. Although

Carnegie was repealed from banishment, he was still censured under the 1649 Act of Classes. Lockhart of Lee and Sir James Montgomery were the relevant two gentry. In addition, Dunfermline, Linlithgow, and Cranston all had their petitions accepted to sit and vote in the House despite their involvement in the Engagement. The political rehabilitation of Engagement nobles was witnessed by the inclusion of Linlithgow and Dunfermline on the Committee for Revising the Acts of the Committee of Estates, and the inclusion of Newburgh and Cranston on the Committee for Overtures. The Committee for Overtures had been established on 27 November. It was not until 4 December that parliamentary sanction was given for Cranston to sit and vote in the House and Cranston did not take his seat until 5 December. Newburgh had sat in the House on 3 December but it was ruled on 4 December that Newburgh was not to enjoy voting powers until he subscribed both the National Covenant and the Solemn League and Covenant.

Therefore both Cranston and Newburgh had been nominated and elected to the Committee for Overtures before they had received official parliamentary sanction to sit and vote in the House. It is therefore inconceivable that both nobles could have even sat on the Committee for Overtures prior to at least 5 December. Therefore the radical leadership both in the Kirk and Parliament sanctioned the political involvement of former Engagement nobles as a pragmatic exercise in the attempt to secure a patriotic accommodation against the occupying Cromwellian force. However, Callander and Lauderdale, the leading Engagers, were still barred from civil office under the 1649 Act of Classes. The rehabilitation of Engagement nobles did not command universal support from the Commission of the Kirk and as early as 30 November seven or eight unspecified members of the commission handed in a petition to Parliament in protest against this development. Instead, further purging of malignants was advocated. This marked the beginning of the Resolutioner-Protestor controversy which was to rage throughout the Church of Scotland in the first six months of 1651. The Resolutioner majority in the Kirk stressed a policy of moderation and compromise in the rehabilitation of Engagers and Royalists, whilst the Protestors refused to adhere to such a policy.[26]

The move towards the political rehabilitation of former Engagers was reflected in the manning and staffing of the Scottish armed forces for the defence of the kingdom. The military defeat of the Western Association by Lambert at Hamilton on 1 December emphasised the urgency of a national co-ordination of military resources. Previous orders for the Western Association to join with the rest of the armed forces had been ignored. Nevertheless, the Western Association was not officially declared null and void until 28 December. On 10 December the Estates were ordered to meet separately primarily to elect representatives (who are not named) to negotiate with the Commission of the Kirk on the issue of admitting men to fight for the country who were currently barred from doing so. Four days later on 14 December Parliament resolved to raise a new unified military force. Following two days of deliberation, on 14 December the Commission of the Kirk issued the 'Public Resolutions' which provided official sanction from the Kirk for the employment of former Engagers in the new army. The Act of Levy for the new force was debated for three days between 20 and 23 December and was not ratified until 23 December. Particular controversy surrounded the nominations and appointments of colonels of the horse and foot. Chancellor Loudoun openly distanced himself from the nominations on the grounds that former adherents of Montrose and former Engagers had been appointed in the ratio of 2:1 compared to other appointees. When the complete Act of Levy was finally approved, 16 nobles were present in the House and were politically balanced between radicals and conservatives/pragmatic Royalists. On 24 December it was enacted that all officers in the new army who had been previously barred from access to the king were now free to do so. Crawford-Lindsay, former President of Parliament and a leading Engager was named as a colonel, as were Atholl and Ogilvie who had been involved in the Northern Rebellion two months previously.[27]

Prior to the close of the parliamentary session on 30 December, the Treaty of Breda was ratified and the king ratified all parliamentary legislation since 1641, except that of the Engagement Parliament. Constitutionally, Charles was still required tbe a covenanted king. Parliament was to reconvene at Perth on 5 February 1651, although the Committee of Estates could alter the location.[28]

3. The Committee Structure of the Sixth Session of the Second Triennial Parliament

The committee structure of the Sixth Session was based on five session committees and two interval committees. Twenty-seven nobles, 34 gentry, and 28 burgesses constitute the total analytical field. Hence there was near parity between the noble and burghal estates, whlist the gentry enjoyed a majority of six in terms of manpower. Eleven of thc 27 nobles (41%), 22 of the 34 gentry (65%), and 15 of the 28 burgesses (54%) were included on only one committee.

Three radical nobles, Cassillis, Burleigh, and Coupar, were nominated to a total of three committees. Gentry committee membership was based on Wauchope of Niddrie (Edinburgh) and Hepburn of Keith (Haddington), each of whom was appointed to a total of three committees. Committee membership for the burghal estate was based primarily on George Garden (Burntisland), who was nominated to a total of five committees. Alexander Bower (Dundee) and James Sword (St Andrews) each gained membership of three committees.

No common membership exists for any of the three estates between the two session committees established with military remits. All nobles included on the Committee for the Bills, the Committee for Overtures, and the Committee for Revising the Acts of the Committee of Estates secured membership of the new Committee of Estates of 30 December 1650. With the exception of William Simpson (Dysart) (Committee for the Bills) and Peter Walker (Dunfermline) (Committee for Overtures), all burgess members of these specialised procedural committees were likewise included on the new Committee of Estates of 30 December. Yet, in marked contrast to the nobility and the burghal estate, only one gentry member of the Committee for the Bills, Scott of Harden (Selkirk), and one gentry member of the Committee for Revising the Acts of the Committee of Estates, Elliot of Stobbs (Roxburgh), were appointed to the Committee of Estates.

In terms of the two interval committees, four of the five nobles, four of the five gentry, and all five burgesses included on the financial interval committee, the Committee for Excise and Accounts, were also nominated to the Committee of Estates.[29]

Therefore limited common membership of parliamentary session and interval committees is prevalent over all three estates in the committee structure of the Sixth Session. In comparative terms, common membership is more marked within the noble and burghal estates, although the gentry had a wider manpower base on which to draw. Committee work appears to have been shared between military and executive committees. However, it is clear that nomination to the Committee of Estates was virtually dependent on having been included on at least one of the other parliamentary committees.

4. The Appointment of Parliamentary Interval Committees

Two parliamentary interval committees were appointed on 30 December; the Committee for Excise and Accounts and the Committee of Estates. Five per estate formed the membership of the Committee for Excise and Accounts and the quorum level was set at one per estate. Membership in terms of numbers and the quorum level had been decided on by 28 December, but the actual personnel was not named until two days later. Noble membership was exclusively radical and was headed by Cassillis.[30] Two nobles, Arbuthnot and Coupar, one laird, Ruthven of Frieland (Perth), and one burgess, Hugh Kennedy (Ayr), apponted to the Committee for Excise and Accounts, 30 December 1650, had also been included on the Excise Commission appointed on 16 March 1649 in the Second Session, which had been renewed on 16 May 1650 in the Fifth Session.

In addition to Frieland and Kennedy, four of the five nobles included on the Committee for Excise and Accounts of 30 December 1650 had also been included on the Committee for Money and Accounts of 14 March 1649 also appointed in the Second Session. Cassillis, Arbuthnot, Torphichen, and Burleigh formed this grouping. Therefore the radical edge was maintained in the Committee for Excise and Accounts of 30 December 1650 and was most marked within the noble estate.[31]

A new Committee of Estates was established on 30 December 1650. It consisted of 26 nobles, 25 gentry, and 24 burgesess (75 individuals in total). Sixteen of the total membership was included as supernumeraries. Near equality per estate is apparent in the composition of the 16 supernumeraries, based on six nobles, six gentry, and four burgesses. Of those Engager and pragmatic Royalist nobles who had been readmitted to Parliament, Dunfermline, Linlithgow, Cranston, and Newburgh gained membership of the Committee of Estates. No Protesters secured membership and the radical regime still maintained its ascendancy.

Compared to the previous Committee of Estates of 7 March, the membership level for the nobility remained identical (in terms of numerical composition), whilst that of the gentry dropped by 25 and that of the burgesses was reduced by eight. Hence the realignment in political power towards the nobility evidenced throughout the parliamentary session was matched in the membership levels of the Committee of Estates. Most notable was the decrease in gentry, membership by 50%. Fifty-eight per cent of the nobles, 56% of the gentry and 50% of the burgesses included on the new Committee of Estates of 30 December, had also been included on the previous Committee of Estates. Therefore personnel was retained over all three estates in virtually equal numbers.[32]

5. The Operation of Parliamentary Interval Committees

Prior to the convening of the Committee of Estates on 2 January 1651, the coronation of Charles II as King of Great Britain had taken place at the traditional Scottish venue of Scone on 1 January. Subjected to a lengthy diatribe by Robert Douglas, Moderator of the General Assembly, against the faults of his father (Charles I) and grandfather (James VI) and a detailed lecture on the necessary virtues of kingship, the new king had been required to re-subscribe the National Covenant and the Solemn League and Covenant. Charles II, as King of Great Britain, had clearly had been crowned as head of the ruling Scottish political faction. Within the wider British archipelago, Charles II was also required by his newfound masters 'to endeavour the reformation of religion in the other two kingdoms, according to the word of God, and the example of the best reformed kirks'.[33] Despite the advance of Cromwellian forces into Scotland and the military fiasco at Dunbar, this religious demand for a truly British reformation, combined with the coronation of Charles as a British king, provided a double whammy to the security of the English Commonwealth and the ascendancy of the English Independents. This dual threat ensured that a decisive struggle between the two godly Protestant kingdoms would be required to determine which of the factions would prevail.

The Seventh Session of the Second Triennial Parliament had been scheduled to meet on 5 February 1651, yet it did not actually convene until 13 March 1651. From 2 January until 6 February the Committee of Estates met at Perth, before moving to Stirling for two days between 10 and 12 February. The committee then returned to Perth until 12 March.

Thirty-four sederunts of the Committee of Estates are recorded between 2 January and 12 March 1651. The king attended 22 out of 34 diets (65%). Cassillis and Chancellor Loudoun were present at all 34 diets. Loudoun also presided at all diets. Of the other leading radical nobles, Eglinton attended 24 diets (71%), Balcarras attended 20 diets (59%), whilst Argyll and Torphichen each attended 19 diets (56%). Conservative and pragmatic Royalist attendance was centred on Roxburgh (22 diets, 65%) and Montgomery (19 diets, 56%).

Six gentry have attendance levels in the region of 17 and 29 sederunts. Three of these gentry represented eastern shires, particularly Edinburgh and its environs; Cockburn of Clerkington (Haddington) is recorded in 29 sederunts

(86%), Hepburn of Keith (Haddington) in 24 sederunts (71%), and Hamilton of Little Preston (Edinburgh) in 19 sederunts (56%). Two of the remaining three gentry within this grouping represented Borders' shires; Belshes of Toftis (Berwick) 18 sederunts (53%) and Scott of Harden (Selkirk) 17 sederunts (50%). Only one western laird had a significant attendance level. Carmichael of Hyndford (Lanark), Treasuer Depute, attended 21 diets (62%).

Compared to the other two estates, burghal attendance was less marked. Sir John Smith (Edinburgh) and Andrew Grant (Perth) are recorded in 25 and 24 diets respectively (74% and 71%). Robert Arnot (Perth) attended 16 diets (47%). With the exception of these three burgesses, the remaining burghal attendance levels were minimal. The fact that the Committee of Estates was residing predominantly at Perth may well explain the high attendance data for Perthshire burgesses.

The commission of 30 December 1650 had set the quorum at nine with two of each estate required to be present. These rules were adhered to at all 34 diets. One noble and three Borders' gentry attended various diets, despite the fact that they were not committee members as per 30 December. The attendance of Elphinstone, Murray of Skirling (Peebles), and Dickson of Hartrie (Peebles) was limited, albeit Kerr of Cavers (Roxburgh) was present at 15 diets (44%).[34]

Three subcommittees were in operation between January and March 1651; a Committee for Grievances, the Committee for Monies, Excise, and Accounts, and the Committee for Provisions and Arms.

The Committee for Monies, Excise, and Accounts was in operation by 10 January, although there are no parliamentary references pertaining to the existence of such a committee. Similarly, no membership details are provided for the Committee for Provisions and Arms which had been established by 14 January. One noble, two gentry, and one burgess were adjoined to the Committee for Monies, Excise, and Accounts on 10 January. In all probability, these additions were made to the parliamentary interval committee, the Committee for Excise and Accounts, which had been established on 30 December 1650. None of the additions of 10 January were members of that interval committee. Additions of two nobles and one laird were made to the Committee for Provisions and Arms on 3 February. Balcarras and Hepburne of Humbie (Haddington) represented a common grouping who were added to both committees.[35]

The Committee for Grievances of 10 January was a complete subcommittee, composed of three nobles, five gentry, three burgesses, and one military official. In common with the other two subcommittees, both Balcarras and Hepburne of Humbie (Haddington) secured inclusion. The services of one further noble member, Angus, and two of the three burgesses, Patrick Ross (Perth) and John Paterson (Perth), had been retained from the Committee for Grievances of 30 November 1650 in the Sixth Session. Both gentry and burghal representation on the subcommittee was based largely on specific geographic domains; Hepburn of Humbie (Haddington), Cockburn of Clerkington (Haddington), and Hepburn of Keith (Haddington) for the gentry, whilst burghal membership was composed exclusively of burgesses of Perth.[36]

The trend towards national reconciliation was emphasised by the case of Sir Archibald Primrose. Primrose was a former Clerk of the Privy Council and of earlier Committees of Estates. He had petitioned the Committee of Estates on 7 January, desiring that he be allowed to serve the country. Primrose had been involved in the Engagement and had been duly punished under the 1649 Act of Classes. Having been absolved by the Commission of the Kirk on 4 January of involvement in the Engagement, a vote was taken in the Committee of Estates on 10 January. Thirteen nobles, 13 gentry, three burgesses (yielding a total of 29 individuals) were present at the diet of 10 January. Primrose's petition was granted by a majority of seven votes. Voting data is limited but Cassillis and Torphichen voted against the petition. Nevertheless, the prevalent mood of the bulk of the nobles and gentry present was for continued accommodation of former Engagers.[37]

On 11 March 'a grate meitting'[38] of the Committee of Estates was held to discuss whether or not the parliamentary session which had been prorogued to 13 March should actually convene on that date. Chancellor Loudoun, Cassillis, and 'ther factione'[39] attempted to have the session prorogued to a later date, but when it came to the vote it was carried that Parliament should meet as planned.

Sixteen nobles, 11 gentry, eight burgesses, and three military officials (38 individuals in all) attended the diet of 11 March. Radical strength among the noble attenders was based on Argyll, Eglinton, Cassillis, Burleigh, Loudoun, and Leven. Four gentry and three burgesses in attendance had been members of the Commission of the Kirk of 4 August 1649; Wauchope of Niddrie (Edinburgh), Ruthven of Frieland (Perth), Erskine of Scottiscraig (Fife), and Sir James Arnot of Fernie for the gentry, with Sir John Smith (Edinburgh), John Boswell (Kinghorn), and James Sword (St Andrews) for the burgess. George Garden (Burntisland) was a further noted radical burgess in attendance on 11 March. Ignoring the presence of the military officials whose voting powers are unclear, sufficient gentry and burgesses votes must have been cast in favour of Parliament convening on the proposed date. National interests appear to have outweighed factional interests regarding this specific issue.[40]

The Seventh Session of the Second Triennial Parliament, 13 March-to 31 March 1651

1. The Composition of the Seventh Session of the Second Triennial Parliament

In common with both the Fifth and Sixth Sessions, no official parliamentary rolls are available for the Seventh Session, albeit Balfour has recorded attendance data for 13 March 1651 (see appendix 4a). Gentry and burghal attendance levels were identical, whilst noble membership was marginally lower. Given the contemporary military and political situation, it is most probably the case that the minimum attendance figures are the most likely.

Sixteen of the 17 nobles (94%), 16 of the 21 gentry (76%), and 10 of the 21 burgesses (48%) listed in Balfour's attendance data of 13 March 1651 had also been present in Parliament, 26 November 1650. Three conclusions can be reached. Firstly, there was a core of nobles, gentry, and burgesses in attendance over both sessions. Secondly, the noble estate witnessed the retention of the largest number of common personnel. In political terms the majority of the 16 nobles were radicals. Thirdly, the burghal estate witnessed the most marked change in personnel, although much of this was due to the presence of burghs who had not sent representatives to the session commencing on 26 November 1650.[41]

2. The Proceedings of the Seventh Session of the Second Triennial Parliament

In common with the Sixth Session, the Seventh Session convened at Perth. Its legislative programme consisted of 33 enactments (26 of which were public acts and seven private acts) and two ratifications.[42] After the subscription of the parliamentary oath, Chancellor Loudoun was once again challenged for the position of President of Parliament. Loudoun had been previously challenged by Cassillis in the Sixth Session, but had managed to defeat the challenge from within the radical leadership. A more successful challenge was launched by Burleigh on 31 March and he was elected as President by a majority of 21 votes.[43]

Five parliamentary session committees were then established on 13 March, namely the Committee for Military Affairs, the Committee for the Conference with the Kirk, the Committee for Bills, the Committee for Overtures, and the Committee for Revising the Acts of the Committee of Estates.[44]

Three per estate formed the membership of the Committee for Military Affairs. Noble membership consisted of Argyll, Cassillis, and Balcarras. A core of radical personnel was employed on the committee. A significant number of personnel were retained from the Committee for the Affairs of the Army of 27 November during the Sixth Session. Two nobles, one laird, and two burgesses formed this common membership; Argyll, Cassillis, Belshes of Toftis (Berwick), Andrew Grant (Perth), and James Sword (St Andrews). In addition, all members of the Committee for Military Affairs had been included on the Committee of Estates of 30 December 1650. Furthermore, Argyll, Cassillis, Sir John Smith (Edinburgh), and James Sword (St Andrews) had been members of the Commission of the Kirk established on 4 August 1649.[45]

On 13 March additions were made to the Committee for Grievances which had been established by the Committee of Estates on 10 January. Hence a subcommittee of the Committee of Estates was formalised into a full parliamentary session committee. Three nobles, five gentry, and three burgesses were added. The total membership of the Committee for Grievances now consisted of six nobles, eight gentry, and six burgesses. Therefore there was an imbalance in membership in favour of the gentry. However, one of the nobles (Angus) and two of the burgesses, Robert Arnot (Perth) and John Paterson (Perth), were members of the original subcommittee. This suggests that all three individuals had failed to attend the appropriate diets of the subcommittee. None of the other two nobles added were noted radicals. One of the noble additions (Lord

Montgomery) and two of the burghal additions, David Wilkie (Edinburgh) and Robert Arnot (Perth), had been members of the Committee of Estates of 30 December 1650. None of the additions had been included on the Commission of the Kirk established on 4 August 1649 and indicates that the influence of the Kirk was limited on this committee.[46]

The importance of liaison with the Kirk was emphasised by the formation of the Committee for the Conference with the Kirk, particularly in light of the Resolutioner-Protester controversy. Three per estate formed its membership and close correlations in membership with the Committee for Military Affairs are apparent. Argyll, Cassillis, and all three burgesses, Sir John Smith (Edinburgh), Andrew Grant (Perth), and James Sword (St Andrews), were included on both committees. With the exception of one laird, Kerr of Cavers (Roxburgh), all members of the Committee for the Conference with the Kirk had been included on the Committee of Estates of 30 December 1650. In addition to Argyll, Cassillis, and James Sword (St Andrews), Wauchope of Niddrie (Edinburgh) was also a member of the Commission of the Kirk established on 4 August 1649.[47]

Two procedural session committees were established; the Committee for the Bills and the Committee for Overtures. Common membership between the two committees was marginal and only one burgess, George Jamieson (Coupar), was included on both committees. The Committee for Bills was composed of five per estate. None of the committee members had been included on the previous Committee for the Bills of 27 November 1650. Noble representation on the latter committee of 13 March 1651 was primarily conservative/pragmatic Royalist, with only two radicals, Torphichen and Coupar, being included. All five nobles, three of the five gentry, and four of the five burgesses had also been included on the Committee of Estates of 30 December 1650. Only one member of the Committee for Bills (Lord Coupar) had been a member of the Commission of the Kirk established on 4th August 1649.[48]

A more leaner spread of human resources of three per estate was deployed to the Committee for Overtures in comparison to the Committee for Bills. Only one noble, Weymes, and one laird, Kerr of Cavers (Roxburgh), had been members of the previous Committee for Overtures of 27 November 1650. Noble representation on the latter committee consisted of one conservative/pragmatic Royalist, Linlithgow, and two radicals, Weymes and Buccleuch. Close links were retained with the Committee of Estates of 30 December 1650, all three nobles, two of the three gentry, and two of the three burgesses had been included on that committee. By way of comparison, only two gentry, Wauchope of Niddrie (Edinburgh) and Kerr of Cavers (Roxburgh), and one burgess John Boswell (Kinghorn) had also been members of the Commission of the Kirk established on 4 August 1649.[49]

A further procedural committee was similarly established on 13 March and was allocated the task of revising the legislation of the previous Committee of Estates. The Committee for Revising the Acts of the Committee of Estates consisted of three per estate. No nobles nor gentry included on either the

Committee for the Bills or the Committee for Overtures secured membership on the committee. However, the burghal estate exhibited a high degree of tripartite committee membership of these procedural committees. George Jamieson (Coupar), Robert Whyte (Kirkcaldy), and George Garden (Burntisland) were also members of the Committee for Bills. George Jamieson was included on the Committee for Overtures. Only one member of the Committee for Revising the Acts of the Committee of Estates, George Garden (Burntisland), had been a member of the committee with an identical remit of 14 December 1650 established during the Sixth Session.

The noble and burghal elements of the Committee for Revising the Acts of the Committee of Estates had infact been included on the previous Committee of Estates of 30 December. Eglinton, Lothian, Roxburgh, Robert Whyte (Kirkcaldy), George Garden (Burntisland), and George Jamieson (Coupar) were therefore to consider retrospective legislation of the most important interval committee of which they had all been members. None of the three gentry members, however, had been included on the previous Committee of Estates. In terms of the total committee membership, only two nobles, Eglinton and Lothian, had also been included on the Commission of the Kirk established on 4 August 1649.[50]

Membership of all session committees was further regulated by legislation enacted on 13 March. According to this legislation, any member of Parliament was free to attend the proceedings of any of the parliamentary session committees. This may well have been an attempt to weaken the power of the radical nobles or intimidate them politically in committee proceedings.[51]

One specialised financial session committee was established during the Seventh Session, namely the Committee for Considering the Affairs and Accounts of the Treasury. This was distinct from the Treasury Commission itself and was in effect an audit committee. Indeed, none of the members of the session committee had been included on the Treasury Commission. All nobles, gentry, and burgesses had also been included on the Committee of Estates of 30 December 1650. Only one committee member, John Boswell (Kinghorn) was a member of the Commission of the Kirk established on 4 August 1649.[52]

The move towards a patriotic accommodation, indicated by the access of conservatives and pragmatic Royalists to parliamentary committees witnessed during the Sixth Session, increased dramatically with developments commencing on 19 March. Acting on a motion from the king, the House agreed that the Kirk should be asked its opinion concerning the admittance to the Committee of Estates of those barred from civil office under the 1649 Act of Classes. This provides clear evidence of the reduction in the power of the radical nobles, and their growing alienation from the other two estates. Lothian even advocated the abolition of the Committee of Estates as a means of blocking access for malignants to political power. According to this line of thinking, malignants would still be barred from civil office and the radical nobles could exercise power through the institution of the Privy Council, thereby marginalising the influence of the gentry and the burgesses. Gentry and burghal voting strength, allied to that of conservative/pragmatic Royalist nobles, worked to ensure that Lothian's proposal was defeated. This indicates that national interests were put to the fore by the gentry and burgesses as opposed to the interests of theocracy and religion. The Commission of the Kirk provided its reply on 22 March. It could not provide a definite answer until further consultation took place within that commission. Nevertheless, the Commission of the Kirk suggested that those who had been allowed to serve in the army should also be allowed to serve on any parliamentary committee that dealt with army affairs. In an exercise of supreme pragmatism, this proposal was seized upon by the conservatives/pragmatic Royalists to establish a Committee for Managing the Affairs of the Army. Those still barred from public affairs were to be enabled to be admitted to this committee. The formation of such a committee was agreed on 25 March. The terms of the commission and its membership were debated for four hours on 26 March without any conclusion being reached. Dissent at the formation of the committee was expressed by 10 nobles (including Argyll, Loudoun, Burleigh, Cassillis, and Lothian) and three gentry, but their voting power was insufficient to prevent the adoption of the measure. The lack of support shown by the gentry and burgesses for this dissent emphasises the fact that the radical nobles had lost their support. On 27 March it was stated that the Committee for Managing the Affairs of the Army was to be distinct from the Committee of Estates. The powers which were allocated to the former committee, enshrined in seven articles, were also agreed on 27 March. Nine nobles and three gentry voted against the seven articles. Eight of the nine nobles and two of the three gentry had also voted against the proposals of 26 March. The actual membership of the Committee for Managing the Affairs of the Army was then named on 28 March.[53]

The colonels for the southern shires were appointed on 28 March all of whom were former Engagers and/or Royalists. Such appointments must be viewed within the context of the fact that the traditional power base of the radical regime lay south of the Tay. In particular, Lauderdale was appointed for East Lothian, Dalhousie for Midlothian, and Hamilton and Douglas for Clydesdale. Technically the 1649 Act of Classes was still in force, but these appointments were of a military as opposed to a civil nature. Having secured the admittance of Royalists to the Committee for Managing the War and as military appointees, the House stated on 29 March that consultation should take place with the Commission of the Kirk to repeal the 1649 Act of Classes in order to secure 'a generall vnity in the kingdome'.[54] Having remitted 78 bills to the Committee of Estates, Parliament was adjourned to 17 April 1651, when it was hoped that the 1649 Act of Classes would be repealed.[55]

3. The Committee Structure of the Seventh Session of the Second Triennial Parliament

Seven session committees and two interval committees have been analysed. The analytical committee field was composed of 47 nobles, 46 gentry, and 50 burgesses. Greater numbers of burgesses were therefore deployed to session and interval committees, whilst noble and gentry allocations were almost equal. Of the 38 nobles who gained membership of only one committee, 21 (55%) were included on the Committee of Estates. In addition, all six nobles who were included on two committees each were included on the Committee of Estates. Thirty-four gentry and 39 burgesses were included on two or less committees; 20 of the 34 gentry (59%) and 21 of the 39 burgesses (54%) were members of the Committee of Estates. The Committee of Estates clearly accounted for the vast majority of committee membership for each of the three estates.

Radical noble influence was restricted to Buccleuch (five committees), Argyll, Cassillis, and Balcarras (four committees each), and Eglinton and Lothian (three committees each). All six radical nobles were included on the Committee of Estates and the Committee for Managing the Affairs of the Army. Both Argyll and Cassillis were members of the Committee for Military Affairs and the Committee for the Conference with the Kirk, whereas Lothian and Eglinton were members of the Committee for Revising the Acts of the Committee of Estates. The trend towards the increased political prominence of conservatives and pragmatic Royalists was evidenced by the prominence of conservatives within the committee structure. Roxburgh secured membership of five committees and Linlithgow, Ruthven, and Newburgh three committees. Of this grouping, all were members of the Committee for Managing the Affairs of the Army and the Committee of Estates.

Four gentry were included on four committees each; Wauchope of Niddrie (Edinburgh), Murray of Skirling (Peebles), Hepburn of Keith (Haddington), and Kerr of Cavers (Roxburgh). Eight further gentry were included on three committees; Hepburne of Humbie (Haddington), Hay of Naughton (Fife), Cockburn of Clerkington (Haddington), Belshes of Toftis (Berwick), Scott of Harden (Selkirk), Elliot of Stobbs (Roxburgh), Colquhoun of Luss (Dumbarton), and Renton of Lamberton (Berwick). Particular influence was therefore centred on the east coast and the Borders. Eleven of the above 12 gentry were included on the Committee of Estates, 10 were included on the Committee for Managing the Affairs of the Army, and five were members of the Committee for the Bills.

In common with the gentry, the maximum number of committees to which any burgess was nominated amounted to four. This figure was achieved by four burgesses; Sir John Smith (Edinburgh), James Sword (St Andrews), George Garden (Burntisland), and John Boswell (Kinghorn). This burghal grouping consisted of noted radicals. Three further burgesses were included on three committees each; Andrew Grant (Perth), Robert Whyte (Kirkcaldy), and David Wilkie (Edinburgh). Burghal influence was therefore strongly eastern. All seven burgesses were included on the Committee of Estates, three were included on the Committee for Managing the Affairs of the Army, three on the Committee for Military Affairs, and three on the Committee for the Conference with the Kirk.[56]

4. The Appointment of Parliamentary Interval Committees

Two crucial interval committees were appointed; the Committee for Managing the Affairs of the Army (28 March) and the Committee of Estates (31 March). Twenty-five per estate formed the membership of the Committee for Managing the Affairs of the Army. Only six noted radical nobles were included (Argyll, Eglinton, Cassillis, Buccleuch, Balcarras, and Lothian). The overwhelming bulk of noble members were conservatives or Royalists and included Hamilton, Lauderdale, Crawford-Lindsay, Atholl, Douglas, Glencairn and Dalhousie.[57]

The commission to the Committee of Estates of 30 December 1650 was renewed on 31 March. Only four variations in membership took place. One laird and one burgess who had been members of the earlier committee did not secure inclusion on the new committee of 31 March. In addition, Rollock, younger, of Duncrub (Clackmannan), and Douglas of Cavers (Roxburgh) had not been included on the previous committee of 30 December. As well as renewing the commission of 30 December, four nobles, eight gentry, and five burgesses were added to the renewed Committee of Estates of 31 March 1651. Hence the redefined total membership of that committee amounted to 92, consisting of 30 nobles, 34 gentry, and 28 burgesses. Ten of the 30 nobles (30%), 13 of the 34 gentry (38%), and six of the 28 burgesses (21%) included on the Committee of Estates of 31 March 1651 were also members of the Committee for Managing the Affairs of the Army. Six of the 10 nobles were radicals (Argyll, Eglinton, Cassillis, Buccleuch, Balcarras, and Lothian).[58]

On 31 March the House also stated that additions of four per estate were to be made by the Committee of Estates to the Committee for Monies. However, no reference exists in the parliamentary records for a Committee for Monies for the Seventh Session. Therefore it may well have been the case that the Committee of Estates was to establish a subcommittee, the Committee for Monies, during the interval of Parliament.[59]

5. The Operation of Parliamentary Interval Committees

No registers of the Committee of Estates for this period are available. However, the Register of the Committee for Managing the Affairs of the Army runs from 1 April–22 May 1651. The committee convened at Perth from 1 April–16 May and then at Stirling from 20 May–22 May. A total of 32 sederunts are recorded. The king was only present at nine diets (28%). Attendance data confirms the dominance of Royalists within noble representation. Hamilton attended 30 diets (94%), Lauderdale 23 diets (72%), Crawford-Lindsay 22 diets (69%), Glencairn 20 diets (62%), and Home 19 diets (59%). Crawford-Lindsay was President of all diets that he attended. In terms of radical influence, Argyll and Eglinton did not attend a single diet. However, Lothian is recorded in 20 sederunts (62%). Therefore it would appear that radical influence on the Committee for Managing the Affairs of the Army was represented by Lothian. The remaining 17 nobles attended 10 or less diets.[60]

Gentry influence was centred on the east and the Borders. Wauchope of

Niddrie (Edinburgh) attended 26 diets (81%) and Hepburne of Humbie (Haddington) 23 diets (72%), whilst Belshes of Toftis (Berwick) and Ferguson of Craigdarroch (Dumfries) are recorded in 26 and 23 diets respectively (81% and 72%). In addition, a western laird, Lockhart of Lee (Lanark), was in attendance at 15 diets (47%). Two further lairds, Foullis of Colington (Edinburgh) and Renton of Lamberton (Berwick), each attended 13 diets (41%). The remaining 18 gentry are recorded in 12 or less sederunts.[61]

Burghal attendance levels were minimal compared to the other two estates. Only one burgess had a notable attendance record. Sir John Smith (Edinburgh) was in attendance at 25 diets (78%). John Auchterlony (Arbroath) and John Boswell (Kinghorn) are recorded in 11 and 10 diets respectively (34% and 31%). The remaining 22 burgesses attended nine or less diets. Burghal influence, though limited, was centred on the east. Attendance of the General Officers of the Army was also limited, with Lieutenant General John Middleton attaining the highest figure of four diets. As per the terms of the commission of 28 March, the quorum of the Committee for Managing the Affairs of the Army was set at 11 with two of each estate required to be present. These rules were adhered to at all 32 diets.[62]

The work of the Committee of Managing the Affairs of the Army was dominated by the attempt to co-ordinate military resources and provisions and liaison with the committees of war in the shires. The establishment of numerous subcommittees reflects this preoccupation. Separate subcommittees were formed for provision of the army (1 April) and for the levies (2 April). The main batch of subcommittees (formed between 3 April and 2 May) was concerned with the provision and distribution of meal and victual for the armed forces. Distinct geographic units were formed for this purpose based on the north-east (3 April), the Highlands (3 April), and Fife (5 April). Moreover, a central subcommittee of 2 May was appointed to oversee the logistics and patterns of distribution of this operation.[63]

According to the commission issued to the Committee for Managing the Affairs of the Army, the committee was to restrict itself to military affairs. However, the committee began to take on an overtly political role, especially in its dealings with the Kirk and the demand for the repeal of the Act of Classes. On 1 April a subcommittee, composed of two per estate, was established to correspond with the Kirk. Hamilton and Lauderdale represented the nobility. Correspondence between the Commission of the Kirk and the Committee for Managing the Affairs of the Army reveals tension within that political relationship. By 4 April the Commission of the Kirk was complaining that it was 'much dissatisfied' with the membership of the army committee. The clash between the Commission of the Kirk and the Committee for Managing the Affairs of the Army had been intensified by 13 May when the latter committee was now openly calling for the Kirk's approval for the repeal of the Act of Classes. By 20 May it had been agreed that a conference between the committee and the Commission of the Kirk should take place. Four per estate formed the membership of the subcommittee established for this purpose.

Hamilton, Marischal, Glencairn, and Lauderdale represented the nobility. In addition, Crawford-Lindsay was included as a supernumerary.[64]

Whilst the Committee for Managing the Affairs of the Army met at Perth, the Committee of Estates convened at Stirling. In essence a power struggle was taking place between the two rival committees, staffed by two opposing factions and the Committee for Managing the Affairs of the Army was acting essentially as a Committee of Estates. Although the Eighth Session of the Second Triennial Parliament was due to convene on 17 April, it was prorogued by the Committee of Estates firstly to 21 May and then until 23 May. The first prorogation to 21 May had been achieved by the political management of the Argyll faction which sought to delay the meeting of the Eighth Session for as long as possible in order to avoid the rescinding of the Acts of Classes.[65]

The Eighth Session of the Second Triennial Parliament, 23 May–6 June 1651

1. The Composition of the Eighth Session of the Second Triennial Parliament

No official parliamentary rolls have been recorded for this parliamentary session. Neither has Balfour provided any attendance data for this session.[66]

2. The Proceedings of the Eighth Session of the Second Triennial Parliament

The Eighth Session was described by a contemporary English scribe as 'the Scotch Loyalist Parliament'.[67] Thirteen public enactments constitute the legislative programme of the Eighth Session held at Stirling. No details of ratifications passed during the Eighth Session are provided. However, at the close of the session there is a reference to a 'List of Ratifications past in pliament' but no further information is provided.[68] Moreover, during the parliamentary session, on 27 May, four gentry were appointed to consider which ratifications were to be presented to Parliament. Following the subscription of the parliamentary oaths, Burleigh was elected as President. Hence the office of President of Parliament was still occupied by a leading radical. The primary purpose of the parliamentary session was to secure legislative sanction for the repeal of the Act of Classes and secure a more comprehensive patriotic accommodation. The Commission of the Kirk had been lobbyed and pressurised throughout April and May to give its approval for a formal parliamentary appeal.[69]

It appears that both the Committee for Managing the Affairs of the Army and the Committee for Provisions, a subcommittee of the Committee for Managing the Affairs of the Army, were continuing to sit, at least initially during the parliamentary session, as was the Treasury Commission. The Committee for Managing the Affairs of the Army has its last recorded sederunt before the Eighth Session on 22 May. It met once at Stirling on 2 June (although no sederunt is recorded), but did not start officially meeting again until 9 June, after the close of the Eighth Session on 6 June. References in the parliamentary minutes of 23 May indicate that this was taking place. Furthermore, on 24 May additions were issued to a Committee for Grievances. In common with the Seventh Session, no details exist of a parliamentary session committee, the Committee for Grievances being formed. A subcommittee of the Committee of Estates of 30 December 1650 called the Committee for Grievances had been established on 10 January 1651. Therefore, it might well be the case that that subcommittee was continuing to sit throughout both the Seventh and Eighth Sessions of the Second Triennial Parliament and during the appropriate parliamentary intervals. What is clear, however, is that the distinction between parliamentary session and interval committees was becoming increasingly blurred.

Eight gentry and one burgess were added to this Committee for Grievances on 24 May. Further additions of three gentry and one burgess were subsequently made to the Committee for Grievances on 31 May. One of the lairds added on 31 May, Shaw of Greenock (Renfrew), was appointed as convener of the Committee for Grievances. This appointment provides an indication of the prominence accorded to the gentry over the other two estates. Of the additions of 24 and 31 May, two gentry, Houston of that ilk (Renfrew), and Nicholson of Carnock, Lord Advocate, had been members of the Committee of Estates appointed on 31 March. One of the burghal additions, John Cowan (Stirling), had been a member of the Committee for Managing the Affairs of the Army of 28 March. Therefore it would appear that there were no noble members of the committee, especially in the light of all gentry and burghal additions. The current dominance of eastern representation on parliamentary committees was thus being partly redressed with regard to the Committee for Grievances.[70]

On 23 May the Committee for Managing the Affairs of the Army had handed in its report to the House concerning particulars that were to be represented to the King (probably concerning the repeal of the Act of Classes). The following day a session committee was established to consider the Committee for Managing the Affairs of the Army's report. Three per estate formed its membership. Noble membership was essentially radical and included Argyll and Cassillis, both of whom had been included on the Committee for Managing the Affairs of the Army. None of the gentry or burghal members had been included on that interval committee. In addition to Argyll and Cassillis, one laird, Barclay of Johnstone (Kincardine), and two burgesses, John Forbes (Inverness) and George Garden (Burntisland), had been members of the Committee of Estates of 31 March. Both Argyll and Cassillis had been included on the Committee for the Conference with the Kirk of 13 March in the Seventh Session. One noble, one laird, and two burgesses were added to the committee on 26 May. The two burgesses added, Sir John Smith (Edinburgh) and James Sword (St Andrews), had also been included on the Committee for the Conference with the Kirk of 13 March in the Seventh Session and were noted radicals. The one laird added, Hepburne of Humbie (Haddington), and both burgesses had all been members of both the Committee for Managing the Affairs of the Army of 28 March and the Committee of Estates of 31 March. Balcarras (the noble addition) had been a member of the Committee of Estates of 31 March.

Detailed consideration of four unspecified articles of the report of the

Committee for Managing the Affairs of the Army was delegated to a specialised session committee of 26 May. Two nobles, three gentry, and three burgesses and one noble military official formed its membership. One of the noble members, Arbuthnot, had also been included on the Committee of Estates of 31 March. All three gentry and one burgess, John Boswell (Kinghorn), had been included on both the Committee for Managing the Affairs of the Army of 28 March and the Committee of Estates of 31 March.[71]

In light of the attempts to secure factional and national reconciliation, liaison with the Commission of the Kirk had acquired a new significance. A formal parliamentary session committtee of four per estate was established on 27 May for this purpose. The radical orientation of the parliamentary committee is emphasised by the fact that two nobles, Argyll and Cassillis, one laird, Kerr of Cavers (Roxburgh), and three burgesses Sir John Smith (Edinburgh), Andrew Grant (Perth), and James Sword (St Andrews), had been included on the Committee for the Conference with the Kirk of 13 March in the Seventh Session. Radical strength was enhanced by the presence of Lothian on the new committee of 27 May. Hence the parliamentary session committee to negotiate with the Commission of the Kirk was politically orientated in favour of the radicals, whereas the subcommittee of 20 May established by the Committee for Managing the Affairs of the Army was dominated by conservatives and former Engagers. A political power struggle was clearly taking place regarding the repeal of the Act of Classes.[72]

Negotiations with the Commission of the Kirk had been finalised by 24 May when that body gave its approval to those who had been censured under the Acts of Classes could have their fines and punishments rescinded by Parliament. Whilst not openly stating that the 1646 and 1649 Acts of Classes could be repealed, the Kirk was clearly giving indirect sanction to such a measure. By 29 May the draught of an act anent the securing of religion and the work of reformation was remitted to the consideration of the three estates separately. This act was approved by each of the three estates and received full legislative sanction on 30 May. This legislation represented a compromise to the Commission of the Kirk. All legislation establishing and promoting religion and the work of reformation was ratified. The current parliamentary session and any future session was barred from repealing any such legislation. Former Engagers and Royalists who might be admitted to Parliament were to be required to subscribe a band indicating that they would not endeavour to repeal such legislation and that they would not seek revenge for any censure or punishment they had received by the radical regime. Neither were they to purge the present occupants of public offices. Finally, on 2 June the respective Acts of Classes of 1646 and 1649 were repealed, although the permission of the Kirk was still required before any former malignant could be admitted to the House.

The repeal of the Acts of Classes appears to have had an immediate effect. In the afternoon session of 2 June the parliamentary oath and the band for securing religion and the work of reformation was subscribed by five nobles who had come to the House; Hamilton, Crawford-Lindsay, Lauderdale, Atholl, and

Huntly. Seven further nobles subscribed the band on 3 June; Douglas, Winton, Annandale, Callander, Tullibardine, Hartfell, Lindores, and Belhaven. The fact that the parliamentary oath was required to be subscribed indicates that they were primarily former Engagers or Royalists. On 3 June Douglas, Tullibardine and Hartfell each subscribed the band for security of religion and on 5 June Lord Madertie subscribed that band along with the parliamentary oath.[73]

Between 31 May and 2 June the House undertook a programme of legislative revision. In common with previous sessions, a session committee was established on 31 May to revise and consider the whole acts of the Committee of Estates. It would appear that the remit of that session committee was not confined to the legislation of the last Committee of Estates but of all previous Committees of Estates. This would then cover all previous legislation relating to censuring of malignants (the Acts of Classes) on the one hand, and the securing of the position of the Kirk (regarding the National Covenant and the Solemn League and Covenant) on the other hand. If such a scenario is correct, then the membership of the session committee is surprising. Two per estate formed the committee membership. Leading radicals, conservatives, and pragmatic Royalists did not secure inclusion for the noble estate, whose representation was based on Arbuthnot and Roxburgh. Arbuthnot had been a member of the Committee of Estates of 31 March, whilst Roxburgh had been included on the Committee for Managing the Affairs of the Army of 28 March. The nominations for all three estates, as per current parliamentary tradition and procedure, were made by each estate itself. Given the political mood and trend towards national reconciliation, the leading nobles may have avoided nomination to avoid arousing political controversy and further factionalism. Furthermore, radical nobles were not politically strong enough within the noble estate to secure nomination to such an important committee. One of the lairds, Colquhoun of Luss (Dumbarton), had been a member of both the Committee for Managing the Affairs of the Army of 28 March and the Committee of Estates of 31 March, whilst one burgess, John Forbes (Inverness), had been a member of the Committee of Estates. Further additions of one noble, two gentry, and one burgess, were made to the committee on 2 June. One noble, two gentry, and one burgess constituted the additions. The one noble addition, Newburgh, had been included on both the Committee for Managing the Affairs of the Army of 28 March and the Committee of Estates of 31 March. One of the lairds added, Belshes of Toftis (Berwick), had also been a member of both these interval committees, whilst the other, Nicholson of Carnock, Lord Advocate, had been a member of the Committee of Estates of 31 March. Given the crucial remit of the committee, it is surprising that only one committee member (including additions), Roxburgh, had been included on the Committee for Revising the Acts of the Committee of Estates of 13 March established during the Seventh Session.[74]

An alternative scenario to the above interpretation is that the scribe recording the parliamentary minutes associated the Committee for Managing the Affairs of the Army with being a Committee of Estates. The former committee had operated virtually like a Committee of Estates between the Seventh and Eighth Sessions. According to this scenario, the session committee appointed on 31 May revised all legislation enacted by the Committee for Managing the Affairs of the Army of 28 March and the Committee of Estates of 31 March. Indeed, on 2 June there is a reference to the existence of a Committee for Revising the Books of the Committee for the Affairs of the Army. Once again, this may have been confused with the session committee of 31 May. According to the minutes of 2 June, Arbuthnot was added to the Committee for Revising the Books of the Committee for the Affairs of the Army. However, Arbuthnot had already been included on the session committee as per 31 May. The phenomenon of a committee member being appointed to a committee of which he was already a member was not unprecedented in parliamentary terms and may only serve to indicate that Arbuthnot had not attended any of the diets of the session committee between 31 May and 2 June.[75]

Having secured the repeal of the Acts of Classes on 2 June, Royalists were now free to infiltrate and exert their authority on the membership of the Committee of Estates to sit after the close of the Eighth Session. On the same day that the Acts of Classes were repealed, a session committee was formed to consider the number of parliamentary interval committees to be established. Three per estate formed the session committee's membership. Noble representation was concentrated in the hands of Hamilton, Lauderdale, and Balcarras. Hamilton and Lauderdale had obviously been included on the Committee for Managing the Affairs of the Army of 28 March, whilst Balcarras had been included on the Committee of Estates of 31 March. This marks the final defeat for the radical nobles as they now had no control over the number and types of interval committees which were to be established. Two of the gentry representatives, Hepburne of Humbie (Haddington), and Hepburne of Keith (Haddington), had been members of both the Committee for Managing the Affairs of the Army of 28 March and the Committee of Estates of 31 March, whilst Hay of Nauchton (Fife) had been a member of the Committee of Estates. All three burghal members had been included on both the Committee for Managing the Affairs of the Army and the Committee of Estates and all three had radical political records; Sir John Smith (Edinburgh), James Sword (St Andrews) and Hugh Kennedy (Ayr).[76]

The move towards not only national but also factional rehabilitation was continued on 3 June with the passage of the Act against the Western Remonstrance. The Remonstrance was condemned and all those who failed to renounce it were to be regarded as seditious persons. Nevertheless, no further proceedings were to be taken against adherents of the Remonstrance, as long as they renounced it. Those in the shires of Stirling, Perth, Dumbarton, Edinburgh, Linlithgow, Lanark, Renfrew, and Ayr were to appear personally before the Committee of Estates before 20 June to renounce the Remonstrance, whilst those in the remaining shires were to appear before 1 July. When the Act against the Western Remonstrance was passed, three radical nobles and three burgesses based in the west and the central belt dissented from the passage of the act; Argyll, Chancellor Loudoun, Cassillis, Robert Barclay (Irvine), Hugh Kennedy (Ayr), and John Short (Stirling) formed the grouping of dissenters.[77]

Following the appointment of the appropriate parliamentary interval committees, the parliamentary session was adjourned to 3 November 1651.[78]

3. The Committee Structure of the Eighth Session of the Second Triennial Parliament

Ten committees, consisting of eight session committees and two interval committees, have been analysed. A total of 51 nobles, 54 gentry, and 49 burgesses form the analytical membership fields. Therefore near parity per estate again exists in the numbers of nobles, gentry, and burgesses employed within the committee structure of the Eighth Session. Almost identical numbers were employed by the nobility and the burgesses respectively, whilst a slightly greater number was employed by the gentry.

Balcarras secured membership of six committees, the largest number of committees that any noble was included on. Argyll was nominated to on three committees and Cassillis to four committees, although Lothian and Arbuthnot were each included on two committees. Lauderdale and Roxburgh, on the other hand, were nominated to three committees. A Royalist grouping of Hamilton, Tullibardine, Glencairn, Dunfermline, Barganie, Cochrane, and Newburgh were also included on two committees.

In common with the noble estate, the largest number of committees that any laird was included on was six. This was achieved by Hepburne of Humbie (Haddington). Three further lairds, Belshes of Toftis (Berwick), Nairn of Strathuird, and Hepburne of Keith (Haddington), were included on four committees each. Blair of Ardblair (Perth), Barclay of Johnstone (Kincardine), and Nicholson of Carnock (Stirling) gained membership of three committees each, whilst 12 gentry were nominated to two committees. For the burghal estate, Sir John Smith (Edinburgh) and James Sword (St Andrews) were each included on a total of five committees. Alexander Douglas (Banff) was included on four committees. John Forbes (Inverness), John Boswell (Kinghorn), and Sir Robert Farquhar (Aberdeen) were included on three committees each, whilst six burgesses secured membership of two committees each.

Thirty-eight nobles (74%), 35 gentry (65%), and 36 burgesses (74%) were included on only one committee each. In terms of the total analytical field, 32 of the 51 nobles (63%), 26 of the 54 gentry (48%), and 30 of the 49 burgesses (61%) were included solely on the Committee of Estates. Almost identical numbers of nobles and burgesses were nominated to the Committee of Estates only, whereas a smaller amount of gentry fall into that category.[79]

4. The Appointment of Parliamentary Interval Committees

Three parliamentary interval committees were appointed in the Eighth Session; the Committee of Estates, the Committee for Taking Inspection of the King's Rents, and the Committee for Monies, Accounts, and Excise. No specific membership details have been provided for the Committee for Monies,

Accounts, and Excise, although that committee was to consist of seven per estate and the quorum was set at five.[80]

A new Committee of Estates was established on 3 June. Forty-two per estate formed its basic membership. In common with previous Committees of Estates, the committee was to divide into two sections, one for governing the kingdom and the other for accompanying the king and the army. No details of individual membership of each section are provided, although the army section was to consist of 16 per estate and the central section of 24 per estate. This indictates that there was to be considerable crossover in personnel between the two sections.

Including supernumeraries of three nobles and two gentry, the final membership consisted of 45 nobles, 44 gentry, and 42 burgesses. Hence the total membership of the Committee of Estates of 3 June 1651 amounted to 131. Compared to the previous Committee of Estates of 31 March, this represents a rise of 15 nobles, 10 gentry, and 14 burgesses (yielding a total rise of 39). A limited degree of retention of personnel existed between the two Committees of Estates. Fifteen of the 45 nobles (33.3%), 21 of the 44 gentry (48%), and 19 of the 42 burgesses (45%) included on the Committee of Estates of 3 June had also been included on the previous Committee of Estates of 31 March.

Closer correlations in membership of the Committee of Estates of 3 June exist with the Committee for Managing the Affairs of 28 March. All 25 nobles, 25 of the 26 gentry, and 21 of the 25 burgesses on the Committee for Managing the Affairs of the Army gained membership of the Committee of Estates of 3 June. These figures represent 25 of the 45 nobles (56%), 25 of the 44 gentry (57%), and 21 of the 42 burgesses (50%) of the total membership of the Committee of Estates of 3 June. Balfour states that the Committee of Estates of 31 March and the Committee for Managing the War of 28 March were amalgamated to form the Committee of Estates of 3 June. Based on the above data, Balfour's assertion appears to be generally correct. What is apparent is that the membership of the Committee for Managing the Affairs of the Army diluted the membership of the Committee of Estates of 3 June. This emphasised the conservative and Royalist nature of the latter committee. Indeed the composition of the new Committee of Estates had aroused the hostility of the Commission of the Kirk, who argued that 'so many persons notourly knowne to us and to all that knowes them are named who are void of the qualifications'.[81]

Sixteen of the 45 nobles (36%), 13 of the 44 gentry (30%), and 13 of the 42 burgesses (40%) who were members of the Committee of Estates of 3 June had *not* been members of the Committee for Managing the Affairs of the Army of 28 March nor of the Committee of Estates of 31 March. These nobles, gentry, and burgesses formed the new manpower employed on the Committee of Estates of 3 June. The 16 nobles were exclusively conservative and Royalist and included Huntly, Tullibardine, Callander, Hartfell, Haddington, and Southesk. The English Royalist noble, Buckingham, was one of the 16 nobles. The admittance of an English peer to an interval committee of the Scottish Parliament was in contravention of the Scottish constitutional settlement of 1639–41. No apparent protest was made to Buckingham's inclusion. Parliamentary procedure had probably been subordinated to the national interest of defence against Cromwell. This grouping of 16 nobles added to the conservative and Royalist bias of the Committee of Estates, provided by the personnel from the Committee for Managing the Affairs of the Army. A significant number of the 13 gentry and 13 burgesses had previous parliamentary experience, including Dundas of Maner (Linlithgow) and Grierson of Lag (Dumfries) for the gentry, and Sir Patrick Leslie (Aberdeen), Sir Robert Farquhar (Aberdeen), Alexander Douglas (Banff), James Pedie (Montrose), James Lentron (St Andrews), and David Spence (Rutherglen) for the burghs.[82] In overall terms, therefore, the membership of the new Committee of Estates 'did diminish the Power of the Church, who were not consulted so much in Civil affairs as before.'[83]

The second parliamentary interval committee, the Committee for Taking Inspection of the King's Rents, was established on 6 June. Four per estate formed its membership. Radical nobles were excluded from noble representation of the committee and noble membership was based on Tullibardine, Barganie, Cochrane, and Balcarras. All committee members were included on the Committee of Estates of 3 June. Although officially a distinct parliamentary interval committee, the Committee for Taking Inspection of the King's rents was in effect a subcommittee of the Committee of Estates.[84]

5. The Operation of Parliamentary Interval Committees

Thirty-five sederunts of the Committee of Estates (Army) are recorded between 9 June and 22 July 1651. The commission to the Committee of Estates of 3 June stated that the committee was to divide in two sections, although no details are provided of the membership of the two sections.[85] All 35 diets were held at Stirling. Nevertheless, the committee continued to meet until 28 August when it was captured by Cromwellian forces at Alyth in Perthshire. Cromwellian forces had entered Perth on 2 July. The Scottish armed forces had invaded England on 6 August and were eventually routed at the Battle of Worcester on 3 September.[86]

Charles II was present at 20 of the 35 diets (57%). Hamilton has the highest attendance record of all noble members with a figure of 28 diets (80%). Yet Hamilton's influence did not extend to securing the position of President of the committee. That office was filled by Chancellor Loudoun, who attended 19 diets (54%). Loudoun was recorded as President of the Committee of Estates (Army) at 18 of these 19 diets (Lauderdale presided at the additional diet). The fact that Hamilton did not attempt to secure the post of President himself may have signified a desire to avoid further antagonism between Hamilton and Argyll, or at least accommodate the radical faction in general and the House of Argyll in particular. Argyll was in attendance at 21 of the 35 diets (60%). On the other hand, the appointment of the Chancellor as President may have been primarily a constitutional appointment in the eyes of the king. Seven further conservative or Royalist nobles attended between

17 and 23 diets (Annandale, Cardross, Crawford-Lindsay, Barganie, Belhaven, Cochrane, and Duffus). The remaining 34 nobles attended 15 or less diets.[87]

Only four gentry have significant attendance records. Murray of Skirling (Peebles) attended 24 diets (69%), Dundas of Maner (Linlithgow) and Stirling of Carden (Stirling) 17 diets (49%), and Drummond of Riccarton 16 diets (46%). The remaining 40 gentry, are recorded in 14 or less sederunts. In common with the gentry only four burgesses have significant attendance records. John Cowan (Stirling) attended 30 diets (86%), although his regular attendance can be explained by the fact that the committee was convening at Stirling. James Monteith (Edinburgh) attended 17 diets (49%), whilst James Roughead (Edinburgh) and John Milne (Edinburgh) each attended 16 diets (46%). The remaining 38 burgesses attended 12 or less diets. According to the commission of 3 June, the quorum of the Committee of Estates (Army) was set at seven, with one per estate required to be present. These rules were adhered to at all 35 diets. One noble, Torphichen, and one laird, MacDowall of Garthland (Wigtown), each attended one diet although they were not officially committee members.[88]

Conclusion

Military defeat at Dunbar had emphasised that national political rapprochement involving the king was necessary in order to mount and sustain an effective military defence of the kingdom against the Cromwellian occupying force which was steadily gaining ground in Scotland. Tentative steps towards rapprochement were initiated in October and November 1650, although the Western Remonstrance had indicated that there was a militant hard core of extreme radicals who refused to acknowledge the king. Facilitated by the Resolutioner majority in the General Assembly, the rehabilitation of former Engagers and Royalists was initiated by the issuing of the Public Resolutions on 14 December 1650 and continued throughout the Sixth, Seventh, and Eighth Sessions of the Second Triennial Parliament. Nevertheless, radical nobles still dominated the parliamentary agenda until the establishment of the Committee for Managing the Affairs of the Army on 28 March 1651, which marked the admission of former Engagers and Royalists, with the Kirk's permission, into the Scottish armed forces. From this point on the parliamentary power of the radical nobles was in terminal decline, as conservative and Royalist nobles increased their parliamentary power, particularly after the repeal of the Acts of Classes on 2 June 1651. It had also become clear that the radical nobles had become politically isolated. Nevertheless, military defeat at Worcester on 3 September 1651 subjected Scotland not only to military occupation by a foreign force, but also to the loss of national independence and subjugation by the English Commonwealth which was to endure until 1660. Cromwell's triumph at Worcester effectively ended the 'Wars of the Three Kingdoms' and ensured that the southern kingdom had now become dominant within the British archipelago.[89]

NOTES

1. Balfour, *Historical Works*, IV, 123; R. Hutton, *Charles II, King of England, Scotland and Ireland* (Oxford, 1989), 56–57; Stevenson, *Government Under the Covenanters*, xxxii; Hewison, *The Covenanters*, volume two, 20–21.
2. Balfour, *Historical Works*, IV, 123; *Records of the Kirk*, 549–550.
3. Balfour, *Historical Works*, IV, 125.
4. Ibid, 131; BL Egerton MS 2542, Nicholas Papers, folio 58.
5. Balfour, *Historical Works*, IV, 129–130, 131, 160.
6. Ibid, 135–137, 166, 168, 169; Dow, *Cromwellian Scotland*, 9; Stevenson, *Revolution and Counter-Revolution in Scotland*, 188–189; Brown, *Kingdom or Province?*, 135; Hutton, *Charles II*, 57–58.
7. Balfour, *Historical Works*, IV, 169–170. Lothian was the remaining noble on the committee of 23 November. Hepburne of Humbie (Haddington) and Nicholson of Carnock (Stirling), Lord Advocate, represented the gentry, whilst Sir John Smith (Edinburgh) and James Sword (St Andrews) represented the burgesses; Rait, *Parliaments of Scotland*, 73.
8. Ibid, 171–172; *Records of the Kirk*, 549–550.
9. Balfour, *Historical Works*, 173; *Records of the Kirk*, 549–550.
10. Balfour, *Historical Works*, 172, 174; Cassillis, Arbuthnot, and Burleigh were the three noble dissenters. Johnston of Wariston (Edinburgh), Clerk Register, Carmichael of that ilk (Lanark), Treasurer Depute, Scott of Harden (Selkirk), Ruthven of Frieland (Perth), Hope of Hopetoun (Stirling), and General Quartermaster William Stewart were the six gentry dissenters. Robert Lockhart (Edinburgh), John Jaffray (Aberdeen), and John Denholm, General Commissioner, were the three burgess dissenters. According to a contemporary manuscript copy of the Act of the Committee of Estates, opposing the Remonstrance, 25 November 1650, four additional gentry and one additional burgess are included in the list of dissenters; Adair of Kinhilt and Dickson of Busbie are included in the figures for the additional dissenters, along with Hepburne of Humbie (Haddington) and Ferguson of Craigdarroch (Dumfries). Patrick Ross (Perth) is the additional burgess included (SRA, Stirling Maxwell of Pollock Papers, T-PM 109/26).
11. Balfour, *Historical Works*, IV, 115, 116, 117, 166, 171. No manuscript committee register of the Committee of Estates is available for this period.
12. Balfour, *Historical Works*, IV, 115, 116, 117–118, 166, 171–172.
13. Ibid, 79, 98, 109, 127, 166; *Correspondence of Sir Robert Kerr, first Earl of Ancrum and his son William, third Earl of Lothian*, volume two, 302; Hewison, *The Covenanters*, volume two 23. The four dates of prorogation listed by Balfour are as follows. On 10 September Parliament was adjourned to meet at Stirling on 1 October. On 1 October the session was adjourned to be held at Stirling, Perth or St Andrews on 22 October. On 17 October the session was adjourned to meet at Perth on 30 October. On 15 November the session was adjourned from 20 November to 22 November at Perth. Two further adjournments must have occurred; firstly, before 10 September, and secondly, after 17 October but before 15 November. According to NLS MS 2263, History of Events 1635–1662, ff 214–216, Parliament actually met at Perth on 30 October and then adjourned to 20 November. It then met again at Perth on 20 November and then adjourned to 22 November. When it reconvened on 22 November it was again adjourned, this time to 26 November. The scribe states that these adjournments were carried out

at the desire of the Commission of the Kirk. Nicoll attributes the prorogation from 15 August to 10 September to the fact that Edinburgh was surrounded by two rival military armies (*Diary*, 23).

14. *APS*, vi, ii, 562, 608; Balfour, *Historical Works*, IV, 179–182.
15. *APS*, vi, ii, 555–556, 562; Balfour, *Historical Works*, IV, 179–182; Hutton, *Charles II*, 59, notes the under-representation of the south-west in this parliamentary session.
16. *APS*, vi, ii, 608–640.
17. Ibid, 608; Balfour, *Historical Works*, IV, 182.
18. *APS*, vi, ii, 609, 613, 621.
19. Ibid, 536–537, 561, 609, 617. On 30 November additions of two per estate were ordered, although no membership details were provided.
20. Ibid, 563, 609.
21. Ibid, 609; *Records of the Kirk*, 549–550. The order of the coronation had been under discussion from at least 22 November, when a specialised subcommittee of the Commission of the Kirk had been formed to negotiate with the Committee of Estates on this issue (*RCGA*, iii, 117). Indeed, as early as 28 June, shortly after the king's arrival in Scotland, an earlier subcommittee of the Commission of the Kirk had been established to revise the 'superstitious solemnities' in the coronation (*RCGA*, ii, 440).
22. *APS*, vi, ii, 536–537, 561, 566, 567, 609; *Records of the Kirk*, 549–550; Balfour, *Historical Works*, IV, 187.
23. *APS*, vi, ii, 388, 536–537, 561, 613; *Records of the Kirk*, 549–550.
24. *APS*, vi, ii, 536–537, 561, 614, 621; Balfour, *Historical Works*, IV, 193; *Records of the Kirk*, 549–550.
25. *APS*, vi, ii, 608, 614, 620; Balfour, *Historical Works*, IV, 181, 182, 188, 189.
26. *APS*, vi, ii, 616, 618, 619, 628; Balfour, *Historical Works*, IV, 188, 189, 195, 196, 198, 198–199, 200, 205, 206, 207, 221; Stevenson, *The Covenanters*, 57–58; Donnachie and Hewitt, *A Companion to Scottish History*, 167; Dow, *Cromwellian Scotland*, 9.
27. *APS*, vi, ii, 617–618, 624–626; 630; Balfour, *Historical Works*, IV, 192–193, 195, 196, 197–198, 202–203, 210–211, 211–212, 212–214, 216, 224, 227; Dow, *Cromwellian Scotland*, 9; Brown, *Kingdom or Province?*, 135; Hutton, *Charles II*, 58–59; Hewison, *The Covenanters*, volume two 25; Stevenson, *Revolution and Counter-Revolution in Scotland*, 193–194.
28. *APS*, vi, ii, 640; Balfour, *Historical Works*, IV, 228–229.
29. *APS*, vi, ii, 609–663.
30. Ibid, 629, 631.
31. Ibid, 294–296, 321, 631.
32. Ibid; Stevenson, *Revolution and Counter-Revolution in Scotland*, 197.
33. *The Form and Order of the Coronation of Charles II, King of Scotland, England, France and Ireland* (reprint, Glasgow, 1741), printed in J. Kerr (ed), *The Covenants and the Covenanters. Covenants, Sermons, and Documents of the Covenanted Reformation* (Edinburgh, 1895), 349–398; J. Morrill, 'The National Covenant in its British Context', in *The Scottish National Covenant in its British Context*, 21; Hutton, *Charles II*, 59; Brown, *Kingdom or Province?*, 135.
34. SRO PA. 11/10, Register of the Committee of Estates, 2 January–12 March 1651, ff 1–107. *APS*, vi, ii, 631–633. Eight military officials also attended various diets; Lieutenant General David Leslie, Lieutenant General Middleton, Quartermaster

General William Stewart, Colonel James Weymes, General of the Artillery, Major General Montgomery, Major General Massie, Major General Holburne, and Major General Brown. Elphinstone and Dickson of Hartrie each attended one diet. Murray of Skirling attended two diets.

35. SRO PA 11/10, ff 20 and 56; *APS*, vi, ii, 631; Balfour, *Historical Works*, IV, 242. Lothian was the remaining noble added to the Committee for Provisions. Hamilton of Little Preston (Edinburgh) and David Wilkie (Edinburgh) were the remaining gentry and burghal additions to the Committee for Monies, Excise, and Accounts.
36. SRO PA 11/10, folio 19. The military representative was Quartermaster General William Stewart. Ruthven of Frieland (Perth) and Scott of Harden (Selkirk) were the remaining gentry on the Committee for Grievances.
37. Balfour, *Historical Works*, IV, 235, 327; Stevenson, *Government Under the Covenanters*, 191–192; SRO PA 11/10 folio 18; *RCGA*, iii, 190–191.
38. Balfour, *Historical Works*, IV, 253–254.
39. Ibid, 254; Stevenson, *Revolution and Counter-Revolution in Scotland*, 198.
40. SRO PA 11/10, folio 10; *Records of the Kirk*, 549–550. Neither Elphinstone, Murray of Skirling (Peebles), Dickson of Hartrie (Peebles), nor Kerr of Cavers (Roxburgh) attended the diet of 11 March. Therefore there was no political 'loading' of these individuals for the specific issue of convening the Seventh Session.
41. *APS*, vi, ii, 640; Balfour, *Historical Works*, IV, 258–262.
42. *APS*, vi, ii, 640–661.
43. Ibid, 640; Balfour, *Historical Works*, IV, 262.
44. *APS*, vi, ii, 642–643; Balfour, *Historical Works*, IV, 262–263.
45. *APS*, vi, ii, 631–633, 640; *Records of the Kirk*, 549–550.
46. SRO PA 11/10, folio 18; *APS*, vi, ii, 631–633, 643; *Records of the Kirk*, 549–550. Balfour asserts that the Committee for Grievances was to consist of three per estate and that its commission was to endure until the next parliamentary session (*Historical Works*, IV, 262). It would appear, however, that Balfour's membership details are wrong.
47. *APS*, vi, ii, 631–637, 643; *Records of the Kirk*, 549–550.
48. *APS*, vi, ii, 609, 631–633, 642; *Records of the Kirk*, 549–550.
49. *APS*, vi, ii, 609, 631–633, 642–643; *Records of the Kirk*, 549–550.
50. *APS*, vi, ii, 621, 631–633, 643; *Records of the Kirk*, 549–550.
51. *APS*, vi, ii, 642.
52. Ibid, 321, 631–633, 647; *Records of the Kirk*, 549–550; Balfour, *Historical Works*, IV, 266.
53. Balfour, *Historical Works*, IV, 266, 270, 273, 274–275, 276, 277; *RCGA*, iii, 344–345, 356–358; Hutton, *Charles II*, 61; Stevenson, *Government Under the Covenanters*, 105–106; Stevenson, *Revolution and Counter-Revolution in Scotland*, 199–200; Dow, *Cromwellian Scotland*, 10; *APS*, vi, ii, 647, 654–655. The five remaining nobles who expressed their dissent were Linlithgow, Weymes, Torphichen, Coupar, and Cranston. The three gentry who also expressed their dissent were Scott of Clerkington (Selkirk), Belshes of Toftis (Berwick), and Ruthven of Frieland (Perth) (Balfour, *Historical Works*, IV, 275). Eglinton and Campbell of Lundie (Forfar) were the respective noble and laird who had not voted against the proposals of 26 March (Balfour, *Historical Works*, IV, 275, 277).
54. Balfour, *Historical Works*, IV, 277–278, 281.
55. Ibid, 281; *APS*, vi, ii, 661; *RCGA*, iii, 361.
56. *APS*, vi, ii, 640–661.

57. Ibid, 654–655; Stevenson, *Government Under the Covenanters*, 105–106; Stevenson, *Revolution and Counter-Revolution in Scotland*, 200.
58. *APS*, vi, ii, 631–633, 654–655, 662–663.
59. Ibid, 661.
60. Stevenson, *Government Under the Covenanters*, 105–173.
61. Ibid.
62. Ibid; *APS*, vi, ii, 654–665. By 25 April the Committee for Managing the Affairs of the Army had become concerned about the non-attendance of burgesses. Letters were written to five specified burgesses demanding their attendance; Sir Alexander Wedderburne (Dundee), Andrew Glen (Linlithgow), Patrick Thomson (Peebles), and Robert Bell (Linlithgow). The committee expressed concern at the attainment of quorum levels due to non-attendance of burgesses. Analysis of sederunts, however, reveals that the quorum levels were adhered to (*Government Under the Covenanters*, 134, 168–173).
63. Stevenson, *Government Under the Covenanters*, 109, 111, 112–113, 113–114, 115, 144, 145.
64. *APS*, vi, ii, 654–655; Stevenson, *Government Under the Covenanters*, 109, 129–130, 154, 160–161; *RCGA*, iii, 368. One laird and both burgess members of the subcommittee to correspond with the Kirk had in fact been members of the Commission of the Kirk of 4 August 1649; Kerr of Cavers (Roxburgh), Sir John Smith (Edinburgh), and John Boswell (Kinghorn). In addition to John Boswell, one further member of the Committee for the Conference with the Kirk, namely Scott of Harden (Selkirk), had also been included on the Commission of the Kirk of 4 August 1649 (*Records of the Kirk*, 549–550).
65. Stevenson, *Government Under the Covenanters*, 107; Stevenson, *Revolution and Counter-Revolution in Scotland*, 200–201; Balfour, *Historical Works*, IV, 297; Nicholl, *Diary*, 51; *RCGA*, iii, 1652, 387–388.
66. *APS*, vi, ii, 667; Balfour, *Historical Works*, IV, 301.
67. BL Egerton MS 2542, Nicholas Papers, ff 75–88.
68. *APS*, vi, ii, 667–687, 687.
69. Ibid, 667, 669; *RCGA*, iii, 361, 387–388, 405–406. Nicholson of Carnock (Stirling), Lord Advocate, Hepburne of Humbie (Haddington), Hepburne of Keith (Haddington), and Belshes of Toftis (Berwick) were the four gentry appointed to consider on the ratifications to be presented to Parliament.
70. SRO PA. 11/10, folio 18; *APS*, vi, ii, 643, 654–655, 662–663, 667, 675.
71. *APS*, vi, ii, 643, 667–668, 668.
72. Ibid, 643, 667–668, 668, 669.
73. Ibid, 671, 672–673, 676–677, 678, 681; *The Diary of Mr John Lamont of Newton*, 30; Stevenson, *Revolution and Counter-Revolution in Scotland*, 202; Balfour, *Historical Works*, IV, 301–306, 306–307; Rait, *Parliaments of Scotland*, 73–74; *RCGA*, iii, 432, 439–441, 441–442, 442–443, 458–459.
74. *APS*, vi, ii, 643, 654–655, 662–663, 675–676, 678.
75. Ibid, 675–676, 678.
76. Ibid, 654–655, 662–663, 678.
77. Ibid, 683–684; Stevenson, *Revolution and Counter-Revolution in Scotland*, 202–204; Balfour, *Historical Works*, IV, 309.
78. Balfour, *Historical Works*, IV, 308.
79. *APS*, vi, ii, 667–686.
80. Ibid, 679–681, 681, 685–686.

81. *RCGA*, iii, 476–479; *APS*, vi, ii, 654–655, 662–663, 679–681; Balfour, *Historical Works*, 308. Parliamentary minutes for 5 and 6 June contain lists for all three estates of those nobles, gentry, and burgesses who were included on the Committee of Estates after voting. Two nobles, Linlithgow and Cranston, are included in the Committee of Estates of 3 June, but not the list for the nobility of 5 June. Two gentry, Robert Bruce of Broomhall and Drummond of Riccarton, are included in the lists for the gentry but not in the commission of 3 June. Three burgesses, Andrew Glen (Linlithgow), Alexander Douglas (Banff), and George Morrison, are included in the commission of 3 June but not in the list for the burgesses of 6 June. For the purposes of the analysed data all figures and details of membership have been based on the commission to the Committee of Estates of 3 June (*APS*, vi, ii, 679–681, 684, 685).
82. *APS*, vi, ii, 654–655, 662–663, 679–681.
83. EUL, Dc 5. 44, Memoirs of Scots Affairs, folio 338.
84. *APS*, vi, ii, 679–681, 685–686.
85. SRO PA 11/11, Register of the Committee of Estates (Army), 7 June–22 July 1651, ff 48–104; *APS*, vi, ii, 679–681. The section to accompany the army and the king was to consist of 16 per estate and the quorum was set at seven with one per estate required to be present. The section to govern the kingdom was to consist of 24 of each estate, the quorum was set at 11 and two per estate were required to be present. No membership details for the separate army section are provided in SRO PA. 11/11.
86. Lynch, *Scotland, A New History*, 279; Brown, *Kingdom or Province?*, 136; Dow, *Cromwellian Scotland*, 11; Hutton, *Charles II*, 63–64; Balfour, *Historical Works*, IV, 314.
87. SRO PA 11/11, ff 48–104; *APS*, vi, ii, 679–681. On 10 June it was decided that Glencairn was to preside at all diets when Chancellor Loudoun was absent. Glencairn subsequently presided at eight of the 23 diets which he attended. That the radical Loudoun was appointed as President may have been an exercise in realpolitik by Hamilton. Radicals would thus exercise influence on the committee, whilst there was no possibility of Argyll being appointed President.
88. SRO PA 11/11, ff 48–104; *APS*, vi, ii, 679–681. Nine military officials also attended various diets.
89. Abbott, *Writings and Speeches of Oliver Cromwell*, volume two, 468.

12

Scottish Representation in the Cromwellian Parliaments

> Such was the calamitous issue of a series of wars, undertaken from principles of civil and religious liberty; an ancient nation, till then unconquered, was subdued by a party hardly perceptible in England when the wars commenced.[1]

The Aftermath of Worcester

Following military defeat at Worcester and the capture of the Committee of Estates at Alyth, Scotland was left without a legally constituted government as well as being a conquered nation. Attempts led by Loudoun to reconvene the Committee of Estates within Scotland and hold a Parliament near Loch Tay had failed drastically (the Estates having failed to turn up with only a few exceptions). The political future was set out in *A Declaration of the Commonwealth of England*, concerning Scotland of October 1651 whereby it was declared that Scotland was to be incorporated within the English Commonwealth. On 23 October the Committee for Scotch and Irish Affairs of the Council of State nominated commissioners to be sent to Scotland who subsequently arrived at Dalkeith on 15 January 1652. On 24 January summons were issued to the shires and burghs to elect representatives to attend the Cromwellian commissioners at Dalkeith where their agreement to union was required. Those Scottish representatives were then to elect 21 of their number (14 gentry and seven burgesses) who were then to proceed to London ostensibly to negotiate on the terms of incorporation. In reality, however, the Scottish deputies were subjected to a political settlement imposed by the Cromwellian regime.[2]

The Scottish Representatives at Dalkeith and Edinburgh

According to the summons of 24 January 1652, each shire was to elect two deputies and each burgh one deputy, with the exception of the burghs of Glasgow, Aberdeen, and Edinburgh who were to elect two deputies. Only 18 shires and 24 burghs actually sent representatives to Dalkeith, although 29 out of 30 shires and 44 out of 58 burghs eventually agreed to the Tender of Incorporation. Although the Tender had been referred back to the shires and burghs for their approval, the political and military reality of the situation ensured that there was no other option but to accept the Tender.[3]

On 16 March 1652 the Tender to Parliament of the Cromwellian commissioners in Scotland was presented to Parliament. That document stated that provision should be made for Scottish representation. It also stipulated that 14 deputies from the shires and seven deputies for the burghs which had accepted the Tender of Incorporation were to be elected to proceed to London to settle the details of Scottish representation. According to the *Declaration of the Parliament of England, in order to the Uniting of Scotland into one Commonwealth with England* of 25 March, the persons to be elected were to be 'of known Integrity, and such as have declared their Consent to the said Union'.[4] Elections were to be held before the end of July 1652 and those elected were to convene at Edinburgh before 20 August.[5]

Nine of the 42 gentry (21%) and 14 of the 37 burgesses (38%) elected had Scottish parliamentary experience, 1639–51.[6] The 21 deputies to proceed to London had been chosen by 20 August. Three of the 14 gentry elected and five of the seven burgesses elected had served in Parliament, 1639–51. Of the 28 shires which had agreed to the Tender of Incorporation at Dalkeith (albeit only 18 actual commissioners had been sent), only 19 voted at the election of the Scottish deputies at Edinburgh. The comparative figures for the burghs are 34 out of the 44 burghs (although only 24 sent commissioners) which had agreed to the Tender of Incorporation at Dalkeith.[7]

The Scottish Deputies at London, October 1652–April 1653

The 21 Scottish deputies arrived in London on 6 October. Between 14 October 1652 and 8 April 1653 negotiations with a specialised committee of the Long Parliament took place on 35 occassions. However, at 13 of the diets the committee sat without the Scottish contingent. Arguments over the exact number of Scottish representatives were finally resolved on 2 March 1653 when the Long Parliament set the level of Scottish representation, in common with that of the Irish, at 30. The Instrument of Government of December 1653, which established the Protectorate, included this provision for Scottish members but did not provide for their distribution. The terms of distribution were not settled until 27 June 1654 which allowed for 20 seats for groups of shires and 10 seats to groups of burghs. The 20 seats for shires consisted of 11 districts of one shire, five districts of two shires, and four districts of three shires. Nine of the 10 groupings of burghs were located in the close vicinity of army garrisons.[8]

Although Scottish representation had been settled by March 1653, the Bill of Union still required legislative sanction by the Long Parliament. The Bill of Union had reached the stage of a second reading by April 1652 but had not progressed any further from that date. Indeed the dissolution of the Long Parliament in April 1653 witnessed the end of that particular proposed Bill of Union. A further Bill of Union was read in the Barebones' Parliament in October 1653 but had not been passed by the time of its dissolution in December 1653. Although the union received legislative sanction in an ordinance of 12 April 1654, it was not until the Second Protectorate Parliament that an Act of Union became law in April 1657. The Protectorate was formally established on 4 May 1654.[9]

Scottish representation in the Cromwellian Parliaments, 1653–59

Following the dissolution of the Long Parliament in April 1653, no elections had taken place for the Barebones' Parliament. Instead all members had been nominated to that Parliament. Five Scottish members, consisting of four gentry and one burgess, were nominated. William Lockhart of Lee (Lanark), Hope of Hopetoun (Stirling), Swinton of that ilk (Berwick), and Brodie of that ilk (Elgin) were nominated for the gentry, whilst Alexander Jaffray (Aberdeen) was nominated for the burgesses. All took their seats bar Brodie of that ilk. With the exception of William Lockhart of Lee, all had experience of the Scottish Parliament, 1639–51. Hope of Hopetoun and Swinton of that ilk, in particular, were noted enthusiasts of and participants in the radical regime of 1649–50.[10]

The first Parliament of the Protectorate convened on 3 September 1654. Hence the elections of the Scottish representatives took place throughout August 1654 against the background of the Glencairn Rising and in the wake of the military campaign against a Royalist uprising. Under the terms of the Instrument of Government known Royalists had been disfranchised and therefore could not vote in elections. Despite the fact that Scottish representation was set at 30 members, only 21 constituencies (including Edinburgh) returned members. Scottish representation in the 1654 Parliament therefore amounted to only 22. Hence there was limited Scottish collaboration. Nine of the 22 were English and eight of these nine held either a military or civil office in Scotland under the regime. The remaining 13 representatives were Scots, six of whom had been elected as deputies to negotiate with the Long Parliament between October 1652 and April 1653. Swinton of that ilk (Berwick), Lockhart of Lee (Lanark), MacDowall of Garthland (Wigtown), Hamilton of Orbiston (Renfrew), Sir Alexander Wedderburne (Dundee), and James Sword (St Andrews) constituted this grouping of six. Swinton of that ilk and Lockhart of Lee had been two of the Scottish nominees in the Barebones' Parliament. The bulk of the Scots also enjoyed employment in an office of trust under the regime. Hence Scottish representation in the 1654 Parliament consisted solely of safe men.[11]

In contrast to the 1654 elections, the elections held in August 1656 for the Second Protectorate Parliament produced a full quota of 30 members. English influence still prevailed. Sixteen of the 30 representatives were English, whilst 14 were Scottish. All 16 English members were either army officers, civilian office holders, or were networked to influential figures under the regime. Of the 14 Scots, five had been elected to the First Protectorate Parliament; David Barclay of Urie, Lockhart of Lee, MacDowall of Garthland, and Sir Alexander Wedderburne. Five of the remaining nine Scots possessed parliamentary experience, 1639–51. Tweeddale, Cochrane, Weymes of Bogie (Fife), Kerr of Newton (Roxburgh), and Alexander Douglas (Banff) formed this grouping. Eight of the 14 Scots had been appointed as Justices of the Peace earlier in 1656. The relationship between military and civil employment in the offices of the Protectorate and election as one of the 30 Scottish representatives was therefore continued.[12]

Following the death of Oliver Cromwell on 3 September 1658, political power within the Commonwealth passed to his eldest son, Richard Cromwell. Under the terms of the Humble Petition and Advice of 1657, the proportion of Scottish representatives was to be reviewed before the dissolution of the Second Protectorate Parliament. However, such a review had not been achieved before the dissolution of that Parliament on 4 February 1658. The Council of State decided during December 1658 to maintain the system of Scottish representation which had been applied in both the First and Second Protectorate Parliaments. Election writs for Scotland were issued on 14 December and reached Edinburgh on 21 December. Throughout November and December 1658 preparations were being made for the management of the Scottish parliamentary elections in order to provide for a body of political creatures amenable to the Protectorate. This stemmed from an intelligence network which was indicating that Scots, notably Argyll, were planning to get themselves elected. Throughout the Cromwellian era Argyll had adopted a somewhat ambivalent attitude towards the regime, but had always maintained a credible working relationship with that regime. In addition, Johnston of Wariston, Cassillis, and Sir William Lockhart of Lee were all members of the Upper House of the Second Protectorate Parliament, 1656–58. Both Johnston of Wariston and Cassillis had been radical allies of Argyll, 1639–51, and continued to represent the 'Argyll interest'.[13]

In common with the elections of 1654 and 1656, the English interest predominated in the 1659 elections to Richard Cromwell's Parliament. Despite the fact that all 30 Scottish constituencies returned a member, only 26 individuals formed the actual Scottish parliamentary grouping. Two Englishmen were elected twice for different Scottish districts, whilst another two Englishmen were also elected for English constituencies and sat for them instead. Only 11 Scots were elected and this figure was reduced to 10 when Archibald Murray of Blackbarony (Selkirk) refused to serve and was replaced by an English nominee. Of the 17 Englishmen elected in their own right, all were either army officers, had connections with the Protectoral interest in England or had connections with the civil administration in Scotland. Six of the 11 Scots elected had served in either or both of the First and Second Protectorate Parliaments. Linlithgow, Tweeddale, Swinton of that ilk (Berwick), MacDowall of Garthland (Wigtown), George Lockhart (Lanark), and John Lockhart (Lanark and adjacent burghs) constituted this grouping. Kerr of Greenhead (Roxburgh) was employed in the civil administration. Of the remaining three Scots, two had experience of the Scottish Parliament, 1639–51; Argyll (Aberdeen) and Gibson of Durie (Fife). Argyll successfully employed his network of influence in Aberdeenshire to secure election without opposition.[14]

When Richard Cromwell's Parliament actually convened, the right of the Scottish representatives to take their seats was challenged, primarily because they were identified so closely as a faction of Protectorate interests. This was possible because neither the Humble Petition and Advice nor the Second

Protectorate Parliament had settled the issue of Scottish representation. In the power struggle which arose between the army and civilian interests of the Protectorate after the death of Oliver Cromwell, the Scottish representatives were identified with the latter interest. Thus by attacking the rights of Scottish representation, it was Richard Cromwell's Protectorate itself which was being challenged. On 8 March 1659 the exclusion of the Scottish members was moved in the House, but when the vote was taken on 21 March the motion was defeated by 211 to 120 votes. By the time an alliance of army officers led by General Charles Fleetwood and anti-Protectorate republicans had forced the dissolution of Richard Cromwell's Parliament on 22 April 1659, the nature of the Cromwellian Union, let alone the issue of Scottish representation, had failed to be settled.[15]

The Issue of Union and Moves Towards the Restoration in England, May 1659–May 1660

The Rump Parliament which was restored on 7 May 1659, following the resignation of Richard Cromwell, delegated the issue of the union to a specialised committee of the Council of State. It recommended that a former Bill for Union, which had been twice read previously, should be revived. Such a bill was required to be revived due to the dissolution of Richard Cromwell's Parliament on 22 April. The fall of the Protectorate and the restoration of the Long Parliament cancelled the Ordinance of Union. This advice of the committee of the Council of State was refused by the House and on 25 June a new bill was ordered to be prepared. Following two readings, a committee of the whole House was in the process of considering the bill throughout August, September, and October 1659, when the Rump Parliament was dissolved by the 'Wallingford House' faction of army officers on 13 October. It was the dissolution of the Rump Parliament that forced General George Monck's hand in declaring that he would act in military terms to defend the authority of Parliament. Even before the collapse of the 'Wallingford House' group on 24 December and the resumption of the Rump on 26 December military preparations were underway by Monck and his forces in Scotland for an invasion of England. Following Monck's march on London on 1 January 1660 and the readmittance of those members who had been expelled by Pride's Purge in 1648 on 21 February, the way was now open for the restoration of the monarchy in England. On 16 March the Long Parliament was dissolved in order to elect a Convention Parliament, which convened in April and was composed of a majority in favour of the Restoration of the monarchy, a mood enhanced by Charles's conciliatory tone as expressed in the Declaration of Breda of 4 April. The fact that Scottish representatives were banned from the Convention Parliament indicated that Scotland's constitutional future would be different from that experience since 1651. On 8 May the Convention Parliament reaffirmed Charles II as king (having been proclaimed as king by the Scottish Parliament of 1649).[16]

Conclusion

Scottish representation in the Protectorate Parliaments was determined by the political needs of a regime which had conquered and defeated Scotland as a nation in military terms. The terms of union and the terms of Scottish representation were basically imposed from above on the remanents of the Scottish political nation. The predominance of English influence regarding Scottish representation in all the three elections of 1654, 1656, and 1659 is therefore hardly surprising. Particularly in 1658–59, the open emergence of the 'Argyll interest' became more pronounced. The issues of the union and Scottish representation became entangled in the power struggle within the English political nation throughout 1659 and 1660. Nevertheless, the Restoration was determined primarily by English political events and it had become clear that the political and constitutional future of Scotland would be relegated to a subordinate place.

NOTES

1. Laing, *History of Scotland*, III, 479.
2. Donaldson, *James V–James VII*, 343–344; Brown, *Kingdom or Province?*, 137–138; Dow, *Cromwellian Scotland*, 30, 32, 36; D. Stevenson, 'Cromwell, Scotland and Ireland' in *Oliver Cromwell and the English Revolution*, J. Morrill (ed.), (1990), 165; C.H Firth (ed.), *Scotland and the Commonwealth 1651–53*, SHS, 18, (Edinburgh, 1895), 21–27; *APS*, v, introduction page vi.
3. Dow, *Cromwellian Scotland*, 36, 38; Donaldson, *James V–James VII*, 344; Lynch, *Scotland, A New History*, 283.
4. Dow, *Cromwellian Scotland*, 45, 46.
5. Ibid.
6. Terry, *The Cromwellian Union*, 185. Those gentry and burgesses with experience of the Scottish Parliament, 1639–51, have been drawn from the parliamentary rolls and Young, PhD thesis, volumes two and three.
7. Ibid, 183–185; Dow, *Cromwellian Scotland*, 47–48; The three gentry who had served in Parliament were MacDowall of Garthland (Wigtown), Stirling of Keir (Stirling), and Gibson of Durie (Fife). The five burgesses who had served in Parliament were John Jossie (Edinburgh), John Milne (Edinburgh/Queensferry), Sir Alexander Wedderburne (Dundee), James Sword (St Andrews), and Andrew Glen (Linlithgow).
8. Dow, *Cromwellian Scotland*, 50; P.J. Pinckey, 'The Scottish representation in the Cromwellian parliament of 1656', *SHR*, 46, (1967), 95–96, 99–100; Stevenson, 'Cromwell, Scotland and Ireland', 165; E.D. Goldwater, 'The Scottish Franchise: Lobbying During the Cromwellian Protectorate', *HJ*, 21, (1978), 29–30; J.A. Casada, 'The Scottish Representatives in Richard Cromwell's parliament', *SHR*, 51, (1972), 124; *The Stuart Constitution 1603–1688*, (ed) J.P Kenyon, 2nd edition, (Cambridge, 1987), Number 91, 308–313; Donaldson, *Source Book of Scottish History*, III, 248; *APS*, vi, ii, 823–4.
9. Ibid, 51; Donaldson, *James V–James VII*, 345; Lynch, *Scotland, A New History*, 283; Hewison, *The Covenanters*, volume two, 48.

10. Dow, *Cromwellian Scotland*, 148; Stevenson, 'Cromwell, Scotland and Ireland', 165; Goldwater, 'The Scottish Franchise: Lobbying During the Cromwellian Protectorate', 29–30.
11. Dow, *Cromwellian Scotland*, 149–153; Pinckney, 'The Scottish representation in the Cromwellian parliament of 1656', 96–97, 104–111; Donaldson, *James V–James VII*, 346; Lynch, *Scotland, A New History*, 284–285; NLS MS 2263, History of Events 1635–1662, folio 231.
12. Dow, *Cromwellian Scotland*, 185–186; Donaldson, *James V–James VII*, 346.
13. Dow, *Cromwellian Scotland*, 237; Casada, 'The Scottish Representatives in Richard Cromwell's parliament', 128–130; Hewison, *The Covenanters*, volume two, 53–55.
14. Dow, *Cromwellian Scotland*, 238–239, 329; Casada, 'The Scottish Representatives in Richard Cromwell's parliament', 130–142; Brown, *Kingdom or Province?*, 138; NLS MS 2263, History of Events 1635–1662, folio 236; H. N. Mukerjee, 'Scottish Members of Richard Cromwell's Parliament', *Notes and Queries*, clxvi, (1934), 65.
15. Dow, *Cromwellian Scotland*, 230, 239; Casada, 'The Scottish Representatives in Richard Cromwell's parliament', 144–145; *CSPV*, 1659–1661, 1.
16. Dow, *Cromwellian Scotland*, 230–231, 241, 249, 259; Hutton, *Charles II*, 130–131; Lynch, *Scotland, A New History*, 286; NLS MS 2263, History of Events, 1635–1662, folio 237; *The Stuart Constitution*, Number 97, 331–332; D.L. Smith, 'The Struggle for New Constitutional and Institutional Forms', in J. Morrill (ed.), *Revolution and Restoration. England in the 1650s* (London, 1992), 32.

13

The Restoration Settlement in Scotland, 1660–1661

Our redemption from slavery is very near.[1]

Scottish Political Developments in the Context of the Three Estates and the Scottish Parliament, October 1659–August 1660

Political developments in Scotland from October 1659 to April 1660 were focused on meetings of the representatives of the shires and burghs. These had been initially summoned on General George Monck's authority, but were increasingly held on the initiative of the nobility. On 27 October Monck decided that each shire and burgh should elect a representative to meet at Edinburgh on 15 November, at which time they would be informed on the state of the nation. When the commissioners convened, the nobles and gentry elected the Royalist Glencairn as their President, whilst the burgess representatives elected the former Remonstrator, Sir James Stewart (Edinburgh). The election of Glencairn indicates the Royalist intentions of the bulk of the representatives from the shires, whilst the election of Stewart indicates that the burgesses were less so inclined. At the close of the meeting provision was made for the next stage of consultation between Monck and the Scottish political community. A further diet was to convene at Berwick on 12 December to discuss appropriate measures to secure the peace in Scotland. Each shire was to elect one representative, whilst burgess representatives from only Edinburgh, Haddington, and Linlithgow were to proceed to Berwick. On 12 December five of the elected commissioners were nominated to negotiate with Monck directly. Glencairn, Rothes, Weymes, Eglinton, and Alexander Bruce, brother to the Earl of Kincardine, constituted this grouping and Glencairn was once more the dominant figure.[2]

The consultation process was continued on 2 January 1660 when Monck sent permits from Northumberland, having crossed the border on the previous day, for a meeting in Edinburgh in February 1660. Each shire was to elect one noble or laird and each burgh was to elect one burgess. Ostensibly the purpose of the diet was for the commissioners to present Monck with a list of grievances which he could present to the English Parliament. Only around 50% of the shires and burghs sent representatives to the meetings of 2 and 3 February 1660. The commissioners of the shires and burghs met separately, although they did liaise, and the proceedings of the former were dominated by a majority grouping of nobles who had been elected as commissioners. Glencairn was again elected as President.[3]

The growing confidence of the Royalist nobility was evidenced on 5 April 1660 when it, along with some of the gentry, convened without the permission of Monck. The diet was formally convened on 6 April when it was claimed that the commissioners could legally meet under the terms of the warrant issued to the shire commissioners in February. Twenty-three nobles and 10 gentry attended the diet. The influence of the nobility was to the fore again and Rothes was appointed as President. Six Royalist nobles, including Glencairn, and two gentry present at the diets of 2 and 3 February were also present at the diet of 6 April. Liaison existed with the burgesses; Robert Murray (Edinburgh) and James Borthwick (Edinburgh) were appointed for this purpose. Four commissioners, led by Glencairn and including two gentry, who had been appointed to proceed to London at the February diets, had their commissions renewed on 6 April. The marked Royalist tone of the proceedings was emphasised by correspondence sent to the king which indicated that they were waiting for instructions on how they could serve him. In spite of the acceptance of the Declaration of Breda by the Convention Parliament on 1 May and the proclamation of the king in Edinburgh on 14 May, the actual government of Scotland was delegated to four commissioners who had been appointed by the Republican regime. On 11 May a proclamation was issued which stated that all those who held offices of trust since 4 April 1659 were to be continued in office. In theory, it was these commissioners who governed Scotland until August 1660.[4]

Following the restoration of Charles II in England, large numbers of the Scottish nobility and gentry flocked to London in an attempt to cultivate royal influence. Charles had been petitioned in June 1660 to summon a Parliament in Scotland, but this did not find favour with the king, whose sphere of interest was focused firmly on England. Instead the Scottish political community at London was asked to present proposals for the administration of Scotland in the interim. The Scottish nobility and gentry therefore advocated the recall of the 1651 Committee of Estates which was to sit until Parliament could meet. It was also recognised that the sole power of summoning and convening Parliaments lay with the king alone. Therefore the constitutional legislation of 1639–41 was ignored, despite the fact that it was still legally viable. On 2 August Charles ordered the Committee of Estates to meet at Edinburgh on 23 August and act as a provisional government until the holding of Parliament on 23 October 1660, when, Charles declared, the royal prerogative would be reasserted.[5]

Shortly after approval had been given for the Committee of Estates to meet, Charles wisely proceeded to fill the offices of his Scottish ministry before the committee met. Middleton was appointed as King's Commissioner for the Scottish Parliament, primarily through the support of the English Chancellor Hyde, on account of his Middleton's Royalist leanings. A contemporary observed that Middleton was 'judged a fitt instrument to cow Scotland'.[6] Lauderdale was appointed as Secretary of State and Glencairn as Chancellor. Hyde had attempted to have the chancellorship filled by Lauderdale in order to remove the Lauderdale's political influence at Court. As a counterweight against Hyde's ploy, Lauderdale decided to reside at London and so the post went to Glencairn. Lauderdale similarly defeated Hyde's influence by securing the office of Secretary despite the backing of both Hyde and Middleton for Newburgh. Crawford-Lindsay retained the post of Treasurer, whilst Cassillis secured the office of Justice-General, Marischal the post of Lord Privy Seal, Rothes that of President of the Privy Council, and Leven that of Governor of Edinburgh Castle. Sir John Fletcher, through the patronage of Middleton, was appointed as King's Advocate, Sir Archibald Primrose as Clerk Register, and Sir William Bellenden as Treasurer Depute. Of the major offices, the only former radicals to secure a post were Cassillis and Rothes, although Loudoun received a substantial pension. Fletcher had also collaborated with the Cromwellian regime, but was now closely allied to Middleton. Primrose not only owed his appointment to his political allegiance to Middleton, but also because he had bribed Sir William Fleming, who had been promised the position when the king had been in exile. The bulk of offices went to former Engagers, although it is clear that the king did not want to rely exclusively on that grouping at that point in time.[7]

Prior to the convening of the Committee of Estates on 23 August, it had become evident that the nobility was in the process of reasserting its political power, as reflected in its domination of shire representation in the meetings of late December 1659 and February and April 1660. Furthermore, the Scottish ministry appointed in July 1660 was amenable to the royal interest, although a political balancing act of the various factions of the 1640s and collaborators had been achieved. It was against this background that the Committee of Estates finally convened.

The Operation of the Committee of Estates, August-December 1660

Sederunts of the Committee of Estates are recorded in two separate committee registers, firstly from 23 August to 13 October and secondly from 9 October to 8 December. Forty-six enactments (10 of which were public acts and 36 private legislation) were passed between 23 August and 13 October, whilst 17 enactments (three of which were public acts and 14 private legislation) are recorded in the second register.[8]

Thirty-one sederunts of the Committee of Estates are recorded between 23 August and 13 October. Only four of the 44 nobles included on the 1651 Commission attended between 20 and 30 diets; Glencairn (who attended all 31 diets), Wigtown, Cardross, and Roxburgh. Glencairn also appears to have taken on the role of President of the Committee of Estates (instead of Loudoun who had been President of the 1651 Committee). Eight further nobles are recorded between 12 and 17 sederunts. Of the remaining 32 nobles included on the 1651 Commission, 25 did not attend at all (some were dead), whilst the remaining seven nobles on the original commission attended less than 12 diets. Significantly, Burleigh was the only noble with a respectable attendance figure who had a political background aligned with the radicals.

Only five of the 44 gentry included on the 1651 Commission attended between 20 and 31 diets. Stirling of Carden (Stirling), Foullis of Colington (Edinburgh), Murray of Skirling (Peebles), Nairn of Strathuird, and Innes of that ilk (Elgin) formed this grouping. Ten further gentry are recorded in the range of 12 and 18 diets. Of the remaining 29 gentry included on the 1651 Commission, 22 did not attend at all, whilst seven attended less than 12 diets.[9]

Of the 42 burgesses included on the 1651 Commission, six have attendance levels between 20 and 30 diets; Sir Robert Farquhar (Aberdeen), John Milne (Queensferry), David Spence (Rutherglen), John Scott, George Garden (Burntisland), and Alexander Cunnigham (Crail). Eleven further burgesses have attendance levels between 12 and 18 diets. Of the remaining 25 burgesses included on the 1651 Commission, 22 did not attend at all, whilst three attended less than 12 diets.

Therefore attendance trends over all three estates adhere to that of small groups of nobles, gentry, and burgesses who collectively formed the provisional government of Scotland until Parliament met. Moreover, large numbers of members of the Committee of Estates initiated on 3 June 1651 did not attend any of the proceedings. Three explanations can be forwarded for non-attendance; firstly, death of many members, secondly, withdrawal from political life to concentrate on their personal affairs and thirdly, the fear of former radicals of political retribution from a regime which was clearly going to be Royalist.

In addition, three nobles, 12 gentry, and eight burgesses who attended diets of the Committee of Estates between 23 August and 13 October were not official members of the 1651 Committee. Dumfries, Seaforth, and Mar constitute the grouping of three nobles. The latter two nobles only attended a small number of diets, but Dumfries attended 24 diets (77%). Of the 12 gentry, four attended ten or more diets; Murray of Polmais (Stirling), Livingstone of Kilsyth, Mercer of Aldie, and Home of Plandergaist (Berwick). Of the eight burgesses, seven attended more than ten diets; William Cunningham, Robert Murray, John Jossie, John Paterson, William Seaton, John Bell, and Sir Andrew Ramsay.[10]

Therefore non-commissioned gentry and burgesses outweighed the noble estate with regard to non-constituted members who were attending diets of the Committee of Estates between August and October. Nevertheless, non-commissioned burgesses were in attendance on a more regular basis compared to non-commissioned nobles and gentry. Given the contemporary political temper, the majority of this grouping was probably pro-Royalist.

Under the terms of the commission to the 1651 Committee, that body was to split into two separate sections (although membership details of both sections were not provided). The quorum of the section for governing the kingdom had been set at 11, with two of each estate required to be present. The quorum of the army section was set at seven, with one per estate required to be present. These rules for both sections were adhered to at all diets of the Committee of Estates between 23 August and 13 December 1660.[11]

The political intentions of the Committee of Estates were made apparent almost immediately. On 23 August a meeting of the leading Protesters had convened in Edinburgh as a rival gathering to that of the Committee of Estates. The Protesters had issued a declaration emphasising the obligation of Charles II to the Covenant, not only in Scotland, but throughout the British Isles. The Protesters also made clear their hostility towards the trend towards the restoration of episcopacy in England. In response to this, the arrests of the 11 Protesters who had gathered were ordered and a subcommittee was established to draw up a proclamation against the holding of meetings without royal approval. The proclamation was subsequently issued by the Committee of Estates on 24 August.[12]

Between 23 August and 13 October the political muscle of the Committee of Estates had been flexed to crush, both in practice and in legislative terms, any form of seditious meetings which challenged the king's authority.

The second committee register records 19 sederunts between 9 October and 8 December 1660. Seven of the 44 nobles included on the 1651 Commission attended 11 or more diets; Loudoun, Haddington, Rothes, Cardross, Cassillis, Wigtown, and Linlithgow. The remaining 37 nobles included on the 1651 Commission were included in nine or less sederunts and 24 did not attend at all.

Ten of the 42 gentry included on the 1651 Commission attended between 10 and 18 diets. Of this grouping, Hamilton of Preston, Foullis of Colington (Edinburgh), Murray of Skirling (Peebles), and Hepburn of Keith (Haddington) were particularly to the fore. The remaining 32 gentry included on the 1651 Commission attended less than 10 diets and 20 did not attend at all.

Eight of the 42 burgesses included on the 1651 Commission attended between 10 and 16 diets. David Wilkie, Sir John Smith (Edinburgh), Archibald Sydserf (Edinburgh), John Milne (Queensferry), and John Burnside were the noted dominant burgesses. The remaining 34 burgesses attended less than ten diets and 16 did not attend at all.[13]

Comparison between the attendance data contained in the two registers reveals that those nobles, gentry, and burgesses who had been in regular attendance between August and October were also in regular attendance between October and December 1660. Therefore there was a continuity of personnel in the attendance trends of the commissioned Committee of Estates between August and December 1660.

In addition, five nobles, 12 gentry, and eight burgesses who attended diets between October and December 1660 were not members of the 1651 Commission. All had attended diets between August and October except for two nobles, one laird, and one burgess. The respective quorums, as per 1651, for the army section and the section for governing the kingdom were observed at all diets.[14]

Ten influential subcommittees were established by the Committee of Estates from August to December 1660. Seven were concerned with the punishment and imprisonment of Protesters, the banning of meetings not approved of by the king, and persons cited to appear before the Committee of Estates. Two subcommittees related to the levying of the excise, whilst the remaining committee dealt with the burghs.[15]

Three distinguishing features are apparent regarding the operation of subcommittees. Firstly, membership tended to be dominated by a small clique of nobles, gentry, and burgesses. Noble membership was focused on Wigtown, Tullibardine, and Rothes. Gentry common membership centred, although not exclusively, on Stirling of Carden (Stirling), Foullis of Colington (Edinburgh), and Sir George MacKenzie of Tarbet. Burghal common membership was concentrated on Archibald Sydserf (Edinburgh) and John Bell (Glasgow). Secondly, non-commissioned members of the Committee of Estates (as per 1651) were securing admittance to subcommittees on a regular basis. Both Sir George MacKenzie and John Bell come into this category. Thirdly, the balance in membership levels between the three estates was tilted towards the gentry and burgesses. A subcommittee of 24 August issued with the remit of considering the reasons for the imprisonment of the Protesters (23 August) consisted of three gentry and three burgesses. Two subcommittees of 9 October concerned with the excise consisted of four nobles, five gentry, and four burgesses, and three nobles, three gentry, and five burgesses respectively. The nobility did not enjoy numerical dominance on any of the subcommittees established.[16]

The Restoration Parliament of Charles II, 1 January–12 July 1661

The parliamentary session which convened on 1 January 1661 constituted the first meeting of the Scottish Parliament in nearly ten years. The session convened after having been originally scheduled for 12 December 1660 and only after the King's Commissioner, Middleton, had arrived in Edinburgh on 31 December. 'Cerainly his great design and business was to make the king absoulute'.[17]

1. The Composition of the Restoration Parliament of Charles II

Seventy-five nobles, 59 gentry representing 31 shires, and 61 burgesses representing 60 burghs (195 members in total) constituted the membership of the Restoration Parliament as per 1 January 1661. Three of the nobles (Chancellor Glencairn, Crawford-Lindsay Treasurer, and Bellenden, Treasurer Depute) and three of the commissioners of shires are recorded in the parliamentary rolls as Officers of State. In strictly constitutional terms, this was a violation of the Scottish constitutional settlement of 1639–41 which was still legally valid.

In terms of membership per estate and total membership, the attendance figures for the Restoration Parliament as per 1 January 1661 were higher than all previous sessions of Parliament, 1639–51 (see appendices 2a, 3a, and 4a). Analysis of common membership between the Restoration Parliament and parliamentary sessions, 1639–51, reveals that 34 of the 75 nobles (45%), 15 of the 59 gentry (25% including Officers of State), and 12 of the 61 burgesses (20% including Officers of State) in the Restoration Parliament had served in previous parliamentary sessions, 1639–51. The noble estate exhibited the highest retention of personnel from the 1639–51 Parliaments in comparison to the other two estates. Allowing for death, this figure is perhaps unsurprising given the comparative lack of radicalism among the noble estate as a whole during the period of Covenanting hegemony. Given the management of elections to the Restoration Parliament, the majority of the 16 gentry and 15 burgesses can be labelled as supporters of the Crown. Nevertheless, a small radical rump was still present in the Restoration Parliament.[18]

Elections had taken place from late November throughout December and were managed by the Royalists. Scrutiny of parliamentary commissions reveals that 47 of the 59 gentry (80%) and 59 of the 61 burgesses (97%) commissioned to sit in the Restoration Parliament actually took their places. The strong correlation in election to and membership of Parliament indicates effective Royalist management of elections. This is supplemented by evidence of disputed elections. On 4 January four cases of disputed elections in the shires of Peebles, Dumfries, Elgin, and Inverness were considered. Throughout November 1660, Rothes had been courting the burghs to secure political support for Lauderdale and had secured the services of Sir Alexander Wedderburne (Dundee), prominent in burghal circles 1639–51, to promote that cause. According to Baillie, 'the chancellor so guided it, that the shyres and burroughs' elected only those 'that were absolutely for the king'.[19]

2. The Proceedings of the Restoration Parliament

The legislative programme enacted (303 enactments, 127 of which were public acts, and 70 ratifactions) not only reasserted royal authority and the royal prerogative in an unprecedented manner, but also revoked the constitutional settlement of 1639–41. Instructions had been issued to Middleton on 17 December in which he had been authorised by the king to assert the royal prerogative. Those instructions had also stressed that because the Crown possessed the right to call and dissolve Parliaments and Conventions of Estates, then Middleton was to secure the repeal of the 1643 Convention of Estates (the mother of the Solemn League and Covenant) and the radical Parliament of 1649. Furthermore, the legislation of 1640–41 relating to the nomination of Officers of State, Privy Councillors, and Lords of Session was also to be repealed. Before the opening of the Restoration Parliament, a Royalist constitutional agenda had already been set out. The fact that the elections had been successfully managed by the Royalists indicated that such an agenda had a favourable chance of successful implementation. Moreover, when the Scottish nobility had petitioned the king they had acknowledged the sole right of the king to call Parliaments and were willing for the royal prerogative to be reasserted. This enhanced the prospects of the successful implementation of the Royalist agenda.[20]

The Royalist backlash against the constitutional settlement of 1639–41 commenced immediately. The legislation of 16 November 1641 concerning the election of the President of Parliament and all other subsequent acts relating to the parliamentary election of President were annulled. It was enacted henceforth the offices of Chancellor and President of Parliament would be complementary. This marked a return to the constitutional tradition of the Chancellor presiding in Parliament. The Chancellor was now also to preside in the Exchequer, instead of the Treasurer, Crawford-Lindsay. In the first six sessions of the Second Triennial Parliament, 1648–51, Chancellor Loudoun had also been President of Parliament, although that had been through election by the three estates and not because he was Chancellor. Therefore the merging of the offices of Chancellor and President of Parliament can be interpreted as a direct attack on the independence of the three estates to elect their own President, who from now on would be a royal nominee.[21]

Just as members of Parliament during the Covenanting era had been required to subscribe the parliamentary oath pledging to defend the authority and freedom of Parliament, the Royalists used this precedent to establish an Oath of Allegiance to be pledged by all parliamentary members. Not only did the Oath of Allegiance demand personal loyalty to the king alone above all public judicatories and acknowledge the king as 'Supream Governour', but parliamentary members were required to defend royal authority. All previous legislation concerning parliamentary oaths (especially that of 18 August 1641) was annulled. Therefore the Oath of Allegiance constituted not only an effective tool of party management, but was also an oath of personal loyalty to the Crown alone.[22]

The Royalist political affiliation of the parliamentary membership was reflected in only one vote of dissent by Cassillis to the Oath of Allegiance. Cassillis refused to take the Oath of Supremacy, primarily because it allowed for crown supremacy in ecclesiastical issues, and he consequently withdrew from the House.[23]

The traditional device of royal control of Scottish Parliaments, the Lords of the Articles, was restored on 5 January (albeit this did not include the clerical estate as yet). This had been instigated by the king who was keen to ensure that the conduct of parliamentary business 'be als conforme as conveniently may be to the antient customes and formes vsed in the Parliaments before these troubles'. Middleton was to preside in Articles. Twelve per estate, plus the Officers of State, formed the membership of the Lords of Articles. The numerical composition of the Articles did not adhere to its traditional format (eight per estate) and the greater number employed may have been used as a sweetener to placate the Estates. The method of the nomination of the commissioners to be on the Lords of Articles was as follows; each estate separately elected its own commissioners, who were then approved by Middleton. This indicates that the Articles were staffed by suitable Royalist personnel.

Apart from the noble Officers of State, Rothes appears to have been the most influential noble. Marischal, now Lord Privy Seal, and a noted radical from 1639–51, also secured inclusion, and had probably now transferred his loyalty to the Crown. With the exception of Dumfries, all noble members of the Lords of the Articles (including Officers of State) were also Privy Councillors. This indicates a strong degree of Royalist parliamentary management. Including

Officers of State, eight gentry on the Lords of the Articles were also Privy Councillors. Eight of the 12 gentry (67%) and six of the 12 burgesses (50%) on the 1661 Lords of Articles had previous parliamentary experience, 1639–51. This does not necessarily imply that those gentry and burgesses had been previous supporters of the Crown. More realistically, it reflects the desire of the political nation to react to changing political circumstances and the wishes of certain gentry and burgesses to retain political power, both in their localities and on the national stage. Gentry representation on the 1661 Lords of the Articles was heavily biased in favour of the east and was concentrated in the Edinburgh, Haddington, and Fife areas. Seven of the 12 burgesses represented eastern burghs. Therefore there was a broader geographic spread among the burgess representatives.[24]

Three specific items of Covenanting legislation were repealed in the commission to the Lords of the Articles; firstly, the third act of the 1640 Parliament which provided for the choosing of parliamentary committees out of every estate, secondly, the 23rd act of the 1640 Parliament which had required all grievances to be presented in open Parliament, and thirdly, the act of 26 July 1644 relating to the choosing of commissioners out of the parliamentary members. Parliamentary political power was to be invested in the Lords of the Articles. The Articles were to receive all papers, overtures, and the like for weekly preparation to the full Parliament and the King's Commissioner. The 1661 Lords of the Articles did not therefore adhere to the tradition of presenting legislation en bloc to Parliament to be enacted in one day. They were also ordered to prepare and call all processes and indictments (including examining of witnesses) before presentation to the full Parliament. The commission allowed for any member of Parliament to present any overture, proposal, or petition to the King's Commissioner and the Estates (which were to meet twice per week during the sitting of the Articles), if the Articles did not present that overture, proposal, or petition to Parliament. Again this may have been a device used to placate the parliamentary membership (particularly the gentry and burgesses) but it did not disguise the fact that the preparation of parliamentary business lay with the Articles and not the Estates.[25]

That royal influence was predominant in the Articles was reflected in the bulk of legislation enacted in favour of the Crown throughout January 1661. In essence the Scottish constitutional settlement of 1639–41 was rescinded. The 'sole choice and appointment' of Officers of State, Privy Councillors, and Lords of Session was placed in the hands of the Crown. The legislation of 1641 governing appointments to these offices was annulled on 11 January. This constitutes a remarkable surrender of parliamentary power to the Crown in light of the experience of the 1640s and the fact that the parliamentary session was only 11 days old.

The Ordinary and Extraordinary Lords of Session were officially named on 5 April, although their nominations had been put forward by the king and decided on months earlier. Fifteen Ordinary and four Extraordinary Lords of Session were appointed. All four Extraordinary Lords were nobles and three were also Officers of State (Crawford-Lindsay, Rothes, and Lauderdale). The remaining noble, Cassillis, was removed for his opposition to the Oath of Allegiance, which he described as 'ane oathe...of a dubious sense'. Five of the Ordinary Lords of Session were also members of the Lords of Articles; Gilmore of Craigmillar, Sir Archibald Primrose (in the capacity as an Officer of State), Lockhart of Lee, MacKenzie of Tarbet, and Stirling of Carden.

Thirty-six nobles, 12 gentry, and one representative of the burghal estate formed the membership of the reconstituted Scottish Privy Council of 1661. In terms of numerical composition, membership adhered almost identically to that of the 1641 Privy Council (36 nobles, 14 gentry, and one burgess). Alexander Bruce, brother of the Earl of Kincardine, was included on the Privy Council Commission. Alexander Bruce represented the burgh of Culross in the Restoration Parliament. It would appear, therefore, that Bruce represented burghal interests on the Privy Council, although it is also the case that the burghal estate was politically marginalised within that body. The noted common membership between the Privy Council and the Lords of the Articles, especially regarding the nobility, provides evidence of the concentration of Royalist parliamentary management within a small group of noble and gentry Officers of State. This would suggest that the lessons of the oligarchic centralism of the Covenanting Movement had been taken on board. On the orders of the king, five additions were made to the 1661 Privy Council. Hyde (the English Chancellor), Albemarle, Ormond, Manchester, and the Principal Secretary in England constituted the five additions. These additions must be viewed in light of Hyde's political objective of controlling Scottish affairs from London, principally in the form of the Scottish Council at Whitehall staffed predominantly by English members. The inclusion of Hyde and the other four additional members on the Scottish Privy Council was not only designed to tighten the control of Scottish affairs from Whitehall, but also to marginalise Lauderdale's control of Scottish business. The Royalist nature of the new Privy Council was also highlighted by the fact that influential radical nobles of the Covenanting era were deliberately excluded, most notably Lothian and Loudoun. This was clearly emphasised in correspondence between Rothes and Lauderdale:

> I am never desirous that persons who has been so eminently active against His Majesty and his Royal Father, without great and eminent signs of repentance, should be admitted to be on the eminentest judicatory of the Kingdom.[26]

The surrender of parliamentary power was continued by further legislation of 11 January which stipulated that the calling and dissolving of Parliaments and Conventions of Estates resided with the king alone. This had a further effect in the sense that it was deemed that any parliamentary legislation passed without the approval of the king or his commissioner would be null and void. Such legislation can be interpreted as a safeguard against the experience of the 1640s when the June 1640 session had met without royal approval and when the 1643 Convention of Estates had also been convened without royal consent. The political assertion of the royal prerogative was compounded by the fact that national acceptance of the above legislation was demanded under pain of treason. Related enactments were passed on 16 and 22 January. Firstly, on 16 January legislation passed in the reign of James VI was renewed whereby conventions, assemblies, and councils were declared illegal without royal consent, as was the subscription of bands and leagues. Not only was this a reaction against the precedent of the meeetings of the Tables in 1638 and the Covenanting bonds of the 1640s but also against the 1643 Solemn League and Covenant. Unauthorised subscription was to be punished under the charge of sedition. Many members of Parliament, including Hamilton (son of William, 4th Marquis and second Duke of Hamilton who had been killed at Worcester in 1651), absented themselves from the House when this vote was taken, Balmerino and Coupar withdrew completely, whilst George Garden (Burntisland) was a vociferous vocal opponent. In total there were six or seven dissenting voices. Secondly, on 16 January, the control of the making of foreign policy and the raising of the militia was invested solely in the king at the expense of Parliament. Thirdly, on 22 January, the 1643 Convention of Estates was annulled as was the act of 5 July 1644 in the First Triennial Parliament which had ratified the acts of the Convention. In technical terms the Solemn League and Covenant had now been rescinded.

Nevertheless, the importance of the ramifications of the Solemn League and Covenant warranted the initiation of a separate enactment on 25 January. Future renewal and swearing of the Solemn League and Covenant was to require the king's approval. It was also stipulated that the Solemn League and Covenant and any related legislation did not now provide any form of obligation for the pursuance of the reformation of religion in England and Ireland. That the political tone of this enactment was tame compared to the aggressive assertion of the royal prerogative throughout January 1661 can perhaps be explained by the fact that it had not yet been decided by the king and his circle of policy advisers whether presbyterianism or episcopacy should be the appropriate form of the government of the Church of Scotland. At this stage, it was therefore imperative that the king should not overtly alienate or arouse the opposition of the Kirk. In British terms it had become clear, however, that presbyterianism would not be imposed in either England or Ireland. The lack of prospects for the reassertion of presbyterianism within Scotland was to become clear by 28 March when it was enacted that the appropriate government of the Kirk would be that which was most suitable to monarchical government, that is episcopacy.[27]

The retrenchment of Crown power continued throughout February and March 1661. The Engagement was approved of and ratified on 9 February. In addition the proceedings of the Committee of Estates which convened from September 1648 to January 1649, following the Whiggamore Raid, and the radical Parliament of January 1649, were declared unlawful. All legislation passed by those two bodies was rescinded. Justification for this was provided by the fact that they had been convened (according to the king and the Royalists) without a lawful warrant. The act was read three times in the House and provoked sustained debate, although it was passed unanimously. That the act was successfully passed, can perhaps be explained by the fact that all those who had sat in the 1649 Parliament and any of its committees were not to be proceeded against, bar those who were to be specified in a future Act of Indemnity. Related legislation enacted on 20 February condemned the settlement of January 1647 whereby Charles I had been delivered into the hands of the English army at Newcastle. Not only was parliamentary legislation of 16 January 1647 ratifying that agreement rescinded and annulled, but the enactment of 20 February acknowledged that there had been a loyal opposition to that agreement which had been the work of a minority political faction and not that of the kingdom of Scotland as a whole.[28]

All constitutional enactments of January and February in favour of the Crown were incorporated into legislation passed on 27 February. That legislation firstly required national subscription of the Oath of Allegiance by all who held public office. Secondly, it required compulsory acknowledgement of the royal prerogative as had been legislated for in the parliamentary session. Those who refused to subscribe the Oath of Allegiance and acknowledge the royal prerogative were declared incapable of holding public office. Action was ultimately taken against Cassillis, who had refused the Oath of Allegiance at the opening of the parliamentary session. Cassillis was removed from the post of Extraordinary Lord of Session on 10 April and barred from holding any other public office. On 30 May further legislation required the Oath of Allegiance to be sworn by the magistrates and Council in each burgh. Hence the Oath of Allegiance can be interpreted as a Royalist alternative to the Covenants as a political point of reference.[29]

Almost one month later, on 28 March, the General Act of Rescissory was enacted. Instigated by MacKenzie of Tarbet and backed enthusiastically by Hyde despite a lukewarm response from Middleton, that act rescinded and annulled en bloc the Parliaments of 1640, 1641, 1644, 1645, 1646, 1647, and 1648 (the 1649 Parliament had already been annulled). That this enactment had not been passed much earlier in the parliamentary session, now nearly four months old, can be attributed to several considerations. Firstly, it would have been politically insensitive and arrogant to introduce legislation at the outset of the session, when Parliament had not met for nine years. It would also have provided invaluable ammunition to the opponents of royal authority and at the very least would have aroused political unease amongst the parliamentary membership, especially the gentry and burgesses, even though the elections had been managed. Secondly, technical problems existed with regard to several items of pre-1660 legislation, but the Engagement had now been ratified, the 1650 ratification of the 1643 Convention of Estates, passed with the king's authority, had been repealed on 22 January, as had the ratification of the 1649–50 Parliaments of the radical regime on 9 February. Thirdly, the political atmosphere of the Estates by 28 March had proven to be more than amenable to the interest of the Crown in constitutional terms. Fourthly, an Act of Indemnity had not yet been forthcoming and members may have been wary of arousing the opposition of the king if they had opposed such a measure. In political terms, the General Act of Rescissory appears also to have been used as a device by Hyde to facilitate the restoration of episcopacy by the back door, because all legislation of the 1640s guaranteeing the presbyterian nature of the Kirk had now also been repealed. Indeed, the Act concerning Religion and Church Government, in which the restoration of episcopacy was hinted at, accompanied the Rescissory Act. The Act of Rescissory provoked the opposition of both Crawford-Lindsay and the new Duke of Hamilton and two other unspecified members of the Lords of the Articles, but it was still passed by a substantial majority, which was observed to be in favour of the bringing back of episcopacy. Unease had nevertheless been felt by some parliamentary members of the annulling of the Engagement Parliament and the 1641 Parliament when Charles I had actually been present. This would seem to suggest that there was a dissenting presence of the former radical mainstream.[30]

The political mood of the Restoration Parliament wholly in favour of the king was also reflected in its willingness to grant him an exuberant financial allowance for the remainder of his life. On 22 March it voted to the king an annuity of £40,000 sterling (£480,000 Scots) per annum for life, the sum having been agreed on by the Committee of Estates in 1660 following a deal struck between Lord Cochrane and the king. £98,000 Scots of this sum was to be raised by customs duties upon specified products, whilst the remaining £382,000 were the proceeds of excise duties on domestic and imported alcohol.[31]

Middleton's instructions of December 1660 had contained orders that loyal Royalists of the Covenanting and Cromwellian periods were to be rewarded, particularly those whose estates had been confiscated. These orders were implemented in two particular stages. Firstly, between February and May 1661 forfeitures of Royalists which had been enacted in the 1640s were rescinded. Eleven such forfeitures were rescinded, the most notable being that of James, 1st Marquis of Montrose, and his successors. Secondly, on 5 July an interval committee was appointed to consider the losses and debts of those who had been loyal to the Royal cause. The commission was to endure until the next parliamentary session. Therefore Covenanting procedure was being employed to compensate noted opponents of the Covenanting Movement. The estates and losses of 24 individuals were specified in the commission, 22 of whom were nobles. Two nobles, five gentry, and three burgesses, as well as all Officers of State, formed the membership of the interval committee. In addition to the Officers of State, one noble (Rothes, President of the Privy Council and Extraordinary Lord of Session), four gentry (all of whom were Ordinary Lords of Session), and one burgess included on the interval committee were also members of the Lords of the Articles.[32]

Outwith the political and constitutional arena, two particular committees were established; the Committee for Trade and Complaints and the Committee for Plantation of Kirks and Valuation of Teinds. In the interests of the efficiency of the processing of parliamentary business relating to the promotion of trade and manufacturies and for hearing of private complaints between parties, the

Committee for Trade and Complaints was established on 5 January. Two specific remits were therefore incorporated into one session committee. The assignment of judicial powers was attributed to the fact that justice courts had not been in operation for the past two years. Twelve per estate, plus the Officers of State, formed the membership of the Committee for Trade and Complaints. Excluding Officers of State, there was no common membership over all three estates between the Lords of the Articles and the Committee for Trade and Complaints. Two explanations can be forwarded for this. Firstly, the Lords of the Articles were already faced with an intensive workload. Secondly, the employment of non-members of the Articles allowed for a more widespread use of parliamentary personnel, which was politically important for keeping the parliamentary membership content. Lord Cochrane, who had been responsible for securing the annuity of £40, 000 sterling for the king, was elected President of the committee at the first diet.[33]

The Committee for Plantation of Kirks and Valuation of Teinds was established on 6 March and marks the retention of one of the few parliamentary formats from the Covenanting era. Including Officers of State, 26 nobles, 25 gentry, and 15 burgesses constituted its membership. The burghal estate had been marginalised in terms of representation compared to the other two estates. Five of the nobles and four of the gentry (one of whom was a member of Parliament) were Officers of State, whilst six of the gentry (four of whom were members of Parliament) were Senators of the College of Justice. According to the terms of the commission, it is unclear whether or not the commission was to endure only until the close of the parliamentary session or whether or not it was also empowered to continue its proceedings as a parliamentary interval committee.[34]

By the close of the parliamentary session on 12 July, which had now lasted for over six months, an Act of Indemnity had still not been passed. On 12 July the King's Proclamation anent the Indemnity had stated an Act of Indemnity would be passed at the close of the next parliamentary session. Prior to this, Commissioner Middleton had been previously reprimanded by Charles II because 'Privat barganes' had been struck and 'money receaved from too many who are represented to have been abominable complyres'. Middleton had been ordered to put a stop to this immediately. Nevertheless, from the time of the meetings of the nobility in London in 1660 it had become clear that Argyll was to be made an example of and he had been arrested almost immediately on arrival at Court in 1660. Johnston of Wariston, the notorious radical laird of the Covenanting era aligned to Argyll and prominent Cromwellian collaborator, was likewise destined to be severely dealt with.

Throughout the parliamentary session six individuals had decrees of forfeiture passed against them. The four most prominent cases were those of Argyll (summoned on a charge of treason on 31 January), Johnston of Wariston (declared a fugitive and rebel having failed to appear on charges of treason having been summoned by the Committee of Estates), Swinton of that ilk (having been already found guilty of treason in 1651 for collaboration with

Cromwell), and James Guthrie, minister at Stirling, the prominent Protester minister. The political atmosphere was so Royalist that the prominent Edinburgh lawyer, John Nisbet (who later became Lord Advocate), refused to represent Argyll. Despite the attempts of Argyll's son, Lorne, at Court and the influence of Lauderdale to save Argyll from the scaffold, Middleton, Glencairn, and Rothes contrived to secure the king's agreement that all of Argyll's defence petitions should be rejected and Argyll must die. When Argyll was found guilty of treason, there was no support in the House for a delay of execution. This indicates once more the extent of Royalist support in the House. It is also indicative of the the desire of Middleton, Glencairn, and Rothes that Argyll had to be executed in order to end his political influence once and for all. Argyll was eventually executed on 27 May 1661. A contemporary scribe bitterly lamented this despicable act (in his opinion) and looked back to the king's coronation in 1651:

> it was the Marquis of Argyles part that day to put the Crown on the Kings head, who had acted the chieff part in bringing him home and how he was rewarded for that service by that same King, the Histories of these times make plain; for he took his head from his Shoulders for putting the Crown upon his.[35]

The other five individuals were all to suffer the same fate as Argyll, although three of them, including Wariston, had not yet been caught.[36]

On 12 July an Act of Adjournment was passed and Parliament was ordered to reconvene on 12 March 1662. In the interests of factional management, there were to be no new elections in the shires and burghs, except in cases of death. Given the combined voting power of the gentry and burgesses, it was essential that the same commissioners should be retained for the next parliamentary session, particularly because they had been more than amenable in supporting the restoration of the royal prerogative. The nobility, as an estate, had learned the lesson of the 1640s of the importance of the combined voting strength of the other two estates, which had previously curtailed the parliamentary power of the nobility.[37]

3. The Committee Structure of the Restoration Parliament

Three session committees, one interval committee, and the Lords of the Articles have been analysed. Thirty-five nobles were employed on these committees. Noble common membership was concentrated on Crawford-Lindsay (Treasurer), Glencairn (Chancellor), and Lauderdale (Secretary) who all served on four committees. Rothes, President of the Council, was included on three committees. With the exception of three nobles (Erroll, Mar, and Hartfell), all noble members of the Lords of the Articles served on more than one committee. Of those nobles, not included on the Lords of the Articles, the highest figure was that of Cochrane who served on three committees. Control and staffing of parliamentary committees was therefore centred on noble members of the Lords of the Articles, who in turn were almost exclusively Privy Councillors.[38]

Thirty-six gentry constitute the total field of gentry analysed. Four gentry served on a total of four committees. Three of these gentry were Officers of State (Sir Robert Moray, Justice Clerk, Sir Archibald Primrose, Clerk Register, and Sir John Fletcher, Lord Advocate), whilst the other was a Lord of Session (Sir John Gilmore of Craigmillar). All four gentry were also Lords of the Articles, as well as Privy Councillors. Four further gentry served on three committees each. Three of this grouping of gentry were included on the Lords of the Articles as well as being Lords of Session (Lockhart of Lee, Stirling of Carden, and MacKenzie of Tarbet), whilst the remaining laird was an Officer of State (Sir William Bellenden). Lockhart of Lee was also a Privy Councillor. Only three of the gentry on the Lords of the Articles (Wedderburne of Gofford, Hamilton of Preston, and Murray of Garth) did not serve on more than one committee. Gentry common membership was centred on the relationship between the Lords of the Articles, Officers of State, Lords of Session, and Privy Councillors. This ensured Royalist parliamentary control of the gentry in the staffing of committees. Eleven gentry analysed were not members of Parliament as per 1 January 1661, although three were Officers of State.[39]

Fewer burgesses (29) than gentry were employed within this committee structure. Three burgesses secured membership of three committees each. Two of these burgesses (Sir Robert Murray and John Bell) were members of the Lords of the Articles. The other burgess (Sir Andrew Ramsay, Provost of Edinburgh) was neither a member of the Lords of Articles, nor a member of Parliament as per 1 January 1661. Eight of the 12 burgess members of the Lords of the Articles were included on more than one committee.[40]

Whilst near parity per estate is apparent in the employment of nobles (35) and gentry (36) within the committee structure, the same cannot be applied to the burghal estate. That Parliament was to be controlled by the king's ministers and not the Estates was emphasised in the close relationship between employment on the Lords of the Articles, the Privy Council, Officers of State, and Lords of Session. Nevertheless, it was the gentry who were the ongoing beneficiaries of Covenanting procedures.

Conclusion

By the close of the parliamentary session on 12 July 1661, the royal prerogative had been firmly re-established and the constitutional settlement of 1639–41 had been annulled and rescinded. The elections to the Restoration Parliament of commissioners of the shires and burghs had been succesfully managed to produce a grouping largely amenable to the Royalist cause. This was recognised by the refusal to allow new elections to be held for the 1662 parliamentary session. The nobility at Court in 1660 had expressed its desire for the royal prerogative to be restored in Scotland. The king now had sole power in the calling and dissolving of Parliaments and in the naming of Privy Councillors, Officers of State, and Lords of Session and also had been granted a handsome annuity. The management of legislation and the operation of the parliamentary committee structure was centred on common membership between the Lords of the Articles, the Privy Council, Officers of State, and Lords of Session. However, Covenanting procedures were adopted rather than rescinded and the gentry still maintained an influential political role. Argyll, the radical leader of 1639–51, had been executed as an example of what usurpers of royal authority could expect. However, an Act of Indemnity had still not been passed and the government of the Church of Scotland had still not been settled. Whereas political power in Scotland, 1639–51, had resided in the Scottish Parliament that power had now been transferred firmly to the Crown and was becoming increasingly controlled from London.

NOTES

1. EUL, Dc 4.46, Transcript Letters to the Earl of Lauderdale from John Leslie, 7th Earl of Rothes, 1660–1664, Rothes to Lauderdale, 6 April 1660.
2. Dow, *Cromwellian Scotland*, 254–256; J. Buckroyd, 'Bridging the Gap: Scotland 1659–1660', *SHR*, 66, (1987), 8–9.
3. Dow, *Cromwellian Scotland*, 258–259; Buckroyd, 'Bridging the Gap', 14; NLS MS 3423, Lauderdale Correspondence, 1656–1662, Number 25, lists the details of the meetings of the commissioners of the shires. Eighteen shire representatives in total were present at the diets of 2 and 3 February 1660. Buckroyd notes the policy differences between the nobles and the burgesses ('Bridging the Gap', 14–15) as does Dow (*Cromwellian Scotland*, 258).
4. Dow, *Cromwellian Scotland*, 262, 264, 268; NLS MS 3423, Lauderdale Correspondence, 1656–1662, Number 25; NLS MS 597 Watson Collection, folio 24A.
5. Dow, *Cromwellian Scotland*, 268; Hutton, *Charles II*, 136; Lynch, *Scotland, A New History*, 287; NLS MS 597 Watson Collection, folio 26; SRO Dalhousie Muniments, GD 45/14/110/(2); NLS MS 3423, Lauderdale Correspondence, 1656–1662, ff 52–53; NLS MS 2263, History of Events 1635–1662, folio 240; SRO Dalhousie Muniments, GD 45/14/110/(2); O. (ed.), *The Lauderdale Papers*, (Camden Society, 1884–1885), I, 32–33; Nicholl, *Diary*, 297; The 1651 Committee of Estates could be revived in technical terms because the Parliament which had appointed it had met by royal summons and the 1651 Commission had been ratified by Charles II in 1651 (Rait, *Parliaments of Scotland*, 380).
6. Kirkton, *History of the Church of Scotland*, 35–36.
7. Dow, *Cromwellian Scotland*, 269; Hutton, *Charles II*, 136–137; Lynch, *Scotland, A New History*, 287; SRO Dalhousie Muniments, GD 45/14/110/(3). St Andrews University, Institute of Scottish Studies, Kincardine Papers Project, Number 122; SRO GD 45/14/110/(3). Sir G. MacKenzie, *Memoirs of the Affairs of Scotland* (Edinburgh, 1821), 9–10; Nicholl, *Diary*, 298.
8. SRO PA. 11/12, Register of the Committee of Estates, 23 August–13 October 1660, ff 1–67; SRO PA. 11/13, Minute Book of the Committee of Estates, 9 October–8 December 1660, ff 1–18.
9. SRO PA. 11/12, ff 1–67.
10. *APS*, vi, ii, 679–681; SRO PA. 11/12, ff 1–67.
11. Ibid.
12. SRO PA. 11/12, folio 4; Hewison, *The Covenanters*, volume two, 69; Donaldson, *James V–James VII*, 361; Dow, *Cromwellian Scotland*, 269; *CSPD*, 1660–1661, 277; Nicholl, *Diary*, 298.

13. SRO PA. 11/13, ff 1–18; *APS*, vi, ii, 679–681.
14. Ibid.
15. SRO PA. 11/12, ff 4, 6, 7, 8, 16, 19–20, 51; SRO PA. 11/13, ff 2, 6, 9–10.
16. Ibid; *APS*, vi, ii, 679–681.
17. Kirkton, *History of the Church of Scotland*, 47; NLS MS 2263 History of Events 1635–1662, folio 241; Dow, *Cromwellian Scotland*, 270; NLS MS 597 Watson Collection, 33; MacKenzie, *Memoirs of the Affairs of Scotland*, 19; Nicholl, *Diary*, 304–305, 310.
18. *APS*, v, 251–252, 258–259, 300–301, 303–304, 305–306, 308, 331–332; *APS*, vi, i, 3–4, 95–96, 284–285, 429–430, 440–441, 474–475, 612–613; *APS*, vi, ii, 3–4, 124–126, 277–278, 555–556; *APS*, vii, 3–4; MacKenzie, *Memoirs of the Affairs of Scotland*, 19.
19. Baillie, *Letters and Journals*, III, 463; SRO PA. 7/25/2–101; *APS*, vii, 3–4. Airy, *Lauderdale Papers*, I, 38. According to Sir George MacKenzie, effective royal management was secured by the use of gentry in each shire favourable to the Royalist cause. Letters were sent to the most influential Royalist laird in each shire indicating who was to be elected. Each Royalist laird would then convene the electoral meeting to secure the election of the nominated laird,(*Memoirs of the Affairs of Scotland*, 12). The commissions to William Murray of Stanehope and the laird of Blackbaronie younger (both Peebles), James Crichton of St Leonards and Ferguson of Craigdarroch (both Dumfries), Sir John Urquhart of Cromarty and Colin MacKenzie of Ridcastle (both Inverness), and Innes of that ilk (Elgin) and Thomas MacKenzie of Pluscarden (both Inverness), were approved on 4 January (*APS*, vii, 2). On 8 January legislation was passed ordaining the Stewartry of Kirkcudbright to elect a commissioner. David MacBrair subsequently took his place in Parliament for the Stewartry on 13 February (Ibid, 10, 32).
20. *APS*, vii, 1–367, appendix page 1; Airy, *Lauderdale Papers*, I, 39–40; NLS MS 3423 Lauderdale Correspondence 1656–1662, folio 82. The long duration of the parliamentary session (6 months) can be attributed to the bulk of business which had to be attended given the re-establishment of the 'monarchical constitution' (Rait, *Parliaments of Scotland*, 76); *CSPV*, 1659–1661, 246; Nicholl, *Diary*, 318; Ferguson, *Scotland's Relations with England*, 150; NLS MS 3423 Lauderdale Correspondence, 1656–1662, folio 53.
21. *APS*, vii, 7; *APS*, vi, ii, 5, 89, 126, 378–379, 556, 562, 608; Stevenson, *Government Under the Covenanters*, 175; MacKenzie, *Memoirs of the Affairs of Scotland*, 19; J. Buckroyd, 'The Monarchy Restored', *The Sunday Mail Story of Scotland*, 18, (Glasgow, 1988), 489; Kirkton, *History of the Church of Scotland*, 49.
22. *APS*, vii, 7; Kirkton, *History of the Church of Scotland*, 50.
23. Rait, *Parliaments of Scotland*, 76; MacKenzie, *Memoirs of the Affairs of Scotland*, 23; Airy, *Lauderdale Papers*, I 1, 62. Hutton, *Charles II*, 161. According to Cassillis, 'I resolve to leave this his counsells and dominions which is as ill as any thing Oliver ever threatened me with' (NLS MS 3423 Lauderdale Correspondence, 1656–1662, ff 112, 114, 188). NLS MS 2263 History of Events, 1635–1662, folio 242; SRO RH2/2/15/62.
24. *APS*, vi, ii, 8–9; NLS MS 2263 History of Events, 1635–1662, folio 242; Nicoll, *Diary*, 316–17, 325–26; Rait, *Parliaments of Scotland*, 76; Hutton, *Charles II*, 161.
25. *APS*, vi, ii, 8–9; Rait, *Parliaments of Scotland*, 77.
26. EUL, Dc 4.46, Transcript Letters to the Earl of Lauderdale from John Leslie, 7th Earl of Rothes, 1660–1664, c. 12 March 1661; *APS*, v, 388; *APS*, vii, 3–5; SRO

RH 2/2/15/62; Nicoll, *Diary*, 325–326; Kirkton, *History of the Church of Scotland*, 51; Ferguson, *Scotland's Relations with England*, 151.

27. *APS*, vii, 10, 10–11, 12–13, 13, 16, 18, 87–88, 123–124, appendix, page 3. MacKenzie, *Memoirs of the Affairs of Scotland*, 21–22; *Treatises on the Laws of Scotland, and Pleadings Before Its Supreme Judicatories; With Their Decisions by Sir George MacKenzie*, 399–400 in *The Works of Sir George MacKenzie of Rosehaugh*, I, (1716); Hutton, *Charles II*, 161; SRO RH 2/2/15/61; NLS MS 3423 Lauderdale Correspondence, 1656–1662, ff 121, 124, 166; NLS MS 2263 History of Events, 1635–1662, folio 242; Hewison, *The Covenanters*, volume two, 79, 81; Airy, *The Lauderdale Papers*, I, 62, 63–64; Kirkton, *History of the Church of Scotland*, 51–52.
28. *APS*, vi, ii, 30–32, 35. On 15 February Crawford-Lindsay had been exonerated by the House for his role in the parliamentary decision of 16 January 1647 (Ibid, 33). Crawford-Lindsay had been President of Parliament and had objected to the decision. MacKenzie, *Memoirs of the Affairs of Scotland*, 25–26.
29. *APS*, vi, ii, 44–45, 162–163, 236; NLS MS 3423 Lauderdale Correspondence, 1656–1662, folio 188.
30. *APS*, vii, 86–87, 87–88; Rait, *Parliaments of Scotland*, 317–318; Hutton, *Charles II*, 161–162; Airy, *The Lauderdale Papers*, I, 76–77; J. Patrick, 'A Union Broken? Restoration Politics in Scotland' in *Scotland Revisted*, ed. J. Wormald (London, 1991), 123; NLS MS 3423 Lauderdale Correspondence, 1656–1662, folio 166; NLS MS 2263 History of Events, 1635–1662, folio 243; *CSPD*, 1660–1661, 492; Hewison, *The Covenanters*, volume two, 81; *Treatises on the Laws of Scotland, and Pleadings Before Its Supreme Judicatories; With Their Decisions by Sir George MacKenzie*, 400, 401 in *The Works of Sir George MacKenzie of Rosehaugh*, I, (1716); MacKenzie, *Memoirs of the Affairs of Scotland*, 28–29; Buckroyd,'The Monarchy Restored', 489; Ferguson, *Scotland's Relations with England*, 150; Kirkton, *History of the Church of Scotland*, 53.
31. *APS*, vii, 78; Rait, *Parliaments of Scotland*, 498; MacKenzie, *Memoirs of the Affairs of Scotland*, 18.
32. *APS*, vii, 8–9, 29–30, 102, 102–103, 123–124, 162–163, 163–164, 164, 197–198, 232, 232–233, 294–295. The four gentry on the interval committee who were also Lords of Articles were Gilmore of Craigmillar, Lockhart of Lee, Stirling of Carden, and MacKenzie of Tarbet. The one burgess was Sir Robert Murray.
33. Ibid, 8–9, 9; MacKenzie, *Memoirs of the Affairs of Scotland*, 21; Nicholl, *Diary*, 318.
34. *APS*, vii, 3–5, 48–50. The one laird who was an Officer of State and a member of Parliament was Gilmore of Craigmillar (Edinburgh). The four gentry who were Senators of the College of Justice and members of Parliament were Lockhart of Lee (Lanark), Foullis of Colington (Edinburgh), Stirling of Carden (Linlithgow), and MacKenzie of Tarbet (Ross).
35. EUL. Dc 5. 44, Memoirs of Scots Affairs, ff 301–302.
36. *APS*, vii, 7, 346–347, appendix, 7–11, 69–70, 71–72, 72–73, 74–75, 75, 82–84. Lauderdale Papers, I, 92–93; SRO Dalhousie Muniments GD 45/14/110/(2); NLS MS 3423 Lauderdale Correspondence, 1656–1662, ff 140, 177; NLS ADV.MS 19.1.28 Papers Relating to Cromwell and the Regicides, folio 9; NLS Watson Collection, folio 56; NLS MS 2263 History of Events 1635–1662, folios 243–244; *Diary of Sir Archibald Johnston of Wariston*, III, 1655–1660, J.D Ogilvie (ed.), (SHS, third series, 34, Edinburgh, 1940), 181–183; Hewison, *The Covenanters*, volume two, 83–84, 87; I.B. Cowan, *The Scottish Covenanters 1660–88*, (London, 1976), 40;

Baillie, *Letters and Journals*, III, 466; Nicoll, *Diary*, 321, 334; MacKenzie, *Memoirs of the Affairs of Scotland*, 34, 37–41; Kirkton, *History of the Church of Scotland*, 55–62.

37. *APS*, vii, 367. On 30 May the House had clarified the qualifications of electors in the shires. Three qualifications were established. Firstly, all heritors who held 40 shillings land of the king could vote. Secondly, all heritors, life-renters and wadsetters holding of the king, whose yearly rent was equivalent to 10 chalders of victual or £1000, after the appropriate deduction of feu duties could vote. The second qualification provided voting rights for feuars who had paid taxes since 1597 and had not qualified under the 1587 act. The third qualification applied to feuars who had held directly from the Crown (Rait, *Parliaments of Scotland*, 211–212).
38. *APS*, vii, 8–295; Nicoll, *Diary*, 325–326.
39. *APS*, vii, 3–5, 8–295; Nicoll, *Diary*, 325–326.
40. Ibid.

Postscript: the European Dimension

Within a broader European perspective, the Covenanting rebellion and the administrative, political, and parliamentary ascendancy of the Covenanters occurred within the historical and chronological timespan of what has now been commonly regarded as the European 'General Crisis'. Whilst it is true that historians should be wary of employing this term on a pan-European basis to define and describe the nature and outcomes of widespread European rebellions, it is also the case that several of these rebellions did have common features, albeit with the historian's advantage of the benefit of hindsight. Thomas Munck has identified a 'causal connection' between the revolts of Catalonia-Portugal, Palermo-Naples, and Scotland-Ireland, England.[1] Monarchical rule over 'multiple kingdoms', the 'composite structures of states', and the clash between the 'metropolitan' and the 'outer states' presented common problems throughout Europe.

Within the British archipelago, the dynastic union of 1603 had created the problem of monarchical government of three kingdoms whose clear focal point of interaction was the monarchy itself. The rebellions of Catalonia (1640–59) and Portugal (1640–68) against the Castilian monarchy and the Scottish experience of rebellion against Charles I present the most appropriate continental comparison.[2] Within a particular British structural context, the Covenanting rebellion conforms to Charles Tilly's recent definition of a 'revolutionary situation' and a 'revolutionary outcome'. Tilly also differentiated between 'state-led nationalism' and 'state-seeking nationalism' within the context of revolts.[3] The Covenanting Movement did not simply constitute a religious reaction against the ecclesiastical policy of Charles I towards Scotland, but represented a wider national movement which sought to reassert traditional Scottish rights against an anglicised, absentee monarch.[4] In this respect, the Scottish experience of rebellion corresponds to Tilly's definition of 'state-seeking nationalism'. Moreover, as Koenigsberger observed in terms of 'revolutionary parties' in France and Netherlands in the sixteenth century, opposition movements to the crown often operated through Parliaments or representative assemblies.[5]

Compared to contemporary continental assemblies, the Scottish Parliament was remarkably powerful as a constitutional forum. In common with a comparative analytical approach to the concept of a 'General Crisis', Richard Bonney has wisely noted that each continental institution should be 'viewed in terms of its own relative successes or failure'.[6] There was no standard form of European assembly; one-chamber, two-chamber, three-chamber, four-chamber, and provincial assemblies were all in existence.[7]

Yet, with the exception of the Swedish riksdag and the States General of the United Provinces, the general continental trend is that of relatively weak representative institutions. Prior to 1632, the Swedish risksdag had secured the principle of redress before supply and all parliamentary legislation now required full plenary approval as opposed to that of parliamentary committee alone. The Additamentum (addition to the Form of Government of 1634) had also secured the principle of triennial diets. Throughout the minority of Queen Christina and prior to her abdication in 1654, the powers of the Swedish riksdag continued to increase. Not only was a monopoly of legislation obtained and consent of the riksdag required for new taxation and conscription, but financial grants were awarded to the Crown for only limited periods. Moreover, the riksdag of 1650 had insisted that its grievances were met before it would grant taxation, and had also witnessed attempts by the three lower estates (clergy, burghers, and peasants) to combat the power of the nobility.[8] The States General of the United Provinces was regarded by contemporaries as 'the most effective representative institution in early modern Europe'.[9] Based on a conferderation of the seven provinces of the Dutch Republic, the States General was a permanent assembly of deputies and represented the 'loose embodiment of Dutch sovereignty'.[10]

The Swedish riksdag was by far the most powerful of Scandanavian representative institutions. In contrast, the Estates General of Norway and Denmark were both hardly 'ever more than an occasional and dispensable institution'.[11] The Danish Estates General of 1648 'proved to be the last opportunity for the estates to take on a permanent political existence'.[12] In 1648 the Danish estates had allowed the nobility to present a joint demand of guarantees which aimed at securing the power of granting taxation and undertaking legislative initiatives for the Estates General at meetings to be held annually. Political pressure exerted by the Danish royal council, however, had resulted in the nobility withdrawing these demands in return for the extension of noble privileges. The capitulation of the nobility destroyed any political potential for the Estates General. Absolutism was later established in Denmark in the Estates General of 1660 and in complementary legislation enacted in 1661, later reaffirmed and enhanced in the Royal Law of 1665.[13]

Both the Estates General of France and the Reichstag of the German States were weak representative institutions. No formal meeting of the Reichstag took place between 1613 and 1640 and during the course of the Thirty Years' War (1618–48) it met on only one occasion. Despite the fact that the Peace of Westphalia (1648) had sought an increased role for the Reichstag, the Reichstag only convened once (in 1653–54) prior to the formation of a permanent diet at Regensburg in 1663. The French Estates General had last met in 1614 and did not reconvene until 1789. Since its support in 1593 for the Catholic rival to Henri IV during the French religious wars, the French Estates General had enjoyed no real constitutional pedigree and had only met on five occasions between 1560 and 1614 anyway. The marginalisation of the French Estates General was reflected in the calling of Assemblies of Notables in 1617–18 and 1626–7 to discuss programmes of reforms.[14]

The general decline of European representative institutions is confirmed by a brief survey of other parliamentary assemblies. The Diet of Bohemia failed to meet between 1620 and 1848, primarily because it had backed the wrong side in the rebellion of 1618–20. The Polish diet (the Sejm) was the most frequently summoned European assembly (on 159 occasions between 1493 and 1661). The Sejm was a bicameral (two-chamber) assembly; the lower chamber was dominated by the provincial nobility. Based on the Nihil Novi of 1505, the lower chamber had gained a veto over legislation. In turn this had ensured that co-operation was essential between the magnates in the upper chamber and the provincial nobility in the lower chamber to secure the effective operation of the Sejm. Following the union between Poland and Lithuania in 1569, this co-operation became difficult to maintain, especially with the development of the veto of Poland. The Polish veto became more pronounced after 1652, and combined with national rivalries between Polish and Lithuanian nobles, resulted in the increased suspension of meetings of the Sejm. The Assembly of the Land (Zemskii Sobor) of the Muscovite kingdom, although achieving a more cohesive form in 1648–49, failed to meet on a regular basis, and was not summoned after 1653.[15]

Yet what marks off the continental perspective from the British archipelago is the role of provincial assemblies from Estates Generals per se. Thus the Parlement of Paris possessed a powerful political role and was at the forefront of the rebellion of the Fronde (1648–52). Nevertheless, provincial estates were not summoned in the Dauphine after 1628, nor in Normandy after 1635, whilst in Provence the estates were replaced by a single chamber Assembly of Communities after 1639. Provincial estates enjoyed a powerful role in the Dutch Republic, especially the Estates of Holland. In the German states the Reichstag enjoyed an inferior role to provincial assemblies, albeit many were subject to royal control and met on an ifrequent basis. The Bavarian estates did not meet between 1612 and 1669, whilst those of Saxony failed to convene between 1640 and 1657. The Thirty Years' War had provided an excellent opportunity for the German estates to enhance their powers in return for political support. The failure of the German estates to enhance their powers was reflected in the levying of taxation by decree without the approval of estates. Thus the Great Elector levied taxation in this manner in Brandenburg, Cleves, and Mark during the War of the North (1655–1660).[16]

One particular continental parliamentary concept which was adopted as a constitutional model for the Scottish Parliament was the use of standing committees between parliamentary sessions. This was especially apparent in the Cortes of the kingdoms of Aragon (once more indicating the appropriateness of an Iberian comparison with Scotland). Indeed, the standing committee of the Cortes of Catalonia (the Diputacio) defended the privileges of Catalonia and was at the forefront of the dispute with Castile which ultimately led to the revolt of the Catalans in 1640. The Scottish Committee of Estates, which acted essentially as a provisional government between parliamentary sessions, must therefore be regarded as a Scottish constitutional device adopted along continental lines. Moreover, the Committee of Estates of 1641 was central to the diplomatic negotiations with the English Parliament and the States General of the United Provinces for a tripartite political confederation.[17]

Without doubt, the most advanced constitutional development of all European parliamentary assemblies belonged to the English Parliament.[18] The House of Commons undertook the leading role in the conflict against Charles I.[19] Perez Zagorin noted the development of English parliamentary control through its executive committees in response to the collapse of royal power during the civil wars. Thus, in 1640 the English Parliament was 'utterly without corporate experience as an executive body' and was forced to 'assume the functions of government which until then had been exercised by the king, the privy council, and a host of royal officials'.[20] Zagorin also aptly observed that the 'committee system was the method Parliament employed to carry on its government'.[21] Zagorin's comments can also be applied to the Scottish parliamentary context. Firstly, an elaborate committee structure (based on session and interval committees) developed in the Scottish Parliament to deal with military involvement in the British Civil Wars, civil war within Scotland, and the effective government of the kingdom of Scotland itself. Secondly, the Scottish Committee of Estates, founded on continental trends, appears also to have acted as a model for the English Committee of Safety founded in July 1642. Thirdly, shire committees of war and specialised session and interval committees appear to have provided an efficient operational structure for the system of county committees in England. Fourthly, the Scottish constitutional settlement of 1640–41 provided an excellent example of constitutional reform for the English Long Parliament.[22]

In terms of the history of the Scottish Parliament itself, the period between 1639 and 1651 ranks alongside the years 1689 to 1707 as the zenith of its powers. The royal prerogative was severely weakened with effective political power transferred to Parliament. Procedural innovation occurred in terms of the passage of legislation and the development of a sophisticated committee structure, primarily as a result of the abolition of the Lords of the Articles. Although the Scottish Parliament was unicameral (single chamber), the commissioners of the shires and burghs collectively played a powerful parliamentary role and challenged the traditional power of the nobility in the House. The doubling of the vote of the commissioners of shires in 1640 was of profound political and parliamentary importance in terms of voting strength. That the gentry and burgessses provided the backbone of the Covenanting Movement was reflected in the personnel provided for the staffing of session and interval committees (especially the latter). Collectively, the increased power of the shires and burghs amounted to the development of a 'Scottish Commons', a theme heavily emphasised throughout this monograph.[23] This does not mean that the nobility was weak, but in relative terms the parliamentary strength and powers of the shires and burghs had increased at the expense of the nobility. Similarly, this does not amount to a 'rise of the gentry' scenario within a Scottish socio-economic context, nor does it necessarily correspond to the 'rise of the middling sort' within Scottish society. Such themes require more detailed Scottish regional studies. Rather, within the political and constitutional confines of the Scottish Parliament, a Scottish Commons clearly emerged. The increased parliamentary power of the gentry (in particular) in the late sixteenth century has been observed by other scholars, whilst government support in the 1621 Parliament had proved extremely difficult to secure.[24]

Placing the achievements of the English Revolution within a longer historical perspective, Zagorin noted that although the English Parliament lost many executive functions at the Restoration,

> the effect wrought upon it by the experience of the revolutionary years was of permanent importance ... the legislation of 1641 which deprived the king of his most important prerogative powers remained operative after the Restoration. As the ease with which James II was overthrown in 1688, Parliamentary government had won. Never after 1660 could the crown act successfully in defiance of the two Houses.[25]

By way of comparison, the Scottish Parliament had experienced unprecedented constitutional development and maturity, yet surrendered all such gains back to the crown in the Restoration Parliament of 1661. The 1661 Restoration Parliament is therefore of central importance to the later history of the Scottish Parliament in the Restoration period. Why did the Scottish Parliament fail to develop along the lines of its English counterpart? First and foremost, Scotland was a conquered nation in 1651 and was subjected to constitutional subjugation and an army of occupation until the Restoration. Within the balance of power within the British archipelago, the Scottish Restoration settlement ensured that Scottish parliamentary developments, 1639–51, would be nullified and the northern kingdom of Charles II would henceforth be politically controlled from London. A strong and powerful Scottish Parliament presented a threat to English dominance within the British archipelago and was inconsistent with a powerful British monarchy.[26]

NOTES

1. Munck, *Seventeenth Century Europe*, 199–203, 235–236; R. Bonney, *The European Dynastic States 1494–1660* (Oxford, 1991), 188. For a recent discussion of Ireland and the 'General Crisis' see J.H. Ohlmeyer, 'Introduction. A failed revolution?', in J.H. Ohlmeyer (ed), *Ireland from Independence to Occupation 1641–1660*, (Cambridge, 1995), 1–24. For an alternative view, within a Scottish and continental perspective, which argues that there was no 'General Crisis' see M. Lee jr, 'Scotland, the union and the idea of a "General Crisis"', in R.A. Mason (ed), *Scots and Britons. Scottish Political Thought and the Union of 1603*, (Cambridge, 1994), 41–57.
2. MacInnes, *Charles I and the Making of the Covenanting Movement*, 43–45, 183; H.G. Koenigsberger, *Politicians and Virtuosi. Essays in Early Modern History* (London, 1986), x-xi, 12, 21, 159, 166; Russell, *The Fall of the British Monarchies*, 27.

3. C. Tilly, *European Revolutions 1492–1992* (Oxford, 1993), 10, 14, 47, 116, 123–126, 131–133, 237, 241–242.
4. MacInnes, *Charles I and the Making of the Covenanting Movement*, 43–45, 183–184.
5. H.G. Koenigsberger, *Estates and Revolutions. Essays in Early Modern History* (London, 1971), 126, 225.
6. Bonney, *The European Dynastic States*, 316.
7. Ibid, 137; Munck, *Seventeenth Century Europe*, 32.
8. Bonney, *The European Dynastic States*, 326–327; Munck, *Seventeenth Century Europe*, 32, 33, 61–62, 231–232; M. Roberts, *Essays in Swedish History* (London, 1967), 8, 27–28; S. Dahlgren, 'Estates and Classes', in M. Roberts (ed), *Sweden's Age of Greatness, 1632–1718* (London, 1973), 107, 110, 117; D. Kirby, *Northern Europe in the Early Modern Period. The Baltic World 1492–1772* (London, 1990), 205–207.
9. Bonney, *The European Dynastic States*, 330.
10. Munck, *Seventeenth Century Europe*, 34.
11. T. Munck, *The Peasantry and the Early Absolute Monarchy in Denmark 1660–1708* (Copenhagen, 1979), 41.
12. Kirby, *Northern Europe in the Early Modern Period*, 205.
13. Ibid, 207, 211–212, 213; Munck, *The Peasantry and the Early Absolute Monarchy in Denmark*, 10, 39, 40–41, 45–46.
14. Bonney, *The European Dynastic States*, 319–320, 322–323.
15. Ibid, 318–319, 320–323.
16. Ibid, 320–323; Munck, *Seventeenth Century Europe*, 34–35, 212–213.
17. Bonney, *The European Dynastic States*, 323–324; Russell, *The Fall of the British Monarchies*, 68.
18. Munck, *Seventeenth Century Europe*, 32.
19. The ascendant role of the Commons has been recently challenged by J.S.A. Adamson in both 'Politics and the nobility in Civil-War England', *HJ*, 34, (1991), and 'Parliamentary management, men of business and the House of Lords, 1640–9', in C. Jones (ed), *A Pillar of the Constitution* (1989).
20. P. Zagorin, 'The English Revolution, 1640–1660', in H. Lubasz (ed), *Revolutions in Modern European History*, (2nd edn, London, 1968), 34.
21. Ibid, 35.
22. Ibid, 36–38.
23. Macinnes, 'Early Modern Scotland: the Current State of Play', *SHR*, 73, (1994), 41–42; See also J.R. Young, 'The Scottish Parliament and the Covenanting Revolution: the Emergence of a Scottish Commons', in J.R. Young (ed), *Celtic Dimensions of the British Civil Wars* (forthcoming).
24. For a recent commentary on the 'middling sort' in Scotland see M. Lynch, 'Response: Old Games and New', *SHR*, 73, (1994), 52–53; J.M. Goodare, 'Parliament and Society in Scotland, 1560–1603', (University of Edinburgh, PhD thesis, 1989), 58–62, 462–464; J.M. Goodare, 'The Scottish Parliament of 1621', *HJ*, 38, (1995), 29–51. Historians should take heed of Koenigsberger's comments: 'any precise correlation between the social structure and the formal institutions of a society is not at all easy to establish' (*Politicians and Virtuosi*, 22). For an alternative viewpoint concerning the powers of the Scottish nobility see Brown, *Kingdom or Province?*, x, 14, 44–45.
25. Ibid, 38–39.
26. For an assessment of the Scottish Parliament in a wider seventeenth century context,

see J.R. Young, 'The Scottish Parliament and National Identity from the Union of the Crowns to the Union of the Parliaments, 1603–1707', in D. Broun, R.J. Finlay, and M. Lynch (eds), *Image and Identity: The Making and Remaking of Scotland* (forthcoming).

Appendix 1: Sessions of Parliament and Conventions of Estates, 1639–1661

Second Parliament of Charles 1, 1639–1641

Session 1	30 August–14 November 1639
Session 2	2 June–11 June 1640
Session 3	15 July–November 1641

Conventions of Estates, 1643–1644

Session 1	22 June 1643–26 August 1643
Session 2	3 January 1644–3 June 1644

First Triennial Parliament, 1644–1647

Session 1	4 June 1644–29 July 1644
Session 2	7 January 1645–8 March 1645
Session 3	8 July–11 July 1645
Session 4	24 July 1645–7 August 1645 (Perth)
Session 5	26 November 1645–4 February 1646 (St. Andrews)
Session 6	3 November 1646–27 March 1647

Second Triennial Parliament, 1648–1651

Session 1 (i)	2 March 1648–11 May 1648
Session 1 (ii)	1 June 1648–10 June 1648
Session 2	4 January 1649–16 March 1649
Session 3	23 May 1649–7 August 1649
Session 4	7 March–8 March 1650
Session 5	15 May 1650–5 July 1650
Session 6	26 November 1650–30 December 1650 (Perth)
Session 7	13 March 1651–31 March 1651 (Perth)
Session 8	23 May 1651–6 June 1651 (Stirling)

Restoration Parliament

	1 January 1661–12 July 1661

Notes:

1. Details have been extracted from D. Stevenson, *Government under the Covenanters, 1637–1651*, (Scottish History Society, 1982) pp. 174–175.
2. All sessions were held at Edinburgh unless otherwise indicated.

Appendix 2a: The Numerical Composition of the Three Estates, 1639–1643

Date	*Reference*	*Nobility*	*Gentry*		*Burgesses*		*Total Membership*
			No. of Shires	*No. of Commissioners*	*No. of Burghs*	*No. of Commissioners*	
31 August 1639	*APS*, v, 251–252	50	25	47	51	52	149
2 June 1640	*APS*, v, 258–259	36	23	43	51	52	131
19 November 1640	*APS*, v, 300–301	22	17	22	34	35	119
14 January 1641	*APS*, v, 302	22	17	22	34	35	119
13 April 1641	*APS*, v, 303–304	11	11	13	5	5	29
25 May 1641	*APS*, v, 305–306	16	13	22	21	22	60
15 July 1641	*APS*, v, 308	43	28	49	56	57	149
17 August 1641	*APS*, v, 331–332	56	29	50	56	57	163
22 June 1643 (Convention of Estates)	*APS*, vi, 3–4	56	26	44	53	54	154

Appendix 2b: Movement in the Numerical Composition of the Three Estates, 1639–1643

Date	*Nobility*	*Gentry*	*Burgesses*	*Total*
31 August 1639–2 June 1640	−14	−4	0	−18
2 June 1640–19 November 1640	−14	−21	−17	−12
19 November 1640–14 January 1641	0	0	0	0
14 January 1641–13 April 1641	−11	−9	−30	−90
13 April 1641–25 May 1641	+5	+9	+17	+31
25 May 1641–15 July 1641	+27	+27	+35	+89
15 July 1641–17 August 1641	+13	+1	0	+14
17 August 1641–22 June 1643	0	−6	−3	−12

Appendix 3a: The Numerical Composition of the Three Estates, 1643–1647

Date	*Reference*	*Nobility*	*No. of Shires*	*Gentry*	*No. of Burghs*	*Burgesses*	*Total Membership*
22 June 1643 (Convention of Estates)	*APS*, vi, i, 3–4	56	26	44	53	54	154
4 June 1644	*APS*, vi, i, 95–96	41	25	44	42	43	128
7 January 1645	*APS*, vi, i, 284–285	43	25	44	46	47	134
8 July 1645	*APS*, vi, i, 429–430	34	14	21	19	20	75
24 July 1645	*APS*, vi, i, 440–441	38	23	38	33	34	110
26 November 1645	*APS*, vi, i, 474–475	33	20	37	32	32	102
3 November 1646	*APS*, vi, i, 612–613	48	28	50	48	56	154

Appendix 3b: Movement in the Numerical Composition of the Three Estates, 1643–1647

Date	*Nobility*	*Gentry*	*Burgesses*	*Total*
22 June 1643–(Convention of Estates) 4 June 1644	−15	0	−11	−26
4 June 1644–7 January 1645	+2	0	+4	+6
7 January 1645–8 July 1645	−9	−23	−27	−59
8 July 1645–24 July 1645	+4	+17	+14	+35
24 July 1645–26 November 1645	−5	−1	−2	−8
26 November 1645–3 November 1646	+15	+13	+14	+52

Appendix 4a: The Numerical Composition of the Three Estates, 1648–1651[1]

Date	*Reference*	*Nobility*	*Number of Shires*	*Gentry*	*Number of Burghs*	*Burgesses*	*Total Membership*
2 March 1648	*APS*, vi, ii, 3–4	56	29 (Maximum)	53 (Maximum)	56 (Maximum)	57 (Maximum)	166 (Maximum)
			26 (Minimum)	47 (Minimum)	48 (Minimum)	49 (Minimum)	152 (Minimum)
4 January 1649	*APS*, vi, ii, 124–126	16	29 (Maximum)	52 (Maximum)	57 (Maximum)	58 (Maximum)	126 (Maximum)
			26 (Minimum)	46 (Minimum)	50 (Minimum)	51 (Minimum)	113 (Minimum)
23 May 1649	*APS*, vi, ii, 277–378	20	30 (Maximum)	53 (Maximum)	58 (Maximum)	59 (Maximum)	131 (Maximum)
			28 (Minimum)	49 (Minimum)	49 (Minimum)	50 (Minimum)	119 (Minimum)
7 March 1650	*APS*, vi, ii, 555–556	23	30 (Maximum)	57 (Maximum)	57 (Maximum)	58 (Maximum)	138 (Maximum)
			16 (Minimum)	29 (Minimum)	24 (Minimum)	25 (Minimum)	77 (Minimum)
26 November 1650	Balfour, 18 *Historical Works*, IV, 179–182		23 (Maximum)	39 (Maximum)	19	20	77 (Maximum)
			17 (Minimum)	27 (Minimum)			65 (Minimum)
13 March 1651	Balfour, 17 *Historical Works*, IV, 258–262		27 (Maximum)	55 (Maximum)	52 (Maximum)	52 (Maximum)	124 (Maximum)
			15 (Minimum)	21 (Minimum)	21 (Minimum)	21 (Minimum)	59 (Minimum)

Formulae:

Maximum figures for number of shires/burghs	=	number of shires/burghs listed with commissioners	+	number of shires/burghs listed with no commissioners
Maximum figures for numbers of commissioners of shires/commissioners of burghs	=	number of commissioners of shires/commissioners of burghs listed	+	maximum possible number of unlisted commissioners (1 for each burgh listed, but with no commissioner named) (2 for each shire listed, but with no commissioners named)
Minimum figures for number of shires/burghs	=	number of shires/burghs listed with commissioners		
Minimum figures for number of commissioners of shires/commissioners of burghs	=	number of commissioners of shires/commissioners of burghs listed.		

Notes:

(1) For further details see J.R. Young, 'The Scottish Parliament, 1639–1661: A Political and Constitutional Analysis', (University of Glasgow, PhD Thesis, 1993), volume three, pp 1207–1210.

Appendix 4b: Movement in the Numerical Composition of the Three Estates, 1648–1651[(1)]

Date	*Nobility*	*Gentry*	*Burgesses*	*Total*
2 March 1648–4 January 1649	–40	–1 (Maximum)	+1 (Maximum)	–40 (Maximum)
		–1 (Minimum)	–1 (Minimum	–39 (Minimum)
4 January 1649–23 May 1649	+4	+1 (Maximum)	+1 (Maximum)	+5 (Maximum)
		+3 (Minimum)	–1 (Minimum)	+6 (Minimum)
23 May 1649–7 March 1650	+3	+4 (Maximum)	–1 (Maximum)	+7 (Maximum)
		–20 (Minimum)	–25 (Minimum)	–42 (Minimum)
7 March 1650–26 November 1650	–5	–18 (Maximum)	–38 (Maximum)	–61 (Maximum)
		–2 (Minimum)	–5 (Minimum)	–21 (Minimum)
26 November 1650–13 March 1651	–1	+16 (Maximum)	+32 (Maximum)	+47 (Maximum)
		–6 (Minimum)	+1 (Minimum)	–6 (Minimum)

Notes:
Movement figures for the gentry and burgesses have been calculated on the basis of the maximum and minimum figures listed in Appendix 4(a). For example, the maximum movement figure for the gentry between the sessions of 23 May 1649 and 7 March 1650 = 57 (Maximum) –53 (Maximum) = +4. Likewise, the minimum movement figure for the gentry for the same period = 29 (Minimum) –49 (Minimum) = –20.

Bibliography

1. MANUSCRIPT SOURCES

Scottish Records Office

Gifts & Deposits
GD 25, Ailsa Muniments
GD 16, Airlie Muniments
GD 37, Airth Writs
GD 112, Breadalbane Collection
GD 45, Dalhousie Muniments
GD 128, Fraser MacKintosh Collection
GD 39, Glencairn Muniments
GD 406, Hamilton Papers
GD 26, Leven and Melville Muniments
GD 220, Montrose Papers
GD 157, Scott of Harden Papers

Parliament

(i) Supplementary Warrants and Parliamentary Papers
PA 7/2, Supplementary Parliamentary Papers, 1606–42
PA 7/4/6, Minutes of the Committee of Estates, 20 March–2 April 1646
PA 7/4/21, Minutes of the Committee of Monies and Processes, 5 March–29 August 1646
PA 7/7/10, Minutes of the Committee of Dispatches, 16 May–5 June 1650
PA 7/25/2–101, Parliamentary Commissions (Shires and Burghs)

(ii) Registers and Minute Books of the Committee of Estates
PA 11/1, Register of the Committee of Estates, 28 August 1643–31 May 1644
PA 11/2, Register of the Committee of Estates, 4 December 1643–23 November 1644 (Army)
PA 11/3, Register of the Committee of Estates, 29 July 1644–6 January 1645
PA 11/4, Register of the Committee of Estates, 10 March 1645–31 March 1646
PA 11/5, Register of the Committee of Estates, 29 March 1647–28 February 1648
PA 11/6, Register of the Committee of Estates, 12 May 1648–1 September 1648
PA 11/7, Register of the Committee of Estates, 22 September 1648–2 January 1649
PA 11/8, Register of the Committee of Estates, 19 March–22 May 1649
PA 11/9, Register of the Committee of Estates, 4 December 1649–26 February 1650
PA 11/10, Register of the Committee of Estates, 2 January–12 March 1651
PA 11/11, Register of the Committee of Estates, 7 June–22 July 1651
PA 11/12, Register of the Committee of Estates, 23 August–13 October 1660
PA 11/13, Minute Book of the Committee of Estates, 9 October–8 December 1660

(iii) Other Parliamentary Committees

PA 14/1, Register of the Committee for Common Burdens and the Commission for Receiving the Brotherly Assistance, 19 November 1641–10 January 1645

PA 14/2, Proceedings of the Scots Commissioners for Conserving the Articles of the Treaty, 22 September 1642–8 July 1643

PA 14/3, Register of the Committee for Monies (South), 3 February 1646–26 October 1646

PA 14/4, Register of the Committee for Monies (North), 9 March 1646–28 October 1646

PA 14/6, Minute Book of the Committee for Monies and Accounts, 1649–1650

Transcripts and Photocopies

RH2/1/42, Transcripts of the Committee of Estates, 4 December 1648–26 February 1650

RH2/2/14, Transcripts of Cosmo Innes, volume II

RH2/2/15, Miscellaneous Transcripts

RH2/8/15, Minutes of Parliament, 11 March–8 April 1648

National Library of Scotland

Advocates' Manuscripts

Adv MS 32.4.8, A Short History of the Reformation of Religion in Scotland, England & Ireland and of the Wars carried on by King Charles the First in these Three Kingdoms

Adv MS 34.2. 10, Copies of State Papers and Political Pamphlets

Adv MS 19.1.17, Papers Concerning the Covenanters

Adv MS 29.2.9, Papers Concerning the Covenanters

Adv MS 19.1.28, Papers Relating to Cromwell and the Regicides

Adv MS 22.1.15, Transactions at Edinburgh of affairs between the Parliament and Committee of Estates, 1647

Wodrow Manuscripts

Folios LXIV, LXII, LXVII, LXXXVII,

Quartos LXXVII, LXXII

Other Manuscript Collections (National Library of Scotland)

MS XIII, Denmilne Collection

Acc 175, Gordon Cumming Papers

MS 3423, Lauderdale Correspondence, 1656–1662

MS 8482, Minute Book of the Convention of Estates

MSS 79–84, 573, 597, 7144, Morton Chartulary Papers

MS 2263, Salt and Coal: Events, 1635–1662

MS 597 Watson Collection

British Library

Egerton MS 2542, Nicholas Papers

Add MSS 34, 713, Historical Collections, 1642–1796

Add MSS 37, 978, Letter-book of the Scottish Commissioners in London, 1645–1646

Edinburgh University Library

Dc 5. 44, Alexander Hamilton of Kinkell, Memoirs of Scots Affairs from the Death of King Charles I to the Restoration

Dc 4. 16, Transactions of the Committee of Estates of Scotland, August 1640–June 1641
Dc 4. 46, Transcripts of Letters to the Earl of Lauderdale from John Leslie, 7th Earl of Rothes, 1660–1664

Glasgow University Library
David Murray Collection 147, Notes of What Passes in Parliament, 1641. From The Time of the King's Coming, 17 August. (Nineteenth century transcription).

St Andrews University, Institute of Scottish Studies
Kincardine Papers Project

Strathclyde Regional Archives
T-PM 109, Stirling Maxwell of Pollok Collection

Private Muniments
Argyll and Bute District Archives, Argyll Papers
Blair Atholl Castle, Manuscripts of the Duke of Atholl
Dumfries House, Cumnock, Loudoun Papers, Manuscripts of the Marquiss of Bute

2. *PAMPHLETS & BROADSHEETS*

Glasgow University Library, James Dean Ogilvie Collection
An Act for the Abolishing the Kingly Office in England, Ireland, and the Dominions thereunto belonging (London, 1648)
A Declaration of the Army of England, Upon their March into Scotland (London, 1650)
The Analysis, Explication and Application, of the Sacred and Solemne League and Covenant, For the Reformation, and Defence of Religion, the Honour and Happinesse of the King, and the Peace and Safety of the three Kingdomes of England, Scotland, and Ireland (London, 1643)
A Declaration of the Lords of His Majesties Privie Councell, And Commissioners for conserving the Articles of the Treatie: For the Information of His Majesties good Subjects of this Kingdome (Edinburgh, 1643)
A Declaration of the Proceedings of the Parliament of Scotland (London, 1641)
A Declaration of the Reasons for assisting the Parliament of England, Against the Papists and Prelaticall Army. By the Generall Assembly of the Kirke of Scotland (London, 1643)
A Message from the Estates of Scotland to the English Commissioners at Edinburgh (London, 1648)
A Relation of the Kings Entertainment into Scotland, on Saterday the 14 of August 1641. As also the Copy of a Speech which the Speaker for Scotland spake to His Majesty (1641)
A True Account of the great Expressions of Love from the Noblemen, Ministers & Commons of the Kingdom of Scotland unto Lieutenant General Cromwel, and the Officers and Soldiers under his command. Whose mutual love each to other is hoped to be the beginnings of a happy Peace to both Nations. Declared in a Letter to Friend (London, 1648)
An Unhappy Game at Scotch and English. Or A Full Answer from England to the Papers of Scotland (Edinburgh, 1646)
News from Scotland: Or the Result of the Generall Assembly of that Kingdome in order to England's Peace; But opposed by the sub-committee of that Kingdome, called, A Committee for the preventing of Danger (London, 1648)
Plaine Scottish, or, Newes from Scotland (London, 1643)

Scotland's Alarme: Or, Some considerations tending to demonstrate the necessity of our speedie marching to the assistance of our Brethern in England, notwithstanding all difficulties, reall or pretended (Edinburgh, 1643)

Scotland's Holy War. A Discourse Truly, and plainly remonstrating, How the Scots out of a corrupt pretended zeal to the Covenant have made the same scandalous, and odious to all good men: and How by religious pretexts of saving the Peace of Great Brittain they have irreligiously involved us all in a most pernitious Warre (London, 1651)

Some few Observations by the Committee of Estates of Parliament, upon the Declaration of the General Assembly of the last of July (Edinburgh, 1648)

Some papers given in by the Commissioners of the Parliament of Scotland, to the Houses of Parliament of England. In answer to their votes of the 24th Sept. 1646, concerning the disposing of His Majesties person. To which is added the speeches of the Lord Chancellour of Scotland (Edinburgh, 1646)

The Desires of the Commissioners of the Kingdom of Scotland: That Both Houses of Parliament may sit in freedome for setling of Religion according to the Covenant. That King Charls the Second (Upon just satisfaction given) May be admitted to the Government of these Kingdoms. Together with their Protestation against all proceedings to the contrary (1649)

The Lord Loudoun's Speech to the English Commissioners at Edinburgh, with the Treaty between the Grand Committee of Scotland, and the Commissioners from the Parliament of England (London, 1648)

The manifold Practices And Attempts of the Hamiltons, And particularly of the present Duke of Hamilton Now Generall of the Scottish Army to get the Crown of Scotland (1648)

The Scots Cabinet Opened. Wherein you have a short and full Account of the secret Transactions of the late affaires, by the Scots Commissioners with the King and Parliament, and the invisible steps, by which wee are brought to a new warre (London, 1648)

The Truth of the Proceedings in Scotland containing the Discovery of the Late Conspiracie. With divers other Remarkable Passages. Related in a Letter written from Edinburgh, 19th October 1641 (1641)

Two Speeches spoken at a Common Hall Octob. 27 1643. Wherein is shew'd the readynesse of the Scots to assist the Kingdome and Parliament of England to the vtmost of their power (London, 1643)

Glasgow University Library, Special Collections

The Differences in Scotland Still on Foot. Or, The late Proccedings between the Parliament and Kirk (London, 1648)

The Dissolution of the Parliament in Scotland (Edinburgh, 1641)

To the Honourable The Knights, Citizens and Burgesses, Now assembled in Parliament. The humble Propositions of William Ball, alias Bennet, Gentleman. Concerning the Forts of this Kingdome with some other Considerations of State (undated)

3. PRINTED TEXTS

A Collection of Original Letters and Papers, Concerning The Affairs of England, From The Year 1641 to 1660. Found Among The Duke of Ormonde's Papers , two volumes, T. Carte (ed), (London, 1739)

A Source Book of Scottish History, III, (1567–1707), W.C. Dickinson & G. Donaldson (eds), (Edinburgh, 1961)

Aberdeen Council Letters, volumes I-II, (1544–1644), L.B. Taylor (ed), (London, 1950)

The Acts of the Parliament of Scotland, T. Thomson, & C. Innes (eds) volumes, v-vii (Edinburgh, 1814–1872)

Baillie, R., *Letters and Journals, 1637–1662,* D. Laing (ed), three volumes, (Bannatyne Club, Edinburgh, 1841–42)

Balcanqual, W.A. *A Declaration concerning the Late Tumults in Scotland* (Edinburgh, 1639)

Balfour, Sir James, *Historical Works,* four volumes, J. Haig (ed), (Edinburgh, 1824–25)

Borough, Sir John, *Notes on the Treaty carried on at Ripon between King Charles and the Covenanters of Scotland, A.D. 1640,* J. Bruce (ed), (Camden Society, London, 1869)

Burnet, G. *The Memoirs of the Lives and Actions of James and William, Duke of Hamilton and Castleherald* (London, 1838)

Calendar of State Papers Domestic (1639–1661), sixteen volumes, W.D. Hamilton & M.A. Everett Green (eds) (London, 1873–1886)

Calendar of State Papers and Manuscripts, Relating to English Affairs, Existing in the Archives and Collections of Venice, and in other Libraries of Northern Italy, volumes XXIV-XXXII, A.B. Hinds (ed) (London, 1923–1931)

Carlyle, T., *Oliver Cromwell's Letters and Speeches,* three volumes, volume I, (London, 1857)

Charters and Documents Relating to the City of Glasgow, 1175–1649, J.D. Marwick (ed), (Glasgow, 1897)

Constitutional Documents of the Puritan Revolution, S.R. Gardiner (ed), (3rd Edition, Oxford, 1906)

Correspondence of Sir Robert Kerr, first earl of Ancrum, and his son William, third earl of Lothian, D. Laing (ed), two volumes, (Edinburgh, 1875)

The Correspondence of the Scots Commissioners in London, 1644–1646, H.W. Meikle (ed), (Roxburghe Club, 1917)

Crawford, G. *The Lives and Characters of the Officers of the Crown and of the State in Scotland, from the beginning of King David 1st to the Union of the kingdoms* (1726)

The Cromwellian Union, C.S. Terry (ed), (SHS, 1902)

Dalrymple, Sir David, Lord Hailes, *Memorials and Letters relating to the History of Britain in the reign of Charles I* (Glasgow, 1766)

Diary of Alexander Jaffray, J. Barclay (ed), (Spalding Club, Aberdeen, 1856)

Diary of Sir Thomas Hope of Craighall, 1634–45, T. Thomson (ed), (Bannatyne Club, Edinburgh, 1843)

Diary of Sir Archibald Johnston of Wariston, III, 1655–1660, J.D. Ogilvie (ed), (SHS, third series, Edinburgh, 1940)

The Diary of Mr John Lamont of Newton, 1649–71, G.R Kinloch (ed), (Maitland Club, 1830)

The Diplomatic Correspondence of Jean de Montereul and the Brothers De Bellievre, French Ambassadors in England and Scotland, 1645–1648, J.G. Fotheringham (ed), (SHS, Edinburgh, 1898)

Dumbarton Burgh Records, 1627–1746 (1860)

Dumbarton Common Good Accounts, 1614–60, F. Roberts & I.M.M Macphail (eds), (Dumbarton, 1972)

Extracts from the Records of the Royal Burgh of Stirling, 1519–1666, R. Renwick (ed), (Glasgow, 1887)

Extracts from the Records of the Burgh of Aberdeen, 1625–1642, J. Stuart (ed), (Scottish Burgh Records Society, 1872)

Extracts from the Records of the Burgh of Edinburgh, 1642–1655, M. Wood (ed), (Edinburgh, 1938)

Fragment of the Diary of Sir Archibald Johnston of Wariston, 1639, G.M. Paul (ed), (SHS, Edinburgh, 1896)

Gordon, J. *History of Scots Affairs, 1637–41*, three volumes, J. Robertson & G. Grub (eds), (Spalding Club, Aberdeen, 1841)

Gordon, P., *A Short Abridgement of Britane's Distemper, 1639–1645*, J. Dunn (ed), (Spalding Club, Aberdeen, 1844).

Gordon, R., Sir, 'Anent the Government of Scotland as it wes befor the late troubles' in W. MacFarlane (ed), *Geographical Collections Relating to Scotland*, (SHS, Edinburgh, 1907), 391–401.

The Government of Scotland under the Covenanters, 1637–51, D. Stevenson (ed), (SHS, Edinburgh, 1982)

Haig, D. & Brunton, G., *The Senators of the College of Justice* (1832)

The Hamilton Papers, S.R. Gardiner (ed), (Camden Society, London, 1880)

Historical Collections, J. Rushworth (ed), vols I-IV, (London, 1680–91)

Historical Fragments, Relative to Scottish Affairs, from 1633 to 1664, J. Maidment (ed), (Edinburgh, 1833)

HMC, 9th Report, part ii, appendix, *Traquhair Muniments* (London, 1887)

HMC, 11th Report, appendix, *The Manuscripts of the Duke of Hamilton* (London, 1887)

Hyde, Edward, earl of Clarendon, *The History of the Great Rebellion and Civil Wars in England*, volume IV (Oxford, 1836)

The Journal of Thomas Cunningham of Campvere, 1640–54, E.J. Courthope (ed), (SHS, 3rd series, Edinburgh, 1927)

Kirkton, J., *A History of the Church of Scotland 1660–1679*, R. Stewart (ed), (Lampeter, Dyfed, Wales, 1992)

The Lauderdale Papers, O. Airy (ed), (Camden Society, 1884–1885)

MacKenzie of Rosehaugh, Sir George, *Memoirs of the Affairs of Scotland* (Edinburgh, 1821)

MacKenzie of Rosehaugh, Sir George, *A vindication of his Majesties government and judicatures in Scotland; from aspersions thrown on them by scandalous pamphlets and news-books: And especially, with relation to the late Earl of Argyle's process* (London, 1683)

The Memoirs of Henry Guthry (Glasgow, 1747)

Memoirs of the Marquis of Montrose, two volumes, (Edinburgh, 1856)

Menteith of Salmonet, Robert, *The History of the Troubles of Great Britain* (1734)

Miscellaneous State Papers, 1501–1726, II, P. Yorke, earl of Hardwicke (ed)

The Nicholas Papers, Correspondence of Sir Edward Nicholas, Secretary of State, G.F. Warner (ed), two volumes (Camden Society, London, 1886)

Nicholl, J., *Diary of Public Transactions and Other Occurences, Chiefly in Scotland, from January 1650 to June 1667*, D. Laing (ed) (Bannatyne Club, 1836)

The Parliaments of Scotland. Burgh and Shire Commissioners, two volumes , M. Young (ed) (Edinburgh, 1992–3)

Proceedings of the Short Parliament of 1640 (Camden Society, 4th series, 1977)

Records of the Commissioners of the General Assemblies of the Church of Scotland, 1646–52, A.F. Mitchell & J. Christie (eds), three volumes (SHS, Edinburgh, 1892–1909)

Records of the Kirk of Scotland, containing the Acts and Proceedings of the General Assemblies, 1630–54, A. Peterkin (ed), (Edinburgh, 1838)

Records of the Privy Council of Scotland, P.H. Brown (ed), 2nd series, i, (1625–1627), (Edinburgh, 1899); iv (1630–1632), (Edinburgh, 1902); vi (1635–1637), (Edinburgh, 1905); vii (1638–1643); viii (1544–1660), (Edinburgh, 1906)

Register of the Great Seal of Scotland, 1620–1633, J.M. Johnson (ed) (Edinburgh, 1894)

Registrum Magni Sigilli Regum Scotorum, 1634–1651, J.M. Thomson (ed), (Edinburgh, 1897)

Rutherford, S. *Lex Rex* (1644)

The Ruthven Correspondence, W.D Macray (ed), (Roxburghe Club, London, 1828)

Scotland and the Commonwealth, 1651–53, C.H. Firth (ed), (SHS, Edinburgh, 1895)

Spalding, J. *The History of the Troubles and Memorable Transactions in Scotland and England, 1624–45*, two volumes, J. Skene (ed), (Bannatyne Club, Edinburgh, 1828–29)

The Stuart Constitution, Kenyon, J.P., (ed), (2nd edition, Cambridge, 1987)

Turner, Sir J., *Memoirs of His Own Life and Times*, T. Thomson (ed), (Bannatyne Club, Edinburgh, 1829)

The Works of Sir George MacKenzie of Rosehaugh, I (1716)

The Writings and Speeches of Oliver Cromwell, W.C. Abbott (ed), volumes one and two, (Harvard, 1937–1939)

4. REFERENCE WORKS

A Companion to Scottish History, Donnachie I., & Hewitt, G., (eds), (London, 1989)

A List of Books Printed in Scotland before 1700, H.G. Aldis (ed), (NLS, Edinburgh, 1970)

Black, G.F., *A List of Works Relating to Scotland* (1916)

Collins Encyclopaedia of Scotland , Keay J. & Keay, J. (eds),(London, 1994).

Handbook of British Chronology, Sir F.M. Powicke & E.B. Fryde (eds), (Royal Historical Society, London, 1987)

Stevenson, D. & W.B., *Scottish Texts and Calendars: An Analytical Guide to Serial Publications* (SHS, Edinburgh & Royal Historical Society, London, 1987)

The Scots Peerage, Sir J. Balfour-Paul (ed), nine volumes, (Edinburgh, 1904–1914)

Williams, E.N., *The Penguin Dictionary of English and European History, 1485–1789* (Suffolk, 1980)

5. THESES

Brown, J.J., 'The Social and Economic Influences of the Edinburgh Merchant Elite, 1600–1638', (University of Edinburgh, PhD thesis, two volumes, 1985)

Goodare, J.M., 'Parliament and Society in Scotland, 1560–1603', (University of Edinburgh, PhD thesis, 1989)

MacInnes, A.I., 'The Origin and Organization of the Covenanting Movement during the reign of Charles I, 1625–41; with a particular reference to the west of Scotland', (University of Glasgow, PhD thesis, two volumes, 1987)

Scally, J., 'The Career of James, 3rd Marquess and 1st Duke of Hamilton (1606–1649) to 1643' (University of Cambridge, PhD thesis, 1993)

Shepherd, W.S., 'The Politics and Society of Glasgow, 1648–74', (University of Glasgow, PhD thesis, 1978)

Young, J.R., 'The Scottish Parliament, 1639–1661: A Political and Constitutional Analysis' (University of Glasgow, PhD thesis, three volumes, 1993)

6. COMMENTARIES

Ashton, R., *The English Civil War. Conservatism and Revolution 1603–1649* (London, 1989)

Bonney, R., *The European Dynastic States 1494–1660* (Oxford, 1991)

Brown, K.M., *Kingdom or Province? Scotland and the Regal Union, 1603–1715* (London, 1992)

Campbell, W.M., *The Triumph of Presbyterianism* (Edinburgh, 1958)

Carlton, C., *Charles 1st: The Personal Monarch*, (London, 1984).

Carlton, C., *Archbishop William Laud* (London & New York, 1987)

Cooper, J.P. (ed), *The Decline of Spain and the Thirty Years War, 1609–59*, The New Cambridge Modern History, volume IV (Cambridge, 1970)

Cowan, I.B., *The Scottish Covenanters 1660–88* (London, 1976)

Cowan, E.J., *Montrose: For Covenant and King* (London, 1977)

Donald, P., *An Uncounselled King. Charles I and the Scottish troubles, 1637–1641* (Cambridge, 1990)

Donaldson, G., *Scotland, James V–James VII* (2nd edition, Edinburgh, 1987).

Donaldson, G., *Scotland: The Shaping of a Nation* (Newton Abbot, 1974)

Dow F.D., *Cromwellian Scotland, 1651–1660*, (Edinburgh, 1979).

Elllis, S.G., & Barber, S., (eds), *Conquest and Union. Fashioning a British State 1485–1725* (London, 1995)

Ferguson, W., *Scotland's Relations with England: A Survey to 1707* (Edinburgh, 1977).

Fitzpatrick, B., *Seventeenth-Century Ireland* (Dublin, 1988)

Fissel, M.C., *The Bishops' Wars. Charles I's campaigns against Scotland 1638–1640* (Cambridge, 1994)

Fletcher, A., *The Outbreak of the English Civil War* (London, 1981)

Gardiner, S.R., *The Fall of the Monarchy of Charles I, 1637–42*, two volumes (London, 1882)

Gardiner, S.R., *History of England from the Accession of James I to the Outbreak of the Civil War 1603–1642* , ten volumes, IX (1639–1641), X (1641–1642), (London, 1884)

Gentles, I., *The New Model Army in England, Ireland and Scotland, 1645–1653*, (Oxford, 1992)

Guizot, M., *History of the English Revolution from the Accession of Charles I*, two volumes, (London, 1838)

Hewison, J.K., *The Covenanters. A History of the Church in Scotland from the Reformation to the Restoration*, two volumes, (Glasgow, 1908)

Hill, C., *God's Englishman. Oliver Cromwell and the English Revolution* (London, 1970)

Hill, J.M., *Celtic Warfare 1595–1763* (2nd, edn., Edinburgh, 1995)

Hughes, A., *The Causes of the English Civil War* (London, 1991)

Hutton, R., *Charles II, King of England, Scotland and Ireland* (Oxford, 1989)

Hutton, R., *The British Republic 1649–1660* (London, 1990)

Kaplan, L., *Politics and Religion During the English Revolution: The Scots and the Long Parliament, 1643–1645* (New York, 1976)

Kerr, J., *The Covenants and the Covenanters. Covenants, Sermons, and Documents of the Covenanted Reformation* (Edinburgh, 1895)

Kirby, D., *Northern Europe in the Early Modern Period. The Baltic World 1492–1772* (London, 1990)

Koenigsberger, H.G., *Estates and Revolutions. Essays in Early Modern History* (London, 1971)

Koenigsberger, H.G., *Politicians and Virtuosi. Essays in Early Modern History* (London, 1986)

Laing, M., *The History of Scotland from the Union of the Crowns on the Accession of James VI to the Throne of England, to the Union of the Kingdoms in the Reign of Queen Anne*, four volumes, III (3rd edn., London, 1819)

Lee, jr., M., *The Road to Revolution: Scotland Under Charles I, 1625–1637* (Urbana & Chicago, 1985)

Levack, B.P., *The Formation of the British State. England, Scotland, and the Union 1603–1707* (Oxford, 1987)

Loades, D.M., *Politics and the Nation 1450–1660. Obedience, Resistance, and Public Order* (London, 1974).

Lockyer, R., *The Early Stuarts. A Political History of England 1603–1642* (London, 1989)

Lynch, M., *Scotland. A New History* (Edinburgh, 1991)

Mackie, J.D., *A History of Scotland* (1st edn., Harmondsworth, Middlesex, 1964)

MacInnes, A.I., *Charles I and the Making of the Covenanting Movement 1625–1641*, (Edinburgh, 1991)

MacKenzie, W.C., *The Highlands and Islands of Scotland* (revised edn., Edinburgh, 1949)

Makey, W., *The Church of the Covenant 1637–1651* (Edinburgh, 1979)

Morrill, J.S., *The Nature of the English Revolution* (London, 1993)

Morrill, J.S., *Revolution and Restoration. England in the 1650s* (London, 1992)

Morrill, J., (ed), *The Scottish National Covenant in its British Context 1638–51* (Edinburgh, 1990)

Mullan, D.G., *Episcopacy in Scotland: The History of an Idea, 1560–1638* (Edinburgh, 1986)

Munck, T., *Seventeenth Century Europe 1598–1700* (London, 1990)

Munck, T., *The Peasantry and the Early Absolute Monarchy in Denmark 1660–1708* (Copenhagen, 1979)

Ohlmeyer, J., *Civil War and Restoration in the Three Stuart Kingdoms.* (Cambridge, 1993)

Ohlmeyer, J. (ed.), *Ireland from Independence to Occupation, 1641–1660* (Cambridge, 1995)

Pennington, D.H., *Seventeenth Century Europe* (1972)

Rait, R.S., *The Parliaments of Scotland* (Glasgow, 1924)

Reid, J.M., *Kirk and Nation. The Story of the Reformed Church of Scotland* (London, 1960)

Reid, S., *The Campaigns of Montrose. A Military History of the Civil War in Scotland 1639 to 1646* (Edinburgh, 1990)

Roberts, M., *Essays in Swedish History* (London, 1967)

Russell, C., *The Crisis of Parliaments. English History 1509–1660* (9th edn, Oxford, 1990)

Russell, C., *The Causes of the English Civil War* (Oxford, 1990)

Russell, C., *The Fall of the British Monarchies 1637–1642* (Oxford, 1991)

Seaward, P., *The Restoration, 1660–1688* (London, 1991)

Sharpe, K., *The Personal Rule of Charles I* (New Haven & London, 1992)

Smellie, A., *Men of the Covenant* (10th edn., London, 1560)

Stevenson, D., *The Scottish Revolution, 1637–44* (Newton Abbot, 1973)

Stevenson, D., *Revolution and Counter-Revolution in Scotland, 1644–51* (London, 1977)

Stevenson, D., *The Covenanters. The National Covenant and Scotland* (The Saltire Society, 1988)

Stevenson, D., *Alasdair Maccolla and the Highland Problem in the Seventeenth Century* (Edinburgh, 1980)

Terry, C.S., *The Scottish Parliament: Its Constitution and Procedure, 1603–1707* (Glasgow, 1905)

Tilly, C., *European Revolutions, 1492–1992* (Oxford, 1993)

7. ARTICLES

Adamson, J.S.A., 'Parliamentary management, men of business, and the House of Lords, 1640–9', in C. Jones (ed), *A Pillar of the Constitution* (1989)

Adamson, J.S.A., 'Politics and the nobility in Civil-War England', *HJ*, 34, (1991)

Beattie, C., 'The Political Disqualification of Nobleman's Heirs in Seventeenth Century Scotland.' *SHR*, 59, (1980)

Buckroyd, J., 'Bridging the Gap: Scotland 1659–1660', *SHR*, 66, (1987)

Buckroyd, J., 'The Monarchy Restored', *The Sunday Mail Story of Scotland*, 18, (1988)

Buckroyd, J., 'Anti-clericalism in Scotland during the Restoration,' in N. MacDougall (ed), *Church, Politics and Society. Scotland 1408–1929* (Edinburgh, 1983)

Casada, J.A., 'The Scottish Representatives in Richard Cromwell's Parliament.' *SHR*, 51, (1972)

Cowan, E.J., 'The Union of the Crowns and the Crisis of the Constitution in the Seventeenth Century', in S. Dyrvik, K. Mykland, J. Oldervoll (eds), *The Satellite State in the Seventeenth and Eighteenth Centuries* (Bergen, 1979)

Cowan, E.J., 'The Solemn League and Covenant', in R.A. Mason (ed), *Scotland and England, 1286–1815* (Edinburgh, 1987)

Cowan, E.J., 'The Political Ideas of a Covenanting Leader: Archibald Campbell, Marquis of Argyll 1607–1661', in R.A. Mason (ed), *Scots and Britons. Scottish Political Thought and the Union of 1603* (Cambridge, 1994)

Dahlgren, S., 'Estates and Classes', in M. Roberts (ed), *Sweden's Age of Greatness, 1632–1718* (London, 1973)

Donaldson, G., 'The Solemn League and Covenant', *The Sunday Mail Story of Scotland*, 17, (1988)

Glow, L., 'The Committee of Safety', *EHR*, 80, (1965)

Goldwater, E.D., 'The Scottish Franchise: Lobbying During the Cromwellian Protectorate', *HJ*, 21, (1978)

Goodare, J., 'The Scottish Parliament of 1621', *HJ*, 38, (1995)

Hamilton, C.L., 'The Anglo-Scottish Negotiations of 1640–41', *SHR*, 41, (1962)

Hannay, R.K., & Watson, G.P.H., 'The Building of the Parliament House', *Book of the Old Edinburgh Club*, XIII, (1924)

Kaplan, L., 'Steps to War: the Scots and Parliament, 1642–1643', *Journal of British Studies*, 9, (1970)

Lee, jr., M., 'Scotland and the general crisis of the seventeenth century.' *SHR*, 63, (1984)

Lynch, M., 'Response: Old Games and New', *SHR*, 73, (1994)

MacInnes, A.I., 'Early Modern Scotland: the Current State of Play', *SHR*, 73, (1994)

MacInnes, A.I., 'Glasgow: Covenanting Revolution and Municipal Enterprise', *History Today*, 40 (1990)

MacInnes, A.I., 'The Long Road to Edgehill', *The Sunday Mail Story of Scotland*, 16, (1988)

MacInnes, A.I., 'The Impact of the Civil Wars and Interregnum: Political Disruption and Social Change within Scottish Gaeldom', in R. Mitchison & P. Roebuck (eds), *Economy and Society in Scotland and Ireland*, 1500–1939 (Edinburgh, 1988)

MacInnes, A.I., 'Scottish Gaeldom, 1638–1651: The New Vernacular Response to the Covenanting Dynamic', in J. Dwyer, R.A. Mason & A. Murdoch (eds), *New Perspectives on the Politics and Culture of Early Modern Scotland* (Edinburgh, 1982)

MacInnes, A.I., 'The First Scottish Tories ?', *SHR*, 67, (1988)

Mason, R.A., 'The Aristocracy, Episcopacy and the Revolution of 1638', in T.

Brotherstone (ed), *Covenant, Charter and Party. Traditions of revolt and protest in modern Scottish History* (Aberdeen, 1989)

McNeill, P.G.B, 'The Independence of the Scottish Judiciary', *Juridicial Review*, (1958)

Mukerjee, H.N., 'Scottish Members of Richard Cromwell's Parliament.' *Notes and Queries*, 166, (1934)

Mulligan, L., 'The Scottish Alliance and the Committee of Both Kingdoms, 1644–46', *Historical Studies Australia and New Zealand*, 14, (1970)

Mulligan, L., 'Peace Negotiations, Politics and the Committee of Both Kingdoms', *HJ*, 12, (1969)

Notestein, W., 'The Establishment of the Committee of Both Kingdoms', *AHR*, 17, (1912)

Patrick, J., 'A Union broken? Restoration politics in Scotland,' in J. Wormald (ed), *Scotland Revisited* (London, 1991)

Pinckney, P.J., 'The Scottish Representation in the Cromwellian Parliament of 1656', *SHR*, 46, (1967)

Russell, C., 'Why did Charles I call the Long Parliament?', *History*, 59, (1984)

Stevenson, D., 'The King's Scottish Revenues and the Covenanters.' *HJ*, 17, (1974)

Stevenson, D., 'The financing of the cause of the Covenants, 1638–51', *SHR*, 51, (1972)

Stevenson, D., 'The Early Covenanters and the Federal Union of Britain,' in *Scotland and England 1286–1815*, R.A. Mason (ed), (Edinburgh, 1987)

Stevenson, D., 'The Century of the Three Kingdoms', in J. Wormald (ed), *Scotland Revisited* (London, 1991)

Stevenson, D., 'Cromwell, Scotland and Ireland', in J. Morrill (ed), *Oliver Cromwell and the English Revolution* (1990)

Wedgwood, C.V., 'Anglo-Scottish Relations, 1603–40', *TRHS*, 32, (1950)

Williamson, A.H., 'Union with England Traditional, Union with England Radical: Sir James Hope and the Mid-Seventeenth-Century British State', *EHR*, 110, (1995)

Zagorin, P., 'The English Revolution, 1640–1660', in H. Lubasz (ed), *Revolutions in Modern European History* (2nd edn, London, 1968)

Index